Holiday Law

By

PROFESSOR DAVID GRANT,
University of Northumbria

&

STEPHEN MASON M.A., (CANTAB.),
Partner in Stephen Mason, Solicitors,
Visiting Fellow, University of Northumbria,
Holder of Higher Courts (Civil Proceedings) Qualification

LONDON • SWEET & MAXWELL • 2003

Published by
Sweet & Maxwell Limited of
100 Avenue Road, Swiss Cottage
London NW3 3PF
(http://www.sweetandmaxwell.co.uk)

First edition 1995
Second edition 1998
Third edition 2003

Typest by YHT Ltd, London
Printed in Great Britain by, CPD (Wales), Ebbw Vale

A CIP catalogue record
for this book is available
from the British Library

ISBN 0 421 79760 6

No natural forests were destroyed to make this product; only farmed timber was used and replanted

Preface

As we put the finishing touches to the third edition of the book it struck us that the task of writing it was akin to painting the Forth Bridge for no sooner was it finished than the task of writing the fourth edition began—precipitated by an announcement from the OFT that after a two year investigation it was taking no action over the level of cancellation charges levied by tour operators in circumstances where clients decide to cancel their holidays. Unfortunately we were unable to incorporate this important development into the text of the book and all we can do at this late stage is to refer you to the OFT website at www.oft.gov.uk and urge you to place your orders now for the fourth edition which will include a full commentary.

On reflection, however, the analogy with the Forth Bridge is a false one. With the Bridge the task is completed and then begun again; with the book the task is completed and then the job begins of writing a new book—analogous to re-building the bridge in a slightly more modern design—but never quite achieving an entirely contemporaneous look. What might be more apt in a travel law context is that writing the book is more like the coach trip described in *Noble v Leger*—a journey of uncertain duration and uncertain destination where the route changes regularly. Witness the huge impact of the *Club Tour* case from the ECJ and the Court of Appeal case, *Hone v Going Places*, which have dramatically altered the travel law landscape. Whether the subsequent path is uphill or downhill depends perhaps on your perspective. Travel agents may perhaps feel that following the *Club Tour* case they have a mountain to climb whereas tour operators feel that *Hone* (sub title "It's not safe until the fat lady moves") has at least made the path less bumpy. As far as way finding is concerned we hope that this book will assist on a regular basis and that our other venture, the *International Travel Law Journal,* will provide more up to date guidance.

In the last edition we remarked that travel law is generally not a matter of life and death and that the case law demonstrates a lighter side of the law. We hold to that view this time around—a significant body of new case law (unfortunately not all of it reported) seems to be concerned with tourists being attacked or injured by a variety of small and not so small animals—birds, monkeys, husky dogs, donkeys and even a cockroach. (Apparently in this last case the consumer was so frightened by the sight of the creature that he jumped back in alarm and seriously injured his back—a case calling out for that classic defence available to tour operators known technically as the "forgot to pack the brain" defence!) Of an entirely different order is a case brought to our attention by Holiday TravelWatch of a crocodile at the bottom of the garden of a Florida hotel in close proximity to the children's play area! Unfortunately there is also a disturbing increase in the number of personal injury cases coming to court. Whilst these cases contribute significantly to the development of the law it is rather sad to reflect that these are the result of what should be, and usually is, an entirely happy experience.

As usual we owe an enormous debt to friends and colleagues who have encouraged and supported us in our endeavours—and directed us back on to the right path on occasions. We thank them all and we are happy to acknowledge that any mistakes in the text are ours not their's—we just hope you don't find too many.

Our greatest thanks, of course, go to our wives and families who have had to accompany us on our fact-finding missions and who have endured with such good grace the hardships we have encountered—emergency landings in Sicily; Amtrak crashes in the US; being stranded by the insolvency of Sabena; suffering "gyppy tummy" on a Nile cruise; being splashed by whales at Seaworld; to say nothing of delayed flights, lost baggage and innumerable close encounters with death while travelling in third world taxis. It's a hard life being a travel lawyer but someone has to do it and we are fortunate in having them to share the burden. We love them dearly and we dedicate this book to them.

David Grant and Stephen Mason
May 8, 2003.

Foreword

Nothing is more newsworthy than a dream holiday ruined and few events give rise to more indignation and recrimination.

The interest in holiday disaster stories from the media has created a climate where perceptions of right and wrong have been distorted in the eyes of the travelling public. The very words used to describe problems with holidays very often bear little or no relationship with the extent of the difficulty experienced.

More than ever before it is the hard facts and an unemotional legal approach which have to prevail so that justice is seen to be done.

"Holiday Law", now in its third edition, adopts a practical and pragmatic approach to this emotive subject. For the student, the agony aunt, the customer-relations manager and the aggrieved or curious customer, the book provides an easy-to-read and invaluable guide to the complexities of the law relating to the travel industry.

Nothing stands still in the leisure sector and the regulations governing it change at just as fast a pace. The emergence of the Internet as a powerful selling tool has completely changed both the marketing and purchasing of the holiday product. The resulting unpackaging of the inclusive holiday has created new legal concerns and, in many cases, threatens consumer rights. "Holiday Law" brings the reader right up-to-date with recent and forthcoming legal requirements and highlights the cases which are determining the current interpretation of the regulations.

Noel Josephides
Managing Director of Sunvil Holidays,
Chairman of the Association of Independent Tour Operators Trust.

Acknowledgements

The authors and publishers would like to thank the following for permission to reproduce materials from publications in which they have copyright.

Crown copyright. Reproduced with the permission of the Controller of HMSO.

While every care has been taken to establish and acknowledge copyright, and contact the copyright owners, the publishers tender their apologies for any accidental infringement. They would be pleased to come to a suitable arrangement with the rightful owners in each case.

Contents

CONTENTS

CONTENTS

CONTENTS

Table of Cases

TABLE OF CASES

TABLE OF CASES

TABLE OF CASES

TABLE OF CASES

TABLE OF CASES

TABLE OF CASES

TABLE OF CASES

Table of Statutes

Table of Statutory Instruments

TABLE OF STATUTORY INSTRUMENTS

TABLE OF STATUTORY INSTRUMENTS

Table of Treaties

TABLE OF TREATIES

Table of European Legislation

Chapter One
Introduction

This is a book which is predominantly about the law relating to package holiday contracts. In due course we shall be examining these contracts in some detail but before we do that it is necessary to do two other things. First we will explain the scheme of the book and secondly we will endeavour to place package holiday contracts in context. The first is easily done. The second involves an examination of the travel industry and a look at some of the agencies that regulate the industry. It also involves a brief look at what can be broadly called the English legal system—to provide a general background into which to fit the specific rules relating to package holidays.

The Scheme Of The Book

After this introductory chapter the book falls conveniently into a number of sections. First, we look at the definition of a package holiday. Secondly, we look at the law of contract in relation to package holidays. The approach we have taken here is to adopt the conventional scheme used in most major works on contract: How is a contract made? What is in it? Who is a party to it? What can go wrong? How can it be brought to an end? What are the remedies for breach of the contract? In adopting this scheme however, we have chosen to give prominence only to those aspects of contract law that we believe are of practical relevance or of particular importance to package holiday contracts. So for instance purists may notice that we devote very little space to an examination of the rules relating to consideration and none to assignment. It is not that we have overlooked these topics it is simply that we do not think that they are of sufficient practical importance to devote space to them in a book of this kind.

Thirdly, we do spend considerable time looking at the regulation of the package holiday contract by the criminal law. This is a form of regulation which has grown considerably in recent years. First the Trade Descriptions Act 1968, then the Consumer Protection Act 1987 and now the Package Travel Regulations 1992 have all had a major impact on the way package holidays are marketed and sold. No one involved with package holidays can afford to be ignorant of this legislation.

Finally, we look at five important aspects of travel law that do not fit neatly into a contract law/criminal law classification but which are essential for a complete picture of the law in this area. In this part of the book we look at the legal position of travel agents; the protection offered consumers through the bonding and security system established by the Package Travel Regulations; a brief look at the practical aspects of litigation in travel cases; an examination of those aspects of air and sea law of particular interest to holidaymakers and finally, of interest to those increasing numbers of independent travellers who have no tour operator to sue, how to pursue an action against a foreign supplier.

The Package Travel Industry

1. The size and structure of the industry

The Package Holiday Market

In 2001 UK residents made just over 58 million visits abroad, of which, 38.7 million were holiday visits. Out of this figure of 38.7 million inclusive tours accounted for 20.6 million or 53 per cent of the total number of holiday visits. Air inclusive tours accounted for 16.9 million and 43 per cent respectively. Figures like these clearly demonstrate the present state of the "outgoing" holiday industry and the extent to which it is dominated by the package holiday.

The reasons why the inclusive tour in general and the air inclusive tour in particular have reached such a position of pre-eminences are complex, but they can be attributed to a number of factors. These include the fact that the components of a "typical" British holiday abroad—sea, sun and sand—are most readily available only at those destinations which are most easily accessible by air.

Other factors include the continuing technical advances in aeroplane design which have combined to increase capacity and reduce costs; the convenience of buying a ready-packaged holiday rather than putting it together oneself; the gradual relaxation of the regulations governing airlines and charter flights; a corresponding relaxation in currency regulations and passport formalities; and action by successive governments and by the industry itself to protect the position of holidaymakers caught out by the financial collapse of a tour operator. *Jarvis* (p.4) mentions the importance of the credit card and the increased use of air conditioning as other

Table 1. Holiday Visits by UK Residents (Source: Business Monitor, Office for National Statistics)

Year	*All visits*	*Holidays*	*ITs*	*Air ITs*
1980	17.5	11.7	6.2	4.8
1981	19.0	13.1	6.8	5.1
1982	20.6	14.2	7.7	5.8
1983	20.9	14.5	8.0	5.7
1984	22.0	15.3	9.0	6.9
1985	21.6	14.8	8.5	6.4
1986	24.9	17.8	10.6	8.3
1987	27.4	19.7	11.9	9.7
1988	28.8	20.7	12.6	10.3
1989	30.8	21.7	12.5	10.0
1990	31.2	21.3	11.4	8.8
1991	30.5	20.6	10.6	7.9
1993	35.8	24.3	13.3	10.6
1994	39.9	27.3	15.1	12.2
1995	41.9	28.1	15.3	12.2
1996	43.1	27.4	14.1	11.5
1997	45.9	29.1	15.4	12.2
1998	50.8	32.3	17.4	13.8
1999	53.9	35	19	15
2000	56.7	36.6	20	16.4
2001	58.2	38.7	20.6	16.9

All figures in millions

factors promoting the growth of travel. Nor should the success of the tour operators in promoting themselves and their products be forgotten. The names of such companies as Thomson, MyTravel (formerly Airtours), First Choice, Thomas Cook (JMC) and Cosmos are every bit as familiar and reassuring to consumers as other well known High Street brands. In common with other successful consumer-oriented companies they produce standard products at attractive prices thereby setting the standards for the rest of the industry. In so doing they have acquired the trust and confidence of the public upon which their growth and success has been based.

It should also be borne in mind that since the war higher levels of disposable income have contributed to a socio-economic climate where average and below average income earners not only have the earning capacity to purchase an annual holiday abroad but have come to regard it as a product to be enjoyed as a matter of course not as a luxury. It is simply another aspect of consumption to be ranked alongside a car or a mobile phone, digital TV or a broadband internet connection.

Although there is an understandable tendency to think of the package holiday as being two weeks sitting by a hotel swimming pool in Majorca eating chips with paella and drinking cheap Bacardi there is in fact a remarkable diversity of packages available. The mass summer market, concentrating mainly on the Mediterranean basin may correspond to the caricature above, but tour operators rely heavily on other markets for a proportion of their income. Not surprisingly one of the major alternatives to the summer sun paradigm is merely a variation on the same theme—namely the winter sun programmes offered by most large operators. Combined with the skiing packages also offered these holidays contribute to overheads during the thinner winter months. Still in the mass market are those holidays which appeal to particular age groups, *e.g.* holidays offered by "Club 18–30" or Saga. Long haul holidays to the Far East, Africa, Australia and Florida have now become commonplace. Cruising is also a type of holiday that is increasingly popular, casting off its rather staid reputation and appealing to a younger age group.

Smaller operators tend to be specialists, catering for the portion of the market that is unprofitable for large scale operators—often offering tailor-made holidays to more exotic and out of the way destinations. It is in this segment of the market that the theme holidays and special interest holidays are to be found—concentrating mainly on sport and adventure but also encompassing a bewildering variety of hobbies and interests from astronomy to yoga and taking in arts festivals, carnivals, history and literature along the way.

Tour Operators and Travel Agents

Although there are many thousands of tour operators in the UK the package holiday market is dominated by just a handful of companies. Almost 60 per cent of air package holidays are sold by only four companies—Thomson, Airtours, Thomas Cook and First Choice. The top 10 tour operators account for approximately 70 per cent (Keynote, 2001). These are the mass market operators whose brochures are to be found in virtually every travel agency in the country and whose brands are every bit as familiar as Heinz, Ford, Coca-Cola and Persil. At the other end of the scale are the "independent" tour operators who exist by selling only a few thousand holidays a year. Indeed there are some independents who make a comfortable living on the basis of selling only a few hundred holidays a year. Whereas most larger operators belong to

ABTA and in general sell their holidays through travel agencies, the independent operators often do not belong to any trade association and sell their holidays direct to the public.

In much the same way as a handful of companies dominate the tour operating market travel retailing demonstrates similar levels of concentration. The major travel agencies—Lunn Poly, Going Places and Thomas Cook own in excess of 700 branches and First Choice have over 350. Lunn Poly, which is the largest, has 800 branches (Keynote, 2001). Known as "multiples" they are the supermarkets of the travel world, selling mass market holidays at greatly discounted prices using the latest technology and appealing to the consumer not only through low prices but also through advertising and high street locations. Just as the major food retailers drive prices down by requiring discounts from their suppliers—the food manufacturers—so too do the multiples extract discounts from tour operators in the form of higher commission rates, or overrides as they are known, the benefits of which can then be passed on to the consumer.

At the other end of the travel agency market are the independents—one or two agency companies—which exist not by competing with the multiples on price but by offering a more personal service and by offering tailor-made travel arrangements that the multiples find too inconvenient to deal with.

There used to be a medium-sized category falling somewhere in between the multiples and the independents that were christened with the unhappy name of "miniples". These chains of regional travel agencies are now an endangered species and have virtually ceased to exist. One of the few remaining examples is Dawson & Sanderson in the North East.

Vertical Integration

In the last edition we remarked upon the level of vertical integration that exists in the industry. For instance we noted the relationship between the tour operator Thomson Holidays, the charter airline, Britannia, and the travel agency, Lunn Poly. Also that Airtours (now part of the MyTravel Group) had its own airline, Airtours International, and its own travel agency, Going Places as well as cruise line and hotel interests. First Choice was linked to Air 2000. This state of affairs provoked charges of anti-competitive practices (see *Holiday Which?* January 1996, p.13) and the matter was referred to the Monopolies and Mergers Commission (MMC) which reported in 1997 (Cm. 3813). The MMC did not find any major market distortions caused by vertical integration and the recommendations it made did not fundamentally affect the structure of the industry. (See "The Monopolies and Mergers Commission Report on Foreign Package Holidays", Sarah Mercer [1998] ITLJ 6 for a brief account on the report.) The most obvious result of the investigation is The Foreign Package Holidays (Tour Operators and Travel Agents) Order 2001 (SI 2001/2581) which regulates the use of insurance as an inducement in the sale of holidays and outlaws attempts by tour operators to insist on "most favoured customer" status with travel agents. Since the report matters have proceeded apace and the industry has made further attempts, some successful, at concentration. What is significantly different about the recent moves, however, has been the increasing European influence. Thomson are now part of the Preussag group based in Germany trading under the TUI brand and in this respect they followed the lead of Thomas Cook who had earlier become part of the German C&N Turistic Group. In the late 90s First Choice made an abortive bid to take over the Kuoni group and when that failed they were themselves the target of a bid by Airtours which was only thwarted by the intervention of the competition authorities of the European Commission—a decision which was overturned by the European Court of Justice, but only after Airtours had withdrawn from the fray (*Airtours v Commission Case*, T–342/99).

2. Contractual relationships within the travel industry

The legal relationship that this book is primarily concerned with is the one between the tour operator and the consumer—the package holiday contract—but in order to properly understand this relationship it is useful to have a picture of the network of contracts and relationships that lie behind or alongside this main contract and which are responsible for creating many of the problems that bedevil the relationship between tour operator and consumer.

Positioned at the centre of the complex of contracts with a pivotal role is the tour operator. Not only does the tour operator contract with the consumer but also with the suppliers of the elements that go to make up the package—the hotelkeepers, the airlines and the transfer companies and ground operators. (Although known as "suppliers" this is a term which serves only to deceive. In reality they are no more than what would be known as subcontractors in other industries.) It is this role of assembler of other contractors products that commercially is so convenient to the consumer but legally has proved so inconvenient. On the one hand it has permitted the tour operator to reduce his liability on the grounds that defects in the package were not his fault but the fault of an independent contractor (see *Wall v Silver Wing Surface Arrangements* 1981, unreported, which is looked at in detail later; *cf.* Grant & Urbanowicz, "Tour Operators, Package Holiday Contracts and Strict Liability", [2001] JBL 253.) On the other hand it has created a barrier to the consumer effectively suing the supplier in his own right. If the only contract that the consumer has is with the tour operator then to bring an action against a supplier, say for serious quality defects at an hotel or even for personal injury, will mean bringing an action in tort rather than contract—in a foreign jurisdiction. This is not a prospect that appeals to many consumers and even if such an action is pursued the chances of success are limited (see MA Jones, "Tour Operators and the Unfair Contract Terms Act" [1983] *Gazette* 2964; but see also Chapter Eight on Privity and the new Contracts (Rights of Third Parties) Act 1999 and Chapter nineteen on Suing Abroad).

It would be a mistake however to think that the disadvantages of the package holiday contract are all one way. It is certainly the case that as the lot of the consumer has been improved by the Package Travel Regulations the tour operator can be found complaining that he is "piggy-in-the-middle" caught between consumers on the one hand with strong legally protected rights and commercially stronger suppliers on the other hand (airlines in particular) which impose terms on them that leave them having to foot the bill when things go wrong. For instance in the charter agreement between the airline and the tour operator the airline may reserve the right to change timings and schedules and the tour operator may be left with no recourse against the airline while at the same time having to pay substantial compensation to consumers for flight changes. (See Briggs, "Tour Operators and Airlines—Between a Rock and a Hard Place" [1994] T.L.J. 44.) Hotel safety is another issue that causes concern to tour operators. In cases of hotel fires, swimming pool drownings, food poisoning and other injuries which occur abroad the tour operator is liable to the consumer under the Package Travel Regulations for the defaults of their suppliers. However, the domestic safety legislation that these suppliers are subject to may not impose particularly stringent standards—leaving the tour operator to carry the can. (See *Wilson v Best Travel* [1993] 1 All E.R. 353; and Lakin, "Hotel Safety: Can Things Only Get Better" [2002] I.T.L.J. 189).

In Chapter 15 we grapple with the problem of the precise legal status of the travel agent but here it is only necessary to point out that when he acts as agent for the tour operator then he clearly has the capacity to influence (and not always benignly) the content of the contract between the consumer and the tour operator. When not acting as agent for the tour operator he may either be acting as agent for the consumer or, if he has no contractual relationship with the consumer, he may be liable to him in tort for any misstatements that he makes.

3. The business environment

Many of the problems arising from package holidays can be laid at the feet of the unstable environment in which tour operators have to trade. A number of features can be identified that make up this difficult environment. First there is the problem of fluctuating exchange rates which often result in the imposition of unwelcome surcharges and which can radically affect the marketing of certain destinations. One only has to look at the popularity of a destination such as Florida and measure it against the pound/dollar exchange rate to see the effects currency fluctuations can have. Secondly there are the problems associated with political unrest and terrorism. Destinations such as Yugoslavia, China, Sri Lanka, Egypt, South Africa, Indonesia, North America and many others have all been afflicted by political problems that have had a detrimental affect on their tourism industry. Fuel prices, which are affected by both the first two factors, are another important element in the environment that tour operators inhabit. Finally there is the weather itself. Severe weather conditions, either at home or at the holiday destination, can seriously disrupt the best planned schedules. (See Hannigan, "Reservations Cancelled", 1980 *Annals of Tourism Research* VII(3) 366, for a fuller account of the tour operating environment).

4. Trade associations and regulatory bodies

ABTA

It is not possible to have a complete grasp of package holiday law in this country without understanding the role of the Association of British Travel Agents (ABTA; *www.abta.com*). ABTA is the trade association which, confusingly, represents both travel agents and tour operators. Although formed in the 1950s it grew to prominence in the 1960s thanks largely to the introduction of "stabiliser". Stabiliser is, or was, a clause in ABTA's articles of association, introduced in 1966, that provided that ABTA tour operators could only sell their products through ABTA travel agencies and that ABTA travel agencies could only sell ABTA tour operators' products.

Stabiliser created a cartel within the travel industry. The effect of this was quite simple. Membership of the cartel was a licence to trade whereas exclusion from membership amounted to commercial suicide. However the reasons behind stabiliser were more complex than simply establishing a cartel. Although prior to stabiliser ABTA enforced financial controls on members and had established a rescue fund for the clients of failed members it could not of course enforce higher standards on the industry as a whole and there continued to be regular failures of companies who were not members of ABTA—which did nothing to create confidence in the industry as a whole. ABTA was sufficiently large already that by creating stabiliser it meant that virtually all travel companies had to join or risk extinction. This in turn meant that standards could be properly enforced because the ultimate sanction, exclusion from membership, was not a consequence that travel companies could seriously contemplate.

Apart from the enforcement of financial controls on members there were two significant features of ABTA membership that flowed from stabiliser. The first, and most important of these, is the system of financial protection, (backed up by a rescue scheme for holidays not covered by an ATOL), provided for clients of failed tour operators. The second is the Code of Conduct, for tour operators and travel agents that confer a greater degree of consumer protection on clients than would generally be available under the law.

We look at the current bonding and security regime which was introduced by the Package Travel Regulations in Chapter sixteen but the ABTA system which preceded it and which still exists for ABTA members consists of a threefold level of protection. First, all ABTA tour operators are required to take out a bond, representing a certain percentage of their turnover, which can be called in the event of their insolvency to compensate their clients who suffer as a result of the insolvency. In some instances the bond money is used to permit clients to continue their holiday or to repatriate them if necessary. Secondly, there is shortfall insurance and, thirdly, there is the Tour Operators' Fund. These latter two forms of protection can be used in the event of the bond not being sufficient to cover all claims. In addition to the purely financial protection offered by the ABTA scheme there is also a rescue scheme to deal with clients stranded when their tour operator becomes insolvent. The system used to cover both "licensable" and "unlicensable" activities, *i.e.* all holidays whether covered by an ATOL licence or not. However, since 1991 the rescue scheme for licensable activities has been taken over by the CAA. (In practice the rescue of stranded holidaymakers is not a great burden either for ABTA or the CAA as rival companies are happy to step into the breach—comforted by the knowledge that they will be indemnified out of the bond money or by the Air Travel Trust and by their chance of increasing their customer base.)

The Code of Conduct regulates the conduct of travel agents and tour operators both between themselves and, more importantly for our purposes, between themselves and their clients. We shall look at it in more detail at various points in the book but for the present it is sufficient to say that its importance stems from the fact that it confers upon the consumer rights which he is not necessarily entitled to at common law. It does this by requiring tour operators to insert into their contract with the consumer certain mandatory terms. These terms cover many of the most important features of the package holiday contract—cancellation, major changes, surcharges, *force majeure*, liability, etc. The Code (See Appendix Three) is revised at regular intervals, the latest revision being in February 2003 and the degree of protection which it affords has varied considerably over time. Certainly the version which was in existence between 1990 and 1993 was much in advance of the existing law but since then the passage of the Package Travel Regulations has reduced its impact.

Stabiliser was the subject of an action before the Restrictive Practices Court brought by the Office of Fair Trading (*Re Association of British Travel Agents Ltd's Agreement* [1984] ICR 12) on the grounds that it contravened the Restrictive Trade Practices Act 1976. Although ABTA was a cartel the court refused to declare stabiliser to be contrary to the public interest. They arrived at this decision on the grounds that the removal of stabiliser would "deny to the public ... specific and substantial benefits" (section 19(1)(b)). In other words the financial safeguards that ABTA provided to the public made the existence of stabiliser reasonable.

Subsequently ABTA has voluntarily abolished stabiliser. The reason was that the Package Travel Regulations created an environment where consumers are entitled to such a high level of protection under the general law that it was no longer necessary for ABTA to maintain a cartel to protect the consumer interest. If ABTA had not moved to abolish stabiliser in October 1993 the Office of Fair Trading would almost certainly have instituted fresh proceedings against it—this time with a greater chance of success.

Since the abolition of stabiliser ABTA has remained largely intact. The only significant defection since its abolition has been one medium-sized tour operator—Saga. Whether it continues in its present form as both a trade association and a regulator of trading standards remains to be seen. Despite doubts expressed in the second edition of this book about its continuing existence in the long term as a trade association representing both tour operators and travel agents it has continued successfully in this role and the regulatory side of its affairs commands general acceptance (but see *R (on the application of Sunspell) v ABTA* (QBD, Admin Ct, October 12, 2000) for a challenge to its authority).

Other Trade Associations

Apart from ABTA there are a variety of other trade associations in the travel industry. Probably the most important outside ABTA is the Federation of Tour Operators (FTO; *www.fto.co.uk*) formerly known as the Tour Operators Study Group (TOSG). This organisation, for which membership is by invitation only, is chiefly made up of the larger tour operators. It is a forum for the discussion of policy matters which are of mutual concern to the tour operating industry and it lobbies on behalf of the industry. One of its chief functions is in connection with the bonding of its members. Where a package does not include a flight the FTO sets the level of bonding required by members and, if necessary in the event of a member's insolvency, it will call the bond and administer it in favour of the consumers affected as a result of the insolvency. It also helps in formulating policy on health and safety issues.

AITO (*www.aito.co.uk*), the Association of Independent Tour Operators, is a trade association representing independent tour operators—small and medium-sized operators, many of whom are not members of ABTA and who mostly sell their holidays directly to the public. Although small it is increasing in size and has an influential voice. It too exercises a bonding function on behalf of members.

The Travel Trust Association (*www.traveltrust.co.uk*) exists to promote confidence in tour operators who choose to provide security by means of a trust fund (see Chapter 16).

Coach tour operators are represented by the Confederation of Passenger Transport (CPT; *www.cpt-uk.org/cpt*) who have their own bonding scheme—Bonded Coach Holidays (BCH; *www.bondedcoachholidays.co.uk*). Cruise operators are brought together by the Passenger Shipping Association (PSA; *www.psa-psara.org*) which also has a bonding scheme for non-licensable activities. Travel agents have a number of associations to which they may belong including the National Association of Independent Travel Agents (NAITA) and the Guild of Business Travel Agents (GBTA; *www.gbta-guild.com*), and the industry has many other specialist groupings of which ABTOF, the Association of British Tour Operators to France, is perhaps the best known (*www.holidayfrance.org.uk*).

The Civil Aviation Authority

The chief responsibility of the CAA is the economic and safety regulation of civil aviation in the UK. As far as travel law is concerned its chief importance is that it operates the ATOL system. Every tour operator who sells package holidays by air must have an ATOL—an air travel organiser's licence—and it is the CAA that administers the system. Broadly speaking an applicant for an ATOL must be able to satisfy the CAA as to its financial stability and it must take out a bond which can be called and used to protect its consumers in the event of its insolvency. Bonds arranged through ABTA, FTO or AITO are all acceptable to the CAA. Package holidays covered by an ATOL are known as "licensable" activities—to distinguish them from non-licensable activities which are not covered by the CAA regime. Under the Package Travel Regulations a company that has an ATOL is regarded as satisfying the requirements under the Regulations as to the protection of consumers in the event of insolvency for holidays which include an air travel component.

The ATOL system is generally regarded as having been a success. So much so that in the debate preceding the passage of the Package Travel Regulations on how best to protect consumers against the financial failure of tour operators it was strongly suggested that it be used as a model for the licensing of all tour operators. This argument was rejected by the Government and was not one which the CAA itself welcomed given the difficulty of policing such a system.

The ATOL system underwent a major revision in the mid 90s resulting in the The Civil Aviation (Air Travel Organisers Licensing) Regulations 1995 (SI 1995/1054). The main effect of this revision was to bring flight consolidators within the ATOL Regulations and to tighten up the financial scrutiny of ATOL holders. It also saw the introduction of directors' personal guarantees to help counter abuse of the system by individuals repeatedly setting up travel companies which then became insolvent. (See Helen Simpson, "Recent Developments on the ATOL Regulations", [1997] ITLJ 113 for a discussion of the new Regulations.) More recently (August 2002) the CAA issued a consultation document on the issue of "split contracts" (see Chapter Two) with a view to extending the ATOL system to fill the loopholes which exist in the bonding system caused by the fact that the ATOL system and the Package Travel Regulations do not provide complete protection against insolvency. (See also Simpson, "Financial Protection for Scheduled Airline Passengers" [2002] ITLJ 15).

Another problem which occurs in relation to air package holidays but which is by no means confined to them is that sometimes when a tour operator becomes bankrupt the bond which they have in place is inadequate to meet the calls upon it. The solution devised to meet this eventuality is the Air Travel Trust, formerly known as the Air Travel Reserve Fund. This is a fund first established in 1975 by the Air Travel Reserve Fund Act 1975 made up of levies upon air package holidays. The purpose of the fund is to make up the difference when an insolvent tour operator's bond is insufficient to meet the demands upon it. The fund grew sufficiently large after just a few years that it became unnecessary to increase it further and the power to raise the levy was repealed. In recent years it has diminished considerably in size and is now effectively bankrupt—only able to continue in operation by virtue of a guarantee provided by the Treasury. It is uncertain how this difficulty will be resolved without finding the Parliamentary time necessary for primary legislation. Despite its present state the fund has generally been regarded as a success and it is disappointing that in 1992 when the Package Travel Regulations were enacted the Government chose not to use it as a model for a consumer fund to protect holidays other than air holidays.

Other Regulatory Bodies

The Office of Fair Trading (OFT; *www.oft.gov.uk*) was first established by the Fair Trading Act 1973 but now derives its powers from the Enterprise Act 2002. It has a wide responsibility for the promotion of consumer protection as well as wide ranging responsibilities in the field of competition law. It was in this latter capacity that it instituted action against ABTA under the Restrictive Trade Practices Act. The OFT also has the power to undertake initial investigations into monopolies and to make references to the Competition Commisison (formerly the MMC) when it is felt necessary. It was in the exercise of this power that the issue of vertical integration in the travel industry was referred to the MMC in November 1996. Another duty of the OFT, to be found in s.8 of the Enterprise Act, is the promotion of good consumer practice. One way in which this can be achieved is to encourage and approve the use of "consumer codes". The ABTA Code of Practice already referred to was a result of consultation between ABTA and the OFT. It should be noted however that although formerly the Codes were prepared in consultation with the OFT they were not "approved" by the OFT. However under the new regime it is possible to obtain the formal approval of the OFT and the 2003 Code of Practice has been approved.

Trading Standards Departments, sometimes also known as

Weights and Measures Departments or Consumer Protection Departments, are charged with enforcing a wide range of consumer protection legislation of which that affecting the travel industry is a very small part. Of particular relevance to the industry are three pieces of legislation—the Trade Descriptions Act 1968, the Consumer Protection Act 1987 and the Package Travel Regulations 1992. They confer upon Trading Standards Officers wide powers to investigate and prosecute complaints arising under the legislation with corresponding powers of search and seizure and the power to interview suspects. All this legislation is dealt with in detail in later chapters.

The English Legal System

1. Introduction

In this section we hope to do three things. First to explain to you the sources of English law; secondly to explain the difference between civil and criminal law; and thirdly to give you a brief description of the court system. To put it more simply we will tell you where our laws come from, what kinds of laws we have, and where you will end up if you infringe them.

2. Sources of law

Very broadly speaking we have two sources of law—legislation and case law. Legislation is law made by Parliament and is the collective name for what are also known as Acts of Parliament or statutes. Case law is law made by the courts and is also known as the common law or judicial precedent.

Legislation

An Act of Parliament, or a statute, is a law which has been passed by Parliament after being subjected to a rigorous scrutiny by both the House of Commons and the House of Lords (often after an equally rigorous consultation process outside Parliament). This process includes a formal introduction into one House by means of a *first reading*, of what is then known as a *bill*. Then there is a full scale debate on the merits of the bill during the *second reading*. After the second reading the bill goes through the *committee stage* where it is looked at in some detail—often clause by clause. Finally it is returned to the floor of the House where, after a *report stage*, it receives its *third reading*. Then the bill is sent to the other House where it undergoes a similar process. If it survives all this it then receives the *royal assent* and becomes law.

Parliament only has time to deal with about 70 or 80 new statutes a year and most of these deal with social, environmental and economic matters. Examples of statutes passed in recent years that don't fall into these categories but have had a direct bearing on the regulation of the travel industry include two already mentioned, the Trade Descriptions Act 1968 and the Consumer Protection Act 1987. Further examples are the Unfair Contract Terms Act 1977 and the Misrepresentation Act 1967, both of which will be examined in some detail later.

Delegated Legislation

Apart from Acts of Parliament another very important form of legislation is *delegated legislation.* For a variety of reasons, including lack of time, lack of technical expertise or the need for speed, Parliament often delegates the making of legislation to an inferior body—usually a minister but sometimes a local authority. Many former nationalised industries such as British Rail had limited powers to make by-laws which are a form of delegated legislation. Much law is therefore made without proper Parliamentary consideration.

The manner in which this is usually done is for Parliament to pass an enabling Act—which is an Act of Parliament which contains a power enabling a minister, or whoever, to make delegated legislation. One example of delegated legislation with which most in the travel industry should be familiar is the Civil Aviation (Air Travel Organisers' Licensing) Regulations otherwise known as the ATOL Regulations. These were first enacted in 1972 and amended on a number of occasions. They were repealed and re-enacted in 1995 as the Civil Aviation (Air Travel Organisers' Licensing) Regulations 1995 (SI 1995/1054). These Regulations provide that tour operators who offer air-inclusive package holidays must be licensed and bonded by the CAA. The minister responsible for bringing them into force is the Secretary of State for Transport and the Act of Parliament which gives him this power is the Civil Aviation Act 1982.

The most important example of delegated legislation relevant to the travel industry is of course the Package Travel, Package Holidays and Package Tours Regulations 1992 (SI 1992/3288). In this instance the enabling Act is the European Communities Act 1972. This Act was passed when the UK joined the EEC and provides that European legislation can be enacted in the UK by means of delegated legislation. This was how the EC Directive on Package

Travel, Package Holidays and Package Tours 1990 became part of English law.

European Legislation

Increasingly, much of our law comes from Brussels rather than Westminster and it is necessary therefore to give a brief explanation of the types of legislation that we are subject to as members of the European Union.

First of all there are the treaties—the European Community Treaty (the Treaty of Rome), the Single European Act, the Treaty on European Union (the Maastricht Treaty), the Treaty of Amsterdam and the Treaty of Nice. These are all *primary* sources of European law and are *directly applicable* in the UK by virtue of the European Communities Act 1972, s.2(2). This means that they create rights in English law without the necessity for legislation by Parliament.

Secondary sources of European law include *Directives* and *Regulations* (not to be confused with the Regulations mentioned earlier which are forms of delegated legislation made by our own Parliament). In general Directives are not directly applicable in the UK unless Parliament gives effect to them by statute or delegated legislation. As explained above, this is how the Package Travel Regulations came into being. Regulations on the other hand are directly applicable.

Occasionally, Directives are regarded as being directly applicable without Parliament having implemented it by means of domestic legislation. This is only possible once the deadine for implementation of the Directive has elapsed. Moreover, only those provisions in a Directive which are sufficiently clear, precise and unconditional could be so regarded. Additionally, Directives can be regarded as directly applicable, and be relied upon as if they were national legislation in the national courts, only in cases involving disputes between citizens and State authorities. For example, Directive 87/102 on consumer credit was due to be implemented in 1990. However, Spain had not done so when Cristina Blázquez Rivero booked herself a holiday through El Corte Inglés (ECI), a Spanish travel agency. She had to obtain a loan via a company that had an exclusive right to provide loans to ECI's customers. The holiday proved to be very disappointing and Ms Blázquez Rivero stopped repayments on the loan. When an action was brought against her in the Spanish courts, she purported to rely upon certain provisions in the Directive. However, she was unable to do so: although the deadline for implementation had passed, and the provisions on which she was relying were clear, the case did not involve a dispute between a citizen and a State authority (case C–192/94 *El Corte Inglés SA v Blázquez Rivero*).

However, when this happens, people such as Ms Blázquez Rivero can claim compensation from the defaulting Member State instead. Thus, it is now quite clear that if the UK had not complied with its European obligations by bringing Directive 90/314, the Package Travel Directive, into force by December 31, 1992, any clear, precise and unconditional provisions in it would nevertheless have been directly applicable in the UK—but only in disputes between citizens and the government of the UK. However, any UK citizen who had been adversely affected by the failure of the UK government to bring the EC Directive into force could have sued the government for the losses caused by the failure.

Thus if a tour operator had become insolvent before the Government had implemented the requirements about security then the consumers harmed by this failure could claim compensation from the Government. The reason we can say this with such certainty is that this is just the situation that arose in Germany in 1993. A major German tour operator became bankrupt before the German government had implemented the Directive and German consumers commenced an action against their government to recover their money lost in the insolvency. The case of *Dillenkofer and Others v Germany* (Case C–178,179, 188–90/94) eventually reached the European Court of Justice which decided that the German Government should compensate the consumers for their loss which had been caused by the Government's failure to implement the Directive by the required deadline (See Hilda Ann O'Connor, *Advance Deposits and the Package Travel Directive: The Final Judgment* [1997] I.T.L.J. 54).

Note that the Directive is directly applicable against the state—known as *vertical* applicability—but it does not create rights as between individuals—*horizontal* applicability.

Examples of Regulations of relevance to the travel industry include EC Regulation 295/91 on Denied Boarding Compensation and EC Regulation 2027/97 on Air Carrier Liability.

Case Law

A large part of our law is not to be found in statutes at all. It can be found instead in case law—decisions made by the judges in individual cases which create *precedents* which are then *followed* by other judges. At one time our criminal law, tort law and contract law consisted almost entirely of case law and it still remains important today.

English law has developed a system of *binding precedent*

(otherwise known as *stare decisis*)—which means that once a court has decided a case then the rule or principle that it establishes is binding in later cases. The rule that the case establishes is also known by a fancy Latin name—the *ratio decidendi* — the reasons for the decision. The judge in a subsequent case has no choice in the matter, he *must* follow the previous *ratio* no matter how much he disagrees with it. The reason for this is to establish consistency in the law. If a judge could decide a case according to whatever principles he chose then it would be difficult for anyone to know where they stood in any particular situation. They would not be able to order their affairs in accordance with what they believed the law to be. For instance there was confusion for a short time before the law was settled on the issue of whether or not it amounted to contributory negligence not to wear a seatbelt in a car. Some High Court judges (whose decisions are not binding on other High Court judges) believed that failure to wear a seatbelt amounted to contributory negligence whereas other High Court judges took a different view. It required an appeal to the Court of Appeal before the matter was settled and a rule established that had to be followed by all High Court judges.

The disadvantage of such a system of binding precedent is that it creates a rigid system with no flexibility and as a consequence the law is unable to grow or adapt to changing circumstances and unjust decisions are perpetuated. This is to overstate the position however because the system in practice does possess sufficient flexibility to overcome the problems of excessive rigidity.

This is achieved in a number of ways. First, it is possible for a court higher up in the hierarchy of courts to *overrule* a previous decision of a lower court. For instance the Court of Appeal can overrule decisions of the High Court, and the House of Lords can overrule decisions of the Court of Appeal. (A case is *overruled* when a court in a *later* case decides that the *ratio* of the first case is wrong. A case is *reversed* when a court to which *that* case is appealed decides that the decision of the lower court was wrong.) Note that it is higher courts that bind lower courts, not vice versa. A High Court decision binds the County Court but it does not work the other way round.

Secondly, a subsequent court can *distinguish* the decision of a previous court and refuse to follow it. To distinguish a previous case is not to disagree with the principle or rule that it lays down but simply to say that the facts are sufficienty different to justify coming to a decision which is not based on that principle. For instance the case of *Jarvis v Swans Tours* [1973] 1 All E.R. 71 establishes that in holiday cases a plaintiff is entitled to damages for distress and disappointment. But how far does this principle extend? The House of Lords, in *Farley v Skinner* [2001] 3 W.L.R. 899, decided that it extended to situations where only *part* of the purpose of the contract was to provide peace of mind or freedom from distress. So what about a "flight-only" contract to a holiday destination? Does this come within *Jarvis* and *Farley* or does it fall outside? It would be possible for a judge, if he so wished, to distinguish the facts of such a case from either *Jarvis* or *Farley*—giving him the freedom to decide the case as he saw fit. This would not require him to ignore or overrule these decisions—merely to say that the factual situation he is dealing with does not fit comfortably within the principles established by those cases and therefore need not be followed. An indication of how the courts might approach this issue is to be found in *Lucas v Avro* [1994] C.L.Y. 1444.

Finally it is possible, if all else fails, for legislation to be passed to overrule inconvenient or unjust precedents. This is effectively what the Package Travel Regulations have done to large parts of the common law relating to package holidays. For instance the decision in *Wall v Silver Wing Surface Arrangements* (1981, unreported), a High Court decision which was followed in a number of County Court cases, laid down that a tour operator was not liable to clients who were injured on holiday by the negligence of the hotel they were booked into. Now, Regulation 15 of the Package Travel Regulations effectively provides that a tour operator is responsible for the negligence of suppliers (but see the much fuller discussion in Chapter Five).

3. Civil and criminal law

Broadly speaking the criminal law is concerned with offences that are regarded as being sufficiently serious or anti-social that when they occur the state should intervene to maintain order or to protect citizens who may be unable or unwilling to protect themselves. This intervention will usually take the form of an individual being *prosecuted* by the state in a criminal court and if the *defendant* is found *guilty* then *punishment* such as a fine or imprisonment will be imposed. This clearly applies to "traditional" crimes such as murder, manslaughter, arson, rape, theft, etc, but the criminal courts also deal with large numbers of "regulatory" offences such as parking on double yellow lines or dropping litter or failing to label the contents of processed food properly. These are not criminal offences in the traditional sense but in order to regulate a complex modern society it has been necessary to classify such activities as criminal and to impose criminal penalties simply in order to ensure that traffic flows freely, that our streets are not unbearably filthy and that we are properly informed as to what we are eating.

Into this latter category fall a number of statutes that impact heavily on the travel industry—the Trade Descriptions Act 1968, the Consumer Protection Act 1987 and many of the provisions in the Package Travel Regulations relating to the provision of information. Lord Scarman has said of the Trade Descriptions Act:

> "... it is not a truly criminal statute. Its purpose is not the enforcement of the criminal law but the maintenance of trading standards. Trading standards, not criminal behaviour are its concern." (*Wings v Ellis* [1984] 3 All E.R. 577).

The civil law on the other hand is largely concerned with disputes between individuals. In this book we are largely concerned with that branch of civil law known as contract law but occasionally we also mention the law of torts. In these two branches of civil law the dispute will often resolve itself into a situation where a *claimant* (formerly referred to as a *plaintiff*) *i.e.* the person with the grievance, is *suing* a *defendant* in a civil court. If the defendant is found *liable* then the court will endeavour to find a *remedy*—usually financial compensation called *damages* but occasionally an *injunction* or an award of *specific performance*.

Often the same set of facts can give rise to both criminal and civil liability. For instance if a tour operator describes a hotel in a misleading fashion *e.g.*, by stating that the hotel has a children's swimming pool when it doesn't this may give rise to a criminal prosecution under s.14 of the Trade Descriptions Act 1968 or Regulation 5 of the Package Travel Regulations. It may also give rise to a civil action for breach of contract or misrepresentation. If the misrepresentation was deliberate then this amounts to the tort of deceit. The tour operator may end up paying both a hefty fine for the criminal offence and substantial damages for the civil liability.

4. The court system

1. General Features

Should you be unfortunate enough to engage in litigation—an activity that has not contributed notably to the happiness of mankind—you will inevitably encounter the court system. Certain features characterise the system. First, as a general proposition, the courts can be divided into civil courts and criminal courts—

although their functions do overlap on occasions. Secondly there are courts of trial (or first instance) and courts of appeal—but again there are overlaps—some courts have both first instance and appellate functions. Thirdly, just as there is a hierarchy of courts so there is a hierarchy of judges. In the lower courts the judges are less experienced, sometimes part-time and, in the magistrates' court in particular, have no formal legal qualifications. At the other end of the scale judges in the House of Lords are full time and extremely experienced—ranking in quality alongside any final court of appeal in the world.

Finally the whole system is complicated by the fact that on matters of European legislation the House of Lords, our highest domestic court, is no longer the supreme court. Disputes involving a European element now have to go to the European Court of Justice in Luxembourg for decisions on the interpretation of European legislation.

The diagram below is intended to give a broad overview of the court system. We will now look briefly at the important features of each court taking the criminal courts first.

2. Criminal Courts

(a) The Magistrates' Court

Jurisdiction. Magistrates' courts are the workhorses of the criminal court system. Situated in every town (often several of them in the larger conurbations) and open for business every day of the week they deal predominantly with what can be termed "petty crime" although their jurisdiction is very wide indeed—including not only crime but also a wide range of family matters and a miscellaneous jurisdiction that includes liquor licensing and the recovery of certain debts such as gas, electricity and council tax.

Apart from proceedings dealing with children and young offenders in a special youth court the criminal jurisdiction of the magistrates can be broadly divided into two types of proceedings—*summary proceedings* and *committal proceedings*. In summary proceedings the court acts as a trial court and will *try* all *summary* offences and many *indictable* offences. A summary offence is one where the defendant has no right to a jury trial in the Crown Court and must be dealt with by the Magistrates' Court. Indictable offences are ones where the defendant does have such a right to trial by jury but may in certain cases waive that right and choose to be tried by the magistrates. Some indictable offences are so serious, *e.g.*, murder, manslaughter, rape, etc. that they can only be tried in the Crown Court but many are said to be *triable either way*, *i.e.*

Criminal Court System

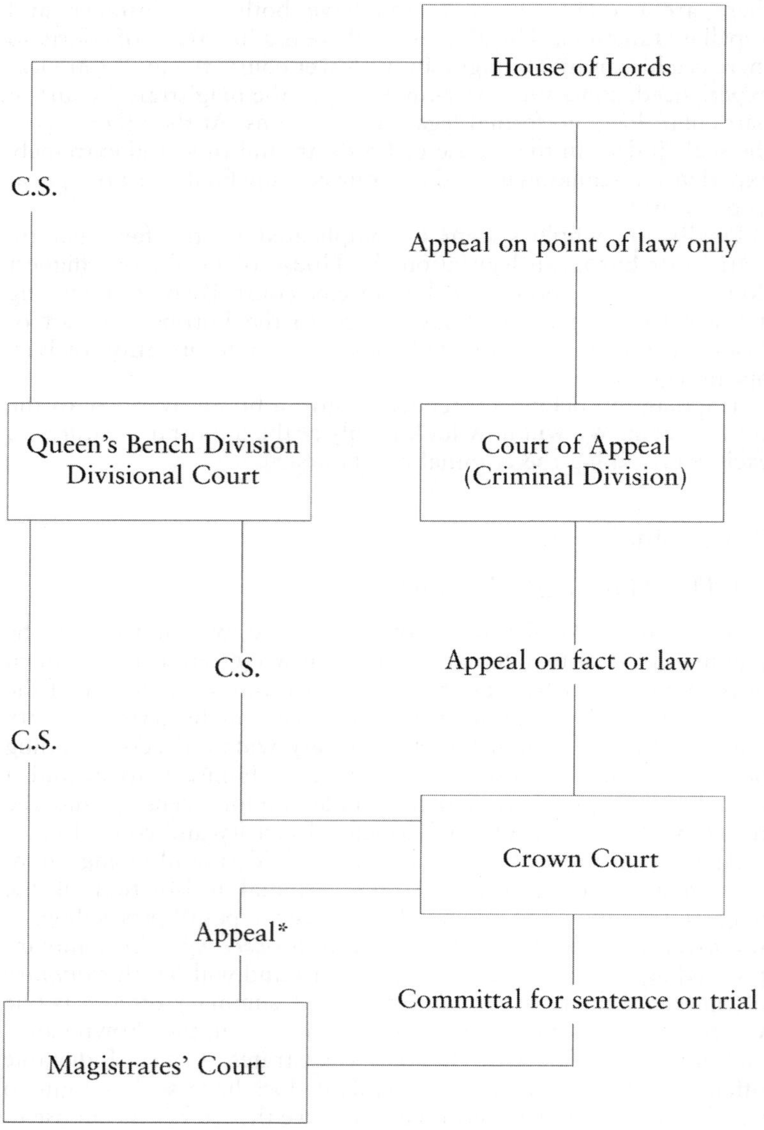

C.S. = Appeal by way of case stated.
* = Appeal against conviction or sentence.

Civil Court System

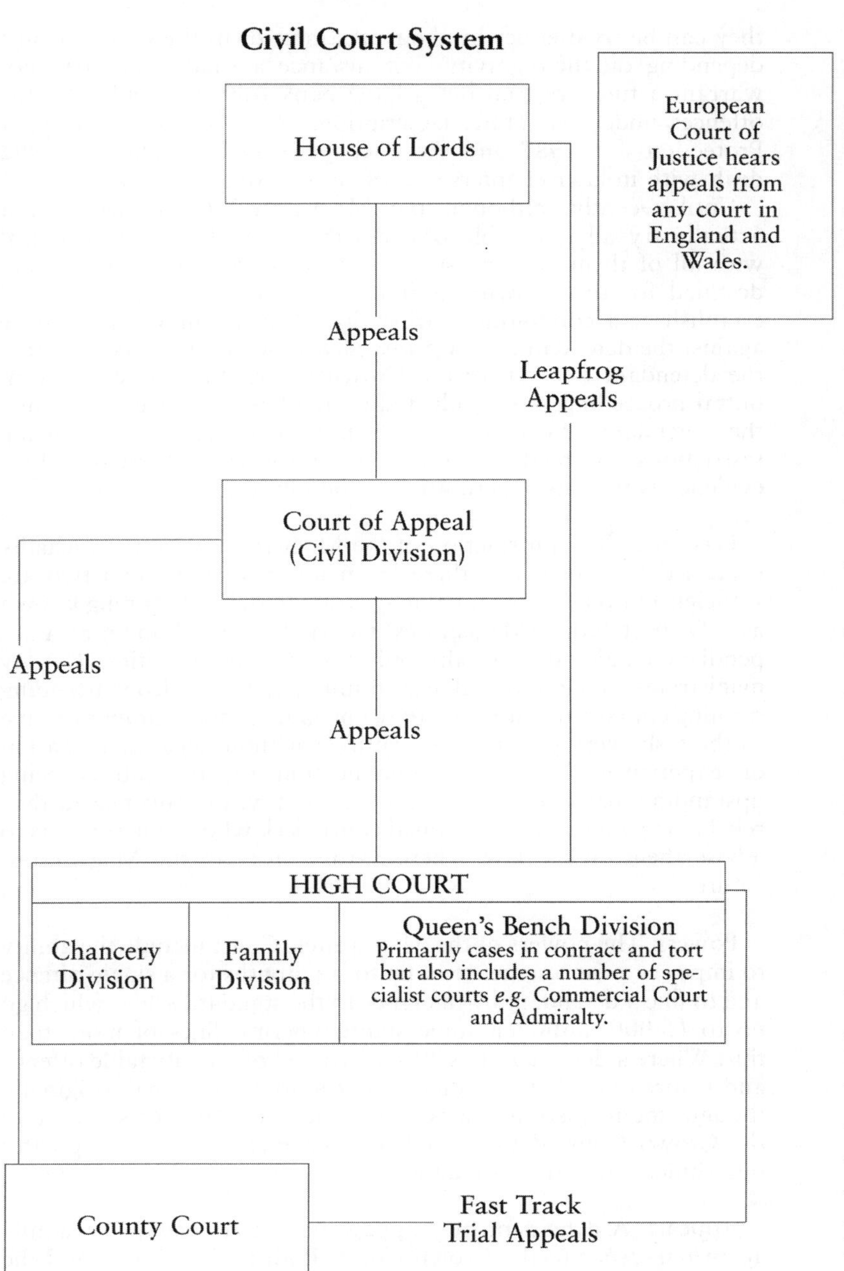

they can be tried either by the magistrates or in the Crown Court depending on their gravity. For instance a small theft may not warrant a full jury trial but a large bank robbery would. All the offences under the Trade Descriptions Act 1968, the Consumer Protection Act 1987 and the Package Travel Regulations 1992 dealt with in later chapters are offences triable either way.

Until recently, although the Magistrates' Court would not actually try all indictable offences they would nevertheless deal with all of them at some stage because in those cases which are destined for the Crown Court the prosecution must first of all establish at a committal hearing that there is sufficient evidence against the defendant, *i.e.* a *prima facie* case, to justify committing the defendant for trial to the Crown Court. In most cases committal proceedings are conducted on the basis of documents only, the defendant offers no defence and there are strict reporting restrictions enforced—something of a formality therefore. Live evidence is no longer permitted at committals.

Personnel. The jurisdiction of the Magistrates's Court is usually exercised by a bench of three lay magistrates (although two are sufficient) or one professional magistrate with legal training known as a District Judge (Magistrates' Court) formerly known as a stipendiary magistrate—usually only found in larger cities. The lay magistrates have no formal legal training and apart from attending training courses and agreeing to devote a minimum amount of time to the task every year they are entirely without legal qualification or experience. Their main qualification for the job is being upstanding members of the local community. For this reason they rely heavily on the legally trained court clerk whose function it is to advise them on the law. There are no juries in the Magistrates' Court.

Powers. The powers of the Magistrates' Court include the ability to impose a prison sentence of up to six months for a single offence and to fine a defendant by reference to the standard scales which go up to £5,000, although some statutes permit fines of more than this. Where a defendant has been convicted of an indictable offence and it turns out that the offence was more serious than originally thought the magistrates can commit the defendant for sentence in the Crown Court if they think the defendant deserves a greater punishment than they are able to mete out.

Appeals. A defendant may appeal against *conviction* or simply against *sentence* to the Crown Court. Both the defendant and the prosecutor can appeal on a *point of law* to the *Divisional Court.*

This latter process is known as an appeal by way of *case stated*. The Divisional Court is the Queens Bench Divisional Court which is a branch of the High Court. In limited circumstances the prosecution can appeal against sentence.

As far as the travel industry is concerned it is offences against the Trade Descriptions Act 1968, the Consumer Protection Act 1987 and the Package Travel Regulations that are most likely to bring them before the Magistrates' Court. Offences under this legislation are offences triable either way but in practice they tend to be dealt with summarily by the magistrates rather than on indictment in the Crown Court.

(b) The Crown Court

The main function of the Crown Court is to try indictable offences. It hears appeals against conviction and against sentence from the Magistrates' Court. It also hears those "either way" offences where the defendant or the court chose to have it heard in the Crown Court. Judges who sit in the Crown Court can be, in order of seniority, High Court judges, circuit judges or recorders. They are all legally qualified and cases are assigned to them according to the seriousness of the offence so for instance High Court judges will hear the most serious cases—murder, manslaughter, rape, etc—and circuit judges and recorders will hear the less serious cases. High Court judges and circuit judges are full time judges but recorders are only part time judges appointed for specific periods. Magistrates also sit in the Crown Court but only with other judges, on appeals.

If the defendant pleads guilty to an offence the court will proceed to sentence him without the aid of a jury but where the defendant pleads not guilty to a charge there will be a full trial with a jury. It is the function of the jury to decide on the facts of the case whether the defendant is guilty and for the judge to advise them on the law. It is no longer necessary for the jury to reach a unanimous verdict; it is possible for the jury to reach a decision on the basis of a majority verdict of not less than 10–2.

A defendant may make an appeal against conviction on a point of law as of right to the Court of Appeal Criminal Division but to appeal on a point of fact or against sentence leave to appeal must be given.

If the defendant has already appealed from the Magistrates' Court to the Crown Court then an appeal by way of case stated on a point of law can be made to the Divisional Court.

(c) The Divisional Court

The Queens Bench Division is a branch of the High Court—a civil court—but two High Court judges of the QBD, or a High Court judge and a Court of Appeal judge, can act as an appeal court to hear appeals by way of case stated from the Magistrates' Court and the Crown Court on points of law only. The appeal is based on documents only accompanied by legal argument from counsel but no witnesses are heard. Many travel cases involving criminal appeals have been heard in the Divisional Court including *Thomson Tour Operations v Birch* 163 JP 465 (1999); *Airtours v Shipley* 158 JP 835 (1994) and *Hotel Plan v Tameside MBC* [2001] EWHC Admin. 154. Despite this, surprisingly few appeals proceed down this simple and effective route.

There is a further right of appeal from the Divisional Court to the House of Lords but only if the case involves a point of law of general public importance and either the Divisional Court or the House of Lords gives leave to appeal.

(d) The Court of Appeal Criminal Division

The Court of Appeal hears criminal appeals against conviction and sentence where the defendant has been tried on indictment in the Crown Court. Appeals are usually heard by three *Lords Justices of Appeal* — although two is sufficient. The president of the Court of Appeal Criminal Division is the *Lord Chief Justice*.

A further appeal is possible to the House of Lords but again, only if a point of law of general public importance is involved and either the Court of Appeal or the House of Lords gives leave to appeal.

(e) The House of Lords

Parliament is made up of two legislative chambers—the House of Commons and the House of Lords. The House of Lords Judicial Committee, which is our final court of appeal is merely part of the House of Lords—but to confuse matters it is usually known simply as the House of Lords. Like the Court of Appeal it hears both criminal and civil appeals. Acting as a final court of appeal in criminal matters it hears appeals on points of law of general public importance from both the Divisional Court and the Court of Appeal Criminal Division. Very few criminal appeals actually reach the Judicial Committee—only about 10 are heard each year. One important travel case which did reach the House of Lords is *Wings Ltd v Ellis* [1985] A.C. 272 which concerned the interpretation of s.14 of the Trade Descriptions Act 1968 (see Chapter Eleven.)

The president of the House of Lords is the *Lord Chancellor* who, for historical reasons, occupies a unique place in our constitution by performing legislative, executive and judicial functions. The other judges in the House of Lords are life peers, known officially as *Lords of Appeal in Ordinary*, or more popularly as the Law Lords. Five judges usually hear an appeal but in important cases a full court of seven is assembled though this rarely happens. The Law Lords are all appointed on the basis of their judicial ability—unlike in the past when any member of the peerage was entitled to be a member of the Judicial Committee.

3. Civil Courts

(a) The County Court

There are about 300 County Courts in England and Wales presided over by Circuit Judges or District Judges (formerly called Registrars). They have a very wide jurisdiction over most civil matters and in most respects the County Court has the same jurisdiction as the High Court. What distinguishes the two is that the High Court deals with those cases which involve more money or which are of greater complexity. So for instance in civil disputes involving a breach of contract or the commission of a tort the County Court has jurisdiction over claims for any amount but in practice, as a general rule, those claims involving over £50,000 will be heard in the High Court. However cases involving amounts in excess of this are frequently heard in the County Court if the issues involved are relatively straightforward. The nature and value of package holiday claims are such that most of them will be heard in the County Court rather than the High Court.

One important aspect of the work of the County Court is what is popularly known as the Small Claims Court. This is where claims for £5000 or less (£1,000 for personal injury claims) are referred to a small claims trial by the District Judge. The procedure is informal and legal costs are not recoverable by either party. Many holiday claims are dealt with by this procedure. We look at it in much more detail in Chapter Seventeen.

In civil courts juries have been almost completely dispensed with and it is very rare indeed to find a jury in a County Court. On the rare occasions where a jury is used it consists of eight members.

Either party who is dissatisfied with the result of the action may appeal from the Circuit Judge to a High Court judge (fast track cases) or to the Court of Appeal Civil Division (multi-track cases). There are limitations on the right of appeal. Permission to appeal must be given. Appeals from the decision of a District Judge at a trial (small claims or fast track) or an interlocutory point are made to a Circuit Judge in the same County Court. Permission is again required. Appeals can only be made if the original decision was wrong, or unjust because of serious procedural or other irregularity (CPR 52.11).

(b) The High Court

The High Court sits mainly in London but also has regular sittings in the provinces. It is divided into three divisions—the Queen's Bench Division, the Chancery Division and the aptly named Family Division. The Queen's Bench Division is the busiest of the three. It hears contract and tort cases and also has specialist courts within the division—the Commercial Court and the Admiralty Court. Most holiday cases which are heard by the High Court will be dealt with in the Queen's Bench Division. The president of the Queen's Bench Division is the *Lord Chief Justice*; the Family Division is led by the President of the Family Division; and the head of the Chancery Division is nominally the Lord Chancellor but in practice he never sits and his functions are carried out by the Vice-Chancellor.

A single High Court judge (known also as a *puisne* judge) will try disputes, usually without the assistance of a jury. The only civil cases today that employ a jury on a regular basis are cases against the police and cases in defamation but even in defamation cases they are under attack for the level of damages they award.

The main difference in practice between the jurisdiction of the High Court and the County Court is that the High Court deals with cases of greater complexity; cases involving larger sums of money; and cases where the remedy required cannot be granted by the County Court. It also has an appeal jurisdiction which the County Court does not have. Each of the divisions of the High Court can sit as a Divisional Court where two judges hear appeals. We have already seen that the Queen's Bench Divisional Court hears criminal appeals from the Magistrates' Court and the Crown Court. There are also Family Divisional Courts and Chancery Divisional Courts.

Appeals against the decision of the High Court are made to the Court of Appeal Civil Division. On rare occasions in special circumstances an appeal can be made direct to the House of Lords which "leapfrogs" the Court of Appeal.

(c) Court of Appeal Civil Division

The Court of Appeal Civil Division hears appeals from the High Court and the County Court. As in the Criminal Division appeals are usually heard by three judges—Lords Justices of Appeal. The president of the Civil Division is the *Master of the Rolls*. Appeals from the Civil Division lie to the House of Lords if permission is given. There is no requirement that the appeal is on a point of law of general public importance but permission to appeal is unlikely to be given if it is not.

(d) House of Lords

Much of what was said about the House of Lords in its capacity as the final court of appeal in criminal cases applies to its function as a court of appeal in civil cases. The main practical difference is that the bulk of its time is spent on civil rather than criminal appeals and that it is possible for it to consider appeals on the facts as well as the law in civil cases.

4. European Court of Justice

For most purposes the House of Lords is the supreme court in the UK but for disputes which involve an element of European Union law the European Court of Justice (the ECJ; *www.curia. eu.int*) has an important function. The ECJ sits in Luxembourg and has 15 judges (and eight Advocates-General who assist the court) drawn from the member states.

The jurisdiction of the court includes hearing disputes between member states; deciding whether member states have fulfilled their obligations under European law; and to determine whether European institutions such as the Council and the Commission have acted illegally. It also has a power under Article 234 of the EC Treaty (formerly Article 177 of the EEC Treaty) to give preliminary rulings, in cases referred to it by domestic courts, on the interpretation of European legislation. What this means in practice is that if say, the Divisional Court was faced with a dispute over the meaning of part of the Package Travel Regulations and whether the Regulations properly reflected the meaning of the EC Directive on Package Travel the Divisional Court could refer the matter to the ECJ. While this was done the case in the Divisional Court would be adjourned until the ECJ gave a ruling on the meaning of the disputed provision. Then the Divisional Court would decide the case in the light of the interpretation provided by the ECJ. Thus the actual decision is made by the English court but only after the ECJ has provided guidance. In the *Dillenkofer* case referred to earlier this was the procedure followed by the German court before which the German consumers brought their case. The German court adjourned the case while the point of law was decided by the ECJ. Apart from the *Dillenkofer* case there have been a number of other cases referred to the ECJ on the intepretation of the Directive, including *AFS Intercultural Programs Finland ry v Kuluttajavirasto* (ECJ Case C–237/97), *Rechberger & Others v Republic of Austria* (ECJ Case C–140/97), *Verein fur Konsumenteninformation v Osterreichische Kreditversicherungs AG* (ECJ Case C–364/96) and: *Club-Tour, Viagens e Turismo Sa v Alberto Carlos Lobo Gonçalves Garrido* (ECJ case C–400/00).

Under Article 234 the position is that only the final court of appeal in the domestic system *must* refer a matter of interpretation to the ECJ. Courts lower in the hierarchy have a discretion whether or not to make a reference. In fact courts at all levels of our system have made references. The decision when to do so depends upon a number of factors including convenience, cost, the difficulty of the point of law, the existing state of the law and whether or not the reference will settle the matter.

Chapter Two
The Package Travel Regulations

Introduction

Until 1993 there was virtually no statutory control of package holidays. The relationship between tour operators and clients was left almost entirely to the common law. However in 1990 the Council of the European Communities (the EC) adopted a Directive—The Package Travel, Package Holidays and Package Tours Directive (90\314\EEC) which had to be implemented by EC members by December 31, 1992. As a consequence the British Parliament passed the snappily entitled Package Travel, Package Holidays and Package Tours Regulations (SI 1992/3288) at the end of 1992. For most purposes it brought the Directive into effect from December 23, 1992.

It is hard to overestimate the effect that these Regulations have had on the travel industry. The provisions in the Regulations created a completely new statutory framework within which tour operators must now work. Important new civil liabilities were imposed and there are a battery of new criminal offences. Additionally a new system of consumer protection was created to protect clients against the insolvency of tour operators. However, having said that it is important to realise that despite their undoubted significance the Regulations are not comprehensive—they do not set out to regulate every aspect of the package holiday contract. Large parts of the contract still remain a matter for the common law. For instance the calculation of damages is one aspect of contract that is largely untouched by the Regulations. Damages are still determined by decisions based on the case of *Jarvis v Swans Tours Ltd* [1973] 1 All E.R. 71; [1973] Q.B. 233. (See Chapter 10). Even here however there is increasing European influence—see *Leitner v TUI Deutschland GmbH & Co. KG* (ECJ Case C–168/00).

What has happened is that a large number of additional rules have been created which operate alongside the ordinary law of contract and impact upon it to a greater or lesser extent. Thus on the one hand the rules on offer and acceptance have not been changed but an operator has to be much more alert to the rules because a number of Regulations require him to provide information to clients before the contract is made—on pain of committing a criminal offence (Regulation 7) or of running the risk that a client can withdraw from the contract (Regulation 9). By contrast the existing law on on privity of contract is greatly changed because the Regulations provide that persons other than the immediate parties to the contract acquire rights under it and can sue.

Those two examples are relatively straightforward but this is not always the case. Take frustration of contract for instance. Nothing in the Regulations specifically excludes the rules on frustration of contract or the Law Reform (Frustrated Contracts) Act 1943 so we must assume that they continue to apply to package holiday contracts. However the Regulations do introduce a new concept to package holidays—the concept of *force majeure*. *Force majeure* resembles frustration of contract in many ways but there are significant differences—not only in its application but also in the consequences that flow from it. The result is not entirely clear but in our view the effect of the new *force majeure* rules is to render the rules on frustration of contract largely redundant (see Chapter 9).

Because of this close inter-relationship between the Regulations and the existing law the Regulations will not be treated as a separate topic. Instead the provisions will be integrated into the appropriate sections of the book wherever they are relevant. However it is important that certain issues arising from the Regulations are dealt with at the outset because they are necessary for a full understanding of what comes later. In particular the scope of the Regulations and some of the more important definitions will be dealt with now rather than later. A brief overview will also be given at this stage so that you can grasp the full import of the Regulations at an early stage.

Scope Of The Regulations

One purpose of the Directive on Package Travel was to regulate conventional package holidays—two weeks of sun, sea and sand in the Mediterranean basin and other similar arrangements. On this everyone is agreed but unfortunately (or fortunately depending upon your perspective), the scope of the definition of a "package" in Regulation 2 is so wide that it goes far beyond conventional package holidays. Much of what it takes in in addition to conventional packages, is uncontroversial, *e.g.* coach trips to London involving overnight accommodation and perhaps a show; or special weekends offered by hotels and guest houses—murder and mystery weekends, etc. Beyond that, however, there are an amazing variety of travel and holiday arrangements over which fierce arguments rage—do they or don't they come within the definition of package, *e.g.* overnight ferry trips to the Continent; business travel; holiday camps and caravan sites; "tailor-made" packages put together by travel agents; sleeper accommodation on the railways; "bareboat" charters; holidays provided by local authority social services departments for their pensioners; "reproductive tourism" for childless couples (*The Independent*, p.11, May 18, 2002); "face-lift safaris" for those wanting a package including cosmetic surgery (*The Independent*, p.5, July 1, 2001); and activity holidays provided by schools or local education authorities? Both the Department for Trade and Industry (DTI), the government department responsible for guiding the legislation through Parliament, and ABTA, the main trade association, issued guidelines on the scope of the Regulations and they disagreed fundamentally on the extent of the definition. LACORS (formerly LACOTS), the Local Authorities Co-ordinators of Regulatory Services Standards, have also issued guidance notes on some of the more difficult aspects of the Regulations. Of much more significance than these commentaries are recent decisions of the European Court of Justice: *AFS Intercultural Programs Finland ry* (Case C–237/97, February 11, 1999); *Rechberger v Austria* (Case C–140/97, June 15, 1999), and *Club Tour Viagens e Turismo SA v Alberto Carlos Lobo Goncalves Garrido* (Case 400/00, April 30, 2002) in which the Court gave its views on what constituted a package. We will give our own views on the above examples in due course. The European Commission has also issued a consultation document (Report on the Implementation of Directive 90/314/EEC on Package Travel and Holiday Tours in the Domestic Legislation of EC Member States, SEC (1999) 1800 final) in which it canvasses opinion on reforms to the Directive.

The problem that the broadness of the definition causes is that a set of rules designed for one purpose may have to be applied to a set of circumstances for which they were not designed. Operators selling non-conventional packages will find themselves square pegs in round holes.

This chapter is concerned with examining the scope of the definitions in the Regulations with a view to determining what falls within the Regulations and is subject to its regime and what falls outside and remains regulated solely by the common law.

1. The definition of package

The Regulations define package in the following manner:

"2(1) 'Package' means the pre-arranged combination of at least two of the following components when sold or offered for sale at an inclusive price and when the service covers a period of more than twenty-four hours or includes overnight accommodation:

(a) transport;
(b) accommodation;
(c) other tourist services not ancillary to transport or accommodation and accounting for a significant proportion of the package,

and

(i) the submission of separate accounts for different components shall not cause the arrangements to be other than a package;
(ii) the fact that a combination is arranged at the request of the consumer and in accordance with his specific instructions (whether modified or not) shall not of itself cause it to be treated as other than pre-arranged;"

This definition poses a large number of problems of interpretation:

(a) "Pre-arranged Combination"

This covers a standard brochured package, *i.e.* an "off the shelf" package and therefore conventional tour operators will clearly be encompassed within this part of the definition. The question arises however as whether it covers "tailor-made" packages put together by travel agents, or indeed by tour operators? Does pre-arranged mean pre-arranged *before the client enters a travel agency* or does it mean that all the components of the package are in place *before the client travels?* It could also mean put together *before the contract is concluded*. If it is either of the latter two then a travel agent or tour operator who puts ad hoc travel and accommodation components together for clients could become liable for the proper performance of the whole arrangement. Not only will the travel agent/tour operator incur liability for the whole package but it will also mean that he is subject to the bonding and insurance regime.

Until recently this was a question that caused considerable difficulty for travel agents but following the *Club Tour* case the position is much clearer. The facts of the case were that the defendant booked a holiday through a travel agency in Portugal. The holiday consisted of accommodation at an all-inclusive resort operated by Club Med in Greece plus flights from Portugal. It was the travel agent who combined the flights with the all-inclusive resort. While on holiday the resort became infested with thousands of wasps which prevented the defendant from enjoying his stay. Despite his complaints, neither the travel agency nor Club Med could provide suitable alternative accommodation. On his return the defendant refused to pay for the holiday and the travel agent sued him. The domestic court in Portugal referred the case to the European Court of Justice for a ruling on two issues. The first of these was whether arrangements put together by a travel agent at the request of, and according to the specifications of, a consumer or defined group of consumers fell within the definition of a package. The second was whether the term "pre-arranged combination" could be interpreted as meaning a package put together at the time when the contract was concluded. In a very brief judgment (see [2002] ITLJ 55) the European Court of Justice held that both questions should be answered in the affirmative. On the first issue the court said that there was nothing in the definition which prevented such arrangements from being a package; and on the second issue it said that, given the answer to the first question, then it necessarily followed that the arrangements were pre-arranged if they consisted of elements chosen by the consumer before the contract was concluded.

It is worthwhile mentioning as an aside that the judgment is in line with the recommendation made in the European Commission consultation document which said:

> "... the word 'pre-arranged' seems to be artificial, of unclear meaning and effect and could be eliminated." (p.8)

Such an approach was also foreshadowed in our own legislation. One modification to the Directive that can be found in the Regulations is Regulation 2(1)(c)(ii) which states:

> "the fact that a combination is arranged at the request of the consumer and in accordance with his specific instructions (whether modified or not) shall not of itself cause it to be treated as other than pre-arranged."

This gives the impression that a tailor made package is within the definition of package but closer examination reveals that this is not so. It is merely stating that there is nothing in the definition of a package that *prevents* a tailor made package from being a package. It does *not* say that a combination that is put together at the request of the consumer *is* a package. However, in conjunction with the *Club Tour* case, there is clearly nothing in the UK legislation to prevent a similar approach being taken by the UK courts.

The consequences of this for travel agents are far-reaching. If, as the case suggests, most travel agents who put tailor-made packages together are within the scope of the Directive then they will have to comply with all the requirements of the Directive. In practical terms this means that they must comply with the information regime; they must be bonded; and they must accept liability for all the components of the package—including all the defaults of the hotels they book for clients in whatever far off place clients choose to go to. (see Chapter fifteen on the legal position of travel agents).

Although the *Club Tour* case goes a long way to clarifying one of the more contentious parts of the law, and it clearly renders redundant much of the discussion that was included in earlier editions of this book, there are nevertheless some types of arrangement which either fall outside the definition or where the answer is not so clear cut. One type of arrangement which falls outside the definition are excursions or other arrangements which are purchased in resort or after the package has been sold. *Gallagher v Airtours Holidays Ltd* [2001] C.L.Y. 4280 is a simple example of such a case. The claimant had purchased a skiing holiday from the defendants and then, while on the transfer bus to the resort, had purchased a "ski-pack". She was injured due to the alleged negligence of the skiing tutor whose services were included in the ski-pack. It was held, amongst other things, that there was no liability under the Package Travel Regulations because the ski-pack was not part of the "pre-arranged combination" that made up the package (see also *Sheppard v Crystal Holidays Ltd* [1997] C.L.Y. 3858). There is nothing however to prevent a tour operator voluntarily accepting liability for excursions which do not form part of a pre-arranged combination. *Waters v Thomson* [2000] 8 C.L. 106 is such a case; where the tour operator did accept liability but was found not liable on the facts. (See also *Excursions: Tour Operators and the Negligence of Local Suppliers*, M Chapman [2002] I.T.L.J. 123).

More difficult are those arrangements which are referred to as "contract splitting". Very broadly what this means is that one party, either the travel agent or tour operator, sells the consumer the elements of a package, most commonly flights and hotel accommodation, but denies that it makes up a package on the grounds that the consumer is not making one contract, with the travel agent or tour operator, but two contracts—with the suppliers of the transport and accommodation. The rationale behind this is apparently that the travel agent/tour operator is not a principal, making a contract in his own right but only an agent making a contract on behalf of others—the suppliers. While this is a perfectly legitimate claim, and can actually be seen as enhancing the rights of the consumer by giving him direct rights against the supplier that he might not otherwise have, it does not necessarily mean that the travel agent/tour operator is outside the scope of the Regulations. Liability is imposed on "organisers" not "principals" and the term "organiser" cuts across the conventional categories of principal and agent. It is possible to be an agent but also an "organiser" and therefore have liabilities under the Regulations. What is important in this context is whether the organiser has put together a package which amounts to a "pre-arranged combination".

At one end of the scale, where the elements of the package are contained in a brochure, and where the consumer can "pick and mix" from a wide offering of transport and accommodation, any statement to the effect that this is not a package because the consumer is merely entering into separate contracts with different suppliers is unlikely to succeed. The travel agent/tour operator who put the brochure together will be regarded as selling a pre-arranged combination every bit as much as the travel agent in the *Club Tour* case, if not more so.

At the other end of the scale much more difficult issues are raised by those internet sites which offer the consumer the facility to book both flights and accommodation by entering into separate contracts with airlines and hotels. Current examples [Spring 2003] include the websites of Ryanair, easyJet and Opodo. After booking the flight the consumer is invited to book a hotel as well and on taking up the invitation a separate site opens up from which the hotel can be booked. When the consumer has completed the booking he will have two contracts with two suppliers represented by two separate debits on his credit card. Does this amount to a "pre-arranged combination" sold by an "organiser"?

Leaving aside for the moment the issue of whether these arrangements are sold at an "inclusive price", which is discussed below, the immediate problem facing the consumer is that the arrangements he has made appear to be separate arrangements with two separate suppliers rather than a combination. This is probably no accident; the separation of the elements may be just what the website host sets out to achieve—in all probability it has been done deliberately so as to avoid creating a package. In commercial terms it produces two benefits that we referred to earlier—there will be no need to incur the cost of bonding the arrangements, nor will liability for the defaults of the suppliers have to be taken on.

What is the difference, it can be argued, between this situation, where the airline, as a convenience to the consumer, provides a link from his website to the site of a separate trader altogether, and the situation where the consumer logs off one site and then proceeds to the other site himself. Where the consumer makes his way independently to the sites could this be regarded as a "pre-arranged combination"? Is it not more akin to the situation where the consumer, using less technologically advanced methods, telephones the airline and books tickets and then, in a separate call, books his hotel room. No one would call this latter arrangement a package so why should the former be one simply because the number of clicks required is fewer?

On the other hand, what is the difference between what these sites can do for the consumer and what a travel agent can do? If I go into a travel agency as an independent traveller the agent can log on to a CRS or a viewdata system and book my flights and then log on to another system and book my hotel rooms—probably accessing the same inventory in the same way as the internet host site. If, according to the *Club Tour* case this would be a package when put together by the travel agent, why would it not be a package when put together by the company hosting the internet site? The travel agent hosts the CRSs in physical premises on the high street whereas the internet operator hosts them in cyberspace but it is essentially the same process.

Another way of looking at it would be to ask what is the purpose of such sites, which permit a consumer to book both flights and accommodation at the same time and also what are the commercial relationships between the host and the other suppliers on the site. A further question might be to ask how the arrangements are viewed by the consumer.

The answer to the first question is that the host, for good commercial reasons, wants to be able to offer the consumer more. Purchasing services over the internet can be a frustrating business and the convenience of buying all ones travel needs via one site is very attractive to the consumer. Putting it another way it means that the host can offer "one stop shopping" for the consumer—permitting him to buy what is to all intents a package.

Looking at the second question it may very well be the case that the host is making money not only on his own product but may also profit from sales made by the other suppliers with links from his site. If this were the case it becomes more difficult to distinguish the conventional travel agent from the internet host in that they both perform similar functions and are rewarded in much the same way. All that the links between the websites do is to make more transparent a process that already takes place in a travel agency.

Viewed from the consumer's perspective, if he gives any thought to the transaction, he may very well consider that by the time he logs off the site he has purchased a combination of elements that could constitute a package. Again, the transparency of the transaction may be an issue. If it is not clear to the consumer that he is leaving the host's website and entering that of another supplier's it could be argued that the host could be seen to be putting a combination together. The more "seamless" the transition is between the sites the more likely this argument is to succeed. Where the transition is clearly flagged up and there are clear indications that the consumer has ceased to deal with one company and is now dealing with another then the argument becomes harder to sustain. But how different is this from the travel agent who says "I have booked you a flight with BA and you now have a contract with them for a transatlantic flight and now I am going to book you a Marriott hotel in New York using another CRS and when I have finished you will also have a separate contract with them?"

It must not be forgotten when looking at these more difficult cases that there are travel websites, such as *Expedia* and *last minute.com*, where the host does acknowledge that they are selling packages and are bonded against insolvency and therefore the problems arising from contract splitting are not an issue.

(b) "Inclusive Price"

Most clients will pay an "inclusive" price for their holiday whether it be "off the shelf" or tailor-made unless perhaps the components of the tailor-made package were purchased at different times. Used in this sense the word inclusive merely means that the price the client pays includes everything he is getting whether the package is off the shelf or tailor-made. It is hard to see what this adds to the definition unless another, special, meaning can be placed on the word "inclusive".

For instance it might be possible to interpret the word restrictively as meaning only those prices where the price is a global price for the whole package and where the individual components of the package are not priced or costed out. In other words where the price of the individual elements is disguised from the client. The argument would be that where a tailor-made package has been put together and the elements are itemised on the invoice before being totalled up the final price would not be an inclusive price. But this raises the problem of conventional packages where certain elements can be priced separately, *e.g.* airport supplements and meal supplements.

If such a distinction can be made then this might be one way of taking tailor-made packages out of the Regulations. However there are limitations on this approach because the Regulation clearly states that:

> "the submission of separate accounts for different components shall not cause the arrangements to be other than a package." (Regulation 2(1)(c)(i))

This reflects the provisions of the Directive (Article 2(1)) which states:

> "The separate billing of various components of the same package shall not absolve the organizer or retailer from the obligations under this Directive"

Clearly that prevents an operator from breaking up an acknowledged package and submitting separate invoices and claiming it is not a package because it is not sold at an inclusive price. But does it prevent a travel agent from separately itemising on one bill the different components of a tailor-made package and arguing that it is not a package as defined in the Regulations on the grounds that he is not selling it at an inclusive price? To go one stage further does it prevent the same agent submitting more than one invoice for the tailor-made package and arguing that this is quite legitimate because it is not a package?

Looked at this way the travel agent is deploying two arguments to buttress his case. First he is saying that this is not a package because it is not a "pre-arranged combination". Then he consolidates that view by issuing an itemised invoice or more than one invoice to reflect the fact that these are separate components not sold at an inclusive price.

The trouble with this approach is that it creates the impression of being a sham. Far from being an effective means of evading the Regulations it would probably have the counter-productive effect of alienating those judges who encountered it. So it will be difficult for a travel agent to convince a court that it is not selling holidays at an inclusive price but to avoid such a conclusion we would suggest that probably the only safe way of not selling at an inclusive price is to demonstrate that the consumer booked components on separate occasions. Even then however there are dangers, as the DTI point out:

> "... someone wanting to book a package holiday could be sold accommodation and told to return later to arrange and purchase the necessary transport. This would create separate bills for each element, but such an artificial arrangement would not mean that a package had not been sold." (*Looking into the Package Travel Regulations*, p.7, note 14, DTI, 1996)

LACORS cites the example of a travel agent who purchased airline tickets to Athens for a client and then contacted an hotel in Athens and arranged for the client to stay for a week. The client gave the travel agent his credit card number to pay for both components. The agent in turn gave the hotel the credit card number and the hotel debited the client's account directly and paid the agent a commission. Acknowledging that this is a grey area LACORS nevertheless advise that the arrangements "had best be treated as a package" on the grounds "that there would be some linking of the two elements—not least in the mind of the consumer." Certainly the fact that the two elements may be linked will go to establish that there is a "combination" but does it satisfy the requirement that the combination be sold at an inclusive price? LACORS answer this by saying that if the consumer was aware of the separate nature of the transactions and therefore aware that the price he would pay was not an inclusive price then it would not be a package. On the other hand, they seem to be saying, if he was not aware that his credit card was financing two separate transactions then he would believe he was paying an inclusive price. (*Package Travel Regulations 1992 "Tailor-Made Packages*, CO 10 94 12, issued April 28, 1994).

This advice was given before the decision in the *Club Tour* case and may not have survived it. If, as seems the case, the travel agent could be seen to have "organised" a "package" then the fact that two separate payments have to be made might simply be regarded as falling foul of Article 2(1) of the Directive. In the Commission's consultation document (paragraph 1.2.1) they suggest that "the element *inclusive price* has only indicative character" and needs clarifying. Given the purposive approach that the ECJ is likely to take if asked to provide such clarification it is quite possible that two separate payments would be regarded as artificial and the arrangements categorised as a package.

This would also have repercussions for the "contract splitting" arrangements discussed above. If an "inclusive price" could be interpreted as encompassing the situation where separate invoices were issued by separate companies who were linked by the same website then such arrangements might very well fall within the Regulations.

In the *Rechberger* case referred to in the introduction the facts were that the claimants had won a prize offered by a daily newspaper. As regular subscribers they were offered the opportunity of a holiday abroad on very advantageous terms. If they travelled alone all they had to pay was an airport departure tax and a single room supplement—flights and accommodation being otherwise free. If they travelled with a companion who paid the full price all the subscribers had to pay was the airport tax. The newspaper left the organisation of the holidays to a tour operator. Unfortunately the offer proved to be far more successful than the tour operator had anticipated, and this caused logistical and financial difficulties which forced it into bankruptcy. The claimants, who had all paid in full, had all had their holidays cancelled and lost their money. The reason for this was twofold. First, the Austrian government had not implemented the provisions in the Directive relating to insolvency in accordance with the deadline laid down in the Directive; secondly when they did implement it, the provisions were not adequate to protect consumers as the bank guarantees required by the Austrian legislation were not enough to cover the losses incurred by the consumers. Thus some of the claimants were suing the Austrian government for non-implementation of the Directive and others for improper or inadequate implementation—depending on whether they had booked their holidays before or after the implementation date.

One of the issues in dispute at domestic level was whether or not those consumers who travelled alone fell within the scope of the Directive. In those circumstances, the national court decided to stay proceedings and refer the following questions to the Court for a preliminary ruling:

> (1) Does the protective purpose of Article 7 of Council Directive 90/314/EEC of 13 June 1990 on package travel, package holidays and package tours also extend to trips for which, on the basis of the contract, the principal contractor has to pay:
>
> (a) if he travels alone, apart from airport security tax (departure tax), only a single-room supplement, or
> (b) if he is accompanied by one or more persons paying the full price, only the airport security tax (departure tax)
>
> and nothing in respect of the flight and accommodation in a room with two or more beds?

The court held that there was a pre-arranged combination of at least two elements and that even though what the consumers paid for the package did not correspond to its value, or even to one component, it was nevertheless a package. To put it another way, the price was inclusive even if the price didn't cover everything that the consumer obtained (see Chapter sixteen on insolvency and security.)

Note that when excursions are bought in resort from tour operators it would be difficult to regard these as being purchased as part of an inclusive price (see the cases mentioned earlier: *Gallagher, Shephard* and *Waters*, and the Chapman article.)

(c) "Two of the Following"

What about "flight only" packages which, at the insistence of some foreign governments, technically include accommodation (not uncommonly a tent in a field a hundred miles from the airport) which in practice is never used? If tour operators are judged according to the strict letter of the law then so long as they offer accommodation, no matter how basic, they appear to be covered by the Regulations. But if they openly recognised the reality of the situation and offered no accommodation at all then they would fall outside the Regulations (so long as they only offered the flight). Thanks however to the liberalisation of air travel within Europe "flight only" which comes with nominal accommodation is very much a thing of the past and it is only for packages outside Europe that this will continue to be a problem.

(d) "Accommodation"

Hotels, dormitories, caravans, chalets and tents—and probably even timeshare exchanges—would all fall within the meaning of accommodation and would form one element of a package but there are marginal forms of accommodation which will cause difficulty. For instance what about a berth on a North Sea ferry or a sleeper on an overnight train? If accommodation is to be equated with sleeping accommodation and if, as is generally the case, extra is paid for this "accommodation" then it would be hard to deny that it fell within the definition. The difficulty is that first, the perception of such arrangements is that the main purpose of such contracts is the transport element and the accommodation is entirely incidental to it. Secondly, although this is not a fatal argument, such arrangements are often not regarded or even purchased as a holiday or for leisure purposes. People do not regard them as "package holidays".

The answer to the first argument is that there is no requirement in the definition that the accommodation makes up a *significant* element of the package—merely that the package includes accommodation. Secondly it should be borne in mind that the Regulations are not concerned exclusively with holidays. They are directed at a wider concept—tourism—which takes in not simply leisure travel but also business travel and other forms of tourism. This might be sufficient to account for the berth on the ferry and the sleeping compartment on the train but what about a couchette on the ferry or the reclining seats in the first class sections on planes that can be turned into beds? Given that all transport requires the provision of accommodation in the widest sense there has to be a line drawn between what is purely accommodation for the purposes of travel—seats—and accommodation which goes beyond this—berths and sleeping compartments.

The Trading Standards Institute (formerly the Institute of Trading Standards Administration) has indicated its view that accommodation incidental to travel to a destination and where the consumer is not participating in a holiday does not create a package. This view can be typified as the "instinctive" or "common sense" approach. Would the man on the Clapham omnibus agree that a passenger who booked a sleeping compartment on the overnight train from Aberdeen to London had purchased a package? Of course not. While not denying that such an approach has its merits it is nevertheless hard to square with the precise words of the definition and it ignores the view that tourism encompasses more than simply holidays and leisure travel. The DTI guidelines endorse the TSI view:

> "For 'accommodation' to be an element in the creation of a package, the Department considers that it needs to represent more than a facility which is ancillary to other aspects of an arrangement. It would regard for example, a berth on a cross-channel ferry or sleeping accommodation on an overnight train as a facility. But a cabin on a cruise ship would, in the opinion of the Department, create a package because the consumer is being accommodated whilst being taken on a pre-arranged itinerary ... "

Interestingly, those companies which run overnight North Sea ferry crossings from England to continental Europe are increasingly emphasising the luxury and comfort of their ships and the nature of the onboard experience. No longer are they simply ferries, they are now "Cruiseferries". (The Pride of Rotterdam is "the largest most luxurious Cruiseferry in the world" *Travel Trade Gazette*, April 30, 2001.)

In the *AFS Finland* case referred to earlier the facts were that AFS was an organisation whose object was to promote international co-operation and exchanges between various cultures. To that end, like its sister organisations in other countries, it organised exchange programmes for students aged between 16 and 18 years of age. To organise these activities AFS relied on the support of various donors and foundations as well as on the work of volunteers. It also received aid from the Finnish State in order to finance its activities. AFS sent students abroad twice a year, usually for a period of six to 11 months. The students attended schools in the host country and lodged with families which put them up free of charge. AFS selected the students and placed them with suitable families selected on the basis of interviews. AFS arranged the students' transport to the host country by scheduled flights and, as a rule, the host family collected the student at the arrival point. Before departure the students had to prepare themselves by following courses on conditions abroad. Ten per cent of the cost of the journey was paid when the student was admitted to the exchange programme, that is to say normally about 10 months before departure. The balance was then paid before the beginning of the visit, in three installments. On departure, the student received a pre-paid return air ticket. Part of AFS's fees went into a reserve fund which ensured, amongst other things, that the student could be transported home in circumstances where the return ticket issued to them could not be used for some reason.

A number of issues arose from the case but the one of particular relevance here is whether or not the stay with the host family could be regarded as "accommodation" within the meaning of Article 2(1)(b) of the Directive (the equivalent of Regulation 2(1) of the Regulations). The court considered that the fact that the accommodation was free, that it was not in hotel or similar accommodation and that it was for a long period of time were not reasons in themselves for saying that the stay with the family was not "accommodation" as defined. However they went on to say that:

> "their combined effect is such that "hosting" which possesses all those characteristics cannot be described as accommodation within the meaning of the Directive."

There is little or no reasoning in support of this view but taken in the context of the whole case the Court seems to be saying that this is not the kind of accommodation that the Directive was intended to cover because it is not "holiday" or "tourist" accommodation. This is a somewhat restrictive view of the scope of the Directive, one which we will return to when we look at the meaning of "other tourist services" below. Interestingly, the Advocate-General's opinion in the *AFS* case, which the court chose not to follow was unequivocal on the question of accommodation. He said:

> "The definition of 'accommodation', in its turn, clearly covers any kind of accommodation, whether it be in a hotel, with a family, in a hostel, or wherever. The duration of the accommodation is of no importance in the scheme of the Directive, which, in this regard, does no more than lay down a minimum

limit: the whole service offered to the consumer must ast not less than 24 hours or must at least include overnight accommodation. By the same logic, the fact that the student is received into the family with which he boards as if he were a child of the family, is also of no consequence."

(e) "Transport"

In general there should be little difficulty with this part of the definition. There may however be doubts over such things as cycling holidays or fly/drive holidays. With the former can it be said that transport is an element of the package when it is the client who actually transports himself from A to B? Does transport mean that the client *is transported* from A to B or can it also encompass a situation where a *means of transport* is provided and the client accomplishes the journey himself. In the cycling holiday example it may not matter because even if the cycle does not qualify as transport it will amount to another "tourist service" and still form one element of a package assuming accommodation is also provided.

On the other hand in a fly/drive holiday if the drive element *is* regarded as transport there is no package but if it can be classified as another tourist service there is a package. A court may very well say that fly/drive "feels" like a package, that car hire is a tourist service, and therefore the consumer has the protection of the Regulations. In practice the distinction may not matter thanks to the tendency of many tour operators using the same set of terms and conditions to cover fly/drive holidays as well as conventional packages and thereby conferring on their fly/drive consumers the same rights as their other clients.

(f) "Other Tourist Services Not Ancillary To Transport Or Accommodation"

What is a *tourist* service? Is there a class of services which are exclusive to tourists? Can a service be distinguished from a facility? When is the service ancillary to transport or accommodation and when is it not? Are meals at an hotel ancillary to the accommodation? All these words cause difficulty and have provoked some of the greatest disagreements about the scope of the Regulations.

"Other". The question implicitly raised by this word is: "Other than what?" And the answer must be "other than transport and accommodation". In other words if the service consists of transport or accommodation then it cannot be another tourist service. The Regulations are drawing a distinction between services which are transport and accommodation and other services. This may very well be the solution to the problem raised above about fly/drive and cycling holidays. Car hire and cycle hire are undoubtedly services but they are transport services and therefore should be classified as transport and not as other tourist services. This problem cries out for an authoritative judicial decision.

"Tourist". If a tourist is regarded as simply someone who travels for pleasure, a holidaymaker in other words, then the ambit of the Regulations is much reduced. The DTI's opinion, as expressed in their guidance notes on the Regulations, takes such a limited view:

> "For example, a conference which included the provision of accommodation would not be a package just because of this, as a conference is not a tourist service. In the opinion of the Department, education is not a tourist service, provided it is undertaken with a view to obtaining a recognised qualification."

It is interesting to see that the Department have softened their line on this. In the first issue of their guidelines they took a much stronger line:

> "Examples of services which are not tourist services are: educational services, business services, conference services etc."

In the *AFS Finland* case the ECJ specifically addressed the question of whether the arrangement of the student visits amounted to "other tourist services". Their answer, albeit brief, was quite categorical. On the issue of the selection of a school they said:

> "In this connection, it should first be observed that selection of a school by the organiser of the package cannot in itself be regarded as a tourist service within the meaning of Article 2(1)(c) of the Directive. The specific purpose of such a service, offered to the students taking part in international student exchanges, is the education of the participants."

And on the issue of selecting a host family they said:

> "Next, the service constituted by the selection of a family to host a student during his stay is in any event an ancillary service within the meaning of Article 2(1)(c) of the Directive and is therefore not covered by the concept of other tourist services."

Thus they are not prepared to extend the meaning of tourist beyond someone who travels for pleasure or leisure—which is consistent with the overall philosophy that they applied to the Directive.

However, any respectable definition of tourist goes much further than "someone who travels for pleasure" (see *Who is a tourist? Issues arising from the Package Travel Regulations,* M Robinson [1995] TLJ 77 for definitions of tourist and tourism). People who travel on business and for educational purposes, or as pilgrims (the original tourists), would all qualify as tourists. Thus a business conference which included hotel accommodation as well as business sessions would constitute a package. More surprisingly an Open University summer school, if purchased as a single transaction, would also be a package. Perhaps the surprise would not be so great if it was accepted that participants in such activities could all be legitimately classified as tourists—every bit as much as the lager lout in Benidorm. Of course many educational or business trips include both transport and accommodation and their status as packages is therefore beyond doubt. However if educational and business services were not tourist services then there is a potential paradox. If the consumer buys only accommodation and an educational or business service then no package exists and there is no recourse against the organiser for defaults in the services under the PTR. However if transport were added to the arrangements then this would constitute a package and the defaults in the non-tourist services would fall within the PTR.

Again, the Advocate-General in the *AFS* case was at odds with the stance eventually taken by the court. On the issue of tourist he had this to say:

> "20. The purposes of the Directive, its wording and the preparatory work leading up to it disclose nothing to suggest that its scope is limited *exclusively* to tourist services. Since the Directive is a measure for the harmonisation of national laws which has as its main objective the protection of the weaker party to the travel contract, it is clear that all package services sold within the territory of the Community are subject to those requirements of consumer protection which justify the application of the protective provisions referred to in the Directive. As for the wording of the Directive itself, it is clear even from its title that is applies to package travel, package holidays and package tours, and this plainly means that there are types of travel included within the Directive's scope of application which are not undertaken for the purpose of holidays in the strict sense. Article 2(4) of the Directive, which contains a definition of 'consumer', also mili-

tates in favour of a broad interpretation of the scope of the Directive. As observed by the Finnish Government, that provision does no more than state that 'consumer' means the person who takes or agrees to take the package, as defined in Article 2, without laying down any requirements with respect to the purposes of the travel, and indeed this is quite different from what one finds in certain other directives aimed at protecting the consumer in which the concept of 'consumer' is expressly limited to 'any natural person who acts for purposes other than those of his professional business'.

21. Moreover, even if one were to concede that the Directive meant only to deal with services in the nature of Tourism, I do not think that this justifies, in any event, the conclusion proposed by the plaintiff in the main proceedings and by the United Kingdom Government. The problem would immediately arise of defining the concept of tourism, the answer to which appears to be anything but clear-cut. It is manifestly not equivalent to that of holidays. There can, of course, be cultural tourism, environmental tourism and so on. Moreover, a single journey may appear in the eyes of the person undertaking it as a holiday or as a form of cultural enrichment, for example. It would therefore seem quite arbitrary to define tourist services by reference to the purpose of the package travel. Consequently, there would be no justification for limiting the protection which the Directive aims to provide to all consumers of package services only to those cases where services are offered to holiday travellers.

22. The scope of the Directive application cannot, therefore, be defined by reference to the purpose of the travel. There is nothing, either in the wording of the Directive or related to its objectives, that can be prayed in aid, to support the conclusion that only 'recreational' travel is protected under the substantive rules of the Directive and that travel for other purposes (business, conferences, family visits, study, to name but a few) is by definition excluded and therefore not subject to the consumer-protection provisions contained in the Directive. Quite apart from the obvious difficulties of identifying the intentions of those who enter into package-travel agreements, the need to prevent the risk, mentioned earlier, of the protection which the Directive aims to provide being evaded militates in favour of not ascribing any importance to the purposes for which the travel is undertaken."

"Services". This is also a word that has provoked discussion. In its guidelines the DTI suggests that a distinction can be drawn between "services" and "facilities". They say: (p.8, note 26)

"There is an important distinction between a service and a facility . Where a facility is available to all, and is provided with one other element of either transport or accommodation, then no package is created. However, where the facility is restricted to only a few who book or pay in advance then it becomes a tourist service and may create a package. As examples: access to fishing rights on a local river would *normally* be a service whereas the provision of a swimming pool at a hotel would be a facility. So the provision of a facility does not automatically amount to a tourist service." [Emphasis added]

Doubtless such a distinction can be made but is it a real one? The DTI itself was sufficiently unsure of its own example to qualify it with the word "normally". If an hotel were asked what services it offered would the answer be different to the one it would have given if it had been asked what facilities it offered? Even if certain things could be classified as facilities—the swimming pool, the golf course, the tennis courts, the health centre—they might all have services connected to them—the pool attendant, the golf professional, the tennis coach, the masseuse, etc., making a nonsense of the distinction. The effect of such a distinction is of course to obscure further a piece of legislation which is already riddled with such difficulties. It is interesting that ABTA have also issued guidelines and on this point they too are unhappy with the distinction between services and facilities. They say that they "are not certain that the DTI are clear on the difference between a facility and a service." Saggerson is equally dismissive of the DTI approach (2nd ed. p.22).

"Ancillary". subsidiary, subservient, subordinate, supplementary or auxiliary. Unfortunately none of these fine words helps to overcome the problem of deciding when a service will be ancillary or not. The problem arises most acutely with the range of services offered by hotels. Are the swimming pool, the golf course, the tennis courts, the health centre ancillary to the hotel? Some guidance can be derived by looking at what ancillary does not mean—distinct, independent, autonomous. Are these services sufficiently distinct to make them a separate part of the package or are they so fully integrated into the accommodation that they can be regarded as one and the same thing. If, when the consumer books the accommodation, all these other services are automatically available without extra charge or without being promoted or marketed as a special feature then perhaps they can be regarded as ancillary to the accommodation. Saggerson suggests the following services at an hotel would be ancillary services: chambermaid and laundry services; concierge facilities; room service; security (2nd ed. p.23). Normal service of hotel meals would also fall into this category. However if the consumer has to pay extra for the services or if a special feature is made of them *e.g.* a "cordon bleu" weekend then the converse applies. Holiday villages are a case in point. Apart from accommodation they offer a range of services—water parks, funfairs, mini-golf, baby-sitting, bars, restaurants, dancing, cabaret, etc. On the one hand all these services could be regarded as ancillary to the accommodation in that they all come as part of the price, they are available to all, they are situated in close proximity to the accommodation, etc. On the other hand they form such a large proportion of the price and they figure so prominently as the reason for choosing this particular kind of holiday that they cannot legitimately regarded as ancillary to the accommodation. The reality is that in many of these villages the accommodation is sometimes so basic that it is not the other services that are ancillary to the accommodation but rather the converse.

It is probably already evident that this part of the definition will have most impact upon the hotel sector. One only has to turn to the small ads in the Sunday papers to see this. There it is possible to find all kinds of short breaks offered by hotels and guest houses with a multitude of added extras—cordon bleu cookery weekends (as distinct from normal meals), drama weekends, mystery weekends, gliding weekends, slimming weekends and even divorce weekends! Virtually all of these would fall into the category of package holidays because the services they offer are not ancillary to the accommodation. As will be discussed in more detail later this will make the hoteliers not only liable for their own acts but also for the acts of their suppliers. In the case of a gliding weekend that goes wrong this liability could be substantial.

But note that rail and coach operators who organise trips to rock concerts or musicals or similar events would not be affected to the same degree as hoteliers because they would not be caught by the Regulations unless the trip lasted for more than 24 hours or there was overnight accommodation.

"Significant proportion of the package". This requirement should pose few problems. Significant can be measured in a number of ways—by the proportion of the price, by the proportion of time spent on it or perhaps, in cases where it costs little and is over quickly, by the importance attached to it. Tour operators often feel that however insignificant the service they fail to provide consumers will always claim that it was the main reason for choosing this particular package. Experience suggests that courts will normally side with the consumer unless he lacks credibility. In the *AFS*

Finland case the court held that the preparation of the documentation and the preparatory courses for the students could not be regarded as a significant proportion of the package.

One issue which arises in this context is the status of holiday insurance. Is it "another tourist service" or not. It is our view that either it is not a "tourist service" or that in any event it is ancillary to the other components of the package.

(f) "Sold or offered for sale". The purchase of a package holiday is generally a commercial transaction and when the organiser provides the holiday in exchange for the consumer's money this can accurately be labelled as a "sale". However there are some packages, where even though money changes hands, it has been suggested that there is not a sale. The DTI say:

> "To fall within the scope of the Regulations a package must be 'sold or offered for sale'. If, for example, members of an organisation not carrying on a trade or business (or any other group of people) come together to share the cost of a package they have decided to undertake and to organise themselves, and they appoint one of their members to arrange the details, then that member is unlikely to be selling or offering for sale the package (even though a surplus may be retained by the organisation to be disposed of as the members may decide).
>
> Similarly, packages organised as part of a course of education (for example a geology field trip) are unlikely to be sold in the normal sense of the word and will probably therefore not fall within the scope of the Regulations."

While recognising that the first example may demonstrate the validity of this argument the second example is not so straightforward. The pupil or the student who purchased the field trip from his school or college might very well argue that they were "sold" a package. They would certainly see it as a commercial transaction and if anything went wrong they would regard themselves as having a contract with the provider whom they could sue if necessary—especially if the existence of a contract with the provider (*i.e.* the school or college) insulated the actual supplier from contractual liability. Note however that under the Contracts (Rights of Third Parties) Act 1999 the members of the party might have a direct action against the suppliers.

Even the first example is not clearcut. If the member of the organisation regarded the package as being put together at arm's length as a commercial transaction by the organisation from whom he then purchased it then again it might be regarded as having been "sold" to him. LACORS discuss just this problem in one of their advice sheets. They were asked to advise on whether or not packages put together by a National Trust Members' Centre was "sold" to members. Their initial comment was that it would depend upon the exact make-up and constitution of the organisation involved but in the case in point they concluded that the packages were "sold"—largely because the packages were also made available to non-members.

Furthermore the very existence of Regulation 21 (trust accounts for packages which are not organised as part of a business) suggests that many of these types of arrangements were intended to be caught as packages.

(g) Excursions

It is appropriate to mention at this point the status of excursions. If an excursion is sold as part of a package then it will be subject to the Regulations and the consumer will get the full protection afforded by the Regulations. However many excursions are not sold as an integral part of the package. They are often purchased in resort while the consumer is on holiday and as such they do not qualify as part of a pre-arranged combination. Apart from anything else they are not "sold or offered for sale in the UK"—but see the section on jurisdiction below. In such cases the consumer would have to rely on the common law for any redress. Against the operator an action based on agency or on a negligent misstatement (*Hedley Byrne v Heller* [1964] A.C. 465) might be a possibility but against the excursion company it would have to be an action in contract brought in a foreign court. In practical terms the chances of success against either would not be high. In the past some tour operators, *e.g.* Thomson, have voluntarily accepted liability in their booking conditions for excursions sold by their representatives overseas (see Chapman, "Excursions: Tour Operators and the Negligence of Local Suppliers" [2002] ITLJ 123).

2. Upon whom is liability imposed?

The Regulations impose liability on "the organiser", upon the "retailer" and upon "the other party to the contract". These terms will be examined in turn.

(a) Organiser

2(1) "Organiser" means a person who, otherwise than occasionally, organises packages and sells or offers them for sale, whether directly or through a retailer.

The test here is how frequently the organiser arranges packages, not, as in other consumer protection legislation, whether the organiser acts in the course of a business. The definition will clearly catch conventional tour operators but there is a fear that some organisations who organise trips might be caught by this definition even though they act in a non-professional non-profit making capacity. For instance what about the local authority which through its social services department organises holidays for pensioners on a regular basis? Also organisations such as the Salvation Army which arranges holidays for its members. Schools which organise a number of trips a year for pupils run the risk also of being caught by the Regulations—but not of course if they sold a ready-packaged trip from a tour operator rather than putting together the coach, accommodation, etc themselves.

The chief significance is that it will catch most travel agents in its net. If "tailor-made packages" are regarded as "pre-arranged" then it will be very rare indeed that a travel agent can say that he does not "otherwise than occasionally" put a package together. In this context it is important to note that the term organiser cuts across the more conventional terms of principal and agent. To be an organiser it is not necessary to be a principal and by the same token an agent is not precluded from being an organiser simply because he is an agent. The criterion is whether a person "organises" a package, not whether they act as principal. Thus a travel agent, who acts as no more than an agent, would still be an organiser if he *organised* a package. For instance if a client asked an agent, without being too specific about precisely what he wanted, to book flights and accommodation for a trip to New York and the agent did just this, in other words he *organised* a package, he would be an organiser. This presupposes that the agent exercised some skill and expertise in the matter, some organisational skills. If however the consumer's instructions were extremely precise, *e.g.* particular flights and a particular hotel then the agent might just escape classification as an organiser. If it couldn't be said that he actually organised anything merely passively followed instructions his function might not be that of an organiser. But even this is dubious. At the end of the day the agent may not have had a very high-level input but nevertheless he did sufficient for it to be said in ordinary everyday English that he had organised the package, albeit on someone else's very specific instructions—after all, he had *some* skills which the consumer chose to use.

Taking the matter one step further it is conceivable that a travel agent who sold a conventional package, say a Thomson or an Airtours package, to a consumer and as part of the same transaction arranged for transport to the airport or hotel to be added to it would be an organiser of a package. The agent would be organiser for the whole package in addition to his more limited responsibilities as retailer of the conventional package (see the *Club Tour* case on this point). Meanwhile Thomson or Airtours would also be liable as organiser for the conventional package. This is yet another controversial area awaiting a court decision.

In the case of *Hone v Going Places* [2001] I.T.L.J. 12 (confirmed by the Court of Appeal, see [2001] I.T.L.J. 153) a retailer was found liable for packages it sold via teletext because they had held themselves out as principals. They were only travel agents but had created the impression that they were tour operators.

Returning to the issue of "contract splitting': Can the company hosting the internet site be regarded as an "organiser"? The answer is just as obscure as with those other parts of the definition of a package we have already examined—"pre-arranged combination" and "inclusive price" but it is quite conceivable that a company which provides the infrastructure from which a package could be put together could be regarded as having "organised" that package. Certainly they have invested heavily in the technology which enables the arrangements to be made and the outcome is one which they desire.

The chief significance of being labelled an organiser is that it is generally believed that the liabilities are much greater that those of a retailer. The organiser is responsible for the performance of the whole package but the retailer's liabilities are much more narrowly defined. There are also additional criminal offences for organisers to fall foul of.

(b) Retailers

"2(1) 'Retailer' means the person who sells or offers for sale the package put together by the organiser."

The definition clearly covers the activities of travel agents. Under the Directive member states had the option of imposing liability on either organisers or retailers or both for failures in the package itself. It is generally believed that the Regulations do not impose such extensive liabilities on retailers but they do make them subject to the provision of information regime (Regulation 5 and possibly also Regulations 7 and 8) and they incur civil liability under Regulation 4 for providing misleading descriptive matter. There is however an argument, which will be explored shortly, that the retailer's liability is concurrent with the organiser's in most respects. If so this represents an unexpected and unwelcome extension of liability for travel agents (see the comments in *Hone v*

Going Places on this issue which appear to adopt our view) but by the same token a considerable degree of extra protection for consumers.

As previously stated a travel agent who puts a package together and sells it in his own name, acting as principal, falls within the definition of organiser rather than retailer and is subject to the more stringent liabilities in the Regulations. Similarly, the agent who packages extra elements with a conventional package is likely to be classified as an organiser rather than a retailer.

It would appear that newspapers which offer reader holidays could also be classified as organisers rather than retailers. Despite the fact that they may have sub-contracted virtually the whole package to a tour operator it could nevertheless be said that they were the organisers of the holiday. They might escape liability by making it clear that they were only agents selling the packages of others but often that is not the way such packages are marketed. The newspaper will commonly use phrases such as "come with us on our Rhine cruise", or "our choice of hotel" or even "we have organised". Meanwhile the "real" tour operator is featured in a minor role. In determining whether the newspaper is an organiser a court will look carefully at the wording of the advertisements and also at how, and to whom, the money is payable by the consumer. Even if the newspaper escapes liability as an organiser it will still be classified as a retailer.

(c) The Other Party To The Contract

"The other party to the contract" is not a term to be found in the Directive itself. It is a term coined by the DTI draftsman to encompass those situations where the Directive invited member states (some of which have very differently constituted tourist industries) to impose liability on either the organiser or the retailer or both. It is defined in Regulation 2(1):

> "the other party to the contract" means the party, other than the consumer, to the contract, that is, the organiser or the retailer, or both, as the case may be.

Taking up the invitation in the Directive the Regulations sometimes impose liability solely on the organiser (*e.g.* Regulations 12, 13 and 14), sometimes on the retailer alone (*e.g.* Regulation 5(2)) but sometimes on "the other party to the contract" (*e.g.* Regulations 7, 8, 9, 10 and 15). The problem that arises is that it is not immediately clear precisely when "the other party to the contract" is intended to mean just the organiser or just the retailer or both.

Take Regulation 7 for instance. It states that the other party to the contract shall provide the consumer with certain information before the contract is concluded. The information concerns passport and visa requirements, health formalities and the protection available to the consumer in the event of insolvency. This is information which the organiser could supply quite readily but it is also information which the retailer could supply and as a matter of practice does so routinely. Is therefore the retailer to be liable as well?

Take also Regulation 15 which imposes liability on the other party to the contract for the proper performance of the contract. In other words civil liability is imposed for defects in the package. Prior to the passage of the Regulations this was a liability which only affected tour operators. If the meaning of "other party to the contract" is extended to cover retailers as well as organisers in this Regulation it would impose a massive extension of liability on travel agents. But does it?

(d) "As The Case May Be"

One clue in the definition is that the retailer will be liable "as the case may be". This effectively leaves the question wide open. Presumably the answer can be found by looking not only at the context in which the definition is employed in the Regulations but also at wider considerations such as the commercial context and the legislative history, *i.e.* the Directive itself.

Looking first at the Directive for guidance three points need to be made. First, the Directive is designed to be a consumer protection measure as well as a harmonising measure. Secondly, a number of Articles in the Directive, as indicated earlier, permit member states to impose liability on the organiser and/or the retailer (see Articles 4 and 5 in particular). Thirdly, Article 7 permits member states to adopt or return more stringent measures to protect the consumer. But as with the Regulations there is no clear guidance on when liability should attach solely to the organiser and when to the retailer as well. The most that can be said is that although member states are free to choose there is a bias towards extending the protection of consumers rather than restricting it.

One explanation given for leaving the choice open for member states is that commercial practice varies from state to state and governments should be free to impose liability on tour operators or travel agents or both—whichever they felt was most appropriate. Applying that kind of reasoning to a UK context it could be argued that it would be more appropriate to impose liability on tour operators rather than travel agents. The justification for this is that tour operators put the package together and market it; they are in a position to influence and monitor its quality; and they are in direct contractual relationship with the consumer. The travel agent on the other hand, so the argument goes, is only an intermediary who has no direct control over the quality of the package and who has no contractual relationship with the consumer.

This is a seductive argument but it does not necessarily correspond to commercial reality. Increasingly the larger chains of travel agencies are using their commercial power to dictate to operators not only the terms on which their brochures will be racked but also to insist on proper quality control. In other words travel agencies have as much influence on what the consumer buys and the quality of what he buys as many tour operators and should therefore be prepared to accept some of the responsibility. It is also the case that the large chains of travel agents are vertically integrated with the major operators, and while legally this means they are distinct entities, commercially they work together closely. It is not too outrageous therefore to suggest that the law should reflect their common commercial purpose.

(e) "The Contract"

What is perhaps more to the point is that the travel agent does not have a contract with the consumer for the sale of the package. Therefore if he is not in fact a party to the contract he should not be classified as "the other party to the contract". There is a simple logic to this which is attractive but it breaks down in the face of the definition of "contract" in the Regulations. It has been given an extended meaning in Regulation 2(1):

> "contract" means the agreement linking the consumer to the organiser or the retailer, or to both, as the case may be.

The significant point here is that a "contract" is not defined in the same way a contract in English law would be defined. It is a much looser definition. It is merely an agreement which *links* the consumer to the organiser or retailer. An agreement *linking* parties in this way is not a term of art known to English law. In ordinary everyday English to link simply means to connect or join. Using the word in this way it is perfectly possible for a package holiday contract to link the consumer to both the organiser\tour operator (with whom he has a contract) and the retailer\travel agent (with whom he does not have a contract). The link is a commercial link rather than a legal one but it is nevertheless a link.

Thus it is perfectly possible for the "other party to the contract" to mean someone who is not in fact a party to any contract with the consumer. The definitions of "contract" and "the other party to the contract" are just a means of extending liability where appropriate—or "as the case may be" to use the words in the Regulations.

It is not beyond the bounds of possibility that even under the same Regulation the liability could vary depending on the facts of the case. For instance under Regulation 15 one court might take the view that if a small travel agency sells a major tour operator's package then only the tour operator should be liable. Conversely, if one of the multiple travel agencies sold a small tour operator's package another court might decide that the travel agent should be liable as well as the tour operator—or maybe only the travel agent.

Little help is derived by looking at the Parliamentary debates which considered the Regulations. In the House of Commons the minister responsible for leading the debate said, in the only direct reference to this matter, "Regulation 15 is important and makes the organiser, *or possibly in certain circumstances the retailer*, strictly liable for the performance of the contract." (December 10, 1992, emphasis added). In the Lords the same form of words was adopted: "Regulation 15 makes the organiser, *or possibly in certain circumstance the retailer*, strictly liable for the performance of the contract". (December 17, 1992, emphasis added). There is a suggestion in the House of Commons debate that the minister was simply saying that the retailer would be liable when he acted as organiser not simply in his capacity as retailer but the matter remains ambiguous. (See the comments of the Court of Appeal in *Hone v Going Places* [2001] I.T.L.J. 153 on this passage.)

Thus a major area of doubt remains as to how far the liability of a retailer extends and no consistent principles can be discerned as to how to resolve this problem. However it is suggested that, in particular, Regulation 15 and the Regulations dealing with insolvency were not intended to include retailers within their scope. The reason for this is not simply because it would represent such an immense extension of liability for travel agents, nor because it cuts across established business and legal practice, but mainly because it would be so unexpected. The basis on which all sides to the debate have proceeded is that in this country the main burden of the liability would be carried by the tour operator rather than the travel agent. To extend that liability would be contrary to everyone's expectations. There is if you like an underlying presumption which is not articulated in the Regulations but forms the basis on which they are to be interpreted that the liability of travel agents is not to be extended beyond the provision of information. The authors do not pretend that this is a satisfactory means of interpreting the Regulations but in the circumstances this "instinctive" approach best reflects the intention of the legislation.

One day a court will be called upon to decide this point. A likely scenario is this: a consumer has had a disastrous holiday but before the matter can be settled the organiser goes into liquidation. The consumer's only recourse is against the retailer. Once again the judge will be under intense emotional pressure to find for the consumer. Time will tell. (See *Minhas v Imperial Travel* [2003] ITLJ 69 for a small claims court decision on just this point).

3. In whose favour is the liability imposed?

The Regulations impose civil liability on the organiser, and, in the light of what has just been said, perhaps the retailer, in favour of "consumers':

"Consumer" is given an extended meaning in the Regulations:

> "2(2) . . . 'consumer' means the person who takes or agrees to take the package ('the principal contractor') and elsewhere in these Regulations 'consumer' means, as the context requires, the principal contractor, any person on whose behalf the principal contractor agrees to purchase the package ('the other beneficiaries') or any person to whom the principal contractor or any of the other beneficiaries transfers the package ('the transferee')."

(a) English Common Law

Before we look in detail at the definition it is necessary to point out that in English law, until very recently, only a party to a contract was entitled to take the benefit of it. A person named in a contract but not party to it (a third party beneficiary) had no rights to sue on the contract. With the advent of the Contracts (Rights of Third Parties) Act 1999 that position has changed radically and there will be many instances now where a third party beneficiary can enforce rights under a contract between two other parties. In package holiday cases however there was case law, which preceded the new Act, on the extent to which members of a client's family who were named on the booking form but who might not have been a party to the contract were entitled to the benefits of the contract—see *Jackson v Horizon* [1975] 3 All E.R. 92 and *Woodar v Wimpey* [1980] 1 All E.R. 571. The problem also extended to members of a party where one person had made the booking on behalf of others. In one unreported case a woman bought a holiday for her cleaning lady which went wrong. The court awarded only nominal damages to the purchaser of the holiday because *she* had suffered no damage. The cleaning lady, who had suffered the damage, was not a party to the contract and had no rights under it.

By making what amounted to a revolutionary change to a long established rule of English law the definition of "consumer" in the Regulations went some way to eliminating those problems before they were tackled more generally by the new Act. However the Regulations go further than the new Act by providing that if a consumer transfers his booking to another person, as he is sometimes entitled to do now under Regulation 10, the transferee stands in the same position as the original consumer.

(b) The Definition

Regulation 2(2) identifies three types of consumer:

- the principal contractor;
- the other beneficiaries; and
- the transferee.

As a broad proposition it could be said that the legislation was intended to cover three types of person:

- a person who buys the package, but may or may not go on it;
- a person who goes on the package, but is paid for by another; and
- a person who acquires a package indirectly from one of the other types of consumer but not directly from the organiser.

Looked at this way anyone who either pays for a package or who goes on a package will get the protection of the Regulations. However, as with the other definitions the wording is a little clumsy and could lead to technical difficulties. The three types of consumer need examining carefully.

(c) The Principal Contractor

The principal contractor is defined as a person who "takes or agrees to take the package". The problem here is the word "takes". It can have at least two meanings. First, it could mean the person who actually goes on the package, or secondly it could mean the person who agrees to purchase the package. At first glance the former meaning appears to fit the word best. To *take* a package holiday usually means to go on a package holiday. However, to adopt this first meaning in preference the second raises the problem of what is meant by the two other definitions—other beneficiaries and transferees. If anyone who goes on a package is a principal contractor then the two other definitions appear redundant. Why is it felt necessary to define "other beneficiaries" and "transferee" if, as appears the case, "principal contractor" encompasses them both?

There is also the problem that if a principal contractor is a person who takes a package, in the first sense, then where does that place the person who purchases a package for another but does not go on the package himself? For instance, what about a company that purchases a package for an employee. The employee is protected by the Regulations but the company is not. This may not matter in most circumstances because when there is a failure in the performance of the contract the employee, as consumer, will have the right to sue, but there may be circumstances where the employee is unable or disinclined to sue and therefore the organiser will not be answerable to the employer—who paid for the package but is unable to obtain redress. This may very well have the effect of removing most purchasers of business travel (and perhaps even their employees) from direct access to the provisions of the Regulations. (It must be remembered however that the employer may still have rights at common law although these might not be as extensive as under the Regulations).

To attribute the second meaning to the word "takes", *i.e.* a principal contractor is someone who purchases a package, would broaden the definition sufficiently to bring in the person who purchased the package but may not have gone on it. This would satisfy the spirit of the legislation although not fitting entirely comfortably with the language employed. It would also accord with the use of the word "contractor" in the definition. To be labelled a contractor implies that the person taking the package has a contract with the organiser. If that is the case then it would also fit better with the definitions that follow.

(d) Other Beneficiaries

If a principal contractor is someone who "takes" a package then why do we need a definition of another beneficiary? What does this second definition of consumer add to the first? If it is not to be redundant then the implication is that the definition of principal contractor is more restricted than simply anyone who goes on a package. It confirms the suggestion above that to be a principal contractor a person has to have a contract with the organiser. By thus narrowing the definition of principal contractor "other beneficiary" can then take on a meaning that is not redundant, *i.e.* a person for whom a package is purchased by someone else—the principal contractor. They are the third party beneficiaries who would not normally have a right of action under English law.

One important point to note here is that the other beneficiary is defined in terms of a principal contractor. There cannot be another beneficiary *unless* there is *also* a principal contractor. Thus where there is no principal contractor there can be no other beneficiary. So if a person cannot be defined as a principal contractor because he does not "take" a package then any person for whom he buys a package will have no rights under the Regulations.

This hinges upon the acceptance of the first interpretation of the word "take" as meaning "going on the package". If the second meaning is accepted, *i.e.* a person who has a contract for a package, whether or not they go on it then the problem ceases to exist. As long as a person has his holiday purchased for him by a person who had a contract with the organiser then they will be an other beneficiary. On the whole this seems a more sensible approach to take as it will extend the protection of the Regulations rather than diminish it. But then there remains the mystery that a principal contractor is a person who "takes" a package whereas the other beneficiary is a person on whose behalf the principal contractor "purchases" a package. Why, if the second interpretation is to be preferred, are two different words used to mean the same thing? If they were intended to have the same meaning why was not the same word used?

Some clue may be found in the preamble to the Directive which states:

> "Whereas the consumer should have the benefit of the protection introduced by this Directive irrespective of whether he is a direct contracting party, a transferee or a member of a group on whose behalf another person has concluded a contract in respect of a package."

The language used in the preamble takes a much broader approach than that found in Regulation 2(2) (which reflects exactly the wording of Article 2.4 of the Directive) and if a purposive interpretation is adopted then the second interpretation of "takes" is entirely consistent with the intent of the preamble.

(e) Transferees

Under Regulation 10 it is possible, in certain limited circumstances, for a consumer to transfer his booking to another person—a transferee. A transferee is defined as being a person to whom a principal contractor or another beneficiary transfers the package.

The transferee then acquires the same legal rights as any other consumer. Again the problem arises that there cannot be a transferee unless there is first a principal contractor or another beneficiary. If a person acquires a package from a person who does not fall into one of those two categories he does not become a transferee and hence acquires no rights under the Regulations.

(f) Variations On a Theme

Proceeding on the basis that the first interpretation is the preferred one it remains the case that care must still be taken to identify just who is a consumer in any particular set of circumstances. Take a conventional package holiday for instance. The tour operator will be the organiser and the consumers will be the persons who go on the holiday. The chances are that there will be one principal contractor and several other beneficiaries. The principal contractor will be the person who agrees to take the package and the other beneficiaries will be the members of his family on whose behalf he purchases the package.

If the tour operator sells the package to a group of adults rather than to a family the position is that everyone named on the booking form is a principal contractor in his own right. This is despite the fact that the wording on the booking form may state that the person who signs it is signing it "on behalf of" everyone else. All this means is that he is acting as their agent and they have given him the authority to make a contract on their behalf. They are just as much a principal as the person signing the booking form.

These are relatively straightforward examples. There are much more complicated ones. Take for instance the case of an Indian ground operator who puts together a package consisting of hotels, bus tours and internal transfers and then sells this to an English tour operator. The English operator then adds international flights to it and sells the whole package through a brochure. The Indian ground operator is an organiser and when he sells his package to the English operator the English operator becomes a consumer. When the English operator then adds on the extra flights and sells it to English tourists he becomes an organiser in his own right and his clients are consumers. However, these clients are not only consumers of the English tour operator's package they are also consumers of the Indian ground operator's package. In the latter circumstances they are other beneficiaries because the English tour operator bought the package on their behalf. Thus the clients will acquire rights against not only the English operator in respect of the whole package but also direct rights against the Indian ground operator in respect of the Indian part of the package. This would be important if the English organiser became insolvent.

(g) Contracts (Rights Of Third Parties) Act 1999

Since the Package Travel Regulations were passed, conferring specific rights on consumers of package holidays the government has passed legislation of a more general nature—the Contracts (Rights of Third Parties) Act 1999—which does for all third party beneficiaries what the PTR has already done for package holiday-makers. To all intents and purposes this has the effect of duplicating the protection already conferred by the PTR.

Its main provision is:

Right of third party to enforce contractual term

1(1) Subject to the provisions of this Act, a person who is not a party to a contract (a "third party") may in his own right enforce a term of the contract if—

(a) the contract expressly provides that he may, or
(b) subject to subsection (2), the term purports to confer a benefit on him.

(2) Subsection (1)(b) does not apply if on a proper construction of the contract it appears that the parties did not intend the term to be enforceable by the third party.

(3) The third party must be expressly identified in the contract by name, as a member of a class or as answering a particular description but need not be in existence when the contract is entered into.

(4) This section does not confer a right on a third party to enforce a term of a contract otherwise than subject to and in accordance with any other relevant terms of the contract.

(5) For the purpose of exercising his right to enforce a term of the contract, there shall be available to the third party any remedy that would have been available to him in an action for breach of contract if he had been a party to the contract (and the rules relating to damages, injunctions, specific performance and other relief shall apply accordingly).

(6) Where a term of a contract excludes or limits liability in relation to any matter references in this Act to the third party enforcing the term shall be construed as references to his availing himself of the exclusion or limitation.

It is clear from this that all the persons on a booking form, subject to express words to the contrary would be able to claim the benefit of the legislation just as they can under the PTR.

4. Jurisdiction

Regulation 3 provides:

> "3(1) These Regulations apply to packages sold or offered for sale in the territory of the United Kingdom."

Thus they would cover:

- purely domestic packages, *e.g.* packages sold in Britain for a holiday confined entirely to Britain;
- purely EC packages, *e.g.* package holidays to Spain sold in Britain;
- packages sold in Britain for destinations outside the EC, *e.g.* packages to the Caribbean or Thailand starting from London;
- packages with no EC connection at all except that they are sold here, *e.g.* an American company which advertises packages confined solely to the US.

In one respect the Regulations are narrower than the Directive. The Directive states that it covers packages "sold or offered for sale in the territory of the Community" (Article 1) whereas the Regulations only cover packages "sold or offered for sale in the territory of the United Kingdom". This means for instance that a tour operator established in the UK who sells packages to the UK but only sells them in Holland would not be covered by the Regulations. This is clearly a contravention of the Directive and if put to the test would be overruled (see the *Dillenkofer* case).

An issue connected with this is the question of what is meant by selling or offering for sale packages *in* the UK? What if for instance a potential client phones up a hotel in the Channel Islands, which is not in the EC, and is informed that not only can the hotel accommodate the client but they can also organise a package for him consisting of flights from his nearest airport, transfers to the hotel, the accommodation and a variety of excursions. Is this a package sold *in* the UK? If the answer to the question depends upon where the contract is made the answer will vary according to how the rules of offer and acceptance are applied to the negotiations.

Thus in some circumstances the client will be protected by the Regulations and in others will not depending upon who had the final say. Alternatively a broader meaning can be attributed to the word "in".

There is a case in criminal law, *Smith v Hughes* [1960] 1 W.L.R. 830, [1960] 2 All E.R. 859, where a woman was accused of soliciting *in* the street. The facts were that she stood at a window and tapped on the pane to attract men in the street below. By a series of gestures she would invite them in and negotiate the price. It was held that she was guilty of soliciting in the street. On appeal it was stated:

> "Everybody knows that this was an Act intended to clean up the streets, to enable people to walk along the streets without being molested or solicited by common prostitutes. Viewed in that way, it can matter little whether the prostitute is soliciting while in the street or is standing in a doorway or on a balcony, or at a window, or whether the window is shut or open or half open; in each case her solicitation is projected to and addressed to somebody walking in the street."

While not for a moment wishing to imply that selling holidays is the same as selling sex it is nevertheless the case that a similar line of reasoning can be adopted. If the purpose of the Regulations is to protect UK consumers in respect of packages which they buy while resident in the UK then the interpretation to adopt is to say that the package was sold over the phone to a consumer *in* the UK. This is a perfectly acceptable interpretation and it should not make any difference that, for technical reasons, the contract was made in the Channel Islands rather than Leeds or Newcastle. Similar issues arise in the context of contracts made over the internet or by email.

Excursions

As indicated earlier many excursions do not form part of a package and therefore a consumer acquires no rights under the Regulations in respect of the excursion. For instance in the case of *Sheppard v Crystal Holidays* (1996) the tour operator was found not liable for injuries sustained on holiday due to the negligence of a ski instructor who had been employed by the claimant while in resort—even though the services has been purchased through the operator's representative. However, some excursions do amount to packages in their own right. If these are sold in the UK, whether on their own or as part of a larger package, then the consumers who purchase them are protected. But if the consumer buys such an excursion while abroad then the protection is not available because it was not purchased in the UK. Take for example a package to Canada consisting of flights to Vancouver, accommodation for two weeks and an excursion by bus for five days into the Rockies. This would be a package sold in the UK and the consumer would be able to sue the operator not simply in respect of the flights and accommodation but also the five day excursion. However if, initially, the consumer only purchased the flights and accommodation in the UK but subsequently purchased the excursion while in Vancouver they would acquire no rights in respect of the excursion under the Regulations despite the fact that it is a package. The point is that the package was not sold in the UK, nor for that matter in the Community.

Many excursions sold by tour operators' representatives in popular Mediterranean resorts amount to packages in their own right. These raise difficult questions of jurisdiction which are dealt with in Chapter 19.

An Overview

Before moving on to the detailed treatment of package holiday contracts it will be useful for readers to have an overview of the full extent of the Regulations. Despite the wide scope of the Regulations it is possible to distinguish particular themes or topics and these will be examined briefly in turn. Full treatment of these issues appears later in the relevant sections of the book.

1. Provision of information

There is a heavy emphasis in the Regulations on the provision of essential information. In a contract where the consumer cannot see or sample the product before he buys it this enables him to make a more rational choice initially and, if he is subsequently disappointed, it gives him a yardstick by which to measure the performance of the tour operator and to assess whether the tour operator is in breach of contract. It should also mean that there are fewer complaints because consumers will be able to make a more informed choice if the information is accurate and are therefore less likely to be disappointed.

Regulation 4 imposes civil liability on both organises and retailers for supplying misleading information. This is a new form of statutory civil liability which resembles both an action for misrepresentation and breach of contract. If a brochure is made available to consumers Regulation 5 requires certain information to be included in the brochure and failure to provide it in a legible, comprehensible and accurate manner amounts to a criminal offence by the organiser, and in some circumstances, the retailer. Regulation 6 reinforces Regulation 5 by elevating *all the particulars* in the brochure into implied warranties, *i.e.* minor terms of the contract.

Regulation 7 provides that information on subjects such as visa and health requirement be given to consumers before the contract is concluded and failure to do so is also a criminal offence. Yet another criminal offence is committed if, in breach of Regulation 8, the other party to the contract fails to provide information on insurance, contact names and addresses and on intermediate stops and accommodation during the journey.

Finally, Regulation 9 requires all the terms of the contract to be communicated to the consumer before the contract is concluded, if possible, and in all cases it must be reduced to writing and a copy supplied to the consumer. The penalty for failure to do so is that the consumer can cancel the package.

2. Changes and cancellation

A package holiday is a complex product which is designed and marketed many months, if not years, in advance of performance. It is not uncommon therefore for circumstances to change in the meantime and for operators to have to make alterations to the holiday or even to cancel it altogether. There are several Regulations which deal with these possibilities. The important thing to note about them is that not only do they label such changes as breach of contract by the operator for which compensation is payable, *i.e.* a financial remedy for the consumer they also provide a range of other remedies, *i.e.* the offer of an alternative holiday; or a requirement that the operator do something practical to put things right; or a right to be brought home early in some circumstances.

Regulation 12 provides that if the organiser makes a significant alteration to a package the consumer is entitled to withdraw from the package or to accept a rider to the contract specifying the alterations made and the impact on the price. If the consumer does withdraw or the organiser cancels the package the consumer is entitled to be offered an alternative package or a refund of his money. Compensation is also payable except in certain limited circumstances. If, after departure a significant proportion of the services is not provided then the organiser is under a duty to make alternative arrangements and if it is not possible to do this the consumer has a right to be taken back to his point of departure.

3. Liability

At common law it was generally, but not universally, accepted, that a tour operator's liability was fault based (see *Wall v Silver Wing Surface Arrangements* (1981) (Unreported). See also *Wong Mee Wan v Kwan Kin Travel Services* [1995] 4 All E.R. 745. Regulation 15 changes all this by introducing a qualified form of strict liability. Subject to certain broad exceptions an organiser is made strictly liable for the "proper performance" of the contract irrespective of whether the failures are due to his own actions or those of his suppliers (subcontractors). The liability is further reduced by provisions which permit the organiser to exclude or limit his liability in certain circumstances. These include circumstances where international carriage is involved or where there is no personal injury.

4. Protection in the event of insolvency

There are extensive provisions in the Regulations intended to protect consumers if the tour operator with whom they are dealing becomes insolvent either before they travel or while they are abroad. To protect consumers' prepayments organisers must adopt one of the options set out in Regulations 17–21. These include bonding, insurance or the establishment of a trust fund. Additionally organisers must also be able to demonstrate that in the event of the insolvency occurring while consumers are abroad they will be repatriated.

5. Other provisions

Apart from the themes just identified there are a number of miscellaneous matters dealt with by the Regulations. Regulation 10 permits a consumer to transfer his booking to another in certain limited circumstances. Regulation 11 preserves the right of an organiser to surcharge consumers but severely circumscribes the circumstances in which this can be done. Regulations 13 permits an organiser to cancel a package for lack of minimum numbers so long as this was expressly stated in the contract and the organiser adheres to the deadlines set out in the contract.

Chapter Three
Offer and Acceptance: Do We Have a Contract?

Introduction

This chapter is concerned with establishing precisely *when* and *how* a contract comes into existence between a tour operator and a client. The importance of establishing this is threefold.

First, so that both the tour operator and the client know precisely when they become legally bound to each other. In other words they know that from that moment they have legal rights and obligations under the contract. So on the one hand the tour operator will know that he will be able to demand payment under the terms of the contract but he will also have to deliver the services he has promised. On the other hand the client knows that he is legally bound to pay for the holiday but he has the right to receive the services he has paid for.

Secondly, knowing how and when the contract is made enables the tour operator to establish procedures so that the contract is made on *his* terms and conditions. For instance, payment clauses often provide for surcharges, and cancellation clauses provide for the payment of cancellation charges. Neither of these provisions would be terms of the contract unless the operator took steps to ensure they were there.

Thirdly, Regulation 9 of the Package Travel Regulations provides that the terms of the contract must be communicated to the client *before* the contract is concluded. The price for failing to do so is that the client may be able to withdraw from the contract without penalty.

The consequences of not knowing the theory and practice of making a contract should be self-evident. First, a tour operator may invest considerable time and effort in a client only to end up with no contract at the end of the day. Secondly, even if a contract appears to be concluded it may be repudiated if the client was not informed in advance of all the terms. Thirdly, even if the client does not wish to cancel, the contract may not include all the carefully drafted terms and conditions in the operator's brochure. All three eventualities could be costly to the tour operator and, in extreme cases, subject him to the even more costly uncertainties of litigation.

What is a contract?

For our purposes a contract can be defined as *a legally binding agreement*. Essentially there are two elements to this definition. First there is the requirement that the agreement between the parties is one which is intended to have *legally enforceable consequences*. In other words the parties envisage that as a last resort, if the contract was broken, they could sue the other party and the courts would enforce the contract—usually by awarding damages. Some agreements of a social or domestic nature, such as an invitation to dinner, are not legally binding but commercial agreements such as those between tour operators and clients are presumed to be legally enforceable. It would be hard to envisage circumstances where a package holiday contract would not be enforced by the courts.

Secondly, there must actually be an *agreement*. If the parties have not come to an agreement then there will be no contract. Most of what follows is concerned with the mechanisms by which agreement is reached but put at its simplest a tour operator will have a contract if the client signifies that he is quite happy to pay £560 per person half board for two weeks in the Hotel Excelsior in the resort of his choice for the first two weeks in August departing from Luton. Conversely there will not be a contract if the client is perfectly happy with all the arrangements except the departure airport—he is not willing to purchase the holiday if he cannot secure a departure from Newcastle but unfortunately the operator does not have a Newcastle departure on the date the client requires.

Other requirements

Apart from the need for an agreement and for the parties to that agreement to intend that it be legally binding there are other requirements for a valid contract. These are that the parties both provide *consideration*; that they both have the legal *capacity* to make a contract; and, that the contract is in the right *form*. The first two of these requirements can be dealt with quite briefly because, although they are important in many types of contract, they are of only minor practical importance in package holiday contracts. The requirement that the contract be in the right form is more important and will be given full treatment.

(a) Consideration

The requirement that both parties provide consideration before the contract is binding means that each must provide the other with something of value. In a package holiday contract the consideration by the client would be the payment for the holiday and the consideration by the tour operator would be the provision of the holiday itself. The consideration need not actually be exchanged for the contract to be binding it is sufficient that each party has *promised* to provide the consideration in exchange for the other's promise. In general no widespread difficulties are likely to arise over the provision of consideration in package holiday contracts although there may be marginal cases where it is relevant. In the past problems have arisen most often where one person has given a holiday as a gift to another with the result that the recipient of the gift cannot enforce the contract because they have provided no consideration. This problem has largely been overcome in package holiday contracts by the wide definition of consumer found in Regulation 2 (see Chapter 2).

(b) Capacity

The parties to a contract must be legally capable of making the contract. Minors, *i.e.* persons under 18, are the largest single group of people that do not have full capacity to make contracts. Given the number of minors that take package holidays there is theoretical potential for difficulties to arise but in practice this rarely occurs and does not justify more than the briefest of mentions.

(c) Form

Although there are very good reasons for putting all but the simplest contracts into writing most contracts are perfectly valid even if they are only oral. However there are a minority of contracts that must be reduced to writing, or at least some of the terms must be put in writing. Contracts for the sale of land and contracts of hire purchase fall into this category. Prior to 1992 there was no such requirement for package holiday contracts and it was possible, although not advisable, to make one without putting it into writing. All that changed when the Regulations were introduced. Regulation 9 requires that consumers be given a written copy of all the terms of the contract—in most cases before the contract is made. This was a major development for both tour operators and consumers and we will deal fully with the impact of it in this chapter.

How is agreement reached?

To establish whether a contract exists or not a lawyer would break down the process of arriving at an agreement into two elements—*offer and acceptance*. For there to be an agreement one party must make an offer to the other party which the other one accepts.

An offer can be defined as a statement by one party of the terms he is *prepared to be bound by* if his offer is accepted. In other words the offeror (as he is known) is *prepared to commit himself* to the terms of his offer.

An acceptance is the *unqualified agreement* to the terms of the offer. In other words the offeree, having received the terms of the offer, is equally prepared to commit himself and does so simply by agreeing, without any strings attached, to what the offeror proposes.

In terms of a package holiday contract what this boils down to is that if a client, after long discussions with his travel agent about all the details of a holiday, finally says "Yes, I would like to buy that particular holiday" this will amount to an offer and if the operator responds by saying "Yes I am prepared to sell it to you" this will amount to an acceptance and from that moment a contract exists.

Two things should be noted about this example. First, the parties themselves did not use the words "offer" or "acceptance". In real life people do not go around talking like lawyers and expressing themselves in the formal language of the law. Ordinary people use words and phrases like "buy" and "sell" and "Do you want it?" and "Yes I'll have it", rather than "I am offering to sell you a holiday" and "I am prepared to accept your offer of a holiday". This does not prevent what they say from being an offer or an acceptance so long as it can be categorised as one or the other. The important thing is not whether the words are formal but whether the words show that the parties are prepared to legally bind themselves.

The second thing to note is that in the example the offeror was the client who was making an *offer to buy* the holiday. The offeree (also called the acceptor in this case) was the tour operator who was accepting the offer by saying that he was *prepared to sell*. These are not fixed categories. If the facts had been slightly different then it could have been the operator who was making an *offer to sell* and the client who was the acceptor, saying he was *prepared to buy*.

Invitations to treat

It is only in the very simplest of contractual situations that the process of arriving at an agreement consists only of an offer followed by an acceptance. In most cases there are preliminary discussions and negotiations before the parties begin making legally binding statements. When one party wants to indicate that he is prepared to enter into negotiations or prepared to commence negotiations with the other party he will often make, what is called by lawyers, an *invitation to treat*. An invitation to treat, as its name suggests is an indication by one party that they are prepared to receive offers from the other. They are inviting the other party to make the first move. Legally speaking they are saying that they are prepared to enter into the bargaining process but they are not yet prepared to commit themselves to a formal offer.

In many cases the distinction between an invitation to treat and an offer is quite clear cut. For instance there is a world of difference between saying "I'm thinking of selling my car. Would you be interested in buying it?" and "I put my car in the paper last night for £4,000 but I'm prepared to sell it to you right now if you give me £3,800". The first statement merely invites the other party to enter into negotiations; the latter is a firm offer which can be accepted by a simple yes.

However, the distinction is not always so clear and it is not uncommon for someone to think that he has been made an offer which he has accepted when in fact it was only an invitation to treat that the other party had made. The difference of course is crucial. In the former case a contract would have been concluded whereas in the latter it would not. One of the most famous cases in English law, *Carlill v Carbolic Smoke Ball Co* [1893] 1 Q.B. 256, turned on just this point.

The defendants, who were manufacturers of smoke balls, placed an advertisement in a newspaper stating that if the public purchased their smoke balls and used them as directed this would protect them from flu. If, despite the use of the smoke balls, a purchaser contracted flu the company was prepared to pay them £100 reward. As an indication of their sincerity in the matter they had deposited £1000 with a bank to meet any claims that might be made. Mrs Carlill had purchased one of the balls from a retailer, a chemist, and used it in the prescribed manner but had nevertheless caught flu. She claimed her reward but the Smoke Ball company refused to pay. One of the defendant's arguments for rejecting liability was that the advertisement was only an invitation to treat not an offer. In such circumstances, the defendant argued, there could be no contract because even if Mrs Carlill's purchase and use of the ball could be interpreted as an offer to enter into a contract with the defendant on the terms set out in the advertisement the defendant had not accepted her offer. Mrs Carlill's contention was that the advertisement constituted an offer which she had accepted by using the ball in the manner prescribed. In upholding Mrs Carlill's view Bowen LJ said of the advertisement:

> "It is an offer to become liable to anyone who, before it is retracted, performs the condition on the faith of the advertisement. It is not like cases in which you offer to negotiate, or you issue advertisements that you have got a stock of books to sell, or houses to let, in which case there is no offer to be bound by any contract. Such advertisements are offers to negotiate—offers to receive offers—offers to chaffer, as, I think, some learned judge in one of the cases has said. If this is an offer to be bound, then it is a contract the moment the person fulfils the condition. That seems to me to be sense ..."

If you doubt the relevance of this case, where the facts are far removed from the travel industry, you need look no further than the case of *Bowerman and Wallace v Association of British Travel Agents Ltd* [1996] C.L.C. 451 (CA). The facts of the case were that the claimants had booking a skiing holiday with Adventure Express, an ABTA tour operator, specialising in skiing holidays for school children. Adventure Express became insolvent shortly before the claimants were due to go on holiday. In accordance with the ABTA scheme set up to protect holidaymakers against the risk of insolvency ABTA refunded the claimants the money they had paid for their holiday. The claimants in turn assigned their right to this money to Skibound, another ski tour operator, which arranged another holiday for them. The problem was, however, that ABTA did not refund the whole of the holiday price. They deducted a small sum to cover the insurance premiums that were part of the price of the holiday. The claimants contended that ABTA should not have deducted this sum—they should have refunded the whole cost of the holiday. The basis of this contention was that a notice published by ABTA, entitled "Notice describing ABTA's scheme of protection against the financial failure of ABTA members", which ABTA required to be displayed prominently at the premises of all travel agents and tour operators who were members of ABTA, constituted a contractual promise by ABTA to refund customers of failed ABTA tour operators *in full*. To put it more simply the claimants said that the notice was an offer by ABTA to members of the public that if they booked with an ABTA tour operator then ABTA would ensure that *all* their money was safe.

The Court of Appeal, by a two to one majority, held that the notice was a contractual document containing the promise contended for by the claimants. This despite the fact that it contained "a remarkable variety of tone and language" (Waite LJ).

Waite LJ approached the interpretation of the document in this fashion:

> "Before analysing the detail in that Notice, it may be helpful to stand aside and look for a moment at the attributes which need to be given to the ordinary member of the public as he or she steps down from the omnibus, enter the travel agency in which the Notice is displayed, and reads it. Such a reader would be aware of the vulnerability of agents and operators in a highly competitive market where failures are not uncommon, and of the disappointment and financial loss which members of the public have experienced in the past as a result of sudden cancellations following financial collapse. The reader would appreciate, too, that ABTA is not a charity or a friendly society, but (as its full name makes clear) an association, for the purposes of trade, of persons and firms carrying on the business of travel agent. He or she would, further, be aware that it is in the interests of such an association to win business for its constituent members by inspiring public confidence. There should also be imputed to the reader common knowledge that those who wish to disclaim legal liability for public representations frequently say so—in large print or in small. Finally it is to be assumed that such a person would read the whole notice—neither cursorily nor with pedantic analysis of every nuance of its wording, but with the ordinary care to be expected of the average customer who is applying money they could not easily afford to lose in buying a holiday which it would be a serious disappointment to forego."

Hobhouse LJ, dealing with how the notice should be interpreted, quoted from the judgment of Bowen LJ in *Carlill*:

> "It was intended to be issued to the public and to be read by the public. How would an ordinary person reading this document construe it?"

His answer to the question was:

> "In my judgment this document is intended to be read and would reasonably be read by a member of the public as containing an

> offer of a promise which the customer is entitled to accept by choosing to do business with an ABTA member. A member of the public would not analyse his situation in legal terms but would clearly understand that this notice would only apply to him if he should choose to do business with an ABTA member and he would also understand that if he did so he would be entitled to hold ABTA to what he understood ABTA to be promising in this document. In my judgment it satisfies the criteria for a unilateral contract and contains promises which are sufficiently clear to be capable of legal enforcement. The principles established in the *Carbolic Smoke Ball* case apply . The plaintiffs are entitled to enforce the right of reimbursement given to them in paragraph 5."

Objective Interpretations

It is worth noting that in *Carlill* the Court of Appeal's interpretation of the advertisement, and in *Bowerman* the interpretation of the notice, was an objective one. They did not ask whether the defendant really intended the document to be an offer or an invitation to treat but whether, objectively, from a disinterested outsider's point of view the words used could be interpreted as conveying the impression that they were willing to be bound or not. In the circumstances, the language used in both documents taken in context led the court to conclude that an offer was being made. This was probably quite contrary to the subjective intention of the defendants who probably thought, in the *Carlill* case they had merely indulged in some harmless advertising which would not be binding upon them, and in the *Bowerman* case that they had retained the discretion to refuse payment when they thought it appropriate.

Legal Status Of The Brochure

Tour operators publicise their holidays in a number of ways including newspaper advertising, TV advertising and, increasingly, the internet but the most important and widespread medium is of course the brochure. The question arises as to the legal status of "offers" made in brochures to "sell" holidays to clients. Are they offers or only invitations to treat? If they are offers then, just like the Carbolic Smoke Ball Co, tour operators may end up with contracts they did not intend to make. If they are invitations to treat then there can be no contract until the tour operator accepts the client's offer to buy the holiday.

It can be said with some certainty that, in the vast majority of cases, such statements are only invitations to treat not offers. The reasons for this are practical. If, for the sake of argument, an operator issues a brochure with special low lead-in prices for early bookers he may be faced with a position where demand outstrips supply many times. If a court interpreted the brochure as meaning that the tour operator was "offering" such holidays for sale then every client who came forward and "accepted" the offer before it was withdrawn would have a contract with the tour operator. In these circumstances the operator could end up with 1000 contracts but only 500 available holidays and no way of making up the difference. The logic of the situation would be that the operator would be in breach of 500 contracts!

A number of cases suggest that a court would be very unlikely to take this line. Where products have been advertised in newspapers or a price list has been circulated the courts have held that no offer was made, only an invitation to treat. In *Grainger & Son v Gough* [1896] A.C. 325 Lord Herschell said:

> "The transmission of ... a price list does not amount to an offer to supply an unlimited quantity of the wine described at the price named, so that as soon as an order is given there is a binding contract to supply that quantity. If it were so the merchant might find himself involved in any number of contractual obligations to supply wine of a particular description which he would be unable to carry out, his stock of wine of that description being necessarily limited."

A court took a similar line in the case of *Partridge v Crittenden* [1968] 1 W.L.R. 1204 where an advertisement was placed in a periodical, *Cage and Aviary Birds*, which stated:

> "Quality British ABCR Bramblefinch cocks, Bramblefinch hens, 25s each."

It was argued that the advertisement amounted to an offer to sell the birds. However, Lord Parker CJ said:

> "... I think that when one is dealing with advertisements and circulars, ... there is business sense in their being construed as invitations to treat and not offers for sale. ... It seems to me ... that not only is that the law, but common sense supports it."

There is a world of difference between a holiday and a crate of wine or a bramblefinch hen, but legally speaking, a brochure, a price list and an advertisement can all be analysed the same way. Invariably they are invitations to treat rather than offers, simply because the product being sold is not available in unlimited quantities. As the judges indicated it would be unrealistic and impractical to categorise them otherwise.

The advertisement in the *Carlill* case was of course an offer but that is simply the exception that proves the rule. The words used in that case were such that they could be interpreted as an offer. It would be possible for a tour operator to phrase his brochure copy or his advertising in such a way that it could be interpreted as an offer. For instance if a major operator which sold hundreds of thousands of holidays a year whipped up public interest just prior to the launch of their summer sun brochure by advertising that when the brochure was published the first 100 clients could purchase any holiday in the brochure for only £10 per head this could easily be equated with the advertisement in *Carlill's* case. It would be a brave operator who argued otherwise.

Stating in the brochure that all holidays are "subject to availability" is a two-edged sword. On the one hand it clearly prevents the operator being saddled with a contract after he has sold out of a particular package but by the same token it may very well imply that if the holidays are available the operator is committed to selling them. In most cases that would not be a problem but there may be circumstances where the operator wants to have the option of refusing a client—whether the holidays are available or not.

Typical Situations

Tour operators contract with their clients in a number of ways. Some use on-line computer systems and clients can conclude a booking in a few minutes in a travel agency. Other operators, who also use travel agents as intermediaries, use the telephone, telex or correspondence to make the contract. Correspondence is also a method chosen by those who deal direct with the public. For last minute bookings the telephone (coupled with the use of credit cards) is often used. As indicated earlier the internet, whether coupled with email or not, is an increasingly important way of doing business for tour operators. The principles of offer and acceptance apply to them all but precisely *who* makes the offer and the acceptance and *when* the contract is concluded varies according to the circumstances. It is proposed to examine some of the most commonly occurring booking procedures and analyse what goes on in terms of offer and acceptance.

(a) On-line Booking Systems Using VDU's In Travel Agencies.

The typical scenario here is that the client, having examined an operator's brochure, or having a vague idea of the kind of holiday he wants, enters the travel agency with a view to booking a holiday. The travel clerk will bring up on the VDU the details of holidays that the client might be interested in. Eventually the client will refine his choice until the screen contains details of a holiday that he wants. All it takes at this stage is for the client to say yes and for the travel clerk to convey this information to the tour operator by pressing the correct button on the keyboard and there will be a contract.

In terms of offer and acceptance the analysis here is that the brochure, if one was used, constitutes an invitation to treat. The client entering the travel agency and asking for details of holidays is indicating that he is interested in a holiday, although, clearly he is not prepared to commit himself at this stage. Any interest he shows at this stage falls far short of making an offer to buy a holiday. Until the choice is narrowed down to precisely what the client wants no offer is made. Once the holiday the client wants is displayed on the screen this can be interpreted as an *offer to sell the holiday* by the tour operator. When the client indicates to the travel agent that he is happy with the choice and the appropriate button can be pressed this amounts to *an acceptance by the client to buy the holiday offered.* The contract is made once the button is pressed.

The display on the screen is an offer rather than an invitation to treat because the circumstances show that the stage in the bargaining has been reached where one party, in this case the tour operator, is prepared to commit himself. There are no problems with availability because otherwise the holiday would not be displayed on the screen and there is nothing else to indicate any qualification to what is being offered on the screen.

Viewed like this the outcome seems to be precisely what the operator wants. He has succeeded in tying the client down to a contract. At this stage he can look forward to collecting his money as it falls due. *But on what terms?* If the travel clerk has done her job properly the client will have signed the booking form in the operator's brochure *before* the button was pushed. This ensures that the contract is made on the operator's terms and all the small print at the back of the brochure has been incorporated into the contract. The case of *L'Estrange v Graucob* [1934] 2 K.B. 394 decided that once a person has *signed* a document they are bound by its terms even though they have not read them.

The analysis of the process of agreement is not affected by the presence of the booking form. The tour operator is effectively saying that he is prepared to sell the holiday displayed on the screen on the terms in the brochure. The acceptance is made by the client signing the booking form and indicating to the travel clerk to press the button. Both the offer and the acceptance have two elements. The offer consists of what is on the screen combined with what is in the booking form. The acceptance is not complete until the booking form has been signed and the button has been pressed.

But what if the travel clerk fails to obtain the signature on the booking form? The position here would almost certainly be that there *is* a contract but *not* on the terms and conditions contained in the brochure. The information displayed on the screen is quite sufficient to form the basis of a contract. It contains everything the client needs to know—dates, price, hotel, mealplan, airport, departure times, etc. Once the button has been pressed a contract exists despite the omission of the operator's terms and conditions. (In an extreme case where the travel clerk's failure resulted in the tour operator being unable to limit his liability under the Warsaw Convention the cost might be the difference between £13,000 and perhaps £2m—see Chapter 6 on Exclusion of Liability). The travel clerk may very well have contravened the tour operator's booking procedures but that will not affect the validity of the contract. That is a private matter between the travel agency and the tour operator.

If the travel clerk obtained the client's signature and deposit *immediately after* the button was pressed this would *probably* not disadvantage the operator. So long as the signature was obtained at roughly the same time as the pressing of the button it could be viewed as part of a single process of offer and acceptance. In *Williams v Thomson Tour Operations Ltd* 1997, Gloucester County Court, unreported, the claimant booked a fly/drive holiday over the telephone via a travel agent; the agent then told the claimant to come down to his shop that day to sign the booking form. It was held that the claimant was bound by her signature to the terms of the contract, including requirements to pay extras for the hire car which were set out in the brochure. The basis of the decision was that the telephone call and the signing of the booking form were all part of the same transaction (the first edition of this book was cited in argument on this point.)

If the travel clerk informed the client before the button was pressed that a signature on the terms and conditions was required but for some reason omitted to obtain the signature the operator would *probably* still not be disadvantaged. The significance of the signature is that it provides *proof* that the client has had the terms and conditions drawn to their attention and has agreed that they form part of the contract. If the client has had the terms and conditions drawn to their attention and it is clear that the contract is being made on the basis of those terms and conditions then the fact that there is no signature does not alter the basic legal position. The problem that arises is that with no signature there is no proof that the client has agreed to what is on the booking form and therefore if a dispute arises later, how is the operator to establish that the client knew about the booking terms? The travel clerk is unlikely to be able to provide convincing evidence simply because she will be unable to remember one transaction amongst hundreds. So although in principle the lack of a signature in these circumstances is not fatal, in practice, the operator, without a signed document, will be hard pressed to make his terms stick.

There are a number of what are called "ticket cases" involving cruise lines and ferries which illustrate the importance of getting booking procedures right to ensure that the operator's terms and conditions are properly incorporated in the contract.

One of these is *Hollingworth v Southern Ferries Ltd (The "Eagle")* [1977] 2 Lloyd's Rep. 70. The claimant had been injured on the defendant's ship due to the defendant's negligence. Their defence was that there was a clause in the contract which exempted them from liability. The facts were that the contract had been made on the claimant's behalf by a friend who was acting as her agent. He had acquired a brochure from a travel agency and then gone back some time later and made a firm booking for the two of them. The booking was made over the phone in the travel agent's office and a booking form was not signed. Nor were the booking conditions in the brochure drawn to the attention of the client at the time of booking, nor indeed was it brought home to the client that the booking was made subject to the booking conditions. There was certainly an exclusion clause on the ticket which the claimant was given prior to departure but that was long after the contract had been made. It was held that the exclusion clause *had not been incorporated* in the contract and therefore the defendants were not protected by it. The fact that there were conditions in the brochure which the claimant's friend had seen was not good enough. The judge said:

> "I do not consider that merely seeing a statement of this kind in a brochure makes that statement in effect of the same import as would be the case if one were shown that document at the time when one was making the contract; the statement in the brochure merely gives an intending passenger advance notice of the terms which he may expect to find when he enters into the contract."

Effectively he was saying that insufficient had been done to bring the conditions to the notice of the claimant so that they were brought home to the claimant *at the time the contract was made*.

He also went on to say that even if he was wrong on this point the conditions in the brochure would still be of no help to the defendants. The brochure did not print the terms and conditions in their entirety it merely said that the voyage was subject to terms and conditions which could be inspected at the defendant's offices in Southampton. In some cases that might be sufficient but in the present case the conditions were so sweeping in nature it was not enough to print a general notice like this. It did not bring home to the claimant the nature of the particular clause which exempted liability.

A contrasting case is *Budd v Peninsular and Oriental Steam Navigation Co* [1969] 2 Lloyd's Rep. 262. In that case the claimant was injured due to the admitted negligence of the defendants. However, in this case when the claimant had entered into the contract at the premises of the defendant's agents the agents had made sure she signed the declaration on the booking form. It stated:

> "... and I understand that all accommodation is offered and fares are quoted subject to the Regulations and Conditions of Carriage as printed on the Passage Ticket of the Line concerned."

One of the conditions on the ticket, which was legible and reasonably comprehensible to the average person, exempted the defendants from liability. The judge said:

> "The law of this country is plain. If you choose to put your signature to a document in which it is made plain that the obligations of the party with whom you are contracting is contained in certain conditions, then you are bound by those conditions ..."

The claimant therefore failed in her action. The difference between the cases is simply that in the former proper procedures were not followed whereas in the latter they were. For a further example of the consequences of failing to follow a proper booking procedure the case of *Fosbroke-Hobbes v Airwork Ltd* [1937] 1 All E.R. 108 discussed in Chapter 6 on Exclusion of Liability is instructive. (Note that since 1977 when the Unfair Contract Terms Act was passed exemption clauses which attempt to exclude liability for personal injury caused by negligence are no longer valid.)

If however the terms and conditions signed by the client at the same time as the button is pressed expressly state that the contract is not concluded until, for instance, confirmation is sent (or received) by the client then the analysis may be different. Here the tour operator is reserving to himself the opportunity of *accepting or rejecting the offer made by the client* to buy the holiday. The conclusion of the contract is being postponed until the tour operator decides he wishes to make the contract—by posting the confirmation, *i.e.* the acceptance. Given the automated nature of the contracting process in these circumstances and the unlikelihood of any human intervention at such a late stage it is a little puzzling why a tour operator would wish to do this. All it seems to accomplish is to give the client an opportunity to reconsider and perhaps withdraw their offer before the tour operator has had a chance to accept. (For withdrawal of offers, see below.) For a practical example of how this might work against the tour operator see "The Problem Page" [1994] T.L.J. 26. See also *Saggerson*, p. 151 on this issue.

(b) Direct Sell Operators Using a Manual System

A typical scenario here would be that the client acquires the brochure, fills in the booking form, posts it off to the operator who then confirms the booking by sending a letter of confirmation to the client. The analysis in this situation would be that the brochure constitutes an invitation to treat. The operator is saying that he has holidays that he wishes to sell and is inviting the public to make an offer to buy them. By filling in the booking form the client makes such an offer and the operator accepts this offer by despatching the confirmation of booking letter. Under this system the operator has the last word. He is in a position to accept or reject the client's offer which he will do according to whether the holiday is available or not.

As far as incorporation of the terms and condition is concerned this is achieved by requiring the client to sign a booking form containing a declaration that he agrees to take the holiday on the terms spelt out in the brochure. If for some reason the declaration is not signed the operator, to protect himself, should send the form back and insist that it is signed. To send a letter of confirmation without first obtaining the signature is to create an avoidable risk.

One problem that arises when dealing with correspondence is that there is necessarily a delay between when the letter of acceptance is posted and when it arrives. Sometimes, as over the Christmas period, that delay can be substantial and in rare circumstances the letter can go missing altogether. The question that this poses is *when* is the contract concluded? When the letter is posted or when it arrives?

The tour operator in fact has control over this situation should he care to take advantage of it. It is open to the operator to provide in the brochure and the booking conditions that acceptance will take effect from the moment the letter of confirmation is despatched. Thus he can be secure in the knowledge that once the letter is posted a contract exists. He is not left at the mercy of the Post Office. The client of course *is* at the mercy of the Post Office. He is left in a state of uncertainty as to whether he has a contract or not until the letter of confirmation arrives, but that is the risk he takes when he contracts on terms and conditions drafted by someone else.

However, even without express words in the terms and conditions providing that the acceptance takes effect on posting, the rule of the common law, known as the postal rule, provides that in the absence of circumstances to the contrary, when the post is the accepted means of communication, the acceptance takes effect when it is posted, *even if it never arrives* (*Household Fire and Carriage Accident Co v Grant* (1879) 4 Ex D 216). This rule, which is entirely arbitrary, is an exception to the general rule that in contract the acceptance does not take effect until it has been communicated to the offeror. In other words there is no contract until both parties know about it. It substitutes a *dispatch* rule for the normal *receipt* rule. Because it is an exception the courts will not apply it if it leads to absurd or inconvenient results. [Note that in the *Carlill* case the claimant did not communicate her acceptance of the offer to the advertisers when she bought the smoke ball and started using it. In the circumstances it was held that the defendants had waived their right to have the acceptance communicated.]

Just as the operator can expressly provide for what the booking procedure will be when using the post so too can the client. Consider the following facts: a client, immediately prior to Christmas, wishes to book a holiday for early in the New Year. Being aware of the difficulties with postal communication at that time of year he phones up in advance to enquire about availability. The operator tells him that a holiday is still available but that no bookings can be taken over the phone, nor will an option be held. The client responds by saying that he will post the booking immediately but in the circumstances he would appreciate a response within the week.

In these circumstances there would be grounds for saying, in the absence of express words on the booking form, that the acceptance would only take effect when communicated to the client and if it arrived outside the time limit laid down by the client it would be too late. The offer was only open for a certain length of time. After that time it is no longer open to be accepted. The client clearly did not want to be left hanging around not knowing whether he has a contract or not. He specified a time limit, after which he would be free to go elsewhere. The operator cannot fall back on the postal rule and argue that there was a contract as soon as the letter was posted. In these circumstances it will be the operator who runs the risk of the delays in the post over Christmas, not the client.

(c) Last Minute, Direct-sell, Telephone Bookings

It is increasingly the case that clients can book holidays or flights over the phone, using a credit card for payment, and perhaps never sign a booking form. The dangers here for the operator are obvious. He may sell the holiday but not on his terms.

Suppose for instance that a client sees a last minute bargain advertised on TV using teletext services such as "Oracle". He can ring up the operator concerned, obtain full details over the phone, pay by credit card and pick up the tickets and accommodation details at the airport. The advertisement on Oracle is only an invitation to treat and many of them make this plain by stating that they are "subject to availability". The initial enquiry by the client will not be an offer simply because the screen does not give enough detail on which to base a firm offer. The offer is probably made by the sales staff describing the holiday and stating that it is available if the client wants it. The acceptance is made by the client agreeing to take the holiday and giving details of his name and address and his credit card number. Unless the sales staff indicate to the client that there are conditions attached to the booking the contract will consist solely of the details described over the phone. Sending written confirmation of the booking later with conditions attached will not change the situation. Conditions added later are not effective. It is not possible for one party to unilaterally insert terms into the contract which the other party did not know of or agree to (see for instance *Olley v Marlborough Court Hotel Ltd* [1949] 1 K.B. 532 discussed in Chapter 6 on Exclusion of Liability).

Note that if the sales staff had indicated that there were conditions attached to the booking then even though the client had not read them they would nevertheless still form part of the contract. It is not necessary for the client to have read them, merely to have had them drawn to his attention. Once he knows of their existence he is bound by them if he goes ahead and makes the contract. But in these circumstances there remains a practical problem. It frequently happens that a travel clerk asserts that attention was drawn to the conditions but the client equally assertively denies that this was done. The courts often find in favour of the client's version of events—often with serious consequences for the operator. There is really no substitute for a signed booking form, although one that goes some of the way to solving the problem might be the use of tape recordings of bookings.

(d) Internet Bookings

Travel companies, particularly airlines and hotels, have found that the internet is an invaluable means of marketing and selling their products. However internet sales are regulated in a way that the other forms of contracting are not. Directive 2000/31/EC, the Directive on Electronic Commerce, which was transposed into UK law by the Electronic Commerce (EC Directive) Regulations 2002 (SI 2002/2013), contains some rudimentary rules which impact upon the process of offer and acceptance over the internet. Before we look at these rules, however, it is useful to examine how a contract might be made over the internet.

In many ways it resembles the way in which a contract is concluded by viewdata except that the client navigates his way through the screens without the assistance of a travel agent. Essentially what happens however is that the client will visit a travel related internet site and having reached a stage where he has selected what he wants he will be prompted to commit himself to the tour operator by clicking on the appropriate part of the screen. From what we have seen already of viewdata bookings this can be analysed, at a very basic level, as an *offer by the tour operator to sell* the selected products, and an *acceptance by the client* of what is on offer. But in practice the situation is often very different because the process usually involves some sort of confirmation or acknowledgement by the tour operator that the order has been received/accepted—suggesting that it is the client who is *offering to buy* and the tour operator who is *accepting the offer*. Often this will be reinforced by the terms and conditions of the tour operator which have been incorporated into the contracting process as the client proceeds through the various screens. For internet bookings this will be very simple for the operator to achieve. All he has to do is to compel the consumer to "click through" a page on which the terms and conditions are displayed or referred to.

What then do the Electronic Commerce Regulations have to say that is relevant to this process? Regulation 9(1) provides that where a contract is to be concluded by electronic means a service provider (in our case a travel company selling over the internet) shall:

"... prior to an order being placed by the recipient of a service [the client] provide to that recipient in a clear, comprehensible and unambiguous manner the information set out in (a) ... below—

(a) the different technical steps to follow to conclude the contract"

And Regulation 9(3) requires that:

Where the service provider provides terms and conditions applicable to the contract to the recipient, the service provider shall make them available to him in a way that allows him to store and reproduce them.

According to Regulation 11(1), if a client places an "order" by electronic means the travel company must acknowledge receipt of the order to the recipient of the service without undue delay and by electronic means. Furthermore, Regulation 11(2) states that:

"... the order and the acknowledgement of receipt will be deemed to be received when the parties to whom they are addressed are able to access them ..." [Emphasis added]

The meaning of "order" is amplified in Regulation 12:

"12. Except in relation to regulation 9(1)(c) and regulation 11(1)(b) where 'order' shall be the contractual offer, 'order' may be but need not be the contractual offer for the purposes of regulations 9 and 11."

So what is the practical impact of this? First, we should note that the Regulations are not prescriptive. They do not require service providers to contract in a particular way, they leave them free to adopt any process they wish so long as they inform the client. However, because travel companies do have to set out the technical steps by which a contract is concluded they should at least have given some thought to the contracting process. This, coupled with the requirement that if they do have terms and conditions, which invariably they do, they have to make them available to the client in a form in which they can be stored and reproduced will make it almost inevitable that somewhere on the site it will say *when* the contract is concluded. Given that it lies within the control of the travel company to dictate the time at which the contract is concluded it would be wise of them to take advantage of the opportunity.

But what is advisable and what happens in practice are two different things. It is entirely conceivable that some travel companies either do not set out the contracting process or do so in a manner which is defective or ambiguous, in which case the answer would have to be determined by recourse to first principles. The problem, as with the post, is that the contract is made at a distance and the question arises, as it does with fax and telex, as to whether the communication by the travel company acknowledging the order of the client, or indeed the order by the client (if it could be construed as an acceptance) should take effect on dispatch or receipt. Some assistance can be found in the wording of Regulation 11(2), quoted above, which suggests that it is a receipt rule.

The same issue has been litigated on a number of previous occasions in relation to contracts made by telex. In *Brinkibon Ltd. v Stahag Stahl und Stahlwarenhandels-Gesellschaft mBH* [1983] A.C. 34 Lord Wilberforce said that there could be no hard and fast rule in such cases:

> "Since 1955 the use of telex communication has been greatly expanded, and there are many variants on it. The senders and recipients may not be the principals to the contemplated contract. They may be servants or agents with limited authority. The message may not reach, or be intended to reach, the designated recipient immediately: messages may be sent out of office hours, or at night, with the intention, or upon the assumption, that they will be read at a later time. There may be some error or default at the recipient's end which prevents receipt at the time contemplated and believed in by the sender. The message may have been sent and/or received through machines operated by third persons. and many other variations may occur. No universal rule can cover all such cases: they must be resolved by reference to the intentions of the parties, by sound business practice and in some cases by a judgment where the risks should lie."

It is probably the case that the same kind of pragmatic approach will be adopted in relation to internet contracts where the travel company has not made it clear in its terms and conditions what the position is.

The impact of regulation 9

Up to now we have seen that the penalty the tour operator pays for failing to incorporate his terms and conditions in the contract is simply that he will not be able to rely upon them. This may be a problem but it is not fatal to the existence of the contract. However, Regulation 9 changes all that. It provides not only that certain information must be incorporated in the contract but also, if practicable, that it must be put in writing and communicated to the consumer *before* the contract is made. In all cases a written copy must be supplied to the consumer. Failure to comply gives the consumer the right to cancel.

Regulation 9 states:

> "9(1) The other party to the contract shall ensure that—
>
> (a) depending on the nature of the package being purchased, the contract contains at least the elements specified in schedule 2 to these regulations;
> (b) subject to paragraph (2) below, all the terms of the contract are set out in writing or such other form as is comprehensible and accessible to the consumer and are communicated to the consumer before the contract is made; and
> (c) a written copy of these terms is supplied to the consumer.
>
> (2) Paragraph (1) (b) above does not apply when the interval between the time when the consumer approaches the other party to the contract with a view to entering into a contract and the time of departure under the proposed contract is so short that it is impracticable to comply with the sub-paragraph.
>
> (3) It is an implied condition . . . of the contract that the other party to the contract complies with the provisions of paragraph (1)."

Regulation 9(1)(b) which requires the information to be provided *before the contract is made* should be read in conjunction with Regulation 9(1)(a) which requires the information to be *in the contract*. For conventional tour operators this should not pose a problem. According to Regulation 5 and Schedule 1 (see Chapter Twelve) a tour operator who publishes a brochure must ensure that the brochure contains certain information. This information is similar, but not identical, to the information required by Schedule 2. On the face of it therefore the brochure can be used to kill two birds with one stone. Regulation 9(1)(b) can be satisfied by putting the information in the brochure; Regulation 9(1)(a) is satisfied by ensuring that when the booking form is signed the consumer agrees that the relevant information from the brochure is incorporated in the contract. But care will have to be taken to communicate some of the requirements of Schedule 2 to the consumer at the appropriate time because the information may not be found in the brochure. Paragraph 2 for instance (means, characteristics and categories of transport to be used and the dates, times and points of departure and return) has no direct equivalent in Schedule 1. Nor has Paragraph 8 (name and address of the organiser, the retailer and, where appropriate the insurer) or Paragraph 11 (special requirements).

The alternative is to produce another standard form contract at the time of contracting, or even to produce a tailor-made or individualised contract at that time. Provision of the information on a confirmation invoice or a computer print out *after* the contract has been made will not be permissible given the requirement in Regulation 9(1)(b) that the information be provided *before the contract is concluded.*

Last Minute Bookings

An exception to this is to be found in Regulation 9(2) in the case of "last minute" bookings. If it is not practicable to comply then the tour operator does not have to supply the information "in writing or such other form ..." before the contract is made. However, given the fact that much if not all the information might be already available in a brochure and given the speed of modern communications it will probably be the exception rather than the rule that this requirement will be waived for conventional tour operators selling holidays from brochures via travel agents.

The real difficulty will be for operators who sell their holidays using telephone credit card sales where the contract is concluded over the phone and where written communication before the contract is made is difficult if not impossible. Given that the Regulation states that the contract should be set out in writing *or such other form as is comprehensible and accessible* then it would be legitimate to provide the information over the phone. The problem, of course, would be the length of time required to provide it. Schedule 2 is not short and several valuable minutes could be consumed just repeating routine information—and then there are the other terms such as exclusion clauses, limitation clauses, cancellation charges, etc. The Regulation will be broken if either the information is provided *after* the contract has been made or if the information is not *communicated* at all.

It is, of course, possible to incorporate terms by reference, *i.e.* by informing the consumer that the contract is subject to terms and conditions without actually spelling out precisely what they are. This is what most transport companies do. On their tickets they state that the ticket is "subject to conditions" (see Chapter 6 on Exclusion Clauses for more on this). Thus, the very least the telesales operator must do to be able to rely on his small print is to inform the consumer over the phone that the contract contains terms and conditions other than the basic details of price, date, destination, etc. But the question arises as to whether or not the tour operator has done sufficient to comply with Regulation 9(1)(b) by merely referring to the small print rather than reading it all out? By using this shorthand method has the operator communicated all the terms in a *form* which is accessible? Although a respectable argument could be made out for saying that such a shorthand form was an appropriate form in the circumstances one has to remember that this is a consumer protection measure and therefore any interpretation that permits less than the full terms of the contract to be communicated is not to be encouraged.

So if reading out all the terms over the phone is impracticable what else is possible? Could the operator be expected to say to the consumer that the contract will not be concluded until the information has been posted or faxed to him? Where time is not of pressing importance this would be entirely reasonable. It would merely place the telesales operator in the same position as other direct sell operators who advertise in papers or other print media and use the post to communicate. However, the nature of telesales is that a large part of the market is "late sales" where it is in the interests of both parties to be able to conclude the contract over the phone. Neither party wishes to lose the sale by having to postpone the conclusion of the contract until the terms have been communicated in full in writing. The reality is that if the consumer were told that he couldn't make the contract there and then he would simply put the phone down and then ring another operator who would be more obliging.

The problem is where to draw the line between "last minute" sales where the operator cannot be expected to comply fully with Regulation 9(1)(b) and other sales where compliance is not a problem. The DTI guidelines suggest that as a matter of "good practice" the dividing line is the one suggested by trade bodies, *i.e.* last minute bookings are those taken within 14 days of departure.

Even if the telesales operator satisfies Regulations 9(1)(a) and (b) by providing the information orally or is not required to provide the information in full because it is a last minute booking Regulation 9(1)(c) still requires them to put all the terms of the contract in writing afterwards. It requires that *a written copy of these terms is supplied to the consumer* although no time limit is placed on this requirement. Presumably a court would imply a term to the effect that the written contract be supplied within a reasonable time after the conclusion of the contract and if the operator did not comply then they would be in breach of Regulation 9.

Mention was made earlier of internet bookings. Given the nature of the technology it is difficult to see how an internet travel company could ever take advantage of the last minute rule—simply because it is so easy for them to comply with the Regulation.

The Penalty For Non-compliance

The penalty for not complying with Regulation 9 is to be found in 9(3). It states that it is an implied *condition* that the operator will comply with the Regulation. Breach of an implied condition gives the client the right to withdraw from the contract. Effectively this means that if a tour operator fails even marginally to comply with the Regulation the consumer will have the right to withdraw. Regulation 9(1)(a) requires *at least* the elements listed in the Schedule to be contained in the contract and Regulation 9(1)(b) requires that *all the terms* of the contract are set out in writing.

This places a premium on getting the paperwork right and at the right time. What the tour operator does not want is large numbers of clients being able to cancel merely because the details were not provided at the right time. Making sure the brochure is as comprehensive as possible is one way. Making sure that agents are aware of their responsibilities is another.

On the face of it the penalty for non-compliance is severe. The operator stands the risk of losing the contract altogether. In practice however the penalty is probably more apparent than real. It depends upon first, the consumer knowing that he has the right to withdraw and secondly, the consumer being prepared to exercise that right. It is doubtful how many consumers are aware of this right and, even when they are, having sufficient confidence to exercise it. They need the confidence to do so because in most cases their money will already be in the hands of the tour operator and they risk losing everything if their decision is wrong. It is unfortunately the case that most telesales operators could probably ignore the provisions of Regulation 9 because the sanction is not likely to be effective.

In *Foster v Dial A Flight Ltd* (1998) Altrincham County Court, unreported, the claimant argued that the tour operator had failed to comply with Regulation 9 and sued for breach of condition and the return of his money. The issue went unresolved however because the court held that the arrangements purchased by the claimant did not amount to a package and therefore the Regulations did not apply. Given the more recent decision of the ECJ in the *Club Tour* case it is likely that if the facts of *Foster* occurred again the consumer would be more successful.

Even where last minute bookings are not an issue a tour operator who fails to comply with Regulation 9 might escape the full impact of the sanction. There is authority to the effect that a victim of a breach of condition may lose the right to withdraw from the contract in circumstances where the common law doctrine of affirmation applies. If the consumer, knowing that a breach of condition has occurred, chooses to affirm the contract then the right to repudiate is lost. Thus, if the consumer knew that by not supplying all the terms of the contract in writing in advance the tour operator was in breach of Regulation 9 and yet still chose to continue with the contract, *e.g.* by paying the balance when it fell due, the consumer would lose the right to repudiate for breach of condition (see the Law Commission Working Paper No. 85 paras. 261-263 and *Chitty on Contracts*, para. 25-002 for further discussion of this point.)

Note that if the tour operator has not drawn the attention of the consumer to the terms and conditions of the contract at all before the contract was concluded then on the basis of the principles already discussed they do not form part of the contract and therefore the tour operator is not in breach of Regulation 9. So for instance, for telephone bookings, as long as the basic details of the contract have been agreed orally over the phone the tour operator may have a perfectly valid contract but he runs the risk of not being able to enforce any of the terms and conditions he may subsequently send to the consumer.

The Other Party To The Contract

Regulation 9 imposes the liability upon "the other party to the contract" *i.e.* the "organiser or the retailer, or both, as the case may be". At first glance one is tempted to say that this seems irrelevant. If the information was not provided does it matter who didn't provide the information? However, closer examination suggests that it may have a practical effect. Where a consumer is buying a holiday at the last minute from a travel agent on the High Street, perhaps with less than 24 hours to go before departure, it might be perfectly justifiable for the tour operator to claim that he could not supply all the information in writing to the consumer. The travel agent on the other hand may be in a position to do so, and failure to comply would result, at least in theory, in the consumer being able to cancel.

Offers, withdrawal of offer and counter-offers

The process of bargaining described above is a little misleading as it gives the impression that the parties proceed from one stage to the next—invitation to treat, followed by offer, followed by acceptance—in a relatively straightforward manner. But life is more complicated than that. Often the bargaining process is much more complicated.

Take for instance the VDU booking. Imagine that at the height of the booking season clients have entered a travel agency and with the assistance of the travel clerk have chosen a holiday. They then ask for just a couple of minutes to deliberate. While this is happening the holiday they chose disappears from the screen because it is now fully booked. When the couple make up their minds to take the holiday it is no longer available. Legally speaking what has happened is that although the operator made them an offer that offer was *withdrawn before it was accepted*. In such circumstances there is no contract. The clients will have to start all over again. The logic of the situation is that if there is no offer on the table there is nothing to be accepted and the parties will have no contract.

This is just a specific example of the general rule that a party can withdraw his offer at any time before acceptance (*Offord v Davies* (1862) C.B.N.S. 748) and there will be no contract (subject to what is said below about options).

What would be the position if a client filled in the booking form for a direct sell operator and despatched it (with deposit) and then immediately afterwards wrote again saying that he is "reconsidering" the hotel he had chosen and would it be possible to upgrade to a higher grade hotel? After receiving both letters the operator writes back explaining that an upgrade is not possible and confirms the original booking. Is there a contract? There is clearly an original offer to buy by the client which has ultimately been accepted by the operator but what is the effect of the intervening enquiry by the client? Is it a withdrawal of his original offer? If so then any attempted acceptance by the operator is to no avail, there is no longer an offer to accept. But what if the second letter is not a withdrawal, merely a request for something different if it can be arranged, but which still leaves the original offer open if the request cannot be satisfied. In this case the operator might successfully argue that he has a contract. It would be a question of what *objective* interpretation a court would place upon the second letter.

It is not unknown in the travel industry for clients to haggle over the price. Take the client who rings up an hotel and asks what the weekend rate for a family room is. He is told that it is £120 per night for a couple. This includes bed, breakfast and evening meal and accommodation in a room which will sleep two adults and two children but the children will have to pay for meals as taken. Knowing that this is the low season for hotels the client manages to bargain the price down to £100 but is still not satisfied and says that unless the children can be accommodated in a separate room he will not make a booking. The reservations clerk has no further discretion in the matter and asks the client to hang on a moment while he consults the manager.

The manager is horrified that the clerk has even considered such a booking because there is a conference booked into the hotel that weekend and almost all the rooms are taken already and the rest can certainly be sold off at full price. The clerk informs the client that there is no way they can accommodate the children in a separate room. The client then backs down and says that he will take the family room for £100 but the clerk informs him that if he wants the room he will have to pay the regular weekend rate. Is there a contract? Probably not.

What has happened here is that the hotel has made an offer to sell the room for £100 per night. The offer was not accepted by the client. The client went so far as to say that he would not have the room at that price and proposed a different arrangement altogether. This amounts to a counter-offer and the legal effect of a counter-offer is to destroy the original offer. The counter-offer was not accepted by the hotel and therefore the client attempted to accept the original offer by the hotel, but this no longer existed. In effect the client was making another new offer and this in turn was rejected by the hotel.

One of the leading cases on this point is *Hyde v Wrench* (1840) 49 All E.R. 132. The facts were that the defendant wrote to the claimant on June 6 offering to sell his farm for £1000. The claimant responded immediately by making an offer of £950 which the defendant refused on June 27. On June 29 the claimant wrote and "accepted" the offer of June 6. On the question of whether there was a contract, Lord Langdale, the Master of the Rolls, said:

> "Under the circumstances stated ... I think there exists no valid binding contract between the parties for the purchase of the property. The defendant offered to sell it for £1000 and if that had been at once unconditionally accepted, there would undoubtedly have been a perfect binding contract; instead of that, the plaintiff made an offer of his own, to purchase the property for £950, *and he thereby rejected the offer previously made by the defendant*. I think that it was not afterwards competent for him to revive the proposal of the defendant, by tendering an acceptance of it; and that, therefore, there exists no obligation of any sort between the parties ..." [Emphasis added]

The important thing to note here is that the response by the claimant amounted to a *rejection* of the original offer. A different response may have kept the original offer open as in the case of *Stevenson v McLean* (1880) 5 Q.B.D. 346. In that case the facts were that in the course of negotiating the sale of a quantity of iron the defendant wrote to the claimants on Saturday saying: "...I would now sell for 40s net cash, open till Monday." On Monday the claimants telegraphed back: "Please wire whether you would accept forty for delivery over two months, or if not, longest limit you would give." After receiving this telegram the defendants sold the iron to a third party and telegraphed the claimants to this effect at 1.25 pm. The telegram did not arrive until 1.46 pm. In the meantime, having received no reply to their original enquiry the claimants had telegraphed the defendant at 1.34 pm accepting the original offer outright.

It was held that the enquiry by the claimants as to the terms on which they could purchase the iron was no more than that, just an enquiry. In the words of Lush J:

> "Here there is no counter proposal. The words are, 'Please wire whether you would accept forty for delivery over two months, or, if not, the longest limit you would give.' There is nothing specific by way of offer or rejection, but a mere inquiry, which should have been answered and not treated as a rejection of the offer."

It was decided therefore that there was an offer which had been accepted by the claimants and therefore the defendant was in breach of contract.

Note that although the defendant had telegraphed the withdrawal of his offer by telegram *before* he had received the acceptance the withdrawal did not take effect until it arrived. This is in accordance with the rule laid down in the case of *Byrne v Van Tienhoven* (1880) 5 C.P.D. 344 to the effect that a revocation of an offer must be communicated before it takes effect.

If we apply *Stevenson v Mclean* to the example used above of the haggling over the hotel room we can see that if the client had been less assertive in his negotiations he might at least have acquired the room for £50. If he had framed his request for a separate room for the children as an enquiry rather than a rejection of the hotel's offer there would still have been an offer on the table for him to accept.

Options

Although this has become uncommon some tour operators permit clients to hold options. An option is simply a willingness to hold an offer open for a specified period of time. With a VDU booking system it allows the client a period of consideration and consultation before having to make a final decision. With a manual system the tour operator may grant an option following a telephone enquiry which will allow the client time to fill in the booking form and post it off.

So long as the offer is still open it can be accepted by the client but it will lapse at the end of the specified period and the client will have nothing to accept. The only problem that arises with options is whether or not the offer can be withdrawn before the time limit has expired and the answer to this is quite straightforward. It was settled in the case of *Routledge v Grant* (1828) 130 All E.R. 920. As with any other offer an option can be withdrawn at any time before it has been accepted so long as the withdrawal is communicated to the other party. The only exception to this, which is unlikely to be found in a travel industry context, is when one party *pays* the other party for an option. In these circumstances the offer must be kept open until the option expires.

Chapter Four
Contents of the Contract

Introduction and Overview

As part of the bargaining process before a contract is concluded the two parties will make a variety of statements to each other, either orally or in writing. Some of these statements may end up as part of the contract and some may not. Those which end up as part of the contract may vary in importance. This chapter is concerned with how to classify these statements. It is important to be able to do this because the rights of the parties clearly depend upon whether a statement is part of the contract or not, and if it is, the relative importance to be attached to it.

This introductory section gives a brief overview of the classification process. The rest of this chapter and Chapters Five and Six amplify what is said here.

1. Terms, representations and mere puffs

The task of classification is complicated by the fact that English law distinguishes between three different types of statement. First, there are those statements which end up as *terms of the contract*, which if broken, give the victim a straightforward action for *breach of contract*. These are the things which the other party has *promised* you will get. In a package holiday context it will be a term of the contract for instance that it is a four star hotel, that the clients will get a balcony and private facilities, that there are three pools and two bars, that it has a children's club, etc. Generally these are all statements which are printed in the brochure and are what the operator has *contracted* to provide.

Secondly, there are statements which *induce* the other party to enter into the contract but do not become terms of the contract. These are known as *representations* and if they are *false* they give rise to an action for *misrepresentation*. An action for misrepresentation is not as straightforward as an action for breach of contract and the remedies available may be inadequate although recent case law suggests that in certain circumstances they may be superior (See *Royscot Trust Ltd v Rogerson* [1991] 3 All E.R. 294

and Chapter 7). Often it is difficult to distinguish between a term and a representation but for example it would *probably* only be a representation if an operator, having described the hotel, then went on to describe the resort as having a "wide range of shops". The operator is contracting to provide an hotel with particular facilities but then in order to encourage the client to enter into the contract he makes other statements which will influence the client's decision but which do not form part of the contract. If the resort turns out not to have a wide range of shops the client can sue for misrepresentation but not for breach of contract. The rules on misrepresentation can be found in Chapter Seven.

Thirdly, there are statements which have no legal force at all. These are known as "puffs" or "mere puffs". A victim of such a statement has no redress at all. In a holiday case, *Hoffman v Intasun* (1990, High Court, unreported), the plaintiff tried to make out that because of the extravagantly worded statements made at the beginning of a "Club 18-30" brochure the defendants, Intasun, had *contracted* that they owed her an especially high standard of care. The judge rejected this approach. He decided that the statements had no contractual effect at all. This is what he said:

> "I am asked to say that because of the advertising—what lawyers call puff—in the early part of the brochure, the Defendants were undertaking to give an especially high standard of care. That is an argument that I reject. Puff is puff, and if that is what lawyers call it, lay people have their own expressions for it which are perhaps less flattering. Everybody knows that travel agents [sic] set out to create an atmosphere on paper of a wonderful holiday and marvellous value for money. It cannot possibly be said that a visitor to the Tyrol can sue the travel company for breach of contract if he fails to have any respiratory defect in regarding the breathtaking views of the mountains there—and so on. I look for example at how the Club reps are described on page 8 of the brochure. Mr Eccles [counsel for Intasun] in his opening drew my attention to it specifically saying that the reps were the life and soul of the party, hard working, good timing, trouble shooting, guitar playing, beach partying, smooth operators. I do not know if Miss Gail Tarburn [the Intasun rep] can even play the guitar and I am certain that it could not form any part of a breach of contract if she cannot."

Much of the advertising that goes into the front of brochures falls into this category—statements that make the holiday sound good but do not amount to specific contractual promises. Open most brochures at the beginning and you are bound to find examples—

"picturesque villages set amidst glorious scenery"—"quality hotels"—"the number one choice for families"—"the holiday of a lifetime"—"the most beautiful locations around the Mediterranean"—"hand picked accommodation"—"a luxury cruise around the glittering Caribbean" and so on. In *Griffiths v Waymark* (Slough County Ct, 1993, unreported, but see [1994] TLJ 122) the judge regarded the phrase "ever-friendly hotel" as not amounting to a legal representation.

Thus not only do terms have to be distinguished from representations, they both have to be distinguished from mere puffs.

2. Conditions, warranties and innominate terms

Terms can be classified into either *conditions* or *warranties*. A condition is a major term of the contract which, if broken, provides the victim of the breach with not only a right to damages but also the right, if they wish, to terminate the contract altogether. A warranty on the other hand only gives rise to an action for damages. There is no right to terminate the contract for what is regarded as a breach of a minor term of the contract. There is also an intermediate form of term—called an *innominate* term—which cannot immediately be classified as either a condition or a warranty. Its classification depends upon the nature and severity of the breach.

3. Express and implied terms

Terms can be further classified into *express* terms and *implied* terms. An express term, as its name suggests is one which is expressed in some way—in writing or orally or even, in the case of brochures, pictorially. An implied term is one where the term is not expressed but can nevertheless be implied into the contract. Terms can be implied in a number of ways: by statute (*e.g.* the requirement that goods be of satisfactory quality implied by s.14 of the Sale of Goods Act 1979); by custom; or by the courts—in which case they can be implied either *in fact* or *in law*. These terms will be explained in due course. However, there is one travel law case, decided before the Package Travel Regulations were passed, *Wall v Silver Wing Surface Arrangements* (1981, unreported), which revolved around the issue of implied terms, and which illustrates the problem vividly. A party of holidaymakers were injured in a hotel fire in Tenerife. They had been unable to escape down the fire escape because the hotel owners had padlocked the gate at the bottom. In the contract between the clients and the tour operators nothing was expressly stated about safety at the hotel but the clients alleged that there was an implied term in the contract that they would be reasonably safe in using the hotel for the purposes for which they had been invited to be there. Ultimately the court held that there was no such term but it had to make a difficult choice between protecting the interests of the clients by implying a term relating to their safety and the interests of the tour operator by not extending their liability to all the components of the package. This case is placed in context in Chapters 5 and 6.

4. The Package Travel Regulations and the classification of terms

The classification of terms in a package holiday contract is no longer simply a matter for the common law. It is heavily affected by the Package Travel Regulations.

For instance Regulation 6 states that all the *particulars* in the brochure (whatever that means) are implied warranties. On the face of it this has two major effects. First it potentially upgrades just about every statement in the brochure to at least a term of the contract—representations and puffs alike. Secondly it appears to classify all statements as minor terms of the contract.

As far as this second effect is concerned closer examination of the Regulations shows that this is not entirely so. For instance Regulation 9 explicitly states that it is an implied *condition* that certain information must be supplied to the consumer before the contract is made. In addition there are other regulations which have the same effect. Regulation 12 permits a consumer to withdraw from the contract if significant alterations have been made to the contract before departure and Regulation 14 effectively gives the consumer the right to terminate a contract if, after departure, a significant proportion of the services cannot be provided.

5. Regulation 4

Regulation 4 creates a new right of action against organisers or retailers who supply misleading descriptive matter to consumers. This new right of action is a statutory action rather than a contractual action and therefore it cuts across the categories already discussed. Insofar as it only gives a right to damages rather than a right to terminate the contract it resembles an action for breach of warranty. However it is available against the retailer as well as the organiser even though the consumer may not have a contract with the retailer. It also covers *any misleading information*, which again extends the action further than any contractual action.

6. Exclusion clauses

One very important type of term, which will be looked at in a subsequent chapter, is the exclusion clause—also known as an exemption clause or an exception clause. These are clauses where one party to the contract endeavours to escape liability for breach of contract by inserting a clause into the contract excluding his liability. There is a considerable body of law on this subject which we will look at in detail. In particular we will examine Regulation 15 which deals specifically with exclusion clauses in package holiday contracts.

Distinguishing Terms From Other Statements

Whether a statement is a term of a contract or not is a matter of intention to be determined by the court. As with offer and acceptance the intention is determined objectively rather than subjectively. As might be expected there are no precise rules for distinguishing terms from other statements but there are some indicators which have been developed by the courts.

1. The importance of the statement

If it can be shown that one party was most unlikely to have made the contract except on the basis of the statement it is likely to be a term of the contract. In the case of *Bannerman v White* (1861) 10 CB (NS) 844 an intending buyer of hops asked the seller whether sulphur had been used in their cultivation because if it had then he was not interested in them. The seller assured him that it had not. It was held that this was a term of the contract.

One can imagine a situation where, say, a disabled client rings up the operator and asks whether a particular hotel featured in the brochure has wheelchair access because if it hasn't then he is not interested. If the operator responds that it has this would be a breach of contract if wheelchair access was not possible.

2. Was the statement verified?

Two contrasting cases illustrate this point. In *Ecay v Godfrey* (1947) 80 Ll L R 286 the seller of a boat stated that the boat was sound but advised the buyer to have it surveyed. In other words he was saying that he could not verify the condition of the boat and was not contracting on the basis that it was sound. It was held that the condition of the boat was not a term of the contract.

In *Schawel v Reade* [1913] 2 IR 64 the purchaser of a horse was about to examine it when the seller told him not to bother looking at it. He said: "You need not look for anything; the horse is perfectly sound. If there was anything the matter with the horse I should tell you." It was held that the statement was a term of the contract.

Again one can imagine a client enquiring of an operator whether it can be confirmed that the water sports mentioned as being available at the hotel will actually be available at the beginning of the season and the operator responding by saying that they always have in the past but it would be better if the client checked with the hotel before booking. These circumstances are similar to *Ecay v Godfrey* and it would probably be the case that it would not be a term of the contract that water sports would be available.

Alternatively, if the operator confirmed in unequivocal terms that the water sports would be available because they had contracted with the hotel for them then it would almost certainly be a term of the contract.

There is an interesting relationship with Regulation 9 in these cases. If a client obtains an express oral promise that the facilities he is interested in exist then these become terms of the contract. Under Regulation 9 these should be reduced to writing before the contract is concluded. Failure to do so gives the client the right to withdraw (see Chapter 3). However, it is very likely, given the circumstances, that the interchange will not be reduced to writing. This opens up the possibility that the consumer may be able to withdraw from the contract—in theory at least. The procedure adopted by many tour operators, of including a term in their contracts stating that they are not prepared to guarantee "special requests" would go some way to averting this problem—but such a term may fall foul of the Unfair Terms in Consumer Contracts Regulations 1999.

3. Did one party have special knowledge?

In *Oscar Chess Ltd v Williams* [1957] 1 All E.R. 325 a private individual sold his car to a garage on the basis of a statement in the log book (which had been forged by a previous owner) that the car was a 1948 model whereas in fact it was much older. It was held that the garage were specialists and as such were in at least as good a position as the seller to know whether the statement was true or not and that therefore the age of the car was only a representation not a term.

The case of *Dick Bentley Productions Ltd v Harold Smith (Motors) Ltd* [1965] 1 W.L.R. 623 can be contrasted with the *Oscar Chess* case. In that case a dealer sold a Bentley car, saying that the car had only travelled 20,000 miles since having a new engine fitted when in fact it had travelled nearly 100,000 miles. It was held that the statement was a term of the contract. The seller in this case was clearly in a better position than the buyer to know the truth of the statement.

Where a long haul tour operator prints in the brochure the average temperatures to be expected in some exotic island in a remote part of the Indian Ocean or where an operator gives the distance from the hotel to the beach a court might say that given the relative knowledge and expertise of the tour operator such statements would be terms rather than representations.

4. When was the statement made?

In *Routledge v McKay* [1954] 1 All E.R. 855 the seller of a motorcycle stated, on October 23, during preliminary negotiations, that it was a 1942 model when in fact it was a 1930 model. A week later on October 30th the motorcycle was sold and the terms of the contract were reduced to writing. The contract made no mention of the age of the motorcycle. It was held that *at the time the statement was made* it was not intended that it would have contractual force. The omission from the written contract, although not fatal in itself, merely reinforced the view that the statement was not intended as a term. The clear time interval between the making of the statement and the final contract assisted the court in coming to the decision.

It is possible to illustrate this point using the facts of a travel law case. *Kemp v Intasun* [1987] 2 F.T.L.R. 234 (CA); [1987] C.L.Y. 1130; (LEXIS) is *not* a case on misrepresentation but it demonstrates the significance of an interval between the stages of negotiation and the importance of bringing important matters to the attention of the other party *at the time the contract is made*. In the *Kemp* case the plaintiff's wife had entered a branch of Thomas Cook and made preliminary enquiries about holidays. She mentioned in passing that her husband was not with her because he was ill. She said that he was suffering from an asthmatic and bronchial attack. It was not until almost four weeks later that she returned the booking form and concluded the contract. On the first night of their holiday, because of overbooking, the Kemps were accommodated in a substandard room. The dirt and dust in the room brought on an asthma attack and the first week of their holiday was ruined as a result. It was held that the casual remark to the travel agent about Mr Kemp's asthma made at an early stage of the negotiations was insufficient to create contractual obligations for Intasun. They were not liable for problems to Mr Kemp's health which they could not foresee and which had not been drawn to their attention.

It would have been different altogether if Mrs Kemp had specifically drawn the asthma attacks to the attention of Intasun at the time the contract was made in such a way as to make it clear that Intasun were accepting a booking from a person with health problems.

Clearly the passage of time between first mentioning the illness and the ultimate conclusion of the contract resulted in the statement having no contractual effect at all. It would be the same with an action for misrepresentation.

These cases and guidelines illustrate the difficulty of distinguishing between terms and other statements. At the margins the distinction is often very difficult indeed to make and can be regarded as more of an art than a science.

If the plaintiff is fortunate then the statement will have been categorised as a term and there will be a straightforward action for breach of contract but if it is not a term there is the further difficulty of distinguishing between statements which are representations and those which are mere puffs.

Distinguishing Between Representations and Puffs

A representation is a statement of fact made by one party to the contract to the other which induces the other to enter into the contract but which does not form part of the contract itself. A misrepresentation is merely a false representation.

From this definition it can be seen that there are two conditions that a statement must satisfy before it can be classified as a representation. First, it must be a statement of fact, therefore statements of opinion or statements as to the future or future intention do not qualify. Secondly, the statement must actually induce the contract. If the statement had no effect upon the other party it will not amount to a representation. Additionally, the statement must be material. In other words the statement must be of some significance to the reasonable person before it can give rise to an action for misrepresentation.

1. There must be a statement of fact

To be a misrepresentation the statement must be one of fact. This branch of the law protects the victim from statements which are false but not against opinions which turn out to be wrong or predictions as to the future which are not realised. However what amounts to a statement of fact has been given a fairly extended meaning in the law of misrepresentation as can be seen from the following cases.

In *Edgington v Fitzmaurice* (1885) 29 Ch D 459 the directors of a company stated in a prospectus that they wanted to raise money to improve buildings and extend the business. In fact they were going to pay off existing debts with the money. On the face of it this was not a statement of existing fact but a statement of future intention. However Bowen LJ said:

> "The state of a man's mind is as much a fact as the state of his digestion. It is true that it is very difficult to prove what the state of a man's mind at a particular time is, but if it can be ascertained it is as much a fact as anything else. A misrepresentation as to the state of a man's mind is, therefore, a misstatement of fact."

On that basis there was a finding of misrepresentation.

In the case of *Smith v Land and House Property Corporation* (1885) 28 Ch. D 7 the owner of a hotel put it up for sale saying that at present it was let to "Mr Frederick Fleck (a most desirable tenant) at a rental of £400 per annum . . . for an unexpired term of 27 years, thus offering a first class investment." In fact Mr Fleck was two quarters behind with the rent. Again, the statement that Fleck was a desirable tenant appears only to be a statement of opinion and therefore not actionable but the court nevertheless held in favour of the buyer. Bowen LJ said:

> ". . . if the facts are not equally known to both sides, then a statement of opinion by the one who knows the facts best makes very often a statement of material fact, *for he impliedly states that he knows facts which justify his opinion*." (Emphasis added)

In *Esso Petroleum Ltd v Mardon* [1976] Q.B. 801 the claimants had represented to a garage owner that his garage would sell 200,000 gallons of petrol a year. In fact sales never reached more than 78,000 gallons. The business went bankrupt and the claimants sought to repossess the garage. It was held that the claimants had made a statement of fact in relation to their prediction as to future sales—that they had exercised reasonable care and skill in arriving at the figure—which in fact they had not.

In contrast is the case of *Bisset v Wilkinson* [1927] A.C. 177 (which was distinguished in the *Esso* case) where the seller of land, which had never been used for sheep-farming, made a statement to the purchaser to the effect that he estimated that it would carry two thousand sheep. This turned out not to be possible. Both parties knew that the land had not been used for sheep-farming previously. It was held that the statement was simply an honest statement of opinion and the purchaser had no action for misrepresentation.

In applying these cases to package holiday contracts one thinks immediately of those brochures where the operator has a section on each resort or hotel where he states what in "Our Opinion" the delights of the resort are. Take the following example for instance:

> "On a peaceful stretch of Kalutara Beach, the Mermaid is a small hotel with a friendly atmosphere, the gardens stretch to the seashore enabling you to relax in the shade of the tall palm trees." [Tradewinds 3 Star Collection brochure published June 1997.]

Clearly this passage is designed to encourage the client to choose that particular hotel but the statements in it probably fall short of being terms of the contract (but see Regulation 6). What then would be the position if the hotel had 500 rooms (as opposed to 72), there were no palm trees to shelter under and no one talked to clients for the duration of the holiday? The statement about the palm trees is a statement of fact which because it is false is an actionable misrepresentation. On the other hand the statement that the hotel is "friendly" is no more than a statement of opinion and so long as the clients cannot prove that the tour operator did not actually hold that opinion there is nothing that can be done about it. "Small" is much more difficult but probably falls into the category of opinion rather than fact—unless again the tour operator can be shown not to actually hold that opinion.

Brochures often contain a statement that a particular resort is "lively". This is obviously inserted to make the resort appeal to younger people. On the face of it it is only a statement of opinion but if the clients arrived to find the resort inhabited entirely by clients of Saga could they justifiably complain? If the statement was solely a statement of opinion nothing could be done—it would be mere puff. However there is a strong argument for saying that *implied* in the statement is a statement of fact, *i.e.* that the tour operator has facts at his disposal that give rise to his opinion that the resort is lively. The statement implies that there are plenty of bars and nightclubs in the resort and that it is filled with young people.

In such circumstances the clients would have a case based on the principle of *Smith v Land and House Property Corporation.*

2. The statement must induce the contract

The statement will have no legal effect if the person to whom it was made did not in fact rely upon it. This point is simply illustrated by the case of *Smith v Chadwick* (1884) 9 App. Cas. 187. The plaintiff in that case bought shares in a company on the basis of a prospectus issued by the company. The prospectus included a statement that a certain person, Grieve, was on the board of the company. Subsequently the plaintiff sought to bring an action for misrepresentation because in fact Grieve was not on the board of the company. The claim was dismissed on the grounds that the plaintiff had never heard of Grieve and the fact that he was supposed to be on the board had not influenced his decision to purchase the shares.

It is not necessary for the representation to be the only reason for entering the contract. As long as it is one of the reasons then it can form the basis of an action. This was the position in *Edgington v Fitzmaurice*. The plaintiff had invested in debentures in the company not only because of the statement that the company would use the money to expand the business but also because he thought that his loan would be secured on the company's assets. It was held that even though the statement as to the uses to which the money would be put was not his only reason for investing he could nevertheless bring an action on the basis of it.

If a brochure states for instance that a wide variety of water sports are available in resort whereas in fact they are not this would not amount to a misrepresentation if the plaintiff was a 70-year-old asthmatic who had no intention of going water-skiing. It may have been a false statement but it was not one of the reasons that particular client chose the holiday. The position would be similar if a brochure which featured both self-catering and hotel holidays falsely stated that there were nearby supermarkets. Clients who were on hotel holidays would probably not be able to show that the existence of a supermarket influenced their decision. On the other hand the self-catering clients would probably have a good case.

3. The statement must be material

The false statement must be of sufficient significance that it would affect the judgment of a reasonable man in deciding whether to enter into the contract or not. If it is not material then it does not matter whether the other party has relied on it or not. For instance it may be the case that a brochure features an outdated picture of an hotel and the windows have shutters painted in a glorious shade of red which the client thinks is just perfect and books the hotel on the basis of the red shutters. On arrival the shutters are discovered to have been painted blue and have been so for the previous three seasons. There may have been a false statement of fact which in fact induced the contract but it is hardly material and the claim is likely to be turned down.

4. Omissions

The general rule is that remaining silent does not amount to misrepresentation. Usually there must be a positive statement of fact before an action can be brought. Occasionally, however, an omission to say something may amount to a misrepresentation. For instance in the case of *Dimmock v Hallett* (1866) 2 Ch. App. 21 the defendant stated, quite correctly, that all the farms on the estate he was selling were let. However this was only a half truth. What he omitted to say was that all the tenants had given notice to quit. It was held that this amounted to misrepresentation. If a tour operator was asked about the beaches at a resort and replied that there was a mile and a half of black sand in front of the hotel he might be guilty of a misrepresentation if he omitted to say that the sand was black because of an oil spill rather than because this was a volcanic island.

Conditions, Warranties and Innominate Terms

In some contracts the terms can be classified as either conditions or warranties in advance. This can be achieved in a number of ways. For instance there are statutes, such as the Sale of Goods Act 1979, where some of the terms in a sale of goods contracts are classified by the statute into conditions and warranties. Section 14, for example, makes it an implied condition that where goods are sold in the course of a business they will be of satisfactory quality.

This approach can be seen in the Package Travel Regulations. Regulation 9 for instance states that if the tour operator does not give a written copy of *all* the terms of the contract to the consumer this amounts to a breach of condition. Regulation 6 states that all the particulars in the brochure are warranties.

Apart from the statutory examples just mentioned the parties themselves are generally free to classify the terms of the contract into conditions or warranties depending upon the importance they wish to attach to them. The courts have also been prepared to classify terms as either conditions or warranties.

The effect of this prior classification means that if a breach occurs then the parties know immediately where they stand. Either it is a breach of condition and one party can terminate the contract at his option as well as claiming damages, or it is only a breach of warranty, in which case the contract must continue but damages must be paid.

This has the advantage of certainty but occasionally causes injustice where for instance there is a minor breach of a condition but the victim of the breach decides to exercise his right to terminate the contract—a drastic step in view of the minor infringement. This is what happened in the case of *Arcos Ltd v EA Ronaasen & Co* [1933] A.C. 470. In that case the buyer ordered a quantity of wooden staves for making barrels. Each of the staves had to be half an inch thick. When they arrived only 5 per cent were the right thickness but the rest were no more than 9/16 of an inch—which made them perfectly usable even though they did not meet the specification exactly. Under the Sale of Goods Act, s.13 it is an implied *condition* that goods must correspond to their description. The buyer was therefore able to reject the goods for what amounted to a mere technicality.

There is a possibility that such a state of affairs could arise under Regulation 9. If a tour operator omits a very minor detail from the written copy of the contract then he will be in breach of condition. For example he may omit some of the hotel facilities that are required to be detailed under Schedule 2 of the Regulations. These facilities may be of no importance to the consumer but their omission from the written contract gives the consumer the right to cancel—a drastic remedy for a minor oversight that has no real significance.

To combat the very rigid approach of classifying terms as either conditions or warranties the courts have developed a third category of terms. These are known as *innominate* terms. An innominate term is one which cannot be pre-classified as either a condition or a warranty. The remedy available will depend upon the severity of the breach. For instance in the case of *Hong Kong Fir Shipping Co Ltd v Kawasaki Kisen Kaisha Ltd* [1962] 1 All E.R. 474 the charterer of a ship wanted to terminate the contract because the ship was "unseaworthy". The charterer said that this was a condition of the contract which automatically gave him the right to terminate. The Court of Appeal said that "unseawothiness" covered a multitude of sins—from minor problems to very serious ones. According to Upjohn LJ the ship would be unseaworthy:

> "if a nail is missing from from one of the timbers of a wooden vessel, or if proper medical supplies or two anchors are not on board at the time of sailing."

It would be wrong for the charterer to be able to repudiate the contract for such trivial defects. The term relating to seaworthiness was therefore only an innominate term and could only be classified as a condition or a warranty once the extent of the breach became clear. The advantage of this approach is that it provides flexibility, *i.e.* a term is not rigidly classified until it is known how serious the breach is. On the other hand it does result in uncertainty—the parties do not know in advance what their rights are and may have to make difficult judgments as to when the breach is serious enough to warrant terminating the contract. If they decide wrongly they might find themselves in breach of condition!

In the case of *The Mihalis Angelos* [1970] 3 All E.R. 125 the Court of Appeal was faced with the problem of classifying the term "expected ready to load" in a shipping contract. A ship which was "expected ready to load" on July 1 had not been ready and the charterers said that this amounted to a breach of condition which entitled them to repudiate the contract—even though it had caused them no loss. Despite the absence of damage the court did classify it as a condition. With time clauses like this in commercial contracts it was important that the parties could predict with some certainty what the consequences of a breach would be and the courts should interpret such clauses consistently—even if in some cases the remedy was out of all proportion to the loss.

The question arises as to how the terms in a package holiday contract are classified—which ones are conditions, which ones are warranties and are there any innominate terms? Or to put it in more practical terms—for which breaches can the consumer repudiate the contract?

The answer is that, at first glance, a very large proportion of them appear to be only warranties, giving the consumer no right to repudiate. The reason for this is that, as we have just seen, Regulation 6 states that all the particulars in the brochure are implied warranties. Given that most of the terms of the contract will be found in the brochure, largely because of the combined requirements of Regulation 5 and Schedule 1, you could be forgiven for concluding that just about everything in the contract is only a warranty. However, you would be mistaken in this belief because Regulation 6 has to be read in conjunction with other Regulations, in particular Regulation 12.

Regulation 12, which is dealt with in more detail in Chapter 10, provides that where an organiser is constrained before departure to "alter significantly an essential term of the contract" then the consumer has the right not only to accept the change subject to a rider specifying the impact on the price but also to *withdraw* from the contract. This *appears* to create a term which is a condition but on closer examination the position is less clear.

The regulation actually describes the term as an *implied* term. It does not classify the term one way or the other. This suggests that it might be either a condition or a warranty depending upon the circumstances, *i.e.* it is more akin to an innominate term. In practice this is how it will work out. The consumer has two hurdles to overcome before he can withdraw. First he must show that there is a change to an *essential* term but then he must show that the alteration is a *significant* alteration. If he can show that there is such an alteration he can withdraw—but not otherwise. Thus if he can show a major change this will be treated as a breach of condition but if it is only a minor change it will be treated as simply a breach of warranty.

Regulation 14 is similar. It creates implied terms to the effect that the organiser must make *suitable* alternative arrangements if a *significant* proportion of the services cannot be provided after departure. Failure to do this gives the consumer the right to be taken home. Thus, depending upon the severity of the breach, the consumer can terminate the contract and come home or must remain on holiday and be content with damages.

The practical effect of all this is that the consumer will have a right to terminate for serious breaches but will have the difficult task of judging when it is sufficiently serious to do so.

Express and Implied Terms

1. Express Terms

An express term, as indicated earlier, is a term which has actually been expressed, either orally or in writing, or perhaps even in the form of a photograph or diagram. Regulation 9 requires an organiser to reduce *all* the terms to writing. Thus in theory all the terms of the contract will be express terms. Therefore the only problems that should arise will concern the interpretation of the express terms in the written contract. For instance what does "private pool" mean? Does it mean that the clients will have exclusive use of the pool or that the pool is not overlooked or that it will shared but only by a few families but not the general public? If a garden is described as "private" does it comply with its description if occupants are shielded from public view by a high hedge but is severely affected by the noise coming from the four lane highway on the other side of the hedge? What appliances does a "self-catering apartment" have to include—a microwave as well as a cooker; a dishwasher as well as a washing machine; a freezer as well as a fridge? In practice, however, there will be many cases where there will also be additional express terms in the form of oral statements and many cases where there will also be implied terms. It is important therefore to know the circumstances where the courts will imply terms into a contract.

2. Implied Terms

In English law terms can be implied into a contract in three ways: by custom, by statute, or by the courts. Terms implied by custom are not relevant to package travel contracts but statutory and judicial implied terms are. Note that this section is concerned with giving a broad overview of *how* and *why* the courts imply terms *in general* whereas Chapter 5, which covers much of the same ground, is more concerned with how the law has been applied *specifically* in a package holiday context.

Terms Implied By Statute

Package holiday contracts contain terms implied by the Package Travel Regulations. Regulation 12, for instance, implies a term into package holiday contracts that if the tour operator makes significant changes to essential terms of the contract then the consumer has the right to withdraw from the contract. Regulation 13 implies a term into the contract about the remedies available to the consumer following such a withdrawal and Regulation 14 implies a term about the consumer's rights in the event of the tour operator being able to perform the contract as promised. All these terms are dealt with in greater detail in Chapter 10.

Another statutory implied term sometimes referred to in holiday cases is s.13 of the Supply of Goods and Services Act 1982 to the effect that:

> "In a contract for the supply of a service where the supplier is acting in the course of a business, there is an implied term that the supplier will carry out the service with reasonable care and skill."

In both *Wilson v Best Travel* [1993] 1 All E.R. 353 and *Wong Mee Wan v Kwan Kin Travel Services* Ltd [1995] 4 All E.R. 745, which were both cases involving the implication of terms, the court discussed the effect of section 13.

Terms Implied By The Courts

These fall into two types: they can be implied *in fact*, *i.e.*, based upon the presumed intention of the parties, or they can be implied *in law* irrespective of the presumed intention of the parties.

The test for whether a term can be implied in fact is known as the "officious bystander" test (*Shirlaw v Southern Foundries Ltd* [1939] 2 K.B. 206). In attempting to find the presumed intention of the parties the courts use a mythical third party, the officious bystander, who intervenes during the making of the contract and asks whether the parties intended the disputed term to be a term of the contract, and if he is testily suppressed by both parties with a common "oh, of course" then this is sufficient to establish the term as part of the contract. On the other hand if the parties disagreed fundamentally about the existence of the term when questioned about it then a court would conclude that the term could not be implied in fact.

When terms are implied in law the basis of implication is that the courts consider that it is desirable that in certain types of contract the law should impose duties on the parties irrespective of their presumed intention. In the words of one leading textbook:

> "In all these cases the court is really deciding what should be the content of a paradigm contract of hire, of employment, etc. The process of decision is quite independent of the parties except that they are normally free, by using express words, to exclude the

> terms which would otherwise be implied. So the court is in effect imposing on the parties a term which is reasonable in the circumstances." (Cheshire, Fifoot and Furmston, *Law of Contract*, 14th ed. p.155)

The operation of these two rules can be seen in the case of *Wall v Silver Wing Surface Arrangements* (1981, unreported).

The facts of the case were that Mr and Mrs Wall and Mr and Mrs Smith and their son David booked a 14-day holiday with Enterprise Holidays at the Martina Apart Hotel in Puerto de la Cruz in Tenerife. They had rooms on the third floor. One night a fire broke out at the hotel. The plaintiffs could not use the lift to escape from their rooms so they tried to use the fire escape, which was made out of concrete and ran down the side of the hotel. Unfortunately, for reasons which did not emerge from the case, the hotel management had padlocked the gate at the bottom of the fire escape and it could not be used. The party therefore returned to their rooms and made a makeshift rope out of sheets. In using the rope, three of the party fell and were injured; one very seriously.

The hotel had been inspected regularly by a representative of Enterprise who had noted that it had an excellent fire escape. He had used it himself late one night and not found it obstructed. There was no suggestion in the case that Enterprise had failed to take reasonable care. They were not at fault and the Judge said as much.

In the absence of any negligence on behalf of the tour operator the plaintiffs pleaded their case on the basis of an implied term in the contract that they "would be reasonably safe in using the hotel for the purpose for which they were invited to be there".

When the Judge applied the officious bystander test the conclusion he reached was that:

> "... if an officious bystander had suggested either to the tour operator or, I think, to most customers, that the tour operator would be liable for any default on the part of any of these people [hotel keepers, airlines, taxi proprietors etc] both would, to put it mildly, have been astonished."

The judge also decided not to imply a term in law. His decision relied heavily upon the judgment of Lord Wilberforce in the case of *Liverpool City Council v Irwin* [1977] A.C. 239. This House of Lords case decided that as a matter of law a term could be implied in a contract for a tenancy in a high rise block of flats that the landlords (the council) should be under an obligation in respect of the common areas to exercise reasonable care to keep the means of access in reasonable repair. The term was implied on the basis that it was a "necessity". In the words of Lord Wilberforce:

> "In my opinion such obligation (in respect of the common areas), should be read into the contract as the nature of the contract implicitly required, no more, no less; a test in other words of necessity."

Applying this line of argument the judge in the *Wall* case said that in his view there must be:

> ". . . a requirement that there be some form of necessity before the court will impose upon the parties obligations which they have not expressly entered into. In my judgment the relationship of customer and tour operator is not one of the type . . . as would justify the courts in imposing obligations upon the parties as a matter of general law."

Although views may differ about the correctness of the decision in *Wall* (see Grant, "Tour Operators' Liability for Hoteliers' Negligence", *Trading Law* 6(2), 1988 p.44) the judgment is to be applauded for the clarity of its approach to implied terms—dealing both with terms implied in fact and term implied in law in a manner which exposes the issues plainly and clearly.

Two other travel cases involving implied terms are *Wilson v Best Travel* [1993] 1 All E.R. 353 and *Wong Mee Wan v Kwan Kin Travel Services* [1995] 4 All E.R. 745. (See also the extensive discussion of *Hone v Going Places* [2001] E.W.C.A. Civ. 947 in Chapter 5.) The former is an English case decided on facts which occurred before the passage of the Package Travel Regulations, but as we shall see in Chapter 5 there is nothing in the Regulations which requires that the case would be decided differently today. The latter is a Hong Kong case decided by the Privy Council on common law grounds as the Regulations are not applicable in Hong Kong.

The facts in the *Wilson* case were that the plaintiff, who had bought a package holiday from the defendants, had fallen through a glass patio door at the accommodation where he was staying. The glass in the door complied with Greek but not British standards. The issue at stake was what liability would be imposed on the tour operator in respect of the quality of the glass in the patio door. There was no express term in the contract about the quality of the glass and therefore the court had to imply a term. The judge rejected a term that the hotel would be reasonably safe, basing his decision on the judgment in *Wall*. The conclusion he came to was that the tour operator was under a duty, based upon s.13 of the Supply of Goods and Services Act 1982, to exercise reasonable care in respect of the glass. What this amounted to was that as long as the glass complied with local standards and those standards were not so low as to cause a reasonable holidaymaker to decline to take a holiday at the hotel in question then the duty was satisfied.

The judge said:

> "What is the duty of a tour operator in a situation such as this? Must he refrain from sending holidaymakers to any hotel whose characteristics, in so far as safety is concerned, fail to satisfy the standards which apply in this country? I do not believe that his obligations in respect of the safety of his clients can extend this far. Save where uniform international regulations apply, there are bound to be differences in the safety standards applied in respect of the many hazards of modern life between one country and another. All civilised countries attempt to cater for these hazards by imposing mandatory regulations. The duty of care of a tour operator is likely to extend to checking that local safety regulation are complied with. Provided that they are, I do not consider that the tour operator owes a duty to boycott a hotel because of the absence of some safety feature which would be found in an English hotel unless the absence of such a feature might lead a reasonable holidaymaker to decline to take a holiday at the hotel in question. On the facts of this case I do not consider that the degree of danger posed by the absence of safety glass in the doors of the Vanninarchis Beach Hotel called for any action on the part of the defendants pursuant to their duty to exercise reasonable care to ensure the safety of their clients.
>
> It is perhaps significant that Mr Norris did not expand on what action the defendants would have taken. It was not suggested that they had a duty to warn clients of this characteristic or that such warning would have prevented the accident in this case. What was, I think, implicit in the plaintiff's case was that the defendants should not have permitted the Vanninarchis Beach Hotel to feature in their brochure. If that contention were valid, it would, on the evidence of Mr Vanninarchis, apply to many, if not the majority, of the other hotels, pensions and villas featured in the defendants' brochure and no doubt the brochures of the other tour operators who send their clients to Greece."

The facts of *Wong Mee Wan* were that the plaintiff's daughter had purchased a package holiday from the first defendants, who were a Hong Kong company. The holiday consisted of a tour of mainland China and included both accommodation and transport. The highlight of the tour was a visit to a lake in China which also involved a lake crossing. The first defendants had subcontracted the performance of the tour to the second defendants. When the plaintiff's daughter reached the lake with her party they were not able to make the crossing by ferry as originally planned. Instead the second defendants arranged for the third defendants to convey the party across by speedboat. To transport the whole party across the lake involved making three return journeys. On the third journey, due to the negligence of the boat driver, the boat collided with a junk and sank. The plaintiff's daughter was drowned.

The Privy Council held the first defendants liable for the death. The approach they took is found in this passage from Lord Slynn's judgment:

> "The issue is thus whether in *this particular contract* the first defendant undertook no more than that it would arrange for services to be provided by others as its agent (where the law would imply a term into the contract that it would use reasonable care and skill in selecting those other persons) or whether it itself undertook to supply the services when, subject to any exemption clause, there would be implied into the contract a term that it would as supplier carry out the services with reasonable case and skill..." [Emphasis added]

After a careful analysis of the contract in this case their Lordships concluded that:

> "Taking the contract as a whole their Lordships consider that the first defendant here *undertook to provide and not merely to arrange* all the services included in the programme, even if some activities were to be carried out by others. The first defendant's obligation under the contract that the services would be provided with reasonable skill and care remains even if some of the services were to be rendered by others, and even if tortious liability may exist on the part of those others." [Emphasis added].

What weighed particularly heavily in favour of liability was the wording of the brochure which emphasised the role of the first defendants at the expense of the second and third defendants. Throughout the brochure and the itinerary there were statements to the effect that "we", the first defendants were responsible for the provision of the various elements of the package:

> "Throughout the detailed itinerary it is always 'we' who will do things—board the bus, go for lunch, live in the hotel. Their

> Lordships do not think that 'we' is to be read simply as referring to the customers—*i.e.* in an attempt to lay the foundations for a friendly atmosphere on the tour. 'We' includes the company offering the tour and integrates the company into each stage of the tour. At Zhu Hai it is 'our staff' who will handle the customs formalities for you. There is nothing to indicate that 'the tourist guide' who is accompanying the group to the Village is other than an employee of the first defendant and in para 7 it is the 'escorts of our company' who may request a member to leave the tour."

On the question of the status of *Wall v Silver Wing* their Lordships had this to say:

> "In their Lordships' view it was an implied term of the contract that those services would be carried out with reasonable skill and care. That term does not mean, to use the words of Hodgson J in *Wall v Silver Wing Surface Arrangements Ltd* that the first defendant undertook an obligation to ensure 'the safety of all the components of the package'. The plaintiff's claim does not amount to an implied term that her daughter would be reasonably safe. It is a term simply that reasonable skill and care would be used in rendering the services to be provided under the contract. *The trip across the lake was clearly not carried out with reasonable skill and care in that no steps were taken to see that the driver of the speedboat was of reasonable competence and experience and the first defendant is liable for such breach of contract as found by the trial judge.*"[Emphasis added. Note the confusion here in the reasoning.]
>
> "... if the tour operator agrees that services will be supplied, whether by him or others on his behalf, to imply a term that those services will be carried out with reasonable skill and care is not imposing on the tour operator a burden which is 'intolerable' as the Court of Appeal thought. Nor is it wholly unreasonable, as Hodgson J thought in *Wall v Silver Wing Surface Arrangements Ltd.*"

Note that although the defendants were made liable for the defaults of one of their subcontractors this was because they had assumed this more extensive liability by the wording of their brochure. Less extravagant prose would probably have saved them from liability. Note also that the court was not required, as in *Wall* and *Wilson*, to decide upon a term of strict liability—that the consumer would be reasonably safe. It is not clear whether the Privy Council would have been prepared to go that far if asked to do so. See the section below for the competing arguments for and against strict liability.

3. Express and implied terms and the level of liability

As we have just seen, the obligations contained in the package holiday contract will be a mixture of both express and implied terms. However, with both express and implied terms difficult questions arise not only about their interpretation and existence but, more importantly, about the level of liability (or the standard of duty) that they impose. This can be illustrated by the use of a simple example. Let us say that the brochure states expressly that the hotel has a swimming pool. By virtue of Regulation 6 this is undoubtedly a term of the contract. If the consumer arrives and finds no pool then is the tour operator liable? One's instinctive reaction is to say yes. They have promised a pool and there isn't one. One is inclined to argue that not only is the term a warranty, *i.e.* a minor term of the contract (Regulation 6), but also that the tour operator *warrants* that it will be there—in the sense that he guarantees that it will be there. Arguments advanced by the tour operator that he had contracted with the hotel for the provision of the pool and was only informed by the hotelier at the last minute that it had been turned into a sunken garden would fall on deaf ears. This is a strict liability obligation. (See *Cook v Spanish Holiday Tours, The Times*, February 6, 1960.)

However, if we were to take a variation on this theme then the answer may not be quite so apparent. Let us say that although the pool did exist it was entirely inadequate for the numbers wishing to use it—in other words it was not fit for its purpose. Again one's instinctive reaction is to say that the tour operator is liable. But what if the reason for its inadequacy was that during the close season the hotelier had built a large new wing onto the hotel with the result that the pool was simply overwhelmed with guests wanting to use the pool? Can the tour operator's express promise that a pool will be *provided* be extended to include an implied obligation that it will be *fit for its purpose*—even in circumstances where the operator is not at fault? Probably yes.

Finally, take a third variation. Let us say that a pool is provided and that it is of adequate size but because of a failure in the chlorination system it becomes contaminated with life-threatening micro organisms and clients suffer death and illness as a result. Is the tour operator liable? If this was not the fault of the tour operator then, according to the *Wall* case there will be no liability and even according to *Wong Mee Wan* there will be no liability so long as the tour operator worded his brochure in such a way that it diminished his liability to that of a mere arranger.

Coincidentally, a variation on this illustration was adopted in *Hone v Going Places* by Longmore LJ:

> "If the brochure or advertisement, on which the consumer relies, promises a swimming-pool, it will be a term of the contract that a swimming-pool will be provided. But, in the absence of express wording, there would not be an absolute obligation, for example, to ensure that the holiday-maker catches no infection while swimming in the swimming-pool. The obligation assumed will be that reasonable skill and care will be taken to ensure that the pool is free from infection."

This leaves a situation where the courts now say that the question of the *existence* of the pool and perhaps its *fitness for purpose* are strict liability obligations but when it comes to issues of *safety* then the obligations are fault based. Why this distinction? Why is it that strict liability, a higher burden, is imposed in respect of the provision and adequacy of the pool but a lesser obligation in respect of the safety—which is surely more important? To put it more bluntly why does the tour operator warrant the existence of the pool but not its safety?

To this question there is no easy answer, and certainly Longmore LJ did not explore it in *Hone*. According to Collins (*The Law of Contract*, Weidenfeld and Nicolson, 1st ed., 1986, p.165):

> "In the absence of statutory guidance, the courts must decide whether or not a party is strictly liable for any defect in performance, and if not, what standard of care should have been expected from him.
>
> In tackling this issue, the courts avoid the enunciation of general principles. They consider each contract in its social context and the particular facts of the case."

Other commentators confirm this pragmatic approach adopted by the English courts (see JW Carter, *Breach of Contract*, The Law Book Company, 1984, p.22; PS Atiyah, *An Introduction to the Law of Contract*, Clarendon Press, Oxford, 1995, p.214). This makes it difficult to predict how a court would view the implication of a term in a novel situation where, as in most holiday cases there was until recently no body of case law to offer guidance—where, not to put too fine a point upon it, the courts are making the law rather than applying it.

If we accept this then what we also have to accept is that the decision to imply a term or not is a policy decision, *i.e.* the courts are deciding what the law *should* be as opposed to what it *is*. Support for this view can be found in the case law. In his decision in the *Wall* case, Hodgson J, relied heavily on the judgment of Lord Wilberforce in the House of Lords case *Liverpool City Council v Irwin* [1977] A.C. 239. In that case Lord Wilberforce hinted that "wider considerations" may be taken into account when implying a term—by which he meant policy considerations.

Looking at the existing case law we can see some of the emerging policy reasons. In *Wall* itself the judge felt that it would be "unreasonable" to impose strict liability on a tour operator to guarantee the safety of the accommodation in a package holiday, particularly as the holidaymaker would have direct rights against the suppliers of the services which failed. In *Wilson* the judge considered that to impose a duty on tour operators not to send consumers to hotels which did not comply with the same safety standards as British hotels was too onerous. Implicit in his judgment was that this would be impracticable. To impose such a standard would result in most accommodation in places such as Cyprus being removed from brochures altogether. In *Wong Mee Wan* the Privy Council felt that it was not "wholly unreasonable as Hodgson J thought in [Wall]" to imply a term that the services promised in a package holiday contract would be carried out with reasonable care and skill even though carried out by others. However, underlying the *Wong* decision is the clear suspicion that if the brochure in that case had not been so extravagantly worded then the tour operator would have escaped liabilty. The decision appears based on the reasoning that the defendants had taken on or assumed liability for the whole of the package and that if they hadn't volunteered so much then they may not have been found liable.

Despite the weight of case law being in favour of fault liability rather than strict (see Chapter 5 and in particular the discussion of *Hone v Going Places*) there are powerful arguments the other way. They find voice in the writing of two American commentators. In the following passage taken from a cogently written article on the legal status of travel agents Wohlmuth discusses the liability of travel agents to their clients when the services booked on their behalf (hotels, airlines, etc.) have proved defective. The reasons he gives for imposing liability on travel agents seem equally applicable to tour operators:

> "In particular courts in the future may ask whether there is any less reason to hold the travel agent liable for faulty accommodations than to hold a retailer liable for imperfections in

goods sold to the consumer in the original sealed container. The parallel between these two cases is obvious. Just as the travel agent cannot adequately control the quality of performance of the hotel or carrier, so the retailer cannot adequately protect himself against imperfections in goods sold to the consumer in the original sealed container. Many of the justifications for finding the latter liable appear applicable to the former. Just as the stocking by a retailer of goods on his shelf, even though in the original sealed package, is some indication to the consumer that the retailer stands behind them, so the booking of reservations by the travel agent at a particular hotel or on a particular carrier is some indication that he stands behind the performance of that hotel or carrier. Just as the accessibility of the retailer to suit by the consumer makes good sense from a policy standpoint because of jurisdictional problems in suing the manufacturer, so making the travel agent available to suit by the client makes good policy sense in terms of the difficulties inherent in obtaining jurisdiction over the carrier or hotel. Finally, both the retailer and the travel agent have ultimate recourse against the person whose 'product' they sell, and he, after all, is the one best able to bear the risk of loss by passing it on to the consumer through higher prices." (*The Liability of Travel Agents: A Study in the Selection of Appropriate Legal Principles* [1966] Temple Law Quarterly 29)

Dickerson makes the same point:

"Although the courts have been willing to find a duty to deliver specific travel services, such a duty has not yet been extended to the provision of 'safe transportation' or 'safe accommodations'. There is no justification nor rationale for so holding, however, since travelers have a right to expect the delivery of travel services which do not cause physical injuries. In such cases the courts may refer to the responsible party as an independent contractor whose tortious conduct should not be shifted to the tour operator-principal. In many of these cases however, the responsible party is out of the jurisdiction of local courts and unavailable to satisfy access to any recovery even though the tour operator made a profit on the transaction. The inequity of these cases is surely obvious and it is likely that future cases will, indeed, find tour operators liable for the misconduct of suppliers resulting in physical injuries." (*Travel Law*, 5–62, 5–63)

From these two pieces a number of countervailing policy reasons can be identified: considerations of consumer protection; the ability to pass liability up the chain of supply to the person ultimately responsible; considerations of loss spreading and identifying who is best placed to bear the risk; access to courts within the local jurisdiction; making a trader responsible for the services he sells; and, as with the arguments deployed by the other side, considerations of what is "just" and "reasonable".

Given the present weight of case law in favour of fault liability, it would be incorrect at present to suggest that a tour operator is under a general duty of strict liability to clients, but it would be possible to construct a respectable argument, deploying the policy reasons just mentioned, to show that a tour operator *should* be under such a liability. (See "Tour Operators, Package Holiday Contracts and Strict Liability" Grant & Urbanowicz, [2001] JBL 253 for a longer discussion of these issues.)

4. Regulation 9

According to Regulation 9 all the terms of a package holiday contract must be reduced to writing before the contract is concluded. But what if the tour operator does not do this? (And cases such as *Wall v Silver Wing* and *Wilson v Best Travel* suggest that this may very well happen.) Does this mean that any term which has not been reduced to writing will not be a term of the contract? Does it mean the end of the implied term in package holiday contracts?

The answer to this must be no. The fact that the tour operator has not reduced all the terms to writing will not mean that statements not in the written contract will not be part of the contract. All it will mean is that the tour operator will be in breach of Regulation 9. A court would still accept that there could be other express and implied terms which the tour operator had omitted from the contract for some reason—either through poor contracting procedures or lack of foresight. The logical consequence of this however is that once an implied term is found to exist a client automatically has the right to rescind for breach of Regulation 9, even though by definition an implied term is never reduced to writing!

Regulation 4

As indicated in the introduction to this chapter, Regulation 4 creates a statutory right to compensation for the consumer that cuts across the traditional boundaries of the common law. It imposes civil liability on both organisers and retailers if they supply misleading information. It states:

> "4(1) No organiser or retailer shall supply to a consumer any descriptive matter concerning a package, the price of a package or any other conditions applying to the contract which contains any misleading information.
>
> 4(2) If an organiser or retailer is in breach of paragraph (1) he shall be liable to compensate the consumer for any loss which the consumer suffers in consequence."

The liability that this imposes is very extensive, going in many cases beyond normal contractual liability. It will be examined in more detail in Chapter 5 on liability.

Regulation 6

Regulation 6 provides:

> "6(1) ... the particulars in the brochure (whether or not they are required by regulation 5(1) above to be included in the brochure) shall constitute implied warranties ... for the purposes of any contract to which the particulars relate."

This is a little puzzling. First, what is meant by the word "particular", which is not a term of art known to English law. Secondly, and more fundamentally, what does Regulation 6 add to the existing common law.

In trying to ascertain the answer to the first question some assistance can be obtained by tracing the derivation of the provision. Article 3.2 of the Directive states:

> "When a brochure is made available to the consumer, it shall indicate in a legible, comprehensible and accurate manner both the price and adequate information concerning:
>
> (a) the destination and the means, characteristics and categories of transport used;
> (b) the type of accommodation, its location, category or degree of comfort and its main features, its approval and tourist classification under the rules of the host Member State concerned;
> (c) the meal plan;
> (d) the itinerary;

(e) general information on passport and visa requirements for nationals of the Member State or States concerned and health formalities required for the journey and the stay;
(f) either the monetary amount or the percentage of the price which is to be paid on account, and the timetable for payment of the balance;
(g) whether a minimum number of persons is required for the package to take place and, if so, the deadline for informing the consumer in the event of cancellation.

The particulars contained in the brochure are binding on the organizer or retailer . . .

The first part of Article 3.2 is enacted in UK law by Regulation 5, which makes it a criminal offence not to provide the listed information in a comprehensible, legible and accurate form (see Chapter 13). It is from the second part of Article 3.2 that Regulation 6 is derived, *i.e.* that the particulars in the brochure are legally binding. It is possible to say with some certainty therefore that "particulars" relate to those statements in the brochure which are listed in Article 3.2. Thus if there is a statement about the number of meals or the classification of the hotel or the places the bus tour visits these are all contractual warranties, which if broken, give rise to an action for damages.

However, Regulation 6 goes further than Article 3.2 by stating that any of the particulars in the brochure, whether required by Regulation 5(1) (*i.e.* Article 3.2) to be included or not are to be regarded as warranties. This might cover holidays where the brochure states that the holidays are exclusively for couples or singles; or that the guides have particular qualifications; or that the temperature will be within a particular range. All these are factual statements, going beyond Article 3.2, but perfectly capable of giving rise to contractual liability and should cause no difficulty. More problematic, however, are photographs. If a photograph shows an hotel with windsurfing equipment drawn up on the beach in front of it does this mean that consumers will be able to sample windsurfing at that hotel, and if so, for the whole season or only part of it? Does the picture *promise* the opportunity to go windsurfing? Suitably crafted text to go with the photograph may go some of the way to resolve the problem but certainly tour operators should examine their photographs carefully to ensure they do not give the wrong message to the consumer.

It may not simply be what the photograph shows that could cause a problem but what it omits. What if there is a photograph of a picturesque hotel beside the Mosel in Germany showing all the rooms with balconies facing onto the river accompanied by text that all rooms have river views. However part of the top half of the picture has been cropped and what has been omitted are the top floor rooms which do not have balconies. Consumers might be understandably upset if they were put into an upper floor room without a balcony. The picture suggests that they will get a balcony. But is it a "particular" in the brochure that all the rooms have balconies if what gives rise to that belief is the photograph rather than the text? The dictionary definition of a "particular" is that it means "a distinct or minute part; a single point; a single instance; item; detail" (Chambers). Certainly the photograph contains "details" about the hotel and therefore is probably within the scope of Regulation 6.

Although photographs could be interpreted as containing factual information that amount to particulars and therefore covered by Regulation 6 where does this take us in terms of the second question: What impact, if any, does Regulation 6 have on the existing common law? It seems perfectly possible to arrive at the conclusion that the photographs of the windsurfing and the balconies are capable of being interpreted as terms of the contract without the necessity of invoking Regulation 6. In answer to that question there are at least two possibilities as to the effect of Regulation 6.

First, its purpose may be to settle that the statements in the brochure capable of being terms are *only* warranties, not conditions (unless stated otherwise). In other words it is solely to categorise terms that already exist, not to create contractual liability for statements that are not terms at common law. Thus its effect would not be to extend liability to statements which are not terms. The second approach is to say that Regulation 6 might be going further and is saying that some statements, described as "particulars", are to be regarded as terms even though at common law they might not be.

If it is possible to find a situation where the brochure contains "particulars" that would not normally amount to terms of the contract then perhaps there is a case for saying that Regulation 6 extends the law beyond its present limits. For instance if we look at the kind of purple prose found in *Hoffman v Intasun* quoted earlier could this be categorised as "particulars" and therefore become legally binding on the tour operator. The answer, we venture to suggest, is no. However if we look at statements that might only amount to representations or puffs at common law then the answer might be different. What about all-inclusive resorts described as "elegant and sophisticated" (supported by pictures of men and women in formal evening wear) that, contrary to expectations, are largely patronised by groups of drunken youths? Such statements, while probably not amounting to terms at common law, might give rise to liability under Regulation 6.

Note also that Regulation 6 provides that if the brochure contains an express statement that changes may be made in the particulars before a contract is concluded, and such changes are clearly communicated to the consumer before a contract is concluded, then those particulars are not binding on the organiser. However once a contract is concluded Regulation 6 further provides that particulars are binding unless the consumer consents to a variation.

SURCHARGES

One term which is frequently found in a package holiday contract is a surcharge clause. We have chosen to deal with it here rather than elsewhere largely because it does not fit neatly into any particular category.

Surcharging is a practice which has caused a great deal of controversy over the years. No one likes to have to pay extra at the last minute and this feeling of grievance is often exacerbated by a suspicion, not completely unfounded, that tour operators, certainly in the past, have included an element of profit in the surcharges. More recently the worst excesses of surcharging seem to have been largely eliminated by low inflation and ABTA's surcharging policy. Nevertheless the issue was considered so important that there are specific provisions in the Regulations to govern it. We also examine the provisions in the 2003 ABTA Code of Conduct on surcharges.

Regulation 11

Regulation 11 preserves the right of the tour operator to surcharge but restricts the circumstances in which this can be done. It provides:

> 11(1) Any term in a contract to the effect that the prices laid down in the contract may be revised shall be void and of no effect unless the contract provides for the possibility of upward or downward revision and satisfies the conditions laid down in paragraph (2) below.
>
> (2) The conditions mentioned in paragraph (1) are that—
>
> (a) the contract states precisely how the revised price is to be calculated;

(b) the contract provides that price revisions are to be made solely to allow for the following variations in:—

(i) transportation costs, including the cost of fuel,
(ii) dues, taxes or fees chargeable for services such as landing taxes or embarkation or disembarkation fees at ports and airports, or
(iii) the exchange rates applied to the particular package; and

(c) the contract provides that—

(i) no price increase may be made in a specified period which may not be less than 30 days before the departure date stipulated; and
(ii) as against an individual consumer liable under the contract, no price increase may be made in respect of variations which would produce an increase of less than 2%, or such greater percentage as the contract may specify, ("non-eligible variations") and that the non-eligible variations shall be left out of account in the calculation.

This reflects the existing common law position which permits price variation clauses so long as they are built into the contract. The difference is that the Regulation circumscribes the items which can be surcharged. It permits surcharging for variations in transport costs, exchange rates and taxes but not for hotel costs. It requires the first 2 per cent of any surcharge be absorbed by the operator. There is no corresponding provision that the consumer be given the right to cancel if surcharges reach more than a particular amount but this is provided for in Regulation 12 which permits the consumer to cancel for "significant changes" to essential terms. Price is specifically referred to as an essential term. Just how large the increase has to be before it is regarded as significant is left open.

Unlike the provisions in successive versions of the ABTA Code there is no notification and monitoring system to ensure that tour operators do not indulge in profiteering. An attempt to overcome this problem is reflected in Regulation 11(2)(a) where it is provided that the manner in which any price revision is made must be stated *precisely* in the contract. The greater the precision the less likely it is that a tour operator will be able to include an element of pure profit in his surcharges. ABTA operators currently publish the rates of exchange on which their prices are based and this serves as a good indication for calculating surchages.

According to Regulation 11(1) any price rise will be of no effect if it does not comply with the Regulation. Additionally there may be criminal liability under the Consumer Protection Act 1987 if the means of calculating the price increase is misleading.

In previous editions we said that some Trading Standards Departments have interpreted Regulation 11 as meaning that if the contract does not provide for *both* an upward *and* a downward revision then the term is void. In other words if the tour operator is prepared to raise prices for currency fluctuations that move against him he must also be prepared to reduce them if the fluctuation is in the consumer's favour.

Such an interpretation depends upon interpreting the word "or" in Regulation 11(1) as meaning "and" *i.e.* "upward *or* downward revision" could be interpreted as meaning "upward *and* downward revision" *i.e.* the "or" is conjunctive rather than disjunctive. Such an interpretation is not beyond the bounds of probability. For instance in the following sentence the word "or" can be interpreted as meaning "and": "It is possible to travel from Newcastle to London via Leeds or York or Manchester." But is this a proper interpretation in the circumstances? Use of the word "or" *usually* means one or the other but not both. Given that it was open to the draftsman to use the word "and" so as to make the position clearer and given also that the commercial context is that price revision clauses have always been used to put prices up rather than down it is reasonable to conclude that the Regulation does not require tour operators to allow for downward revisions. However it seems that this view is wrong. In October 2002 the OFT, exercising its powers under the Unfair Terms in Consumer Contracts Regulations 1999, required all four of the major tour operators: Thomson, MyTravel, Thomas Cook and First Choice to make changes to their standard terms and conditions. The surcharge clauses had to be changed so that if the operators wished to impose surcharges for rises in costs they also had to offer consumers a reduction if there was a reduction in cost.

There is some ambiguity about Regulation 11(2)(b)(ii) which states that a surcharge can be levied for:

> "dues, taxes or fees chargeable for services such as landing taxes or embarkation or disembarkation fees at ports and airports . . ."

Are the words "dues" and "taxes" qualified by what follows—"chargeable for services such as . . ." or do they stand alone. In other words can a tour operator levy a surcharge for any rise in taxes or dues or can he only levy it if the tax is raised for services such as landing taxes etc? In the first edition of the book we inclined to the latter view, and indeed can still see some justification for such an interpretation, but on balance we now prefer the former. To interpret it otherwise would put tour operators at the mercy of changes in taxes which did not relate to the services listed in Regulation 11(2)(b)(ii) such as the imposition of APD and its subsequent increase.

Following the events of September 11, 2001 a number of airlines increased their level of security and passed the increase on to tour operators. Some tour operators, who had already set the price of their holidays and sold them at that price, endeavoured to pass the increase on to consumers by levying a surcharge under their surcharge clause. It is an open question whether they could bring such charges within the rubric of Regulation 11(2)(b)(ii); but the typical charge (£7 per person) combined with the requirement to absorb the first 2 per cent of price rises made this fairly academic. Industry attempts to lobby the government to suspend the 2 per cent requirement fell on deaf ears.

2. Under the Code

The ABTA Code has a separate and extensive section devoted to the imposition of surcharges. Most of it is concerned with the authorising and monitoring of surcharges by ABTA. The system established by the Code is that tour operators must first of all notify ABTA of what their surcharge policy is. Secondly they must obtain authorisation from ABTA if in fact they wish to surcharge. Thirdly their policy will be subject to monitoring by the ABTA Legal Department. ABTA also requires members to include in their brochures one of two mandatory clauses set out in the Code. The first of these clauses is a no surcharge guarantee clause and the second provides a range of items which the tour operator may surcharge for.

Despite the fact that the Code supposedly "recognises and embodies the relevant parts of those Acts and Government Regulations which relate to the travel industry" some differences do remain between the Code and the Regulations. For instance the range of items for which tour operators may surcharge under the Code is expressed differently from the corresponding provisions in the Regulations. Under the Code tour operators can surcharge for:

(a) transportation costs e.g. fuel, increases in scheduled fares and any other airline surcharges which are part of the contract between airlines (and their agents) and the Member.

(b) government action as defined in Section 3 of these Standards; and

(c) currency in relation to exchange rate variations.

Government action is amplified in Section 3:

> "For the sake of clarity Members should note that government action relates to the imposition of new taxes and the variation of existing taxes or any other Government imposed increase such as an increase in VAT. Government action does not cover currency variations and Members should specify the exact items for which they reserve the right to surcharge as shown in the mandatory paragraphs . . ."

As with other parts of the Code where differences occur between the Code and the Regulations one wonders why this is the case and why the Code could not simply have adopted the wording of the Regulations verbatim? All it does is cause unnecessary complications. Take the phrase "government action" for instance. It is not a phrase which is used in the Regulations and therefore is not one of the permitted exceptions to the no surcharge rule. However it is defined in such a way in the Code that it *almost* corresponds to Regulation 11(2)(ii) which permits surcharging for "dues, taxes or fees . . ." The problem is that if a tour operator simply states that he can surcharge for government action he may not succeed. It could be argued that this is not one of the permitted exceptions.

There is a greater danger however for tour operators. An attempt to surcharge for items which are not permitted may result in not being able to surcharge even for those items which are permitted. Regulation 11 provides that price revision terms in a contract will be void unless the contract satisfies certain conditions. One of those conditions is that price revisions can be *solely* for the variations listed in Regulation 11(2)(b). Thus if a tour operator attempts to surcharge for increases in hotel costs not only will he not be able to do so he will not be able to surcharge for legitimate items such as currency fluctuations and transport costs.

The upshot of this is that the ABTA Code, by encouraging tour operators to claim for non-permissible items, is effectively invalidating all surcharges—whether legitimate or not. In the short term at least this is a technicality that consumers could benefit from.

Chapter Five
Liability

Introduction

We have seen in Chapter Three how the parties to a package holiday contract agree on the terms of the contract and in Chapter Four we looked, in *general* terms, at the sources of those terms and about how they are classified. In this chapter we will be looking much more closely at the content and extent of the obligations imposed upon tour operators, and to a lesser extent travel agents, by the Package Travel Regulations. This will involve an examination of Regulation 15 on the "proper performance" of the contract; Regulation 4 which imposes liability for misleading statements; and also the interesting obligations imposed by the Regulations and the ABTA Code of Conduct requiring tour operators to offer assistance to consumers in circumstances where there is no breach of contract.

1. Strict and fault liability

Before we examine Regulation 15 in detail it will be worthwhile explaining again the difference between obligations imposing fault liability and those imposing strict liability.

Fault liability is where a court will only hold a party to be in breach of contract if it can be shown that they were at fault in some way. For instance in the case of *Wall v Silver Wing* (1981, unreported) which we discuss below the tour operator was found not liable for the injuries to their clients because they were not at fault. The hotelkeeper was at fault but the tour operator was not liable for the faults of others, as the law stood in 1981. Strict liability on the other hand is where a party will be held to be in breach of contract even though they are not at fault. For instance under s.14 of the Sale of Goods Act 1979 a seller of goods is under a strict obligation to ensure that the goods he sells are of satisfactory quality and it is no defence to say that it was not his fault. As long as the buyer can show that the goods are defective in some way then the seller is liable. This means that in many instances a perfectly innocent retailer must compensate consumers for defects caused by the manufacturer of the goods—defects which the retailer didn't know about and which he might not have been able to detect even if he had looked for them.

The example given by Longmore LJ in *Hone v Going Places* quoted in Chapter 4 about the swimming pool is worth quoting again as a good illustration of the difference:

> "If the brochure or advertisement, on which the consumer relies, promises a swimming-pool, it will be a term of the contract that a swimming-pool will be provided. But, in the absence of express wording, there would not be an absolute obligation, for example, to ensure that the holiday-maker catches no infection while swimming in the swimming-pool. The obligation assumed will be that reasonable skill and care will be taken to ensure that the pool is free from infection."

The reason why it is important to distinguish between strict and fault liability is that this has been the major battleground between consumers and tour operators over the years. Tour operators have argued that they are only subject to fault liability whereas consumers have contended that strict liability should prevail. (See Saggerson [2001] ITLJ 159).

2. Early development

At first, the law moved in a direction which was favourable to the package holiday tour operators. An early case was *Wall & Smith v Silverwing Surface Arrangements Ltd*, decided by the High Court in 1981. This case does not appear to have been formally reported, but transcripts exist and the case is referred to in the reported cases dealt with below of *Wilson v Best* and *Wong Mee Wan*. In *Wall*, the holidaymakers had booked a package holiday to Tenerife. They were staying in a modern hotel. A fire broke out one night. The four claimants attempted to exit the hotel by the fire door, only to find it locked (this had apparently been done by a security guard because of problems with local troublemakers). The claimants returned to their room and endeavoured to exit the hotel buy means of climbing down a series of sheets which they had tied together. Not surprisingly, during this risky enterprise, two of them fell and were seriously injured. They sued the defendant tour operator (which traded as Enterprise Holidays). The case came before Hodgson J., as he then was. He said:

> "Tour operators who provide so called package holiday are a comparatively recent and very welcome arrival on the holiday

scene... the tour operator puts together a number of holiday which are then included in this brochure for that year. The brochure typically contains—as did the brochure in this case—a booking form. Each holiday offered includes for a fixed sum travel arrangements, hotel accommodation, and usually some provision for a representative at the holiday resort to see that the customers of the tour operator are being looked after and obtaining that which they bargained for. The tour operator, by making block bookings on aeroplanes and at hotels, can offer its customers holidays which are far cheaper than could be obtained by individual reservations. In the normal way it is perfectly well known that the tour operator neither owns, occupies or controls the hotels which are included in his brochure, any more than he has any control over the airlines which fly his customers, the airports whence and whither they fly and the land transport which conveys then from airport to hotel. It is of course also true that the customer makes no contract himself with the hotel, airline, taxi or coach proprietor... it is clear, I think, that the agreement contained in the booking form and brochure is perfectly efficacious in a business sense, standing on its own. It needs no additional terms to make it work and, if injury is caused by the default of the hotel owners and occupiers, the airline, the airport control as well as the taxi proprietor, the customer will have whatever remedy the relevant law allows.

"It is also I think clear, despite the heroic efforts by [counsel for the plaintiff] to persuade me to the contrary, that if an officious bystander has suggested either to the tour operator or, I think, to most customers that the tour operator would be liable for any default on the part of any of these people both would, to put it mildly, have been astonished".

The judge concluded that tour operator had a duty to make a reasonable choice of subcontractor and to inspect the hotel. In this case the hotel had a perfectly satisfactory fire escape which was open at the time it was inspected by Enterprise. Therefore, the defendants were held not liable for the injuries suffered.

The reasoning in *Wall v Silver Wing* was adopted in a number of County Court decisions including *Gibbons v Intasun Holidays* [1988] CLY 168; *Kaye v Intasun Holidays* [1987] CLY 1150; *Toubi v Intasun Holidays* [1988] CLY 1060 and *Usher v Intasun Holidays* [1987] CLY 418. *Wilson v Best Travel* [1993] 1 All E.R. 353, a High Court case decided on common law principles, decided that the tour operator was not simply under a duty to take reasonable care (as in *Wall*) but arguably had a duty to see that care was taken. It should be pointed out however that the decisions were not all one way. There were notable exceptions including *Tucker v OTA* [1986] CLY 383 and a much overlooked Court of Appeal decision *Cook v Spanish Holiday Tours*, *The Times*, Feb 6, 1960, both of which imposed strict liability on tour operators.

Regulation 15

1. The scope of regulation 15

Regulation 15 provides:

> "15(1) The other party to the contract is liable to the consumer for the proper performance of the obligations under the contract, irrespective of whether such obligations are to be performed by that other party or by other suppliers of services but this shall not affect any remedy or right of action which that other party may have against those other suppliers of services.
>
> (2) The other party to the contract is liable to the consumer for any damage caused to him by the failure to perform the contract or the improper performance of the contract unless the failure or the improper performance is due neither to any fault of that other party nor to that of another supplier of services, because—
>
> (a) the failures which occur in the performance of the contract are attributable to the consumer;
> (b) such failures are attributable to a third party unconnected with the provision of the services contracted for, and are unforeseeable or unavoidable; or
> (c) such failures are due to—
>
> (i) unusual and unforeseeable circumstances beyond the control of the party by whom this exception is pleaded, the consequences of which could not have been avoided even if all due care had been exercised; or
> (ii) an event which the other party to the contract or the supplier of services, even with all due care, could not foresee or forestall.
>
> (3) In the case of damage arising from the non-performance or improper performance of the services involved in the package, the contract may provide for compensation to be limited in accordance with the international conventions which govern such services.
>
> (4) In the case of damage other than personal injury resulting

from the non-performance or improper performance of the services involved in the package, the contract may include a term limiting the amount of compensation which will be paid to the consumer, provided that the limitation is not unreasonable.

(5) Without prejudice to paragraph (3) and paragraph (4) above, liability under paragraphs (1) and (2) above cannot be excluded by any contractual term.

(6) The terms set out in paragraphs (7) and (8) below are implied in every contract.

(7) In the circumstances described in paragraph (2) (b) and (c) of this regulation, the other party to the contract will give prompt assistance to a consumer in difficulty.

(8) If the consumer complains about a defect in the performance of the contract, the other party to the contract, or his local representative, if there is one, will make prompt efforts to find appropriate solutions.

(9) The contract must clearly and explicitly oblige the consumer to communicate at the earliest opportunity, in writing or any other appropriate form, to the supplier of the services concerned and to the other party to the contract any failure which he perceives at the place where the services concerned are supplied.

In very broad terms Regulation 15 does a number of things. First, Regulation 15(1) provides that a tour operator shall properly perform the obligations under the contract and shall be liable for breach of those obligations irrespective of who had to perform those obligations—the tour operator or his subcontractors such as transport or hotel companies. Secondly Regulation 15(2) provides that in cases where neither the tour operator nor his suppliers are at fault there is no liability. Thirdly Regulations 15(3)-(5) govern the use of exclusion and limitation clauses in package holiday contracts. Fourthly Regulations 15(6)-(8) require the tour operator to offer assistance to consumers in difficulty. Finally Regulation 15(9) deals with making complaints. In this section we are concerned with Regulations 15(1) and Regulation 15(2). Rendering assistance is also dealt with in a later section of this chapter. Exclusion clauses are discussed in the next chapter and Regulation 15(9) is examined in the section on mitigation of loss in Chapter Ten.

There was general agreement after the passage of the Package Travel Regulation that all had changed and that by virtue of Regulation 15 of the Package Travel Regulations tour operators are now under a form of qualified strict liability—by which we mean that their liability has been extended beyond fault liability but falls some way short of full strict liability. (See Saggerson p.54; Nelson-Jones and Stewart pp.47–48; Cordato p.29; Chitty pp.634

and 701; Atherton, "Tour Operator's Responsibility for Package Holidays: Common Law takes the EC Directive Model Global", [1996] TLJ 90; and also the first edition of this book pp.112-115.) Whether this is in fact the case we hope to demonstrate shortly, but in brief it appears that the law may not have advanced as far as some have hoped (or feared).

2. Regulation 15(1). Proper performance of the obligations under the contract.

Regulation 15(1) does two, related, things. First it states that a tour operator must properly perform the obligations under the contract and secondly makes it clear that if the obligation is broken by virtue of some default by a "supplier" the tour operator is nevertheless still liable to the consumer. How the Courts have interpreted this we shall examine shortly.

"Supplier" is not a term of art but would certainly encompass direct subcontractors such as transport companies and hoteliers and perhaps also sub-subcontractors such as independent contractors hired by the immediate subcontractors to perform part of the services making up the contract—courtesy bus providers, tennis coaches, entertainers, etc. The Regulation expressly reserves the right of the tour operator to sue "suppliers" directly (assuming there is such a right). Of course the consumer may also have a claim against the supplier. This may not be a right which is much exercised. In practice it would entail a consumer suing a foreign company in a foreign court in the local equivalent of the law of tort—not a prospect which the average holidaymaker would relish. It probably explains why in the *Wall* case the plaintiffs chose to sue their tour operator in an English court rather than embark upon litigation in Spain against the hotel. (Jones, "Tour Operators and the Unfair Contract Terms Act" [1983] Gazette 2964. See also Chapter 8 on privity and the Contracts (Rights of Third Parties) Act 1999.)

3. Regulation 15(2). Qualified strict liability.

After ascertaining what the tour operator's obligations are under the contract it is necessary (at least in cases of strict liability—see passage on *Hone v Going Places* below) to look carefully at Regulation 15(2) which contains a number of sweeping qualifications to the tour operator's liability. However the extent of those qualifications is not immediately apparent. Regulation 15(2) states that the tour operator will be liable:

> "unless such failure to perform or improper performance is attributable neither to *any* fault of theirs nor to that of another supplier of services, *because* ..." (Emphasis added)

It then goes on to specify the situations in which the organiser will not be liable. Are the words quoted above general words providing that the organiser will never be liable if there is no fault on his behalf or the suppliers' behalf and the categories which follow merely examples of situations of no fault and the list is not exhaustive? Or are the categories a closed list and if a situation arises where there is improper performance which is not the fault of the organiser or the supplier and yet is not provided for in the list then the operator is still liable.

The use of the word "because" suggests the latter, *i.e.* the interpretation to be placed upon it is that the organiser will not be liable if the failure is not his fault *for the following reasons only*, suggesting that if it is not for the following reasons then the operator remains liable.

On the other hand the use of the word "any" suggests that if there is *no* fault on the operator's behalf or by the supplier then the operator is not liable and the list is merely illustrative of the situations where the operator escapes liability. (See Saggerson, p.125)

If in fact the list encompasses every situation where there is failure of performance and yet the operator is not at fault then the problem may be a little academic. To answer this requires an examination of the four relevant provisions.

The first is where the failure is attributable to the consumer. It is difficult to see why it was felt necessary to include this. On simple principles of causation a tour operator would not normally be held liable for damage caused to the consumer if the consumer was the author of his own downfall. One reported case that would fall into this category is *Hartley v Intasun* [1987] C.L.Y. 1149. The plaintiff in that case arrived at the airport a day late. Intasun put him on the next available plane and he arrived in resort to find that his room had been re-let and he had to accept inferior accommodation. On his return he sued for breach of contract. It was held that his failure to turn up at the airport on time amounted to a cancellation of the contract and therefore the defendants were under no obligation to do anything for him. They should not be penalised for doing their best to patch up some kind of holiday for him.

The second exception is where the failure is attributable to a third party unconnected with the provision of the services *and* was unforeseeable or unavoidable. Thus if the hotel swimming pool was unusable for a number of days because vandals had broken into the hotel grounds and put dye in the water then certainly this would have been due to third parties unconnected with the provision of the services but would it be unforeseeable or unavoidable? If it had happened before on a regular basis and if it could have been avoided by more stringent security it might be the case that the operator would still be liable.

What if a tour operator books a party into a downtown Miami hotel in an area frequented by drug addicts and a child in the party is injured when she steps on a hypodermic needle in the grounds of the hotel? Such an injury may have been caused by a third party unconnected with the provision of the services but could it be said to be unforeseeable or unavoidable? But there again, has there been a failure of performance of contractual obligations? Perhaps so if the hotelier knew of the risk but failed to do anything about it.

If the dye had been put in the pool by a disaffected employee would this be a "third party unconnected" with the provision of the service? In English law an employer is usually vicariously liable for the wrongful actions of his employees but only if they are committed in the course of their employment even if they are carrying out that employment in a way contrary to instructions. Depending on the facts, such an act of vandalism could be regarded as outside the course of employment. The Regulation however appears to encompass such a case. The employee is probably not a "third party" nor is he "unconnected" with the contract. Much the same problem might arise with air traffic controllers strikes. Are they third parties *unconnected* with the provision of the services contracted for?

The third exception to strict liability is where there is a *force majeure* event. *Force majeure* is examined in detail in Chapter 9 and therefore only a brief explanation is necessary here. For the exception to apply the failure must be due to *unusual and unforeseeable circumstances beyond the control of the organiser, the consequences of which could not have been avoided even if all due care had been exercised.*

The requirements are cumulative and therefore will be difficult for an operator to satisfy. How many things that go wrong with a package are unusual *and* unforeseeable *and* beyond the control of the operator *and* he could not have avoided them by the exercise of reasonable care? Apart from acts of God such as earthquakes and hurricanes and sudden outbreaks of war or civil unrest, *e.g. Charlson v Warner* (see Chapter 9 on *force majeure*) it appears that this exception will not be available to the organiser—but see the surprising decision in *Hibbs v Thomas Cook* (1999, Reigate CC) where a mechanical failure of a ferry was held to be *force majeure*.

The fourth exception is where the failure is due to an event which the operator or the supplier could not have foreseen or forestalled even with all due care.

Unlike the third exception this provision will have the effect of drastically narrowing the operator's liability. It would cover things such as air traffic controllers' strikes which if not unforeseeable are unavoidable. Waiters' strikes might fall within this exception as well. Whether it would cover technical breakdown of aircraft is more debatable. Are such events foreseeable or avoidable? (See [1997] I.T.L.J. 117 on charter airline delays.) One County Court case *Bedeschi & Holt v Travel Promotions Ltd* (Central London County Court, January 1998) demonstrates how significant this exception can be. The plaintiffs had suffered from vomiting and diarrhoea attributable to the food and drink they consumed on the defendant's Nile cruise boat. On the basis of expert evidence that standards of hygiene in Egypt were such that the risk of infection could not be eliminated the court held that the plaintiffs' illness might have been foreseeable but could not have been forestalled. (Following *Hone v Going Places*, below, however, the judge would not now have needed to look at the exception, as the Claimant could not prove improper performance). Two contrasting cases are *Hayes v Airtours* [2001] 2 C.L. 436 (hurricane not an event which could be forestalled, or even predicted) and *Bensusan v Airtours* (original decision at [2001] 7 C.L. 432, but overturned on appeal August 8, 2001, unreported but available at *http://tlc.unn.ac.uk*). In the latter case, discussed below, the judge held that a cumulative series of minor reasons for delay could be regarded as one "event", which in the circumstances was preventable. Judge Edwards said:

> "In my judgment . . . the word 'event' comprises a chain or series of separate events as well as each separate event itself. Each one of a number of events may be separately foreseeable or forestallable but their combination may not."

4. Development of the law to date

As we have said, the initial view of the effect of the Regulations was this: that now, for the first time, tour operators were strictly liable for the proper performance of the holiday. If a consumer is on the holiday, using the hotel provided, and is injured (*e.g.* by a glass door) or made ill (for example by the food), then the tour operator will be liable. He cannot escape by blaming his suppliers, however creditably that supplier had performed in the past. The only way in which the tour operator could escape liability was by demonstrating that he came within one of the exceptions to Regulation 15(2), set out above, for example by showing than an accident on a transfer coach was caused by a third party driver, or by showing a *force majeure* event.

The high point of this line of thinking was the case *Jordan v Thomson Holidays Limited* a decision of a district judge at Bristol County Court reported at [1999] 11 C.L. 389. It is not in fact a personal injury case. What happened was this: some days into their holiday the Jordan's returned to their apartment to find workmen repairing a burst pipe in one bedroom. As a result of the burst pipe, the Jordan's suffered a flood and had to move apartments twice. They claimed compensation.

The district judge held that, to escape liability Thomson would have to rely on Regulation 15(2)(c), an occurrence which was unusual and unforeseeable. It was held that pipes can and often do burst without warning and the burden of proof was on Thomson that it came within Regulation 15(2)(c). They could not discharge that burden and accordingly were held liable for the spoilt holiday.

The Privy Council Weighs In

The decision which appeared to support the above line of thinking was the Privy Council decision in *Wong Mee Wan v Kwan Kin Travel Services Limited* [1995] 4 All E.R. 745. This was an appeal from the Hong Kong Court of Appeal and therefore, obviously, not subject to any European directives. The (first) defendant was a Hong Kong tour operator. It is a tragic case. What happened was this: Miss Yee contracted to take a package tour in China. There was a party of 24. They left Hong Kong first by ferry and then by coach. They were accompanied by a tour leader employed by Kwan Kin. There was a delay at the border. Once in China they were accompanied by a tour guide from a Chinese tour company. The coach took them to the guest house where they were to spend the first night. The tour guide told them that they should leave their luggage quickly as, because of the delays, they were late to visit the ethnic village at the lake. When they got to the pier at the lake they were told by the guide that the coach and ferry had already gone and there was no alternative to the group but to cross the lake in a speed boat. Since the speed boat took only eight persons, three trips were involved each taking 15 minutes. After two trips, the speed boat employee refused to do the third. A volunteer from the boat company was found to drive the boat. It seems that the boat went very fast, perhaps racing another speed boat, and hit a fishing junk. The occupants were thrown into the water and two, including Miss Yee, were drowned. The Hong Kong Court of Appeal had held, in respect of the Defendant, that it:

> "It must have been clear to all members of the tours that it could not provide all those services itself but would delegate to other companies in China its duty to provide the bulk of them ... It would in my view impose an intolerable burden if the firm which put the tour package together was to be held liable for the negligence of a transport operator in another country".

The Privy Council disagreed. They concluded that:

> "The first defendants obligation under the contract that the services would be provided with reasonable skill and care remains even if some of the services were to be rendered by others ...
>
> In their Lordships' view it was an implied term of the contract that those services would be carried out with reasonable skill and care. That term does not mean ... that the first defendant undertook an obligation to ensure 'the safety of all the components of the package'. The plaintiff's claim does not amount to an implied term that her daughter would be reasonably safe. It is a term simply that reasonable skill and care would be used in rendering the services provided under the contract."

Unfortunately, for those seeking clarity in this area of law, this apparently helpful definition in the judgment of Lord Slynn is undermined in two ways. First of all, immediately after the above quoted passage, he muddies the waters by adding:

> "the trip across the lake was clearly not carried out with reasonable skill and care in that no steps were taken to see that the driver of the speed boat was of reasonable competence and experience and the First Defendant is liable for such breach of contract."

Surely, on the test which the judge had laid out, one would have expected him to say: "the trip across the lake was clearly not carried out with reasonable skill and care in that the driver of the speed boat drove recklessly"; instead, by making the breach of contract refer to the question of monitoring the quality of the driver, the judge appears to take us straight back to the test in *Wall v Silverwing* (a decision with which, by the way, Lord Slynn was unimpressed).

A second problem is this: Lord Slynn starts his analysis by referring to the contractual terms, namely the promises in the brochure, including: ". . . we will firstly gather at ... we will board the deluxe double jet hydrofoil ... our staff will handle the customs formalities for you ... we will board the deluxe coach ... we will visit the rustic and beautiful holiday village . . . " and so on and so on with repeated use of the word "we". Lord Slynn says:

> " 'we' includes the company offering the tour and integrates the company into each stage of the tour ... taking the contract as a whole their Lordships consider that the First Defendant here undertook to provide and not merely to arrange all the services included in the programme, even if some activities were to be carried out by others."

One gets the clear impression that if the tour operator had not so clearly taken obligations on themselves with the word "we", the decision might have been different. Consequently, this case has generally been regarded as turning on its own facts and has been cited but rarely applied in subsequent holiday cases.

The Tide Turns

The impetus to clarify the law once and for all has in fact come from a different line of cases. These cases are targeted at the following question, which inevitably arises when British tourists sue a British tour operator in respect of injuries sustained abroad. It is this: when deciding whether or not an hotel (or other holiday service) fulfils the necessary health and safety requirements, which standards should it be measured by? British standards or the local standards where the hotel is situated? For many years, the leading case has been *Wilson v Best Travel Limited,* decided in April 1991 but not reported until [1993] 1 All E.R. 353. It is a classic glass door case. On the first morning of their holiday on the Greek island of Kos, the plaintiffs party were in a hotel bedroom. The plaintiff tripped and fell against the glass patio door. The door shattered and the plaintiff fell through it sustaining lacerations from the broken glass to shoulder, elbow, hand and in particular to the right leg. "The gravity of the consequences was attributable to the fact that the glass fragmented into fragments of razor edged sharpness."

Phillips J. (as he then was) held:

> "I am satisfied, having read their brochure, that the service provided by the Defendants included the inspection of the properties offered in their brochure ... in my judgment one of

the characteristics of accommodation that the Defendants owed the duty to consider when inspecting properties included in their brochure was safety. The Defendants owe their customers, including the plaintiff, a duty to exercise reasonable care to exclude from the accommodation offered any hotel whose characteristics were such that guests could not spend their time there in reasonable safety. I believe that this case is about the standard to be applied in assessing reasonable safety."

Five millimetre annealed glass of the type used in this hotel was common in Greece. British Standards require the use of safety glass in doors and large panels although (at least in 1991) these were not mandatory by law, but "it is nonetheless the practice in England to comply with the relevant standards".

As we have previously seen the judge went on to say:

"What is the duty of a tour operator in a situation such as this? Must he refrain from sending holidaymakers to any hotel whose characteristics, in so far as safety is concerned, fail to satisfy the standards which apply in this country? 1 do not believe that his obligations in respect of the safety of his clients can extend this far. Save where uniform international regulations apply, there are bound to be differences in the safety standards applied in respect of the many hazards of modem life between one country and another. All civilised countries attempt to cater for these hazards by imposing mandatory regulations. The duty of care of a tour operator is likely to extend to checking that local safety regulations are complied with. Provided that they are, I do not consider that the tour operator owes a duty to boycott a hotel because of the absence of some safety feature which would be found in an English hotel unless the absence of such a feature might lead a reasonable holiday maker to decline to take a holiday at the hotel in question."

Thus it can be seen that local safety standards apply unless:

- There are contrary international regulations; or
- The absence of the safety feature would lead a reasonable holiday maker to decline to go. A glass door did not come within this exception. One can however imagine how the parents of a toddler might decline a holiday in an upstairs bedroom with a balcony whose railings were wide enough for the child to slip through, not withstanding any argument that such a balcony complied with local safety standards; or
- There are express provisions in the contract to the contrary.

Over the years since *Wilson v Best Travel* was decided, there has been much debate as to whether it was correctly decided, whether it would survive a challenge in a suitable case to the Court of Appeal; in particular whether the Package Travel Regulations 1992, not in force at the time of *Wilson v Best Travel,* would change the outcome. These questions have now been answered.

The Latest Developments

The Wilson principle was tested in the Court of Appeal in the case of *Codd v Thomson Holidays Limited, The Times* October, 20, 2000. This case arose out of an accident suffered by a ten-year old child with the glass lift door of his hotel in Majorca. The lift had an outer door which was hinged and an inner sliding door which closed automatically when the outer door had been closed. The claimant and his sisters went into the lift and neither of the doors shut. It appears that the outer door had for some reason jammed before it reached its proper resting place in the door frame. The claimant put his right hand round the door and pulled it towards him. The door then shut quickly and caught his right middle finger as a result of which he sustained a serious injury to it.

By the contract terms, Thomson agreed that they would be liable for injuries caused by the negligence of their suppliers, in this case the hotel.

The court had before it documentation which showed that in accordance with Spanish law, the lifts at the hotel were examined on a monthly basis by engineers. There was evidence that the lifts were working satisfactorily prior to and after the accident and there were no regulations in Spain which required safety signs to be posted in a lift or the requirement that there should be an these emergency alarm or emergency procedure in the lift if the door did not close or the lift became stuck. There is such a requirement in English law. The lift did not comply with those regulations but complied with Spanish legislation.

> "Accordingly [the trial judge] arrived at the conclusion that negligence had not been established against the hotel owners or managers and in consequence it was not established against the tour operator."

The claimant challenged this decision in the Court of Appeal on a variety of grounds which included "that the onus of proving that the accident did not result from the negligence of the hotel or Thomson was upon them and not on the Claimant" and "that the judge was in error in not applying the British Standards to this particular lift."

The Court of Appeal rejected both of these submissions. Swinton Thomas L.J., on the first point, said:

> "... this is not a case in which, in my view, it is appropriate to say that the hotel or the tour operator is liable for this accident without proof of negligence. In order to succeed, the claimant must prove that the hotel management was negligent either in relation to the maintenance of the lift or in relation to the safety procedures."

On the second point, that British Standards should apply, he said:

> "that is not a correct approach to a case such as this where an accident occurred in a foreign country. The law of this country is applied to the case as to the establishing of negligence, but there is no requirement that a hotel for example in Majorca is obliged to comply with British Safety Standards".

and he approved *Wilson v Best Travel.*

Although this answered many of the outstanding questions, it left one: because the case proceeded on the basis of Thomson's booking conditions, the Package Travel Regulations were never mentioned. Do they make a difference? One County Court judge thought not see *Logue v Flying Colours* [2001] 6 CL, a case with facts very similar to *Wilson.*

Hone v Going Places

The latest piece in the jigsaw has now been slotted in by another Court of Appeal decision, *Hone v Going Places Leisure Travel Limited,* [2001] E.W.C.A. Civ. 947. The facts were rather unusual. First of all, Going Places (as is perhaps well known) is a travel agent, and not a tour operator. This was an issue in the original High Court trial, where the judge concluded that they had held themselves out as a tour operator and were therefore potentially liable on the contract. This issue was not revisited in the Court of Appeal. (See Chapter Fifteen on travel agents).

Turning to the more important issue, the claimant and his family were on their way home by aeroplane from a holiday in Turkey. Shortly after takeoff there was a bomb scare on board and the pilot decided to divert to Istanbul. The passengers were instructed to prepare for an emergency landing and then for a crash landing, after which, the passengers would have to descend from the aeroplane by emergency chute. When the claimant was at the top of the chute he noticed a large lady, who had also been on holiday, at the bottom of the chute. In the course of his descent, Mr Hone realised that she was stuck at the bottom of the chute and unable to move away. He opened his legs wide enough to avoid striking her back but collided with her. His fiancée followed him down the chute and struck his back with her shoes, causing a spinal injury which was exacerbated when he tried to assist the large lady to stand up.

Mr Hone sued the defendant relying entirely on Regulation 15 of the Package Travel Regulations. The Court of Appeal were called upon to decide two points: whether Regulation 15 imposed strict liability; and whether the onus of proving fault was with the claimant, rather than on the defendant to disprove fault.

Longmore LJ. said:

> "The starting point must in my view be the contract which Mr Hone made with the Defendant ... in the absence of any contrary intention, the normal implication will be that the service contracted for will be rendered with reasonable skill and care. Of course, absolute obligations may be assumed. If the brochure or advertisement on which the consumer relies promises a swimming pool, it will be a term of the contract that a swimming pool will be provided. But in the absence of express wording, there would not be an absolute obligation for example to ensure that the holidaymaker catches no infection while swimming in the swimming pool. The obligation assumed will be that reasonable skill and care will be taken to ensure that the pool is free from infection."

He went on:

> "Going Places is ... liable for 'the proper performance of the obligations under the Contract'. But Regulation 15(1) says nothing about *the content of that performance* [our emphasis]
>
> "Regulation 15(2) provides for [the tour operator] to be liable for any damage caused to the consumer by failure to perform the contract or by the improper performance of the contract. The present case is not a case of failure to perform. It can only be a case of improper performance. It is only possible to determine whether it is a case of improper performance by reference to the terms of the contract which is being performed. *To my mind, Regulation 15(2) does not give the answer to the question, 'what is improper performance?' rather, it is a requirement of the application of Regulation 15 (2) that there should be improper performance* [our emphasis]. That can only be determined by

reference to the terms of the contract . . . I would not, for my part, accept that the existence of the fault based exceptions in Regulation 15(2) makes it otiose or nonsensical for the Claimant to have to prove fault in an appropriate case. The exceptions will, in any event, come into play if the other party to the contract assumes obligations which are themselves not fault-based."

This case gives the lie to the simplistic formulation that the effect of the PTR's is this: that if the supplier is liable, then the tour operator is liable under Regulation 15. In *Hone* the airline *was* liable by virtue of the strict liability regime in the Warsaw Convention. However, Longmore LJ expressly rejected the idea that a strict liability similarly applied to the tour operator.

In summary, therefore, a Claimant must go through the following process:

- He must establish the terms of the contract.
- Unless they are expressed in terms of strict liability, there will only be fault-based obligations.
- The burden of proof is on the claimant to prove that fault.
- Nothing in Reg.15(2) switches the burden of proof in such circumstances. Indeed, in fault liability cases, the exceptions in Regulation 15 will always be irrelevant. Either the Claimant can prove fault, in which case, of course, it is impossible for the Defendant to prove lack of fault; or the Claimant cannot prove fault, the case fails, and the exceptions never come into play.

For further commentary on *Hone* see Saggerson at [2001] ITLJ 159.

Strict Liability Terms

Hone v Going Places is a case where the court held that liability was fault based and the burden of proof was on the claimant to prove fault. By way of contrast *Bensusan v Airtours* mentioned above is a case where the judge decided that the duty on Airtours to fly the claimants to Jamaica in time to join their cruise was an obligation of strict liability. It therefore fell upon Airtours to prove that one of the statutory defences applied, in this case that the delays could not have been foreseen or forestalled with all due care. This they failed to do.

Final Thoughts

The terms of the contract are therefore now king. (See also further support for this view in the case of *Williams v Travel Promotions Ltd, The Times*, March 9, 1998 (CA) where the Court of Appeal adopted the approach later found in *Hone*.) It seems clear that once the obligations under the contract have been established, the tour operator cannot escape liability for those obligations by blaming his subcontractors. The following question could however be asked: what is to stop a tour operator from defining his obligations in the contract, using the formula from *Wall v Silverwing*? In other words, a tour operator would say that its obligations under the contract extend only to making a good choice of subcontractor and (perhaps) monitoring its performance. Any defect in performance by the subcontractor is not then a breach of the operator's contracted obligation to make a good choice, and as the subcontractor had no part in discharging the "good choice" obligation, Regulation 15 is circumvented. All we can say is that courts are likely to strive for a method of rejecting such an attempt to restrict liability, although this type of philosophy seems to underpin the decision of Reading County Court in *Grahame v JMC Holidays* [2002] 8 CL 505 whereby JMC were found not liable for aircraft delay because they had used reasonable skill and care in selecting the airline.

5. Specific issues

Dangerous Destinations

In one case, Torquay County Court decided that where illness is known by the tour operator to be prevalent in a resort there is a duty to warn customers—*Davey v Cosmosair* 1989 CLY 2561. In *Beales v Airtours* (1996, CA) the plaintiffs had booked a holiday whereby they chose to go to the Algarve but the precise location of the resort and hotel were left to the tour operator. Whilst in the resort of Vilamoura the plaintiff and his wife were mugged. They sued the tour operator for sending them to a dangerous destination. It was held by the Court of Appeal (on an application for leave to appeal) that the plaintiffs had no case. LJ Saville said:

> "To my mind the starting point of the claim advanced by Mr Beales must be that Vilamoura was at the material time a resort in the Algarve marked out as one of special danger to holiday-makers from the activities of street robbers. The reason for this is that it is Mr and Mrs Beales themselves who chose to go to a resort in the Algarve, leaving only the specifice choice of resort to

> the tour operators. Having themselves chosen that part of the world for their holidays, it seems to me, really as a matter of common sense as much as a matter of law, that Mr and Mrs Beales could hardly complain of the state of affairs in resorts in the Algarve generally. Thus, apart from anything else, it seems to me that Mr Beales, to have any chance of success, has to demonstrate that Vilamoura, as opposed to resorts in the Algarve generally, fell into a special category of danger to holiday-makers of such a marked kind that either the tour operator should have refrained from sending holiday-makers to that resort at all or at least should have given more than the general warnings that they did give to holiday-makers and to Mr and Mrs Beales." (See [1996] TLJ 167 for a short commentary on this case.)

This can be seen as a case where the tour operator was held not liable for the actions of a third party. Pushing the logic of the case to its extremes it appears that a tour operator can never be liable for sending a client to a dangerous destination *which the client has chosen*. However in our view tour operators cannot afford to be complacent—a slightly different set of facts could very well produce a different result.

Contributory Negligence

Whilst it can be said that individual cases are fact sensitive, nonetheless there are enough cases to enable us to distinguish trends.

In *Brannan v Airtours* CA, *The Times*, February 1, 1999, Airtours had organised an entertainment evening. They pointed out to customers the overhead fans. The Claimant was hemmed into a corner and, having been plied with alcohol all evening, needed to go to the toilet. He climbed onto the table and was injured by the fan. Airtours had put him in this difficult position where injury was foreseeable; on the other hand, the danger was patent, not hidden, and warning had been given. Not surprisingly, perhaps, the Court of Appeal decided that Airtours were liable but with 50 per cent contributory negligence by the Claimant.

Contrast this with *Williams v First Choice* [2001] 8 CL 437 a plate smashing evening which resulted in injury to the Claimant. Here it was held that the Defendants had taken all necessary precautions to warn customers about their behaviour, and to avoid the risks.

In *Logue v Flying Colours* [2001] 6 CL 454, a case similar on its facts to *Wilson v Best Travel,* the Defendant was found not liable for the injuries caused when the Claimant went through a glass patio door; but the Judge commented that had he found the Defendant liable, he would have reduced the Claimant's damages by 75 per cent for contributory negligence as he was considerably affected by alcohol.

In *Isle and Dean v Thomson Holidays Limited* 2000 QBD, unreported, the Claimants, also to some extent inebriated, were looking for somewhere to relieve themselves late at night and fell down an insufficiently guarded cliff. The Defendants were held liable, but with 60 per cent contributory negligence by the Claimants, who had been at the hotel for two weeks and knew the layout of it.

Similar considerations led to a finding of 33 per cent contribution against a Claimant who slipped on a marble ramp on the 10th day of his holiday. The anti-slip tape on the marble was missing, but the Claimant was aware of the hazard (*Shore v First Choice* [2002] Bristol County Court, unreported).

Children and Parents

Unfortunately, accidents on holiday sometimes befall children. The duty of care of a tour operator towards children is that of the reasonable parent, particularly where children are participating in organised "children's club" activities. Where a parent has authorised participation by the child in an activity, there is therefore unlikely to be liability on the tour operator if injury to the child results (unless of course there was a defect in the delivery of the activity, *e.g.* the hotel had failed to maintain playground equipment properly in a way which may not have been obvious to the parent).

Thus in one unreported case, at Liverpool County Court, Thomson Holidays were found not liable to a child who fell and was injured whilst dancing the "hokey cokey", with which the daily children's mini disco always ended. The parents had watched their child on a number of previous occasions, knew exactly what was involved, and had approved it.

A case which vividly and tragically illustrates the circumstances in which the tour operator is liable, the parents are liable, or maybe both are liable to a child, is *Roberts v Ibero Travel Limited QBD,* February 14, 2001 (2001 12 CL 409). The Roberts family consisted of Mr and Mrs Roberts, their son Kevin (the Claimant) aged six, and other sons aged nine and one. They arrived at their Spanish hotel late one night. The next day the family visited the pool. Kevin could not swim. He did not have his arm bands. Kevin was in the pool in the company of his nine-year-old brother, and his parents were elsewhere. It was the first day of the holiday. What exactly happened is not known, but two teenage girls pulled Kevin's body from the water and a doctor eventually arrived and resuscitated him; but not in time to prevent serious brain damage. Kevin sued the tour operator Ibero Travel. The damages in this case were very substantial, well into seven figures. The Judge decided that liability depended upon two separate questions and each would attract an equal half share of the damages:

1. Why did Kevin get into difficulty?
2. Why was he not rescued sooner?

On the first point the Judge held the tour operator liable because the pool shelved too steeply and it had insufficient warnings about depth, suitability for children, etc. The parents had been made Part 20 Defendants. The Judge (Gibbs J) said

> "the fact remains that Kevin was permitted into the pool unaccompanied, save for his nine-year-old brother. If the pool was unsafe for use by a child who could not swim, it was not in my judgment a reasonably sufficient safeguard to leave him with a child of nine, even one who could swim .... Kevin's parents had used armbands for him previously. If he was to be left, even temporarily unattended, then the use of armbands though not a complete safeguard would have been a reasonable and sensible precaution. The reasonableness of the parent's actions has to be seen in a context that the depth and dimensions of the pool were completely unknown to them. It was a foreign country. It was their first visit to it. I regret that I am driven to the conclusion that to allow Kevin into the pool in those circumstances did fall short of the reasonable standard of care to be accepted of them".

In respect of how Kevin got into difficulty, the Judge held that the tour operator was 50 per cent to blame and the parents were 50 per cent to blame.

In respect of the failure to rescue Kevin more quickly, the Judge held, following *Wilson v Best Travel*, that the tour operator was 100 per cent to blame; because in breach of Spanish regulations there was no lifeguard on duty.

Defective Furniture

For a typical case of a collapsing sun lounger or plastic chair, see *McRae v Thomson Holidays* [2001] 5 CL 572. The *Hone* principle was applied: did the hotel act with reasonable skill and care in maintaining the chair, or should they have spotted the defects? In this case Thomson were found not liable.

Illness

Illness contracted while on holiday tends to fall into three broad categories:—

- Legionnaires disease: applying the *Hone* principle, we believe that these claims will often go well for the Claimants. As we understand it, a hotel run with reasonable skill and care should not have legionella bacteria in its water supply/ air conditioning and the claimant should have little difficulty proving this.
- Food poisoning: a large outbreak of food poisoning in a hotel, with many people affected, and not duplicated in the rest of the resort, is again suggestive of liability on the part of the hotel and therefore the tour operator. It is likely that there has been some lack of reasonable care and skill in preparation or handling of food. Individual one off cases are more of a problem. Where only one person in the hotel suffers food poisoning, *e.g.* salmonella, it is suggested that the source of the illness may be elsewhere and the tour operator not liable; alternatively that there has been no sufficient lack of care and skill.
- Cryptosporidiosis: in the UK this illness is most commonly associated with water supplies; in a holiday context, the swimming pool is a common culprit. Because of the way in which the organisms enter the water (faecal accident), such infection can be contracted from the best run pool. However, a poorly run pool, particularly with a poor filtration system, can make matters a lot worse.

In all cases of illness, attention needs to be paid to the incubation periods when considering the issue of causation.

6. The liability of travel agents under regulation 15(1)

Up to this point we have worked on the assumption that Regulation 15(1) imposes liability upon tour operators only. However that may be incorrect. Regulation 15(1) imposes liability not upon organisers alone but upon "the other party to the contract". In Chapter Two we have already seen that this term includes not only tour operators but also travel agents. The question arises therefore as to whether a consumer could sue his travel agent as well as, or instead of, his tour operator in the event of a breach of contract. As indicated in Chapter Two, the question is still open, and although we think this is an unlikely direction for the law to take, nevertheless it still remains a possibility. It would be a particular temptation in circumstances where the tour operator had become insolvent and was unable to meet claims from consumers. On this point see *Minhas v Imperial Travel* [2003] ITLJ 69. However two areas of potential liability—by a travel agent holding itself out as operator (*Hone v Going Places* 2000 QBD) and under a "split contract" arrangement (*Club Tour v Garrido* 2002) are discussed further in chapter Fifteen.

7. The ABTA Code of Conduct

The provisions on liability in the ABTA Code (February 2003 version) corresponding to Regulation 15 are to be found in paragraphs 2.6(i)–(iii):

(i) A principal shall include, as a term of any contract for the sale of Packages, a provision accepting responsibility for the proper performance of the contract. A Principal shall not be required to accept responsibility where the failure to perform the contract or the improper performance of the contract is due neither to the fault of the Principal nor to that of his employees, agents, sub-contractors or suppliers because the failure—

(a) is attributable to the Client, or
(b) is attributable to a third party unconnected with the provision of the services contracted for *and* is unforeseeable or unavoidable, or
(c) is due to

(i) unusual and unforeseeable circumstances beyond the control of the Principal the consequences of which could not have been avoided even is all due care had been exercised, or
(ii) an event which the Principal, his employees, agents suppliers and subcontractors could not, even with all due care, have foreseen or forestalled.

(iii) Where the contract services referred to in Clause 2.6 (i) consist of carriage by air, by sea, or by rail or the provision of accommodation, the Principal shall be entitled to limit his

> liability in accordance with the international conventions which govern such services.

The provisions of the ABTA code have undergone fundamental revisions since the last edition of this book. Some of these changes appear to be a response to *Hone v Going Places*. The reason for others is less clear. Gone are previous provisions distinguishing between quality complaints (for which there was strict liability) and injury/illness claims (for which ABTA members were required to accept responsibility for the negligence of suppliers and sub-contractors).

In their place comes wording which follows the Package Travel Regulations more closely. The important point about the ABTA code is that it *requires* ABTA tour operators to express this state in their contract that they accept a certain level of liability. The first point to be noted is that a Principal is required to include "as a term of any contract for the sale of packages, a provision accepting responsibility for the proper performance of the contract". (We should add that although Principal has a complex definition, it is simplest for present purposes to regard the word as meaning much the same as "organiser" under the Regulations). In some ways this is a rather circular provision, as it would be a very odd term of any contract that provided that a Principal was not responsible for the proper performance of the contract! To paraphrase Longmore LJ in *Hone*, the Code says nothing about the content of the performance of the contract. The writers have indeed seen booking conditions of some tour operators which provide that they are responsible for the proper performance of the contract, without ever stating what, in practice that means.

The ABTA code goes on to set out the exceptions to liability as found in Regulation 15 (2) PTR. In conclusion, we suppose that the effect of this change to the code is exactly that of *Hone v Going Places*, namely:

> In the case of absolute obligations (*e.g.* a promise to supply a swimming pool), there will be strict liability unless the organisers/Principal can make out one of the exceptions to liability; but that where there is fault based liability (*e.g.* an obligation to use reasonable care and skill in maintaining the hotel), the burden of proof will be upon the consumer to show the fault; and if he can, the exception has become irrelevant.

One small interesting point to note is that in paragraph 2.6(iii) of the code, it envisages permission for tour operators to limit their responsibility under International Conventions (*e.g.* Warsaw,

Athens, etc) in a wider way than that envisaged by the Regulations. Regulation 15(3) only allows the organiser to limit the *compensation payable* in accordance with the conventions; paragraph 2.6(iii) provides for the possibility of limiting *liability* in accordance with the Conventions. Thus, the code would seem to allow tour operators to rely on the exclusion of mental distress/discomfort claims which are not bodily injury, and to deny liability where there has been no "accident" as defined (see chapter 18 for a detailed discussion of these topics). Having said that, the Code cannot make legal that which the Regulations appear to make impermissible.

In our last edition we admired the way in which the Code forced its members to give wider measures of consumer protection than were required by the Regulations; this merit appears to have been lost. The only consumer bonus now found in the Code is paragraph 2.5 which requires an organiser to notify (and re-accommodate) consumers where building work will seriously impair enjoyment of the holiday, regardless of whether the building work is a breach of the contractual obligations or not (*e.g.* if work was on neighbouring premises to the hotel); *cf. Griffiths v Flying Colours Holidays* [1999] 5 CL 473).

8. Rendering assistance—(1) The Regulations

If consumers are injured or mugged on holiday or if their money and passports are stolen they are clearly going to be in some difficulty. Even if they have insurance which will cover the financial consequences of such a disaster they are nevertheless often a long way from home and the support of family and friends. They may not be able to speak the language of the country they find themselves in and they may not understand the complexities of the legal or medical systems they have to contend with. It is for reasons like this that Regulation 15 provides that even in situations where the tour operator is not at fault the operator must nevertheless offer assistance to consumers. This is an area where the ABTA Code of Conduct also contains provisions to protect the consumer. However, there are significant differences between the Regulations and the Code. For the sake of completeness therefore we will look first at the Regulations and then at the Code of Conduct.

(a) Prompt Assistance

If there has been some failure in the contract but the organiser is not liable under Regulation 15(2)(b) and (c) he is nevertheless under an obligation to render prompt assistance.

Regulation 15(7) provides:

> "15(7) In the circumstances described in paragraph (2)(b) and (c) of this regulation, the other party to the contract will give prompt assistance to a consumer in difficulty."

The Regulation requires that there be a *failure in the performance of the contract* before this provision is triggered—not simply a misadventure as in the ABTA Code which will be examined shortly. So for instance if the consumer was run down by a drunk driver while coming back from the beach the organiser would be under no obligation to do anything. The accident may have been caused by a third party unconnected with the provision of the services but it did not result in "failure to perform" or "improper performance" of the contract. It would be different if vandals had wrecked the air-conditioning system of the hotel or if a transfer bus had been hit by a drunken driver. In those circumstances there would be failure of performance of the contract. The organiser would not be liable but would have to render assistance. (See *Josephs v Sunworld* [1998] C.L.Y. 3734 for a decision on this point which seems clearly wrong; see also *Coughlan v Thomson Holidays Ltd* [2001] C.L.Y. 4276 for a case where the court held that assistance should have been given more promptly.)

No financial limit is placed on this assistance and it is difficult to establish to what lengths the tour operator is obliged to go to in order to comply. Does it merely extend to the giving of advice or making appropriate telephone calls or does it go further. If more concrete help is extended e.g. taking the client to hospital or putting them on a flight home can the tour operator charge for this? The answer is far from clear but some indication may be gained from an examination of Regulation 15(8) which is dealt with below.

(b) Finding Appropriate Solutions

Regulation 15(8) provides:

> "15(8) If the consumer complains about a defect in the performance of the contract, the other party to the contract, or his local representative, if there is one, will make prompt efforts to find appropriate solutions."

This is the corollary to Regulation 15(9) which imposes a duty on the consumer to complain if he finds fault with the package. If the consumer complains then the organiser must endeavour to do something about it. The difficulty is in establishing whether it adds anything to the requirement in Regulation 15(7) to render "prompt assistance". The answer seems to be that Regulation 15(7) only covers situations where the organiser is *not liable* to the consumer whereas Regulation 15(8) covers all situations where the consumer has a complaint about defects in the performance of the contract—whether it amounts to a breach of contract or not. The interesting point is that in cases of no breach of contract covered by 15(7) the organiser seems to be under a more onerous duty—to render "assistance"—than when there is a breach of contract where the duty is to make "efforts" to find an appropriate solution. The answer probably lies in the fact that Regulation 15(7) refers to consumers *in difficulty*. This suggests a more serious level of need and therefore greater efforts need to be taken to remedy the situation.

Neither Regulation 15(7) nor Regulation 15(8) imposes a limit on the efforts the organiser is required to make unlike the ABTA Code with its £5000 limit which is at the organiser's discretion. One can envisage a situation where a tour operator has thousands of clients waiting at the airport because of an air traffic controllers' strike. Clearly the organiser is *obliged* to do something, either under Regulation 15(7) or 15(8). But if this means providing bed and board for them at great expense is this cost to be borne by the organiser or the consumer? Under Regulation 15(7) the answer would point to the consumer. If the organiser is not in breach then even though he must render assistance he may be able to claim an indemnity should he so wish. Under Regulation 15(8), assuming a breach of contract, the answer may be different. Here the Regulations are saying that as the organiser is in breach then he must mend that breach, not by the payment of damages, but in some more practical form by putting the problem right.

This view of Regulation 15(8) corresponds with the provisions of Regulation 14 with which it overlaps. Where there is a non-provision of services after departure, Regulation 14 provides that the organiser *must* make suitable alternative arrangements and may also have to pay damages. In cases therefore of *non-provision* the consumer would make his case under Regulation 14 whereas for *improper* provision the claim would be made under Regulation 15(8). It would be strange if the remedy under Regulation 15 were to be different than under Regulation 14.

9. Rendering assistance—(2) The ABTA Code of Conduct

The first thing to say is that the Code contains no precise equivalent of Regulation 15(7) or (8). What it does have are paragraphs 2.6(iv) (a) and (b):

(iv) A Principal shall include as a term of any contract for the sale of a package holiday or tour provisions stating that, where appropriate and subject to the Principal's reasonable discretion:—

(a) general assistance shall be afforded to clients who, through misadventure, suffer illness, personal injury or death during the period of their holiday arising out of an activity which does not form part of the contracted services nor of an excursion offered through the Principal.

(b) where legal action is undertaken by the client, with the prior agreement of the tour operator, initial costs associated therewith shall be met by the Principal, always provided clients request such assistance within 90 days from date of misadventure.

(a) Misadventures

Paragraph 2.6(iv)(a) only covers the client if they suffer misadventure arising from an activity *which does not form part of the contracted services*. The essence of the paragraph is that the tour operator shall lend assistance to clients in circumstances where the tour operator is not contractually liable to them but nevertheless they are deserving of help. For instance if the client is injured by a drunken driver while walking back from the beach or mugged while shopping or hit by a pedalo while swimming these are misadventures arising from activities which do not form part of the services contracted for but where the operator would be required to render assistance. It only applies however if they suffer death, illness or personal injury. Technically it would not cover mere illness not arising from misadventure or loss of a passport or theft of valuables or false imprisonment or other incidents not involving personal injury although it is hard to imagine tour operators actually turning a blind eye in such circumstances.

Any assistance given is only at the operator's reasonable discretion. Thus if the assistance is likely to be prohibitively expensive or if the client has been the cause of his own downfall it may be that it would be reasonable to refuse assistance. For instance what if a client who had been warned about his behaviour had nevertheless become so drunk that he had fallen into the swimming pool and ended up in hospital—without insurance. Would it be reasonable in the circumstances to refuse assistance?

(b) Legal Assistance

Under paragraph 2.6(iv)(b) a tour operator is required, at his reasonable discretion and with his prior agreement, to meet a client's initial legal costs if he undertakes legal action. This would cover situations where the consumer wanted to sue the drunken driver who knocked him over on the street or the restaurant which gave him food poisoning.

However it would not extend to being given support to sue the driver who damaged not the consumer but his camera because the misadventure must cause personal injury or death not damage to property.

(c) Limits on Assistance

A £5000 limit is placed on the assistance that the operator must provide under paragraphs 2.6(iv)(a) and (b) and in the event that the client claims successfully against either a third party or an insurance policy the tour operator will be entitled to recover this money from the client.

Regulation 4

We turn now to Regulation 4 which creates a statutory right to compensation for the consumer that cuts across the traditional boundaries of the common law. It imposes civil liability on both tour operators and travel agents if they supply misleading information. It states:

> 4(1) No organiser or retailer shall supply to a consumer any descriptive matter concerning a package, the price of a package or any other conditions applying to the contract which contains any misleading information.
>
> (2) If an organiser or retailer is in breach of paragraph (1) he shall be liable to compensate the consumer for any loss which the consumer suffers in consequence.

The elements of the Regulation are that if:

- an organiser or a retailer
- supplies
- descriptive matter

- to a consumer
- containing misleading information
- concerning a package
- compensation will be payable for any losses suffered as a consequence.

We shall examine these elements in turn.

1. Organiser or retailer

The significant point here is that the travel agent retailer as well as the tour operator could incur liability. (Remember that retailers also include newspapers or magazines selling "Readers Offers" type trips). Not only that but there is also the possibility that it is the agent who will be first in the firing line. If the consumer has a complaint about a misleading brochure then the chances are that he will take it up first with his agent, who is local, rather than the operator who will usually not be as accessible. It may be that the agent can deflect complaints by blaming the operator but this may not always be possible. The Sale of Goods Act for instance has educated many consumers to the concept of the retailer being liable to them rather than the manufacturer. The true difficulty for the travel agent however is that the liability appears absolute; there is no defence. In the equivalent criminal legislation such as the Trade Descriptions Act 1968 and the Consumer Protection Act 1987 there is a due diligence defence but it appears that under Regulation 4 once it can be shown that the travel agent did the supplying then he will be liable without fault. It is as well for travel agents that the public have as yet shown little appetite to target them instead of tour operators.

It is hard to over emphasise the effect Regulation 4 could have on travel agents. It creates civil liability for every detail in a tour operator's brochure that is misleading—the location, the price, the meal plan, the hotel facilities, the resort facilities, the availability of excursions, the availability of car hire etc etc. The only way to combat this liability is to ensure that the agency agreements they have with operators contain indemnity clauses. Whether they do may very well be a matter of bargaining power (see Chapter Fifteen on travel agency); but an indemnity will be valueless in the likely event that the consumer exercises his right to sue the retailer because the tour operator is insolvent, which is perhaps the most likely scenario in which the consumer will prefer to pursue the retailer. (See *Minhas v Imperial Travel* [2003] ITLJ 69 on this point).

2. Supplies

It is beyond doubt that a tour operator is the person who supplies the brochure to the consumer, even though it is distributed via an intermediary, but the question arises as to whether the travel agent is also a supplier. In the sense that he is not the originator or publisher of the brochure and is only the means by which the tour operator supplies the consumer with the brochure it could be argued that he is not the supplier—any more than a vending machine is the supplier of cigarettes or confectionery. On the other hand the travel agent does exercise some judgment in the matter—he chooses which tour operators to deal with; he decides which brochures to rack; and he decides which brochures might appeal to the consumer. As such he is not simply a passive conduit and therefore should bear responsibility. This was surely the intention of the Regulation.

What about the client who acquires a misleading brochure from Agent A but then books his holiday through Agent B? Although B has booked the holiday he is not liable under Reg. 4 because he did not supply the brochure (although ironically he may very well have dozens of other such brochures in his agency). Agent A has supplied the brochure but has not had the advantage of making a sale. Is he to be liable even though he has no connection with the contract which ultimately results? On the one hand he has aided in the deception by racking the brochure in the first place, on the other it seems a little harsh to penalise him when he has not profited from the transaction.

Closer examination of Regulation 4 may provide the answer. For liability to be imposed it must be shown that the misleading descriptive matter concerned:

> "a package, the price of a package or any other conditions applying to *the contract* ..." [Emphasis added]

"Contract" is further defined in Regulation 2(1) as meaning:

> "the agreement linking the consumer to the organiser or to the retailer or both, as the case may be;"

Taking these together it suggests that Agent A will escape liability because although he was a retailer who supplied a brochure he was not a retailer who supplied it in relation to a contract which linked him to the consumer and the organiser.

One way in which Regulation 4 is wider than an action in

misrepresentation is that there seems no requirement that the information be supplied *before* the contract is concluded or that it induced the contract. It might be the case that after the contract is concluded the consumer returns to the travel agency and asks for clarification about the features of the resort where he has booked his holiday and the travel agent photocopies a page from a gazetteer for the consumer which contains misleading information. This would appear to be a contravention of the Regulation. Alternatively the client may have booked the holiday without the benefit of a brochure, using viewdata alone, and then subsequently returns to the travel agency and acquires a misleading brochure. Traditionally the ticket wallet supplied by the tour operator shortly before departure contains much information about the resort and the itinerary, all of which could potentially ground a claim if misleading. More complex cases might arise. Take for example the case of a Mediterranean cruise calling at a number of ports where shore excursions are possible. Let us say that when the ship docks in Malaga and passengers are given a sheet of tourist information that states, amongst other things, that the castle in Malaga is open for the duration of the ship's stay. A consumer, in reliance on this information, hires a taxi to take him to the castle only to find it closed for renovation works. He has been supplied with misleading descriptive matter and suffered in consequence. It would appear he had a good case for compensation. Whether the courts will be happy to extend liability to post-contractual matter in this way remains to be seen.

3. Descriptive Matter

The liability is imposed for supplying misleading descriptive *matter* not simply the supply of misleading *information*. The implication here is that it will cover written matter but not oral statements. The word matter suggests something tangible. It will obviously cover brochures and other brochure-like leaflets and it would most probably extend to videos of holiday destinations. It probably does not extend to window displays or window cards because the requirement is that the matter be *supplied to* the consumer and it cannot be said that such matter is supplied to the consumer. Press advertisements are a different matter. It is a moot point whether it can be said that the operator or the retailer have supplied the matter. It comes in a paper or journal supplied by a publisher or newsagent.

Now that many tour operators and travel agents have websites on the Internet there exists the possibility that Regulation 4 could

be broken by placing misleading information on the website. But does this involve the supply of misleading descriptive *matter*? In the light of what has been said above it appears that the Regulation will only be broken when the consumer downloads the information and prints it off—simply reading it on the screen may not be enough—a rather unsatisfactory distinction. A consumer excluded in this way would have to rely on narrower rights in Misrepresentation. See Chapter Seven.

4. A consumer

The extended meaning of consumer would apply here. Thus a tour operator might find himself liable to holidaymakers with whom he did not originally have any contractual relationship, *e.g.* transferees and other beneficiaries—so long as it could be shown that there was a supply by the operator to these other consumers.

5. Containing misleading information

Misleading is a word which goes much further than "inaccurate" or "false" which form the basis of the criminal offences under Regulation 5 of the PTR and s.14 of the Trade Descriptions Act 1968. The clear indication here is that although the information may be technically correct, if it gives rise to a false impression then liability will result; the emphasis is thus on the impression reasonably created in the mind of the consumer, whereas "false" refers to matters which are more objectively measurable. Cropped photographs are an example. Technically the photograph may be accurate in that it correctly depicts the hotel sited right on the seafront skirted by golden sands, but by failing to show the shanty town just next door it conveys a misleading impression. One adjudication by the Advertising Standards Authority concerns misleading photographs. The ASA received a complaint from a holidaymaker who had booked a holiday with Airtours from their "Golden Years" brochure. The brochure claimed "Thousands more holidays for the over 50s" on the front cover and contained photographs of groups of middle-aged and elderly people. The complainant, who found that the age of guests at her resort ranged from 10 months to 86 years, objected to the misleading impression that holidaymakers at the resorts featured would be over 50 years old. In upholding the complaint the ASA agreed that the photographs in the brochure could give readers the overall impression that the accommodation was exclusively for the over-50s. (ASA Monthly Report No. 78 p.7). We hasten to add that this is not a decision under Regulation 4 but it shows how photographs can be misleading.

One wonders, however, at what point the courts would cease to hold the information misleading and say that it amounted to mere puff with no legal effect. For example take a brochure which sold holidays to India and which featured a photograph of the Taj Mahal on the front cover. In front of the Taj Mahal is the reflecting pool and behind it is a red sun, low on the horizon, bathing the monument and the pool in a rosy glow. What could be more romantic? The truth however may be a little more prosaic. When tourists arrive they find that the rosy glow is rather more permanent than they anticipated because it is caused by the effect of viewing the sun through the acrid stifling smog that smothers the area for much of the year. This is not a sunset but a by product of an environmental disaster. But is it misleading? Technically of course the information is correct; it is possible to see such a sight at the Taj Mahal. It is the impression created by the photograph that is misleading—it leads consumers to believe that this is a sunset, viewable only at certain times of the day when in fact, due to the smog, it is visible all day and very disappointing because of that. But are consumers misled? Or do they in fact take such pictures with a healthy pinch of salt, knowing that this is not much more than advertising hyperbole—a photograph carefully chosen by the tour operator to show the Taj Mahal in the best possible light but not necessarily an accurate reflection of what the average holidaymaker might see? Presumably the test will be the same as with the Trade Descriptions Act—what would the reasonable consumer understand by the picture and would they be misled? (See *Thomson Travel v Roberts* (1984) 148 JP 666 for an application of this test in a Trade Descriptions Act context—and the section below on *Mawdsley v Cosmosair 2002*, which shows how wide "misleading" can be.)

But what of the tourist who rises at dawn to see the sunrise over the Taj Mahal and discovers that the reflecting pool is no more than a glorified mud puddle because the stream that feeds it has temporarily run dry. Can he complain that the photograph is misleading? Probably no more so than the consumer who rises early to reserve his sun bed beside the hotel pool (featured prominently in the tour operator's brochure) to find that the pool has been drained for essential maintenance. The fact that the photograph depicts a feature does not necessarily mean that that feature will always be just as it is shown in the photograph—circumstances change and even consumers can be expected to know and understand this. A pool is not always full; the waiters in a restaurant do not always hover attentively; and a bar is not always crowded. So long as the pool is not always, or mainly, empty; the restaurant has an adequate quota of staff; and the bar has a regular clientele then the consumer will not have been misled.

Disclaimers may also have a bearing on the question of what is misleading. Tour operators frequently state that facilities and services may not be available or may be temporarily out of order. This is a typical example:

> "All due care and diligence has been exercised in the production of this brochure. All of the information in this brochure concerning resorts, hotels and their facilities has been compiled as accurately as possible by our own staff and has been checked at the time of going to press. However there may be times when certain amenities are temporarily not available and it is possible, particularly in the low season, that a facility we have described in our brochure may have been modified or is not available. For example electrical equipment and lifts may break down and some of the shops, restaurants and night-clubs may not be in full operation. Such situations may be dictated by local circumstances, unsuitable weather conditions , necessity for maintenance or redecoration, local licensing regulations or government fuel saving legislation ... There may be a charge made payable locally for some facilities e.g. cots, sauna, gymnasium. tennis, squash courts, TV in rooms etc ..." (Direct Cruises, Summer 1998 brochure, 2nd edition—note this should be read in the context of the pressure from the OFT, accepted in 2002 by major tour operators, no longer to rely upon the "low season" exception).

To be effective we would suggest that a starting point would be the Trade Descriptions case of *Norman v Bennett* [1974] 1 W.L.R. 1229 where Lord Widgery CJ said that a disclaimer which was "as bold, precise and compelling" as the original description would be effective to negate the effect of a false odometer reading on a car. The case of *R v Clarksons Holidays Ltd* (1972) 57 Cr. App. R 38 might also be a useful pointer. That case, which was also a false trade descriptions case, turned upon what meaning was conveyed by a brochure picture which consisted of an artist's impression of an hotel. The court held that it was a reasonable conclusion for a jury to come to that the picture was a statement that the hotel actually existed even though there was a disclaimer in the brochure that where there was an artist's impression of an hotel it meant that the hotel had not been built yet.

One point to mention here, which helps to bring home the extent to which a consumer of package holidays is now protected, is that the same false or misleading description in a brochure could give rise to prosecutions both under the Trade Descriptions Act 1968 and the Package Travel Regulations (see Chapters Eleven and Thirteen) as well as forming the basis of civil actions under Regulation 4, for breach of contract or for misrepresentation.

There is nothing in the Regulation which expressly provides for the situation where the information in the brochure is initially correct but subsequently becomes misleading. To supply the information after it has become misleading is clearly a breach but can a tour operator be held retrospectively liable to a consumer if the information was correct when given but later becomes misleading? We are inclined to think not. The reason being that the breach is committed when the descriptive material is *supplied* and if at that moment it is not misleading then there is no breach. Under the Trade Descriptions Act 1968 (see Chapter Eleven) the courts have interpreted the offence of making a false statement as capable of being a repeated offence i.e. every time someone reads a brochure then potentially an offence is committed but in that legislation the offence is couched in different words - the offence is to *make a statement* whereas in Regulation 4 the breach is *to supply descriptive matter*.

6. Suffers as a consequence

The other qualification is that liability is only imposed where the consumer, as a result of the misleading information, *suffers in consequence*. For the consumer to show that as a consequence of the descriptive material he suffered loss there will have to be some evidence of cause and effect. He will have to show that he relied upon the information otherwise how can it be said that he suffered loss as a consequence.

The issues of causation, and indeed the full impact of the words "misleading", were considered by the Court of Appeal in the case of *Mawdsley v Cosmosair Plc* [2002] E.W.C.A. Civ. 587. In a nutshell, this case seeks to answer the question; "Can reading a brochure cause you to fall down stairs?" (other, that is, than by walking downstairs whilst reading the brochure!).

The claim was put under Regulation 4, and also for negligent misrepresentation and/or breach of contract. It was agreed by the Court that the words "suffered in consequence" in Regulation 4 did not mean anything different from the established concept of causation.

The facts are these: Mr and Mrs Mawdsley and their two children then aged 3½ years and six months went on holiday to a hotel described as a village complex, with accommodation either in bungalows in the grounds, or in the main block. The brochure from which the Claimants made their booking showed photographs of the hotel and pool area. To the rear of the hotel, viewing it from the sea, was the main building. To the front of the main building at the lower level was a substantial terrace. The terrace extended underneath the main building and also outward towards the sea. Immediately below that terrace was another terrace which in turn gave access via a single flight of steps to the pool area. The photographs showed two substantial flights of steps leading from the upper terrace to the lower terrace.

The description in the brochure rather curiously did not mention a restaurant at all, but it is clear there must have been one as the holidays were offered on an all-inclusive full-board basis. Among the facilities listed was "lift (in main building)". As it turned out, the restaurant was on the Mezzanine Terrace described above; and although there was a lift in the main building, it stopped at every floor except the Mezzanine Terrace. Thus, to access the restaurant, it was necessary to take the lift to the reception floor above the terrace and walk downstairs, or to the pool level and walk upstairs. On the fifth day of their holiday Mr and Mrs Mawdsley were walking downstairs from reception to the restaurant carrying their baby in a buggy. Mrs Mawdsley was, quoting from the Trial Judge: "holding the handle of the pushchair, which was facing downstairs. Her husband, having his back to the pushchair, was holding the foot area, a position which wives and husbands can regularly be seen to take in carrying a pushchair downstairs". Mrs Mawdsley lost her footing and slipped, suffering a back injury. There was never any allegation that the stairs were in any way defective.

As to whether the brochure was misleading, Jonathan Parker LJ said:

> "The description 'lift (in main building)' in the brochure does represent that all levels in the main building can be accessed directly by lift ... nor does the fact that the brochure makes no specific mention of the restaurant assist in this connection. Absent any such specific mention, a reader of the brochure would, it seems to me, naturally assume that the restaurant was situated somewhere in the main building and consequently accessible directly by lift."

The Trial Judge had further found that the fact that there was no direct access to the restaurant by lift rendered the hotel "unsuitable for parents with young children" but Jonathan Parker LJ overruled that, saying that "it is unrealistic to conclude that the mere fact that access to the hotel involves negotiating stairs renders the hotel unsuitable for young children, the more so when one looks at the nature of the hotel complex as shown in the photographs in the brochure." But as has been seen, on the first point (lifts in main buildings), the Court found there was misleading information under Regulation 4, as well as a misrepresentation and a breach of contract.

On the point of causation, the Court was also against Cosmos. The Court distinguished *Quinn v Birch Brothers Builders* [1966] 2 QB 370 (C.A.), a long established authority on causation in the law of contract. In *Quinn*, the Claimant was a plasterer carrying out work under a subcontract. The Defendants, the main contractors, in breach of contract failed to supply him with a step ladder despite his request for one. In order to complete his work in the absence of a step ladder, the Claimant chose to prop a folded trestle against the wall and used it as a ladder. The foot of the trestle slipped causing the Claimant to fall and suffer injuries. He claimed damages for breach of contract. Jonathan Parker LJ said about *Quinn*:

> "In that case it was truly said that the Defendant's breach of contract provided no more than the opportunity for the Claimant to do what he did. In the instant case there is in my judgment a sufficient causal link between the misrepresentation that the restaurant could be accessed by lift and the accident which occurred on the stairs. ... [T]he misrepresentation served to expose Mrs Mawdsley to the risk of suffering the very type of accident which in the event she suffered. It is not just that "but for" the representation Mrs Mawdsley would not have been in the hotel at all; the misrepresentation related directly to the means of access to the restaurant ... the Judge expressly found that it was reasonable for her to descend the stairs in the way she did".

So it seems that reading a misleading description can be the cause of an accident taking place many months later. This case illustrates the wide ambit which the Courts are prepared to give to Regulation 4 and in particular the words "misleading" and "suffers as a consequence". (Criticism of *Mawdsley* can be found at [2002] LSG May 16, 35.) There is an analogy here with misrepresentation. (See below). For a more conventional approach to causation readers are referred to the case of *Balram Singh v Libra Holidays Ltd* [2003] EWHC 276 (QB) where the defendants were guilty of negligence by failing to warn holidaymakers of the dangers of diving into the shallow end of a swimming pool but escaped liability on the grounds that the breach was not causative of the accident. Largely because the claimant was drunk at the time of the accident and repeatedly ignored advice from staff. (See also *Jones v Sunworld* [2003] All ER D349).

A further complication is that Regulation 4 covers *any loss* suffered as a consequence but does not indicate the basis of calculation of that loss, *i.e.* contractual or tortious. What if for instance the brochure stated wrongly that an hotel had a children's pool and it only had a pool suitable for adults? Clearly, damages for distress and disappointment would be recoverable in such circumstances if a consumer's young children had a miserable time as a consequence of not being able to use the adult pool. However a scenario could be imagined where a child, in defiance of a parent's express instructions, entered the adult pool and was drowned. Is such a loss suffered as a consequence of the misleading information? A case could be made out for compensation in such circumstances. This is a problem which is in part concerned with *remoteness of damage* which is explored in more detail in Chapter Ten on remedies, but also see the passage on *Mawdsley v Cosmosair*, above.

It was indicated earlier that there was no requirement that the misleading information be supplied before the contract has been concluded but where it has been supplied afterwards problems may arise when trying to ascertain whether the consumer suffered as a consequence. For instance what if the consumer booked a holiday without the benefit of a brochure using teletext alone, perhaps it was a late booking and no brochure description was available, and no mention of a swimming pool was made. If, when the consumer arrives at the hotel he discovers that there is no pool, he has no right of action against the tour operator because he had not been promised a pool. However, *after* making the booking he may have asked the travel agent if the agent had any further details about the hotel and the agent might have supplied him with a photocopy of an out of date brochure which said that the hotel had a pool. Clearly this is misleading but does the consumer suffer as a consequence? In strict contractual terms probably not. If he had not paid for a pool how can he complain that he suffered as a consequence of not having one? He is not out of pocket as a consequence. But this is to view the issue as a contractual issue when this is not strictly the case. Regulation 4 creates a *statutory* right to damages and it may be possible to show losses arising from the breach of Regulation 4 which would not give rise to damages in contract but which might still be recoverable. For instance, as a consequence of relying on the misleading information, the consumer might have purchased swimming costumes and bathing towels and this expenditure would be wasted. This would not be recoverable as damages for breach of contract but may very well be in an action based on Regulation 4. More debatable in these circumstances would be recovery of damages for distress and disappointment (*e.g.* as a result of the heightened anticipation of enjoyment caused by reading the photocopy). While such damages are clearly recoverable in an action for breach of contract (see Chapter Ten on remedies) there is no authority for their recovery in an action for breach of statutory duty. On the other hand the Regulation does provide for the recovery of "any loss which the consumer suffers in consequence" which is a form of words wide enough to cover distress and disappointment.

7. Exclusion of liability

Regulation 4 creates a statutory duty rather than a contractual duty and therefore the ability of the tour operator to contract out of liability under the Regulation by the use of an exclusion clause is probably not possible. The reasons for this are twofold. First it is a general principle of the law that if Parliament has created a duty then the parties to a contract cannot contract out of it by private bargain. Secondly, in Regulation 15(5), which provides for limitation of liability in certain circumstances, exclusion of liability is only permitted for breaches of Regulations 15(1)and (2) *i.e.* for breaches of the *obligations under the contract*—not for breach of Regulation 4.

8. Regulation 4 and misrepresentation

There are clear similarities between an action under Regulation 4 and misrepresentation, as clearly demonstrated by *Mawdsley*. However it should not be supposed that an action under Regulation 4 would be the same as an action for misrepresentation. Although the two actions would be similar in that both require the consumer to have relied upon the statement an action under Regulation 4 would go further because it covers *any misleading information concerning a package*. This could be given a very wide interpretation by the courts to include, for example, resort descriptions as well as hotel descriptions. A tour operator might try to argue that the beautiful sandy beach he described as being a mile from the hotel, but which was in fact shingle, was not part of the package and therefore not covered by the Regulation (but see *Jones v Sunworld* [2003] All ER (D) 349). An action for misrepresentation is narrower because it only covers false statements of *fact*.

Statements of opinion and statements as to the future do not give rise to liability in misrepresentation but they would under Regulation 4. On the other hand an action in misrepresentation would cover oral statements whereas Regulation 4 probably does not (but see *Minhas v Imperial Travel* [2003] ITLJ 69). (See Chapter Seven for a full discussion of Misrepresentation.)

Chapter Six
Exclusion of Liability and Unfair Contract Terms

Introduction

There are a number of ways in which a tour operator can reduce his liability for breach of contract. The first way is to supply a product of the right quality. It may be stating the obvious but if there is nothing wrong with the product and the client gets precisely what he contracted for, then there will be no breach of contract. It is for this reason that the consumer relations department should always have an input into a tour operator's quality control function. Prevention is always better than cure and a consumer relations department which is solely concerned with sorting out the problems created by others will soon become demoralised. (See Grant and O'Cain, "Lies, Damn Lies and Holiday Brochures" [1995] T.L.J. 4 for an example of the tensions created by marketing defective products.)

Secondly the tour operator can endeavour to reduce his liability by promising less in the first place. Prior to the 1990 revision of the ABTA Code of Conduct for Tour Operators and the passage of the Package Travel Regulations it was possible for a tour operator with a set of suitably drafted terms and conditions to escape with only fault liability. In *Wall v Silver Wing Surface Arrangements* (1980, High Ct) (Unreported), which has been discussed in some detail already in relation to implied terms, that is precisely what the tour operator succeeded in doing. In cases such as *Gibbons v Intasun Holidays* [1988] C.L.Y. 168; *Kaye v Intasun Holidays* [1987] C.L.Y. 1150; *Toubi v Intasun Holidays* [1988] C.L.Y. 1060 and *Usher v Intasun Holidays* [1987] C.L.Y. 418 tour operators also succeeded on this basis. The passage of the Package Travel Regulations and the 1990 revision of the ABTA Code of Conduct made significant changes to the liability of tour operators but as we have just seen in Chapter Five there remains the possibility that a tour operator, by adopting a suitably drafted set of terms and conditions, may get away with fault liability, or little more, in many cases.

The third means by which a tour operator can seek to reduce or limit his liability, and which forms the subject matter of this chapter, is by the use of exclusion clauses.

The conventional approach to exclusion clauses is to see them as terms in a contract by which one party seeks to exclude or limit or restrict his liability for a breach of contract. Viewed in this way an exclusion clause is a *defence mechanism* used by a party to a contract to protect himself when in breach of a *proven liability*. There are other ways of viewing exclusion clauses and these will be examined later but for the moment the conventional approach will suffice.

One's first reaction to such a device is perhaps to ask how come they are acceptable. How is it that one party to a contract is permitted to break the contract and then escape liability by relying on the small print? The immediate answer to such a question is that acceptability does not come into it. It is simply a matter of making a contract with the appropriate terms in it. If one party offers to make a contract on certain terms and the other party accepts such terms then the courts will enforce the agreement they have made.

In reality the answer to the question is much more complex. First of all the courts, and then Parliament, recognised that in many cases the *agreement* between the parties was often more illusory than real. Exclusion clauses are typically to be found in standard form contracts drafted by a commercially stronger party and offered to a weaker party on a take it or leave it basis. There is no question of being able to negotiate over the terms and conditions (even if you could find someone to negotiate with) and the only freedom of choice available is to go to a rival who offers much the same package of terms and conditions.

Lord Reid summed up the situation in the case of *Suisse Atlantique Societe D'Armement Maritime SA v NV Rotterdamsche Kolen Centrale* [1966] 2 All E.R. 61. He said:

> "Exemption clauses differ greatly in many respects. Probably the most objectionable are found in the complex standard conditions which are now so common. In the ordinary way the customer has no time to read them, and, if he did read them he would probably not understand them. If he did understand and object to any of them, he would generally be told that he could take it or leave it. If he then went to another supplier, the result would be the same."

Given this lack of real agreement and the ability of one party to exploit their bargaining position to the detriment of the other party, the courts, without ever going so far as striking out exclusion clauses simply because they were unreasonable, developed a number of techniques to curb some of the worst excesses of exclusion clauses. Admirable though these efforts were the common law was simply unable to cope adequately with the problems created by exclusion clauses and it became necessary to legislate against them. The Unfair Contract Terms Act 1977 (UCTA) was a major piece of legislation which made many types of exclusion clause void altogether and made most of the rest subject to a test of reasonableness.

The common law rules and those contained in UCTA apply generally to all contracts but the Package Travel Regulations contain rules about exclusion clauses which are of specific application to package holidays. In addition to these rules there are also the Unfair Terms in Consumer Contracts Regulations 1999 ("UTCCR")(SI 1999/2083) which are derived from the Directive of the same name (93/13/EEC) and which was first implemented in the UK in 1994. As the name suggests, the UTCCR apply not only to exclusion clauses but also to clauses which are unfair—a much wider concept.

All four sets of rules will now be examined in turn. Before proceeding however it is necessary to point out two things. First, the rules are not exclusive of each other—they can be applied concurrently. Although this chapter will examine the rules in order of historical development a party seeking to avoid an exclusion clause would usually look first to the Package Travel Regulations or the UTCCR for specific assistance and only then turn to UCTA or the common law. In some circumstances all four sets of rules would provide assistance.

Secondly, although the Package Travel Regulations do permit certain limited exclusions, it is worth indicating at the outset that there is such a battery of weapons that can now be deployed against exclusion clauses that a tour operator will find cold comfort in what follows. What has made the climate even more unwelcoming for tour operators is that in October 2002, the Office of Fair Trading agreed with the four largest UK tour operators and ABTA, that a whole range of standard terms and conditions were unfair and would have to be re-drafted. These terms will be examined later but a number of them had been used routinely for many years and were previously regarded as unexceptional by the industry.

The Common Law

As indicated above, the attitude of the courts to exclusion clauses was somewhat ambivalent. On the one hand the courts could never bring themselves to say that exclusion clauses should be rejected simply because they were unreasonable but on the other hand, recognising that many such clauses were unreasonable, they created a set of technical rules which could be invoked to oust them. These rules fall into two categories.

First, the clause will not be effective unless it has been *incorporated in the contract*. In other words if the clause does not form part of the contract then it cannot be relied upon. The clause will be incorporated in the contract by the process of offer and acceptance. (See Chapter Three) Secondly, even if the clause has been incorporated in the contract, the courts will examine it very carefully and it will be equally ineffective if it does not cover the breach that occurred. This is a matter of *construction* or *interpretation* and such clauses are interpreted very strictly—*contra proferentum*—against the person proffering the clause.

1. Incorporation

There are three ways in which an exclusion clause can be incorporated in a contract—by signature, by notice or by a course of dealing.

Signature

The surest way of incorporating a term in a contract is to have a contractual document signed by the other party. The leading case on this point is *L'Estrange v Graucob* [1934] 2 KB 394. The facts of the case were that the plaintiff bought an automatic vending machine from the defendants. When the machine failed to work properly she sued them. It was held that they were protected by an exclusion clause in their "Sales Agreement" which she had signed when she bought the machine. Although the clause was "in regrettably small print" it was still quite legible. Scrutton LJ said:

> "When a document containing contractual terms is signed, then, in the absence of fraud, or, I will add, misrepresentation, the party signing it is bound, and it is wholly immaterial whether he has read the document or not."

It is for this reason that tour operators place so much emphasis on obtaining the client's signature on a booking form. Once it has been signed the tour operator has effectively incorporated not only any exclusion clauses in the contract but all the other terms as well.

An example of a travel case where this principle worked to the advantage of the travel company is *Budd v Peninsular and Oriental*

Steam Navigation Co [1969] 2 Lloyd's Rep. 262. In that case the plaintiff was injured due to the admitted negligence of the defendants. However the plaintiff had entered into the contract at the premises of the defendant's agents and the agents had made sure she signed the declaration on the booking form. It stated:

> "... and I understand that all accommodation is offered and fares are quoted subject to the Regulations and Conditions of Carriage as printed on the Passage Ticket of the Line concerned."

One of the conditions on the ticket, which was legible and reasonably comprehensible to the average person, exempted the defendants from liability. The judge said:

> "The law of this country is plain. If you choose to put your signature to a document in which it is made plain that the obligations of the party with whom you are contracting is contained in certain conditions, then you are bound by those conditions ..."

The plaintiff therefore failed in her action. The significance of the case is that the agent followed the procedures laid down and thereby protected the interests of the shipping company. Failure by the agent would have led to the liability of P & O, who in turn would probably have sought an indemnity from the agent for breaching the agency agreement. (Since 1977 exemption clauses such as these which attempt to exclude liability for personal injury caused by negligence are no longer valid because of UCTA.)

Note that under the Package Travel Regulations there is increased emphasis on the provision of information to the client both before contracting and in the contract itself. One way of proving that the information has been supplied is to have a signed booking form. It is therefore the case that a signed booking form has grown rather than diminished in importance.

Notice

Many contracts are concluded using documents which are not signed but merely handed over at the time of contracting or simply displayed at the place where the contract is made. If the document contains an exclusion clause the question of whether it has been incorporated in the contract depends upon whether *reasonable notice* of it has been given to the other party.

What amounts to reasonable notice is of course a question of fact and will vary according to the circumstances. Relevant circumstances include: the kind of document containing the clause; the amount of notice given; and the type of clause.

The document. In *Chapelton v Barry UDC* [1940] 1 KB 532 the plaintiff hired a deck-chair from the defendants. He was given a receipt on the back of which were printed conditions which exempted the defendants from liability for any damage caused by the chair. When he sat on the chair it collapsed and he was injured. It was held that the defendants could not rely upon the exclusion clause because the receipt was simply a document showing that the plaintiff had paid for the chairs. It was not a document with contractual force.

On the other hand a document will be treated as having contractual force if the other party knows that this was the intention or it was the kind of document that usually contains contractual terms. Most tickets for travel will fall into this latter category. In fact in this area of the law there are a body of cases collectively known as the "ticket cases" in which railway and ferry companies feature prominently and in general it can be said that such tickets are regarded as contractual documents.

Amount of notice required. The leading case here is *Parker v South Eastern Railway Company Ltd* (1877) 2 CPD 416 (CA). The facts of the case were that the plaintiff had deposited a bag in a cloakroom at the defendant's station. He had been given a ticket on the front of which were printed the words "See back". On the back was an exclusion clause limiting liability to £10 per item. Due to the negligence of the defendant's employees the bag was lost. The plaintiff claimed the value of his bag, £24, but the defendants, relying on the exclusion clause, offered him only £10. In the Court of Appeal, Mellish LJ said the test as to whether the exclusion clause was binding on the plaintiff was:

> "... that if the person receiving the ticket did not see or know that there was any writing on the ticket, he is not bound by the conditions; that if he knew there was writing, and knew or believed that the writing contained conditions, then he is bound by the conditions; that if he knew there was writing on the ticket, but did not know or believe that the writing contained conditions, nevertheless he would be bound, if the delivering of the ticket to him in such a manner that he could see there was writing upon it, was ... reasonable notice that the writing contained conditions."

A case in which this line of reasoning was applied was *Thompson v London, Midland and Scottish Railway Company* [1930] 1 KB 41 (CA). The plaintiff in that case had purchased an excursion ticket. On the face of the ticket were printed the words "For conditions see back", and on the back were the words "Issued subject to the conditions and regulations in the company's timetables and notices and excursion and other bills." If the plaintiff had purchased a company timetable (for 20 per cent of the price of the ticket!) she could have discovered that the ticket was issued subject to the condition that the defendant was not liable for any personal injury, howsoever caused. The plaintiff was injured when the carriage in which she was travelling pulled up just short of the platform and she slipped and fell when alighting.

It was held by the Court of Appeal that the exclusion clause protected the defendant. Lord Hanworth MR said:

> "... it appears to me that when that ticket was taken it was taken with the knowledge that the conditions applied, and that the person who took the ticket was bound by those conditions."

He also said:

> "... it has not ever been held that the mere circuity which has to be followed to find the actual condition prevents the passenger having notice that there was a condition."

Treitel, in *The Law of Contract* (10th edition, 1999), suggests that the decision was a harsh one on the facts but nevertheless supports the principle that terms can be incorporated in such a fashion on the grounds that otherwise many contracts would become impossibly bulky documents.

Another travel case which illustrates the principle of reasonable notice is *Richardson, Spence & Co v Rowntree* [1894] AC 217. In that case the plaintiff had booked a passage on the defendant's steamer and had been handed a ticket for the voyage which was folded in such a way that no writing was visible on it. It was held by the House of Lords that reasonable notice had not been given to her of the conditions on the inside, one of which excluded liability for personal injury. Applying the three questions in *Parker v South Eastern Railway* Lord Herschell said that although the plaintiff knew that there was writing on the ticket she did not know that they contained conditions relating to the contract of carriage and that the defendants had not done what was reasonably sufficient to bring them to her notice.

Type of Clause. Some cases seem to suggest that where the clause is particularly unusual then greater steps should be taken to draw it to the attention of the other party. For instance in *Thornton v Shoe Lane Parking Ltd* [1971] 2 Q.B. 163 (CA) it was held that inadequate notice had been given of a clause on the back of a car parking ticket which excluded liability for personal injury. The notice might have been adequate if the clause had merely related to damage to the car. Such a clause would not have been unusual.

In *J Spurling Ltd v Bradshaw* [1956] 1 W.L.R. 461 Denning LJ said:

> "Some clauses I have seen would need to be printed in red ink on the face of the document with a red hand pointing to it before the notice could be held to be sufficient."

Time. It should also be mentioned that the giving of reasonable notice means that the notice must be given *before* the contract is concluded. Once the contract is made the courts will not permit terms to be added retrospectively. This point is graphically illustrated by the case of *Olley v Marlborough Court Hotel Ltd* [1949] 1 KB 532. The plaintiff in that case had belongings stolen from her hotel room due to the negligence of the hotel staff. The defendant relied upon a notice on the wall of the bedroom which excluded liability in such circumstances. The Court of Appeal held that the contract had been concluded at the reception desk when the plaintiff had booked into the hotel and that notice of the exclusion clause came too late. It would have been a different matter if the notice had been prominently displayed at the reception desk.

Fosbroke-Hobbes v Airwork Ltd [1937] 1 All E.R. 108 is a travel case which vividly illustrates the importance of giving notice at the right time. The plaintiff in the case was a member of a party who had hired an aeroplane. The aeroplane was owned by the second defendants but hired out by the first defendants. The contract, which was negotiated some days before the flight was due to take place, was between the leader of the party and the first defendant. The plaintiff was killed when the pilot (employed by the second defendants) negligently crashed it just after take-off. Just before take-off the leader of the party had been handed an envelope containing a "ticket". The ticket was in fact a "special charter". It contained a number of contractual terms including an exclusion clause which exempted the second defendants and their employees from liability for negligence.

It was held that as far as the first defendants were concerned they were not liable to the plaintiff because as he was not a party to the contract of hire he had no rights against them. (See Chapter Eight on Privity of Contract for a fuller discussion of this principle.) If they had had a contract with the plaintiff then the exclusion clause would not have helped them because it had not been incorporated in the contract in time. Handing the "ticket" over as the aeroplane was about to taxi off was too late—long after the contract had been concluded.

The second defendants, however, were liable. The action against them appears to be in the tort of negligence rather than contract but similar principles apply to the giving of notice. Their employee, the pilot—for whom they were vicariously liable, had been negligent and the notice that they endeavoured to give, excluding their liability, was not communicated in time to the plaintiff. The plaintiff had not had time to even see the contents of the envelope before take-off, far less read and understand them and certainly not enough time to realise that he was being carried on the basis that the owner of the plane would not be liable to him in negligence.

Course of Dealing

Where the exclusion clause has not been incorporated in the contract by signature or notice it may nevertheless form part of the contract if it can be shown that there was a course of dealing between the parties. In other words the parties had dealt with each other on previous occasions and on those previous occasions the exclusion clause had formed part of the contract. If on one occasion the term was omitted it could nevertheless be said that it was part of the contract because that was the expectation of the parties—they always dealt on the same terms.

In *Spurling v Bradshaw* the plaintiff had stored some goods in the defendant's warehouse but they were damaged due to the negligence of the defendant. The contract had been made over the phone and no mention of an exclusion clause had been made. However the defendant had subsequently sent the plaintiff a set of his standard terms and conditions, which included an exclusion clause. The terms were the same as had been used over a long period and on many previous occasions. It was held that a course of dealing had been established and that the term had been incorporated in the contract despite the fact that on this occasion the terms had been sent retrospectively.

However a different result was reached in *McCutcheon v David MacBrayne Ltd* [1964] 1 W.L.R. 125. In that case the plaintiff had shipped his car from Islay to the Scottish mainland on the defendant's ferry. The car was lost when the ship ran aground due to the negligence of the ferry captain. When the contract was made it was entirely oral. No documents were handed over except for a receipt after the money had been paid. On previous occasions however the defendant's practice had been to obtain the plaintiff's signature on a "risk note" which excluded liability. The defendant endeavoured to show that there was a previous course of dealing which established that on this occasion the exclusion clause was part of the contract. However the evidence established that the previous dealings were inconsistent. On some occasions a risk note had been signed but on other occasions it had not. Therefore the only course of dealing that could be established was that sometimes the clause was in the contract and sometimes it wasn't.

It is interesting to note that the failure in this instance was that of the booking clerk. It was his omission or carelessness that exposed his employers to a liability they had thought they had avoided. All the fine words on the risk note could not protect them if they did not ensure that proper booking procedures were followed. It serves as an object lesson for tour operators and travel agents of the importance not only of proper systems but also of proper training.

2. Construction

Clauses Interpreted Contra Proferentum

Prior to 1977, the courts, as part of their general disapproval of exclusion clauses, interpreted them strictly against the party trying to rely upon them. If there were any ambiguities or omissions the courts would give the benefit of the doubt to the innocent party.

Given that one party had made certain promises in the contract which he had then broken and was then trying to escape from liability by the use of the small print then it was perfectly logical for the courts to say that unless the words excluding liability were clear and unambiguous then the liability remained intact. However the courts often went to extremes in their interpretation of exclusion clauses and given the flexible nature of the English language it was usually possible for a particularly determined court to find an ambiguity somewhere and use this as a reason for striking out the clause.

For instance in the case of *Houghton v Trafalgar Insurance* [1954] 1 Q.B. 247 a car insurance policy excluded liability if the car was carrying an excessive *load*. The car, which was only constructed to carry five people, was involved in an accident when carrying six people. It was held that the word load applied to luggage not to passengers and the insurance company was held liable.

In *Wallis, Son & Wells v Pratt & Haynes* [1911] A.C. 394 liability was excluded for breach of any *warranty* in the contract (a minor term of the contract). It was held that this did not protect the defendant against breach of a *condition* (a major term of the contract). Similarly in *Andrews Bros (Bournemouth) Ltd v Singer & Co Ltd* [1934] 1 KB a clause limiting liability in respect of *implied* conditions and warranties did not protect against breach of *express* conditions and warranties.

The problem with this kind of approach is that every time the court strikes out a particular type of clause the legal draftsman learns from his mistakes. The next time he is called upon to draft a clause he drafts a better one eliminating the previous loophole.

One tour operating case which shows the dangers of poor or inappropriate drafting is *Spencer v Cosmos Air Holidays Ltd* (1989, CA) (Lexis). The plaintiffs had been thrown out of their hotel by the management for alleged rowdy behaviour. They sued Cosmos for breach of contract on the grounds that they had not been provided with the promised accommodation. Unfortunately for Cosmos it could not be *proved* that the girls had been rowdy because the evidence was not sufficiently strong. If it could have been proved this would have been a complete defence. However Cosmos also tried to rely on their exclusion clause. It stated:

> **"Liability**
>
> We are travel and holiday organisers only. We do not control or operate any airline neither do we own or control any shipping company, coach or coach company, hotel, transport or any other facility or service mentioned in this brochure. We take care in selecting all the ingredients in your holiday, but because we only select and inspect them and have no control in the running of them, we cannot be responsible for any injury, death, loss or damage which is caused by any negligence of the management or employees of an independent contractor arising outside our normal selection and inspection process."

The Court of Appeal held that the clause simply did not cover what had happened. Farquharson LJ said that the words "injury, death, loss or damage" were not appropriate to cover what had happened to the plaintiffs. Mustill LJ said that the clause would not help the defendants, not because of inapt drafting, but because:

> "... the clause does not even set out to exclude claims in contract for failure to provide the services comprised in the holiday."

Another, more briefly reported, travel case which deals with exclusion clauses is *Askew v Intasun North* [1980] C.L.Y. 637. There the plaintiffs had been told on arrival in resort that they were being allocated to a different hotel. The court held that the exclusion clause that the defendants relied upon:

> "was poorly worded and difficult to interpret, and did not exclude liability in this case."

Clearly the clause was so badly drafted it offered an open invitation to the court to avoid it. Another example of drafting that caught the tour operator out is *Williams v Travel Promotions Ltd (trading as Voyages Jules Verne)* (1998, CA, *The Times*, March 1998). In that case the defendants had moved the plaintiff from his chosen hotel to another hotel on the day before departure. They claimed to be able to do this and not offer compensation because this was a minor change as defined in their terms and conditions for which compensation was not payable. The Court of Appeal, in a masterly judgment which managed to sidestep all the major issues raised in respect of the Package Travel Regulations and the Unfair Contract Terms Act, resolved the case on a simple interpretation of the defendant's terms and conditions. They found that the terms and conditions expressly stated that minor changes could only be made if they were "necessary" and as the defendants had not proven that this was a necessary change they were in breach of contract and had to pay compensation. (For a further example of hapless drafting, although not involving an exclusion clause, see *Marsh v Thomson* [2000] C.L.Y. 4044, where the tour operator shot itself in the foot over the drafting of their "money back guarantee".)

Negligence

In many contracts one party may be under both strict liability and fault liability. For instance in *White v John Warwick & Co Ltd* [1953] 2 All E.R. 1021 the defendant hired a cycle to the plaintiff. The plaintiff was injured when the saddle tipped forward due to the negligence of the defendant. The contract excluded liability for personal injury. The defendant in these circumstances is not only liable for negligence he is also strictly liable to the plaintiff for any defects in the bike—whether caused by negligence or not. The court held that the words used in the exclusion clause were sufficient to protect against the strict liability but not the fault liability—that should have been spelt out more clearly.

Main Purpose Rule

A further rule of construction developed by the courts to deal with exclusion clauses is the "main purpose rule". In other words an exclusion clause would not assist a party in breach to alter the main purpose or substance of the contract. If a person contracts to deliver peas and instead substitutes beans an exclusion clause will not help him. What he has delivered is so different that it can be said that he is not performing the contract at all. The exclusion clause relates to the delivery of peas not beans.

One leading case on this point is in fact a travel case, *Anglo-Continental Holidays Ltd v Typaldos Lines (London) Ltd* [1967] 2 Lloyd's Rep. 61. The plaintiffs were travel agents who had booked a party onto the defendant's ship, *Atlantica*, for a cruise to Israel. With less than two weeks to go the defendants substituted a much inferior ship, the *Angelika*, and an equally inferior itinerary. The plaintiffs cancelled the cruise, refunded their clients' money and sued the defendants for breach of contract. The defendants relied on an exclusion clause which stated:

> "Steamers, Sailing Dates, Rates and Itineraries are subject to change without prior notice"

Lord Denning MR said:

> "In my opinion a steamship company cannot rely on a clause of this kind so as to alter the substance of the transaction. For instance, they could not say: 'We will change you from this fine modern ship to an old tramp'. Nor could they say: 'We are putting the sailing dates back a week'. Nor could they say: 'We are taking you to Piraeus instead of to Haifa'. . . . No matter how wide the terms of the clause, the Courts will limit it and modify it to the extent necessary to enable effect to be given to the main object and intent of the contract.
>
> Applied to this case we have to ask ourselves: Was the proposed trip by the Anjelika in substance a performance of the contract or was it a serious departure from it? To my mind there is only one answer. It was a radical departure."

Russell LJ was equally clear the clause was ineffective:

> ". . . a reasonable construction must be put upon such a term, and as a matter of construction the defendants were not enabled thereby to alter the substance of the arrangement. Whether they attempted to so must be, in a sort of package deal like this, a

question of degree and perhaps to some extent of general impression. But in my view a combination of all the matters which were in fact involved in the substitution of the *Angelika* for the *Atlantica* together did constitute an alteration of the substance of the arrangement."

3. Common law developments since 1977

The impression that is gained from the discussion above is that the courts have often strained the meaning of words and created excessively technical barriers in their enthusiasm to combat exclusion clauses. Such an impression would be entirely justified. However since the advent of UCTA in 1977 the courts have taken a more restrained view on the interpretation of such clauses. Now that there is legislation to deal with unfair and unreasonable exclusion clauses the courts no longer feel the need to stretch or bend the rules to achieve a just solution. In *Ailsa Craig Fishing Co Ltd v Malvern Fishing Co Ltd* [1983] 1 All E.R. Lord Wilberforce said that:

> "... one must not strive to create ambiguities by strained construction. ... The relevant words must be given, if possible, their natural plain meaning."

In *George Mitchell (Chesterhall) Ltd v Finney Lock Seeds Ltd* [1983] 2 All E.R. 737 Lord Diplock said that recent legislation had:

> "removed from judges the temptation to resort to the device of ascribing to the words appearing in exemption clauses a tortured meaning so as to avoid giving effect to an exclusion or limitation of liability when a judge thought that in the circumstances to do so would be unfair".

Two reservations, however, need to be expressed. First, the statements made by the House of Lords in the *Ailsa Craig* and *George Mitchell* cases were made in the context of limitation clauses rather than outright exclusion clauses. In *Ailsa Craig* Lord Wilberforce said:

> "Clauses of limitation are not regarded by the courts with the same hostility as clauses of exclusion; this is because they must be related to other contractual terms, in particular to the risks to which the defending party may be exposed, the remuneration

> which he receives and possibly also the opportunity of the other party to insure." (At p.102)

And Lord Fraser said in the same case:

> "There are . . . authorities which lay down very strict principles to be applied when considering the effect of clauses of exclusion or of indemnity. . . . In my opinion these principles are not applicable in their full rigour when considering the effect of conditions merely limiting liability. Such conditions will of course be read contra proferentem and must be clearly expressed, but there is no reason why they should be judged by the specially exacting standards which are applied to exclusion and indemnity clauses. The reason for imposing such standards on these conditions is the inherent improbability that the other party to a contract including such a condition intended to release the proferens from a liability that would otherwise fall on him. But there is no such high degree of improbability that he would agree to a limitation of the liability of the proferens especially when, as explained in condition 4(i) of the present contract, the potential losses that might be caused by the negligence of the proferens or its servants are so great in proportion to the sums that can reasonably be charged for the services contracted for." (At p. 105)

These statements indicate that where it is felt necessary the courts will continue to interpret exclusion clauses just as strictly as previously. (See also *Williams v Travel Promotions Ltd* referred to above.)

Secondly, in *Interfoto Picture Library Ltd v Stiletto Visual Programmes Ltd* [1989] Q.B. 433 the Court of Appeal appeared to extend rather than relax the rules on incorporation. Dealing with a particularly onerous clause Dillon LJ said:

> "In the ticket cases the courts held that the common law required that reasonable steps be taken to draw the other parties' attention to the printed conditions or they would not be part of the contract. It is in my judgement a logical development of the common law into modern conditions that it should be held, as it was in *Thornton v Shoe Lane Parking Ltd* [1971] 2 Q.B. 163 that, if one condition in a set of printed conditions is particularly onerous or unusual, the party seeking to enforce it must show that that particular condition was fairly brought to the attention of the other party."

He then went on to hold that sufficient notice had not been given of this particular term. This approach, though orthodox, nevertheless represents a highly technical application of the rules on incorporation.

In the same case Bingham LJ took a more novel approach. He held that where a clause was unreasonable and extortionate, as in this case, it was necessary for the party relying on the clause to draw it "fairly and reasonably" to the attention of the other party. Opening his judgment he introduced the civil law notion of good faith and suggested that in civil jurisdictions the matter might be decided by holding that:

> "... the plaintiffs were under a duty in all fairness to draw the defendant's attention specifically to the high price payable if the transparencies were not returned in time, and ... to point out to the defendants the high cost of continued failure to return them."

Later he said:

> "The tendency of the English authorities has, I think, been to look at the nature of the transaction in question and the character of the parties to it; to consider what notice the party alleged to be bound was given of the particular condition said to bind him; and to resolve whether in all the circumstances it is fair to hold him bound by the condition in question. This may yield a result not very different from the civil law principle of good faith, at any rate so far as the formation of the contract is concerned." [Emphasis added]

It is difficult to divine precisely the basis of the judgment but he appears to be saying that even if a term could be incorporated into a contract by the normal operation of the rules of offer and acceptance the party seeking to rely upon it would have to demonstrate good faith.

This approach suggests that, far from relaxing the rules on incorporation, the courts are quite prepared to bolster them with new concepts when they judge it appropriate.

The Unfair Contract Terms Act 1977

1. Preliminary points

Contrary to what the name of the Act suggests UCTA is not aimed at *unfair* contract terms in general, that is left to the UTCCR. Its focus is much more limited. What it does do is to curb the worst kinds of *exclusion* clause. It makes some exclusion clauses void altogether and it makes others subject to a test of reasonableness.

Two particular features of the legislation can be identified. First, there is an outright ban on clauses which exclude liability for negligence which gives rise to personal injury. Secondly there is comprehensive protection given to consumers, *i.e.* those who are worst placed and least able to protect themselves.

2. Business liability

One restriction on the scope of the Act is that it only applies to business liability. This is defined in section 1(3):

> 1(3)In the case of both contract and tort, sections 2 to 7 apply (except where the contrary is stated in section 6(4)) only to business liability, that is liability for breach of obligations or duties arising—
>
> (a) from things done or to be done by a person in the course of a business (whether his own business or another's);
>
> or
>
> (b) from the occupation of premises used for business purposes of the occupier;
>
> and references to liability are to be read accordingly.

This is of only marginal importance because private individuals who make contracts tend to do so orally rather then in writing. Exclusion clauses are usually only found in printed standard form contracts or notices produced by businesses. Thus most exclusion clauses will be covered by the Act.

3. Clauses Excluding Liability For Negligence

Section 2 of the Act imposes strict limitations on the ability to be able to exclude liability for negligence.

Definition of Negligence

There is a comprehensive definition of negligence in s.1(1):

> 1(1)For the purposes of this Part of this Act negligence means the breach—

(a) of any obligation, arising from the express or implied terms of a contract, to take reasonable care or exercise reasonable skill in the performance of the contract;
(b) of any common law duty to take reasonable care or exercise reasonable skill (but not any stricter duty);
(c) of the common duty of care imposed by the Occupiers' Liability Act 1957 or the Occupiers' Liability Act (Northern Ireland) 1957.

Essentially what this means is that whether you negligently break a contract or negligently injure or cause loss to people on your premises or simply commit the tort of negligence this will be covered by the Act.

Negligent breach of contract is easily illustrated. This is what happened in both *Thompson v LMS* and *Richardson, Spence & Co v Rowntree*. In the former the plaintiff was injured due to the train pulling up short of the platform. In the latter the plaintiff was injured because the chair she fell off was not suitably constructed to withstand the rolling caused by rough seas. In both cases the actions of the defendants were negligent.

The Occupiers' Liability Act 1957 imposes a duty on occupiers of premises to take reasonable care of visitors. If a client visiting a travel agency tripped and fell on a badly fitted carpet this would amount to a breach of the Act. The position would be similar if a hotel guest was injured if the bedroom ceiling collapsed due to the negligence of the hotelier. (Note that the issue of whether this Act applies outside England and Wales was left undecided *Hoffman v Intasun* above.)

Most negligence occurs outside the context of a contract or the Occupiers Liability Act. A very common example of the tort of negligence is when one driver negligently injures another by careless driving. Most injuries at work which lead to litigation are caused by negligence and lead to an action in tort rather than contract. The definition of negligence stops short of imposing liability for the negligence of independent subcontractors.

Death and Personal Injury Caused by Negligence

Section 2(1) states:

> 2(1) A person cannot by reference to any contract term or to a notice given to persons generally or to particular persons exclude or restrict his liability for death or personal injury resulting from negligence.

Thus in any case where the defendant is proved to be negligent it will be impossible for him to exclude liability where death or personal injury has been caused.

The immediate effect of this section is to reverse the effect of cases like *Thompson v LMS*. Irrespective of whether the clause had been incorporated in the contract it would be of no effect. The railway had negligently caused personal injury and no matter what it said on the ticket they would now be unable to exclude their liability. The result would be the same with *Richardson, Spence & Co v Rowntree*. There would be no need to deal with the small print on the ticket at all because it would count for nought. Examples of case law subsequent to 1977, particularly involving travel cases, are hard to find but on the European Database on Case Law about Unfair Contractual Terms (CLAB) maintained by the Health and Consumer Protection Directorate of the European Commission (*https://adns.cec.eu.int/CLAB*) there is one example. It refers to an unreported County Court decision from 1994 in which a client of Aspro was injured by the defective condition of the private transport provided by the holiday firm to transport her from her home to the airport (Ref: GB000028). One of the booking conditions stated:

> "Liability will only be accepted if you can prove that the death, injury or illness was caused by the negligence or breach of contract of Aspro, its servants, agents, suppliers or contractors. In all cases our liability is limited to twice the price of the holiday."

The court held that this condition "in all cases" was ineffective as it breached section 2 of UCTA.

Other Loss or Damage Caused by Negligence

Section 2(2) covers loss or damage which is caused by negligence but does not result in death or personal injury. Section 2(2) states:

> 2(2) In the case of other loss or damage, a person cannot so exclude or restrict his liability for negligence except in so far as the term or notice satisfies the requirement of reasonableness.

The kind of damage envisaged here would occur if for instance an hotel negligently left a client's room open and personal belongings were stolen as in *Olley v Marlborough Court Hotel Co*. If a travel agent negligently failed to notify clients of important changes to a holiday this would also be covered by section 2(2). If a tour operator's representative sends clients' luggage to the wrong hotel and it gets lost this too would be subject to s.2(2).

The major difference between section 2(1) and section 2(2) is that the former prevents the exclusion of liability altogether whereas the latter is subject to a test of reasonableness. Precisely what this means will be dealt with later but what it means in practice is that once a client can prove that his loss or damage is caused by the negligence of the other party it is up to that other party to prove that it is reasonable for him to exclude liability. Given that it will already have been determined that he has acted without reasonable care this will not be easy to establish.

4. Clauses excluding liability for any breach of contract

As explained above a party may be under different kinds of liability, strict or fault, and the contract may try to exclude liability for both or either. Section 2 deals with negligent breaches of contract, as well as the tort of negligence and breach of the Occupiers' Liability Act, but section 3 deals with any kind of breach of contract whether it be a breach of a strict obligation or was caused by negligence.

Section 3 states:

> "3(1) This section applies as between contacting parties where one of them deals as consumer or on the other's written standard terms of business.
>
> (2) As against that party, the other cannot by reference to any contract term—
>
> (a) when himself in breach of contract, exclude or restrict any liability of his in respect of the breach; or
>
> (b) claim to be entitled—
>
> (i) to render a contractual performance substantially different from that which was reasonably expected of him, or
>
> (ii) in respect of the whole or any part of his contractual obligation, to render no performance at all,
>
> except in so far as (in any of the cases mentioned above in this subsection) the contract term satisfies the requirement of reasonableness."

Broadly speaking this section will protect a person if they can establish two things: first that they are the victim of any one of three types of unreasonable exclusion clause; secondly if they can establish that they fall into one of two categories—either they "deal as consumer" or they deal on the other party's "written standard terms of business". These two categories and the three types of term will now be dealt with in turn.

"Dealing As Consumer"

A client will get the benefit if he can show that he "deals as consumer". This is defined in section 12:

> "12(1) A party to a contract 'deals as consumer' in relation to another party if—
>
> (a) he neither makes the contract in the course of a business nor holds himself out as doing so; and
> (b) the other party does make the contract in the course of a business; and
> (c) in the case of a contract governed by the law of sale of goods or hire-purchase, or by section 7 of this Act, the goods passing under or in pursuance of the contract are of a type ordinarily supplied for private use or consumption."

Holidays are services rather than goods and therefore section 12(1)(c) is not relevant in this context.

The conventional package holiday is sold by a tour operator, who makes the contract in the course of a business, to a client who does not make it in the course of a business. In these circumstances if the contract contained an exclusion clause the client could claim the benefit of section 3. In the case of business travel however the client would be making the contract in the course of a business and therefore does not qualify as a consumer.

Section 12(3) places the burden of proof on the tour operator in these circumstances to prove that the client is not a consumer rather than for the client to prove he is.

Note that the term "consumer" used in section 3 of UCTA has a different meaning to the same term in the Package Travel Regulations and the two should not be confused. The definition is different again in the UTCCR.

Dealing on Written Standard Terms of Business

"Written standard terms of business" is not defined in the Act but it can be taken to include the small print at the back of a tour operator's brochure in which the terms and conditions are set out. They are certainly written; they are terms of business; and they are standard in the sense that these are the terms and conditions which the tour operator invariably deals on. They are not subject to negotiation. They are simply presented to the client on a take it or leave it basis. They always form the basis of the contract.

Thus any client signing a booking form which incorporates such a standard set of conditions will qualify for the protection offered by section 3. Note that the average client will qualify for protection under both categories whereas a business traveller would only qualify in the latter category.

An early case on the meaning of "written standard terms of business" case is *McCrone v Boots Farm Sales* Ltd 1981 SLT 103. This is a Scottish case and in the part of the Act that applies to Scotland a slightly different form of words is used—"standard form contract" instead of "written standard terms of business" but to all intents and purposes the meaning is the same. In *McCrone* Lord Dunpark said:

> "... the section is designed to prevent one party to a contract from having his contractual rights, against a party who is in breach of contract, excluded or restricted by a term or condition, which is one of a number of fixed terms or conditions invariably incorporated in contracts of the kind in question by the party in breach, and which have been incorporated in the particular contract in circumstances in which it would be unfair and unreasonable for the other party to have his rights so excluded or restricted. If the section is to achieve its purpose, the phrase 'standard form contract' cannot be confined to written contracts in which both parties use standard forms. It is in my opinion wide enough to include any contract, *whether wholly written or partly oral*, which includes a set of fixed terms or conditions which the proponer applies, without material variation, to contracts of the kind in question." [Emphasis added]

Thus, according to Lord Dunpark, the contract does not have to be wholly written, it can include oral terms just so long as there are fixed terms in it. He would also permit minor alterations to the fixed terms without them losing the characteristics of a standard form contract.

The "Flamar Pride" [1990] 1 Lloyd's Rep. 434 is a case involving the breach of a ship management contract. It was argued by the owners of the vessels concerned that the management contract was made on written standard terms of business and therefore UCTA applied. The judge rejected this argument. He said that although the starting point for negotiating the management contract had been the standard form contract used by one of the parties it had been subjected to a number of individually negotiated alterations to fit the particular circumstances of the case. In these circumstances it could no longer be said to be on written standard terms.

The issue was discussed at some length in *The Chester Grosvenor Hotel Co Ltd v Alfred McAlpine Management Ltd* (1991) 56 Build LR 115 where Judge Stannard had this to say on the meaning of written standard terms:

> "In my judgment the question is one of fact and degree. What are alleged to be standard terms may be used so infrequently in comparison with other terms that they cannot realistically be regarded as standard, or on any particular occasion may be so added to or mutilated that they must be regarded as having lost their essential identity. What is required for terms to be standard is that they should be regarded by the party which advances them as its standard terms and that it should habitually contract in those terms. If it contracts also in other terms, it must be determined in any given case, and as a matter of fact, whether this has occurred so frequently that the terms in question cannot be regarded as standard, and if on any occasion a party has substantially modified its prepared terms, it is a question of fact whether those terms have been so altered that they must be regarded as not having been employed on that occasion."

Apart from a package holiday contract itself there are innumerable standard form contracts in the travel industry. Tour operators contract with airlines and hotels on a regular basis and invariably these will be on standard terms. Hotels themselves will have any number of supply contracts.

In such cases the tour operator or hotel may be contracting on their own standard terms or they may be contracting on the other party's. In the case of their own they need to be aware that any exclusion clause will be subject to a test of reasonableness. On the other hand if the terms have been imposed upon them by the other party they can take the benefit of section 3. For instance a tour operator dealing with a charter airline is likely to be faced by a standard contract which is non-negotiable. In these circumstances if the airline broke the contract and wished to rely upon an exclusion clause they would have to prove that it was reasonable to do so. (For more on standard terms in tour operator/airline contracts see Briggs, [1994] T.L.J. 20 and 44.)

The relevance of cases like *McCrone, The Flamar Pride* and *The Chester Grosvenor Hotel* however is that once the parties depart from the standard form contract and begin negotiating terms on an individual basis the contract ceases to be covered by section 3. The logic of this is that if the parties are able to negotiate on the terms then it is less likely that the terms will be unreasonable. It will be more likely that any exclusion clause will have been part of a genuine bargaining process.

Breach of Contract

Once a party has qualified for the protection of section 3 then he will get that protection against three kinds of exclusion clause—so long as the term cannot be shown to be reasonable. The first of these is to be found in section 3(2)(a). If a person deals as consumer or on the other's written standard terms then:

> "3(2) As against that party, the other cannot by reference to any contract term—
>
> (a) when himself in breach of contract, exclude or restrict any liability of his in respect of the breach;"

This is relatively straightforward. If a tour operator has made certain promises in his contract which he fails to keep then he will be in breach of contract. Any term which purports to exclude or limit that liability will not be entirely void but will have to be justified as being reasonable. So for instance if the tour operator has promised the client that he will be accommodated at the four star Grand Hotel and then at the last minute substitutes the three star Rustic Hotel this will be a simple breach of contract and the tour operator will have to prove that any exclusion clause is reasonable.

Substantially Different from what was Reasonably Expected

Section 3(2)(b)(i) covers an entirely different kind of clause. Subject again to the test of reasonableness it states that where one party deals as consumer or on the other's written standard terms of business then:

> "3(2) As against that party, the other cannot by reference to any contract term—
>
> (a) . . .
> (b) claim to be entitled—
>
> (i) to render a contractual performance substantially different from that which was reasonably expected of him."

If a tour operator says that he will take you on a one day trip to Lapland at Christmas to see Santa Claus and you will fly there by Concorde he will be in breach of contract if he substitutes a 747 instead. It is a term of the contract that you will fly by Concorde and he has broken it. In these circumstances section 3(2)(a) will apply if his terms and condition include an exclusion clause.

However he might have drafted his terms and conditions in a more sophisticated manner. What they might have said is that if he cannot get you there on Concorde then he has the right to substitute another kind of aircraft. In other words the small print is not *excluding* his liability it is *defining* it. The tour operator is saying that when he supplies a 747 instead of Concorde he is not breaking the contract he is actually fulfilling his contractual obligations as set out in the contract. Those obligations are drafted in such a way that they impose a very low level of liability on the tour operator.

It is against this kind of clause that section 3(2)(b)(i) will protect the consumer. What it says is that even if the tour operator has managed to define his liability in such a way that it could be said that providing a 747 instead of Concorde is to actually "render a contractual performance" nevertheless if this amounts to something *substantially different* from what the client *reasonably expected* it will be subject to a test of reasonableness.

There is an argument (see Yates, *Exclusion Clauses in Contracts,* 2nd ed. p.104) which says that if the tour operator has actually managed to draft his terms and conditions in such a way that he could actually convince a court that he was entitled to substitute a 747 for Concorde and not be in breach of contract then how could anyone "reasonably expect" anything else. If it is reasonable to interpret the contract as meaning that how is it possible to say it means something else? It is difficult to argue with the strict logic of this but it assumes of course that the other party has actually read the contract, which many clients don't, and it also assumes that one's expectations are created solely be reading the contract.

In its *Second Report on Exclusion Clauses*, No. 69, 1975, the Law Commission included a draft bill which eventually became the Unfair Contract Terms Act 1977. In the commentary accompanying the draft clause which became section 3(2)(b)(i) they said:

> "In deciding what was reasonably expected under the contract the terms of the contract will not be decisive: regard will be had to all the circumstances."

They justified this view in the body of the report.

> "... [Definitional clauses] ... have been the subject of complaint

> on the ground that they deprive the persons against whom they are invoked of contractual rights which those person legitimately expected to enjoy. They can be so expressed that the promisee may think that the promisor is undertaking an obligation which is more valuable to the promisee than in fact it is . . ."
>
> ". . . it is the likelihood (in the light of the surrounding circumstances including the way in which the contract is expressed) that the promisee might reasonably have misunderstood the extent of the promisor's obligation." (Para. 143)
>
> "The flaw in the weapons that the courts now have at their disposal for dealing with cases of the sort under consideration is that they are not sufficiently flexible to deal with what appears to us to be the essential danger, namely that the relatively unsophisticated or unwary party will not realise what or how little he has been promised, although the legal scope and effect of the contract may be perfectly clear to a lawyer." (Para. 145)

Thus, the Law Commission is saying that although the contract can legitimately be interpreted as meaning one thing nevertheless it is possible to have a reasonable expectation that something different has been promised.

This can arise not only from the words of the contract itself but also from the presentation of the information in the rest of the brochure. In fact it is from the body of the brochure that a client is most likely to derive his expectations. It is here that the operator sets out his stall and gives the impression perhaps of being able to deliver more than he actually promises in the small print.

To qualify for protection under section 3(2)(b)(i) the performance must not only be contrary to the client's reasonable expectations it must also be *substantially different*. This is a question of degree and there will obviously be room for argument at the margins but to return to the Concorde example that would clearly be a substantial difference. If however the trip was to be made in a 747 to start with and the operator substituted a DC 10 that would probably not amount to a substantial difference.

A case mentioned earlier, *Anglo-Continental Holidays Ltd v Typaldos Lines (London) Ltd*, is one which today would probably be decided using section 3(2)(b)(i). Russell LJ said of the exclusion clause that:

> "It is not an exemption clause. . . . It is a clause under which the actual contractual liability may be defined, and not one which will excuse from the actual contractual liability."

In cases like this the courts could take the line that even though the ship owners were not actually in breach of contract nevertheless they were offering a performance substantially different from that which was reasonably expected and therefore could not rely upon the clause in the contract to protect themselves.

It is conceivable, however, on the facts of the case that a court could say that although the performance was substantially different it was still within the realms of what the plaintiff *in this case* could reasonably expect. Remember that this plaintiff was not an innocent consumer requiring the protection of the law but someone in the travel business who could perhaps be expected to know and understand the terms of the contract and moreover be aware that this kind of thing goes on regularly.

One common problem that arises with package holidays is that flight times are often changed substantially—frequently at the last minute—but unless the change involves more than a 12 hour time difference compensation is not usually payable. First of all is a change of say only 10 or 11 hours *substantially different*? Secondly is it a performance substantially different from what was *reasonably expected*? The answer to the first question must surely be yes. A difference of almost half a day when the typical package holiday only lasts one or two weeks is a substantial difference by anyone's reckoning. On the other hand if the change only amounted to some two or three hours the answer would almost certainly be different.

As far as the second question is concerned it could very well be argued that such a change was to be expected—partly because the terms will say as much and partly because transport delays are a fact of life to be expected by all travellers. But whether it is reasonable to expect such substantial delays is debatable.

Of course the answer to such clauses may be that they are not definitional clauses at all, to be dealt with under section 3(2)(b)(i), but merely traditional exclusion clauses falling under section 3(2)(a), *i.e.* the consumer would argue that the operator was under an obligation to depart at a particular time and failure to depart on time amounted to a simple breach of contract—which the clause dealing with delays simply excludes.

To Render no Performance at All

Section 3(2)(b)(ii) covers the situation where the tour operator is under a contractual obligation but a clause permits him to render no performance at all.

> "3(2) As against that party, the other cannot by reference to any contract term—
>
> (b) claim to be entitled—

(i) ...
(ii) in respect of the whole or any part of his contractual obligation, to render no performance at all,

except in so far as (in any of the cases mentioned above in this subsection) the contract term satisfies the requirement of reasonableness."

This is a provision which has puzzled most commentators because it is hard to see what it adds to the existing provisions. If a term in the contract gave a party the right not to perform at all then it could be argued that there was no contract at all. If on the other hand it gave the right not to perform part of the contract then this would be covered by section 3(2)(b)(i). Poole (*Textbook on Contract,* 6th ed. p.204) describes it as a "red herring" and Yates (*Exclusion Clauses in Contracts*, 2nd ed. p.94) says that "It is ... doubtful if section 3(2)(b)(ii) adds anything but confusion ... ".

There is one example given in Cheshire, Fifoot and Furmston's *Law of Contract* (14th ed., p.202) that would probably be covered by section 3(2)(b)(ii):

"Suppose for instance a supplier of machine tools provided in his standard printed conditions that payment terms are 25% with order and 75% on delivery and that he should be under no obligation to start manufacture until the initial payment is made."

Such a term would literally be within section 3(2)(b)(ii) but it is doubted whether it was intended that such situations would come within its scope. Treitel, *The Law of Contract,* makes a similar comment.

In a package holiday context it would probably apply to those situations where a consumer turns up at the airport late, as the plaintiff did in *Hartley v Intasun*, and the flight has already gone. In these circumstances an operator's terms and conditions often explicitly state that the operator will be under no liability. As with the example above it is hard to see this as an exclusion clause at all but now, by virtue of Regulation 15(2)(a) (failures wholly attributable to the consumer) it is entirely redundant.

5. Varieties of exclusion clause

A straightforward exclusion or limitation clause is not the only way of reducing liability. It can be done in a variety of other, more subtle, ways. To combat this section 13 provides:

> 13(1) To the extent that this Part of this Act prevents the exclusion or restriction of any liability it also prevents—
>
> (a) making the liability or its enforcement subject to restrictive or onerous conditions;
> (b) excluding or restricting any right or remedy in respect of the liability, or subjecting a person to any prejudice in consequence of his pursuing any such right or remedy;
> (c) excluding or restricting rules of evidence or procedure;
>
> and (to that extent) sections 2 and 5 to 7 also prevent excluding or restricting liability by reference to terms and notices which exclude or restrict the relevant obligation or duty.

This would include, for instance, imposing very short time limits for the receipt of claims as in *RW Green Ltd v Case Bros Farm* [1978] 1 Lloyd's Rep. 602 (see below); threatening to blacklist consumers if they complain; offering only replacements rather than full refunds; etc.

ABTA tour operators routinely provide in their terms and conditions that consumers must submit claims within 28 days of the end of the holiday. The reasonableness of such clauses is discussed shortly but it seems to have been accepted without argument that the time limit was a variety of exclusion clause.

6. The test of reasonableness

Both section 2 and section 3 impose a test of reasonableness on exclusion clauses which do not involve negligence causing death or personal injury.

A number of issues are involved with this test: who has to prove the reasonableness or unreasonableness of the clause? When is the reasonableness to be measured? How will the courts decide whether a clause is reasonable? These issues will be examined now.

The Burden of Proof

Section 11 provides:

> "11(5) It is for those claiming that a contract term or notice satisfies the requirement of reasonableness to show that it does."

Thus it is not for the client to establish that the clause is unreasonable but for the tour operator to show that it is reasonable.

When the Reasonableness is Measured

This depends upon whether the exclusion is included in a contract or not. If, as is most likely in travel cases, the exclusion is contained in a contract then section 11(1) applies.

> "11(1) In relation to a contract term, the requirement of reasonableness for the purposes of this Part of this Act . . . is that the term shall have been a fair and reasonable one to be included having regard to the circumstances which were, or ought reasonably to have been, known to or in the contemplation of the parties when the contract was made."

This means that the courts will not take into account any events occurring after the contract was made. It is the state of mind and the circumstances existing at the time the contract was made that are relevant to the reasonableness of the clause.

In particular the courts will not be able to take into account the extent or seriousness of the breach if that was not something which could have been foreseen by the parties.

If the claim is being made in tort rather than contract then section 11(3) applies:

> "11(3) In relation to a notice (not being a notice having contractual effect), the requirement of reasonableness under this Act is that is should be fair and reasonable to allow reliance on it, having regard to all the circumstances obtaining when the liability arose or (but for the notice) would have arisen."

Thus in a tortious claim the reasonableness of the notice is to be measured when the tort took place—not necessarily when the plaintiff was given notice of the exclusion.

In *Monarch Airlines Ltd v London Luton Airport Ltd* [1998] 1 Lloyd's Rep. 403 the claimant's aircraft was damaged by the defective state of the runway caused by the negligence of the defendant airport. The defendants had a set of standard terms and conditions which contained an exclusion clause which, on its proper construction, protected them against negligence. However there was some doubt as to whether the clause was a contractual clause, incorporated into a contract between the two parties, or whether it was a notice which operated to exclude the defendant's liability under the Occupiers' Liability Act 1957, *i.e.* was the defendant's liability contractual or tortious? A further complication was the issue as to whether, if it was a contractual clause, the contract had been concluded at the beginning of the season or on the day of the accident. Unfortunately the case does not give us the answer to these questions because it was only concerned with deciding some preliminary issues. However the judge did say that *if* the contract was concluded at the beginning of the season then the clause was a reasonable one to include:

> "Having tried to take all the circumstances of the case into account I have reached the conclusion that, if cl. 10 is considered as at say March or April, 1992, it was a fair and reasonable term to include in the terms and conditions. As already stated, it was generally accepted in the market, including the insurance market. Indeed, so far as I am aware, there has been no suggestion in the market (whether it be from the airlines, the airports or the insurers) that the clause be amended in any way. It was accepted by the plaintiff without demur. It has a clear meaning and the insurance arrangements of both parties could be made on the basis that the contract was governed by standard terms which had already been held to be reasonable in principle. It follows that, judged as at the beginning of the year in April, the terms did not fall foul of the Unfair Contract Terms Act, as issue 3 puts it. It does not, however, necessarily follow that the answer is the same if the question is posed as at the day of the accident." [Because the claimant alleged that the defendant had made an inspection which revealed the state of the runway just a few days prior to the making of the contract.]

The judge further said that if the liability was tortious, then the reasonableness of the notice would be measured at the time of the tort not the giving of the notice, *i.e.* if circumstances had changed between giving the notice and the tort being committed these could be taken into account.

Determining Reasonableness

There is no comprehensive definition of reasonableness in the Act but since its passage there have been a number of cases from which guidance can be obtained. Before looking at these cases however it is necessary to point out that the Act is not entirely silent about the reasonableness test. Section 11(4) for instance sets out factors which are to be taken into account if the clause restricts liability to a sum of money rather than excludes liability outright. It states:

> "11(4) Where by reference to a contract term or notice a person seeks to restrict liability to a specified sum of money, and the question arises (under this or any other Act) whether the term or

notice satisfies the requirement of reasonableness, regard shall be had in particular (but without prejudice to subsection (2) above in the case of contract terms) to—

(a) the resources which he could expect to be available to him for the purpose of meeting the liability should it arise; and
(b) how far it was open to him to cover himself by insurance."

Many tour operators have clauses limiting their liability to specified sums of money in various circumstances. In particular they have scales of compensation covering major changes and cancellation before departure. This is not the kind of situation where a breach of contract gives rise to a liability out of all proportion to the price of the service and therefore the tour operator should have the resources to meet the claims in full.

This provision is intended to cover a much different kind of situation far removed from travel cases where say a client asks a surveyor to do a valuation of a property for a relatively small fee. If the surveyor overlooks a major defect and the property turns out to be worthless then there may be insufficient resources available to meet the claim. Not only that but the risk in relation to the remuneration is disproportionate. Is it reasonable to expect a professional to take on that kind of risk for that level of fee?

On the other hand the second limb of section 11(4) may count against the surveyor in such circumstances. This is indeed what happened in the case of *Smith v Eric S Bush* [1990] 1 A.C. 831. The House of Lords decided that one of the reasons for an exclusion clause being unreasonable in such circumstances was the fact that insurance was available on reasonable terms to cover the surveyor's risk.

Apart from section 11(4) there is also a schedule to the Act which sets out guidelines for determining the reasonableness of an exclusion clause. These guidelines in Schedule 2 relate specifically to the sale and supply of goods not to contracts for services such as package holidays. However the Act does not say that the guidelines cannot be applied to contracts for services and it is clear that the courts are adopting the guidelines in non-sale of goods cases. The reason for this is quite straightforward. Most of the guidelines are as applicable to services as they are to goods—an approach which was adopted in *Phillips Products Ltd v Hyland* [1987] 2 All E.R. 620. The guidelines provide that when assessing the reasonableness of a clause regard should be had to:

(a) the strength of the bargaining positions of the parties relative to each other, taking into account (among other things) alternative means by which the customer's requirements could have been met;

(b) whether the customer received an inducement to agree to the term, or in accepting it had an opportunity of entering into a similar contract with other persons, but without having to accept a similar term;

(c) whether the customer knew or ought reasonably to have known of the existence and extent of the term (having regard, among other things, to any custom of the trade and any previous course of dealing between the parties);

(d) where the term excludes or restricts any relevant liability if some condition is not complied with, whether it was reasonable at the time of the contract to expect that compliance with that condition would be practicable;

(e) whether the goods were manufactured, processed or adapted to the special order of the customer.

Applying these guidelines to a typical package holiday contract it can be seen that (a) will probably favour the client. The bargaining power is all with the tour operator rather than the client.

It is difficult to see how (b) applies but Cheshire, Fifoot & Furmston (14th ed., p.206) give the example of what used to happen under the Railway and Canal Traffic Act 1854. Under that Act carriers used to offer two tariffs to passengers, a cheap one excluding liability and a more expensive one without exclusions. This was held to be reasonable. In *Woodman v Photo Processing* (1981) N.L.J. 933, a case decided under UCTA, a County Court judge held that it was unreasonable for a film processing company to exclude liability when accepting films to be developed. One factor which weighed heavily with the judge was that it was possible for the defendants to have offered a two tier system of liability but had failed to do so. Another factor was the difficulty of finding any company at all which did not exclude liability.

In both *Love v Arrowsmith* [1989] C.L.Y. 1187 and *Usher v Intasun Holidays* [1987] C.L.Y. 418 the court held that as the exclusion clause was one which was almost universal in package holiday contracts then this was grounds for establishing its reasonableness. Although it is possible to see the merit in this argument, *i.e.* if it is generally accepted it must be reasonable it nevertheless seems to fly in the face of (b) in that the consumer is faced with the situation that no matter where he goes he will have to accept the same kind of clause.

In relation to (c) it has been pointed out by Cheshire, Fifoot &

Furmston that unless the other party had reasonable notice of the term in the first place it would not even be part of the contract. They suggest that what it means is that if a party is not only aware of the term but understands the full consequences of it then this will point to the reasonableness of the term.

Guideline (d) applies in situations where one party says to the other that if he wishes to assert his rights then he must complain within a certain time limit. In *RW Green Ltd v Cade Bros Farm* [1978] 1 Lloyd's Rep. 602 the plaintiff bought seed potatoes which were not of merchantable quality. There was a term in the standard form contract which required complaints to be made within three days of receipt. The justification for this was that the goods were highly perishable and could easily deteriorate rapidly after delivery, especially if not stored properly. However the particular defect with the potatoes was not discoverable by inspection. It was held that the time limit was unreasonable in the circumstances.

In the past most tour operators imposed a time limit of 28 days for the receipt of complaints, after which no claims would be entertained. Two cases raised the issue of whether such a limit would be reasonable. In *Davison v Martyn Holidays* (1990, Leeds County Court, unreported) the court held that the 28 day rule was unreasonable. This was largely because it was contained in a clause which imposed other conditions relating to the complaints procedure and which taken as a whole was unreasonable because of the unreasonable burdens it placed upon consumers who wished to complain. In *Sargant v CIT* [1994] C.L.Y. 566 however another county court held that the 28 day rule was reasonable. The judge chose not to follow the *Davison* case on the grounds that the decision in that case was based upon a concession by counsel that the clause should stand or fall as a whole. The judge in the *Sargant* case felt that the concession should not have been made and it was possible to consider the 28 day rule in isolation from the rest of the complaints procedure. Although the decision was not based on the Package Travel Regulations he also went on to say that the clause was reasonable in the light of Regulation 15(9) and Schedule 2 of the Regulations which permits time limits to be placed on the making of complaints.

These cases have almost certainly been superseded by the action of the OFT under the UTCCR in October 2002. In a series of decisions announced in that month the OFT required two of the major operators, MyTravel (Airtours) and Thomas Cook, to remove this "exclusion". (See below for further discussion.)

Guideline (e) also seems to have no immediate relevance to the travel industry. However, the principle can perhaps be applied to tailor-made packages. For instance a client may approach a travel agent and ask him to put together a specific package to some remote third world country consisting of airlines, hotels and excursion companies the travel agent has never heard of. In such circumstances it might be reasonable for the agent to say that he cannot guarantee the quality of the products he is selling.

Moving away from the guidelines it must be remembered that whether a term is reasonable or not is largely a question of fact rather than law and therefore what is reasonable in the circumstances of one case may not be so in another. For instance in *Wight v British Railways Board* [1983] C.L.Y. 424 a court held that it was reasonable for British Rail to limit their liability for loss of luggage by reference to the weight of the luggage. The reason for this was that BR had no means of knowing how valuable the contents were whereas the owner did and could insure them. Moreover BR's competitors used similar or less generous terms. In contrast in the earlier case of *Waldron-Kelly v British Railways Board* [1981] C.L.Y. 303 the court held that it was unreasonable to limit the liability by weight. The plaintiff recovered the full value of the contents rather than the amount he was limited to by the contract.

These are both only County Court decisions of little value as precedents. They demonstrate not only how very similar circumstances can give rise to very different decisions but also that counsel for British Rail must have learnt from their earlier set-back and prepared a new set of arguments for the later case!

Lord Bridge, in *George Mitchell Ltd v Finney Lock Seeds* [1983] 2 All E.R. 737 explained how a court should approach the application of the reasonableness test and in particular how an appellate court should treat an appeal that the decision was wrong. He said:

> "... the court must entertain a whole range of considerations, put them in the scales on one side or the other and decide at the end of the day on which side the balance comes down. There will sometimes be room for a legitimate difference of judicial opinion as to what the answer should be, where it will be impossible to say that one view is demonstrably wrong and the other demonstrably right. It must follow, in my view, that, when asked to review such a decision on appeal, the appellate court should treat the original decision with the utmost respect and refrain from interference with it unless satisfied that it proceeded on some erroneous principle or was plainly and obviously wrong."

This is a clear warning to contracting parties that appeals on the question of reasonableness will not be entertained unless an obviously perverse decision has been reached.

Before leaving the test of reasonableness it is necessary to point out that the court will assess reasonableness in relation to the *particular contract* that is under consideration. It does not matter that the clause could be regarded as reasonable in most situations if in a particular contract it was not reasonable—bearing in mind the circumstances "which were , or ought reasonably to have been, known to in the contemplation of the parties *when the contract was made*" (section 11(1)). That was the decision in *Phillips Products Ltd v Hyland* [1987] 2 All E.R. 620.

It was mentioned earlier that if a tour operator imposed a 28 day time limit for the receipt of complaints then this might be regarded as reasonable as a general rule. This does not mean, however, that because it was generally reasonable that it would be regarded as reasonable in all cases. There will be circumstances where, for instance, clients are injured on a skiing holiday and spend weeks or months afterwards in hospital. Would it be reasonable in such a case, where injuries are not uncommon, to impose a 28 day limit on the receipt of claims arising from the incident. (But note that if the injury was caused by the negligence of the tour operator itself liability could not be excluded at all (section 2(1) and see also Regulation 15(5) below on the extent to which such claims can be excluded.)

THE PACKAGE TRAVEL REGULATIONS

The Regulations contain not only many new obligations but also sweeping provisions preventing tour operators from excluding liability if they break these new obligations.

1. Exclusion of liability in general

Regulation 15 regulates the ability of a tour operator to exclude his liability. The three relevant paragraphs are:

> "15(3) In the case of damage arising from the non-performance or improper performance of the services involved in the package, the contract may provide for compensation to be limited in accordance with the international conventions which govern such services.
>
> 15(4) In the case of damage other than personal injury resulting from the non-performance or improper performance of the services involved in the package, the contract may include a term limiting the amount of compensation which will be paid to the consumer, provided that the limitation is not unreasonable.

> 15(5) Without prejudice to paragraph (3) and paragraph (4) above, liability under paragraphs (1) and (2) above cannot be excluded by any contractual term."

Regulation 15(5) is of general application and will be examined now. Regulation 15(3) and (4) will be examined shortly.

The importance of Regulation 15(5) is that it imposes an outright prohibition (subject to Regulation 15(3) and (4)) on any term of a contract which excludes liability for a breach of any of the obligations under the contract. This is the approach taken by the judge in *Lathrope v Kuoni Travel Ltd* [1999] C.L.Y. 1382. Kuoni argued that an exclusion clause in their contract excluded liability for a 26 hour delay on the outbound leg of a seven day package holiday to the Bahamas. Failing that, their liability was limited to £50 per head. The court held that the exclusion clause was caught by Regulation 15(5) and therefore ineffective. The limitation of liability was caught by Regulation 15(4) and as the sum was unreasonably low it too was ineffective.

Thus on the one hand the Regulations impose potentially greater liability on tour operators than ever before while on the other they prevent the exclusion of that liability.

Note, however, that the tour operator will only need to invoke an exclusion clause if there has been a breach of contract. If there has been no breach the existence or the effectiveness of any exclusion clause is irrelevant. A clear example of this is the case of *Wilson v Best Travel* [1993] 1 All E.R. 353 which we have already examined in relation to implied terms (see Chapter Four and Chapter Five). The issue in that case was whether or not the glass in the patio door should conform to British or Greek standards. It was held that it was sufficient that the glass complied with Greek standards and therefore there was no breach of contract. This was a case decided at common law before the passage of the Package Travel Regulations but the outcome would probably be the same today. It would probably be the case that a court would decide that there had been no breach of Regulation 15 *i.e.* the tour operator had properly performed his obligations under the contract. Therefore there would be no need for the tour operator to have to rely on any exclusion clauses in his contract with the consumer—which is just as well because they would have been ineffective. (See also Schedule 2, paragraph 3 of the Package Travel Regulations.)

We have already looked briefly at the case of *Sargant v CIT* [1994] C.L.Y. 566 where a court held that a client who did not complain within 28 days of return was barred from making a claim by a term in the contract. This was upheld as being reasonable under the Unfair Contract Terms Act. However the case could have been decided entirely differently under the Regulations if they had been applicable. *Sargant* was a case involving personal injury and therefore the blanket prohibition on exclusion clauses in Regulation 15(5) may catch the 28 day rule and make it ineffective in such cases (although it must be said that the combined effect of Regs. 15(9) and Schedule 2, Paragraph 12 conflicts with this view—which in turn seems to conflict with the view of the OFT).

This is dependent of course on a 28 day limit for receipt of claims being regarded as an exclusion clause. Views may differ on this. One way of looking at such a clause is to say that it is an exclusion clause because failure to comply has the effect of denying the consumer rights he would otherwise have but for the clause. Another way is to say that there is no denial of rights at all, merely a justifiable encouragement to act on those rights in a timely fashion. In both *Sargant* and in *Davison v Martyn Holidays* the view taken by the court was that the clause was an exclusion clause. In adopting this stance the courts were guided by s.13 of UCTA, which as we have already seen regards the imposition of "restrictive or onerous conditions" as a variety of exclusion clause. The thrust of this provision however is that the imposition of such a condition is only an exclusion clause if it is *restrictive or onerous*. In other words such conditions are not automatically to be regarded as exclusion clauses—only if the condition is too stringent. Thus UCTA imposes a twofold test. First, is the condition restrictive or onerous?—in which case it can be regarded as an exclusion clause. Secondly, if it is an exclusion clause is it unreasonable?

If we adopt this kind of approach to a time limit that falls to be decided under the Regulations we would have to say first whether it was restrictive or onerous. If not then it would not be regarded as an exclusion clause at all and the tour operator could rely on it. If it was regarded as restrictive then it would automatically fail because it would be caught by the blanket restriction under Regulation 15(5). It must however be remembered that although it would be convenient to adopt the wording from UCTA, "restrictive or onerous", that is merely a shorthand version of the real question: is it an exclusion clause? But if that approach is adopted it is difficult to deny that a 28 day limit is *restrictive*.

2. Limitation in accordance with international conventions

Regulation 15(3) permits a tour operator to limit his liability in accordance with international conventions. The Regulations do not actually specify which international conventions are being referred to. However, the preamble to the Directive does refer to the Warsaw Convention on Carriage by Air, the Berne Convention on Carriage by Rail, the Athens Convention on Carriage by Sea and the Paris Convention on the Liability of Hotelkeepers. It can be assumed therefore that these conventions at least will be relevant to Regulation 15(3) and perhaps others as well because the list contained in the preamble is not exhaustive.

These conventions permit the relevant carriers and hoteliers to limit their liability to the sums specified in the conventions. The situation could conceivably arise where the organiser was held liable under the Regulations for some fault of his supplier, say an airline, and would have to pay full compensation whereas the supplier himself would be able to limit his liability under the Warsaw Convention even though he was the one at fault. The purpose of this provision is to restore the balance between supplier and organiser. If the supplier can limit his liability then so should the organiser be able to.

The choice of words, however, is a little unfortunate. The Regulations provide that Member States may allow compensation to be limited *in accordance* with the relevant international convention. Strictly speaking to allow an organiser to limit his liability for deficiencies with the air travel would not be *in accordance* with the Warsaw Convention because the Convention does not apply to tour operators. [Although there is an argument to the contrary which has not been tested. (See Grant, "Tour Operators, the Package Travel Regulations and the Warsaw Convention", *The Aviation Quarterly* October 1999.) Presumably what the Regulations mean to say is that the organiser can limit his liability under the Regulations *as if he were a carrier* under the Warsaw Convention.

A problem arises for the tour operator when a flight is not covered by the Warsaw Convention but where the airline is able to limit its liability by other means. For instance in India airlines can limit their liability for domestic flights and passengers can recover little by way of compensation (see Nelson-Jones and Stewart on this point). In such cases a consumer could very well make a claim against the tour operator under Regulation 15 and recover the full amount of compensation because the tour operator would be unable to limit his liability using Regulation 15(3), unless he could rely on Regulation 15(4) if it was a non-personal injury case. The tour operator would be thrown back on any indemnity he had negotiated in his contract with the airline—which in turn would depend on the kind of leverage that could be brought to bear during contract negotiations.

There is a great danger here for travel agents and other organisers who put tailor-made packages together involving international carriage if they are not in the habit of using standard form contracts. Unless they have a set of terms and conditions which restrict their liability in accordance with the relevant convention they may find themselves first in the firing line when it comes to compensation. The ECJ decision in the *Club Tour* case makes this much more of an issue for travel agents.

Take the example of a travel agent who organises a tailor-made package for an internationally renowned brain surgeon who is subsequently badly injured in a plane crash. He will never work again and requires round-the-clock nursing care. The damages in such a case will be huge. The airline involved will be able to restrict its liability under the Warsaw Convention but the travel agent without an appropriate set of terms and conditions may be fully liable. Even when the agent does have a set of his own terms and conditions it will still probably be necessary to obtain the consumer's signature on a booking form to ensure that the terms can be *proved* to be incorporated in the contract. It follows that yet again we see the vital importance for tour operators and travel agents to obtain a signed booking form.

Regulation 15(3) permits the tour operator to limit the *compensation* payable in accordance with the relevant international conventions. This clearly permits the *amount* of compensation to be limited but the question of whether the *type* of compensation payable, *e.g.* for mental distress, is limited is more dubious. In *Reid v Ski Independence* 1999 S.L.T. (Sh Ct) 62 the court held that damages for distress and disappointment caused by aircraft delay could be recovered from the tour operator. However the basis of the decision is that it could have been recovered anyway under the Warsaw Convention. Thus the case does not provide an answer to the question of whether, if such damages could not be recovered under the Convention, they could therefore be denied under the PTR by virtue of Regulation 15(3).

Regulation 15(3) also has nothing to say on other provisions. For instance under the Warsaw Convention there is a two year limitation period and no claims can be brought outside this period. There is nothing in Regulation 15(3) to suggest that the tour operator can take advantage of this shorter period.

One problem that may occur is that with air travel in particular there is more than one convention to apply. Although the Warsaw Convention, as amended by the Hague Protocol, has been adopted in over 100 countries its ratification is not universal. The US for instance has not signed the Hague Protocol and airlines flying to the US are subject only to the original Warsaw Convention. Other countries, *e.g.* Thailand, have not signed either convention and therefore no limit applies. The picture is further complicated by a complicated web of licensing conditions and voluntary agreements that the world's airlines have to comply with. Airlines flying to the US must comply with the Montreal Agreement by virtue of which the basic Warsaw limits are substantially raised. Australian airlines also have much more generous limits because of domestic legislation. Japanese airlines have voluntarily raised their limits and airlines which are members of IATA have signed up to the IATA Intercarrier Agreement (IIA) and thereby raised their limits of liability. Many European countries have imposed licensing conditions on their airlines requiring them to raise the limits of liability. None of these are international conventions and therefore they will have no impact on tour operators. More recently, however, the EU has passed Regulation 2027/97 on Air Carrier Liability in the event of Accidents which came into force in 1998, and which applies to all EU registered airlines. This will have the effect of waiving all limits on liability and reducing the circumstances in which the defences under the Warsaw Convention will be available to carriers. It is arguable whether this Regulation will fall into the category of "international convention". If it does it will apply to tour operators. In time, the Montreal Convention of 1999, which also waives the upper limits of liability for personal injury and substitutes more generous compensation for loss or damage to baggage, will probably sweep away the existing patchwork of liability when it comes into force but until that happens the liability regime remains extremely complicated. (See Chapter Eighteen for a fuller discussion of the liability regime in international air carriage.)

In practical terms what will this mean for tour operators faced with such a patchwork of provisions? First, the tour operator will not be able to invoke the limitation of liability if it is not contained in an international convention so this rules out domestic licensing conditions and domestic legislation as well as voluntary agreements. This leaves the Warsaw Convention as amended by the Hague Protocol and possibly the EU Regulation (and certainly, when it comes into force, the Montreal Convention). Secondly it makes sense that the tour operator cannot simply choose to limit his liability according to the convention that suits him best, *i.e.* the unamended Warsaw Convention which imposes the lowest limits. The limitation that the operator has to abide by will be the limitation that applies to the flight (or "governs the service" as the Regulation provides) on which his clients were carried—which will vary according to the destination of the flight and the registration of the carrier—just as it does for ordinary passengers. Admittedly this is a complicated business but no more so than for air travel as a whole.

The CCV

There is a much overlooked international convention—the International Convention on Travel Contract (CCV) (Brussels 1970)—which deals specifically with the liability of tour operators and travel agents. Unfortunately the drafting was seriously defective and only seven countries ever ratified it, but they include two EU countries, Belgium and Italy. The importance of the CCV for our purposes is that it does permit a limitation of liability to 50,000 francs for personal injury, 2,000 francs for damage to property and 5,000 francs for other damage. Thus if a tour operator fell within the definitions in the Convention it could take advantage of these limitations. (See Bogdan, *Travel Agency in Comparative and Private International Law* and Vanderperren, *European Transport Law*, 1968, 226 for a full discussion of the Convention.)

3. Limitation in cases of non-personal injury

Regulation 15(4) permits the organiser to limit his liability for non-personal injury *provided that the limitation is not unreasonable.*

It is difficult to assess what impact this is having on an organiser's liability. Conceivably it could be of immense benefit to an organiser. Given that most breaches of contract do not give rise to personal injury the potential for limiting liability is extensive. The problem lies in calculating when the limitation of liability is unreasonable and indeed how the organiser arrives at a figure at all.

Two situations come to mind when thinking about limitation of liability. The first is where the client on a "square-deal" holiday loses his luggage which he asserts contains designer clothes, a Rolex watch and a very expensive camera. Usually this is an insurance problem but occasionally the blame is laid at the door of the tour operator. In such circumstances a limit on liability would be of assistance—in much the same way that the insurance companies' liability is limited.

The second situation is where the consumer is claiming damages for distress and disappointment. In the past tour operators have complained vociferously that such damages are often excessive and out of all proportion to the value of the holiday. Setting a limit on such damages would go some way to satisfying these complaints.

But at what level is the limit to be set? The Regulations state that the limit is not to be "unreasonable". One could argue that any limit is unreasonable if it is less than the consumer would be entitled to if the damages were assessed by a court. If one is entirely cynical then the answer depends upon whether the limit accords with what the judge assesses the damages to be. If the limit is less than his assessment then the limit is unreasonable.

Such an approach of course thwarts the intent of the Regulation which does permit a *limitation* on the compensation in appropriate cases. This means that in some cases the consumer will not be compensated for all his losses. Perhaps what the courts will do is set a "tariff" or "going-rate" for various kinds of damage and these will become the limits of liability accepted by both the courts and the industry. What the draftsman probably had in mind are the kind of arbitrary limits imposed under the Warsaw Convention. It might have been better therefore if limits had been set and it had not been left either to Member States or organisers themselves to determine what limits would not be unreasonable.

One case where a tour operator would have benefited from a limitation on liability is *Clarke & Greenwood v Airtours* [1995] C.L.Y. 1603. In that case the clients paid £2058 for their holiday but were awarded damages of £8040. This included £800 for damages for distress for each member of the group of eight—including each of the three children. Admittedly it was a disastrous holiday but the award of damages, which included nothing for personal injury, was very much out of line with other awards. In practice what it meant is that the family could purchase four more identical holidays with the damages they were awarded for one disastrous holiday. (See Chapter Ten on Remedies.)

One major operator used to have a term in its booking conditions stating that in the case of non-personal injury damages will be limited to three times the price of the holiday. Given that even in the most extreme cases damages rarely exceed twice the price of the holiday it is difficult to see what purpose such a limit serves. It may even have the effect of encouraging larger claims than previously simply because consumers have been given such a generous yardstick by which to measure their loss.

At present most operators, under the influence of the ABTA Code of Conduct, include scales of compensation covering such events as cancellation and major changes. The fact that the compensation is on a rising scale and that it is payable without proof of loss are arguments in favour of the limitation being reasonable. However the generally low level at which the compensation is pitched would count against its reasonableness. Where the tour operator has limited the compensation to a single, low, sum the courts have had no hesitation in rejecting it as unreasonable—see *Lathrope v Kuoni* [1999] C.L.Y. 1382 and *Jervis v Kuoni* [1998] C.L.Y. 3733 (also *Hartman v P&O Cruises Ltd* [1998] C.L.Y. 3732 which was decided under the UTCCR along similar lines).

The Unfair Terms in Consumer Contracts Regulations

1. Introduction

The Unfair Terms in Consumer Contracts Regulations 1999 (SI 1999/2083) are the amended version of The Unfair Terms in Consumer Contracts Regulations 1994 (SI 1994/3159)), which were passed on December 14, 1994 and came into force on July 1, 1995. The Regulations implement the EC Directive on Unfair Terms in Consumer Contracts. (93/13/EEC)·

The key to the Regulations lies in the title. It is a measure designed to protect *consumers* against *unfair* contract terms. We have already seen that there is a whole battery of legislation to protect consumers against exclusion clauses but what is novel about this legislation is that it goes beyond the existing legislation in order to curb not simply exclusion clauses but any contract term which is unfair—a much broader concept than exclusion of liability.

For instance if I say that in the event of a breach of contract by me, *e.g.* by not providing the swimming pool at the hotel that I promised, I will not be liable to pay compensation to you then I am *excluding* my liability. On the other hand if I say that if you wish to cancel your holiday you may do so but you will have to pay an exorbitant amount in cancellation charges this is not a question of me excluding my liability, I am simply relying on a term in the contract which you may regard as *unfair*. UCTA and the PTR might catch the former but certainly not the latter whereas the new Regulations would catch both.

Thus the consumer has, in theory, been protected against unreasonable exclusion clauses since 1977 but as of July 1995 is also protected against a whole range of unfair terms as well. The reason why in many cases the protection has only been theoretical is that many consumers either do not know their rights or for one reason or another are not prepared to exercise those rights. One of the ways in which the Regulations seek to overcome the problem of enforcement is by empowering the Director General of Fair Trading (DGFT) to restrain the use of unfair terms, in the first instance by agreement, but failing that, by applying for an injunction. This is probably the most significant feature of the Regulations and recently it has had a significant impact on package holiday contracts which we will discuss shortly.

2. Limitations on the applicability of the regulations

Consumer

The Regulations only protect *consumers*. A consumer is defined as being "any natural person who, in contracts covered by these regulations, is acting for purposes which are outside his trade, business or profession." The effect of this is to place all contracts made by companies outside the scope of the Regulations as well as all business travel (Regulation 3(1)).

As with other consumer legislation, such as the Trade Descriptions Act 1968, difficulties could arise at the margins as to what is meant by "purposes outside his business". For instance what about the traveller who combines business and pleasure? What is the situation where his primary purpose is to go on holiday but who takes the opportunity of having a business meeting while abroad? (See *London Borough of Havering v Stevenson* [1970] 3 All E.R. 609 and *Davies v Sumner* [1984] 3 All E.R. 831 for a discussion of this issue in the context of the Trade Descriptions Act 1968.)

Terms not Individually Negotiated

Individually negotiated terms are not covered by the Regulations (Regulation 5(1)). The clear intention is to offer protection against the dangers inherent in standard form contracts. Clearly this covers standard form contracts such as for package holidays and therefore most package holidaymakers will, prima facie, obtain the protection of the Regulations. In fact the Regulations go further and say that a term will always be regarded as not being individually negotiated if it has been drafted in advance and the consumer has not been able to influence the substance of the term (Regulation 5(2)). Even if some terms of the contract have been individually negotiated the Regulations will apply to the rest of it if overall it can be regarded as a "pre-formulated standard contract" (Regulation 5(3)). It is for the seller or supplier to show that a term was individually negotiated (Regulation 5(4)).

Thus if I agree with the tour operator at the time of booking that they will provide a cot for my four month old child this will be an individually negotiated term and will not be subject to the Regulations. Furthermore if the tour operator explains orally that they will not be liable if there is no cot this too will be an individually negotiated term and will not be subject to the Regulations.

However if the tour operator does not explain to me on an individual basis what limits it places on its liability, but simply relies upon a standard exclusion clause term then this will not be individually negotiated and the Regulations will apply. (Note that in this example the tour operator had not merely agreed to use its best endeavours to fulfill a special request; it promised to provide the cot.)

The Main Subject Matter of the Contract

No assessment of fairness can be made about a term which relates to "the adequacy of the price or remuneration as against the ... services ... supplied ..." or which relates to "the definition of main subject matter of the contract" (Regulation 6(2)) unless it is not written in plain intelligible language (Regulation 6(2)).

The provision relating to price is relatively straightforward. If the tour operator sells me a full price holiday and I find myself sitting on the plane next to someone who has bought a "late bargain" at a fraction of the price I cannot complain however unfair I may regard it. The Regulations cannot be used to impose a "fair" price—unless the price was not expressed in plain intelligible language.

What amounts to "the main subject matter of the contract" is much more difficult. If I buy a package holiday to Majorca then presumably the main subject matter will be not only the destination but also the duration and the hotel. These are all "core terms" and therefore not subject to the unfairness test. But there will also be a myriad of other terms concerning such things as changes and amendments and cancellation and liability all of which qualify the core terms but which are not core terms in themselves and therefore are subject to the unfairness test.

If we take an example of a "flight-only" package from Gatwick to Orlando then the main subject matter is a flight from Gatwick to Orlando. But what if the ticket has all kinds of restrictions attached to it—validity, duration of stay, refunds, etc. Do these form part of the main subject matter of the contract? Am I buying "a flight to Orlando" or "a flight with restrictions to Orlando"? If it is the former then the restrictions can be attacked as unfair, but if it is the latter then the Regulations do not apply.

It is our view that what the consumer buys is a "flight" and therefore any other terms and conditions relating to the flight do not "define" the main subject matter of the contract they merely qualify it. Whether the terms are actually unfair is another question. When examining the unfairness of the term the court is entitled to take "all circumstances attending the conclusion of the contract" into account including the price (Regulation 4(2)). If I buy a cheap ticket do I expect to get all the benefits of a fully flexible ticket that may cost me several times more?

On the other hand if I say to the tour operator, "I don't care how you get me to Paris, by plane or boat or train or whatever, just get me there" then I probably couldn't complain if he put me on a clapped out bus and took me by road and tunnel. Here the "core" term would be to transport me by any means and that is just what he has done—by the cheapest and most uncomfortable means.

According to the OFT which has published guidance on this aspect of the Regulations the purpose of the provision is to "allow freedom of contract to prevail in relation to terms that are genuinely central to the bargain" (Unfair Contract Terms Guidance (OFT 311) (February 2001) para.19.13)).

Terms Which Reflect Other Statutory Provisions

According to Regulation 4(2) the Regulations do not apply to contractual terms which reflect:

"(a) mandatory statutory or regulatory provisions (including such provisions under the law of any Member State or in Community legislation having effect in the United Kingdom without further enactment);
(b) the provisions or principles of international conventions to which the member States or the Community are party."

The effect of this is that if the terms and conditions faithfully reflect the provisions of another enactment then the UTCCR cannot be used to oust them. Presumably the purpose of this provision was twofold—not to duplicate existing legislation and not to upset well established rules of liability that already have domestic or international approval such as the Warsaw Convention. The prime example here is of course the Package Travel Regulations. Given the comprehensive nature of the PTR it appears that if a tour operator complies with the Regulations there is very little left for the UTCCR to bite on. However, should the terms and conditions not comply then what has happened is that the PTR, by creating a whole raft of new obligations, has created a whole range of possibilities for terms to be regarded as unfair. Prima facie if the terms and conditions do not comply with the PTR then they will be unfair under the UTCCR — at least in so far as they provide less than what the PTR intended. So failure to comply with the following provisions lays the tour operator open to challenge:

- liability (Regulation 15(1) & (2))
- exclusion of liability (Regulation 15(3)(4) & (5))
- surcharges (Regulation 11)

- changes and cancellations by the operator (Regulations 12, 13 &14)
- transfer of bookings (Regulation 10)
- insolvency and repatriation (Regulation 16)

3. Unfair contract terms

If a term can be brought within the Regulations then it will be subjected to an "unfairness" test. An unfair term is one which "contrary to the requirement of good faith causes a significant imbalance in the parties' rights and obligations under the contract to the detriment of the consumer."(Regulation 5(1)). Regulation 5(5) provides that the "indicative and non-exhaustive" list of terms in Schedule 2 "*may* be regarded as unfair" (emphasis added).

Regulation 6(1) states that:

> "... the unfairness of a contractual term shall be assessed, taking into account the nature of the goods or services for which the contract was concluded and by referring, at the time of conclusion of the contract, to all the circumstances attending the conclusion of the contract and to all the other terms of the contract or of another contract on which it is dependent."

Thus to establish that a term is unfair there are three requirements:

(a) a breach of the requirement of good faith; which,

(b) causes a significant imbalance in the parties' rights and obligations;

(c) to the detriment of the consumer.

These three elements will be examined in turn.

Good Faith

In determining good faith the 1994 Regulations provided that regard should be had to the following matters:

(a) the strength of the bargaining positions of the parties;

(b) whether the consumer had an inducement to agree to the term;

(c) whether the goods or services were sold or supplied to the special order of the consumer; and

(d) the extent to which the seller or supplier has dealt fairly and equitably with the consumer.

These provisions (which are almost identical to guidelines found in the Unfair Contract Terms Act. (Schedule 2)) have been omitted from the 1999 Regulations, but very similar words can nevertheless be found in the preamble to the Directive and therefore courts, when seeking guidance, may have recourse to the preamble.

Some guidance on the meaning of good faith can be derived from the House of Lords decision in *Director General of Fair Trading v First National Bank plc* [2000] Q.B. 672 (C.A.); [2001] 3 W.L.R. 1297 (HL). Lord Bingham said:

> "The requirement of good faith in this context is one of fair and open dealing. Openness requires that the terms should be expressed fully, clearly and legibly, containing no concealed pitfalls or traps. Appropriate prominence should be given to terms which might operate disadvantageously to the customer. Fair dealing requires that a supplier should not, whether deliberately or unconsciously, take advantage of the consumer's necessity, indigence, lack of experience, unfamiliarity with the subject matter of the contract, weak bargaining position or any other factor listed in or analogous to those listed in Schedule 2 to the Regulations." [This was a decision under the 1994 Regulations.]

A Significant Imbalance

It is not sufficient that the company is not acting in good faith: the lack of good faith must cause a significant imbalance in the parties' rights and obligations. Guidance on this is also to be found in Lord Bingham's judgment in the *First National Bank* case:

> "The requirement of significant imbalance is met if a term is so weighted in favour of the supplier as to tilt the parties' rights and obligations under the contract significantly in his favour. This may be by the granting to the supplier of a beneficial option or discretion or power, or by the imposing on the consumer of a disadvantageous burden or risk or duty."

Clearly if the contract is riddled with draconian exclusion clauses depriving the holidaymaker of all rights on the one hand while on the other permitting the tour operator to avoid its obligations at will this would be an obvious example of the imbalance the Regulations are designed to curb.

To the Detriment of the Consumer

The third requirement of an unfair term is that it be to the detriment of the consumer. Unlike the other two requirements this should not create undue difficulty. The detriment will be the delayed departure, the dirty room, the non-existent pool, etc., for which there is no compensation.

Examples of Unfair Terms

To assist in the determination of whether a term is unfair guidance is offered in the form of Schedule 2 which provides an "indicative and non-exhaustive" list of terms which may be regarded as unfair. Schedule two does not create a "black list", but a list of terms which *may or may not* be unfair depending on the circumstances. It has been referred to as a "grey list".

Many of the examples given are straightforward exclusion clauses that are already caught by the Unfair Contract Terms Act but there are others which may simply be unfair. For instance examples 1(d) and 1(e) which deal with terms which may require a consumer to pay disproportionately large sums if they choose to cancel a contract. Example 1(n) concerns clauses which limit the supplier's duty to honour commitments undertaken by agents or employees—a type of clause occasionally found in package holiday contracts.

4. Plain English

There is a requirement in the Regulations that written terms must be expressed in plain, intelligible language and if there is a doubt about the meaning of the term then the interpretation most favourable to the consumer will prevail. (Regulation 7). This amounts to no more than the *contra proferentum* rule in statutory form.

Where there is clear ambiguity there should be no problems applying this provision. Problems may arise however because in some cases it could be argued that there is no doubt about the meaning of the term—it only has one meaning—unfortunately it takes a lawyer to find it. Presumably it is open to a consumer to say that he had doubts about the meaning of it because he just couldn't understand it at all. In such circumstances he could go on to say that perhaps it meant this or perhaps it meant that or perhaps it meant the other and then choose the interpretation that was most favourable to him. He might just say that as it was meaningless to all but lawyers then no meaning should be attributed to it at all.

5. The effect of finding a term unfair

If a term is found to be unfair then it will not be binding on the consumer but the rest of the contract will continue to be binding (Regulation 8). The dilemma for individual consumers is that it will often be difficult, and expensive, to contest a term which they consider to be unfair. Often it will be a battle which they will prefer to concede rather than fight—no matter how right they may feel they are.

6. The role of the Director General of Fair Trading

If a complaint is made to the DGFT that a term drawn up for general use is unfair then, unless the complaint is vexatious or it is being considered by a "qualifying body" (see below), it is his duty to consider it (Regulation 10). After considering the complaint, and taking into account any undertakings that have been made to him, he may restrain the use of the term by applying for an injunction (Regulation 12). Given that many consumers are either ignorant of their rights or may not be inclined to pursue them as far as court, this is clearly a very important method of curbing the use of unfair terms. If one consumer complains about a single term in a single contract then the impact of this, even if successful, is likely to be minimal. But if the OFT manages to restrain the use of such a term in all such contracts then the benefit will be felt by all consumers. It is clearly in the interests of holidaymakers to identify terms which they consider unfair and bring them to the notice of the OFT. The success of such a course of action will depend of course on the enthusiasm, and the resources, which the OFT decides to devote to it. There is plenty of evidence that the OFT is pursuing such terms vigorously. Regular bulletins have been published by the OFT listing the terms which have been drawn to their attention and the action they have taken. These frequently feature terms and conditions from tour operators brochures. In October 2002 the OFT published the results of its discussions with all four major tour operators and ABTA and they all agreed to make significant changes to the terms and conditions they used or, in the case of ABTA, recommended. These will be examined below.

Note, however, that although action by the DGFT can be triggered by an individual complaint about an unfair term there is nothing in the Regulations empowering the DGFT to take up individual cases on behalf of consumers. The powers conferred are aimed at restricting the use of unfair terms in general rather than acting on behalf of specific individuals. Nevertheless those powers include the power to seek an injunction not only against the person actually using the unfair term, *e.g.* the tour operator, but also, as we have just seen in the case of ABTA, any person recommending the use of such a term.

Since the Regulations were first brought into force in 1995 a significant change in the enforcement regime has taken place. Whereas formerly it was only the OFT which could seek injunctive relief, now a whole range of "qualifying bodies" have that power. They are listed in Schedule 1 and include every weights and measures authority in Great Britain (trading standards departments); the Rail Regulator; and the Consumers' Association. These qualifying bodies must inform the OFT if they are taking up a complaint and if it is seeking an injunction.

The power of the court to award an injunction extends not only to the particular term it is being asked to consider but also "any similar term, or a term having like effect, used or recommended for use by any person" (Regulation 12(4). Thus it may be possible for the court to restrain the use of one type of clause, in say a Thomson brochure, and at the same time to restrain the same type of clause in MyTravel, First Choice, Thomas Cook and Kuoni brochures.

7. Schedule 2

Schedule 2 includes an "indicative and non-exhaustive" list of terms which may be regarded as unfair. Many of these terms are simply varieties of exclusion clause which would probably be caught by the PTR or UCTA already but some are examples of unfair terms which are not simple exclusion clauses. One of these is Illustrative Term 1(n)

> *"(n) limiting the seller's or supplier's obligation to respect commitments undertaken by his agents or making his commitments subject to compliance with a particular formality"*

It is a fairly common problem for companies to find that employees or agents have exceeded their authority and promised clients more than they should have. It is also the case that, having placed the employee or agent in a position where either they have actual authority or apparent authority to make such promises, the company will have to honour the commitments made (*Freeman & Lockyer v Buckhurst Park Properties (Mangal) Ltd* [1964] 2 W.L.R. 618). To combat this difficulty companies will insert a clause like this into the contract:

> "No agent, employee or representative of the Company has authority to alter, modify or waive any provision of these Conditions of Contract."

The effect of this clause is to place a restriction on the ability of employees and agents to make promises which are beyond their authority to make. The reason the restriction is printed in the terms and conditions is so that the consumer is given notice that the employee or agent has no such authority. It is thus not possible for the consumer to argue that the employee had either express or apparent authority to vary the terms and conditions of the contract (*Overbrook Estates Ltd v Glencombe Properties Ltd* [1974] 1 W.L.R. 1335).

In Practical Terms What Does This Mean?

Perhaps I particularly wish to book an hotel where I can have adjoining rooms with other members of my party. I ask the travel agent if this is possible and he explains that although I can make a "special request" for adjoining rooms tour operators will not guarantee such a request. This does not satisfy me so I ask the travel agent to phone the tour operator to see if something more can be done. The travel agent speaks to someone who is prepared to give such a guarantee and therefore I book the holiday. However what the tour operator's member of staff has done is unauthorised. He should not have guaranteed me adjoining rooms. So what happens when I subsequently arrive at the hotel and find that my party is split between two floors? Can I claim breach of contract? The tour operator might endeavour to rely upon the term in their terms and conditions to the effect that special requests are not guaranteed and that any employee who promised otherwise had no authority to do so. Moreover because I had signed the booking conditions I had had notice that the employee did not have the authority to vary the booking conditions and therefore could not argue otherwise.

This is where the Regulations come in. Is such a term unfair? We think that a good case could be made out for saying that it is—and not just in the example given above but in most cases. Apart altogether from the fact that the tour operator's bargaining position is far superior to the consumer's and that the term is buried in a long document full of legal jargon and that the consumer had no choice but to accept the term we think that most objective observers would say that the term is unfair by any standards.

Tour operators employ people in positions where it is a reasonable expectation that they have the authority that goes with that position. The employees deal with consumers who will rely upon what they say and act upon the advice that they are given. Surely it is right that if such employees make mistakes then the tour operator should be prepared to accept liability for those mistakes and not hide behind the small print in the contract—which they know full well will not be read or understood by the majority of their customers?

Schedule 2 contains other examples of unfair terms which are not exclusion clauses and therefore not entirely within the scope of this chapter. These other terms will be dealt with elsewhere in the book where appropriate. In particular the impact of the UTCCR on cancellation charges is examined in Chapter Ten.

8. The OFT and the Major Tour Operators. October 2002

As indicated above the OFT agreed significant changes to their terms and conditions with the four major tour operators in October 2002. At the same time ABTA agreed to make changes to their recommended terms and conditions. The following types of terms were regarded as unfair and the tour operators concerned agreed to change or delete them:

- Terms which permitted tour operators to impose surcharges if costs rose but denied a reduction if they fell (Airtours, Thomas Cook, Thomson, First Choice, ATBA).
- Terms denying liability if complaints were received more than 28 days after the holiday (Thomas Cook, Airtours). [ABTA's Model Booking Conditions for tour operators, issued in February 2003, now urge consumers to write in within 28 days failing which "this may affect your rights".]
- Terms which gave no cancellation rights after a holiday had started where there was a change to the holiday arrangements if the company offered a "suitable alternative" (Airtours).
- Terms which excluded payment of compensation for significant changes to a holiday before departure above a set scale, even if a consumer could prove a greater loss (Airtours, Thomson, First Choice, ABTA).
- Terms which prevented the transfer of bookings to another person where the consumer is prevented from travelling, on certain types of holiday (Airtours).

- Terms which allowed the imposition of cancellation charges within eight weeks of departure where the consumer wishes to transfer a booking to another where he/she is prevented from travelling even if the cost of making the change was less than the cancellation charge (Airtours).
- Terms which limited liability for lost or damaged baggage to £400 per person. Liability was increased to £1,000 per person (Airtours).
- Terms which excluded liability for the non-availability of facilities outside the peak season. Compensation now offered to consumers, where appropriate, if there is a significant change to the brochure's description of the facilities (Airtours).
- Terms which did not comply with the PTRs requirement that the tour operator should meet the first 2 per cent of any surcharge (Thomson).
- Terms which did not comply with the requirement that if a significant surcharge was imposed (stated in the contract as more than a 10 per cent increase) and the consumer cancels, the tour operator should offer replacement holidays of equivalent/superior quality, if able to, as well as the option of a full refund (as required under the PTRs)(ABTA, Thomson, First Choice, Thomas Cook).
- Terms which required consumers to take out insurance but refused to refund premiums when the consumer cancelled the holiday following a significant surcharge (Thomson, First Choice, ABTA).
- Terms which offered compensation for only certain named significant changes made to the holiday before departure (Thomson, First Choice).
- Terms which required the consumer to pay the difference in price on taking a more expensive substitute holiday when the original holiday was cancelled through no fault of the consumer or when the tour operator significantly altered the holiday (Thomson, Thomas Cook).
- Terms which did not specify that the PTRs require that no surcharge should be made within 30 days before departure (First Choice)
- Terms which failed to provide the consumer with the option of taking a replacement holiday of equivalent/superior

quality, if available, or a full refund, as required by the PTRs, where building work had a significant effect on the consumer's enjoyment of the holiday (First Choice)

- Terms which stated that the contract is governed exclusively by English law and granted exclusive jurisdiction to the English courts which is potentially unfair to consumers in Scotland and Northern Ireland (ABTA, Thomas Cook)
- Terms which failed to make clear the options available under the PTRs when the original holiday is cancelled through no fault of the consumer (ABTA).
- Terms which recommended that a 21-day notice period would be a reasonable requirement for a consumer to request a name change under Regulation 10 of the PTRs. This was changed so that the term now refers to what is reasonable in individual circumstances (ABTA).
- Terms which excluded an insurance premium refund where a consumer cancels as a result of a significant change including an increase of more than 10 per cent of the price, contrary to the PTRs (Thomas Cook)
- Terms which stated that a name change affecting everyone on the booking will be treated as a cancellation and incur cancellation charges. This conflicts with the right under the PTRs to transfer a booking in certain circumstances (Thomas Cook)
- Terms which excluded payment of compensation for significant changes made to a holiday by the tour operator above a set scale, even if the consumer could prove a greater loss. In addition the contract excluded compensation entirely for changes made more than 56 days before departure. Both conflict with the PTRs (Thomas Cook).
- Terms which denied liability for flight delays (contrary to PTRs requirement to be responsible for third party suppliers) (Thomas Cook).

Whether the OFT could have obtained an injunction in respect of every single one of the above points may be debated. But there is no doubt that the agreement reached has the effect that it will benefit over 90 per cent of package holidaymakers.

CHAPTER SEVEN
Misrepresentation

INTRODUCTION

In Chapter Four we saw how representations could be distinguished from terms of the contract and mere puffs. Once that has been done it is necessary to distinguish between different types of misrepresentation. The reason for this is that the type of misrepresentation determines the remedies that are available to the victim. At one end of the scale the victim may end up with no remedy at all whereas at the other end the remedies are quite comprehensive. In this chapter we will look first at the different types of misrepresentation and then at the remedies available.

TYPES OF MISREPRESENTATION

There are three types of misrepresentation—*fraudulent* mispresentation, *negligent* misrepresentation and *innocent* misrepresentation. Prior to 1967 there were only two types—fraudulent and innocent but the Misrepresentation Act 1967 created a third type—negligent misrepresentation. The effect of the Act is relatively limited. Its main effect is to improve the remedies for non-fraudulent misrepresentation. It has no effect upon what amounts to a misrepresentation and what does not.

1. Fraudulent misrepresentation

The accepted definition of a fraudulent misrepresentation is to be found in the case of *Derry v Peek* (1889) 15 App Cas 337. Lord Herschell said:

> "... fraud is proved when it is shown that a false representation has been made (1) knowingly, or (2) without belief in its truth, or (3) recklessly, careless whether it be true or false ..."

The essence of this definition is that the representor is not guilty of fraud if he made the statement with an honest belief in its truth—

no matter how ill founded that belief may be. In *Derry v Peek* itself the directors of a company had issued a prospectus in which they stated that the company had the power to operate steam driven trams rather than horse drawn trams. In fact the company did not have this power but the directors *honestly believed* it did and were therefore not liable for fraud.

At this stage it is necessary to point out that a fraudulent misrepresentation amounts to the *tort of deceit*. In other words when a plaintiff brings an action for fraudulent misrepresentation his action, technically, is not in the law of *contract* but in the law of *tort*. The reason for this is historical. Actions for deceit in the law of tort developed in such a way that they took in fraudulent statements connected to contracts as well as statements which were not related to contracts. The only practical effect this has on the law of misrepresentation is that the damages that are payable are calculated in a slightly different fashion, on a *tortious* rather that a *contractual* basis. The way this works is dealt with in the next section.

If a tour operator deliberately published statements in a brochure which he knew to be false then he would be making fraudulent misrepresentations. So for instance if he published an artist's impression of an hotel and said that this hotel "will be completed" before the commencement of next season when he knows full well that it will not and he will have to move clients to another hotel then in the words of Lord Herschell he makes a false statement "knowingly" and will be guilty of deceit. It would be different if the operator put the statement in the brochure honestly believing that it was true. Even if all the evidence pointed the other way and only somebody who was either excessively optimistic or truly stupid would have believed it, it would nevertheless not amount to fraud. It might very well be negligent but it would not be dishonest. It would always be open to the court however to infer from the circumstances that the statement could only have been made knowingly or recklessly because *no one* could be so optimistic or so stupid!

Note that allegations of fraud must be proved by a plaintiff on the criminal standard *i.e.* beyond reasonable doubt, rather than the civil standard, on the balance of probabilities.

2. Negligent misrepresentation

Prior to 1967 if a misrepresentation was not fraudulent it could only be innocent. An innocent misrepresentation therefore covered a wide spectrum of statements. It encompassed those which were very nearly fraudulent such as in *Derry v Peek* and extended to cover those which were made without any element of fault at all by the representor such as in *Oscar Chess Ltd v Williams* [1957] 1 W.L.R. 370. In that case the seller of the car had only represented that the car was younger than it really was because the log book had been very carefully forged by a previous owner and there was nothing about the model of the car or its mileage or its condition to suggest that the log book was wrong. The injustice this created was that only fraudulent misrepresentations entitled the victim to damages. Even for the most negligent of statements the victim could not be compensated with damages. There was another remedy, *rescission of the contract*, but this might not be available, in which case the victim was left without a remedy altogether.

The Misrepresentation Act 1967 was passed to remedy this situation. Section 2(1) of the Act creates an action for damages for negligent representations. Section 2(1) states:

> "Where a person has entered into a contract after a misrepresentation has been made to him by another party thereto and as a result thereof he has suffered loss, then, if the person making the misrepresentation would be liable to damages in respect thereof had the misrepresentation been made fraudulently, that person shall be so liable notwithstanding that the misrepresentation was not made fraudulently, unless he proves that he had reasonable ground to believe and did believe up to the time the contract was made that the facts represented were true."

This is phrased rather clumsily but what it comes down to is this. If a misrepresentation has been made which is not fraudulent the representor will nevertheless be liable to pay damages *unless he can prove that he had reasonable grounds for making the statement.* Thus the Act creates a right to damages which did not exist before, but, just as importantly, if not more so, it places the onus of proof on the representor. Once it can be shown that there is a misrepresentation it is up to the representor to show that it was reasonable to make the statement not for the victim to show that it was unreasonable.

The difficulties of doing this are clearly illustrated in the case of *Howard Marine & Dredging Co Ltd v Ogden & Sons Ltd* [1978] Q.B. 574. The plaintiffs owned two barges which they hired to the defendants who wanted them to carry waste from excavation works to be dumped at sea. The capacity of the barges was crucial to the defendants. The plaintiff's marine manager misrepresented their capacity to the defendants. The reason for this was that he quoted them the capacity of the barges as stated in Lloyd's Register. In fact, for once, the Register was wrong. The correct capacity was contained in shipping documents which were in the plaintiff's possession but which the marine manager did not refer to. Once the truth was apparent the defendants, claiming misrepresentation, refused to pay any more hire charges and returned the barges. The plaintiffs sued them for breach of contract.

In a split decision the Court of Appeal decided that the plaintiff's marine manager did *not* have reasonable grounds for making the false statement. After reviewing all the evidence Bridge LJ said:

> "But the question remains whether his evidence, however benevolently viewed, is sufficient to show that he had an objectively reasonable ground to disregard the figure in the ship's documents and to prefer the Lloyd's Register figure. I think it is not."

If a tour operator publishes a false statement in his brochure about the facilities at an hotel and based it upon what a very experienced resort manager told him rather than checking with the hotel owner then a similar situation might arise. Did the tour operator have reasonable grounds for making the statement? On the one hand the resort manager is on the spot, is very experienced, is aware of the consequences of getting such things wrong and can usually be trusted. On the other hand it would be probably be just as easy to get the information from the hotel and would be likely to be more accurate (although in practice information from hotels tends to be rather optimistic!). What is reasonable is a question of fact and the amount of care required varies with the circumstances. If it was a matter of detail of no real importance and on which the resort manager could be expected to have a good knowledge then relying on her might be sufficient. On the other hand if it was a matter of some importance which the manager might not be conversant with and which was very easy to check with the hotel then this might not amount to reasonable grounds.

3. Innocent misrepresentation

If the representor can prove that he did have reasonable grounds for making the statement then he will only have made an innocent misrepresentation for which the remedies are not as powerful as for negligent or fraudulent misrepresentation.

Remedies for Misrepresentation

Once it has been established that not only is there a misrepresentation but what type it is then the remedies available can be determined. Basically there are two types of remedy: *damages* and *rescission*. Damages are financial compensation designed to compensate the victim for the harm done by the misrepresentation in so far as money can do this. Rescission of the contract is where the victim of the misrepresentation is permitted to call the contract off and the parties are treated as though the contract never existed. The availability of the remedies is determined by the type of misrepresentation and the stage the contract has reached when the victim discovers the misrepresentation. The remedies will be looked at in turn.

1. Rescission

To rescind a contract means to call the contract off and return the parties to the position they were in before the contract was made as if the contract had never existed (the *status quo ante*). Rescission is a remedy which is available to the victim of a misrepresentation no matter what kind of misrepresentation occurred. However, there are certain limitations on the right to rescind and if the right is lost the victim may find himself in a position where he cannot rescind and no damages are available so he is without a remedy at all.

Affirmation of the Contract

If a party knows of the misrepresentation and chooses to affirm the contract, *i.e.* continue with it, he cannot then turn round and rescind it or ask the courts to rescind it. So for instance in the case of *Long v Lloyd* [1958] 1 W.L.R. 753 the plaintiff purchased a lorry on the basis of a misrepresentation. After discovering the fault with the lorry he nevertheless continued to use it. It was held that this amounted to affirmation and he could not later rescind the contract when the fault proved irreparable.

If a tour operator induced clients to enter into a package holiday contract on the basis of a misrepresentation but then discovered it and sent errata to clients this would entitle the clients to rescind the contract at that stage. However, if they were not initially concerned by the misrepresentation and went on to pay the balance when it became due they could not subsequently rescind. Paying the balance after they knew of the misrepresentation is evidence of affirmation. They had demonstrated that they wanted the contract to continue despite knowing of the misrepresentation.

Lapse of Time

Lapse of time is not in itself a reason for denying rescission, particularly if the misrepresentation has not been discovered. However if the lapse of time is sufficiently long then it may amount to evidence of affirmation and this may give grounds for denying rescission. So for instance, what if a client books a holiday in October to be taken in August of the following year and is informed by an errata notice in November that the brochure is inaccurate? If the client does nothing until the following June when the balance is payable and then claims the right to rescind a court might say that such a long delay before trying to rescind amounts to affirmation and will not be permitted. In *Leaf v International Galleries* [1950] 1 All E.R. 693 a purchaser of a painting discovered after five years that it had not been painted by Constable, as had been represented to him. It was held that rescission was no longer available.

Full Restitution Impossible

The essence of rescission is that the parties can be restored to the position they were in before the contract was made. Therefore if one party has used or damaged or consumed the subject matter of the contract before the misrepresentation is discovered it is impossible to restore the parties to their original positions, the *status quo ante*, and rescission is unavailable.

If a client only discovers the misrepresentation when in resort it will then be too late to rescind. Having already "consumed" the outward flight and perhaps some of the accommodation the client is not in a position to restore the tour operator to his pre-contractual position.

Third Party Rights

This is a bar to rescission which normally applies in situations very different to package holiday contracts. The usual scenario arises where for instance Alan is induced by the fraud of Brian to sell his car to Brian in exchange for a cheque which bounces. Normally the contract could be rescinded for fraud (that is if Brian can be found!). However if Brian acts quickly and sells the car to Charles, an innocent buyer, before the fraud is discovered then the contract cannot be rescinded. The law will not restore Alan to his original position if an innocent third party, Charles, has acquired the subject matter of the contract in good faith before the fraud is discovered.

It is difficult to envisage circumstances where this would be relevant to package holiday contracts but conceivably it might arise in relation to transfers. Under Regulation 10 a consumer may transfer his contract to another in certain limited circumstances. It is possible to imagine circumstances where a tour operator, A, is induced by the fraud of B, to enter into a package holiday contract. B then transfers the holiday to C, who pays him for it, before his fraud is discovered by A. A then wishes to rescind his contract with B but because C has already acquired rights under the contract cannot do so.

Although such a situation is theoretically possible it is hard to see it arising in practice simply because Regulation 10 provides that in the event of a transfer the transferee remains jointly and severally liable with the transferor for the payment of the price of the package. In other words the tour operator has an alternative remedy to rescission which he would exercise in the circumstances.

Where Damages are Awarded In Lieu of Rescission

Section 2(2) of the Misrepresentation Act states:

> "Where a person has entered into a contract after a misrepresentation has been made to him otherwise than fraudulently, and he would be entitled, by reason of the misrepresentation, to rescind the contract, then, if it is claimed, in any proceedings arising out of the contract, that the contract ought to be or has been rescinded, the court or arbitrator may declare the contract subsisting and award damages in lieu of rescission, if of opinion that it would be equitable to do so, having regard to the nature of the misrepresentation and the loss that would be caused by it if the contract were upheld, as well as to the loss that rescission would cause to the other party."

What this means is that if the court considers that it would be fair to do so it can award damages instead of rescission. Thus the right to rescission will be lost but damages will be available instead. It is envisaged that the courts will do this where the misrepresentation is relatively minor and can easily be compensated by a sum of money and where to rescind the contract would be out of all proportion to the damage caused by the misrepresentation. For instance, if a tour operator misrepresented that apartments had a swimming pool when they did not but in fact the hotel just next door had a swimming pool to which the clients had easy access this would be an appropriate case for awarding damages instead of rescission. Note that the discretion to substitute damages for rescission only exists where the misrepresentation is not fraudulent. For cases of fraud the right to rescission exists unfettered by the Misrepresentation Act.

2. Damages

Damages for Fraudulent Misrepresentation

As indicated earlier fraudulent misrepresentation amounts to the *tort of deceit* therefore when the damages are calculated they are measured according to *tortious* rather than *contractual* principles. What this means is that the victim of the tort will be placed, *financially*, in the position he would have been in if the statement had not been made, *i.e.* if the tort had not been committed. In general this means putting him in the position he would have been in if no contract had been made. In contract the position is that the victim will be placed in the position he would have been in if the representation had been true, *i.e.* he will get the full benefit of the contract.

So for example if a client had purchased a holiday for £500 on the basis of a misrepresentation about the quality of the hotel then the damages he would receive in tort would be the difference in value between what he actually got and the price he actually paid. In financial terms he would then be in the same position he was in before the contract was made. So if he was supposed to be accommodated in a four star hotel and was actually accommodated in a three star hotel then he would receive the difference between the value of a three star hotel holiday and what he actually paid. Thus if the difference in value was assessed at £150 that is what he would get.

In contract, using the same example, the figures come out exactly the same although they are arrived at by a different route. To put the client in the position he would have been in if the representation had been true requires the tour operator to make up the difference between what the client got and what he was promised—also £150.

It would be different, however, if the client had bought a late bargain. Say he had paid £400 for a holiday which normally sold for £500. However the hotel is substandard and what he actually gets is something worth only £350. In tort, to put him in the position he would have been in if the representation had not been made would mean giving him £50 in compensation. He is thus not out of pocket but he does not get a £500 holiday. On the other hand, in contract he will be put into the position he would have been in if the contract had been performed. In contract he would be given £150 compensation—the difference between what he actually got and what he had contracted for. He will thus receive the benefit of his bargain. Note that this example depends upon the holiday being valued at £500. There is an argument that the value of a late bargain is only what it can be sold for—in this case only £400—which means that the figures for both tortious and contractual damages would be the same again.

In addition to these damages for difference in value of the holiday itself there are also damages available for *consequential loss*. Consequential losses occur when the misrepresentation not only results in the value of the thing acquired being worth less but the thing itself goes on to cause further loss. In holiday cases the most usual kind of consequential loss is the distress and disappointment caused by the substandard holiday—illustrated by *Jarvis v Swan Tours Ltd* [1973] Q.B. 233 (see Chapter Ten on remedies for a fuller discussion of damages for distress). This was a case of breach of contract rather than misrepresentation but it seems that emotional damage can also be claimed for misrepresentation (See *Chesneau v Interhome Ltd*, discussed below; *cf. Ichard v Frangoulis* [1977] 2 All E.R. 461.)

One problem that arises with consequential losses is that in contract damages are only recoverable if they are a reasonably foreseeable consequence of the breach of contract whereas in the tort of deceit the rule is that all the damages that flow from the fraud are recoverable whether foreseeable or not.

If a contract breaker cannot reasonably foresee that his breach will cause the damage that actually occurred then he is not liable for it. This was precisely the point that the case of *Kemp v Intasun* (1988) Tr. L. 161 turned on. It was held that putting Mr Kemp in a dirty room would be inconvenient and upsetting but that an asthma attack was not foreseeable—in legal jargon the damage was *too remote a consequence* of the breach of contract.

The rule in the tort of deceit that all damages which flow directly from the fraudulent statement are recoverable *whether they are foreseeable or not* is illustrated by the case of *Doyle v Olby (Ironmongers) Ltd* [1969] 2 Q.B. 158.

In that case the seller of a business had fraudulently misrepresented that the turnover of the business was entirely "over the counter" when in fact a large part of it was brought in by a travelling salesman. The accounts did not reflect this. In particular they made no mention of wages for the travelling salesman. Lord Denning MR said of the claim for damages:

> "In contract, the damages are limited to what may reasonably be supposed to have been in the contemplation of the parties. In fraud, they are not so limited. The defendant is bound to make reparation for all the actual damages directly flowing from the fraudulent inducement. The person who has been defrauded is entitled to say:
>
> 'I would not have entered into this bargain at all but for your representation. Owing to your fraud, I have not only lost all the money I paid you, but, what is more, I have been put to a large amount of extra expense as well and suffered this or that extra damages.'
>
> All such damages can be recovered: it does not lie in the mouth of the fraudulent person to say that they could not reasonably have been foreseen. For instance, in this very case Mr Doyle has not only lost the money which he paid for the business, which he would never have done if there had been no fraud: he put all that money in and lost it; but also he has been put to expense and loss in trying to run a business which has turned out to be a disaster for him. He is entitled to damages for all his loss ..."

Thus *if* the tour operator in the *Kemp* case had *fraudulently misrepresented* the cleanliness of the room for some reason then he would have been liable for the asthma attack whether it was foreseen not.

Damages for Negligent Misrepresentation

Until 1967 damages were not available for negligent misrepresentation at all. Now they are, by virtue of s.2(1) of the Misrepresentation Act 1967. It states:

> "Where a person has entered into a contract after a misrepresentation has been made to him by another party thereto and as a result thereof he has suffered loss, then, if the person making the misrepresentation would be liable to damages in respect thereof had the misrepresentation been made fraudulently, that person shall be *so liable* notwithstanding that the misrepresentation was not made fraudulently, unless he proves that he had reasonable ground to believe and did believe up to the time the contract was made that the facts represented were true." (Emphasis added)

After a period of uncertainty the courts have decided that damages for negligent misrepresentation will be calculated on the same principles as for fraudulent misrepresentation, *i.e.* on tortious principles. The emphasised words in the section led to this interpretation. The courts have decided that not only the basis of calculation will be tortious but that the rules relating to remoteness of damage will be tortious also.

Chesneau v Interhome Ltd 134 N.L.J. 341; *The Times* June 9, 1983; LEXIS, CA, is a case involving s.2(1) of the Misrepresentation Act and the calculation of damages under it. The defendants, Interhome Ltd, had misrepresented the state of some accommodation that the plaintiffs had hired from them. The house was not secluded as promised, there was no private pool, and the sleeping accommodation was not as described. The plaintiffs had left the accommodation and found other accommodation but it cost them £209 more. They were suing for this amount plus a sum for distress and disappointment suffered while they searched for alternative accommodation.

In the County Court the judge had decided that as damages under section 2(1) were to be assessed on a tortious basis then he should put the parties in the position they would have been in *if the misrepresentation had not been made*. If the misrepresentation had not been made then the parties would be back in England without a contract. In such circumstances the plaintiffs could probably have found similar accommodation at much the same price and therefore he awarded only £30 in damages for the misrepresentation. The Court of Appeal regarded this approach as entirely inappropriate in the circumstances. Given that the plaintiffs were stuck in substandard accommodation in the middle of France by the time the misrepresentation was discovered it was somewhat artificial to assess the damages as though they were back in England. Their solution to the problem was to say that the sum of £209 represented what the plaintiffs had to spend to *mitigate* the loss caused by the misrepresentation. In tort as in contract a victim is under a duty to mitigate his loss. The Court of Appeal thus neatly sidestepped the problem of how to assess damages in tort for a holiday which has already commenced.

It was mentioned above that where the tort of deceit has been committed the victim can claim all the losses flowing from the fraud whether they were foreseeable or not (*Doyle v Olby (Ironmongers) Ltd*). That seems fair enough if the representor has been fraudulent but what if he has not? What if the false statement had only been made negligently? In *Royscot Trust Ltd v Rogerson* [1991] 3 All E.R. 294, it was decided quite emphatically that even if the false statement is only made negligently the victim can claim all the losses he suffered even if normally they would be too remote. Basing this conclusion on s. 2(1) of the Misrepresentation Act 1967 Balcombe LJ said:

> "With all respect to the various learned authors whose works I have cited above, it seems to me that to suggest that a different measure of damage applies to an action for innocent misrepresentation under the section than that which applies to an action for fraudulent misrepresentation (deceit) at common law is to ignore the plain words of the subsection and is inconsistent with the cases to which I have referred. In my judgment, therefore, the [plaintiff] is entitled to recover from the [defendant] all the losses which it suffered as a result of its entering into the agreements with the [defendant] . . . ., *even if those losses were unforeseeable* . . ." [Emphasis added] [When he refers to innocent misrepresentation this includes negligent misrepresentation.]

The result of this judgment creates an anomalous situation. Someone who suffers from a negligent misrepresentation can claim damages for all the losses he suffers whether foreseeable or not (*Royscot Trust Ltd v Rogerson*) yet if the same statement amounted to a term of the contract only foreseeable losses could be recovered (*Kemp v Intasun*). The decision has come under sustained academic attack but still survives. In *Smith New Court Securities Ltd v Scrimgeour Vickers (Asset Management) Ltd* [1997] A.C. 254 the House of Lords refrained from overruling it, whilst acknowledging the criticisms.

Damages for Innocent Misrepresentation

The only situation where damages can be claimed for innocent misrepresentation is under s.2(2) of the Misrepresentation Act 1967 where the court, at its discretion, can award damages in lieu of rescision. This was discussed above in the section on the availability of rescission. However there is some doubt as to whether a claimant can recover damages in lieu of rescission if the right to rescission has already been lost *e.g.* by affirmation. In *Thomas Witter Ltd v TBP Industries Ltd* [1996] 2 All E. R. 573 the court held that the right was not lost but in *Floods of Queensferry Ltd v Shand Construction Ltd* [2000] BLR 81 and in *Alton House Garages (Bromley) Ltd v Monk* (1981) (LEXIS). the court said it was. This conflict remains to be resolved.

If damages were to be awarded under section 2(2) there is no authoritative answer yet as to whether they would be calculated on tortious or contractual principles.

4. Misrepresentations which become terms

Up to now it has been assumed that a statement can either be a term or a representation but not both. Certainly it is the case that some statements can only be representations and some statements are only terms but it is also possible for a statement which is originally a representation to be incorporated into the contract as a term. For instance a brochure may contain statements about a resort that are only representations but which the client is sufficiently concerned about to ask the operator to confirm and makes it clear that the contract is only being made on that basis, *i.e.* the statement is being incorporated into the contract. So what was originally only a misrepresentation is a term as well.

The practical effect of this is that in some circumstances the victim can only sue for misrepresentation, in others he can only sue for breach of contract and in yet others he can sue for either breach or misrepresentation depending on which is most to his advantage.

Chesneau v Interhome Ltd appears to be the kind of case where the action could have been brought for either breach of a term of the contract or for misrepresentation. There is no indication in the report of why an action in misrepresentation was chosen. It would have seemed easier to have sued simply for breach of contract. A better example is *Mawdsley v Cosmosair* referred to in previous chapters. In that case the statement that the hotel had a lift was found both to be an implied term, to the effect that the lift stopped at all floors, and to be a negligent misrepresentation. For good measure the court also held it to be a misleading statement under Regulation 4 of the Package Travel Regulations.

It used to be the case that when it came to a claim for damages plaintiffs would prefer that a statement be classified as a term rather than a representation because damages were then automatically available for breach of contract rather than subject to the limitations of an action in misrepresentation. However cases such as *Royscot* that have opened up the possibility of damages for unforeseeable losses, coupled with the more favourable burden of proof established by the Misrepresentation Act, mean that actions will arise where the defendant may wish to establish that the statement was a representation rather than a term.

5. Relationship with the package travel regulations

It is worthwhile repeating at this point that an action for misrepresentation cannot be viewed in isolation from the provisions of the Package Travel Regulations. We have already seen in Chapter Five that Regulation 4 creates civil liability for any misleading statements and in Chapter Four that Regulation 6 turns the particulars in the brochure into warranties—as just illustrated by *Mawdsley v Cosmosair* above.

Chapter Eight
Privity of Contract

Introduction

In English law the general rule is that only a person who is a party to a contract can sue or be sued upon it. To put it another way, if I buy a TV from an electrical shop and *give* it to you, if it does not work *you* cannot sue the shop because *you* do not have a contract with them. By the same token if I had bought the TV for you on credit but I was not keeping up the payments the shop could not sue you because they do not have a contract with you. It would make no difference at all even if I had said at the time I bought the TV that I was buying it for you—the fact that the contract was for your benefit, and you were named in it, does not make you a party to it.

In practice this rule has proved to be extremely inconvenient and the most noticeable aspect of it is the large number of exceptions to it. The exceptions to the rule are to be found both at common law and in statute. As we shall see shortly, travel law provides one of the leading and most controversial exceptions at common law (*Jackson v Horizon Holidays Ltd* [1975] 3 All E.R. 92) and one of the newest statutory exceptions can be found in the Package Travel Regulations. In fact we have already looked at this aspect of the Regulations in Chapter Two. There we saw that Regulation 2 defines a "consumer" in such a way that persons who would not normally be regarded as being party to a package holiday contract are in fact treated as parties by the Regulations.

In this chapter we will be looking first of all at the general rule at common law and how it works in practice. Then we will look again at the common law rule specifically in relation to package holiday contracts. Next we shall see how the common law rule has been overtaken and largely replaced by the new rules in the Package Travel Regulations. While looking at the rules in the Package Travel Regulations we will also examine the concept of transferring a package holiday from one consumer to another and the problems this poses. Finally we will look at the Contracts (Rights of Third Parties) Act 1999 which may also have an effect on the rights of package holidaymakers. This Act, which is of general application, was passed following the Law Commission Report on privity of contract: *Privity of Contract: Contracts for the Benefit of Third Parties* (Cm 3329 (1996)).

Privity of Contract—the General Rule

Tweddle v Atkinson (1861) 1 B & S 393 is a case whose facts are far removed from the world of travel law but nevertheless it forms the basis of the rules on privity of contract. In that case William Tweddle, the son of John Tweddle, was marrying the daughter of William Guy. The two fathers drew up an agreement whereby they each promised to pay a sum of money to William Tweddle. Not only was William named in the agreement he was also expressly given the right to sue on the agreement. Unfortunately before William Guy had paid any money to his new son-in-law he died. His estate was taken over by his executor who refused to pay the money so William sued the estate for the money he had been promised. The court refused his claim. It was held that although he had been named in the contract he was not a party to it because he had not provided any *consideration*. We have already mentioned briefly in Chapter Three that for a valid contract to exist the parties to it have to provide consideration. In other words you have to pay for the promises you receive from the other party. In this case although William Tweddle had been promised £200 by his new father-in-law he had promised nothing in exchange and therefore could not enforce the contract.

A more straightforward example is *Dunlop Pneumatic Tyre Co Ltd v Selfridge & Co Ltd* [1915] A.C. 847 where Dunlop sold tyres to a wholesaler, Dew & Co, who in turn sold them to a retailer, Selfridge. Dunlop inserted a term in their contract with Dew & Co that when Dew & Co re-sold the tyres to retailers such as Selfridge the contract should contain a price maintenance clause, *i.e.* the retailer should not sell below Dunlop's list price—and if they did so they would be subject to financial penalties. Although Dew & Co followed Dunlop's instructions Selfridge nevertheless chose to sell below list price and in consequence Dunlop's sued them. The outcome was quite simple. Dunlop had a contract with Dew & Co but they did not have one with Selfridge and therefore they could not insist on the price maintenance clause being enforced. Even though Selfridge had promised in their contract with Dew & Co not to break Dunlop's price maintenance policy Dunlop had not given them any consideration in return.

Privity of Contract—The Impact on Package Holidays

In *Jackson v Horizon Holidays Ltd* the plaintiff, Mr Jackson, had bought a package holiday to Ceylon (now Sri Lanka) for himself, his wife and his two young children. Although Mr Jackson had requested an hotel of the highest standard and was very specific about what he wanted, the hotel provided was woefully inadequate. The children's room was mildewed, there was no bath, the shower was dirty, the toilet was stained and fungus was growing on the walls. In the parents' room there was no bath and the linen was dirty. As for the facilities there was no mini-golf, no swimming pool, no beauty salon, no hairdressing salon and the food in the restaurant was unacceptable. In the County Court the defendant admitted liability and the judge awarded £1100 damages on a holiday that cost £1200. But the judge specifically stated that although he could award damages to Mr Jackson that included an amount for distress and disappointment under the principle established in *Jarvis v Swans Tours Ltd* [1973] 1 All E.R. 71, he could not award anything to the rest of the family for their distress and disappointment. He said:

> "... the damages are the Plaintiff's; that I can consider the effect upon his mind of his wife's discomfort, vexation and the like, although I cannot award a sum which represents her vexation."

Horizon appealed to the Court of Appeal on the grounds that the damages were too high, particularly if they only represented Mr Jackson's own loss. This inevitably raised the issue of whether Mr Jackson could claim damages not only for himself but also for other members of the party.

At this point it is worthwhile quoting extensively from Lord Denning's judgment where the issues are set out:

> "[Counsel for Mr Jackson] submits that damages can be given not only for the leader of the party, in this case, Mr Jackson's own distress, discomfort and vexation, but also for that of the rest of the party.
>
> We have had an interesting discussion as to the legal position when one person makes a contract for the benefit of a party. In this case it was a husband making a contract for the benefit of himself, his wife and children. Other cases readily come to mind. A host makes a contract with a restaurant for a dinner for

himself and his friends. The vicar makes a contract for a coach trip for the choir. In all these cases there is only one person who makes the contract. It is the husband, the host or the vicar, as the case may be. Sometimes he pays the whole price himself. Occasionally he may get a contribution from the others. But in any case it is he who makes the contract. It would be a fiction to say that the contract was made by all the family, or all the guests, or all the choir, and that he was only an agent for them. Take this very case. It would be absurd to say that the twins of three years old were parties to the contract or that the father was making the contract on their behalf as if they were principals... No, the real truth is that in each instance, the father, the host or the vicar, was making a contract himself for the benefit of the whole party. In short, a contract by one for the benefit of third persons.

What is the position when such a contract is broken? At present the law says that the only one who can sue is the one who made the contract. None of the rest of the party can sue, even though the contract was made for their benefit. But when that one does sue, what damages can he recover? Suppose the holiday firm puts the family into a hotel which is only half built and the visitors have to sleep on the floor? Or suppose the restaurant is fully booked and the guests have to go away, hungry and angry, having spent so much on fares to get there? Or suppose the coach leaves the choir stranded half-way and they have to hire cars to get home? None of them individually can sue. He can, of course, recover his own damages. But can he not recover for the others? I think he can."

Lord Denning then went on to give reasons why he thought Mr Jackson could recover which we will examine shortly but in the meantime it is worth looking a little more closely at the situation in the *Jackson* case. What Denning is saying is that although Mrs Jackson and the twins are named on the booking form they are not parties to the contract—they are merely beneficiaries of a contract made by Mr Jackson—and as such they cannot sue in their own right. One way round problems such as this is to make a finding that the person who made the booking was doing so as agent for the others. In other words he was authorised by the others to make a contract with Horizon on their behalf. This may be a possibility in some cases but in this case Denning rejected that idea. So we are left with a situation which is bound to arise constantly in package holiday contracts where a person for whose benefit the contract was made is unable to claim because they have no contract with the tour operator.

The reasoning Lord Denning adopted in *Jackson* to overcome the problem was suspect to say the least and has subsequently been disapproved. He referred to the judgment of Lush LJ in the case of *Lloyd's v Harper* (1880) 16 Ch D 290 where he said:

> "... I consider it to be an established rule of law that where a contract is made with A for the benefit of B, A can sue on the contract for the benefit of B, and recover all that B could have recovered if the contract had been made with B himself."

Taken at face value this appears to settle the matter in favour of Mr Jackson and this was sufficient for Lord Denning. The problem is that the statement was taken entirely out of context. In *Lloyd's v Harper* Lush LJ was describing a situation where A was acting as an agent or trustee for B and not simply making a contract for B's benefit. An agent or a trustee is entitled to sue on behalf of a principal or a beneficiary but an ordinary contractor is not.

A subsequent case, *Woodar Investment Development Ltd v Wimpey Construction UK Ltd* [1980] 1 W.L.R. 227, considered the *reasoning* in the *Jackson* case and strongly disapproved of it but it is difficult to say whether they actually overturned the decision itself. Certainly, however, they indulged in some re-interpretation of what it did decide. Lord Wilberforce said:

> "I am not prepared to dissent from the actual decision in that case [*Jackson*]. *It may be supported either as a broad decision on the measure of damages* (per James LJ) or possibly as an example of a type of contract, examples of which are persons contracting for family holidays, ordering meals in restaurants for a party, hiring a taxi for a group, calling for special treatment." [Emphasis added]

He then went on to disagree with Lord Denning on the interpretation of the passage from *Lloyd's v Harper*. Lord Russell took much the same line over *Lloyd's v Harper* and also said:

> "I do not criticise the outcome of that case [*Jackson*]: the plaintiff had bought and paid for a high class family holiday; he did not get it, and therefore he was entitled to substantial damages for the failure to supply *him* with one."

And Lord Keith said:

> "That case [*Jackson*] is capable of being regarded as rightly decided on a reasonable view of the measure of damages due to

> the plaintiff as the original contracting party, and not as laying down any rule of law regarding the recoverry of damages for the benefit of third parties."

What is happening is that the House of Lords in the *Woodar* case is saying that although they do not agree with the way Lord Denning reached his decision in *Jackson* nevertheless they agree with the result and that they are prepared to support the decision but on other grounds. Those grounds are that the damages that Mr Jackson received were solely for his own distress and disappointment and did not include an element for his family's distress and disappointment. This flies in the face of what was actually said in the *Jackson* case. Lord Denning expressly stated that he thought that £1100 would be excessive if awarded only for Mr Jackson's suffering but would not be so if extended to his wife and family. Orr LJ agreed unequivocally with him. Only James LJ took the line adopted by the House of Lords and he certainly did not dissent from the views of Lord Denning and Orr LJ. We reproduce below what he said in full:

> "In this case Mr Jackson, as found by the judge on the evidence, was in need of a holiday at the end of 1970. He was able to afford a holiday for himself and his family. According to the form which he completed, what was the form of Horizon Holidays Ltd, he booked what was a family holiday. The wording of that form might in certain circumstances give rise to a contract in which the person signing the form is acting as his own principal and as agent for others. In the circumstances of this case, as indicated by Lord Denning MR, it would be wholly unrealistic to regard this contract as other than one made by Mr Jackson for a family holiday. The judge found that he did not get a family holiday. The costs were some £1,200. When he came back he felt no benefit. He said: 'The only thing, I was pleased to be back, very pleased, but I had nothing at all from that holiday.' For my part, on the issue of damages in this matter, I am quite content to say that £1,100 awarded was the right and proper figure in those circumstances. I would dismiss the appeal."

This leaves the status of the *Jackson* case a little unclear. The only certain thing that can be said about it in the light of the House of Lords judgment in *Woodar* is that in a holiday case the person booking the holiday for a family can recover damages for his own distress—which will be that much greater because of the distress of the rest of the party. Whether the novel part of the judgment—that Mr Jackson could claim for other members of the party—has survived the body blows inflicted by *Woodar* is open to conjecture. Given that none of the law lords actually disapproved of the decision in so many words and at least one, Lord Wilberforce, expressly said that he was not prepared to dissent from it then it may still represent the law. At least one subsequent holiday case decided by the Court of Appeal *Kemp v Intasun* [1987] C.L.Y. 1130 C.A.; (Lexis) seems to accept the basis of *Jackson* without question. In that case Kerr LJ proceeded on the basis that the person making the booking could also claim on behalf of the other members of the party. He said:

> "The plaintiff is a Mr Alan Kemp, but he is suing in effect, *as is accepted in these cases*, on behalf of himself and the other members of the family who accompanied him on this holiday: Mrs Kemp and his step-daughter Susan." [Emphasis added]

One thing is clear, however, and that is that the other members of the party cannot sue in their own right. *Jackson* is a means of avoiding the full rigours of the privity of contract rule but it is not a full blown exception to it.

Another point to make is that if the factual situation in *Jackson* had been a little different then the problems of privity would not have arisen. For instance in *The Dragon* [1979] 1 Lloyd's Rep. 257; aff'd [1980] 2 Lloyd's Rep. 415 it was held that where a husband booked tickets on a cross Channel ferry for himself and his children there was a contract of carriage between the wife and the ferry company. The basis on which this was decided is that the husband was regarded as the plaintiff's agent. Such a finding was potentially detrimental to the plaintiff. By holding that she was a party to the contract she could have been bound by exclusion clauses that would have deprived her of compensation. In the event it was held that the exclusion clauses were not binding on her but had they been so she would have received no damages. In such a case she might have preferred a finding that she was a third party beneficiary rather than a party to the contract.

A further variation can be seen in *Lockett v AM Charles Ltd* [1938] 4 All E.R. 170 where the court held that where a husband and wife lunched together at a restaurant they had both made contracts with the restaurant and therefore could both sue on their individual contracts.

The use of the rules of agency can be seen in the case of *Wilson v Pegasus* [1988] C.L.Y. 1059. In that case a party of children suffered a disastrous skiing holiday and each child recovered £125 damages in their own right. It was held that the teacher who had booked the holiday had acted as agent for each of the 31 pupils in the party.

On many booking forms it is common to find a form of words to the following effect:

> "I agree on behalf of all the clients named hereon to accept the booking conditions overleaf." [These were the words used on the booking form in the *Jackson* case itself.]

In most circumstances this has the effect of making the signatory to the booking form the agent of the others in the party. It would not overcome the problem of Mr Jackson's two twin sons who were too young to be contracting on their own behalf no matter what the booking form said but it would probably be sufficient to cover Mrs Jackson and other adult members of a party.

One benefit for a tour operator with such a clause is that it ensures that he has a contract with all the members of the party—so that for instance if they do not pay, or if they cancel, the tour operator can seek cancellation charges not only from the party leader but also the other party members if necessary. But if the clause is sufficient to create a contract between the tour operator and the other members of the party so that the tour operator can sue them then the converse must also apply—the other members of the party can then sue the tour operator.

Finally there remains the issue of whether or not the *Jackson* case and the rules of privity have any relevance any longer to holiday cases now that the Package Travel Regulations have defined a consumer in such a way that it would include members of a family and other members of a party. The extent of this definition has already been examined in some detail in Chapter Two and will be reviewed again briefly in the next section but the position is that although the problems raised by the *Jackson* case will not arise again in the context of package holidays as defined in the Regulations they will continue to arise in other holiday contexts. A "fly-drive" holiday for instance may not be within the scope of the Regulations and therefore there is potential for problems of privity to arise. It would be the same with booking accommodation or ferries or flights or excursions where there was no package but one person made the contract on behalf of others. So although the Regulations may have laid some of the problems to rest others still remain.

Privity of Contract—The Impact of the Regulations

In Chapter Two we explained how the definition of consumer to be found in Regulation 2(1) extended the protection of the Regulations not only to the purchaser of the package but also to other beneficiaries and transferees. For an explanation of those terms and to save duplication we would simply refer you back to the relevant sections of Chapter Two. All that needs to be added to what we said there as far as the other beneficiary is concerned is that the definition would certainly cover Mrs Jackson and the two twins. There is no longer any need for Lord Denning's legal acrobatics to avoid the privity of contract rules. Mr Jackson is a principal contractor and Mrs Jackson and the twins are other beneficiaries because the package was purchased on their behalf by a principal contractor. Therefore the whole family have full rights under the package holiday contract.

In *Henley v Cosmosair plc* (1995) unreported, the plaintiff had refused to disclose holiday photographs to the defence, taken by member of her family who were not themselves plaintiffs but who had accompanied her on holiday. The Circuit Judge, on appeal from the District Judge, ordered that the photographs should be disclosed on the grounds that under the County Court Rules he could order her to do so if he considered they were within her "power". On the question of whether an order could have been made against members of the family because they were all co-plaintiffs, by virtue of the definition of "consumer" in Regulation 2(2) of the Package Travel Regulations, the judge hesitated to do that but there is a clear indication that he would have done so if necessary.

Privity of Contract and Transferees

A much larger breach in the privity rules is to be found in Regulation 10. Under that Regulation the consumer is permitted to transfer his booking to someone else, the "transferee". Thus it is possible for someone entirely uncontemplated by the original contract to become a party to it.

Regulation 10 provides:

> "10(1) In every contract there is an implied term that where the consumer is prevented from proceeding with the package the consumer may transfer his booking to a person who satisfies all

> the conditions applicable to the package, provided that the consumer gives reasonable notice to the other party to the contract of his intention to transfer before the date when departure is due to take place.
>
> (2) Where a transfer is made in accordance with the implied term set out in paragraph (1) above, the transferor and the transferee shall be jointly and severally liable to the other party to the contract for payment of the price of the package (or, if part of the price has been paid, for payment of the balance) and for any additional costs incurred by that other party as a result of the transfer."

One immediate practical consequence of this which tour operators will not find attractive is that if the consumer can find a substitute to go in his place then that deprives the operator of the ability to levy cancellation charges in such a situation.

The right to transfer the booking to another is not unqualified. First the right only arises if the consumer is "prevented" from proceeding with the package. Clearly a prison sentence or a serious illness will fall into this category but what about redundancy or a death in the family? These are occurrences which do not literally prevent a consumer from proceeding with a package but may make it highly undesirable to do so. (See Saggerson p.75 on this point where he argues for a liberal interpretation.) The existence of insurance to cover such eventualities may influence the interpretation of this provision. At the other end of the scale are situations where the consumer has merely changed his mind and does not wish to proceed. The Regulation does not seem to extend the right of transfer in such circumstances. The commentary included in the original DTI Consultation Document also takes this line. It states:

> "A mere change of mind is not interpreted as giving the consumer the rights in this paragraph, because in such a case he would not be *prevented* from proceeding."

Using its powers under the Unfair Terms in Consumer Contracts Regulations the OFT required Thomas Cook (October 2002) to revise a term which required consumers to treat a booking as cancelled and to pay cancellation charges if all the names on the booking were changed. This was regarded as being in conflict with Regulation 10 and had to be changed so that name changes were permitted. At the same time Airtours were also required to change a term which prevented transfers on certain types of holiday.

Secondly the transferee must be someone who "satisfies all the conditions applicable to the package". In broad terms this means that a pensioner would not be qualified to take the place of a person booked on a "Club 18-30" holiday and by the same token a 16-year old could not take her granny's place on a Saga holiday. A married person would not satisfy the conditions for a "singles" holiday and an inexperienced hill-climber would not be eligible for an advanced mountaineering expedition to the Andes. All these are straightforward examples and no one could take exception to a refusal by the tour operator in such circumstances but it may be open to a tour operator to interpret the conditions applicable to the package restrictively so as to deny the right to transfer—thus benefiting from cancellation charges.

If additional costs arise from the transfer these have to be paid for, *e.g.* if a couple sharing a room transfer their booking to two single men who wish to have single rooms then a single room supplement becomes payable for both of them. (There is an argument that the tour operator could refuse such a transfer anyway because this would not amount to a transfer of the booking—it would be a different booking altogether.) This supplement can be claimed by the tour operator from either the transferors or the transferees because both are "jointly and severally liable". "Additional costs" can be interpreted as also covering the administrative costs involved in making the change. As the Regulation only provides for the recovery of "costs" the question arises as to whether any administration fee can include an element of profit. On the one hand the Regulation does not expressly rule it out. On the other hand it would subvert the purpose of the Regulation if the transferee was faced with such large "administration" charges that it discouraged him from taking the holiday. It might be the case that if the administration charge was too great it might also fall foul of the UTCCR.

The final requirement is that the operator is informed within a reasonable time before departure. What is a reasonable time will vary according to the circumstances but it will for instance have to be sufficiently far in advance to satisfy airline and hotel notification requirements. In the DTI guidelines (p.11) it is suggested that 21 days would be a reasonable time. We are inclined to think that in many cases this is excessively cautious. If a tour operator, with all the advantages of modern technology, can take a fresh booking within 24 hours of departure why cannot he effect a name change in under 21 days? This view was vindicated by the OFT in October 2002 when it required ABTA to remove from its recommended terms a recommendation that 21 days would be a reasonable requirement in the case of name changes and to change it to what would be reasonable in the circumstances. When the Directive was transposed in Luxembourg the Grand Duchy also decided on a 21-day-limit but after an intervention by the Commission agreed to change it to a period of "reasonable notice" (Report on the Implementation of Directive 90/314/EEC on Package Travel and Holiday Tours in the Domestic Legislation of EC Member States, SEC (1999) 1800 Final, Para. 1.1).

The Contracts (Rights of Third Parties) Act 1999

As indicated at the beginning of the chapter the common rule on privity of contract could be seen as depriving third parties of benefits to which they had a legitimate expectation. As far as package holidays are concerned the decision in the *Jackson* case went a long way to redressing the balance in favour of holiday-makers and the Package Travel Regulations seem to have filled in the blanks. However there is new legislation of general application on the issue of privity and it is worth examining it to see if consumers of package holidays derive any further benefit from it, as well as the benefit which may accrue to consumers of non-packages. That legislation is The Contracts (Rights of Third Parties) Act 1999 and its most important provision is section 1:

"S.1 Right of third party to enforce contractual term.

(1) Subject to the provisions of this Act, a person who is not a party to a contract (a 'third party') may in his own right enforce a term of the contract if—

(a) the contract expressly provides that he may, or
(b) subject to subsection (2), the term purports to confer a benefit on him.

(2) Subsection (1)(b) does not apply if on a proper construction of the contract it appears that the parties did not intend the term to be enforceable by the third party.

(3) The third party must be expressly identified in the contract by name, as a member of a class or as answering a particular description but need not be in existence when the contract is entered into.

(4) This section does not confer a right on a third party to enforce a term of a contract otherwise than subject to and in accordance with any other relevant terms of the contract.

(5) For the purpose of exercising his right to enforce a term of

> the contract, there shall be available to the third party any remedy that would have been available to him in an action for breach of contract if he had been a party to the contract (and the rules relating to damages, injunctions, specific performance and other relief shall apply accordingly)."

Very broadly, put into a package holiday context, what this means is that a third party, *e.g.* Mr Jackson's wife and children, can enforce the terms of the contract against the tour operator if they can show that the contract:

- Expressly provides that they may, or
- Purports to confer a benefit upon them, unless the parties did not intend the term(s) to be enforceable by a third party.

While it may not be possible to find an express term which confers on the consumer the right to sue the tour operator it is hard to envisage a situation where the contract will not purport to confer a benefit on the third party—be it transport, accommodation, meals, etc. Furthermore, in such cases, it will be equally unlikely to find an intention that the third party cannot enforce the terms—simply because this would be contrary to Regulation 2 of the Package Travel Regulations. But this gets us no further than what the consumer is already entitled to under the PTR; it seems to add nothing to his existing rights. Whether he enforces his rights under the PTR or the Contracts (Rights of Third Parties) Act seem immaterial.

However, there is one situation where the Act may make a difference. When tour operators contract with hotels, or other sub-contractors, they often go into great detail about what the hotel has to provide for the tour operators' clients. These contracts may not confer an express right on the holidaymaker to enforce the terms of the contract but they certainly purport to confer benefits upon the holidaymaker. If, in breach of contract, the hotelier does not provide the number or quality of meals promised then this opens up the possibility of the holidaymaker suing the hotelier. What would make it easier would be the fact that such contracts are often made subject to English law and to the jurisdiction of the English courts.

While the tour operator remains solvent this is not necessarily the most practical way of settling the problem but one might envisage a situation where a tour operator becomes insolvent and the hotelier, fearing he might not get paid, reduces his service to the tour operators' clients or perhaps puts them out on the street altogether. (See *Verein fur Konsomenteninformation v Osterrei-*

chische Kreditversicherungs AG Case 364/96 ECJ for an example of the lengths hoteliers are prepared to go to protect their interests when faced with the insolvency of a tour operator.) In these circumstances, where the clients have little or no hope of recovering damages from the tour operator, a class action on behalf of all the consumers who suffered might offer a reasonable prospect of success. This prospect would be defeated of course if the parties to the contract, the hotelier and the tour operator, expressly provided that the third party would acquire no rights under the contract. What might be a greater bar to success would be the defence which is provided in s.3 of the Act:

> "3 (1) Subsections (2) to (5) apply where, in reliance on section 1, proceedings for the enforcement of a term of a contract are brought by a third party.
>
> (2) The promisor shall have available to him by way of defence or set-off any matter that—
>
> (a) arises from or in connection with the contract and is relevant to the term, and
>
> (b) would have been available to him by way of defence or set-off if the proceedings had been brought by the promisee."

In other words if the hotelier had a defence against the tour operator for failing to provide the services then the same defence could be raised against the third parties—the holidaymakers. What better defence could the hotelier have than not having been paid by the tour operator?

There may also be some doubt as to the efficacy of such an action on the basis of the purported intention to create such a right. Professor Burrows, the Law Commissioner principally responsible for the report which led to the legislation, had this to say:

> "I would anticipate that it would not normally be rebutted [the purported intention] unless there is a term in the contract expressly negating the third party's legal rights, or an express term that is otherwise inconsistent with the third party having legal rights, or *unless the parties have entered into a chain of contracts which gives the third party a contractual right against another party for breach of the promisor's obligations under the alleged 'third party' contract.*" [Emphasis added]

Given that hoteliers, tour operators and consumers enter into such a chain of contracts then it might be argued that the tour operator/

hotelier contract did not confer a right on the third party to sue—for the reason that the consumer already has a perfectly good right to sue the tour operator.

CHAPTER NINE
Frustration of Contract and *Force Majeure*

INTRODUCTION

When terrorists attack the Twin Towers; when clubs are bombed in Bali; when hurricanes hit Florida; when tourists are gunned down at Luxor; or when war breaks out in the Gulf it will almost certainly be the case that tour operators will have clients who will be affected. These clients may already be in their resort or they may be about to travel. In many cases the holiday will have to be cancelled altogether. In other cases it may be physically possible to travel but the holiday would be so severely affected that it would not be worthwhile taking it. In yet other cases the only practicable thing to do is abort the holiday and bring clients home.

Such events are usually unforeseen and beyond the control of the parties to the holiday contract. Neither party is at fault but difficult questions arise as to how the losses caused by the cancellation will be apportioned. If the client has already paid for the holiday does he lose his money? Because the tour operator has not provided the holiday does he have to return the money? What if the client has only paid the deposit and is due to pay the balance—can he be compelled to pay it? What if the client has not paid anything yet but the operator has laid out money in advance for accommodation and flights? Is the tour operator compelled to bring clients home and if he does so who has to pay?

These questions are dealt with by an extremely complex mixture of the common law rules on *frustration of contract*, the rules in the Package Travel Regulations on *force majeure*, and the rules in the ABTA Code of Conduct for ABTA tour operators. Section two of this chapter examines the circumstances in which a court is prepared to say that a contract is frustrated. The third section takes a brief look at how the losses involved in a frustration of contract were apportioned at common law. Section four looks at the Law Reform (Frustrated Contracts) Act 1943 (LR(FC)A 1943) which modified and replaced the common law rules on apportionment. The rules to be found in the Package Travel Regulations 1992 will be examined in section five and finally section six looks at the rules in the ABTA Code of Conduct.

It should be said at the outset however that it is our view that as far as package holidays are concerned the new rules in the Package Travel Regulations on *force majeure* almost entirely, but not quite, supersede the old common law rules on frustration. However for those "packages" such as "fly-drive" or "flight only" which may fall outside the scope of the Regulations the old rules continue to apply. They will also continue to apply to providers of accommodation or transport only and to many other holiday products that fall outside the definition of a package, *e.g.* a visit to Disneyland Paris or to Alton Towers where these are booked separately from accommodation or transport.

When is a Contract Frustrated?

1. Historical background

Historically, apart from some minor exceptions, the obligations in a contract were regarded as *absolute*, *i.e.* the parties to the contract were bound by its terms and if, for whatever reason, they were unable to perform their part of the bargain they would be in breach of contract. This applied even if performance was made impossible by some external intervening event over which they had no control. The logic behind this was that the parties were quite free to determine for themselves the terms of the contract and if they failed to provide for such events they would just have to accept the consequences (*Paradine v Jane* (1647) Aleyn 26).

This view was modified later in *Taylor v Caldwell* (1863) 3 B & S 826. The facts of the case were that the plaintiffs had hired Surrey Gardens and Music Hall from the defendants for the purpose of giving four concerts. Six days before the concerts were due to be performed the hall burnt down and it was impossible to give the concerts. The plaintiffs had not yet paid for the use of the hall but they had incurred considerable expenditure in advertising the concerts and other expenses.

It was held that the defendants were not in breach of contract for failure to provide the concert hall. Blackburn J said:

> "Where, from the nature of the contract, it appears that the parties must from the beginning have known that it could not be fulfilled unless ... some particular specified thing continued to exist, so that, when entering into the contract, they must have

> contemplated such continuing existence as the foundation of what was to be done; there, in the absence of any express or implied warranty that the thing shall exist, the contract is not to be construed as a positive contract, but as subject to an implied condition that the parties shall be excused in case, before breach, performance becomes impossible from the perishing of the thing without the fault of the contractor."

What was decided was that once the contract became impossible to perform the contract was *discharged* and the parties were excused from further performance. The obligations under the contract which were still to be performed were no longer enforceable.

Since *Taylor v Caldwell* the courts have developed a number of categories where the contract can be said to be frustrated and the parties excused from further performance.

2. Impossibility

Apart from *Taylor v Caldwell* there are a number of cases involving impossibility. In *Asfar & Co v Blundell* [1896] 1 Q.B. 123 a contract for the sale of a cargo of dates was frustrated when the cargo was sunk and became so contaminated by water and sewage that it was effectively useless.

Contracts of *personal service* will be frustrated where the contractor dies or is incapacitated. In *Cutter v Powell* (1795) 6 T.R. 320 a sailor had signed on for a three month voyage but when he died half way through the contract it was held to be frustrated. In *Condor v The Barron Knights Ltd* [1966] 1 W.L.R. 87 a member of a pop group became too ill to play regularly and his contract was frustrated.

Unavailability of the subject matter of the contract can cause it to be frustrated. It has been held in numerous shipping cases that where a ship has been seized, or detained or requisitioned then this will frustrate the charterparty. Difficulties arise when the unavailability is only temporary. In *Jackson v Union Marine Insurance Co* (1874) L.R. 10 C.P. 125 a ship had been chartered to sail from Liverpool to Newport and then take on a cargo for San Francisco. The contract did not stipulate any time limit for completion of the task. One day out of Liverpool the ship ran aground and was out of action for eight months for repairs. It was held that the contract was frustrated. A term was implied into the contract that it would be completed within a reasonable time and that therefore the delay involved was so extensive that it served to frustrate the contract.

In such cases it is often a question of degree whether or not the delay will be sufficient to frustrate the contract or not. In *FA Tamplin SS Co Ltd v Anglo-Mexican Petroleum Products Co Ltd* [1916] 2 A.C. 397 a ship was requisitioned during the First World War in February 1915. The charter was to last until December 1917. The House of Lords felt that the war would be over sufficiently soon to allow a substantial period of the charter to be performed as intended and therefore held that the contract was not frustrated!

During the Falklands war cruise ships such as the QE2 and the Canberra were requisitioned by the British Government to be used as troop carriers. As far as clients who were already booked onto the ships were concerned this would frustrate their contracts with Cunard and P&O unless, as would be most likely, the contract provided for frustrating events.

3. Impracticability

In some circumstances events may conspire, not to make the contract impossible to perform, but to make it particularly burdensome on one of the parties. English courts have generally taken the view that simply because the contract becomes more difficult, or expensive, or more time consuming to perform does not frustrate the contract. The leading case on this point is *Davis Contractors Ltd v Fareham UDC* [1956] A.C. 696 in which a builder agreed to build 78 houses in eight months at a fixed price. Because of shortages of materials and skilled labour the contract took 22 months to complete and cost substantially more to perform. The contractors argued that the contract had been frustrated. The House of Lords held that it was not. Lord Radcliffe said:

> "... it is not hardship or inconvenience or material loss itself which calls the principle of frustration into play. There must be as well such a change in the significance of the obligation that the thing undertaken would, if performed, be a different thing from that contracted for."

The same kind of problem occurred when the Suez Canal was closed during the 1956 crisis. In the case of *The Eugenia* [1964] 1 All E.R. 161 a ship was chartered to sail from Genoa, via the Black Sea to India. Both parties assumed that the ship would go via the Suez Canal but the contract did not specify. The Canal was closed after the contract was concluded and after the ship had entered it and the ship was trapped in the Canal. The Court of Appeal held that the contract was not frustrated. The journey could be completed by going via the Cape of Good Hope. This would add 30 days to a voyage that would normally take 108. Although the contract would be more burdensome and expensive it was not impossible and the impracticality was not enough to frustrate the contract. (See below for a discussion of a different aspect of the case.) The rationale behind such cases is that the courts are not willing to come to the aid of parties who are simply faced with a bad bargain. It also serves to encourage parties to expressly provide for such events rather than leaving themselves open to entirely arbitrary consequences—see below.

4. Frustration of purpose

There are situations where the contract is not impossible to perform and neither is it impracticable in the sense that one party would have to face a much greater burden than anticipated and yet performance would be pointless and without purpose. This is what happened in the case of *Krell v Henry* [1903] 2 K.B. 740. The facts were that the defendant had hired a room from the plaintiff from which to watch the coronation procession of Edward VII. The King became ill and the procession was cancelled. The Court of Appeal held that the contract was frustrated. Although the room was still available for hire it would have been a fruitless exercise to make use of it.

One significant feature of that case is that it was stressed that the contract was not simply for the hire of a room but for the hire of a room from which to watch the procession. A contrasting case is *Herne Bay Steam Boat Co v Hutton* [1903] 2 K.B. 683. In that case the contract was for the hire of a boat "for the purpose of viewing the naval review and for a day's cruise round the fleet". The naval review was in fact a royal review at Spithead by the King. The review was cancelled, again because of the illness of Edward VII. On this occasion the Court of Appeal held that the contract was not frustrated. Although the review would not take place nevertheless the fleet was still there to be viewed and the harbour cruise was still possible. The distinction between the cases is fine but the difference seems to be that in the former the whole purpose of the room hire was undermined whereas in the latter one of the main purposes of the boat hire still remained. The result seems to depend upon the extent to which the recipient of the service brings home to the provider the importance of the event. (For a discussion of these cases in the context of a package holiday see Grant "Caribbean Chaos" (1998) 148 N.L.J. 190 and "It's not cricket" [1998] ITLJ 51).

5. Illegality

When war breaks out it is illegal to trade with the enemy. Any contracts affected by such illegality are frustrated. Similarly if the government prohibits certain types of contract or requisitions goods under emergency legislation the contract is frustrated. For example in the case of *Fibrosa Spolka Akcyjna v Fairbairn Lawson Combe Barber Ltd* [1943] A.C. 32 a contract for the supply of machinery to a company in Poland was frustrated by the outbreak of World War II when it became illegal to trade with the enemy.

6. Events provided for

The rules relating to frustration of contract are all about allocating the risk of events over which the parties have no control. If the parties have made no provision in the contract for the event then the contract will be frustrated and the risk will be allocated according to the rules in the LR(FC)A 1943. However, if the parties have expressly stated in the contract what will happen if a frustrating event occurs then the courts will give effect to their express wishes rather than impose an external solution on them. This ability to "contract out" is preserved in s.2(3) of the LR(FC)A 1943:

> "2(3) Where any contract to which this Act applies contains any provision which upon the true construction of the contract, is intended to have effect in the event of circumstances arising which operate, or would but for the said provision operate, to frustrate the contract, or is intended to have effect whether such circumstances arise or not, the court shall give effect to the said provision and shall only give effect to the foregoing section of this Act to such extent, if any, as appears to the court to be consistent with the said provision."

A number of points need to be made about this ability to contract out. First, it is often a very difficult question of interpretation to decide whether a particular clause in a contract effectively avoids a frustration of contract. For instance in *Metropolitan Water Board v Dick, Kerr & Co* [1918] A.C. 119 a company agreed in July 1914 to build a reservoir within six years but they were to be given an extension for delays "however occasioned". In 1916 the government ordered them to stop work and sell their plant. It was held that the clause was intended to cover temporary stoppages because of labour and materials problems, not the kind of delay that actually occurred. In such circumstances the contract was frustrated. In *Jackson v Union Marine Insurance Co* a clause in the contract provided that the ship was to proceed to Newport with all possible dispatch "dangers and accidents of navigation excepted". When the ship ran aground and was out of action for eight months being repaired it was held that the contract was frustrated. The phrase "dangers and accidents of navigation excepted" was not intended to cover such a long delay.

The second point, which arises from the first, is that the contract may provide for the event in a number of ways. For instance it may provide simply that if, say, a strike occurs the contract will not be frustrated. In such circumstances the parties will be assumed to have contracted on the basis that if a strike occurs one or other of them will have to bear that risk. In a package holiday contract if such a clause were inserted it might mean that the tour operator was agreeing to provide a holiday irrespective of strikes and if one occurred and he could not provide it then he would be in breach of contract—and would have to pay damages. Alternatively, the clause might say that the contract is not frustrated in the event of a strike and go on to say that the operator will not be liable for non-performance in such circumstances. The effect of this clause is that the strike neither frustrates the contract nor does it put the tour operator in breach. He is excused from performance but the client is still liable to pay for the holiday. The clause places the whole risk of the strike on the client. (It is unlikely that the tour operator would get away with this because it would be prevented either by Regulation 15(5) of the Package Travel Regulations or s.3(2)(b)(ii) of UCTA or by the provisions of the UTCCR.)

A further variation is where the clause states that the event will frustrate the contract and then goes on to state what the consequences of the frustration will be. For instance the clause might state that the contract will be discharged by the strike and that the operator will be able to retain all the client's money. Such a consequence is different from the consequences provided for in the LR(FC)A 1943 which will be examined shortly. Such a clause will not be caught by UCTA 1977 because it is not excluding liability for *breach of contract* it is providing for the consequences of a *frustration of contract*. However, it could be caught by Regulation 13 or 14 of the Package Travel Regulations.

The third point to make is that tour operators who are members of ABTA do in fact expressly provide in their package holiday contracts for what they call *force majeure* events. The Code of Conduct defines what is meant by *force majeure* and requires ABTA members to expressly provide for such events in certain circumstances.

The ABTA Code of Conduct will be examined in detail at the end of this chapter but it needs to be pointed out now that *force majeure* as defined in the Code is different from frustration of contract and different again from *force majeure* as defined in the Package Travel Regulations. Also the Code does not require a tour operator to provide comprehensively for situations which might amount to force majeure. Broadly speaking the Code applies the *force majeure* provisions to pre-departure but not post-departure events.

7. Events foreseen

Frustrating events are usually unforeseen. The parties have made the contract without taking such eventualities into account just because they are unforeseen and it is for that reason that the doctrine of frustration of contract has to be invoked.

The other side of the coin is that, generally, if the events were foreseen then the parties will be taken to have contracted on that basis and will have to accept the consequences of the risk that they foresaw. For instance take a tour operator who offered packages to Dubrovnik in the summer of 1993 without expressly providing in the contract that he would be discharged from his obligations if there was renewed fighting. It could be argued that if he could not provide the holiday he would be in breach of contract. The risk of such an event can easily be foreseen and the tour operator who contracts in such circumstances could be said to be assuming that risk.

In the case of *Walton Harvey Ltd v Walker & Homfrays Ltd* [1931] 1 Ch 274 the plaintiffs bought the right to display advertising on the side of the defendant's hotel for seven years. Before the period was up the hotel was demolished. The defendants were held liable for breach of contract because they knew of the risk of the building being demolished. The plaintiffs did not know of this risk.

However, there is a big difference between events which are *foreseen* and those which are merely *foreseeable*. If we look at any of the cases on frustration of contract none of the events that occurred were totally unforeseeable. Is it completely beyond the bounds of possibility that a concert hall would burn down or a ship run aground or war break out? The issue here is that foreseeability is a flexible concept encompassing events where there is a strong likelihood that they will occur and other events where the degree of foreseeability is extremely small. Events at the latter end of the scale are regarded as being so improbable that they are capable of frustrating the contract. Those events at the other end of the scale which are readily foreseeable, as well as those which are actually foreseen, are events which will not generally frustrate the contract.

This latter statement is qualified because there are some cases where the courts have suggested that even foreseeable events may frustrate a contract in appropriate circumstances. In *WJ Tatem v Gamboa* [1939] 1 K.B. 132 the defendants chartered a ship for the purpose of evacuating civilians from Spain during the Spanish Civil War. The ship was seized by the Nationalist government and the question arose as to whether the contract was frustrated. Goddard J held that the contract was frustrated. In the course of his judgment he said:

> "I do not feel that I can hold on the evidence which I have before me that a risk of seizure of the description which took place here, and the detaining of the vessel not only for the period of her charter but for a long period thereafter, was a risk which was contemplated by the parties."

However later in the judgment he indicated that even if the parties had contemplated that the ship would be seized the contract would still be frustrated:

> "... it seems to me ... that, if the true doctrine be that ... frustration depends on the absolute disappearance of the contract; or, if the true basis be ... 'the continued existence of a certain state of facts' it makes very little difference whether the circumstances are foreseen or not."

In the case of the *Eugenia* [1964] 2 Q.B. 226 (C.A.) Lord Denning MR made similar statements. The Eugenia had been chartered to take a cargo from the Black Sea to India. It was envisaged that the ship would go via the Suez Canal although there was no term in the contract to that effect and there was no time limit within which the voyage had to be completed. While the contract was being negotiated the Suez crisis arose. The two parties were aware of the risk and each suggested how the matter could be resolved if the Canal were to be closed but they could not agree on a solution and therefore the contract was silent as to the risk. The ship in fact entered the Canal and was caught there for several months.

The actual decision in the case was that the charterers had broken the contract by entering the Canal and had to pay damages to the owners for doing so. However, the court speculated on what the position would have been if there had been no breach. In particular would the contract have been frustrated or not, given that the parties were aware of the risks when the contract was concluded? Lord Denning said:

> "It has frequently been said that the doctrine of frustration only applies when the new situation is 'unforeseen' or 'uncontemplated', as if that were an essential feature. But it is not so. The only thing that is essential is that the parties should have made no provision for it in their contract. The only relevance of it being 'unforeseen' is this: If the parties did not foresee anything of the kind happening, you can readily infer they have made no provision for it: whereas, if they did foresee it, you would expect them to make provision for it. Such was the case in the Spanish Civil War when a ship was let on charter to the republican government. The purpose was to evacuate refugees. The parties foresaw that she might be seized by the nationalists. But they made no provision for it in their contract. Yet when it was seized, the contract was frustrated. . . . So here the parties foresaw that the canal might become impassable: it was the very thing they feared. But they made no provision for it. So there is room for the doctrine to apply if it be a proper case for it."

Despite these comments he then went on to say that if he had been called upon to answer the question as to whether the contract was frustrated he would have said not. The closure of the canal did not bring about a "fundamentally different situation". The voyage would take longer and be more expensive but it could still be accomplished even if the Canal were closed.

8. Anticipatory frustration

Contracts are frustrated when the frustrating event occurs and the parties' obligations cease from that moment. But what would be the situation if an event occurs which does not frustrate the contract immediately but the parties believe that it will in the near future? For instance in the case of *Embiricos v Sydney Reid & Co* [1914] 3 K.B. 45 a Greek ship was chartered for a voyage which would take it through the Dardanelles. War broke out between Greece and Turkey and the charterer decided to treat the contract as frustrated. In fact the Turks unexpectedly permitted vessels to "escape" through the Dardanelles for a period of time and this meant that the voyage would have been possible. Nevertheless the court held that the charterer's decision was justified. *At the time the decision was taken* it was a reasonable decision to take.

Sometimes the event may not be as clear cut as the outbreak of war between Greece and Turkey and the parties will have to wait until the position is clearer. For instance in the Iran-Iraq war a number of ships were detained in the Shatt al Arab. At first it was believed that the war would not last long and that the ships would soon be released. At that stage the contracts for the ships would not be frustrated. Only later when it became apparent that the detention would last much longer were the contracts frustrated.

In the Gulf War of 1991 a number of tour operators had clients in India. The holidays would not be directly affected by the outbreak of war but because flights would have to be re-routed around the prospective war zone it would adversely affect the holiday, adding much more travelling time and costing substantial amounts more to the operator. Assuming that such an event could frustrate the contract (and it is not beyond doubt) the question arises as to the point at which the tour operator would be justified in saying that the holiday was frustrated. Would it be when Kuwait was initially invaded? or when the United Nations decided to take action? or when the allied forces started a build up of forces? or when an outbreak of hostilities appeared imminent? or when war actually commenced? The law seems to be that even if hostilities had never broken out if it appeared to a reasonable person that holidays were about to be affected then a decision to treat the contract as frustrated would be justified. Foreign Office warnings would be relevant here. If they were unequivocal in their advice to avoid the area because of danger to overflying aircraft then a tour operator could rely on this to justify a decision not to perform the contract.

9. Hurricane Georges

In September 1998 Hurricane Georges hit the Caribbean. One of its effects was to disrupt the holidays of clients of Thomson Holidays. (*Norwegian Cruise Line Ltd v Thomson Holidays*, Q.B.D. November 29, 2000, reported on Westlaw) Thomson had a contract for a season with Norwegian Cruise Lines for their ship, the Norwegian Sea, to embark and disembark Thomson clients in Santo Domingo at seven day intervals. On September 27, because of the hurricane, it proved impossible to pick up 208 Thomson clients from Santo Domingo. The ship was, however, able to embark and disembark other Thomson clients at San Juan according to the usual schedule and to sail on an altered itinerary. Thomson claimed that the contract was frustrated because of the hurricane and wished to recover the money that had been pre-paid for the 208 passengers. The court said:

> "... while it may be that the contracts of individual passengers with THL were frustrated by their inability to join the vessel, the frustration of the whole cruise is a rather different concept.
>
> In *The Super Servant Two* [1990] 1 Lloyd's Rep. 1 Bingham LJ set out five truths in respect of frustration. The second and third truths as set out in Chitty at para 24-007 are that "*secondly, frustration operates to 'kill the contract and discharge the parties from further liability under it' and therefore it cannot be 'lightly invoked' but must be kept within 'very narrow limits and ought not to be extended.' Thirdly, frustration brings a contract to an end 'forthwith, without more and automatically.'*
>
> Clearly the ... contract was not killed 'forthwith' and THL does not contend that it was.
>
> While the concept of divisibility may be highly relevant to accrued rights of payment, I do not have the same ease of acceptance where it is sought to make two or more contracts out of one. Contracts are not like earthworms. If one is to have more than one contract, one must start with more than one contract. The ... contract comprised a series of obligations but it did not comprise a series of contracts. Accordingly the frustration claim fails."

Given that the contract extended for the whole season and only part of one cruise was affected the court was essentially saying that the hurricane had not done enough to destroy the contract—it remained largely capable of performance. Interestingly, if asked, the court may have been prepared to regard the individual package holiday contracts as frustrated but that was an issue which did not arise in the case—presumably because the passengers would have had more generous treatment under the Package Travel Regulations.

The Consequences of Frustration—The Common Law

Reasonable though it may seem at first glance to call off a contract because it has become impossible to perform there remains the equally difficult problem of how to sort out the consequences of the frustration. In *Taylor v Caldwell* for instance the owner of the hall would be excused from providing the hall rather than being in breach of contract but what about the hirer? Would he have still to pay for it and what about the losses that he would suffer by not being able to hold the concerts?

At common law the solution to such problems was to say that from the moment the contract was frustrated both parties were excused from any further obligation—but they remained liable for any obligations that had already accrued. The loss would lie where it fell. So for instance in *Krell v Henry* the contract was that £25 was to be paid immediately and another £50 two days before the procession. The procession was cancelled after the £25 was paid but before the £50 became due. It was held that the first payment was made while the contract was still valid and therefore could not be recovered by the hirer. On the other hand the second payment was not due until after the contract was frustrated and therefore need not be paid because the obligation to pay no longer existed.

If for some reason the hirer had not actually paid the deposit before the frustrating event even though he should have done so the owner could have sued him for it. It was an obligation which had arisen when the contract was still valid and therefore it could be validly claimed. The hirer would not have been permitted to take advantage of his own breach of contract.

The way the rule worked was entirely arbitrary. If the schedule of payments had been different then the risk could have fallen entirely on one or the other of the parties depending on just when the frustrating event occurred.

In *Appleby v Myers* (1867) L.R. 2 C.P. 651 the plaintiff had agreed to install some machinery in the defendant's factory. Before the work could be completed the factory burnt down. No money was payable until the job had been completed. The plaintiff therefore recovered nothing.

In *Cutter v Powell* the seaman had completed over half the voyage when he died. He was only due to be paid on completion of the voyage so his widow was entitled to nothing even though a substantial benefit had been obtained by the shipowner.

In 1943 the House of Lords developed an exception to the rule that if money had been paid before the frustrating event it could not be recovered. In *Fibrosa Spolka Akcyjna v Fairbairn Lawson Combe Barber Ltd* [1943] A.C. 32 a manufacturer agreed to sell machinery to the buyer for £4,800. The buyer paid £1000 in advance and the remainder was to be paid on delivery. Delivery was prevented by the outbreak of war and the contract was frustrated. The buyer, having paid £1000 received nothing in return. The House of Lords held that where there is a *total failure of consideration* by one party, *i.e.* the other gets nothing at all in return for his money then the buyer could recover his money.

Although the decision would be welcomed by the buyer it would have the opposite effect on the seller who had incurred considerable expense in building the machinery and would be paid nothing for that expense.

If these rules are applied to a package holiday context the results are quite interesting. If the client pays his deposit on booking and the contract is frustrated before the balance is due then the client will lose the deposit but will not have to pay any more. The tour operator is of course released from his obligation to provide the holiday. The position is much the same if the frustrating event occurs after the balance has been paid (or should have been paid). The client will lose his money but the tour operator will not have to provide the holiday.

But what if the contract is frustrated after the holiday has commenced? Suppose a tour operator had clients who had arrived in Russia for a two centre holiday in Moscow and Leningrad (now St Petersburg) just as the Russian government announced that the Chernobyl nuclear reactor had blown up. It would be impossible to travel to Leningrad for the second part of the holiday and to fly home from Leningrad airport as planned. Such circumstances could amount to a frustration of contract. This would mean that neither party would be under any further obligation to each other. The clients would lose their money and the tour operator could walk away from the contract saying that he was no longer under an obligation to do anything more for them! It is for this reason of course that most holiday contracts provide for what will happen in such circumstances.

The Consequences of Frustration—The Law Reform (Frustrated Contracts) Act 1943

The unsatisfactory position at common law for dealing with the consequences of frustration led to the passage of The Law Reform (Frustrated Contracts) Act 1943. Broadly speaking the Act provides means by which the risks of frustration can be apportioned between the parties. The rules are not entirely free from criticism but they are better than the old common law rules which they replace in most cases. There are contracts which are not covered by the Act but they do not include holiday contracts.

1. Money paid or payable

Section 1(2) provides:

> "1(2) All sums paid or payable to any party in pursuance of the contract before the time when the parties were so discharged (in this Act referred to as 'the time of discharge') shall, in the case of sums so paid, be recoverable from him as money received by him for the use of the party by whom the sums were paid, and, in the case of sums so payable, cease to be so payable:
>
> Provided that, if the party to whom the sums were so paid or payable incurred expenses before the time of discharge in, or for the purpose of, the performance of the contract, the court may, if it considers it just to do so having regard to all the circumstances of the case, allow him to retain or, as the case may be, recover the whole or any part of the sums so paid or payable, not being an amount in excess of the expenses so incurred."

This does two things. First it states that if one party has paid money to the other party, or was due to pay money to the other party, before the contract was frustrated then they can recover the money already paid, and\or keep the money they were due to pay.

Secondly, however, it says that if the other party has already incurred expenses in the performance of the contract these expenses can be claimed out of the money already paid or payable but only if the court thinks it just to do so.

Take for instance the *Fibrosa case*. In that case £1000 had already been paid in advance before the contract was frustrated. Under section 1(2) that money could be claimed back (as it could under the common law) but it would be subject to the court's discretion as to whether it would be just to permit the manufacturer of the machinery to retain some of the money for any expenses incurred. If the machinery had been specially built for the buyer and could not be resold elsewhere then one can imagine that a court would be tempted to make a large deduction for expenses out of the £1000. It would be different if the machinery was in high demand and it could be sold to another buyer without loss.

It should be noted, however, that the maximum that can be claimed for expenses is the amount paid or payable before the frustrating event. Even if the manufacturer had expended almost the whole contract price in building the machinery he would get no more than what was due when the contract was frustrated.

Applying this rule to tour operators what would be the situation if a contract was frustrated after the deposit had been paid but before the balance? First, the client is entitled to recover the amount of his deposit. Secondly the operator is entitled to have any expenses he has incurred taken into account if the court thinks it just to do so. If the operator has already laid out money on transport and accommodation then this could be set against the deposit. Presumably the court would enquire whether this money was recoverable by the operator from the suppliers concerned. If it could be then it would not count as expenses. On the other hand the Act specifically provides in section 1(4) that a reasonable sum for overhead expenses can be taken into account. However establishing that expenses have been incurred is one thing, convincing a court that it would be just to recover them is another. It is not beyond the bounds of possibility to imagine a court saying that the operator is better placed than the client to bear the risk of the frustration and that it would be just to permit the client to recover the whole of his deposit. On the other hand the operator might equally argue that the prepayment is a form of insurance designed specifically to protect him against such eventualities and therefore he should be able to retain all his expenses.

Frustration after departure would increase the chances of the operator having incurred expenses which he would not be able to recover. He would still have to show however that it would be just to recover them. Where the client has not only paid the whole of the holiday price but is stranded abroad and is facing the expense of getting himself home would it be just to permit the operator to claim his expenses from the price of the holiday? In such circumstances it might be necessary to take into account section 1(3).

2. Benefits received

Section 1(3) provides:

> "1(3) Where any party to the contract has, by reason of anything done by any other party thereto in, or for the purpose of, the performance of the contract, obtained a valuable benefit (other than a payment of money to which the last foregoing subsection applies) before the time of discharge, there shall be recoverable from him by the said other party such sum (if any), not exceeding the value of the said benefit to the party obtaining it, as the court considers just, having regard to all the circumstances of the case and, in particular,—
>
> (a) the amount of any expenses incurred before the time of discharge by the benefited party in, or for the purpose of, the performance o the contract, including any sums paid or payable by him to any other party in pursuance of the contract and retained or recoverable by that party under the last foregoing subsection, and
>
> (b) the effect, in relation to the said benefit, of the circumstances giving rise to the frustration of the contract."

What this means is that in cases like *Cutter v Powell* where one party has conferred a benefit on the other party before the frustrating event occurs the value of this benefit can be awarded by the court if it feels it would be just to do so.

Whether it would apply to cases like *Appleby v Myers* is debatable. Although a large part of the machinery had been installed by the plaintiffs it was all destroyed in the fire. In such circumstances it could be argued that the other party obtained no benefit from the contract and therefore could not be awarded anything for it.

In package holidays where the contract is frustrated before departure this section will have little relevance but if the contract is frustrated after departure then it may have some impact. To return to the example of the two centre holiday in Russia. If the client has been transported abroad and spent a week in Moscow before being told that the contract is frustrated it could be said that he had obtained a valuable benefit. If so, a value has to be put on the benefit and the tour operator can make a claim for an amount which does not exceed this value. Whether this will be awarded by the court depends upon whether it is considered just to do so.

However, the court also has to take into account the fact that the client has already paid in full for the holiday and will be reclaiming all this under section 1(2) but that the tour operator will also be claiming his expenses out of this amount. Additionally the fact that the frustrating event has left the client high and dry in Moscow has to be taken into account.

It would be open to the client to say in these circumstances that the tour operator could not claim to be paid both for his expenses under section 1(2) *and* for the part of the holiday that the client received in Moscow under section 1(3) given that the client is now having to make his own way home.

Section 1(3)(a) might have relevance in some cases where for instance, as a requirement of the contract the client had purchased equipment in advance of the holiday, *e.g.* a motor cycle touring holiday that required the client to provide his own motorbike or a skiing holiday that required the client to provide his own skis or the trekking holiday that required hiking equipment. All these would be expenses incurred for the purpose of the performance of the contract. It might also cover situations where the client had to purchase services in advance—such as scuba diving lessons to bring him up to a minimum standard for a diving holiday.

3. Insurance

Section 1(5) provides:

> "1(5) In considering whether any sum ought to be recovered or retained under the foregoing provisions of this section by any party to the contract, the court shall not take into account any sums which have, by reason of the circumstances giving rise to the frustration of the contract become payable to that party under any contract of insurance unless there was an obligation to insure imposed by an express term of the frustrated contract or by or under any enactment."

What this means is that if one party has had the foresight to take out insurance to cover the frustrating event then this will *not* be taken into account when assessing how to apportion the losses *unless* it was an express term of the contract that insurance be taken out.

What this means is that *if* a tour operator makes it compulsory for a client to take out an insurance policy to cover frustrating events and there is a payment by the insurance company then the court may take this into account. So for instance if the policy provides that in the event of a strike by air traffic controllers the client can cancel and get a refund then the operator could argue that in these circumstances they should be able to reclaim their full expenses.

4. Apportionment in practice—the *Guns 'n' Roses* case

There is remarkably little case law on the effect of the Law Reform (Frustrated Contracts) Act but one case which illustrates its operation vividly is *Gamerco SA v ICM/Fair Warning (Agency) Limited* [1995] E.M.L.R. 263. The facts of the case were that the rock group, Guns 'n' Roses were due to perform at a football stadium in Madrid but shortly before the concert took place the stadium was found to be unsafe and use of it was prohibited. This had the effect of frustrating the contract between the promoters of the concert and the first defendants, Guns 'n' Roses. The promoters had promised to pay the group $1.1 million or 90 per cent of the gate receipts, whichever was greater. By the time the contract was frustrated the plaintiffs had paid $412,000 on account and were due to pay another $362,000—both payments net of tax. Both parties had incurred expenses in or for the purpose of the performance of the contract. The judge held that, applying s.1(2) of the Act, the plaintiffs were entitled to the return of the $412,000. However he also had to consider whether the defendants could retain any money out of that pre-payment to cover their expenses under section 1(3). In deciding this question he concluded that the Act gave him a very wide discretion:

> "I see no indication in the Act, the authorities, or the relevant literature that the court is obliged to incline either towards total retention or equal division. Its task is to do justice in a situation which the parties neither contemplated nor provided for, and to mitigate the possible harshness of allowing all loss to lie where it has fallen."

After taking into account a number of matters:

- the defendants had incurred $50,000 of expenses;
- the plaintiff had incurred in excess of $450,000 of expenses;
- neither party had conferred a benefit on the other;
- both parties' expenditure was wasted;
- the plaintiff was only concerned with one contract whereas the defendants had contracts for 20 concerts; and
- although both parties were insured he was not entitled to take account of this by virtue of s.1(5) of the Act

he decided that the defendants could not retain any of the prepayment.

The Package Travel Regulations

The Package Travel Regulations do not mention frustration of contract as such, nor do they state what the relationship between the Regulations and the Law Reform (Frustrated Contracts) Act is. What they do cover are:

> "... unusual and unforeseeable circumstances beyond the control of the party by whom ... [it] ... is pleaded, the consequences of which could not have been avoided even if all due care had been exercised."

These circumstances will be referred to, for the sake of convenience, as *force majeure* events. The EC Directive on which the Regulations are based specifically refers to *force majeure* but this terminology has been omitted from the Regulations. If these circumstances occur then the Regulations provide what the consequences will be. In many cases what would be a frustrating event at common law will also be a *force majeure* event under the Regulations. The position therefore will be that where an event occurs which is both a frustrating event and a *force majeure* event then the Regulations will govern the matter because they were passed specifically to deal with package holidays and will therefore take precedence over the common law and the LR(FC)A 1943 which are more general provisions. If, however an event occurs which is not a *force majeure* event, then the common law and the LR(FC)A 1943 apply.

This section will look first at what a *force majeure* event is and how it can be distinguished from a frustrating event; and secondly at how the consequences of a *force majeure* event are provided for in the Regulations.

1. Force majeure events

The definition of *force majeure* given above is to be found in Regulation 13(3)(b) and Regulation 15(2)(c)(i). It provides limited immunity for a tour operator who cancels a package holiday or fails to perform it properly—but only if the definition can be satisfied. To do this the operator has to show that the circumstances were:

- Unusual;
- Unforeseeable;
- beyond the control of the operator;
- the consequences of which could not have been avoided;
- even if all due care had been exercised.

The requirements are cumulative. It would not be sufficient to show that something was unusual if it was not also unforeseeable.

Many of the frustrating events already examined would probably fall within the definition. For instance if the Suez Canal was closed preventing a cruise ship from proceeding from the Mediterranean to the Red Sea this would be a *force majeure* event which also frustrated the contract. Similarly, war breaking out in Yugoslavia or civil unrest in Beijing or earthquakes in Turkey would fall within both categories. But what about air traffic controllers' strikes? At common law such an event would almost certainly frustrate the contract if it went on long enough but under the much tighter definition in the Regulations it *might* fail to be classified as a *force majeure* event. The reason for this is that it might not be unusual nor even unforeseeable. Such events happen with sufficient frequency that a court might conceivably come to the conclusion that it was not a *force majeure* event. If this was the case the rules to be applied would be the common law rules and the LR(FC)A 1943 but not the Package Travel Regulations.

A problem might also arise in relation to civil unrest in Sri Lanka. For many years there were incidents which have affected the tourist industry. Any tour operator taking clients to Sri Lanka in such circumstances might be unable to plead *force majeure* if the situation deteriorated to such an extent that the holiday had to be cancelled. Could the operator deny that the unrest causing the cancellation was unforeseeable? (See Cons LJ [1994] C555 for an example of how a situation such as this was treated by the German courts.)

The problem arises over the word "unforeseeable". If one uses enough imagination almost nothing is unforeseeable. Even without a lot of imagination most tour operators have experienced sufficient problems in the past to be aware of a whole range of events that could affect a typical package holiday. Does such knowledge and experience mean that any time an event which has occurred in the past occurs again then this was a "foreseeable" event and therefore does not amount to *force majeure*.

For instance, does the fact that hurricanes have happened in the past in Florida and the Caribbean mean that such events are foreseeable to a tour operator? Does the fact that a nuclear reactor once exploded near Leningrad and another almost exploded at Three Mile Island in America mean that it is foreseeable that holidays to both Russia and America could be affected by nuclear explosions?

These events may very well be foreseeable if one thinks about it long enough but on a spectrum of foreseeability they are clearly at the bottom end. They could not be said to be "reasonably foreseeable" and certainly they would not be "foreseen" by a tour operator. Unless the definition is to lose much of its impact it would be better to interpret "foreseeable" as having a more restricted meaning such as "reasonably foreseeable". Not to do so would rob the Regulations of effect in just the kind of circumstances that it was clearly intended to cover. (This passage, which first appeared in the first edition, was noted with approval in the Argentine case—*Giambelluca, Emilia v Nabil Travel Service et al*, L. 342247, Buenos Aires, July 11, 2002.)

The effect of a *frustrating event* is to *discharge* the contract, *i.e.* the contract will cease to exist as far as future obligations are concerned and the parties will be excused from further performance. This is because the whole contract has become impossible to perform. Except in very limited circumstances there is no such thing as a partial frustration of a contract. It is all or nothing. However, when a *force majeure* event occurs although in many circumstances it will be sufficiently serious to discharge the contract nothing in the Regulations states that a *force majeure* event *discharges* the contract. The event may fit within the definition and not actually discharge the contract. For instance what if during a 30-day touring holiday of Europe terrorists occupy the Louvre and clients cannot visit the museum on that day. This would amount to a *force majeure* event but it would not frustrate the contract.

In such circumstances the rules on frustration would not apply at all. Either the rules on *force majeure* in the Regulations would apply or the operator would be in breach of contract.

2. The consequences of a force majeure event

Pre-departure Cancellations and Withdrawals

Regulation 13 provides that where a holiday is cancelled or where the client has withdrawn because the operator has made a major change to the holiday the client will not only be entitled to a full refund or substitute holiday (see Chapter Ten on Remedies) but also compensation. However there are exceptions to this. One is that where the package has been cancelled for reasons of *force majeure* compensation is not payable. This places a client in a much better position than he would be under the LR(FC)A 1943. Under the LR(FC)A 1943 any money already paid over would be subject to a deduction for expenses at the court's discretion. If the event was not a *force majeure* event because it was foreseeable the Regulations would not apply and the client would have to rely on the LR(FC)A 1943 for assistance.

Post-departure Problems

Regulation 14 does not mention *force majeure* or frustration of contract at all but it will clearly have an impact in such situations. It provides that there is an *implied term in the contract* that where a tour operator is unable to provide a significant proportion of the services contracted for he shall make suitable alternative arrangements for the clients and if necessary transport the clients back to their place of departure. In "appropriate" cases compensation should also be paid.

This provision will come into operation whenever a significant proportion of the services cannot be provided—whether that is due to a frustrating event or not. If it is not a frustrating event then what the Regulation does is to provide additional remedies to the client when the operator is in breach of contract. If it is a frustrating event then the position is a considerably more complex and it depends upon the nature of the relationship between Regulation 14 and s.2(3) of the LR(FC)A.

You will remember that what section 2(3) states is that if there is a *term in the contract* that is intended to take effect in the event of a frustrating event occurring then that term will be enforced by the court rather than the court applying the provisions of s.1 of the LR(FC)A—but only if the term is inconsistent with the LR(FC)A.

By virtue of Regulation 14 there is certainly a term (albeit implied) in the contract that states that in the event of the tour operator being unable to provide a significant proportion of the services promised then he will have to make suitable alternative arrangements or bring the consumer home. It is reasonable to assume that this term is intended to take effect in the event of a frustrating event occurring. Therefore the term implied by Regulation 14 will take precedence over the consequences laid down by s.1 of the LR(FC)A—but only where they are inconsistent with those consequences.

That leaves the problem of interpreting the implied term in Regulation 14. Is it in fact saying: "In circumstances where a contract would normally be discharged for frustration this will not happen—the contract will not be discharged. Instead the contract must be performed in a different way by the tour operator, *i.e.* he can fulfill his obligations under the contract by offering you a suitable alternative or by bringing you home?" Or is it saying: "If a frustrating event occurs then the contract will be discharged and the *consequences of the frustration* will be that the tour operator will have to provide a suitable alternative or take you home?" If the former interpretation is preferred then the rules in section 1 of the LR(FC)A cannot be applied at all because what the implied term is saying is that the contract is not frustrated therefore the rules about apportioning the loss in the event of a frustration cannot be applied. If the latter interpretation is preferred then what will happen is that the courts will apply the remedies in Regulation 14 and also the rules in s.1 but only if those rules are not inconsistent with Regulation 14.

In such a complex situation it is difficult to offer any real guidance but if pushed we would prefer the former meaning. First, because Regulation 14 states that the tour operator must offer suitable alternative arrangements for *the continuation of the package*. These words suggest that the contract will continue in existence (although the performance of it will be varied). Secondly the remedies in Regulation 14 apply not only to events which frustrate the contract but also to events which fall short of frustration, *i.e.* circumstances where the contract clearly does continue and therefore it would be better to adopt an interpretation of Regulation 14 that applied consistently to both these circumstances. Thirdly, to adopt this interpretation would be the simpler approach—it would not involve the difficulties of determining whether the provisions of Regulation 14 were consistent with the provisions of s.1 of the LR(FC)A.

So what does all this mean in practice? To go back to the example of the two centre holiday in Russia which is frustrated when Chernobyl blows up. If it were simply a matter of the common law and the LR(FC)A 1943 the position would be that both parties are excused from further performance. Additionally the client is entitled to all his money back subject to deductions for expenses and for benefits already received at the discretion of the court—bearing in mind that the frustration has left the client stranded in Russia without accommodation or flights. However, if our interpretation of the Regulations is correct then the common law and the LR(FC)A becomes irrelevant and all a court would have to do is apply Regulation 14—a much more simple and straightforward situation.

The Regulation also provides that compensation is payable in "appropriate" circumstances. This will mean that the operator will have to pay compensation if the non-provision of the services was somehow due to his fault but not if the reason falls within one of the exceptions to Regulation 15(1) found in Regulation 15(2)—in particular *force majeure*. This is dealt with below.

Faced with a serious *force majeure event* therefore, the tour operator must not abandon his customers but must at least repatriate them. Compensation however would not be appropriate.

Liability for Non-performance and Improper Performance of the Contract

Regulation 15 provides that a tour operator is liable for damage caused to the client by failure to perform the contract or the improper performance of the contract except in certain circumstances. One of those exceptions is when a *force majeure* event has occurred.

We have already seen that where a package holiday contract is cancelled before performance or where major changes have been made and the client has withdrawn under Regulation 13 then if this is caused by a *force majeure* event the client can have a refund but no compensation. Similarly under Regulation 14 if what causes the non-provision of services is a a *force majeure* event then no compensation will be payable because Regulation 15 states that the operator is not liable in such circumstances.

The relationship between Regulation 14 and Regulation 15 and the issue of *force majeure* was discussed in the case of *Charlson & Brooks-Jones v Mark Warner Limited* (West London County Court December 1999) (2000 [ITLJ] 196). The claimants were claiming breach of contract of a skiing holiday because the holiday had to be curtailed by extreme bad weather and they had to be evacuated and flown home early. The breach alleged was that the holiday was not provided as promised. The defendants had included in their terms and conditions a "*force majeure*" clause very similarly drafted to Regulation 15(2)(c)(i). On the facts the judge held that the adverse weather conditions could not have been predicted by the defendants and they were protected by both their standard clause and by Regulation 15(2)(c)(i). He went on to discuss the claimant's argument that they were also protected by Regulation 14:

> "The claimants also rely upon paragraph 14 of the regulations which is the provision giving holidaymakers a right to suitable alternative arrangements at no extra cost if it is not possible to perform the contract. I do not find that this is of any assistance to the claimants. I accept the defendant's submissions that paragraph 14 is dependent upon paragraph 15 and has to be read conjunctively. I accept that paragraphs 14 and 15 provide different remedies but are subject to the same exclusion contained in paragraph 15(2) sub-paragraph (c)."

This seems to bear out the comments above, that compensation is not payable under Regulation 14 if it would not be available under Regulation 15.

The ABTA Code of Conduct

The ABTA Code of Conduct (February 2003 edition) contains provisions relating to *force majeure*. The Code requires ABTA tour operators to insert terms in the contract providing for what will happen if a *force majeure* event occurs. Although the Code refers specifically to *force majeure* and defines what it means it should be noted that it does not mean the same thing as *force majeure* in the Package Travel Regulations. Nor does it mean the same thing as frustration of contract at common law. For this reason and to avoid confusion it will be referred to as "Code of Conduct *force majeure*".

If an ABTA operator has complied with the Code the question arises as to how the clause in the contract is affected by and relates to the LR(FC)A 1943 and the Package Travel Regulations. This will depend in part on how Code of Conduct *force majeure* is actually defined and in what circumstances the provisions will be applied.

1. Meaning of Code of Conduct *force majeure*

Force majeure is defined in the Code as meaning:

> "circumstances where performance and/or prompt performance of the contract is prevented by reasons of war, or threat of war, riot, civil strife, industrial dispute [which is defined elsewhere], terrorist activity, natural or nuclear disaster, fire or adverse weather conditions."

This definition clearly extends further than events which would frustrate the contract at common law because it extends to events which not only prevent the whole of the performance of the contract but also to those which only prevent the prompt performance of the contract. Whereas an air traffic controllers strike which wiped out two days of a long weekend in Paris would frustrate such a contract it is unlikely that it would frustrate a three week holiday to Florida.

2. The consequences of Code of Conduct *force majeure*

Since the Code was re-drafted in 2003 the differences between the Code and the Regulations have considerably narrowed but have not disappeared altogether.

Pre-departure Cancellation

Paragraph 2.1 of the Code provides that if the tour operator has to cancel a package before departure because of *force majeure* the client should be offered either a full refund or an alternative holiday.

Pre-departure Alterations

Paragraph 2.2 provides that if a significant alteration has to be made to a holiday prior to departure for reasons of *force majeure* then the client must be offered the choice of accepting the change or cancelling and receiving a full refund or taking alternative arrangements of a comparable standard.

Post-departure Changes

The Code has no equivalent to Regulation 14 but under Paragraph 2.6 if there is an improper performance of the contract caused by *force majeure* the tour operator need not pay compensation.

3. The relationship between Code of Conduct *force majeure*, frustration of contract and *force majeure* under the Package Travel Regulations

We have already seen that where both the Package Travel Regulations and the LR(FC)A 1943 apply then the Regulations take precedence but there are still situations where only one set of rules applies. The position with the Code of Conduct provisions is that where they are inconsistent with the Regulations the Regulations will take precedence and that where they are inconsistent with the LR(FC)A 1943 the provisions in the Code will take precedence. The reason for this is that, as already discussed earlier in this chapter, where the parties to the contract actually provide for what will happen in the event of a frustrating event occurring the wishes of the parties will prevail (s.2(3) of the LR(FC)A).

Potentially this leaves an extremely complex situation where an event could be governed by only one set of rules or by any combination of two or three sets. In practice however the position is relatively simple. The following examples help to illustrate the situation.

Illustration One

A volcano erupts unexpectedly two days before departure and the resort is destroyed by lava.

Technically this would fall within all three categories. It would be a frustrating event, a *force majeure* event and a Code of Conduct *force majeure* event. However, because the Regulations will apply there is no need to go further. The position would be that under Regulation 13 the client would be entitled to be offered an alternative holiday or a full refund but would not be entitled to compensation.

Illustration Two

On arrival in resort clients cannot be accommodated in their hotel for the first two days of their 14 day holiday because there has been an unexpectedly ferocious storm which flooded the hotel.

This is not a frustrating event because it is not sufficiently serious to discharge the whole contract therefore the common law rules on frustration and the LR(FC)A 1943 do not apply. The provisions of the Code of Conduct do not apply because the Code's *force majeure* provisions do not apply to post-departure problems except to deny compensation, as under Regulation 15.

It is almost certainly a *force majeure* event and therefore the Regulations apply. As this is a post-departure problem it is Regulation 14 and 15 that apply. Regulation 14 requires the tour operator to make suitable alternative arrangements at no cost to the clients when a significant proportion of the services contracted for cannot be provided. Regulation 15 makes the operator liable for damage caused to the clients by failure to perform the contract or the improper performance of the contract. However they are not liable to pay damages where the failure is caused by a *force majeure* event. Thus the client is entitled to have suitable alternative arrangements made but will receive no compensation.

Illustration Three

A group of holidaymakers arrive at Luton airport to be told at check-in that there is an air traffic controllers' strike and they will be 24 hours late taking off for their two week holiday in the Caribbean. This is the third such lightning strike of the summer. The unions involved had warned that they would take industrial action if their pay claim was not settled to their satisfaction.

This is a pre-departure problem. It is probably not a frustrating event because it is not substantial enough to merit discharging the whole contract. Thus the LR(FC)A 1943 will not apply. However Regulations 12 and 13 will apply but only if the days delay can be seen as a significant alteration to an essential term—which it probably will be. An alteration of 24 hours in the time of departure would be regarded as significant by most consumers. This means that the consumer will have the option of withdrawing or being offered a suitable alternative if one is available. At that stage it is unlikely that they will withdraw and it is probably also the case that a suitable alternative cannot be found. Thus they will take off a day late and the tour operator will be faced with a claim under Regulation 15 for improper performance of the contract. Can the tour operator plead *force majeure* as a defence?

It may not be regarded as a *force majeure* event because it is not "unforeseeable". On the face of it therefore the operator has failed to perform the contract properly and is liable under Regulation 15(2) to the consumer for the damage caused. However, even though the strike is not a *force majeure* event it could nevertheless be an event which could not be forestalled by the operator and therefore under Regulation 15(2)(c)(ii) the operator will not have to pay damages.

Under the Code of Conduct it is a *force majeure* event—it is an industrial dispute which prevents the "prompt performance of the contract". As such under Paragraph 2.2 it would give the consumer the right to alternative arrangements or a full refund—essentially placing them in the same position as under the Regulations.

Illustration Four

Consumers purchase a package holiday to Rio to see the Carnival. The package is for flights, accommodation and meals but there is nothing in the contract about the Carnival. Identical packages are available from the same tour operator at other times of the year. The clients, however, specifically stated to the tour operator when booking that their sole reason for travelling was to see the Carnival. When they arrive Carnival is cancelled because of the death of the President and the whole country is in mourning. All the services the tour operator promised in the contract are still available.

Regulations 14 and 15 do not apply. Regulation 14 is only triggered if a significant proportion of *the services contracted for* are not supplied. All the services contracted for will still be supplied. Regulation 15 requires a proper performance of the *obligations under the contract*. There has been no improper performance therefore Regulation 15 is inapplicable. Nevertheless the clients are not getting what they wanted—to see the Carnival. There is an outside chance that under the principle established in *Krell v Henry* the clients may be able to claim the contract is frustrated. In practical terms however this may not be the best way forward. It would leave them with no rights to further accommodation or meals or return flight and subject to the rules on apportionment of loss under the LR(FC)A 1943. It might perhaps be better simply to enjoy the delights of the Copacabana and put it down to experience. (See Grant, "It's not Cricket", [1998] ITLJ 51).

If the Carnival was cancelled before travel then the only difference would be that it would be Regulation 13 that would be inapplicable. This Regulation is only triggered by significant alterations to essential terms of the contract and if no term has been altered then the regulation cannot be invoked. From the clients' point of view they would not have any rights under the PTR and would still be faced with the problem of the LR(FC)A 1943 if they chose not to travel and wanted a refund.

CHAPTER TEN
Remedies

INTRODUCTION

When one of the parties to a contract breaks it the other party, the victim of the breach is entitled to a remedy, *i.e.* the law will require the contract breaker to put things right in some way. By far the most common remedy is when the court orders the contract breaker to pay damages—a sum of money to compensate the victim for the breach of contract. For really serious breaches of contract the victim also has another remedy—the right to terminate the contract—but this can only be done when there has been a breach of condition (a major term of the contract) rather than a breach of warranty. (For the difference between these two terms you should refer back to Chapter Four on Terms of the Contract.) Remember that for misrepresentation the victim has a range of remedies discussed fully in Chapter Seven.

There are other remedies such as specific performance and injunctions but these are highly unlikely to be awarded in a package holiday case. Specific performance is where a court orders one party to the contract to actually perform the contract as promised. An injunction is when the court orders one party not to break the contract. Generally they are only awarded by a court when damages would not be appropriate, where the subject matter of the contract is rare or unique and where there is no element of personal service involved. Given that damages will usually be a sufficient remedy in holiday cases that will almost inevitably rule out specific performance or an injunction. However, having said that, these two remedies will not generally be available to package holidaymakers, the Package Travel Regulations do provide remedies under Regulations 13 and 14 which are remarkably similar to specific performance and there is a further remedy under Regulation 14 which also requires performance in kind rather than cash. Under Regulation 13 if a tour operator has made a significant alteration to an essential term the consumer is entitled to be offered a suitable alternative if one is available. Likewise under Regulation 14 if the tour operator is unable to provide a significant proportion of the services after departure than he must make suitable alternative arrangements for the consumer at no extra cost. Also under

Regulation 14 if the tour operator finds it impossible to make suitable arrangements he must return the consumer to his point of departure.

In this chapter we will look first at the rules governing the award of damages—including the award of damages to the tour operator when the consumer breaks the contract—and then we will examine the remedies available under Regulations 13 and 14.

DAMAGES

Introduction

Damages in holiday cases are awarded under two broad headings. First for the difference in value between what the client was promised and what he actually received. Secondly for consequential loss, *i.e.* further loss caused by the breach of contract. Under this latter heading there are a number of sub-headings. It encompasses not only out of pocket expenses such as the cost of taxis from the airport when the transfer bus is not provided but also damages for distress, damages for physical discomfort and damages for personal injury.

It will become apparent that precise calculation of damages is impossible and even the most able practitioners often come unstuck in their predictions. It is an art rather than a science. The greatest difficulties arise over the award of damages for distress, which are, by their very nature, incapable of measurement in monetary terms. The difficulty of putting any figure at all on distress is compounded by the very subjective nature of the damage. Some clients are phlegmatic in the face of all difficulties whilst others suffer extremes of disappointment when faced with the slightest problem. Often the degree of distress suffered is not apparent to the tour operator until the client enters the witness box where the impression created, whether favourable or otherwise, is sometimes a determining factor in the level of damages awarded. This is one way perhaps of understanding the surprisingly high award made to the plaintiffs in *Clarke & Greenwood v Airtours* [1995] C.L.Y. 1603 and the low award in *Morris v Carisma Holidays* [1997] 4 CL 215.

The problems, however, are not confined to damages for distress. Even a simple calculation of difference in value can be fraught with difficulties. For instance, if the accommodation provided is so abysmal that it ruins the whole holiday how should the loss be calculated? Should the approach be to say that as the accommodation blighted the whole holiday then the whole holiday price should be refunded or could it be said that as the price of the accommodation amounted to say 30 per cent of the cost of the holiday (as is often the case when a flight is also included) then only 30 per cent should be refunded under this head? Often the answer to this question is inextricably bound up with what has been awarded by way of damages for distress and the two cannot be disentangled from each other.

Basic principles

Damages for breach of contract are intended to put the plaintiff "so far as money can do it . . . in the same situation . . . as if the contract had been performed" (*Robinson v Harman* (1848) 1 Ex 850, 855). In other words, damages are compensatory, not punitive. What this means in practice is that if the client can establish that he was promised a room with a balcony and his room did not have a balcony he will be awarded a sum of money equivalent to the value of having the room upgraded. This is intended to put him in the same position, financially, as if the contract had been performed. However, to do this properly he will also need to be compensated for any distress which he suffered as a result of the breach. Only then can he be considered to be in the same position as if the contract had been performed properly.

Coupled with the rule that the client should be put in the same position as if the contract had been performed is another rule on remoteness of damage. This rule was formulated in the case of *Hadley v Baxendale* (1854) 9 Exch. 341 and will be examined in more detail later. For the present it is sufficient to say that a tour operator will have to pay damages for breaches of contract that lead to damage which is within the reasonable contemplation of the parties but not otherwise. For instance, if a breach of contract consisted of failure to provide the promised swimming pool and as a consequence the client decided to swim in the sea and was eaten by sharks this would be regarded as too remote a consequence of the breach. On the other hand it might not be too remote a consequence of the tour operator's failure to provide the swimming pool if it was known to the tour operator that sea water in the resort was contaminated by sewage and clients contracted a nasty disease from swimming in the polluted sea water.

There is one further rule which will be examined and that is on mitigation of loss. If a client suffers from breach of contract he is under a duty to take reasonable steps to mitigate his loss. He cannot just sit back and wait for the damages to roll in; he must endeavour, so far as can reasonably be expected of him, to reduce his losses. So for instance if the holiday is defective in some way then the least that he can be expected to do is to complain. Often a complaint to the representative is sufficient to get things sorted out. Failure to complain in such circumstances, when something could have been done, will result in a loss of compensation for the client.

Difference in value claims

There are numerous cases on diminution in value. One leading example is *Jackson v Horizon Holidays* [1975] 3 All E.R. 92. (For the facts see Chapter Eight on Privity of Contract.) It is very typical of holiday claims and therefore much relied upon by County Courts—more so in fact than its more famous counterpart *Jarvis v Swan Tours*. The plaintiff was awarded £1100 damages on a holiday that cost £1200. The sum was initially awarded by a judge in the County Court who did not break the figure down into component parts. In the Court of Appeal Lord Denning commented upon the award and said:

> "If I were inclined myself to speculate, I think the suggestion of counsel for Mr Jackson may well be right. The judge took the cost of the holiday at £1200. The family only had about half the value of it. Divide it by two and you get £600. Then add £500 for the mental distress."

Another straightforward case is *McLeod v Hunter* [1987] C.L.Y. 1162 where £439 was awarded when the defendant substituted a cramped apartment for a luxurious villa. This was in addition to a sum for distress and disappointment.

In *Levine v Metropolitan Travel* [1980] C.L.Y. 638 the defendants argued that as the holiday was a cheap one then the damages for diminution in value should be correspondingly small. The judge rejected this argument and awarded damages for difference in value at £200 on a holiday costing £323. £200 was also awarded for "assault on feelings". The report is brief and it is difficult to work out precisely the principles the judge was applying. However, reading between the lines, what it seems to be saying is that if you pay £300 for a late-saver bargain holiday that would normally cost, say £400, at full brochure price, then you are entitled to damages based on £400 not £300. To do otherwise would deprive you of your bargain. You bought a holiday worth £400 and therefore if what you are getting is only worth £200 you should get £200 damages because that is the difference between the value of what you purchased and what you received. On the other hand if the holiday is only worth £300 and that is what you paid for it then damages will only be assessed on the lower figure.

Most disputes that arise are connected with the accommodation. Strictly speaking, even if the accommodation is totally inadequate, the court should only award the cost of the accommodation under this head of damages. However the cost of the accommodation doesn't necessarily bear any relation to its importance to the success of the holiday. The holiday might be totally ruined by the lack of suitable accommodation yet it may nevertheless amount to only 30 per cent of the holiday price. Refunding this to the client will not appear adequate in his eyes for accommodation which blighted the whole holiday.

There are two ways of approaching this problem. One is to view the holiday as a whole and to say that a holiday which is so blighted is worth nothing, therefore the whole holiday price should be returned. Damages for distress and disappointment would be awarded in addition to this. The other is to say that the damages for loss of accommodation should be calculated by awarding the value of the accommodation but the loss should also be reflected in the damages for distress and disappointment.

Consequential loss—out of pocket expenses

The client will be able to recover reasonable out of pocket expenses incurred because of the breach of contract by the tour operator. Obvious examples include the cost of meals taken in local restaurants where the hotel food provided as part of the package was inedible; or alternative accommodation where the original was uninhabitable. In *Harris v Torchgrove* [1985] C.L.Y. 944 the plaintiff received £40 for car parking fees because the promised parking at the apartment was not available and £300 was awarded for the cost of extra meals because the apartment had no oven and the fridge was "eccentric". In *Davey v Cosmos* [1989] C.L.Y. 2561 an award included a sum for ruined clothing when the plaintiffs suffered from diarrhoea and dysentery on holiday.

Note that where, for instance, the client purchases meals from a restaurant because the hotel meals are inedible he will not be able to claim both for the difference in value and for the out of pocket expenses. If this were permitted he would be compensated twice over.

One claim often included in this category is loss of earnings. A plaintiff is not entitled to claim loss of earnings for the time he was on holiday, on the alleged ground that the holiday was a waste of time and used up their holiday leave entitlement. This point was specifically addressed in *Jarvis v Swans Tours Ltd* [1973] 1 All E.R. 71 by Stephenson LJ who said

> "I would add that I think the judge was right in rejecting the plaintiff's ingenious claim, however it is put, for a fortnight's salary." (But see Grant, Damages for Distress, Trading Law, Vol 5 No 7, 293; see also *Hartman v P&O* [1998] C.L.Y. 3732).

However, there is authority that where a plaintiff genuinely has salary deducted because a flight delay or overbooking made him late back for work they are likely to be able to recover this (*Harvey v Tracks Travel* [1984] C.L.Y. 1006; *Graham v Sunsetridge* [1989] C.L.Y. 1189; *Taylor v ITS* [1984] C.L.Y. 1023).

Where a holiday has been cancelled by the tour operator before departure, and in breach of contract, the Plaintiff will commonly have a claim for a variety of out of pocket expenses—kennel fees, locum booked to cover the Plaintiff's business, clothes bought for the holiday, suntan lotion, etc, etc. Provided the Plaintiff can show that these costs were genuinely incurred, they are in principle recoverable; alternatively the Plaintiff may have been able to re-book a holiday; in that event the Plaintiff will have been able to use the clothes, suntan lotion, etc, but may instead have a claim for the additional cost of the substitute holiday—subject to the rules on mitigation of loss.

Consequential loss—mental distress

The origin of this head of damages is generally regarded as the case of *Jarvis v Swans Tours* [1973] 1 All E.R. 71 (but see *Feldman v Allways* [1957] C.L.Y. 934). The facts were these: Mr. Jarvis, a solicitor, booked a holiday with the Defendants which their brochure described as a house party in Switzerland with special resident host. It promised "Welcome party on arrival. Afternoon tea and cake. Swiss dinner by candlelight. Fondue party. Yodeller evening. Farewell party". It also promised a wide variety of ski runs, the hire of ski packs, an atmosphere in the hotel of geniality, comfort and cosiness, a hotel owner who spoke English, and a bar that would be open several days a week. The brochure added "You will be in for a great time when you book this house party holiday". (Tour operators these days rarely make the mistake of promising consumers enjoyment.) Mr. Jarvis paid £63.45 for a two week holiday over Christmas and New Year. In the first week, the house party consisted of only 13 people and for the whole of the second week, the Plaintiff was the only person there. There was no welcome party. The ski runs were some distance away and full length skis were only available on two days. The hotel owner did not speak English, so in the second week, the Plaintiff had no-one to talk to at all. The cake for tea was potato crisps and dry nut cake. There was little night time entertainment. The yodeller evening consisted of a local man in his working clothes singing a few songs very quickly. The bar opened only one evening. For the second week, there was no representative at the hotel.

At the original hearing at Ilford County Court, the Judge calculated the Plaintiff's compensation only on the basis of a "difference in value claim". He felt that by means of the transport and accommodation provided, the Defendants had given about half the value of the contract, and consequently awarded Mr. Jarvis £31.72. He felt that he could not award anything for the disappointment or loss of enjoyment because such damages were irrecoverable in principle for breach of contract.

This last point caused the Plaintiff to appeal to the Court of Appeal. On what was then the novel question of damages for distress Lord Denning MR said:

> "In a proper case damages for mental distress can be recovered in contract. ... One such case is a contract for a holiday, or any other contract to provide entertainment and enjoyment. If the contracting party breaks his contract, damages can be given for the disappointment, the distress, the upset and frustration caused by the breach."

This view was supported by Stephenson LJ who said:

> "I agree that ... there may be contracts in which the parties contemplate inconvenience on breach which may be described as mental: frustration, annoyance, disappointment; and ... the damages for breach of it should take such wider inconvenience or discomfort into account."

The third judge, Edmund Davies LJ, also supported damages for distress. He said:

> "In determining what would be proper compensation for the defendants' marked failure to fulfil their undertaking I am of the opinion that ... "vexation" and "being disappointed in a particular thing which you have set your mind upon" are relevant considerations which afford the court a guide in arriving at a proper figure.

> When a man has paid for and properly expects an invigorating and amusing holiday and, through no fault of his, returns home dejected because his expectations have been largely unfulfilled, in my judgment it would be quite wrong to say that his disappointment must find no reflection in the damages to be awarded."

Since then virtually all holiday cases have included a sum to compensate for distress and disappointment (although *Morris v Carisma Holidays* 1997 mentioned above is a rare exception). Just how much will be awarded however remains a little of a mystery, although some guidance was offered in *Scott and Scott v Blue Sky Holidays* [1985] C.L.Y. 943 where it was said that damages for distress and disappointment should not be related to the price of the holiday. The intangible nature of the damage makes accurate prediction almost impossible. This has been recognised in a number of cases including *Jarvis v Swans Tours* itself where Lord Denning said:

> "I know that it [distress] is difficult to assess in terms of money, but it is no more difficult than the assessment which the courts have to make every day in personal injury cases for loss of amenities." (An almost identical statement was made in *Stedman v Swan's Tours* 95 Sol. Jo 727 (1951) by Singleton LJ.)

In *Adcock v Blue Sky Holidays* (1980, Lexis) Bridge LJ also likened the process to awarding damages in personal damages cases. He said:

> "The assessment of damages in a case of this nature is not a mathematical exercise. It is not dissimilar from the assessment of damages in personal injuries cases, although perhaps it can be said in this kind of case it is even more difficult than in a personal injuries case to arrive at the appropriate figure with any degree of precision."

The difficulty is such that the issue is often fudged, quite explicitly. Eveleigh LJ in *Adcock v Blue Sky Holidays* said:

> "I would not in the present case find it necessary to assess in detail the effect of these conditions upon each of the people concerned. I would prefer to take the broader approach and say: What is the kind of holiday they were entitled to expect, what is the kind of holiday they got, and what do I think that that is

> worth in damages ... and I for myself would award the sum of £500."

Although the Jarvis decision is now beyond question as far as holiday cases are concerned, the precise ambit of damages for distress in general have been reviewed recently in a number of cases. In *Hayes v Dodd* [1990] 2 All E.R. 815, the Court of Appeal was concerned to confine damages for distress within fairly narrow limits. It held that such damages were available only if the object of the contract was to provide peace of mind or freedom from distress and were not recoverable for anguish and vexation arising out of the breach of a purely commercial contract. On the face of it this merely re-affirms the existing position as far as holidays are concerned. A package holiday contract is one designed to provide peace of mind and therefore clearly falls within *Hayes v Dodd.*

Some extension of the principle is to be found in *Ruxley Electronics v Forsyth* [1996] A.C. 344 in which a swimming pool constructed at a house turned out to be not quite as pleasing as contracted for and the House of Lords felt that damages for loss of amenity was more appropriate than the disproportionate cost of rebuilding the pool. In another important House of Lords case, *Farley v Skinner* [2002] 2 A.C. 732, a surveyor who had been asked to advise on whether a house was affected by aircraft noise, negligently gave it the "all clear". The House of Lords felt that this was an appropriate case to award damages for distress—even though only one of the purposes of the contract had been to provide pleasure, relaxation or peace of mind. Interestingly the decision was made in the teeth of a scathing attack by the Court of Appeal on the whole principle of damages for distress/disappointment).

However, problems arise with "flight-only" holidays. Is a flight a contract to provide peace of mind or freedom from distress? There are those who might suggest quite the opposite! On the other hand the context in which such contracts are made may need to be taken into account. Clients buying such flights usually do so as part of a holiday and if the contract is broken then they will suffer just the same distress as a client who books the flight as part of a package—in fact they could be sitting next to them on the plane (or delayed with them in the departure lounge as the case may be). The client who buys the flight-only simply to get from A to B, as with the businessman who buys a scheduled flight ticket, may be regarded as making a purely commercial contract and on that reasoning would not be eligible for damages for distress. This was certainly the view of one court—see *Lucas v Avro* [1994] C.L.Y. 1444. A similar decision was in *Noble v Leger Holidays* [2000] 6 CL 476 about a coach trip to Disneyland Paris. Only the coaching was unsatisfactory, so the Court awarded the diminution in value, but not claims for distress/disappointment. Damages for mental distress as a general rule are still not recoverable for breach of contract and *Jarvis* (as extended in *Ruxley* and *Farley*) must be seen as an exception, albeit a now well established one, to the general rule. However, maverick cases do emerge from time to time. See *Graham v Sunsetridge* [1989] C.L.Y. 1189 where damages for distress were awarded for what appears to be a delay in a "flight only" contract.

As indicated earlier most complaints concern accommodation. Damages for distress will be awarded where substandard accommodation is provided but the level of award may vary according to the kind of accommodation and the type of holiday. For example, in a summer holiday where the accommodation is in a complex with swimming pools, sports facilities, entertainment etc all on site it may be expected that the client will spend a great deal of time in or near the accommodation, so that poor accommodation will severely spoil the holiday. On the other hand, on a skiing holiday the party may scarcely see their rooms except when sleeping, so the damages for an identical breach of contract should be the same when assessing difference in value claims but different when assessing damages for distress.

By contrast, it will be noticed that in the *Jarvis* case, the Defendants had promised to keep the Plaintiff entertained all day, by means of the skiing during the day time and the house party at night. Since the Plaintiff was hardly provided with any of this, this may help to explain why a total award of twice the holiday price was considered appropriate. By contrast, the *Jackson* case was a more typical summer holiday case, in which the defective accommodation caused serious disappointment but did not undermine the entire purpose of the holiday. In that case a total award of £1,100 was made as against a price of £1,200 (the award broken down as £600 for difference in value, and £500 for disappointment). *Jackson* is, as has been stated, more typical of the run of the mill holiday claim, and is often found helpful by county court judges as a benchmark against which to measure the facts of any particular case which the Judge has to decide; however it is not uncommon in cases of truly disastrous holidays for the court to award damages of twice the price of the holiday—representing a full refund and damages for distress and disappointment of another 100 per cent. As already mentioned *Clarke & Greenwood v Airtours* is an extreme example of such awards, which strays from compensation of Claimants to improper punishment of defendants (see the judicial attention it received in "Benchmarks" 1998 LSG June 17, Judge Geoffrey Martin).

Further criticism has been levelled at the seemingly high awards for distress and disappointment in some cases. Tomlinson and Wardell ("Damages in Holiday Cases," (1988) 85 L.S.Gaz. 28) make a comparison with personal injury cases:

> "We submit that, in awarding distress damages, the courts should bear in mind the well established conventional scale of figures to cover matters such as pain and suffering in personal injury cases. A person who suffers an agonising and debilitating injury from which he recovers completely after a period of two weeks would be unlikely to recover more than £500 pain and suffering damages. It would be inconsistent for courts to award substantially greater damages for the pain and suffering caused by a ruined holiday for a similar period." [Of course, inflation will now have some impact on these figures.]

An illustration of just this point is the case of *Hoffman v Intasun Holidays* (1990, High Court, unreported). The plaintiff in the case suffered 26 hours of great pain because the defendant's representative failed during that time to obtain the medication the plaintiff should have had. An award of only £100 was made for that period.

Regulation 15(4) of the Package Travel Regulations provides that organisers can limit damages for non-personal injury to a sum which is "not unreasonable". Given the unpopularity of damages for distress amongst tour operators it is not surprising that some at least attempt to limit this head of liability—perhaps by saying that total damages cannot exceed a conventional sum such as the price of the holiday or twice the price.

In *Lathrope v Kuoni Travel Ltd* [1999] C.L.Y. 1382 Kuoni had fixed a sum of £50 per day of holiday lost through flight delay regardless of the cost of the (quite expensive) holiday. The Court held that such an inflexible limit never likely to be a "not reasonable" limit. See also *Jervis v Kuoni* 1998 C.L.Y. 3733, a similar decision where the breach of contract was defective accommodation.

Consequential loss—physical discomfort

Prior to *Jarvis v Swan Tours* it was well established that damages could be claimed for a breach of contract resulting in physical discomfort. Lord Denning referred to a number of these cases in *Jarvis*. He said:

> "The courts in those days only allowed the plaintiff to recover damages if he suffered physical inconvenience, such as having to walk five miles home, as in *Hobbs v London & South Western Railway Co* (1875) LR 10 QB 111; or to live in an overcrowded house: see *Bailey v Bullock* [1950] 2 All E.R. 1167." (See also *Stedman* v *Swan's Tours* and *Farley v Skinner* on this issue.)

In *Cook v Spanish Holiday Tours* (CA) *The Times*, February 6, 1960 the plaintiffs were awarded £25 damages for disappointment which included a sum to compensate them for the inconvenience of having to spend the first night of their honeymoon on a park bench! Perhaps not as distressing but more common would be the physical inconvenience of being stuck at an overcrowded Gatwick or Luton airport for many hours.

More recently, the issue of discomfort in long haul flights in economy class has resulted in an award of £500 to the Claimant in the case of *Horan v JMC Holidays* 2002 Chester County Court—regardless of the fact that the seat pitch and layout had been approved by the CAA. But other Courts have refused identical claims see *Watt v First Choice Holidays* February 20, 2002, Liverpool County Court, unreported. See also *Grahame v JMC Holidays* [2002] 8 CL 505 Reading County Court for a case in which CAA approval was discussed.

Consequential loss—physical injury

There is nothing exceptional about claiming damages for personal injury, including psychiatric/stress injuries (see *Griggs v Olympic Holidays Ltd* (No.1) [1996] C.L.Y. 2184) in breach of contract cases. It is a recognised and well established head of damages. Fortunately it is a category which arises in only a minority of cases. *Wall v Silver Wing* (1981, High Ct, unreported) is a case in which substantial damages would have been awarded had the plaintiffs been able to establish liability. *Hoffman v Intasun* (1990, High Ct, unreported) is another case where a personal injury claim was made but the plaintiff failed to establish liability except in the limited way mentioned earlier.

One case where the plaintiffs succeeded is *Davey v Cosmos* [1989] C.L.Y. 2561. In that case the plaintiffs suffered from dysentery and diarrhoea because of the negligence of the defendants. Damages were awarded which included a sum for the pain and suffering of the illness.

The cases of *Wilson v Best Travel Limited* [1993] and *Wong Mee Wan v Kwan Kin Travel Services Limited* [1995], discussed in

Chapter 4, are further examples of personal injury claims arising out of package holidays, which typically raise questions about the appropriate safety standards imposed on tour operators.

The assessment of damages for personal injuries is a major topic in its own right and readers are referred to the standard texts or Current Law. A huge volume of case law exists, making it easier for the parties to calculate the court's likely award in advance, and so settle the case. It further assists defendants that a Claimant must file a medical report with any court action. This contrasts sharply with the position already described in relation to claims for disappointment and distress, which are so subjective and impressionistic.

Remoteness of damage

As explained above a plaintiff can only recover damages which are not too remote a consequence of the breach of contract. The rule in *Hadley v Baxendale* was formulated by Alderson B:

> "Where two parties have made a contract which one of them has broken, the damages which the other party ought to receive in respect of such breach of contract should be such as may fairly and reasonably be considered either arising naturally *i.e.* according to the usual course of things, from such breach of contract itself, or such as may reasonably be supposed to have been in the contemplation of both parties at the time they made the contract, as the probable result of the breach of it."

The test lays down that any damage which results from the breach of contract which is not in the reasonable contemplation of the parties at the time they made the contract is not recoverable. The test in fact has two limbs or branches. This was explained by Asquith LJ in a later case, *Victoria Laundry (Windsor) Ltd v Newman Industries Ltd* [1949] 2 KB 528. He said:

> "In cases of breach of contract, the aggrieved party is only entitled to recover such part of the loss actually resulting as was at the time of the contract reasonably foreseeable as liable to result from the breach.

What was at that time reasonably so foreseeable depends on the knowledge then possessed by the parties or, at all events, by the party who later commits the breach.

For this purpose, knowledge "possessed" is of two kinds; one imputed, the other actual. Everyone, as a reasonable person, is taken to know the "ordinary course of things" and consequently what loss is liable to result from a breach of contract in that ordinary course. This is the subject-matter of the "first rule" in *Hadley v Baxendale*. But to this knowledge, which a contract-breaker is assumed to possess whether he actually possesses it or not, there may have to be added in a particular case knowledge which he actually possesses of special circumstances outside the "ordinary course of things", of such a kind that a breach in those special circumstances would be liable to cause more loss. Such a case attracts the operation of the "second rule" so as to make additional loss also recoverable." (See *Kemp v Intasun* below on what is meant by natural consequences).

So for instance, if a tour operator places clients in a 14-storey hotel and the lift breaks down the damage that flows from that "in the ordinary course of things" is that many clients will suffer physical inconvenience from having to climb the stairs. The effects will be short lived however for most of the population. Once they have recovered their breath they will be alright. There should be no problems fitting this within the first rule or limb of *Hadley v Baxendale*. If, however, the clients are elderly or disabled then it may not simply be discomfort they suffer if they attempt to climb the stairs. They may suffer further physical injury or exacerbate their disabilities in the attempt. If they are known to be elderly or disabled then the second rule in *Hadley v Baxendale* applies. In this case there are special circumstances actually known to the tour operator which put the effects of the breach within his contemplation. (See *Causby v Portland* [1995] C.L.Y. 1604.)

In the *Victoria Laundry* case Asquith L.J. talked about the damage being reasonably foreseeable as liable to result. However later cases, in particular the House of Lords case, *The Heron II* [1969] 1 A.C. 350, have narrowed the scope of the test. Now it can be said that the test is not one of reasonable foresight but one of reasonable contemplation. The practical effect of the difference in terminology is that a plaintiff must prove a higher likelihood of the damage occurring under a reasonable contemplation test than under a reasonable foresight test. In The Heron II the judges used phrases such as "not unlikely" and "quite likely" and "a real danger" or "a serious possibility" to describe the degree of foresight required of the defendant before he was liable for the damage.

This was an issue which the courts had to face in *Kemp v Intasun Holidays Limited* [1987] C.L.Y. 1130; [1987] B.T.L.C. 353; 7 Tr Law 161. The facts were that Intasun, in breach of contract, placed Mr Kemp, an asthmatic, in a dirty, dusty room. He was moved out of the room after the first night but the whole of the first week of his holiday was blighted by an asthma attack brought on by the dirty room. It was held that the family were entitled to damages for the breach of contract for being placed in a disgustingly filthy room for 30 hours but these damages were for difference in value and for distress and disappointment not for the asthma attack. On the question of damages for the asthma the Court of Appeal held that it did not occur in the ordinary course of things for a person placed in a dusty room to have an asthma attack. Asthma was a sufficiently rare illness for it not to be regarded as the natural consequence of sleeping in a dusty environment. Thus Mr Kemp failed to recover damages under the first rule in *Hadley v Baxendale*. (See *Waters v Thomson* [2000] C.L.Y. 879 for a case on asthma where remoteness was not an issue.)

This is what the court had to say on what would amount to the ordinary course of things in a package holiday case:

> "[The tour operator] must also accept liability for any other consequences which should have been in the reasonable contemplation of the parties if these flowed naturally from his breach and caused additional foreseeable loss or damage. Such liability would be equally within the rule expressed in the passage from the headnote which I have read and which is often referred to as the first rule in *Hadley v Baxendale* (1854) 9 Exch 347, [1843-60] All E.R. Rep. 461. For instance, if the consequence of not providing the contractual accommodation is not merely the loss of its enjoyment and so forth, but also the fact that the plaintiffs has to sleep out on the beach, with the result that their health suffered in a natural and ordinarily foreseeable way because they caught colds or even pneumonia, then that would be a natural and foreseeable additional consequence which would equally flow from the tour operator's breach. In such circumstances his liability would not be limited to the basic damages on account of disappointment and loss of enjoyment to which I have referred." (Kerr LJ)

The question then arose as to whether Intasun had any special knowledge that put the asthma attack within their reasonable contemplation. There was evidence that prior to making the booking Mrs Kemp had made a preliminary visit to the travel agency and while she was choosing the holiday she explained to the travel clerk that her husband was not with her because he was suffering from an asthma attack. It was not until a month later that the holiday was booked. If it could be shown that the knowledge of the travel agency could be attributed to Intasun there were grounds for arguing that Intasun had the knowledge that made the asthma attack an event which could be reasonably contemplated. The court avoided this difficult problem by saying first that the travel agents were not the agents of Intasun at the time the conversation took place. Secondly, that a casual conversation such as took place between Mrs Kemp and the travel clerk could not give rise to contractual obligations on the part of Intasun. In other words the special knowledge has to be "brought home" more forcibly than in a passing conversation. This is a view which is endorsed by Treitel (*Law of Contract*, 10th ed, p.903).

Contrast, however, the position where at least *some* personal injury is foreseeable; the full amount of injury can then be recovered even though the tour operator could not have anticipated that full extent without special knowledge being brought home—see *Brown v Thomson Tour Operations* [1999] C.L.Y. 1412 Sheffield County Court and also Ward, "Case Commentary: Brown v Thomson Tour Operations" [1999] ITLJ 170.

It is worth mentioning again at this point that in cases of misrepresentation as opposed to breach of contract the rule on remoteness is that damages are recoverable even where the loss was not foreseeable (*Royscot Trust v Rogerson* [1991] 3 All E.R. 294); but note that *McGregor on Damages*, 16th ed., 1997 paragraph 2002 questions whether this case was correctly decided and suggests that it may not be upheld in future.

Mitigation of loss

A disappointed client who suffers from breach of contract cannot just sit back and let the damages roll in. He is under a duty to mitigate his loss, *i.e.* take reasonable steps to reduce his loss. The rule is an aspect of the rules on remoteness—the defendant can foresee that the reasonable plaintiff will act reasonably to minimise his loss. The two most common practical applications in travel law involve first, the choice faced by a consumer who is offered some alternative to his booked arrangements; and secondly the duty to complain when things go wrong.

The rule has three aspects. First, the plaintiff cannot recover for loss which he could have avoided by taking reasonable steps to do so. Secondly, the plaintiff can recover for expenses incurred in taking reasonable steps to avoid loss. Thirdly, the plaintiff cannot recover for loss which he has succeeded in avoiding.

The first principle was explained in *British Westinghouse & Manufacturing Co Ltd v Underground Electric Rly Co of London Ltd* [1912] A.C. 673. Lord Haldane LC said:

"The fundamental principle is thus compensation for pecuniary damage naturally flowing from the breach; but this first principle is qualified by a second which imposes on the plaintiff the duty of taking reasonable steps to mitigate the loss consequent on the breach, and debars him from claiming any part of the damage which is due to his neglect in taking such steps."

In *Payzu v Saunders* [1919] 2 K.B. 581 a seller of goods had contracted to provide the goods on credit but broke the contract and refused to supply them except for cash. The buyer refused to pay cash and sued for breach of contract. It was held that he should have mitigated his loss by taking the goods for cash:

"... in commercial contracts it is generally reasonable to accept an offer from the party in default."

There are a number of reported cases on just this point. In *Tucker v OTA* [1986] C.L.Y. 383 a flight was overbooked but when an alternative was offered it was held that the client had refused it on reasonable grounds. Similarly in *Rhodes v Sunspot Tours* [1983] C.L.Y. 984 the plaintiff was held to have acted reasonably in refusing an alternative apartment because of the atmosphere of distrust that existed between the parties by that stage. Other examples of reasonable grounds for refusing an offer of alternative accommodation are: small villa offered with shared pool and no compensation—*Buhus-Orwin v Costa Smerelda Holidays* [2001] 11 C.L.R. 360; hotel over 10km away and holidaymakers to bear own expenses—*Currie v Magic Travel Group* [2001] 9 CL 446. (See also *Askew v Intasun* [1980] C.L.Y. 637; *Abbatt v Sunquest* [1984] C.L.Y. 1025; *Corbett v Top Hat Tours* [1989] C.L.Y. 1194.)

On the other hand in *Toubi v Intasun Holidays* [1988] C.L.Y. 1060 it was held unreasonable for a plaintiff to refuse the offer of an alternative hotel when the original one was overbooked. He preferred to cancel his holiday. He did receive a full refund of the holiday price but he was refused damages for distress and disappointment.

It is difficult to draw any general conclusions from any of these cases other than the fact that they illustrate the general principle. This is simply because what amounts to a reasonable refusal depends upon the facts of the particular case.

The second principle is illustrated by the case of *Banco de Portugal v Waterlow & Sons Ltd* [1932] A.C. 452. The defendants printed banknote for the plaintiffs. In breach of contract they delivered them to a criminal who put them into circulation. The plaintiffs withdrew the issue from circulation and undertook to exchange all the old notes for new ones. It was held that the defendants were liable not only for the cost of printing the original notes but also for the cost of exchanging the notes when they were withdrawn from circulation. This was expenditure incurred in reasonable mitigation of their loss, having regard to the bank's commercial obligation to the public.

In *Chesneau v Interhome* (1983) 134 N.L.J. 341 the defendants provided the plaintiffs with inferior accommodation. The plaintiffs incurred further expenditure by finding more suitable accommodation. This was regarded as a reasonable mitigation of loss in the circumstances. Similarly in *Trackman v New Vistas Ltd*, *The Times*, November 24, 1959 it was held that the plaintiff was entitled to mitigate his loss by booking into an hotel which would provide the standard of accommodation he had been promised. However, the case of *Ruxley Electronics* referred to above is authority for the proposition that the cost of reinstatement must not be wholly disproportionate to the damage which it is sought to mitigate.

The *British Westinghouse* case also illustrates the third principle that the plaintiff cannot claim for loss that he has succeeded in avoiding. The facts of the case were that the plaintiffs had bought a turbine that was less efficient than promised. As a result of the breach they later bought new turbines which were so efficient that the savings in running costs compared to the original machines exceeded the cost of replacing them. On that basis the plaintiffs could not claim the cost of replacing the turbines because that loss was more than offset by the efficiency savings on the new turbines.

So if, by booking themselves into an acceptable hotel, consumers have therefore enjoyed their holiday they cannot claim for distress and disappointment for that period as well as the cost of the new hotel. This is the most common type of holiday case where damages for disappointment are inappropriate. (See *Hartman v P&O* above.)

Most tour operators are aware of the client's duty to mitigate his loss and specifically provide for this in the terms and conditions. They expressly state that in the event of problems arising the client should inform the representative so as to give the tour operator the opportunity to put things right. An example of this policy operating to the benefit of the tour operator is the unreported case of *Czyzewski v Intasun* (1990, County Court). Intasun had provided the plaintiff with a room with an "offensive" toilet. He complained, and after unsuccessful attempts were made to repair the toilet he was offered an alternative room—which he refused. It was held that this was an unreasonable refusal to mitigate his loss and he was awarded only £50 damages—based on the limited time he would have suffered had he accepted the alternative.

Another case where damages were reduced because of a failure to mitigate by the client is *Scott and Scott v Blue Sky Holidays* [1985] C.L.Y. 943. The plaintiffs had not complained to the tour operator's representative about the food and this failure operated to reduce what would otherwise have been substantial damages. As Tomlinson and Wardell point out the report does not say so but there must have been a finding of fact that if the clients had complained the representative would have been able to put things right.

The rule on mitigation is enshrined in Regulation 15(9) which provides:

> "(9) The contract must clearly and explicitly oblige the consumer to communicate at the earliest opportunity, in writing or any other appropriate form, to the supplier of the services concerned and to the other party to the contract any failure which he perceives at the place where the services concerned are supplied."

This Regulation should be read in conjunction with Regulation 8(2) which obliges the operator to provide the client with contact names and addresses, and with Schedule 2, Paragraph 12 which requires the operator to incorporate into the contract the periods within which the client must complain (presumably, although not expressed, this means the follow up letter of complaint on return home).

Thus the organiser is under a contractual duty to inform the consumer that he in turn is under a contractual duty to complain. It also seems that the consumer must complain to both the operator and the supplier in writing or other appropriate form—presumably an oral complaint would be appropriate in some circumstances, *e.g.* if the transfer bus was being driven recklessly an oral complaint might have more impact than a written one—especially if delivered with appropriate emphasis! If he does not complain at the earliest opportunity or does not complain to both then he will be in breach of contract. In practical terms this means that the consumer is under a contractual duty to mitigate his loss and if he fails to do so in the manner provided in the Regulations he will have to suffer the consequences—loss of compensation for those defects in the holiday which could have been remedied if the consumer had complained promptly.

There will be no loss of compensation where failure to complain would have made no difference or where it was sufficient to complain to just the organiser or supplier—on the grounds that the breach of contract does not cause the organiser any loss.

Given that there is already a common law duty to mitigate loss it is difficult to see what this provision adds to the law except perhaps to drive home to the consumer more forcefully that he should complain. Where it might make a difference is where a complaint is made some weeks or months after the consumer has returned home and the organiser has no record of what happened and is unable to assemble the evidence to combat the complaint. It might be the kind of problem that could not have been mitigated at the time, *e.g.* food poisoning, but if the organiser has notice of it at the time he may be able to defend himself more ably at a later date.

If the organiser does not inform the consumer of his obligation to complain then the immediate effect of this is to permit the consumer to repudiate the contract. Regulation 9 states that all the terms of the contract must be set out in writing or other appropriate form before the contract is made. Failure to do so is a breach of condition which entitles the consumer to cancel the contract.

But what is the effect if the statement is not included but the consumer does not repudiate, takes the holiday and does not complain promptly? Can the consumer argue that he has no obligation to complain promptly because the organiser has failed to inform him of this? On the one hand the consumer is in breach of the term imposed by Regulation 15(9) whereas on the other the organiser is in breach of Regulation 9. If the two obligations are regarded as being linked—that the obligation to complain promptly is dependent upon being informed of this duty then the consumer is excused his failure and will suffer no penalty for it. On the other hand if the two are regarded as separate obligations the consumer cannot hide behind the organiser's failure—he must complain promptly regardless of the organiser's breach. This latter view is the one to be preferred if only because it should be a matter of commonsense to complain promptly. Also because the common law duty to mitigate probably exists independently of the Regulations and the consumer will have to comply with this independent duty regardless of the Regulations.

One other minor point about making complaints is the interpretation of the phrase "at the place" in Regulation 15(9). Does this mean that the consumer must complain promptly at the place where he is on holiday or does it mean that if there is a problem at the place where he is on holiday then he must complain but it does not necessarily have to be there and then so long as it is done promptly? In most circumstances it will come down to the same thing. There will be a complaint about the holiday and it will be possible to complain there and then but in some cases that may not be practicable. For instance what if the consumer is on a gite holiday in deepest provincial France and the local owner is either not known or not contactable or speaks only French? How is the consumer to complain "at the place" where the services are supplied. The answer probably lies in Regulation 8(2)(b) which makes it a criminal offence for the organiser not to provide the consumer with, at the very least, a contact number where the organiser can be reached during the stay.

See also Chapter 6 on the subject of failure by the consumer to write in after the holiday within the time limit set out in the contract for making complaints and the OFT's views on the 28-day time limit recommended by major tour operators.

Eviction cases

There are a group of cases in which the consumer is bringing an action against the tour operator for damages where the hotelier has evicted the consumer from the hotel for misconduct. Although it is the tour operator who is being sued for breach of contract the essence of the action is whether the consumer's conduct was sufficient to justify an eviction. If so then the tour operator is not in breach of contract.

It has been held by the Court of Appeal that provided the tour operator can prove the consumer is guilty of serious misconduct justifying eviction the consumer cannot claim compensation for the fact that accommodation was not provided for the full period of the holiday. However the burden of proof is on the tour operator (*Spencer v Cosmos*, *The Times*, December 6, 1989). It is not sufficient for the tour operator to rely on the judgment of the hotelier alone. Other evidence will usually be required but often this is difficult to acquire. Incidents justifying eviction frequently take place late at night when only a night porter or a sub-contracted security guard is on duty and it is often impossible to bring them to the UK to act as witnesses at a trial.

An interesting variation on this theme came in the unreported case of *Hickman v CIT Ltd* (Willesden County Court, 1991). In that case the plaintiffs were evicted for misconduct. The judge found their conduct was "boorish" but not serious enough to warrant their eviction from the hotel. He, therefore, awarded them damages for loss of part of their holiday but felt he was entitled to reduce the damages because of the contribution they made to their own problems. It is difficult to fit this decision precisely into legal principle but it is a form of rough justice.

Conclusions

In our first edition, we attempted to offer some rules of thumb for the assessment of damages in practice. However, cases reported since that time have only served to emphasise how individual the decisions in these cases are. In *Rebello v Leisure Villas* [1995] 10 CL 320 the party were overbooked from a private detached villa into a very small studio apartment with numerous other defects. Blackburn County Court awarded them something less than the full holiday price, and this case is very much in line with *Jackson v Horizon Holidays*. In *Clarke & Greenwood v Airtours* [1995] C.L.Y. 1603, the Plaintiff was overbooked from hotel rooms to self catering apartments which were by all accounts of a disgraceful standard. Whilst it is clear that their problems were greater than in the *Rebello* case, the award to them by Staines County Court of four times the cost of the holiday seems a disproportionate response and is out of line with any other known decision—can it really be said that the Plaintiffs in effect required four more holidays to recover from that one? There again, in *Morris v Carisma Holidays* [1997] 4 CL 215, the Watford County Court decided that the Defendants were in breach of Regulation 6 of the Package Travel Regulations (see Chapter Four) where the luxury holiday home on a camp site turned out to be dirty, inadequate and overcrowded; but awarded only one quarter of the cost of the holiday. We can only repeat that the impact made on the Judge by the live evidence of either party is a major factor in determining the award; and by commending to Courts a greater consistency by using *Jackson v Horizon Holidays* or *Jarvis v Swans Tours*, both Court of Appeal cases, as benchmarks, as many Courts already do.

In fact, a braver soul than us has ventured some guidelines. District Judge Geoffrey Martin, who frequently writes and lectures on Holiday Law issues, suggested in the *Law Society's Gazette*, June 17, 1998:

> "As a rough guide and ignoring the extremes, total damages for an inordinately bad holiday tend to hover around two to two and a half times the total cost. Damages for a holiday when a few things go wrong range from half up to the total cost. A series of petty complaints can justify a small award for diminution but nothing for distress and disappointment".

A search for cases at the top end of Judge Martin's scale revealed *Carter v Thomson* [1986] C.L.Y. 976; *Glover v Kuoni* [1987] C.L.Y. 1151; *Charles v Trans Air* [1994] C.L.Y. 1476; and *Hal-*

pern v Somak [1998] C.L.Y. 1428. However there are no others to our knowledge which come remotely near *Clarke & Greenwood v Airtours*—which remains on its own on the issue of damages. *Harvey v Tracks Travel* is a high award case which seems much more justified than *Clarke & Greenwood*.

Cancellation by the Client

Introduction

Most tour operators include a clause in their booking conditions stating that if the client cancels the holiday then he must pay compensation to the operator according to a scale of charges. Usually the charges are on a sliding scale commencing with just the deposit and getting larger as the date of departure draws near and ending up with a charge of 100 per cent on or about the actual date of departure. The charges are designed to cover the operator against the risk of not being able to resell the holiday. If this is all they do then they are unexceptionable but in some cases the scale is particularly steep, rising quickly to a peak long before the departure date. In such circumstances the suspicion is that the scale is not simply designed to compensate the operator for the loss he will suffer but there may also be an element of profiteering in the scale. If this is the case the question arises as to whether or not the client has to pay the full scale charge or can get away with paying less?

The answer to this question is that it depends upon which of two quite distinct categories the clause falls into.

A cancellation clause will be placed in the first category if the cancellation is regarded as a breach of contract by the client. In such cases the cancellation charges represent what are called agreed or liquidated damages. These will be enforced unless they amount to a penalty. Cancellation clauses are placed in the second category if they are seen as giving the client an option to terminate the contract. If the client chooses to exercise this option then the contract provides that he must pay a price for doing so—the cancellation charges. In such circumstances the client is not breaking the contract he is merely exercising his rights under it and the sum he pays in these circumstances does not amount to damages for breach and does not attract the rules about penalties.

These two categories will be examined in turn and the consequences of categorising a cancellation clause one way or the other will be considered. The impact of the Unfair Terms in Consumer Contracts Regulations 1999 will also be considered.

Liquidated damages

This section will proceed on the assumption that cancellation charges amount to agreed damages which are payable because the client breaks the contract when he cancels.

Generally speaking the courts are favourably disposed to the parties to a contract agreeing between themselves what the consequences of a breach of contract will be. There are numerous reasons for this. First, it means that the parties have a clear idea of what their liabilities will be in the event of a breach because they have assessed them in advance. It means they go into the contract with their eyes open as to the risks they run if they do break the contract. It is simply an aspect of good contract planning. Secondly, because the sum is fixed in advance difficult problems of quantification and remoteness do not arise. Thirdly, the payment of the damages is not complicated by having to prove actual loss; agreed damages are payable automatically on proof of breach. Finally, it avoids litigation. Going to court is an expensive, wasteful, time-consuming, unsatisfactory business and anything which eliminates or reduces this possibility is welcomed—even by the courts.

Therefore if the cancellation charges can be classified as agreed damages the courts will uphold the clause. On the other hand if it amounts to a penalty clause the cancellation charges are not payable and only the actual losses incurred by the tour operator are payable. (Note that if greater damages are incurred than are provided for in the liquidated damages clause the victim of the breach is still bound by the clause and cannot claim the higher amount—*Diestal v Stevenson* [1906] 2 KB 345. Note also however that where the agreed damages clause is imposed on the consumer by the tour operator to cover breaches by the tour operator then this may be treated as an exclusion clause or an unfair contract term—see Chapter Six). So what distinguishes an agreed damages clause from a penalty?

An agreed damages clause exists when the sums involved amount to a genuine pre-estimate of the losses that might flow from the breach of contract. On the other hand a penalty clause exists when the sum is greater than any genuine pre-estimate of loss and is inserted into the contract to punish the other party for breach rather than simply compensate the victim. One phrase commonly used is that a penalty clause is inserted "in terrorem", to frighten the other party into performing although the phrase has been criticised by Lord Radcliffe, who said in the case of *Bridge v Campbell Discount Co Ltd* [1962] 1 All E.R. 385:

> "I do not think that that description adds anything of substance to the idea conveyed by the word "penalty' itself, and it obscures the fact that penalties may quite readily be undertaken by parties who are not in the least terrorised by the prospect of having to pay them and yet are, as I understand it, entitled to claim the protection of the court when they are called on to make good their promises."

There have been a number of cases where the distinction has been discussed and the most important of these is *Dunlop Pneumatic Tyre Co Ltd v New Garage & Motor Co Ltd* [1915] A.C. 79 where Lord Dunedin stated the principles by which penalty clauses can be distinguished from agreed damages clauses:

> "(a) It will be held to be a penalty if the sum stipulated for is extravagant and unconscionable in amount in comparison with the greatest loss that could conceivably be proved to have followed from the breach.
> (b) It will be held to be a penalty if the breach consists only in not paying a sum of money, and the sum stipulated is a sum greater than the sum which ought to have been paid.
> (c) There is a presumption (but no more) that it is a penalty when a single sum is made payable by way of compensation, on the occurrence of one or more or all of several events, some of which may occasion serious and others but trifling damage.
> (d) It is no obstacle to the sum stipulated being a genuine pre-estimate of damage, that the consequences of the breach are such as to make precise pre-estimation almost an impossibility. On the contrary, that is just the situation when it is probable that pre-estimated damage was the true bargain between the parties."

The facts of the case itself were that Dunlop had contracted to sell tyres to the defendants who had agreed not to tamper with the marks on the goods, not to sell or offer the goods to any private customers or to any co-operative society at less than the plaintiffs' current list prices, not to supply to persons whose supplies the plaintiffs had decided to suspend, not to exhibit or export without the consent of the plaintiffs, and to pay the sum of £5 by way of agreed damages for every tyre sold in breach of the agreement. The purpose of the agreement was to maintain prices. Although illegal now this practice was not so in 1915.

The court accepted that any of the practices outlawed by the contract would contribute to undermining the price maintenance agreement and would damage the plaintiffs' business. Lord Dunedin, in holding that the clause was not a penalty said:

> "But though damage as a whole from such a practice [selling below list price] would be certain, yet damage from any one sale would be impossible to forecast. It is just, therefore, one of those cases where it seems quite reasonable for parties to contract that they should estimate that damage at a certain figure, and provided that figure is not extravagant there would seem no reason to suspect that it is not truly a bargain to assess damages, but rather a penalty to be held in terrorem."

If we apply these principles to cancellation charges the question to be answered is whether or not the tour operator, in setting the charges, has made a genuine pre-estimate of the loss that would flow from the cancellation? On the face of it the type of scale usually employed, which imposes a higher charge the nearer the departure date, seems to take into account the greater risk that the operator runs of not reselling the holiday the nearer to departure the cancellation is. But what evidence is there for such a scale? Are the figures plucked out of the air at random or are they based on exhaustive research? Are they just a guess based on incomplete information or are they simply adopted because everybody else uses just about the same figures therefore they must be OK? Clearly if they are based on actual booking and cancellation patterns and losses have been calculated precisely and the scale accurately reflects the average loss that the operator would incur for cancellations at particular times before departure then the scale would be unimpeachable. On the other hand the operator might be in real difficulties if the scale was merely guesswork.

Prior to the restrictive practices case that was brought by the Office of Fair Trading against them, ABTA recommended a scale of cancellation charges that was adopted by most tour operators. The scale was as follows:

Period before departure within which cancellation received by company	**Charge**
More than 42 days	Deposit
29–42 days	30 per cent of holiday price
15–28 days	45 per cent of holiday price
1–14 days	60 per cent of holiday price
On or after day of departure	100 per cent of holiday price

No one quite knows how this scale came to be adopted by ABTA and it was in fact abandoned by them as a result of the pending action. However, Alan Milner, Dean of Trinity College, Oxford and former legal correspondent of the *Travel Trade Gazette*, did some empirical research at a leading tour operator to test the accuracy of the scale and although his findings are a little tentative because of the relatively small sample size he employed the good news for tour operators is that the money recouped in cancellation charges almost exactly equalled the actual losses suffered by the tour operator. (See Milner "Liquidated Damages: An empirical study in the Travel Industry", (1979) 42 M.L.R. 508). In other words it could be demonstrated that the scale was not imposing a penalty for breach that was "extravagant and unconscionable" in relation to the actual losses. Moreover it could also be argued that the imposition of a scale like this was appropriate in an industry where precise calculation of actual loss might be very difficult.

Unfortunately as Milner concedes, the findings do not necessarily hold true in all cases because they were specific to a particular company for a particular season, a particular resort and for a particular scale of charges. Given the volatility and complexity of the package holiday market there is no guarantee that the scale could be applied by other companies with destinations in other countries. Simply adopting the scale would not necessarily protect the operator against a charge that he was not making a genuine pre-estimate of his losses. Something more might be required. But given that precise calculation of the losses in advance is almost impossible and that losses could vary from season to season then probably the tour operator would not have to do more than show he had taken an intelligent stab at the scale based upon the information available to him.

The Milner article, however, contains much more good news for the operator. He identifies a number of reasons why tour operators are unlikely to be seriously challenged over cancellation clauses. First, the money involved is usually in the hands of the tour operator and any client who wishes to recover it must sue to do so. Most clients are not prepared to do this, either because they believe that the charges are legally enforceable anyway, or because they are simply not prepared to embark upon legal proceedings and all the trouble that that involves. Secondly, when the money has not been paid, tour operators are in fact quite prepared to issue proceedings, which are usually undefended. Thirdly, there is the role of insurance. Where clients are insured for cancellation they will claim against their insurance company, thereby deflecting any desire they may have to challenge the scale of charges. The insurance companies themselves could challenge the scale but Milner found no evidence of this at the time he wrote the article. He believed this was because the level of claims for cancellation was so low that it was not a significant problem for them. (This position may have changed recently and at the end of this section we look at how insurance companies might combat the high level of cancellation charges that are increasingly being levied.)

Finally, even if the matter does come to court it is not for the tour operator to prove his scale is a genuine pre-estimate of loss but for the client to show that it is not; that it is in fact extravagant and unconscionable. Moreover the law is such that the tour operator can hide behind the fact that it is impossible to calculate his losses precisely and need not show therefore that his calculations are accurate!

Thus it would appear that only in the most extreme of cases is the tour operator not going to be able to defend his cancellation charges.

On the other hand if the charges are shown to be a penalty the operator will then have to be able to prove his actual loss and this might in fact be difficult to do. It is for this very reason of course that agreed damages clauses attract the approval of the law in the first place. No one who could possibly avoid it would want to embark upon difficult questions of quantification and remoteness.

Options to terminate

The alternative approach to cancellation charges is to regard the clause as giving the client the option to terminate the contract early if he chooses to do so. In which case he is not breaking the contract, he is abiding by it and exercising one of his rights under it—the right to escape from it short of completion—but having to pay a price to do so.

The context in which this problem has usually arisen is in cases of hire purchase. In a typical hire purchase contract the owner of the goods lets it out on hire to the hirer on the terms that if a certain number of hire payments are made the hirer can then purchase the goods for a further small payment. Invariably the contract also provides that if the hirer wishes to terminate the agreement before he has made all the payments he may do so provided he makes up the payments to a certain minimum. This minimum payment clause often amounted two thirds of the value of the goods and was intended to cover "depreciation". In fact these minimum payments often far exceeded any conceivable depreciation and merely amounted to profit for the owner. As such they closely resembled penalty clauses—they were extravagant and unconscionable and were imposed in situations very similar to breach.

The argument came to a head in the Court of Appeal in the case of *Campbell Discount Co Ltd v Bridge* [1961] 2 All E.R. 97. Mr Bridge had acquired a car from the Campbell Discount Company on hire purchase. He paid £105 deposit and agreed to make monthly payments of approximately £10 until he had made up the total payments to £482. After making only one monthly payment he found he could not keep up the payments and wrote to the company saying:

> "... I am very sorry but I will not be able to pay any more payments on the Bedford Dormobile. Will you please let me know when and where I will have to return the car? I am very sorry regarding this but I have no other alternative."

He later returned the car to the garage where he had first acquired it. The company then invoked clause 6 of the hire purchase contract which provided:

> "The hirer may at any time terminate the hiring by giving notice in writing to the owners, and thereupon the provisions of clause 9 hereof apply."

Clause 9 stated that upon exercising the option to terminate the hirer had to make up the payments to two thirds of the total hire purchase price.

Holroyd Pearce LJ said:

> "The hirer exercised his option under clause 6 by giving notice. Clause 9 then applied. Under clause 9 ... he has to pay such sum as will make up the rentals to two third of the purchase, viz., the sum here claimed. No breach of contract or damages are in question for the hirer is simply exercising his right to return the car with all the incidents set out under clause 9. Therefore the doctrine of penalties does not apply."

Stated like this the law is quite straightforward. If the hirer is exercising an option to terminate this does not amount to breach and therefore the court will not investigate the question of whether the minimum payments clause is extravagant or unconscionable. Put another way the owner can put whatever amount he likes into the minimum payments clause and get away with it. (Note that such clauses in hire-purchase contracts are now heavily regulated by the Consumer Credit Act 1974 and the courts have a wide discretion to disallow them in consumer credit contracts.)

However, the matter did not end there. The case was appealed to the House of Lords under the name *Bridge v Campbell Discount Co Ltd* [1962] 1 All E.R. 385. There the court proceeded on a completely different basis. They said that the circumstances showed that Mr Bridge was not exercising his right to terminate he was actually breaking the contract. Lord Morton said:

> "I am of opinion, however, that the appellant [Bridge] never had the slightest intention of exercising the option contained in clause 6, and the terms of his letter show that he did not have clause 6 in mind. He frankly and simply informs the respondents that 'I will not be able to pay any more payments on the Bedford Dormobile.' There is no reference to any option, and I cannot reconcile the statement just quoted with the view that he intended to exercise an option, the terms whereof put him under an immediate obligation to pay a further large sum to the respondents. To my mind, the letter means that the writer feels reluctantly compelled to break his agreement, and the apologetic terms of the letter confirm me in this view. Why should the hirer apologise so humbly, twice, if he thought that he was merely exercising an option given to him by the agreement?"

If it was a breach then clauses 7 and 8 applied. By virtue of these clauses the company could retake possession of the vehicle, terminate the agreement because of the hirer's breach and claim the payments due under clause 9. In these circumstances the doctrine of penalties applied. The court went on to decide that the payments under clause 9 in the event of a breach did amount to a penalty and Mr Bridge only had to pay the company's actual losses as opposed to the charges laid down in clause 9.

Thus the case turned on the interpretation placed upon Mr Bridge's actions. The Court of Appeal interpreted what he was doing as an option to terminate therefore the doctrine of penalties did not apply. The House of Lords put a different interpretation on his actions and said he was in breach and therefore the doctrine did apply.

As Lord Denning pointed out in the House of Lords this leads to a paradox. The conscientious hirer who has difficulties making the payments and who does the right thing under the contract and exercises his option to terminate has to make up the payments as laid down in the minimum payments clause whereas the unconscientious hirer who falls behind with his payments but does nothing until the owner comes along and repossesses the car and then sues only has to pay the actual losses for his breach.

Although the court was not actually called upon to solve this paradox it did not stop four of their lordships expressing an opinion on the matter. What they said however was not helpful because two of them said that if the option had been exercised then the minimum payment clause was valid whereas the other two expressed the opinion that they would have applied the doctrine of penalties to an option clause. In effect this meant that on this point the Court of Appeal judgment was still valid because it had not been overruled.

A later House of Lords case, however, *Export Credits Guarantee Department v Universal Oils Products Co* [1983] 2 All E.R. 205 has confirmed that the doctrine of penalties does not apply to sums which are payable on the occurrence of an event which is not a breach.

What this means in practice for tour operators' cancellation clauses is that *if* operators want to ensure that the clauses are enforceable without having to prove that the sums involved are a penalty then they should be drafted in such a way that they can only be interpreted as conferring an option to terminate not as imposing damages for breach. Wordings should be tightened up. Instead of using a clause such as this:

> "If you cancel your booking ... [w]e will ask you to pay cancellation charges on the scale shown below. These charges reflect our estimated loss as a result of dealing with your booking to the point of cancellation and any other losses we may have to pay." (Airtours 2002)

or one like this:

> "Because we start to incur costs in relation to your arrangements from the time we confirm your booking, if you cancel we have to make a charge, and the nearer to your departure date you cancel, the more the charge will be." (Olympic 2002)

an operator should choose a much more explicit form of words to make it clear that the cancellation is the exercise of an option not a breach *e.g.*:

> "You have an option to cancel your holiday which must be exercised in writing ... The fees for the exercise of this option are ..." (Balkan Holidays 1992)

The first two clauses leave open the possibility that a court could interpret a cancellation as either a breach or an option to terminate. The third can only reasonably be interpreted as an option. If a court accepted it it would mean that the operator could put what figures he liked in the scale of charges and it could not be questioned by the courts! (Subject to the application of the VTCCR).

But getting the drafting right is only half the answer. The client must actually exercise the option. If, as in the *Bridge* case his actions could be interpreted as a breach of contract then the clause will not apply at all because it doesn't cover breach. In which case the operator is back to proving his actual loss—or also having an agreed damages clause in the contract on a scale which is less fierce than the option to terminate clause. This of course would look very peculiar in the brochure—having two different scales for essentially the same thing.

Anyone advising a client who is having difficulties making the payments and who is considering cancelling would be well advised to look carefully at the cancellation clause and determine whether it is an agreed damages clause or an option to terminate clause. If it was the latter and the charges seemed excessive the advice to the client should be to make it clear that he is not exercising an option but is repudiating the contract altogether and simply refusing to pay any more and if the tour operator wants his money he will have to sue for it. If it is the former then again the adviser should carefully consider whether the scale of payments it excessive or extravagant and if it is advise the client not to pay. It would then be up to the operator to sue.

At the end of the day, unless the operator succeeds in getting the client to exercise a genuine option to terminate, the client will not have to pay an amount which is extravagant or unconscionable so long as he is prepared to exercise his legal rights. On the one hand, faced with an option to terminate clause with extravagant payments attached to it the client should just ignore it and inform the operator he is in breach. On the other hand, faced with an agreed damages clause which is in reality a penalty he should be prepared to challenge it.

From the operator's point of view if he wants to avoid difficulties he would be well advised not to rely upon a scale which is excessive. Additionally he should provide for both breach and an option to terminate so that all possibilities are covered and the likelihood of litigation is minimised.

There are two travel cases which involve the issue of cancellation charges. The first is *Global of London (Tours and Travel) Ltd v Tait* 1977 SLT 96. Having made her booking and paid her deposit in January the client did nothing further. On August 4, only five days before she was due to depart the tour operator wrote to her and said: "Your attitude to the whole matter has now entailed your booking's complete cancellation", and claimed cancellation charges. The court held that clause 4 of the contract permitted the tour operator to cancel in writing—but she had not done this and the court would not imply a cancellation when the clause clearly required written cancellation. Alternatively clause 2 permitted the tour operator to cancel if the balance was not paid within 56 days of travel. In this latter case however they would be restricted to retaining the deposit but no more. The lesson here for the tour operator was either to act more quickly when faced with default or to draft a clause which imposed a sliding scale of charges—which most tour operators now do.

The second travel case which deals specifically with cancellation charges is *Thomson Travel Ltd v Hall* (1981, County Court, unreported). Mr Hall had booked his holiday on July 19 and then cancelled it on July 21 because his employers wanted him to go abroad on business during his holiday. Mr Hall refused to pay the 60 per cent cancellation charges due under the contract. The judge held, relying on the Court of Appeal judgment in the *Bridge* case, that the cancellation clause was an option to terminate clause and that therefore the doctrine of penalties did not apply. As Mr Hall had exercised his option and was not in breach he was therefore liable to pay the whole sum. The judge said:

> "The first important matter to emphasise is that there was no breach of contract here. Under the contract which Mr Hall signed he was entitled if he wished to do so to cancel and he exercised that option, and that option it is stated in the contract is to be exercised at a price."

If Mr Hall had not followed the procedure under the contract but had simply intimated that he was not going to pay any more then he might have been regarded as being in breach in which case the clause would not have applied.

The impact of the Package Travel Regulations

Earlier in this section we mentioned that insurance companies were becoming increasingly concerned at the high level of cancellation charges they were having to pay. One way of combatting this that has been mooted is to utilise the opportunity created by Regulation 10.

Under Regulation 10 if a consumer is "prevented from proceeding" with a package then he can transfer the package to someone who "satisfies all the conditions applicable to the package". The immediate effect of this is that a consumer who would otherwise have to cancel and pay cancellation charges will be able to minimise his loss if he can find someone suitable to take his place. However if he cannot find a substitute he will still have to pay the cancellation charges. Often these charges will be paid for by the client's insurance company.

The question arises as to whether the insurance company can utilise Regulation 10 in an effort to reduce their costs. Could they for instance have the package transferred to them so that they could then sell it on to another transferee at a price which allowed them to recoup at least some of the cancellation charges? Alternatively could they use their right of subrogation under the insurance contract to keep the contract alive and compel the consumer to sell it to a transferee?

The first of these alternatives may not be possible under the Regulations. Regulation 10 states that the consumer can transfer his booking to a person who satisfies the conditions of the package. Although an insurance company is regarded as a legal person the wording of the Regulations suggests that the transferee must be a real person. However this is not beyond doubt and it may very well be that the insurance company could qualify as a transferee.

The second alternative seems a much more realistic possibility. Under their right of subrogation the insurance company would inform the client that they were exercising their rights under the contract to take over the contract in the client's name and they would require him to transfer the holiday to anyone else who was suitable. Thus if a transferee could be found the company may lose less on the resale than they would have done on the cancellation charges.

At first sight there seem to be two major disadvantages from the insurance companies' point of view. First, how are they to find the transferees to take up these cancelled holidays? Even if they set up a market for such holidays they would probably have to sell them at substantial discounts to make them attractive.

Secondly, they will have to sell the holidays very quickly because as long as the contract is kept "alive" the clock is running and greater and greater cancellation charges are accruing. If the holiday is not sold the company is left with even greater losses than originally.

But this may not be the drawback it first appears. Major tour operators now impose such high cancellation charges for such long periods before departure that it would be possible for insurance companies to offer substantial discounts on the holiday and yet still make significant savings on the cancellation charges. For instance, until quite recently, one major operator imposed 100 per cent cancellation charges for cancellations made within three weeks of departure. Another imposed 90 per cent charges for cancellations made within 14 days of departure. Among major tour operators the norm was to charge at least 60 per cent for cancellations within 4 weeks of departure. Even if the insurance company offered as much as 40 per cent off the holiday they would still lose less than the operator would charge for cancellation.

The Unfair Terms in Consumer Contracts Regulations

We referred in Chapter Six on exclusion clauses to the Unfair terms in Consumer Contracts Regulations 1999. These regulations cover not simply exclusion clauses but any kind of unfair terms in contracts which have not been individually negotiated and which contravene the requirement of good faith. As has been seen, Schedule 3, lists terms which may be regarded as unfair. The list includes terms:

> "permitting the seller or supplier to retain sums paid by the consumer where the latter decides not to conclude or perform the contract, without providing for the consumer to receive compensation of an equivalent amount from the seller or supplier where the latter is the party cancelling the contract.
>
> Requiring any consumer who fails to fulfil his obligation to pay a disproportionately high sum in compensation."

Both these provisions appear targetted at cancellation charges. Consumer groups believe that both these provisions apply to some of the higher levels of cancellation charges required by tour operators. They also suggest a more promising line of argument for insurance companies than those explored above. One answer given by tour operators is this: that in the event that they cancel a holiday, they refund a sum which is more than 100 per cent of the price, *i.e.* a full refund plus compensation calculated on a scale which varies according to the time before departure the holiday was cancelled; whereas if the consumer cancels, he or she must forfeit a sum which is a maximum of 100 per cent, and usually less.

The problem with taking this approach however is that the sums are not necessarily comparable. The sum payable by the tour operator is a full refund—because the consumer didn't get a holiday at all—*plus* a sum for distress and disappointment and any out of pocket expenses—which is why it adds up to more than 100 per cent. On the other hand when the consumer cancels the tour operator has to be compensated for the lost sale. This should only be 100 per cent if he fails to sell the holiday again. In many cases the loss will be substantially less because of the operator's ability to make late sales—which suggests that compensation should be payable on much gentler scales than presently employed.

One case, referred to earlier, *Hartman v P&O Cruises*, looked at the issue of cancellation charges in the light of a decision by P&O to cancel the claimants' cruise and to refund the money plus £40 per head compensation. According to the brief report the court held:

> "that the 1992 Regulations could not be considered in isolation, because they did not deal with unfair contract terms which were governed by the 1994 Regulations [now the 1999 Regulations], in particular Reg. 4(1) and Reg. 4(2) and Sch. 3 para. 1(d). If the terms relied upon by P were reasonable then H entered into a binding contract to restrict their damages to GBP 40 each. P were clearly in the stronger bargaining position and the restriction of compensation to GBP 40 per person was unfair, particularly when compared with the sum that P would have kept had it been H who had cancelled the cruise the day before departure. Therefore, there was no limit on the award of damages."

Significantly, when the OFT announced in October 2002 that it had reached agreement with all the major operators and ABTA to modify their terms and conditions, cancellation clauses did not figure in the list of terms. Presumably this is not because the OFT do not think they are reasonable but because they have not yet managed to convince the tour operators to reduce their charges. It must be said, however, that compared to the former draconian levels that were levied the current levels are not so severe—evidence perhaps that OFT pressure is succeeding.

Remedies Under Regulation 13

Regulation 13 provides that in certain circumstances, when the organiser is unable to provide the promised package, the consumer is entitled to be offered an alternative package—as well as or instead of damages. On the face of it this is a radical departure from the remedies traditionally available from the law but in reality it is a practice which had become quite commonplace in the travel industry long before the advent of the Regulations. Tour operators, faced with the inevitable fact that a service designed and marketed many months, if not years, in advance of performance, could not always be delivered as promised, would often offer an alternative holiday to clients rather than cancel the holiday altogether and have to pay substantial damages. Clients on the other hand were often grateful to be offered a substitute package if the alternative was not to go abroad at all. The offer of an alternative package is the equivalent in the travel industry of a car dealer offering to repair your new car instead of taking it back and returning your money. The main difference now is that the package holidaymaker has a right to demand an alternative package whereas the car owner cannot demand a repair—he will only get one if he can negotiate it with the car dealer (although this is due to change).

The right to be offered an alternative package is to be found in Regulation 13 but it is dependent not only on the provisions in Regulation 13 but also the provisions of Regulation 12. Regulation 12 gives the consumer a right to withdraw from the contract is there are significant alterations to essential terms. If the consumer does withdraw under Regulation 12 then under Regulation 13 he has the right to be offered an alternative holiday. This right exists not only if the consumer withdraws under Regulation 12 but also, under Regulation 13, if the tour operator cancels the package for other reasons.

Regulation 12 provides:

"12 In every contract there are implied terms to the effect that—

(a) where the organiser is constrained before the departure to alter significantly an essential term of the contract, such as the price, he will inform the consumer as quickly as possible in order to enable him to take appropriate decisions and in particular to withdraw from the contract without penalty or to accept a rider to the contract specifying the alterations made and their impact on the price; and
(b) the consumer will inform the organiser or the retailer of his decision as soon as possible."

A number of difficulties present themselves here regarding the interpretation of this Regulation. First what is meant by "essential terms"? Are they the terms found in Schedule 2 of the Regulations which are compulsory terms of the contract? They seem to be regarded as essential by the drafters of the Directive otherwise they would not feature as compulsory terms of the contract. But are these the only terms that are essential? For instance the operator might have advertised the package as suitable for singles only but then at the last minute decided to throw it open to married persons as well. It could very well be an essential term of the contract that the package is only open to singles but it doesn't feature in the Annex—in which case it might not be governed by Regulation 12.

Are the terms in the Schedule to be regarded as essential simply because they are in the Schedule? Are they all to be regarded as sufficiently important as to give rise to the right to withdraw from the contract if significantly altered? On balance the answer seems to be yes.

This raises a second problem. What is meant by "significant"? At present tour operators tend to classify changes into major and minor changes in their terms and conditions and in some cases permit the consumer to cancel in the event of major changes. Changes in the day of departure, resort, hotel and airport frequently feature in such lists and there is no reason to believe that under the Regulations the situation will be different. There may be other changes however which may appear insignificant initially but when viewed from the perspective of the consumer are much more important. For instance if the brochure promises that water sports are available in resort this may not be a vital element of many clients' holidays but in individual cases they may have built their whole holiday around it. It may in those circumstances amount to an "essential" term of the contract. (Note that in October 2002 when the OFT required major tour operators to change some of their standard terms and conditions Thomson were required to change the term that only offered compensation for certain named significant changes. Thus it appears that it is irrelevant how the tour operator classifies the term it may still be regarded as significant.)

Some idea of what amounts to a significant term can be gleaned from *Golby v Nelson's Theatre and Travel Agency* (1967) 111 Sol Jo 470, a case which pre-dates the Package Travel Regulations by some years. In that case the Court of Appeal had to decide whether a flight change gave rise to the right to cancel a holiday to Israel. A booking had been made on a non-stop scheduled BOAC flight, BA 316, to Tel Aviv. A day before travel the claimant was informed that the flight number had been changed to BA 924 and the flight would be leaving 75 minutes later. In the mistaken belief that this was not a non-stop flight, and without listening to the travel agent, the claimant repudiated the contract and claimed the return of his deposit. The court held that this did not amount to a breach of condition, nor even to a breach of contract at all, and denied him the return of his deposit.

Regulation 12 applies where the operator is *constrained* to alter the essential terms of the contract. The term originally used in the draft Regulations was *compelled*—a term which is more restrictive than constrained. Compelled suggests that alterations can only be made for events beyond the control of the operator and where he has no choice in the matter but the use of constrained implies that changes can be made on financial grounds alone. This broadens the range of situations where the operator can "legitimately" make alterations but it also broadens the circumstances where the consumer is entitled to additional remedies. *Hayes v Airtours* [2001] C.L.Y. 4283, a case arising out of Hurricane Georges which devastated parts of the Dominican Republic held that the tour operator was not in breach of Regulation 12. Although the hurricane hit the resort only two days after the claimants arrived the nature of hurricanes is so uncertain that even with only two days to go its path was unpredictable and the best estimate was that it would have avoided the island. (See Kilbey, "Of Holidays and Hurricanes" [1999] I.T.L.J. 46 for a discussion of this issue.)

Note that the operator is under a duty to inform the consumer as quickly as possible of the changes in essential terms. This means that the operator cannot keep the information to himself and only divulge it to the client at the last moment—when the client will have no choice but to accept. Two cases involving First Choice Holidays illustrate the consequences for tour operators for failing to comply with this requirement. In *Graham v First Choice Holiday & Flights Ltd* [1997] C.L.Y. 1771 the tour operator knew two days prior to departure that the claimants' accommodation was not available (two weeks at the most expensive hotel offered them) but failed to inform them. As a consequence the claimants were accommodated for part of the time in a business hotel with few tourist facilities 80km from where they wanted to be. They asked to be returned home but that was not possible. On their return First Choice returned the whole of the holiday price to them and the court awarded them a further £500 for distress and disappointment. The report is a brief one and Regulation 12 is not mentioned, nor is Regulation 15, but the case seems a straightforward application of the two.

In *Hook v First Choice Holiday & Flights Ltd* [1998] C.L.Y. 1426 the tour operator knew four days before the claimants departed on holiday that their hotel was not available and did inform them of this. They were told that the alternative being offered them was in the same resort and of equivalent quality. They were further told that if they chose to cancel they would only receive a 10 per cent refund. The claimants reluctantly agreed to the change. The hotel, although of the same star rating, was of inferior quality. It was decided that the claimants' holiday had not been entirely ruined and they were entitled to a 20 per cent discount on the price for diminution of value (£200) and £250 for distress and disappointment. Of more significance however is that the judge said that the claimants had not been "properly informed" of their full rights under Regulation 12, including the right to withdraw without penalty, and that in such circumstances tour operators should inform consumers in writing of the options available to them. In this case he felt that there had been "an element of H being duped into believing he had no right to cancel". (See also *Crump v Inspirations East* [1998] C.L.Y. 1427 for a case where the tour operator failed to inform the consumer of significant problems in resort which they knew about before departure.)

It is not just the operator who is under an obligation in Regulation 12. It is also an implied term that the consumer notifies the operator or agent as soon as possible of his decision. It is not specified what the penalty will be but it could very well be that the consumer would lose his right to withdraw if he did not act quickly enough. But note that the client is under no obligation to take the decision quickly—merely to inform the operator as quickly as possible once the decision has been made.

If the consumer does withdraw from the contract under Regulation 12 his rights will be governed by Regulation 13. This offers the consumer the choice of either an alternative package or a full refund and, in most circumstances, compensation.

Regulation 13 provides:

> "13(1) The terms set out in paragraphs (2) and (3) below are implied in every contract and apply where the consumer withdraws from the contract pursuant to the term in it implied by virtue of regulation 12(a), or where the organiser, for any reason other than the fault of the consumer, cancels the package before the date when it is due to start.
>
> (2) the consumer is entitled—
>
> (a) to take a substitute package of equivalent or superior quality if the other party to the contract is able to offer him such a substitute; or
>
> (b) to take a substitute package of lower quality if the other party to the contract is able to offer him one and to recover from the organiser the difference in price between the price of the package purchased and that of the substitute package; or
>
> (c) to have repaid to him as soon as possible all the moneys paid by him under the contract.
>
> (3) The consumer is entitled, if appropriate, to be compensated

by the organiser for non-performance of the contract except where—

(a) the package is cancelled because the number of persons who agree to take it is less than the minimum number required and the consumer is informed of the cancellation, in writing, within the period indicated in the description of the package; or
(b) the package is cancelled by reason of unusual and unforeseeable circumstances beyond the control of the party by whom this exception is pleaded, the consequences of which could not have been avoided even if all due care had been exercised, provided that it is not open to that party to rely on this exception in cases of overbooking."

As already indicated the obligation to offer a substitute package if available corresponds with existing practice and, for ABTA members, had already been formalised in the ABTA Code. It appears that the duty to offer an alternative if available is not optional—the consumer is entitled to the offer if the organiser is able to offer it. The organiser does not appear to have the choice of simply refunding the consumer's money rather than offering an alternative. In practice this is unlikely to happen because in most circumstances the operator would prefer to hold on to the booking but it may be that with a particularly "difficult" client who is already unhappy with the alteration the operator may not wish to offer an alternative even if one was available. Regulation 13(2)(a) seems to preclude this possibility.

One problem that arises under Regulation 13(2)(a) is what is meant by a substitute package of equivalent or superior quality? Put at its simplest this means that if the tour operator is unable to offer two weeks in the chosen resort at the four star Grand Hotel then he could offer the same two weeks at the four star Excelsior Hotel just a couple of hundred yards down the beach. This would clearly be a package of equivalent quality. Likewise if the operator couldn't offer a four star alternative but was able to upgrade the consumer to a five star hotel in the same resort this would be a substitute of superior quality.

But difficulties could arise if for instance the operator was unable to offer an equivalent or near equivalent package to the consumer but nevertheless was able to offer a far superior one to a different destination. Let's say that the consumer had booked a two night city break in Paris at a two star hotel at the height of the season and at the last minute the tour operator was unable to provide this. Not only that but there was no further availability in Paris at all—but the operator still has four night breaks available in Vienna in a four star hotel—or, if we push this example to the limits—a 14 day package to a deluxe hotel in Rio.

The problem from the tour operator's point of view is that the consumer is entitled to take a substitute package of equivalent or superior quality if the tour operator is able to offer him such a substitute. Clearly the operator is able to offer the alternatives in Vienna and Rio and clearly the Regulations envisage that the consumer will get a superior holiday in some circumstances. So why should the consumer not be entitled to the packages in Vienna or Rio?

One answer which has a certain superficial attraction is that of course the consumer can have the package to Vienna or Rio just so long as he is prepared to pay the difference in price. This is certainly a solution which some tour operators have successfully adopted but it may not be sanctioned by the Regulations. The Regulations are in fact silent as to whether or not the operator can charge extra for a superior substitute but there is one indication that they cannot. Regulation 13(2)(b), which deals with the right to an inferior package, does actually say that the consumer is entitled to the difference in price when offered an inferior quality package. The inference that can be drawn from this is that if the Regulations do provide for a financial adjustment in Regulation 13(2)(b) but do not in Regulation 13(2)(a) then this must be for a reason—and the reason is that the operator is not allowed to charge extra for the superior package. If it had been intended that the tour operator could charge extra then this would have been provided for in the Regulation—as it was in Regulation 13(2)(b).

On the other hand, an opposing argument can be constructed. As we shall see, under Regulation 14, where alternative arrangements are made for a consumer after departure, it is expressly stated that these shall be at no extra charge to the consumer. If it is expressly stated there, why not in Regulation 13? One answer is that, after departure, the consumer can almost be likened to a prisoner of the tour operator who must be protected from being ripped off with extra charges; whilst before departure, the consumer is in a much stronger position to decide whether or not to pay any proposed extra charges.

Consumers who felt compelled to pay the extra might be able to recover it in some circumstances if it could be seen as a payment made in order to mitigate loss in the face of a breach of contract.

It may be that argument on this point is now moving towards the consumer. In October 2002 the OFT required both Thomson Holidays and Thomas Cook to remove terms in their standard conditions requiring consumers to pay the difference if a superior holiday was offered when the holiday was cancelled through no fault of the consumer or when the tour operator made significant changes—*because this conflicted with the Package Travel Regulations.*

If the tour operator is able to offer an equivalent or slightly superior holiday, as they will be able to do in most cases, then this remains an academic problem, but it is nevertheless the case that on occasion the operator will be faced with a dilemma like this and will have to solve it. One way is to argue that the words should be interpreted in context. If the operator is required to provide a substitute for a city break holiday to Paris then the substitute must also be a city break holiday to Paris. To require the operator to offer holidays to Vienna or Rio would be so different from the original package that it could not be a reasonable interpretation of the Regulations.

Failing that the only recourse for the operator would simply be to refuse to supply the alternative. This would place the operator in breach of the implied term but it would probably not increase the damages. Ultimately it would be a financial decision for the operator—will it cost me more to upgrade the client from Paris to Vienna or Rio than to cancel the holiday altogether and pay damages for distress and disappointment? There will also be the loss of goodwill to take into account as well.

If the operator is unable to offer an alternative package, or the consumer rejects it and decides to withdraw from the contract anyway then the operator is required to repay "all the moneys paid by him under the contract". Whether this includes insurance premiums will depend upon whether the insurance was paid as part of the package or whether it was purchased separately.

Whether or not the consumer withdraws or takes an alternative package he is entitled to damages for the non-performance of the contract (Regulation 13(3)). Nothing is said about the manner in which the damages are to be calculated (although Regulation 15(4) does permit tour operators if they are so minded to provide that damages can be limited to an extent that is not unreasonable) therefore the principles established in *Jarvis v Swans Tours* [1973] 1 All E.R. 71 will still be applicable. So too, will the rules on mitigation of damage. Thus if the operator does offer a suitable alternative and the consumer, for no good reason, refuses it then the consumer will get little or nothing by way of damages. Most tour operators provide a table of compensation in their booking conditions. There is of course nothing wrong with this practice, but the sums concerned are only legally enforceable if they are not unreasonable.

Where a substitute package has been provided the damages are likely to be relatively small and in many cases the consumer may not receive any damages at all—simply because the substitute would be adequate compensation. It will be noted that compensation is payable "if appropriate" and one example where it may not be appropriate is if the substitute package is superior, but no additional charge has been made.

Damages are not recoverable in two circumstances. The first is where the operator cancels for lack of numbers. In such cases as long as this is expressly provided for in the contract and the operator complies with the time limits the consumer is limited to recovering the price of the holiday (or substitute arrangements). Note that ABTA operators cannot cancel for lack of minimum numbers after the balance of the price has been paid. (Paragraph 2.3 (i) of the Code).

The second situation where the consumer is denied compensation is where the contract is cancelled by reason of unusual and unforeseeable circumstances beyond the control of the party by whom it is pleaded, the consequences of which could not have been avoided even if all due care had been exercised. This is the *force majeure* defence and for a more detailed examination of the *force majeure* provisions you should refer back to Chapter Nine.

In *Josephs v Sunworld* [1998] 7 CL 395, in a muddled report where the remedies under Regulations 12, 13 and 14 seem to have been confused, it was held that there had been a breach of both Regulation 12 and Regulation 13 and that the tour operator had failed to offer the consumer the alternative of continuing with the holiday and claiming compensation or returning home. (*Westerman v Travel Promotions* [2000] C.L.Y. 4042 is another case where there seems some confusion over the remedies under Regulations 12 & 13 and those under Regulation 14.)

Remedies Under Regulation 14

Regulation 14 covers the situation where major changes to the package occur after departure. It provides:

> "14(1) The terms set out in paragraphs (2) and (3) below are implied in every contract and apply where, after departure, a significant proportion of the services contracted for is not provided, or the organiser becomes aware that he will be unable to procure a significant proportion of the services to be provided.
>
> (2) The organiser will make suitable alternative arrangements, at no extra cost to the consumer, for the continuation of the package and will, where appropriate, compensate the consumer

for the difference between the services to be supplied under the contract and those supplied.

(3) If it is impossible to make arrangements as described in paragraph (2), or these are not accepted by the consumer for good reasons, the organiser will, where appropriate, provide the consumer with equivalent transport back to the place of departure or to another place to which the consumer has agreed and will, where appropriate, compensate the consumer."

This Regulation appears to cover the non-provision of service whereas Regulation 15, which also has a bearing on this Regulation, covers the improper provision of the services as well as the non-provision of the services. In some cases this may be a difficult distinction to make. For instance if the brochure states that rooms are air-conditioned and the air-conditioning system is not working is that a case of non-provision or improper provision? The same argument could be applied where the hotel does provide the advertised meals but they are inedible.

As with Regulation 12 the requirement in Regulation 14 is that a "significant" proportion of the services not be provided before the consumer is entitled to the benefit of the Regulation. How large a proportion amounts to significant will be a question of fact in each case. If for instance the consumer finds that the hotel he booked is not available then, prima facie, this would amount to a significant proportion of the services. It would be the same if in a package consisting of transport to London, overnight accommodation and tickets to "Les Miserables", the tour operator found that he could not provide the tickets to the theatre. It would not be regarded as "significant" if on a 10 day package to Paris the bottle of champagne was not in the bedroom as promised.

If the failure is significant then the organiser is first obliged to make "suitable" alternative arrangements. This could mean booking the consumer into an alternative hotel, arranging for meals to be taken elsewhere, arranging for the promised boat trip on the Seine to be taken on the second day of the holiday rather than the first. Even if the alternative is "suitable" it is provided that the consumer is entitled to compensation for the difference between the service offered and the service actually supplied "where appropriate". Presumably this means that if the service supplied is cheaper than that offered then the consumer is entitled to a refund of the difference in price. It is not entirely clear whether the compensation is only to cover difference in value or whether it also encompasses compensation for the distress and disappointment suffered because of the difference. Even if it does cover the latter the amounts involved are not likely to be large simply because the alternative could not be called suitable if it caused a significant amount of distress.

The obligation placed on the organiser is that he "will" make suitable alternative arrangements and only if it is "impossible" to do so will he be able to offer transport home. Suppose for instance the consumer has contracted for a two star hotel in Paris on July 14 and the tour operator cannot offer this but there is a suite available in the most expensive hotel in Paris. Is this a suitable alternative? Certainly it is suitable to the consumer. Is it impossible to arrange? Certainly not, all it takes is a phone call. Is the operator obliged to book it? Nothing in the Regulation seems to give him any alternative, no matter what the cost to him. This is similar to the dilemma facing the operator under Regulation 13 already discussed where there alternative packages available but at much greater cost. *Thompson v Airtours Holidays Ltd (No.1)* [1999] C.L.Y. 3819 is authority for the proposition that the onus is on the tour operator to to make an offer to find alternative accommodation. Airtours knew what was available but an offer was not made.

When considering the cost of upgrading it should be borne in mind that the alternative could be much more costly. The Regulations provide that if the organiser does find it impossible to make alternative arrangements or they are not accepted by the consumer for good reasons the organiser is under an obligation to return the consumer to his starting point, where appropriate. At common law the consumer was able to mitigate his loss by returning home under his own steam and could reclaim the cost as part of his damages but there was no obligation on the tour operator to assist him. This is a major departure from the common law and from the ABTA Code. Cases such as *Booth & Ingram v Best Travel* [1990] C.L.Y. 1542, *Abbatt v Sunquest* [1984] C.L.Y. 1025 and *Bragg v Yugotours* [1982] C.L.Y. 777 are all pre-1992 cases which would now fall to be decided under Regulation 14 and where the tour operator, having failed to provide suitable alternative arrangements, would be under an obligation to repatriate the consumers. *Marsh v Thomson Tour Operators* [2000] C.L.Y. 4044 is a case where the tour operator went beyond what is required in Regulation 14. The brochure promised that if consumers was not satisfied with the holiday then they could ask to be repatriated and would be given a full refund. After failing to satisfy the expectations of the claimant Thomson reluctantly agreed to fly him home but did not offer the promised refund on the grounds that his request was not reasonable. The court held:

> "... that the guarantee did not specify that a customer's dissatisfaction had to be 'reasonable', and such a term could not be

implied. The guarantee was included by Thomson as a sales gimmick, to provide something extra to set it apart from the competition. If the operation of the guarantee was limited to situations where it was reasonable for a customer to request to be flown home, it would be worth little."

The obligation to repatriate is only imposed where it is "appropriate" to do so. If the failure to provide the services occurred with only two days of a 21-day holiday to Australia remaining then it might be deemed inappropriate for the organiser to have to book the consumer on to an expensive scheduled flight home. Perhaps the organiser might not have been able to provide the two day trip to the Great Barrier Reef which was regarded as the highlight of the package. Even though this might be regarded as significant and the organiser might not have been able to make suitable alternative arrangements nevertheless the remedy might be out of all proportion to the fault of the organiser. Slightly different considerations would apply on Majorca where there is a wide choice of cheap flights back to the UK on most days.

The consumer is not entitled to reject the alternative arrangements without good reason. If he has no good reason then the organiser is not obliged to transport him home. Presumably if he then chooses to go home at his own expense the tour operator would not be obliged to compensate him in such circumstances. Having offered a suitable alternative and the consumer having rejected it for no good reason then the organiser could argue that the alternative should have been accepted as a reasonable mitigation of loss and the decision to go home was not a reasonable decision in the circumstances.

There is a suggestion that even if the alternative is suitable the consumer may yet have good reasons for rejecting it. It is hard to envisage such a case but they might occur in circumstances such as occurred in *Harvey v Tracks Travel* [1984] C.L.Y. 1006. In that case the plaintiff had suffered such privations already that no matter what alternative she was offered it might have been reasonable for her to say: "Enough is enough. I want to go home now. I no longer have any confidence in your ability to provide me with the rest of the holiday. Nor do I have any confidence that the alternative you are offering me will be any better than what you have already provided—no matter what assurances you give me." A similar situation arose in *Rhodes v Sunspot Tours* [1983] C.L.Y. 984 where the consumer was offered a succession of sub-standard apartments.

Where the consumer has been transported home the organiser "shall, where appropriate, compensate the consumer". Thus a consumer would receive compensation on a pro rata basis for the truncation of his holiday and also damages for distress. In most cases compensation would be appropriate under Regulation 14; indeed, a consumer who returns home almost as soon as the holiday has begun, will expect a full refund of the holiday price plus damages for disappointment etc of an equivalent amount. An exception would be where the disruption of the holiday arrangements has been caused by *force majeure*, *e.g.* the outbreak of war or circumstance falling within Regulation 15(2)(b)(ii). It will be noted, that unlike Regulation 13, there is no exception under Regulation 14 for *force majeure*. Thus at the very least the tour operator remains under an obligation to transport the consumer home; but alternative arrangements or compensation may not be appropriate. (This does of course raise a further question about the overlap between Regulations 14 and 15, where *force majeure* is permitted as an exception. On this point see *Charlson v Warner*, referred to in Chapter Nine).

One recent case on Regulation 14 is *Martin v Travel Promotions Ltd* [1999] 4 CL 434. In that case the delay of an internal flight in India meant that the plaintiffs missed a connecting international flight to Heathrow. The court held that the tour operator was under a duty under Regulation 14 to make suitable alternative arrangements. Their solution was to book the plaintiffs on a flight the next day. In the meantime the plaintiffs had gone out and purchased first class airfares on the same flight. It was held that the defendants were in breach of contract but that the loss to the plaintiffs was not caused by that breach but by the plaintiffs' hasty and disproportionate actions in purchasing the first class fares. Another case is *Hibbs v Thomas Cook Group Ltd* [1999] C.L.Y. 3829. After 10 days of a 15 day trip around the Rocky Mountains the tour operator found that a ferry had been suddenly withdrawn from service because of "entirely unforeseen" mechanical problems and the tourists in the group has to be re-routed. They complained about the new itinerary but the court held that the ferry breakdown amounted to "*force majeure*" which would have excused the tour operator from its obligation to perform the entire contract and they could simply have flown the claimant back to the UK. The decision is suspect for a number of reasons. First there is the question of whether mechanical problems amount to *force majeure*. Secondly, *force majeure* does not necessarily release the tour operator from its obligation to perform the contract. Thirdly, there is a clear duty to make suitable alternative arrangements unless it is impossible to do so.

An interesting illustration of the problems arose early in 1998 when tour operators took a number of British tourists on a package which included tickets for a test match between the West Indies and England. The match was abandoned on the first day because the pitch had been prepared so poorly. The law has long made clear that a consumer has no remedy where a cricket match is rained off, but here the situation was different—incompetence was involved. For those consumers unable to extend their holiday in order to view the next match, no suitable alternative arrangements could be made and, harsh as this is for the tour operator, it appears that compensation may be appropriate—although this was denied in a case that was decided under the ABTA arbitration scheme. (See Grant "Caribbean Chaos" (1998) 148 NLJ 190 and "Its not Cricket" [1998] ITLJ 51).

A gap in the Regulations?

Regulation 13 provides that where the tour operator cancels the holiday "before the agreed *date* of departure" the consumer is entitled to the remedies in that Regulation, *i.e.* an offer of alternative packages or a full refund. Regulation 14 on the other hand provides for remedies if a significant proportion of the services contracted for cannot be provided "after departure". It is possible to envisage a consumer caught between these two provisions and being denied a remedy. What if, for example, a consumer turns up at the airport on the agreed date but because of industrial action is prevented from departing. The next day, after clients have been hanging around the airport for 24 hours, the tour operator decides to cancel the package because he believes it will be impossible to perform the contract. This cancellation happens *after* the agreed date of departure but *before* any actual departure. The consumer therefore is not entitled to the benefits he would otherwise have under Regulations 13 or 14. Regulation 15 is of no immediate assistance either because in cases of *force majeure* or events which cannot be forestalled by the operator there is no right to compensation. However the ABTA Code of Conduct does provide that if a tour operator cancels a tour "for reasons of *force majeure before departure*" [emphasis added] then an alternative holiday or a refund must be offered. If the ABTA Code did not apply then arguably the common law rules on frustration could be invoked. For a discussion of these points see Kilbey, "Delayed Departure, Cancellation and the Package Travel Regulations" [1998] ITLJ 110 and Saggerson, "Delayed Departure and Cancellation. Hope for Consumers this Side of Midnight", [1999] ITLJ 6.

Rectification

Rectification is a remedy available to the parties to a contract when they have reached agreement but by mistake they have failed to express the agreement correctly in writing. For instance a tour operator may have agreed with a client that the price for a particular holiday will be £1000 but when the confirmation invoice arrives it states £100. In these circumstances the tour operator can apply to have the document rectified to reflect the true position. The basis of this principle is that if there has been a mistake then the other party cannot take advantage of it if the mistake is obvious. In *Craddock Brothers v Hunt* [1923] 2 Ch 136 the owner of property agreed to sell it exclusive of its adjoining yard. Unfortunately the document in which this oral agreement was expressed stated that the yard was included in the sale. In these circumstances the court ordered that the contract should be rectified to express the true agreement between the parties. It is of course necessary to be able to prove that the written document did not represent what the parties had truly agreed which may not always be easy.

The situation described above needs to be distinguished from a slightly different situation, also involving mistake but which proceeds on a different basis. What if a tour operator, by mistake, indicates that the price of a holiday is only £100 when it is really £1000, *e.g.* if the viewdata information has been corrupted? If this can be interpreted as an offer by the operator to sell at that price (see Chapter Three on this point) and the client accepts this offer does the client have a contract at the lower price? The operator would argue that the holiday at £100 was not on offer at all and therefore was not open for acceptance by the client. The distinction between the two situations is that in the former there is a common mistake which has resulted in an acknowledged agreement being incorrectly expressed but in the latter there is a unilateral mistake by the operator resulting in a dispute as to whether a contract exists at all.

In *Hartog v Colin and Shields* [1939] 3 All E.R. 566 the two parties had been negotiating for the sale of some hareskins and throughout the negotiations the price had been expressed as so much per piece—which was customary in the trade. The seller then, by mistake, quoted a price per pound which in the circumstances was absurdly low. The buyer purported to accept this offer but the seller refused to sell. When it came to court Singleton LJ said:

> "The plaintiff could not reasonably have supposed that the offer contained the offerors' real intention."

Note that the test is not whether the seller had made a genuine mistake but whether the buyer should have known this.

The problem facing tour operators is of course that such absurdly low offers are not unknown in the industry and the problem would be to convince a court that the client did not really suspect that the offer was just too good to be true; this is not such a problem in practice because the problem usually arises in the following form: travel agents surf through Viewdata looking for unlikely low prices and then make bookings for themselves or their friends. In such a case it would be easier for the tour operator to demonstrate that the buyer should have known that the offer did not contain their real intention.

Chapter Eleven
The Trade Descriptions Act 1968

Introduction

There are three sets of statutory provisions which have progressively imposed upon tour operators the duty to make their advertising (and many other statements they make to the public) honest, truthful and accurate. The three are the Trade Descriptions Act 1968, the Consumer Protection Act 1987 and the Package Travel Regulations 1992 (Regulations 5, 7 and 8). The Trade Descriptions Act is examined now. The Consumer Protection Act is dealt with in Chapter Twelve and the offences created by Regulations 5, 7 and 8 of the Package Travel Regulations are dealt with in Chapter Thirteen. There are a number of defences provided by the statutes and these are dealt with in Chapter Fourteen.

It often seems extra-ordinary to the travel industry (although perhaps not to consumers) that so many of the mistakes they make in the normal course of running their businesses can have the result of labelling them as criminals. Sending out an errata letter to clients which is unintentionally ambiguous, or getting the name of your overseas representative wrong, for example, do not feel like crimes. Indeed this point has been recognised by the judiciary. In *Wings v Ellis* [1984] 3 All E.R. 577 Lord Scarman said that the Trade Descriptions Act:

> "... is not a truly criminal statute. Its purpose is not the enforcement of the criminal law but the maintenance of trading standards. Trading standards, not criminal behaviour, are its concern."

To which many tour operators might respond that it certainly feels as if one is being treated like a criminal when facing the full panoply of a tape recorded interview by the investigating trading standards officer conducted under the Police and Criminal Evidence Act; or when facing a bench of magistrates in court.

The Trade Descriptions Act

The origins of the Trade Descriptions Act 1968 can be traced back to the Molony Committee Report on Consumer Protection of 1962 (Cmnd. 1781) which, as one of its findings, identified that consumers needed to be protected against misdescription of goods and services. The Trade Descriptions Act was an attempt to implement the recommendations of the report relating to misdescriptions.

The relevant provisions

The sections of the Act which relate to services and are therefore relevant to tour operators are set out below.

"14(1) It shall be an offence for any person in the course of any trade or business—

(a) to make a statement which he knows to be false; or
(b) recklessly to make a statement which is false;

as to any of the following matters, that is to say,—

(i) the provision in the course of any trade or business of any services, accommodation or facilities;
(ii) the nature of any services, accommodation or facilities provided in the course of any trade or business;
(iii) the time at which, manner in which or persons by whom any services, accommodation or facilities are so provided;
(iv) the examination, approval or evaluation by any person of any services, accommodation or facilities so provided; or
(v) the location or amenities of any accommodation so provided.

(2) For the purposes of this section—

(a) anything (whether or not a statement as to any of the matters specified in the preceding subsection) likely to be taken for such a statement as to any of those matters as would be false shall be deemed to be a false statement as to that matter; and
(b) a statement made regardless of whether it is true or false shall be deemed to be made recklessly, whether or not the person making it had reasons for believing that it might be false.

(3) . . . . . .
(4) In this section "false" means false to a material degree . . .

The requirements of the offence

If a prosecution is to succeed then it has to be established that:

- a statement has been made;
- in the course of a trade or business;
- which relates to one of the categories specified in section 14, and;
- the statement is false; and
- it was made knowingly or recklessly.

Each of these requirements will be looked at in turn.

Making a statement

There is no requirement that the statement be in writing so not only could the text of a brochure amount to a false trade description but also the photographs in it and any oral statements by the tour operator's (or the travel agent's) staff.

The following examples from the case law illustrate the wide variety of statements caught by the Act:

- In *Wings v Ellis* [1984] 3 All E.R. 577, the abbreviation "AC", which meant "air-conditioning", was held to be a false statement when it turned out that the hotel rooms were not air-conditioned.
- In *Yugotours v Wadsley* [1988] Crim. LR 623, a picture of a three masted schooner was held to be a false trade description when a two masted schooner with no sails was provided.
- In *R v Clarksons Holidays Ltd* (1972) 57 Cr App R 38 an artist's impression of an hotel was held to constitute a false trade description.
- In *Herron v Lunn Poly (Scotland) Ltd* [1972] SLT 2 an oral statement made over the phone to the effect that an hotel was complete when it was not. This was held to be a false trade description.

It does not matter whether the statement is made before or after a client books the holiday. In most cases the statement will be made in the brochure and the client will have seen it before the contract is made but in *Herron v Lunn Poly* the statement was made some time after the client booked the holiday and that did not affect the prosecution. There will be cases where information is provided on a confirmation invoice and if it turns out to be false then the potential for a prosecution exists.

In many cases a breach of the Trade Descriptions Act, leading to criminal liability, will also give rise to civil liability for breach of contract. Even if the civil action is settled to the satisfaction of the complainant this will not affect the criminal liability. In *Cowburn v Focus Television Rentals Ltd* (1983) 147 JP 201, DC, the defendant published an advertisement which gave the false impression that if customers rented a video recorder then they would be able to hire 20 feature films absolutely free. Due to an administrative error this advertisement remained in circulation after it had been superseded by another, less generous offer. Under this latter offer customers would only be able to hire six films free of charge and, in addition, they would have to pay postage on them. After a customer complained the defendant was visited by a trading standards officer. Following this visit the defendant took steps to ensure that the customer received 20 films and did not have to pay postage. The magistrates acquitted the defendant on the grounds that when the defendant had belatedly honoured the original offer this rectified the prior false statements. When the prosecution appealed to the Divisional Court it was decided that the subsequent act of honouring the original offer did not prevent the offence being committed. The actions of the defendant were only relevant as mitigating factors when it came to sentencing.

In practice, however, honouring the original promise or making a generous offer of compensation will often remove the threat of prosecution—either because the consumer does not complain to Trading Standards or because the Trading Standards Officer, using his discretion, feels that the full might of the criminal law in not required where the trader has behaved with integrity.

In the course of a trade or business

The Act is designed to catch dishonest businesses not private individuals. Most package holidays are sold by tour operators in the course of a business and therefore this provision is of little relevance. At the margins however it may be difficult to say what constitutes a trade or business. For instance if a lecturer in tourism organised a foreign holiday for staff and students on an occasional basis, say once a year, and on which he made a modest profit, would this amount to a "trade or business"?

In *London Borough of Havering v Stevenson* [1970] 3 All E.R. 609 a car hire firm sold a car with a false mileage. Although the firm was not a car dealer it nevertheless sold off its cars on a regular basis after they had been used for about two years. It was held that the sale was an integral part of the business. The car was not sold *for* the purposes of trade or business or even *by way of* trade or business but nevertheless it was *in* the course of trade or business.

A contrasting case is *Davies v Sumner* [1984] 3 All E.R. 831 where a self-employed courier sold his car with a false mileage on the clock. It showed 18,000 miles instead of 118,000. It was held by the House of Lords that the sale was not in the course of a trade or business. Lord Keith felt that the Act intended there to be some regularity to the sales before they could be in the course of a trade or business. The *Havering* case was distinguished on the grounds that it was their *normal practice* to dispose of the cars after a period of time.

> "... the occasional sale of some worn out piece of shop equipment would not fall within the enactment."

However, he qualified this in one respect. He said:

> "The need for some degree of regularity does not, however, involve that a one-off adventure in the nature of trade, carried through with a view to profit, would not fall within s.1(1) because such a transaction would itself constitute a trade."

Thus a one-off attempt to organise a package holiday if done with a view to profit could be said to be within the course of a trade or business.

Note that there is no requirement that the statement be made to a consumer; thus a statement made by a tour operator to a travel agent is covered.

The statement must fall within the categories listed in section 14

Section 14(1) lists the categories of description which fall within the ambit of the Act. If a description is published which is false it will not constitute an offence if it does not fall within section 14(1). Nevertheless the section is sufficiently wide to catch most descriptions used by tour operators. The case law clearly illustrates this:

- *Herron v Lunn Poly* was a prosecution under section 14(1)(b)(i) for a false statement relating to the *provision ... of any services, accommodation or facilities.* That case concerned an hotel and its facilities which were incomplete when the clients arrived.
- *R v Clarksons* was a prosecution under both section 14(1)(b)(i) and (ii) that is, not only for the *provision* of the services, but also the *nature of any services, accommodation or facilities.* This was also a case involving an incomplete hotel.
- *British Airways Board v Taylor* [1976] 1 All E.R. 65, which concerned a passenger who was "bumped" from a scheduled flight after he had been given a confirmed booking, was a prosecution under section 14(1)(b)(iii) for a false statement as to the *time* at which any services are provided. See also *R v Avro plc* (Court of Appeal, January 14, 1993).
- *Direct Holidays plc v Wirral Metropolitan Borough Council* (Div. Ct., April 28, 1998) was a prosecution under section 14(1)(b) for falsely describing the official classification of some holiday apartments. Although the case does not make it clear it must be presumed that this was contrary to section 14(1)(b)(iv) the *approval or evaluation* of the accommodation.
- *R v Sunair* [1973] 1 W.L.R. 1105, included a count for contravening section 14(1)(b)(v) relating to the *location and amenities of any accommodation* provided. In that case the prosecution concerned the non-availability of promised facilities.

Note that section 14 is not concerned with false or misleading prices. Before the enactment of the Consumer Protection Act 1987 there were a number of unsuccessful attempts to bring misleading prices within the wording of the Act. With the advent of the CPA 1987 such attempts are no longer necessary.

The statement is false

There are a number of issues here. First, before a statement can be said to be false it may be necessary to decide precisely what it means. Second, to be false the statement has to be a statement of fact. A statement of opinion or future intention or a mere promise is in most cases incapable of being held to be false. Third, the statement may not be true or false when originally made but become false at a later date. Fourthly, the Act states that "false" means "false to a material degree".

(i) What Does the Statement Mean?

In most cases this will not constitute a problem. If the brochure states that all rooms have private facilities and they do not this is clearly a false statement. Likewise if it says "200 metres to the beach" and it is 500 this too is a false statement.

On the other hand what if the brochure states that the "hotel is right on the *beach*" [emphasis added] and on arrival the clients find that the beach is a man-made construction consisting of an area of sand approximately 51 yards long and 17 yards wide retained behind a concrete wall bordering the sea. Access to the sea is by ladders down to water level at which point the depth of the sea is equivalent to the shallow end of a swimming pool. The only other area which could possibly be regarded as a beach is an area of about 100 square feet consisting of sand and rock which is out of sight of the hotel and which some clients never manage to find. (The report of the case describes the "beach" as a "large sandpit".)

This is just the situation which arose in *Thomson Travel Ltd v Roberts* (1984) 148 JP 666. The defendants were prosecuted under s.14(b)(v) of the Act for recklessly making a false statement about the amenities of the accommodation. Essentially the problem was whether or not a "beach" existed at the hotel. The magistrates held that:

> "Nothing at the hotel could be described as a beach, as the words would be interpreted by the average person."

On appeal the Queen's Bench Divisional Court upheld the Magistrates' decision. The meaning of the words was a question of fact and the justices came to a perfectly acceptable decision on the evidence.

A similar issue of interpretation arose more recently in the case of *London Borough of Southwark v Time Computer Systems Ltd* (Divisional Court, July 7, 1997) where the Divisional Court was called upon to decide an appeal involving an advertisement for a computer which was represented in a photograph surrounded by boxes of software. The prosecution contended that the advertisement constituted a false trade description on the basis that although the software had been pre-installed on the machine it was not supplied with either the software disks or manuals. It was held by the Magistrates' Court and on appeal that there had been no offence committed. The Divisional Court agreed with the Magistrate that the test to be applied was not whether any individual consumer would be misled by the advert but whether the reasonable customer would be misled. The consumer of computer equipment must be taken to be reasonably sophisticated. Perhaps the same can be said in 2003 of the consumer of foreign holidays.

In interpreting the words "complained of" the court receives guidance from section 14(2)(a) which states (in the most opaque of terms):

> "(a) anything (whether or not a statement as to any of the matters specified in the preceding subsection) likely to be taken for such a statement as to any of those matters as would be false shall be deemed to be a false statement as to that matter;"

Using this provision the court's approach is to look at the wording through the eyes of the ordinary consumer. If, for example, the wording or photograph is ambiguous the trader is still guilty of an offence if the consumer is likely to have been misled even if the trader can argue that the representation is technically true. Indeed the provision goes further than that. In one unreported case a consumer booked a twin-centre holiday to stay a week at Hotel A and a week at Hotel B. A few weeks before departure the tour operator sent a letter to the clients describing a problem at Hotel A. Hotel B was not mentioned in the letter at all. In fact problems had also arisen at Hotel B. It was held by the magistrates that the letter constituted an offence in respect of the description in the brochure of Hotel B because of section 14(2)(a)—a consumer would imagine that the silence about Hotel B in the letter was in fact a representation that everything at Hotel B remained correctly described in the brochure. Whilst it is not known whether such a decision would be supported on appeal the case does demonstrate how widely the provision can apply.

Much the same problem that arose in the *Roberts* case was also an issue in *R v Clarksons Holidays Ltd*. In that case the brochure featured an hotel which was not yet built. On the page giving the holiday details the hotel was depicted by an artist's impression. Nothing else on that page suggested that the hotel was incomplete but at the end of the brochure, a further 160 pages on, it stated:

"Artist's Impressions

> In the case of most hotels which are in the course of construction we are unable to provide photographs which will help our clients see what the new hotel will be like. To give our clients this information we therefore print 'artists' impressions,' which are based on the architect's plans and drawings and other information available at the time this brochure is published. Such 'impressions' are clearly shown on the appropriate pages and are published in good faith and to help our clients with their choice. If some details of construction, surroundings and background are later found to differ, we only accept responsibility to our clients if such differences, if any, are fairly judged to have materially marred our clients' holiday. We constantly seek to improve both the range and standards of hotel accommodation and consequently inaugurate a number of brand new hotels each season. Every effort is made to ensure that new hotels are 100 per cent ready but clients will appreciate that some delay in the completion of some facilities is possible. In such rare instances we will, of course, make an appropriate refund to the client or provide extra facilities, entertainment etc. in lieu."

The brochure was published in Autumn 1969 and Clarksons had a contract to have the hotel built by June 1970. One of the clients who subsequently complained read the brochure on April 17, 1970 and booked his holiday on the strength of it.

When the client arrived in resort on June 4th he found that the hotel was not yet completed and that numerous facilities were not available. On returning home he complained to his local Trading Standards Department. Clarksons were prosecuted on a number of counts relating to the missing facilities. The main issue was whether, as the prosecution contended, the statements made in the brochure meant that the facilities existed in fact on April 17, or whether, as the defence contended, that the brochure merely meant that the facilities would be available when the clients arrived. The crucial point to note is that the charge related to April 17, 1970 and what the statements made on that day meant.

A jury convicted Clarksons on a number of counts. On appeal to the Court of Appeal the convictions were upheld. Roskill LJ said that the trial judge's summing up had been correct and that the Court of Appeal did not find it in the least surprising that the jury had accepted the interpretation placed on the brochure by the prosecution—despite the disclaimer on p.160.

The *Time Computers* case referred to earlier also raised the issue of the relationship of pictorial representations in one part of the brochure and explanatory text in another part. In that case the advertisement for the computer was in a 20-page brochure contained in a specialist computer magazine. Although on the page in the brochure where the photograph appeared there was no specific reference to the fact that no disks or manuals were supplied there were a number of such references in other parts of the brochure. Both the Magistrate and the Divisional Court found that it was reasonable to expect the reasonable customer to consider the brochure as a whole and that taken as a whole the brochure did not contain a false trade description. No real principles can be derived from the *Clarkson* and *Time Computers* cases except to say that what the reasonable consumer understands from a particular set of words and pictures is a question of fact and that it is perfectly possible for different conclusions to be drawn from very similar facts.

Another aspect of this question of interpretation is the House of Lords case *British Airways Board v Taylor*. In this case BOAC had sent a letter to a passenger confirming that he had a reservation on a particular flight at a particular time. In the event the passenger was "bumped" when he arrived at the airport because of the deliberate overbooking policy operated by BOAC in common with other scheduled airlines. It was held by the magistrates that the letter of confirmation meant that *in fact* he had a reserved seat. As this was false and BOAC had acted recklessly when they made the statement the magistrates duly convicted them. The House of Lords approved the reasoning in the case but BOAC actually escaped liability on a technicality. (For further consideration of the legality of over-booking flights, see Mason "Call me old fashioned—but isn't it illegal" [1996] TLJ 145.)

Finally, it would appear to be illogical for a statement to be found to be false where the person reading or hearing it did not rely upon it because, *e.g.*, he knows the truth, having been told by the tour operator or other source.

(ii) Statement of Fact or Statement of Future Intention?

The Act is directed at statements which are *false*. Therefore any statement which cannot be said to be either true or false is not caught by the Act. Statements of intention or promises as to the future are examples of statements which fall into this category. One of the leading cases on this point is *Beckett v Cohen* [1973] 1 All E.R. 120. In that case a builder promised to build a garage within ten days that was similar to an existing garage but failed to do so. He was prosecuted under the Act for making a false statement. When the prosecutor appealed against the magistrates' finding of not guilty the appeal was dismissed. In the Divisional Court Lord Widgery CJ said:

> "... if ... the person who provides the service makes a promise as to what he will do, and that promise does not relate to an existing fact, nobody can say at the date when that statement is made that it is either true or false. In my judgment Parliament never intended or contemplated for a moment that the Act should be used in this way, to make a criminal offence out of what is really a breach of warranty."

This was just the issue in two of the cases just discussed, *R v Clarksons* and *British Airways Board v Taylor*. In each of those cases the defence was attempting to say that the statements were not statements of existing fact, merely promises as to services to be provided in the future, and as such not caught by the Act. As we have already seen the statements in each case were interpreted to be statements of fact.

In *R v Sunair* [1973] 1 W.L.R. 1105, CA, the tour operator published a brochure featuring the Hotel Cadi in Calella. The brochure stated (amongst other things) that the hotel had a swimming pool, that pushchairs could be hired at the hotel and that good food with English dishes was provided at the hotel as well as special meals for children. The brochure was read by a client in January 1970. When the client arrived in resort in May 1970 none of those facilities was available. The company was convicted by a jury at the Crown Court of having contravened the Act. On appeal the Court of Appeal quashed the conviction. The reason being that the judge in the Crown Court had failed to instruct the jury of the difference between a statement of fact and a statement of intention. If he had done so the jury would have had to consider whether the words in the brochure meant that the facilities described already existed *in fact* or whether Sunair were merely *promising* that when the client arrived they would be available. Without this guidance to the jury the conviction could not be regarded as satisfactory.

The Court of Appeal in *R v Sunair* approved what was said in *Beckett v Cohen* about the distinction between statements of fact and statements as to the future. McKenna J who gave the judgment in *Sunair* said of section 14:

> "The section deals with 'statements' of which it can be said that they were, at the time when they were made, 'false.' This may be the case with a statement of fact, whether past or present. A statement that a fact exists now, or that it existed in the past, is either true or false at the time when it is made. But it is not the case with a promise or a prediction about the future. A prediction may come true or it may not. A promise to do something in

> the future may be kept or it may be broken. But neither the prediction nor the promise can be said to have been true or false at the time when it was made. We conclude that section 14 of the Trade Descriptions Act 1968 does not deal with forecasts or promises as such."

Unfortunately the distinction between statements of fact and statements of future intention is not quite as clear cut as this passage makes out. McKenna J recognised this in the passage immediately following. He said:

> "We put in the qualifying words 'as such' for this reason. A promise or forecast may contain by implication a statement of present fact. The person who makes the promise may be implying that his present intention is to keep it or that he has at present the power to perform it. The person who makes the forecast may be implying that he now believes that his prediction will come true or that he has the means of bringing it to pass. Such implied statements of present intention, means or belief, when they are made, may well be within section 14 of the Act of 1968 and therefore punishable if they were false and were made knowingly or recklessly. But, if they are punishable, the offence is not the breaking of a promise or the failure to make a prediction come true. It is the making of a false statement of an existing fact, somebody's present state of mind or present means."

Thus, for instance, if a tour operator's brochure states that clients will be accommodated in twin-bedded rooms then this will be a statement of intention that is neither true nor false when made. But it implies that the tour operator has the present intention to fulfil this promise—which is a statement of fact. If in fact the tour operator knows that the hotel only has double-bedded rooms and he has no intention of providing twin beds then this will be caught by the Act.

Alternatively if the hotel has twin-bedded rooms but the contract which the tour operator has with the hotel provides only for double-bedded rooms; or if the tour operator has no contract with the hotel at all, then again he will be caught by the Act. There have been a number of cases in which tour operators have been convicted because they had no contract with the hotel advertised. Of course the operator always believed that they would have no difficulty obtaining the accommodation for the consumer in due course but in the event such belief turned out to be over optimistic! (See Grant & O'Cain, "Lies, Damn Lies and Holiday Brochures"

[1995] TLJ 4 & 40 for a fuller account of the problems arising when a tour operator advertises accommodation he has no contract for.)

What about the bus tour operator who offers pick-up points at every town between Newcastle and Dover for continental bus tours? Again this would be a statement of future intention not a statement of fact but it does imply that the operator has the intention and the means of making the promise come true and if this is not the case then he could be prosecuted.

Another case which combines both the points made so far—the meaning to be attributed to the statement and whether that meaning is a statement of fact or future intention is *Sunair v Dodd* [1970] 2 All E.R. 410 where the defendants published a brochure describing the facilities offered at an hotel as "all twin-bedded rooms with private bath, shower, WC and terrace". Clients who read the brochure in January 1969 discovered when they arrived at the hotel that their rooms did not have balconies or terraces. At the time the brochure was published Sunair had a contract with the hotel for twin-bedded rooms.

Lord Parker CJ gave the judgment of the Divisional Court which overturned a conviction by the Magistrates' Court. He said:

> "It seems to me that the brochure was intended to convey and does convey to the prospective holidaymaker, *that the twin-bedded rooms that we can offer you at this hotel* have those amenities. Looked at in that way, that statement when it was made was perfectly true. This was not the typical case of a brochure advertising accommodation which did not exist, having a swimming bath that was not constructed, or of hotel accommodation where a hotel was not opened. At the time when the statement was made it was perfectly accurate that the accommodation that they were offering existed. Not only did it exist, but the appellants had a contract with the hotel—I need not go into it—whereby the only twin-bedded rooms which they kept available for the appellants, and were offering to the appellants' clients, were rooms with these amenities, including a terrace. Accordingly, when it was made, it was in my judgment completely accurate." [Emphasis added]

According to Lord Parker the brochure could be interpreted as meaning—this is what we can *offer* you—and that was an intention which they had the means of fulfilling—they had a contract with the hotel to provide just what they were promising to provide.

Tour operators sometimes argue that their booking conditions allow them to make changes to holiday arrangements and that such an express provision means that they are not committing an offence if a brochure description changes. This point was specifically dealt with in *R v Avro plc* (1993) 12 TrLR 83 CA. Avro sold a return air ticket on which the return was to be at 12.55 pm on a flight from Alicante to Gatwick. This was twice changed and in the end the customer had to fly back to Southend. It appeared that the original flight had never existed. Lloyd LJ said:

> "... the ticket when issued contains in reality two statements of fact: first, 'There is a flight which is timed to leave Alicante at 12.55' and, secondly, 'You are booked on that flight'. If either of those statements of fact were known to be false at the time they were made, then the jury would be entitled to convict."

Dealing with the argument that contract conditions might allow the flight to be altered or cancelled the judge quoted with approval the judge at first instance who put it aptly:

> "An alteration implies a starting point of existing fact."

Avro's appeal against conviction failed.

(iii) Continuing Statements?

When a false statement is published in a brochure the problem this poses for the tour operator is that the statement is not made just once. It is made every time a person reads a copy of the brochure. Moreover the statement continues to be made so long as the brochure is in current use. This much is clear from the case of *Wings v Ellis* which will be examined in more detail later but for the present is relevant on the question of the continuing nature of the statements made in a brochure. Lord Hailsham LC said:

> "When, in the course of a trade or business, a brochure containing a false statement is issued in large numbers through a chain of distribution involving several stages, and intended to be read and used at all or some of the stages, it does not follow that it is only 'made' at its ultimate destination. It may be 'made' when it is posted in bulk, when the information is passed on by telephone or in smaller batches by post, and when it is read by the ultimate recipient, provided that at each stage what happens is in accordance with the original intention of the issuing house."

Thus according to Lord Hailsham the statement in the brochure is "made" on a number of different occasions. Lord Brandon in the same case offered a slightly different view. He said:

> "In the present case I regard the false statement about air-conditioning contained in the respondent's brochures as having been a continuing false statement, that is to say a false statement which continued to be made so long as such brochures remained in circulation without effective correction. I should regard a statement made in an advertisement exhibited on a street hoarding in the same way."

If this bold view is correct the practical effect on tour operators would be that if circumstances change then a statement which was outside the ambit of the Act might be brought within it. Take for instance the facts of *Sunair v Dodd*. If, prior to clients arriving at the hotel, the hotel management had indicated to Sunair that clients would not be accommodated in rooms with balconies or terraces, then the statement in the brochure would become false. Sunair would still only be making a promise as to the future but as they knew that the promise could not be fulfilled the implication that they had the ability to carry out the promise would be false.

It would be the same with brochures featuring hotels not yet built but where the tour operator expected it to be complete before the season started and had contracted for an allocation of rooms. So long as the brochure made it clear that the hotel was in the process of being built (unlike the case of *R v Clarksons*) then the statements in the brochure would only be statements of future intention. If it became apparent however as the season approached that the hotel would not be ready in time then the statements would become false. No longer could the tour operator say truthfully that rooms were being offered in the hotel for the start of the season.

Sunair v Dodd contains a passage by Lord Parker CJ which suggests that this approach may be incorrect. He said:

> "Counsel for the respondent has rather faintly suggested that really this statement is a continuing statement, and that it existed when these couples arrived at the hotel. For my part I am quite unable to accept that. This is a statement made on 13th January or at some later date after the brochure had been shown to them, and they had accepted the offer contained in it, and nothing that happened after that can affect the matter one way or the other whether that statement was false and made recklessly."

If he is suggesting that the statement is made only once then he is clearly wrong in the light of the subsequently decided *Wings* case. So long as that particular brochure remained in circulation then the statements in it were made on a repeated basis and if circumstances changed then the truth or falsity of the statements could also change. It may not have contained a false statement when it was first read by the clients who later complained but that is not to say that it could not become false later. The falsity of the statement is not to be measured solely when someone makes a contract on the basis of it. It can be false even though no one acts upon it, and it can become false after someone has acted upon it. In summary therefore the statement is made repeatedly, though possibly not continuously.

(iv) False to a Material Degree

Even though the statement is false no offence will be committed if it is not false to a material degree. This was an issue that arose in the case of *Direct Holidays plc v Wirral Metropolitan Borough Council* (Divisional Court, April 28, 1998). (For another aspect of this case see Stockdale, "Trade descriptions and holiday brochures: Proving falsity and recklessness in the making of statements and the rule against hearsay", [1999] ITLJ 102.) In their brochure Direct Holidays had described the official category of an apartment complex in Tenerife as being "Three keys" when in fact it was only "One key". The defence rather weakly endeavoured to argue that the official Spanish key ratings were of little or no value and therefore not material.

Given that the defendants, when they had discovered the error, had offered clients a full refund, the court found it relatively easy to reject the submission that the false classification was not material. Although this was not a prosecution under the Package Travel Regulations and no reference to the Regulations was made in the case the Regulations must surely be of relevance in TDA prosecutions such as this. Regulation 5 for instance requires the official classification of accommodation to be included in brochures (Schedule 1) and Regulation 9 requires similar information to be included in the written terms of the contract (Schedule 2). In the face of such statutory requirements it would be difficult to make out a case that the classification was not material.

However, if the falsity is so trivial or inconsequential that it really makes no practical difference then the defendant might escape conviction. One can imagine for instance a situation where the brochure features a photograph of an hotel and all the curtains are red. When the clients arrive all the curtains are blue because the management have redecorated the hotel during the off season. In such circumstances it would be difficult to see how it would make a "material" difference to the client. It might be a different matter altogether if there were no curtains at all!

The statement must be made knowingly or recklessly

Unlike the provisions of the Consumer Protection Act or Regulations 5, 7 and 8 where the offences are ones of strict liability, *i.e.* the defendant can be convicted without any fault on his part, section 14 requires that the prosecution prove that the defendant had the requisite state of mind. It must be shown that the defendant made the statement *knowing* it was false or *recklessly* made a false statement. On the face of it these are words which usually imply dishonesty on the part of the defendant. Lawyers call such a state of mind *mens rea* or guilty mind. In many instances however case law has reduced the offence to one of strict liability or "semi-strict liability" according to Lord Scarman in the *Wings* case. Section 14(1)(a), which requires knowledge on the part of the defendant, and section 14(1)(b), which requires recklessness, will be looked at in turn.

Knowledge that the statement is false

The leading case here is the *Wings* case, the facts of which were that the tour operator, Wings, published a brochure in early 1981 advertising holidays for the 1981-82 season. Unfortunately there was a mistake in the brochure. It stated that a particular hotel had air-conditioning when in fact it did not. Wings did not discover this until May 1981. At that point they issued errata to all existing clients and instructed all telephone sales staff to inform travel agents and prospective clients of the error before bookings were made. At least one client, however, was not told of the lack of air-conditioning before travelling. On return he complained to his local trading standards department who subsequently brought a prosecution under section 14(1)(a). [There was also a prosecution under section 14(1)(b) which failed.]

To succeed, the prosecution had to show that at the time the statement was made it was not only false but known to be false by the defendant. The statement was false from the outset because the hotel did not have air-conditioning but that was not enough to convict—the prosecution also has to show knowledge of the falsity. When the statement was first made Wings did not know that the hotel had no air-conditioning so at that stage no offence could have been committed. Only in May 1981 did Wings have the requisite knowledge and at that stage they took steps to ensure that the false statement received no further currency by instructing reservations staff to pass on the correction to enquiring travel agents. As we have already seen, however, the statement in the brochure remains at risk of being a false statement so long as uncorrected brochures remained in circulation to be read. Unfortunately at least one brochure was seen by a client who was not informed of the error. By the time he read it in January 1982 Wings clearly knew the statement was false but they did not know that it was still being made.

When the case came to the House of Lords in 1984 the issue revolved around the question of whether Wings could be properly convicted if they did not know the statement was being made even though they knew it was false. To put it another way could they be convicted even though there was no fault on their part?

The House of Lords upheld the decisions of the lower courts to convict Wings. On a literal interpretation of section 14(1)(a) the offence is "to *make a statement* which he knows to be false", not, as Wings contended, to *knowingly make a statement* which is false. The requirement of knowledge therefore relates to the falsity of the statement, not the making of it. Thus once Wings knew the statement was false they would be guilty every time they made the statement even though they did not know it was being made and had taken active steps to prevent it being made. It was for these reasons that Lord Scarman described the offence as one of "semi-strict liability". Essentially Wings were liable without fault.

The implications of this for tour operators are far reaching. It means that if a mistake has been made in a brochure and this is discovered and brought to the attention of the tour operator then every brochure that remains in circulation uncorrected has the potential to give rise to a prosecution. Given that in some cases the print run may be in the millions the chances of a prosecution being brought may be quite high.

However there is a defence available in such circumstances under s.24 of the Act which will be examined later in Chapter Fourteen. The defence was available to Wings but they chose not to use it for reasons which are not fully revealed in the case.

Although Wings were convicted it is perhaps useful to point out that prior to May 1981 when the mistake was discovered a conviction would not have been secured. Despite the fact that the statement was false it was not *known* by Wings to be false so at that stage they did not have the requisite *mens rea* for a conviction. If there is *no* knowledge of falsity there cannot be a conviction.

It is also worth pointing out that despite this being a criminal conviction the court was at pains to point out that there was no dishonesty on Wings' behalf. Lord Hailsham said, having agreed that Wings were guilty of an offence:

> "Having said all this, I am bound to say that I am not at all happy about the position to which I have felt constrained to come, and, without criticising the authorities who mounted the present proceedings and persisted in the present successful appeal, I would say that there is room for caution by prosecuting authorities in mounting proceedings against innocent defendants ... Whatever else the 1968 Act was meant for it ... was not designed to bring on respectable traders who had acted honestly the reputation of having been guilty of fraudulent conduct of which in fact they were innocent."

He commended to tour operators the idea that a "prompt and generous offer of compensation when the error was first brought to its attention" could possibly have saved a good deal of trouble and anxiety.

A much simpler case turning on the requirement for knowledge under section 14(1)(a) is *Hotel Plan Ltd v Tameside Metropolitan Borough Council* (Divisional Court, February 28, 2001) (See Bragg, [2001] ITLJ 75 for a commentary on the case). The prosecution alleged that clients of the defendants had been promised a hotel with a lift, namely the Hotel Gruberhof in Igls in Austria, which was a statement they knew to be false. The clients had made a late booking and could not be allocated their hotel at the time of booking but could be told the area they were going to. The clients had requested a hotel with a lift and this request was relayed to the defendants in a telephone conversation between the defendants and the clients' travel agent. It was found as a matter of fact that during the conversation a lift or ground floor room had been guaranteed but that the Hotel Gruberhof was not mentioned during this conversation. In the event it turned out that their request could not be satisfied at the hotel they were allocated to, the Hotel Gruberhof.

The Divisional Court found it impossible to convict the company because at the time the telephone conversation took place the Hotel Gruberhof had not been allocated to the clients and therefore no false statement could have been made in relation to that hotel. The language of the judgment however gives the merest hint that had the information been drafted differently then a conviction could have been secured.

Recklessness in the making of the statement

Despite the *Wings* case it is probably true to say that most prosecutions under section 14(1)(a) will involve defendants who not only know that the statement was false but know it from the outset. In other words there will be dishonesty by the defendant as envisaged when the Act was passed. With section 14(1)(b) it is much more difficult to be able to say this. The way the case law has developed means that quite clearly a prosecution can succeed even without evidence of dishonesty. Two of the leading cases are non-travel cases but their relevance to the industry is self-evident.

In *MFI Warehouses Ltd v Nattrass* [1973] 1 All E.R. 762 the defendants had published an advertisement in which the price and delivery terms on which some furniture was available were ambiguous. On one interpretation the advertisement could be understood to mean that the furniture was available on certain terms when in fact it was not. MFI were prosecuted under section 14(1)(b) as having recklessly made a false statement as to the provision of a facility. The advertisement had been drafted by a director of the company and approved by the chairman. The latter had considered the advertisement for five to ten minutes but had not directed his mind as to whether the advertisement contained statements which were false. The magistrates convicted and the defendants appealed to the Divisional Court. The issue on appeal was whether the actions of MFI could be regarded as reckless within the meaning of the Act.

Lord Widgery CJ said that normally recklessness involved dishonesty and that according to the usual meaning attached to the word MFI would not be guilty. However, the Act has its own definition of recklessness in section 14(2)(b):

> "a statement made regardless of whether it is true or false shall be deemed to be made recklessly ..."

Despite existing case law on the meaning of recklessness in other contexts Lord Widgery felt constrained to ignore it and base his decision on the definition in the Act. Taken literally it meant that recklessness amounted to no more than *not having regard to* the truth or falsity of the statement. Seen in this light the actions of the chairman who considered the advertisement for five to ten minutes but did not think about whether it was true or false amounted to recklessness and the company had been properly convicted. As with the *Wings* case the judge justified his decision by saying that this was a consumer protection statute and that it was not unreasonable to impose on the advertiser a positive obligation to have regard to whether his advertisement was true or false.

Dixons Ltd v Roberts 82 LGR 689 takes this development a stage further. In that case an advertisement had been prepared which contained a false statement. This advertisement had been amended by the company secretary. Unfortunately, the amended advertisement also contained a false statement but the company secretary had not considered the possibility that the amended advertisement could be false. Upholding the justices on this point Forbes J said:

> "The justices finding of fact ... indicates quite clearly that they considered that it was this amended statement which he [the company secretary] did not sufficiently think through. ... [T]he explanation of their decision is thus that they considered that the company secretary did not have regard to the falsity or otherwise of the amended statement. ... In my view the justices were right to conclude that the defendants had recklessly made a statement which was false."

It is clear that in neither of these two cases were the defendants reckless in the normal sense of the word. They were in fact no more than negligent or careless. The implications of this for brochure preparation are patent. A tour operator cannot afford any form of sloppy practice to creep in to the process unless he wishes to invite a prosecution.

A straightforward tour operating case which illustrates the requirement of recklessness is *Best Travel Company Ltd v Patterson* (1986) (unreported). This was an unsuccessful appeal from a decision of the magistrates to convict. The facts were that Best Travel, trading under the name of Grecian Holidays, published a brochure in November 1983 featuring the Palace Hotel, Malia, Crete. The brochure stated that the hotel facilities included a bar, lounge and breakfast room. In January 1984 two clients booked a holiday at the hotel for September 1984. Just before they departed they were told that no bar, lounge or breakfast room existed at the hotel. On arrival they discovered that the ground floor of the hotel was no more than a building site.

Best had contracted with the hotel in July 1982 and the contract provided that the facilities would be completed by March 1983. By July 1983 the facilities had not been completed and Best knew this. Best had no further contact with the hotel until April 1984 when they were told that the facilities *would* be ready, *i.e.* they were not ready yet. Thus, between July 1983 and January 1984, when the clients booked, Best had no contact with the hotel and did not investigate whether the facilities had been completed. Yet they went ahead and published the brochure in November 1983 stating that the facilities existed, and the statements in the brochure were still being made, uncorrected, in January 1984.

The Divisional Court had little hesitation in agreeing with the magistrates that the circumstances in which the statement about the facilities was made amounted to recklessness by Best. If they had not investigated then they could not know whether the facilities existed and therefore they were making a statement without having regard to its truth or falsity.

In *Direct Holidays v Wirral* the Divisional Court held that the defendants had been reckless on the facts but Blofeld J who gave the judgment took the opportunity to say that he felt that the distinction drawn by Widgery LJ in *MFI v Nattrass* between the statutory definition of recklessness in the TDA and the common law definition was more apparent than real:

> "At page 768(c) Lord Widgery CJ said:
>
> > 'I have accordingly come to the conclusion that 'recklessly' in the context of the 1968 Act does not involve dishonesty. Accordingly it is not necessary to prove that the statement was made with that degree of irresponsibility which is implied in the phase 'careless whether it be true or false'. I think it suffices for present purposes if the prosecution can show that the advertiser did not have regard to the truth or falsity of this advertisement even though it cannot be shown that he was deliberately closing his eyes to the truth, or that he had any kind of dishonest mind."
>
> In the course of submissions Kennedy LJ [the other judge in this case] queried whether there was in the end a real difference between Lord Widgery's analysis of "recklessly" and the phrase "careless whether it be true or false". The distinction seems, with respect, to be slight. I would prefer to decide this case on the basis of the well known phrase "careless whether it be true or false". It has never been the Respondent's case that the Appellants were acting dishonestly."

It is indeed difficult to see circumstances where someone who is not careless whether the statement is true or false cannot have had *regard* to the truth or falsity of the statement but that is what apparently happened in the *Dixons* case and the court would have been prepared to convict on that basis.

The state of mind of the defendant

To say that the defendant must knowingly or recklessly make a false statement requires that he have a particular state of mind. With most Trade Descriptions Act prosecutions the defendants will be limited companies which do not of course have either minds or bodies. In these circumstances the rule is that a "directing mind" of the company has to have the requisite state of mind. A directing mind means someone in the company of such seniority that he can be regarded as acting as the "brains" of the company. Managing directors, directors, company secretaries etc fall into this category. In a leading Trade Descriptions Act case, *Tesco Supermarkets Ltd v Nattrass* [1972] A.C. 153, Lord Reid said that a company would only be criminally liable for the acts of:

> "... the board of directors, the managing director and perhaps other supervisor officers of [the] company [who] carry out the functions of management and speak and act as the company."

This point is made quite simply by the judge in the *Best* case mentioned earlier. He said:

> "The state of the mind of the company, it is trite law to say, must be the state of mind of a person or persons who were sufficiently in control of the company to act as its mind for this purpose. It is agreed that the human person who filled that role is a gentleman named Mr. Shacalis. [The managing director] For all effective purposes, Mr. Shacalis was the appellant company for the purposes of ascertaining its state of mind."

A case going the other way is *Wings v Ellis* [1984] 1 All E.R. 1046. On a charge of recklessly making a false statement under s.14(1)(b) of the TDA it was said by Mann J in the Divisional Court in a decision which was not appealed:

> "In particular, we reject the respondent's suggestion that Michael Stephen-Jones, who approved the photograph and who variously called himself a 'long haul development manager' and 'the contracts manager', could be inferred to be a member of the relevant class." [*i.e.* the directing minds of the company]

Thus if no one sufficiently senior in the company acted knowingly or recklessly then the company cannot be convicted. That at least is the theory. However, case law has made inroads into this principle.

In *Wings v Ellis* when it came to the House of Lords it was decided that so long as the company knows the statement is false there is no requirement that there be knowledge of it being *made*. Lord Scarman said:

> "The day-to-day business activities of large enterprises, whatever their legal structure, are necessarily conducted by their employees, and particularly by their sales staff. It follows that many of the acts prohibited by the Act will be the acts of employees done in the course of the trade or business and without the knowledge at the time of those who direct the business. It will become clear that the Act does cover such acts . . ."

Yugotours Ltd v Wadsley [1988] Crim LR 623, a case involving a prosecution under section 14(1)(b) for recklessly making a false statement the court came close to dispensing with the requirement of *mens rea* (see the first edition of this book for a full discussion) but in *Airtours v Shipley* (1994) 158 JPN 319 (DC)) this view was rejected. The facts were that Airtours had featured a hotel in one of their brochures that was said to have an indoor swimming pool. This was not the case. The hotel did not have and never had had an indoor swimming pool. Airtours conceded that the false statement had somehow crept into the brochure because of a mistake at head office—which they could not explain. This was despite an errata policy which the court described as an "excellent system". (See Cooper, *Due Diligence—The Tour Operator's View* [1994] TLJ 11 for a discussion of errata systems.) The errata policy, although devised by the directing minds of Airtours, was operated by middle management who were directly responsible to the directors.

A prosecution under section 14(1)(b) for recklessly making a false statement succeeded in the magistrates' court. The magistrates said that although Mrs Bryan, the Overseas Operations Controller at Airtours responsible for the brochure, was not one of the directing minds of the company nevertheless the company could be convicted because the directors had "delegated' their functions to her. In other words she became the directing mind of the company for this purpose.

However on appeal to the Divisional Court the decision was overturned. The court said that the justices reliance on a theory of delegation was based upon a selective reading of the judgments in *Tesco v Nattrass* [1971] 2 All E.R. 127. Although it is perfectly possible for a board of directors to delegate its functions to others, and *Tesco v Nattrass* confirms this, the case actually decided that on the facts no delegation had taken place. The Divisional Court preferred to adopt the reasoning from the *Tesco* case that concluded there was no delegation. McCowan LJ in the Divisional Court quoted the following passage by Lord Morris from the *Tesco* case:

> "My Lords, with respect, I do not think that there was any feature of delegation in the present case. The company had its responsibilities in regard to taking all reasonable precautions and exercising all due diligence. The careful and effective discharge of those responsibilities required the directing mind and will of the company. A system had to be created which could rationally be said to be so designed that the commission of offences would be avoided. There was no such delegation to the manager of a particular store. He did not function as the directing mind or will of the company. His duties as the manager of one store did not involve managing the company. He was one who was being directed. He was one who was employed but he was not a delegate to whom the company passed on its responsibilities. He had certain duties which were the result of the taking by the company of all reasonable precautions and of the exercising by the company of all due diligence. He was a person under the control of the company. . . . He was, so to speak, a cog in the machine which was devised: it was not left to him to devise it."

He also adopted the skeleton argument put up by counsel for Airtours:

> "It is contended by the appellant that Mrs Bryan only had a discretion to produce the holiday brochure in question and that such a discretion was limited by the errata policy of checking for mistakes set up by the directors. The directors of the appellant company had, therefore, not delegated their authority to run and manage the appellant company but had simply employed Mrs Bryan to produce a holiday brochure within set guidelines and procedures. Mrs Bryan had not been given full discretion to act independently of instruction from the directors but had been given a measure of discretion to produce the holiday brochure in question within the framework of instructions embraced by the errata policy document. The directors of the appellant company simply, therefore, employed Mrs Bryan to work within a system that had been created and designed so that the commission of offences would be avoided. Her duties did not involve managing the company but preparing a company brochure. She was, so to speak, a cog in the machine which was devised and it was not left to her to devise it."

Thus Airtours were not guilty on the grounds that any recklessness that occurred was not that of the directing minds of the company or anyone to whom they had delegated any authority to manage the company. The company itself was not reckless because by setting up a proper errata system and ensuring that it operated effectively they were having regard to the truth or falsity of the statements in the brochure (section 14(2)(b)).

On the question of the *Yugotours* case although the court was unable to overrule that decision it went out of its way to cast doubt on its authority. It suggested that the reasoning was a "radical departure from principle and authority'. It also said that insofar as it cast doubt on the decision of Mann J on the issue of recklessness in the *Wings* case it was also wrong. (See Bragg "Recklessness and Authority" [1996] TLJ 97 for a discussion of the *Airtours* case.)

Looking beyond the narrow confines of travel law and the Trade Descriptions Act for assistance on this question of attributing the knowledge of senior managers to their companies the problem was examined in *Meridian Global Funds Management Asia Ltd v Securities Commission* [1995] 2 A.C. 500 by the Privy Council. They said that whether there could be such attribution depended upon the interpretation to be placed upon the statute imposing liability and the policy it sought to achieve and that different statutes might treat the actions of employees differently. However on the issue of the Trade Descriptions Act they seemed content with the approach adopted by the House of Lords in the *Tesco* case.

Multiple prosecutions

In *R v Thomson Holidays Ltd* [1974] 1 Q.B. 592 Thomsons had published a brochure with false statements in it. They were convicted in July 1972 of offences under s.14(1)(b) of the Act by Stockport magistrates. In March 1973 a further prosecution was brought before Manchester Crown Court concerning the same false statements, although on this occasion the prosecution stemmed from different complainants. Thomsons pleaded "autrefois convict", meaning that they had already been tried and found guilty of the offence. This defence depended on whether the statement is made only once or more than once. As already seen in the *Wings* case the statements in a brochure are made at every stage of the chain of distribution and every time someone reads it. Thus an offence is committed every time someone new reads it. The Court of Appeal held therefore that Thomsons could be convicted again in Manchester on exactly the same grounds as in Stockport. They added, however, that if multiple prosecutions were brought then the court had a discretion to stay the prosecution or impose only nominal penalties if it considered that to proceed would be oppressive. However, two prosecutions, as in this case, were not regarded as oppressive.

An interesting position arises from the suggestion in *Wings v Ellis* that the offence can be committed without an actual reading of the words by a consumer (contrary to what is said in the *Thomson* case). If a tour operator were prosecuted more than once in such circumstances, he may well have stronger grounds for arguing "autre fois convict"—it might be very difficult to tell, from reading the Summonses, whether the convictions related to different offences if they were just general, rather than specific to a consumer. In practice, Trading Standards departments avoid this problem by prosecuting cases where a specific named consumer has been misled.

Chapter Twelve
The Consumer Protection Act 1987

Introduction

Part III of the Consumer Protection Act 1987 (the "CPA") is designed to protect consumers from misleading price indications. It should be noted that this is not the only relevant legislation for the travel industry; the Package Travel Regulations also regulate statements relating to prices. Regulation 5 of the Package Travel Regulations lists the price of the package as one of the things to be stated legibly, comprehensively and accurately in any brochure. Regulation 5 is dealt with in the next Chapter. Some Trading Standards officers believe this is a more onerous requirement than the whole of the CPA.

The kind of practices the CPA is designed to outlaw include for instance printing just the basic price of a holiday in a price panel and omitting the airport supplements, the insurance premiums, the airport taxes etc so that the client is misled into believing that the price is much less than it actually is. By the time he realises this it may be too late to turn back. The psychological decision to buy has already been made.

It would also protect clients against such practices as placing cards in the window saying "Majorca. Two weeks self-catering £79" and then when he enters the shop explaining that there had been a mistake and the price was actually £179. Some clients may just walk out but others, whose interest has been aroused, may remain to be sold the holiday at the higher price or another holiday altogether.

The primary rationale of the legislation is to prevent consumers making decisions to purchase based upon false or misleading information. It is not in the economic interests of the consumer to purchase goods or services because he *thinks* they are a bargain when in fact they are not; when in fact he could have bought them elsewhere more cheaply. A second and equally important rationale is that it enables legitimate businesses to compete on equal terms with their less reputable counterparts. If I display the prices in my brochure clearly and comprehensively I do not wish to lose custom to other tour operators who disguise the true price of the holiday behind low lead-in prices or by not mentioning all the hidden extras. The Act is designed to provide a "level playing field" for businesses. There is also the moral argument that false and misleading information is in itself wrong and should be legislated against on that ground. (See *Review of Legislation on False and Misleading Price Information,* the Report of the Inter-departmental Working Party published by the DTI in February 1984.)

One novel feature of the Act is that it is accompanied by a Code of Practice, rather like the Highway Code, which sets out what amounts to good practice for traders who wish to avoid giving misleading price indications. There are several specific references in the Code to the travel industry. The precise status of the Code will be explained later.

The Relevant Provisions

Section 20 of the Act sets out the offences and section 21 defines what is meant by "misleading". Section 22 defines services. These sections are set out below. The defences are contained in sections 24, 25 and 39 and are set out later.

"20. Offence of giving misleading indication

(1) Subject to the following provisions of this Part, a person shall be guilty of an offence if, in the course of any business of his, he gives (by any means whatever) to any consumers an indication which is misleading as to the price at which any goods, services, accommodation or facilities are available (whether generally or from particular persons).

(2) Subject as aforesaid, a person shall be guilty of an offence if—

(a) in the course of any business of his, he has given an indication to any consumers which, after it was given, has become misleading as mentioned in subsection (1) above; and
(b) some or all of those consumers might reasonably be expected to rely on the indication at a time after it has become misleading; and
(c) he fails to take all such steps as are reasonable to prevent those consumers from relying on the indication.

(3) For the purposes of this section it shall be immaterial—

(a) whether the person who gives or gave the indication is or was acting on his own behalf or on behalf of another;

(b) whether or not that person is the person, or included among the persons, from whom the goods, services, accommodation or facilities are available; and
(c) whether the indication is or has become misleading in relation to all the consumers to whom it is or was given or only in relation to some of them.

(4).... .
(5).... .
(6) In this Part—
'consumer'—

(a) in relation to any goods, means any person who might wish to be supplied with the goods for his own private use or consumption;
(b) in relation to any services or facilities, means any person who might wish to be provided with the services or facilities otherwise than for the purposes of any business of his; and
(c) in relation to any accommodation, means any person who might wish to occupy the accommodation otherwise than for the purposes of any business of his;

'price' in relation to any goods, services, accommodation or facilities, means—

(a) the aggregate of the sums required to be paid by a consumer for or otherwise in respect of the supply of the goods or the provision of the services, accommodation or facilities; or
(b) except in section 21 below, any method which will be or has been applied for the purpose of determining that aggregate.

21. Meaning of "misleading"

(1) For the purposes of section 20 above an indication given to any consumers is misleading as to a price if what is conveyed by the indication, or what those consumers might reasonably be expected to infer from the indication or any omission from it, includes any of the following, that is to say—

(a) that the price is less than in fact it is;
(b) that the applicability of the price does not depend on facts or circumstances on which its applicability does in fact depend;
(c) that the price covers matters in respect of which an additional charge is in fact made;

(d) that a person who in fact has no such expectation—

(i) expects the price to be increased or reduced (whether or not at a particular time or by a particular amount); or

(ii) expects the price, or the price as increased or reduced, to be maintained (whether or not for a particular period); or

(e) that the facts or circumstances by reference to which the consumers might reasonably be expected to judge the validity of any relevant comparison made or implied by the indication are not what in fact they are.

(2) For the purposes of section 20 above, an indication given to any consumers is misleading as to a method of determining a price if what is conveyed by the indication, or what those consumers might reasonably be expected to infer from the indication or any omission from it, includes any of the following, that is to say—

(a) that the method is not what in fact it is;

(b) that the applicability of the method does not depend on facts or circumstances on which its applicability does in fact depend;

(c) that the method takes into account matters in respect of which an additional charge will in fact be made;

(d) that a person who in fact has no such expectation—

(i) expects the method to be altered (whether or not at a particular time or in a particular respect); or

(ii) expects the method, or that method as altered, to remain unaltered (whether or not for a particular period); or

(e) that the facts or circumstances by reference to which the consumers might reasonably be expected to judge the validity of any relevant comparison made or implied by the indication are not what in fact they are.

(3) For the purposes of subsection (1)(e) and (2)(e) above a comparison is a relevant comparison in relation to a price or method of determining a price if it is made between that price or that method, or any price which has been or may be determined by that method and

(a) any price or value which is stated or implied to be, to have been or to be likely to be attributed or attributable to the goods, services, accommodation or facilities in question or to any other goods, services, accommodation or facilities; or

(b) any method, or other method, which is stated or implied to be, to have been or to be likely to be applied or applicable for the determination of the price or value of the goods, services, accommodation or facilities in question or of the price or value of any other goods, services, accommodation or facilities.

22. Application to provision of services and facilities

(1) Subject to the following provisions of this section, references in this Part to services or facilities are references to any services or facilities whatever including, in particular—

(a) ...
(b) the purchase or sale of foreign currency

...

(4) In relation to a service consisting in the sale or purchase of foreign currency, references in this Part to the method by which the price of the service is determined shall include references to the rate of exchange.

Requirements of the offence

Section 20 creates two offences. The first is giving a misleading price indication (section 20(1)) and the second is giving a price indication which subsequently becomes misleading (section 20(2)).

The elements of an offence under section 20(1) are that:

- a person in the course of a business of his
- gives
- a misleading indication about
- the price or
- the method of calculating the price
- of goods, services, accommodation or facilities
- to a consumer

The elements of an offence under section 20(2) are that:

- a person in the course of a business of his

- gives
- an indication of the price or its method of calculation
- which subsequently becomes misleading; and
- some consumers might still be relying upon the original indication; and
- he has not taken reasonable steps to correct the indication.
- These requirements of the section 20(1) offence will be looked at first.

A person in the course of any business of his

Just as in the Trade Descriptions Act the offence can only be committed in the course of a business. For the meaning of this provision you are referred back to Chapter Eleven.

However there is one difference between the provisions. Unlike the Trade Descriptions Act the CPA provides that the price indication be given in the course of a business *of his*. The effect of this is to take employees out of the scope of the CPA. (See *R v Warwickshire CC ex parte Johnson* [1993] 1 All E.R. 299, HL). This is not the case under the TDA although it is not the policy of Trading Standards Departments to prosecute junior employees under the TDA. However under section 40(2) of the CPA if the offence is shown to be committed with the "consent or connivance of, or to be attributable to any neglect on the part of any director, manager, secretary or other similar officer of the body corporate ... he, as well as the body corporate, shall be guilty of that offence ..."

Although the indication must be given by a person in the course of a business of his it does not have to be his business that is selling the goods, services, accommodation or facilities. This is made clear by section 20(3)(a) which states:

> "(3) For the purposes of this section it shall be immaterial—
>
> (a) whether the person who gives or gave the indication is or was acting on his own behalf or on behalf of another;"

This is of crucial importance of course to travel agents. They are in the business of selling holidays but in the majority of cases it is not their product that they are selling and it is not their price but nevertheless they can be prosecuted for giving a misleading price indication in the course of a business of theirs.

Giving an indication

It does not matter how the indication is given. The Act expressly provides that the indication can be given "by any means whatever". We have already seen in Chapter Eleven the remarkable diversity of ways in which a "statement" can be made under the TDA and the CPA is much wider. As well as oral indications over the phone or in person it will cover price panels in brochures, prices on teletext and on the internet, prices emailed to consumers, "late bargain" cards in travel agency windows, prices in newspaper advertisements and on television and quotations written down for clients by travel agency staff.

However, it is the defendant who has to *give* the indication and the question arises in relation to prices set by tour operators as to the circumstances when it can be said that it is the travel agent who is giving the price. Thus where they put "late bargain" cards in the window or advertise tour operators' prices in the local paper it is they who are giving the indication and it is not unknown for agents to be prosecuted whose cards were wrong or badly out of date. It is debatable whether simply handing over a brochure with prices already printed or showing the client the price on the viewdata screen would be regarded as the travel agent giving an indication. Even here, however, there may be grey areas. What if the client asks the price of holidays in say, the Thomson brochure, and the travel agent reads the price out of the brochure to the client. In these circumstances who is *giving* the indication—the operator only or the agent as well? In many cases this will be a purely academic question because the agent will have a defence but in some cases the defence might not be available and the agent could be convicted.

The offence is committed when the defendant "gives . . . to any consumers" a misleading price indication. This suggests that the offence is complete when the indication is communicated to the consumer—not necessarily when the price is first displayed. For many practical purposes this may not matter because if the price has been displayed but no consumer has been misled there is unlikely to be a complaint.

The price

The price is defined in section 20(6) as meaning the aggregate of the sums required to be paid or the method of calculating that aggregate. Thus in a situation where a client is required to take the operator's compulsory insurance but this is not made clear then an offence will be committed.

Misleading indications

Section 20 creates the offences of giving misleading price indications and s.21 defines what is meant by misleading price indications. It does so by identifying five situations where a price indication is misleading (section 21(1)(a)–(e)) and another five where a method of calculating the price is misleading (section 21(2)(a)–(e)). There is some doubt about whether the definition is exhaustive. According to Lowe and Woodroffe (5th. ed., 1999) the list of situations *is* exhaustive and they are quite categorical on this point. On the other hand the Act leaves open the possibility of other categories of misleading indication being illegal by the use of the word "includes" in the definition—a non-exclusive term. This would permit an interpretation of the section as meaning that the categories listed are only illustrative of the general offence. The practical effect of this is that if a trader finds a way of misleading consumers about prices in a manner not covered by section 21 then under the Lowe and Woodroffe view he will escape prosecution but not if section 20 is regarded as creating a *general* offence covering *all* misleading price indications—whether specifically identified by section 21 or not. See below for a category which does not fit the categories listed in section 21.

The definition of misleading contains both objective and subjective elements. On the one hand section 21(1) talks about "what is conveyed by the indication"—clearly an objective test. On the other hand it also talks about "what those consumers [*i.e.* those to whom the indication is given] might reasonably be expected to infer from the indication". This is a subjective test. While it might be expected that most people today would realise that prices in brochures are usually quoted on the basis of two people sharing a room there are still those who may not realise this and therefore the tour operator should spell out such things explicitly or be prepared to run the risk of misleading *some* of its clients.

It is not necessary to prove that the indication is misleading to all the consumers to which it was given. Section 20(3)(c) states that it is immaterial whether the indication is misleading to all or only some of the consumers to which it was given. On the other hand, if the facts are that only one or two out of a large number of consumers were misled, it may be difficult to prove that the indications was "misleading" as defined.

Section 21(1) expressly states that what is misleading depends not simply on what the indication conveys but what any omission from the indication conveys. This is particularly relevant for tour operators and travel agents because holiday prices tend to be calculated on a low basic price with a large number of supplements to cover a wide variety of options—airport supplements, single room supplements, half and full board, insurance, surcharges, balconies, seaviews, etc, etc. The danger is that if these are not displayed clearly or explained thoroughly the client may be misled into believing that he is getting a particular service or facility as part of the basic price when in fact he has to pay for it.

The advent of a tax on airport departures led to a highly publicised argument in 1997 as to whether APD should be included in the prices of packages (and indeed scheduled air fares), or can be shown as a separate item. The effect of section 21(1) surely requires that the tax be part of the all-inclusive price, and not shown separately. (See the ASA Monthly Report No. 79, December 1997 for their decisions on airline pricing.) On this issue the ABTA Code of Conduct (February 2003 edition) has this to say:

> "1.3(vii) A Member shall include within the Basic Price quoted in Advertising and Promotions for all Travel Arrangements, all non-optional costs for example, but not limited to, all airport and seaport fees, charges and taxes (except those that cannot be paid in advance by the Principal) insurance and ticketing costs."

In *Toyota (GB) Ltd v North Yorkshire County Council* (Div. Ct., March 11, 1998; (1998) 162 J.P. 794) the defendants published an advertisement for a car which gave a headline price of £11,655 but included in very small print at the bottom of the advertisement further obligatory charges of £445 for taxes and delivery charges, etc. It was confirmed on appeal that despite the qualifying words the advertisement amounted to a misleading price indication under section 20(1) because it conveyed that the car was available for £11,655 when it was not.

The categories of misleading indications

Section 21(1) sets out the categories of indication that are misleading. It is proposed to examine them in turn.

(a) "The Price Is Less Than In Fact It Is"

This is one of the simplest of ways to mislead clients. For instance a tour operator may print the wrong price mistakenly in the brochure, *e.g.* £279 instead of £379. Any client reading the brochure is misled into believing that the holiday is £100 cheaper than in fact it is. Unless the tour operator can claim the benefit of one of the defences he will have committed an offence. Note that regardless of whether the client buys the holiday or not the offence will have been committed. Even if the tour operator admits to the mistake when it is pointed out and permits the client to have the holiday at the lower price the offence is still committed. The tour operator's actions can be used in mitigation of the sentence but will not prevent the offence occurring in the first place. Of course a client who is treated in such a way is unlikely to complain to a Trading Standards Department in which case no prosecution will be brought.

The position would be the same if a travel agent placed a card in the window with the wrong (low) price on it. In those circumstances it would be the travel agent who would have misled the client into believing that the price was less than in fact it was.

However, the situation may be different if the trader takes care. After all, the offence is committed by giving a misleading indication as to the price at which services etc *are available*. In the case of *Toys R Us v Gloucestershire County Council* (1994) 158 JP 338, toys were on display on the shelves together with their prices. However it sometimes happened that at the till, when the bar code was read, a higher price appeared. The Company were found guilty of a number of offences by the Magistrates, but were successful in their appeal to the Divisional Court. Kennedy LJ said:

> "[Toys R Us] did require cashiers to check price tickets, and if they found the price lower than the price displayed on the [till] to charge the lower price. Life being what it is, it is not surprising that cashiers did not always check as they should have done. ... In my judgment ... the relevant time is the time at which the indication as to price is given, that is to say in the context of this case when the item was on the shelf with a ticket attached to it. ... The statute does not require ascertainment of 'the correct price'. All it requires is ascertainment of the price at which the goods were available, bearing in mind that prices defined in Section 20(6) as the sums 'required to be paid by a consumer'. ... As it was the policy and practice of [Toys R Us] to charge the price on the ticket, that was the price at which the goods were available. If a customer had asked a passing store manager 'what sum will I be required to pay for this article?', the reply would have been the price on the ticket, and if the store manager knew that there had been a price increase he might have added 'make sure the cashier does not charge you the new price' ... [the Prosecutor] submits that because cashiers make errors, the price

> ticket is not really the price at which the goods are available, it is only the price at which they are available on a conditional basis, the condition being that either the cashier or the customer notices the discrepancy. The condition could of course be put the other way round, namely that the goods are available at the ticket price unless the cashier or customer fails to notice the discrepancy. . . . It seems to me that the Magistrates should have started from the standpoint that an offence under Section 20 (1) could only be established if it could be shown that despite the policy, in reality goods were not available at the ticket price . . . what happens in practice is important".

Thus, Toys R Us were found not guilty because in practice, and by their policy, any discrepancy in the price was operated in favour of the consumer. In other words the goods were *made available* at the price on the ticket.

It is interesting that this case was *not* decided on the basis of whether or not the Company operated a due diligence system to avoid offences.

The lesson for tour operators and travel agents is clear. Discrepancies most frequently arise between brochure prices and viewdata prices, or between window card prices and prices given at the desk. If a Company operates a policy (which should be demonstrable by reference to a written booking policy and confirmed by financial records) that any such price discrepancy is operated to the benefit of the consumer, who therefore gets the lower price, then offences will be avoided. However, repeated breaches of the policy would be evidence that in reality the holidays were not available at the brochure price and the tour operator could be convicted.

In *Berkshire CC v Olympic Holidays* (1993, Divisional Court, unreported) a confirmed booking was made between a client and a tour operator on the basis of a computer print out which displayed a price which was £182 lower than the actual price. In other words there had been an error on the screen so that a price was displayed which was £182 lower than the brochure price—which Olympic asserted was the actual price. Olympic were charged with a breach of section 20(1) of the CPA. Ultimately they were found not guilty by the Divisional Court on the grounds that they had exercised all due diligence to prevent the offence occurring (see section four) but it is interesting to note that the Magistrates felt that Olympic had brought the case on themselves by refusing to honour the price quoted on the screen. It is also interesting to speculate that regardless of the position under the CPA and the criminal law the client may actually have had a contract at the lower price. There was clearly full agreement between the parties as to the subject matter of the contract and the price and it was only later that Olympic chose not to honour the price.

How then can a tour operator ever legally increase his prices in a buoyant market?

- Withdraw the brochure; but this is a prohibitively expensive operation;
- Put no prices at all in the brochure—but does this breach Regulation 5, which requires an accurate indication of the price in brochures?;
- Change the price on Viewdata and rely on a combination of warnings in the brochure, travel agency "shelf-talkers" and other techniques as a due diligence defence;
- Operate the system which has been mis-named "Fluid Pricing"; the price in the brochure is the maximum price to be charged to the consumer, and the tour operator is free to vary the price up and down below that ceiling. Very careful wording is required to explain this to the consumer and it may yet infringe Reg. 5 of the PTR. (See section three.) In 2001 LACORS indicated that as a concession they would not prosecute cases where the maximum price was shown and never exceeded.

Compared to the supermarket which can change prices easily, the tour operator can be seen to be trapped between the expensive old technology of the brochure and the flexible new technology of viewdata and its successors. Perhaps the days of the brochure are numbered. One day, when the practice becomes that brochures are downloaded from the Internet or accessed via interactive television, it will be easy to keep the prices accurate and up to date.

(b) "The Applicability Of The Price Does Not Depend On Facts Or Circumstances On Which Its Applicability Does In Fact Depend"

Most holiday prices are based on two people sharing a hotel room but occasionally operators publish brochures which feature rooms accommodating four people and if two people want to share it they will have to pay more per person. If this was not made clear in the brochure it would be perfectly reasonable for a client to believe that the price quoted was based on two sharing rather than four sharing. In other words the price does not make it clear that it does not depend on facts (an occupancy rate of four to a room) on which it does in fact depend. It would be the same where a travel agent did not make it clear that the prices quoted were for payment by cash and there was an extra charge for paying by credit card. A suggestion in a brochure that discounts are only available to early bookers would offend if the truth is that holidays for unpopular dates or destinations were discounted throughout. Another example would be if the tour operator offered free insurance but did not make it clear that this was only available on holidays over £1000.

(c) "That The Price Covers Matters In Respect Of Which An Additional Charge Is In Fact Made"

This is another straightforward category that many tour operators could easily fall into. Prices in brochures tend to be based on a basic price onto which various supplements are added, *e.g.* single room supplement, airport supplements, full board supplements, etc. Unless the pricing panel is quite clear it would be relatively easy to mislead a potential client into believing that the basic price covered matters (the supplements) for which in fact an additional charge was made.

(d) "That a person who in fact has no such expectation;"

(i) expects the price to be increased or reduced (whether or not at a particular time or by a particular amount); or
(ii) expects the price, or the price as increased or reduced, to be maintained (whether or not for a particular period);

The first of these two categories covers the situation where a travel clerk says "I would buy the holiday now if I were you because the price will go up next week". The second covers statements such as "There is no point hanging on for late bargains this year because there won't be any. I would buy now". If in fact the people making these statements do not believe that what they are saying is true and this can be proved then this amounts to an offence.

This category would also cover "special low price introductory offers" where the operator had no intention of putting the price up at all.

The problem with this category is that it requires proof of a state of mind—which is always much more difficult to establish. It therefore creates an odd exception to the basic rule that *mens rea* is not required for offences under the CPA. That this is so is confirmed by the case of *Thomson Tour Operations Ltd v Birch* (Divisional Court, January 26, 1999). The facts of the case were that a Mrs Baxter had bought a holiday from Thomson in November 1997 for £1712. Mrs Baxter had chosen the holiday from Thomson's brochure which included their Fair Trading Charter. One of the provisions in the Charter stated: "... if Thomson's reduce the price of the holiday after it has been booked, the new lower price will be charged." Subsequently Thomson reduced the price of holidays like her's by 10 per cent but when she applied for a refund she was initially refused it. Only after she had complained to the Thomson head office was she given a refund—some several months after her return from holiday. In the meantime she had informed Herefordshire Trading Standards Department of the position and they brought a prosecution under s.20(1) of the CPA on the basis that she had been given a price indication which was misleading in the manner provided in section 21(1)(d). The essence of the case was that Thomson had misled consumers by indicating that they expected the price to be reduced but that was not, in reality, their expectation, because events proved that they had not in fact honoured the price reduction in Mrs Baxter's case. What the prosecution had to establish therefore was that Thomson had given an indication that they *expected* the price to be reduced and that *when the indication was given* Thomson *had no such expectation*.

The court found that the language used in the Fair Trading Charter was not sufficient to establish that Thomson had an expectation that they would reduce prices and as there was no other evidence as to their state of mind then the prosecution failed. All the Fair Trading Charter established was a promise by Thomson that *if* they reduced the price then Mrs Baxter would receive a refund. This they had belatedly agreed to do. If they had failed to do so then "Mrs Baxter would have had an unanswerable case for damages for breach of warranty" but this did not amount to the commission of an criminal offence under the CPA.

(e) "That the facts or circumstances by reference to which the consumers might reasonably be expected to judge the validity of any relevant comparison made or implied by the indication are not what in fact they are"

This deals with price comparisons. Essentially it is saying that if you make a price comparison then you should make clear the factual basis on which the comparison is being made. If an operator advertises that he is selling two weeks in La Siesta hotel in Playa de las Americas for £473 per person half board whereas a rival is selling it for £617 per person half board but the advertisement does not make it clear that the comparison is between low season and high season prices this is misleading. The consumer is entitled to believe that the operator is comparing like with like but the operator is not doing this.

More commonly this will cover comparisons with the tour operators own prices, *e.g.* "up to 50% off" or misleading use of words such as "bargain" or "special offer".

Misleading methods of determining a price

Section 21(2) deals with *methods of determining* a price that are misleading. The immediate relevance to the travel industry is of course the imposition of surcharges and how the surcharges are calculated. As in section 21(1) there are five different categories of misleading price calculations and again it is proposed to deal with them in turn.

(a) "That The Method Is Not What In Fact It Is"

If a tour operator states that the cost of the holiday is subject to surcharges and that the surcharge will be calculated according to rates of exchange prevailing on a particular day when in fact this is not the case then this is a misleading indication of how the price is determined.

This provision was addressed in passing in a case involving an internecine travel industry dispute—*Association of British Travel Agents & Others v British Airways & Others* [2000] 1 Lloyd's Rep. 169; aff'd [2000] 2 Lloyd's Rep. 209. In January 1999 IATA airlines changed the basis on which their fares were calculated in such a way that travel agents received less commission. What they did was to ask travel agents to represent the Passenger Service Charge (PSC) on tickets as a tax. The PSC is a charge levied on airlines by airports for the provision of certain airport services and is calculated according to the volume of passengers the airline puts through the airport. It is important to note that the PSC is *not* a tax and it is *not* a charge on passengers, it is merely one of the overheads of airline operation. However, by calling it a tax the airlines would not then have to pay commission on that element of the fare!

One of the issues that arose out of the case was whether there was an implied term in the standard contract between IATA airlines and ABTA tour operators to the effect that the airlines would not require travel agents to commit an illegal act—*i.e.* give a misleading price indication as to the *method of calculating* the price of an airline ticket. On the point the judge in the High Court had this to say:

> "Under s. 20(1) of the 1987 Act, it is an offence to give to 'any consumers an indication which is misleading as to the price at which any ... services ... are available'. Since the definition of 'misleading' in s.21(2) encompasses an indication which is misleading as to a 'method' of determining a price, it seems clear enough that a document which states that the total price includes an ingredient for tax when it does not, conveys an indication that the method of determining the price 'is not what in fact it is' within s. 21(2)(a)."

(b) "That The Applicability Of The Method Does Not Depend On Facts Or Circumstances On Which Its Applicability Does In Fact Depend;"

A tour operator may state prominently at the front of the brochure that surcharges will be levied in a range of circumstances. In the small print in the terms and conditions at the back it may repeat the circumstances in which the surcharges will be levied but to include circumstances which are wider than those indicated at the front. For instance it may not mention fuel price increases at the front although it does at the back. It could be argued that the indication at the front is misleading because it leads the consumer to believe that the method of determining the price does not depend on fuel increases when in fact it does.

(c) "That The Method Takes Into Account Matters In Respect Of Which An Additional Charge Will In Fact Be Made";

There is a degree of overlap here with category (b). If the surcharge information at the front of the brochure appears to list all the matters which go into the calculation of surcharges but omits certain matters which are in fact listed in the small print at the back and for which additional charges are made then this will be misleading. (*Toyota v North Yorkshire* referred to earlier is an example of this illustration.)

(d) "That a person who in fact has no such expectation;"

- (i) expects the method to be altered (whether or not at a particular time or in a particular respect); or

(ii) expects the method, or that method as altered, to remain unaltered (whether or not for a particular period); or

If a travel agent encourages clients to "book now" because he expects surcharges to be applied to all future bookings when in fact he does not believe this at all then this will be an offence. He is saying that he expects the method of determining the price to be altered when he has no such expectation.

(e) "That The Facts Or Circumstances By Reference To Which The Consumers Might Reasonably Be Expected To Judge The Validity Of Any Relevant Comparison Made Or Implied By The Indication Are Not What In Fact They Are."

If a travel agent makes a comparison between tour operators as to how they calculate their surcharges and misleads a client by indicating that one is better than the other because it excludes certain factors when in fact it does not then this will be an offence. He is indicating that the facts by reference to which the comparison is made are not what in fact they are. For example the travel agent might mistakenly believe that Operator X has a "full price guarantee" as defined by ABTA when in fact they have the same "partial price guarantee" as Operator Y.

Another category?

The issue of whether the list of categories of misleading price indications in the Act is exhaustive was mentioned earlier. This is only significant if there is some other way of misleading consumers not covered by the list. There may in fact be such a category: that the price is higher than in fact it is. Take for instance the following example. The Smith family acquire a range of brochures to study at home. They discover that calculating how much they will have to pay is a very complex business once all the supplements and "free child places" have been taken into account. However, they come to the conclusion that the holiday they want will cost say £1500 from operator A but only £1450 from operator B so they book with operator B. Subsequently they discover that they had done their calculations wrong and in fact the holiday from operator A only cost £1400. As a result of the misleading fashion in which operator A had displayed their prices the Smith family believed that the price was higher than in fact it was—resulting in a loss of £50 to the Smiths, and also, ironically, a loss of £1400 for operator A.

Goods, services, accommodation or facilities

Services and facilities are defined in section 22(1) to include "any services or facilities whatever". It can be assumed that accommodation will include accommodation provided by tour operators as part of a package. The same word is used in s.14 of the Trade Descriptions Act 1968 and has been held to include holiday accommodation.

Services are specifically defined to include "the purchase or sale of foreign currency" so any travel agency dealing in foreign currency will be subject to the Act. There are in fact specific regulations dealing with Bureaux de Change—The Price Indications (Bureau de Change) Regulations 1992—which impose particular obligations on foreign currency dealers as to the kind of information they must provide to consumers and how it must be displayed.

Consumer

In relation to services and facilities a consumer is defined in section 20(6)(b) as being:

> "any person who might wish to be provided with the services or facilities otherwise than for the purposes of any business of his"

Thus the Act appears at first sight to be aimed at protecting private individuals rather than traders. However, once it has been demonstrated that a misleading indication has been made to a consumer there is nothing to prevent a trader who feels he has been harmed by a rival from complaining to a trading standards officer. It does not have to be shown that a consumer has suffered harm merely that a misleading indication has been made to him. There is certainly no requirement that there actually be any supply of the services. Section 20(6)(b) makes it clear that a consumer is any person *who might wish to be* supplied with the services. A Trading Standards Officer can in effect be the consumer who complains. This was considered in the *Toys R Us* case where it was said:

> "Was the trading standards officer a consumer?
>
> Mr Matheson also submitted that a trading standards officer on duty is not a consumer for the purposes of the 1987 Act, because

s 20(6) defines consumer in relation to any goods as 'any person who might wish to be supplied with the goods for his own private use or consumption'. Mr Treacy's response is that an important word is 'might'. The fact that a trading standards officer does not in fact wish to be supplied is not material, and of course if he visits a supermarket during opening hours ticket prices which he sees will be seen by others too, because they are an indication to consumers as to the price. In my judgment Mr Treacy is right in relation to this issue. As he points out the definition of consumer is probably formulated as it is to exclude retailers buying from wholesalers, but for our purposes that is of little relevance."

This decision was cited in *MFI Furniture Centres Limited v Hibbert* (1995) *The Times* July 21, which arrived at a similar decision on this point. Indeed that case went further by saying that there need be no evidence of any particular consumer being misled. If evidence from an actual consumer were required it would hamper the operation of the Act.

Price indications which subsequently become misleading

Section 20(2) provides for situations where prices are initially correct but subsequently become misleading for some reason. A tour operator might perhaps publish a second edition of a brochure with new prices in it but the first edition remains in circulation with the old, now misleading, prices in it. What is the position if someone relies upon the old edition? The meaning of section 20(2) was examined in the case of *The Link Stores Ltd v The London Borough of Harrow* (Divisional Court, December 21, 2000).

The facts of the case were that a Mr Reynolds went to a Link store in Harrow to buy an Easylife mobile phone. It cost £89.99. Before he made his purchase he saw displayed at the store a notice in these terms:

"We won't be beaten on price. If you find exactly the same package cheaper in local store within seven days we will refund the difference."

Within the seven day period Mr Reynolds saw the same package on sale in another local store at a price of £69.99. However, when he returned to the appellant's store to ask for a £20 refund it was refused. He complained to the Harrow Trading Standards

Department and the store was prosecuted under s.20(2) of the CPA. Although convicted by the Magistrates the Divisional Court quashed the conviction. The reasons are set out in the judgment of Waller LJ:

> "... the question is whether the facts as found constitute an offence under Section 20(2).
>
> In my view that subsection is designed to deal with a situation (a) in which a seller of goods or services gives an indication that becomes misleading after it was given but before a contract is entered into; and (b) where consumers can be expected to rely in entering into the contract on the indication after it has become misleading; and (c) where the seller fails to take steps to prevent consumers relying on the indication after it has become misleading and before they enter into the contract.
>
> The ingredients of the offence are cumulative, and thus the statement must at one time not have been misleading; must then have become misleading before the consumer relies on it and enters into the contract; and between the time of it becoming misleading and it being relied on there must have been a failure to take reasonable steps to prevent reliance.
>
> In this case, there is no evidence that the indication changed its character from the moment it was given until the moment it was relied on when the goods were brought. Indeed the charge asserts that it became misleading when the customer returned to obtain a refund within seven days after purchase.
>
> If the indication was misleading from the outset because the seller never intended to honour the indication, then it did not in my view become misleading after it was given, and clearly, it did not become misleading simply when the customer tried to claim a reimbursement. If it was intended to be honoured when originally given, then in the absence of evidence establishing that the seller changed his mind before sale, and did nothing to withdraw the indication before sale, no offence would be committed under this subsection. Since as already said the charge stated that the indication became misleading only at the time when the customer sought to obtain a refund, it is unsurprising that evidence was not called or available to establish the change of heart prior to sale.
>
> The plain fact is that an allegation that an indication only became misleading after the sale, unfortunately demonstrates an absence of what in my view is an essential ingredient under this subsection that the customer relied in making his purchase on an indication that had become misleading where the seller had failed to take steps to prevent him relying on the same."

It is a common practice amongst travel agents to advertise that they will not be beaten on price and this case indicates that they might be able to renege on such promises with impunity. Indeed it suggests that if the indication is misleading from the outset then any prosecution under section 20(2) will fail. However Waller LJ prefaced his decision by saying that there might be other provisions of the Act under which a prosecution might have been brought. Presumably what he had in mind was the offence under section 20(1) which as we have seen deals with indications which are misleading from the outset.

Indeed, in the case of *R v Warwickshire County Council ex parte Johnson* mentioned above, the House of Lords had no doubt that when a manager of Dixon's refused to honour an offer stating that "We will beat any TV, Hi-Fi and Video price by £20 on the spot" this amounted to an offence under section 20(1). On appeal from the Divisional Court they were required to answer the question:

> "Whether for the purposes of section 20(1) of the Consumer Protection Act 1987 a statement, which in itself is not misleading on the face of it, can be rendered misleading by virtue of the fact that, even in the absence of evidence to show a general practice or intention to dishonour the offer, contained therein, on one occasion the person making the statement declined to enter into a contract within the terms of the statement."

Their answer on this issue was unequivocal:

> "As to the first question, it was strenuously argued that because the notice was not misleading on its face it could not subsequently become misleading by a refusal to honour its terms. It was said that it never ceased to be a genuine offer. Overcharging could not of itself convert that notice, itself not misleading, into a notice which was misleading. Counsel for the appellant frankly admitted that Mr Thomas was misled. I ask: by what was Mr Thomas misled? There can only be one answer. Mr Thomas was misled by the notice. I find myself in complete agreement with the reasoning of the Divisional Court on this issue (156 JP 577 at 580):
>
>> The notice is a continuing offer and whether it is misleading or not can only be tested by somebody taking up the offer. It was misleading because [the appellant] did not in accordance with the terms of the notice beat any t.v., hi-fi, video price by £20 on the spot.
>
> To hold otherwise would be seriously to restrict the efficacy of

this part of the consumer protection legislation. Seemingly innocent notices could be put up and then when such notices were followed by a refusal to honour them by a person acting in the course of his business no offence would be committed. I would therefore answer the first certified question Yes."

Where tour operators have published a brochure and then subsequently changed the prices in it the Code of Practice offers some helpful advice on what can be done in these circumstances. These will be looked at in the next Chapter which is concerned with the defences to all the statutory provisions imposing criminal liability on tour operators and travel agents.

There has been at least one attempt by a prosecutor to circumvent the ease with which a defendant may be able to secure acquittal under section 20(2). Where a Tour Operator decided to increase prices but could show that no consumers relied on the old price, a charge was brought under section 20(1). The result was a not guilty verdict, probably because innocence under section 20(2) amounts to due diligence under section 20(1) in these circumstances—*Oldham MBC v Sun Express Holidays* (1997 Oldham Magistrates Court, unreported).

Tickets and car hire

Regulations under the CPA, the Price Indications (Resale of Tickets) Regulations 1994 (SI 1994/3248) came into force on February 20, 1995. They require that anyone other than the promoter of an entertainment who in the course of a business gives to consumers a price indication about tickets for entertainment must disclose the face value of the tickets as well as accurate details about the seat's location, etc. However, Regulation 3(3) provides that this does not apply to packages covered by the Package Travel Regulations. So tour operators selling package holidays which include for example tickets for the opera at Verona or for the Olympic Games or the World Cup do not have to comply. However, one day coach trips to a rock concert or a musical will be caught because they are not "packages" as defined.

One further small point. ABTA's Standards on Brochures contain a requirement for members to make it clear in brochures what any offer of car hire includes, *e.g.* insurance, collision damage waiver, etc. Whilst the ABTA rules do not create a criminal offence as such this rule does tackle a price problem which has caused many an unpleasant surprise for consumers over the years and which has the potential to give rise to criminal charges if the brochure misleads the consumer about the price of the car hire.

Chapter Thirteen
Criminal Offences Under The Package Travel Regulations

Introduction

As we have seen in Chapters 11 and 12 the Trade Descriptions Act and the Consumer Protection Act cover an extremely large range of possible false trade descriptions about every aspect of a holiday and an equally wide range of misleading prices. The Trade Descriptions Act in particular does not require the organiser to give any information; but if the information is given, it must not be false.

Regulations 5, 7 and 8 of the Regulations take this a stage further. They provide that certain important information *must be given* to the consumer at various points in the contracting process *and* must be accurate.

Brochures—Regulation 5

The Regulations do *not* require a brochure to be made available to consumers, but where a brochure *is* made available it lays down stringent requirements as to what must be included.

Regulation 5 provides:—

(1) "Subject to paragraph (4) below, no organiser shall make available a brochure to a possible consumer unless it indicates in a legible, comprehensible and accurate manner the price and adequate information about the matters specified in Schedule 1 to these Regulations in respect of the packages offered for sale in the brochure to the extent that those matters are relevant to the packages so offered.

(2) Subject to paragraph (4) below, no retailer shall make available to a possible consumer a brochure which he knows or has reasonable cause to believe does not comply with the requirements of paragraph (1).

(3) An organiser who contravenes paragraph (1) of this regulation and a retailer who contravenes paragraph (2) thereof shall be guilty of an offence and liable:—

(a) on summary conviction, to a fine not exceeding level 5 on the standard scale; and
(b) on conviction on indictment, to a fine."

The effect of this Regulation is to ensure that certain information goes into the brochure—on pain of incurring a criminal penalty. As to the defences available and other general provisions, see Chapter Fourteen below.

Thus the elements of the offence are that:

- if a brochure
- is made available
- to a possible consumer
- by an organiser
- it must contain certain information
- which must be legible, comprehensible, accurate and adequate.

and therefore the offence is committed if either the brochure does not contain the information required or it is not legible, comprehensible, accurate and adequate. For tour operators, as with the CPA, this is a strict liability offence but for travel agents there is an additional requirement that they must know or have reasonable cause to believe that the requirements of paragraph 1 have not been complied with.

(a) A Brochure

Regulation 5 is concerned with the information provided in a *brochure*. We all know a brochure when we see one but at the margins there are some forms of advertising that may or may not be brochures. Some brochures are little more than leaflets or pamphlets and others amount to only a single sheet or two. Do all these amount to brochures? The Regulations are no help at all. Brochures are defined in Regulation 2(1) in the following manner:

"brochure" means any brochure in which packages are offered for sale;"

A dictionary definition is not much more help:

"Booklet, pamphlet, esp. giving information about place". (The Concise Oxford Dictionary).

The dictionary does state that the word is derived from the French word "brocher" meaning a stitch and that brochure literally means "stitching". This suggests that to be a brochure it must be substantial enough or contain enough pages to require stitching, or, given that most brochures are not now stitched but stapled or thermal bound, to have required stitching in the past. This would raise difficulties with those smaller "brochures" consisting simply of a single sheet of paper folded in concertina fashion. It would be hard to dispute that such things are brochures even though they might not fit within a conventional definition of one.

Even more difficult would be newspaper advertisements; for example, Readers Travel Clubs and other similar features found in many local and national newspapers and magazines. Frequently they contain considerable amounts of information, including booking conditions, itineraries and booking forms and are intended to fulfil the function of brochures yet one would be hard pressed to call it a brochure. However the European approach to statutory interpretation is to take a much broader, purposive, approach and it may be that even newspaper advertisements would be caught by the term brochure.

Another pitfall for the operator in relation to brochures is when a supplement to a main brochure is published which may not contain all the relevant information. To avoid being caught by Regulation 5 the quickest solution is to ensure that the supplement does contain the required information. Another possible solution is to state clearly that this is only "part" of the brochure and if the consumer wishes to obtain all the relevant information he must read it in conjunction with the main brochure.

A photocopy of a page of a brochure handed to a consumer by a travel agent is probably not, on its own, a brochure.

Since May 2001 ABTA's Code of Conduct has provided their own definition of a brochure:

> "**Brochure:** a communication in any printed, viewable, audible or other form which specifies the contents of Travel Arrangements offered by a Member in sufficient detail to allow a Client to reliably book the Travel Arrangements without obtaining additional information from the Member."

Clearly this is intended to cover more than the conventional printed brochure. In particular the definition would encompass internet travel sites so long as the information provided was sufficiently detailed. Whether a court would accept that the Regulations went so far is a moot point but the fact that the industry itself is prepared to admit that this is a brochure would probably go a long way to convincing them.

(b) Is Made Available

As we have seen the TDA makes it an offence to *make* a false statement and in the leading case of *Wings v Ellis* [1985] A.C. 262 the House of Lords held that a statement was made every time it reached the next link in the chain of distribution and every time a consumer reads it. Although Regulation 5 does not employ the same words the ones it does use are sufficiently similar to give rise to the same interpretation. It could be said that the operator was making the brochure available to a consumer if he sends him one direct or if he distributes it to agents to make available to consumers. So long as a brochure was intended for public consumption it would not matter how it came into the hands of a consumer—it would all count as being made available to the consumer. Strictly speaking the offence could be committed even where a consumer had not read the brochure. It could even be argued that the offence is committed where the consumer had not yet acquired one; it would still be available to him when sitting on the travel agent's shelf. In the real world, however, the prosecution need a complainant of some sort to give evidence in Court. It must be remembered also that criminal statutes must be strictly construed in favour of the defendant.

If the brochure was not legible, comprehensible or accurate when first made available then an offence will be committed. But what if it subsequently becomes inaccurate? For instance what if it states that UK nationals do not need visas to visit the USA but after publication the rules are changed and visas are required. If the brochure is still being racked by travel agents then, unless the operator has told the agents not to display it, the brochure is still being made available *by the operator* and it is inaccurate and therefore the operator is committing an offence. This is a difficulty that tour operators face under both the Trade Descriptions Act 1968 in relation to false statements and the Consumer Protection Act 1987 in relation to misleading prices. The problem is that the brochure has a life of several months and yet the information in it can change from day to day—(see Chapter Fourteen, the section concerned with whether errata are effective, for guidance on this point).

(c) To a Possible Consumer

One departure that the Regulation makes from the Directive is to make it an offence to make the brochure available to a *possible consumer* whereas the Directive only refers to *the consumer*. The practical effect of this is to considerably widen the potential scope of the offence. A consumer is defined in the Directive and the Regulations as a person 'who takes or agrees to take the package'. Thus a consumer is only someone who has a contract with the operator or who actually goes on the package. But a *possible consumer* could be anyone who might wish to go on the package. Whether this will make any real difference is debatable. Although it is foreseeable that there will be possible consumers who discover brochures which may not be legible, comprehensible and accurate it is unlikely that they will complain. Even if they do so will a prosecution be brought? It is likely that only those consumers who suffer from a breach of the Regulation will complain and only serious breaches will give rise to a prosecution. However, Trading Standards sometimes make enquiries posing as "possible consumers" in order to bolster their evidence; the Court has approved such tactics, at least under the different wording of the Consumer Protection Act 1987 (see previous Chapter).

(d) By an Organiser

The term organiser will cover conventional tour operators but following the *Club Tour* case (see Chapter Two) will also encompass travel agents who put ad hoc packages together, so long as they publish a brochure.

(e) Which Contains Certain Information

The first thing to say about Regulation 5 is that many tour operators already provide the required level of information as a matter of routine in their brochures therefore this requirement should not impose any additional burdens on them. The only difficulties which should arise will be over matters of detail, in particular the itinerary. Health and visa requirements may also be a problem. However the need to give passport and visa information applies to UK nationals only when the brochure is made available in the UK. The requirement to advise on health formalities applies to everyone.

The information which must be included in the brochure is set out in Schedule 1 to the PTR. Most of the items in the schedule are self-explanatory. However we will deal with a few points from the Schedule and most importantly, the issue of the price of the package.

(i) The Price

In the early days after the Package Travel Regulations came into force, no-one got very excited about the fact that the "price of the package" was one of the items required by Regulation 5 to be stated in a legible comprehensible and accurate manner. This simple requirement appeared to add nothing to the much more complex and sophisticated requirements of the Consumer Protection Act (see previous chapter).

As time has gone on, however, Regulation 5 has been revealed as having real teeth. The way in which it has been interpreted by Trading Standards has certainly irritated the holiday industry, distorted the market and put tour operators at a serious disadvantage to the likes of low cost airlines, who vary their prices minute by minute.

The reason is this: as we have already seen, an offence is committed under Regulation 5 if information is given but in a way which is say inaccurate (or incomprehensible); it is also committed if the information is not given at all.

The requirement is for the price to be indicated. The industry has tried to argue that "indicate" merely means that a vague clue is given as to what the price might be. For details ask elsewhere. However Trading Standards, not unreasonably interpret the words as meaning simply "to state the price".

Therefore, the price must be given. It must be given accurately. Thus, for the life of the brochure, the price stated in the brochure must be the actual price. It cannot be changed (or at least it cannot be increased—Trading Standards as a concession say they will not prosecute where the price is reduced). There is no Code of Practice, as under the CPA, permitting changes to brochure prices to be made in certain circumstances (see Chapter Fourteen on this, and also on the issue of whether the CPA Code of Practice can be used as part of a "due diligence" Defence to a Regulation 5 Offence).

Furthermore, tour operators cannot get round the Regulation by omitting prices altogether from the brochure, but merely suggesting that the consumer enquires at the travel agency desk, or on the internet, or wherever. As we have seen, it is equally an offence to omit the price from the brochure.

Brochures are extremely expensive to produce and cannot be replaced to reflect ever changing market conditions. Thus this requirement of Regulation 5 imposes a straightjacket on the normal workings of the market.

An interesting argument has been run that Regulations 5 and 6 should be read together as the emanate from one article of the Directive, namely Article 3.2. That permits changes in certain circumstances as we have seen under Regulation 6 (see Chapter Four). In English Law, Article 3 has been transposed as two different things, the Civil Section (Regulation 6) and the Criminal Section (Regulation 5). The response of Trading Standards to this argument is that there is nothing to prevent the UK Government legislating in a way which is more tough than the directive; and that the words in Regulation 5 are clear.

The requirement for prices to be stated comprehensively probably adds nothing to the requirement under the CPA that prices not be misleading.

(ii) The Means, Characteristics and Categories of Transport

The DTI in its guidelines has indicated their view that these words are to be taken in the general sense and that it is not necessary to specify for example the type of aircraft in a package involving air travel. Although perhaps a holidaymaker of a nervous disposition going to one of the smaller Caribbean islands for a holiday might prefer to be told in advance that the second leg of the journey from Barbados to St Vincent was not by wide-bodied jet but a much smaller propellor-driven aircraft.

(iii) The Type of Accommodation etc,

Again the DTI indicates its view that the tourist classification under the Rules of an EC Member State can only be given where such rules exist. Where a classification system exists but is not mandatory (as is the case in the UK) then the organiser is free to use it or not as he pleases; but the category or degree of comfort must be indicated by one means or another. The "main features" of accommodation is a rather vague concept—does the hotel have en suite bathroom facilities, a bar, a restaurant, a swimming pool? A consumer, however, might feel that many other smaller facilities were main features as far as he was concerned! To whom are the features main? The organiser, the bulk of consumers or the individual consumer? This is particularly important bearing in mind that the offence is not confined simply to inaccuracy; but to omission of the "main features" as well. In *Inspirations East Limited v Dudley MBC 1997 DC*, unreported, the Divisional Court failed to make an express finding that an offence of stating matters in a brochure inaccurately could only be committed if it would also have been an offence to omit the same information; however they proceeded on the assumption that this was correct. In the early pages of their brochure Inspirations had indicated that the standard wheelchair/disabled logo against a hotel meant that the hotel was most suitable for those with walking difficulties or who use a wheelchair and that the lift, room and bathroom doors had been measured and there were ramps to every public area. This was under a heading in large bold type saying "Holidays for the Elderly and Disabled". The complainant booked a holiday at a hotel in the brochure which exhibited the logo, because she wished to take her wheelchair bound daughter. They found that, while the swimming pool area was accessible from the hotel via a ramp and across a patio, there were five steps down to the pool itself from the patio and no ramps. Pill LJ and Garland J made the point that the "main features" of a hotel might vary from case to case. The information must be stated accurately where relevant to the packages on offer; and that by virtue of the use of the logo and the bold paragraph on the introductory pages "Holidays for the Elderly and Disabled", "the brochure was plainly intended, it seems to me, to encourage disabled people . . . to go on holidays offered in the brochure. That is made relevant by the presence of the disabled logo".

Inspirations, it seems, had made "suitability for the disabled" into a main feature by the boldness of their claims. It remains to be seen in future cases where a line might be drawn. The second author has seen prosecutions alleging such matters as "weekly Turkish night" as being a main feature of a hotel, but no such cases had come to trial at the time of going to press.

Note that all this information needs to be given only "where relevant to the package". There will be no need to name a hotel, for example, for the type of economy holiday sold on the basis that the hotels are allocated by the tour operator on arrival—but the main features expected must still be named. The DTI feels this may apply also to the type of package which is an extended tour of a number of cities.

(iv) Passport/Visa/Health Formalities

After the 1998 amendments the requirement applies to "general information about passport and visa requirements which apply to nationals of the Member State of States in which the brochure is made available." For most British tour operators this will be British nationals; though a catch for the unwary are the different visa requirements for "British citizens" and for "British subjects". Also some tour operators distribute brochures in Eire and this will have to be taken into account too. Note also the different criteria under Regulation 7 below.

(v) Cancellation for Minimum Numbers

The number need not be stated, but the deadline date for cancellation must be stated and adhered to. Organisers bound by ABTA's rules, however, are unable to stipulate any date for cancellation after the date when payment of the balance of the price is due.

(vi) Arrangements in Event of Delay

It appears that complete silence on this point will not suffice. The organiser must either state the arrangements (*e.g.*, refreshments, meals, hotel) or must specify that no arrangements apply in the event of delay—the idea being that the consumer will know what he is getting for his money and can make an informed choice. ABTA operators are already under such an obligation.

(f) Which is Legible, Comprehensible, Adequate and Accurate

Legible and comprehensible should cause no real problem to a tour operator. Presumably "legible" refers to the type size in the brochure. If the print is so small it cannot be read even by someone with good eyesight it would fail this requirement. As far as "comprehensible" is concerned this test will presumably be similar: could the text be readily understood by a person of average intelligence? (In this context the requirement in Regulation 3 of the Unfair Terms in Consumer Contracts Regulations 1999 that contracts be written in intelligible language might be of relevance.) For instance it is a requirement that information about the price be comprehensible and this will include information about surcharges. If a tour operator tried to explain his surcharge policy in the kind of language found in Regulation 11 he would surely fail the test! The real meat is in the word "accurate". This appears to put a premium on precise and express information, and is harder to satisfy than a mere requirement that the words be "not misleading". Although the information will have to be "accurate" it will probably be subject to a *de minimis* test. If the inaccuracy is not material it will probably not constitute an offence. It is not possible to be dogmatic on this point because, unlike the Trade Descriptions Act, the Regulations do not actually say that the offence is only committed if the inaccuracy is material. Even if courts were to take a strict line it is unlikely that minor inaccuracies would be prosecuted—either because consumers would not complain or because Trading Standards Officers have better things to do with their time.

There has been a view that the words "legible comprehensible and accurate" are requirements only as the price of the package;

whilst only "adequate information" is required as to the matters in Schedule 1. However, in the case of *Inspirations East Limited v Dudley MBC* (1997) DC (See [1998] ITLJ 16 for a report of the case.) the court rejected that view. Pill LJ agreed that the wording was "clumsy" but said "it is clear to me that the words legible, comprehensible and accurate are intended to govern not only the price but the information; and the word adequate is included as a means of strengthening the protection which the Regulations provide".

Packages offered for sale

A technical point that arises from the wording of the Regulation is that it speaks of "packages *offered for sale* in the brochure". On the face of it an operator could escape liability simply by saying that he was not *offering for sale* the packages in the brochure. A tour operator's brochure does not usually constitute an offer for sale. The brochure is merely an invitation to treat and it is for the consumer to make an offer to buy. However this eventuality is covered by Regulation 2(1) which provides:

> " 'an offer' includes an invitation to treat whether by means of advertising or otherwise, and cognate expressions shall be construed accordingly."

Similar provisions exist in the Trade Descriptions Act and they are aimed at preventing the tour operator escaping criminal liability on the basis of a technicality of the law of contract such as occurred in the case of *Fisher v Bell* [1961] 1 Q.B. 394. In that case a shopkeeper who displayed a flick knife in his window escaped conviction for *offering* a dangerous weapon for sale as the display was only an invitation to treat not an offer. The effect of Regulation 2(1) will be to deprive tour operators of a similar defence.

Travel agents

Regulation 5(2) creates criminal liability for travel agents but, in a change from the original consultation document, only if the agent "knows or has reasonable cause to believe" that the brochure does not comply with Regulation 5(1) *i.e.* it is an offence, like s.14 of the TDA, that requires *mens rea*. For corporate defendants this will mean that the prosecution will have to show that a "directing mind" of the company had the requisite knowledge. (See Chapter Eleven on the TDA for this.) As long as the agent does not know or have reasonable cause to believe then he escapes liability but once he does then he can be convicted. On the face of it this seems eminently fair but on reflection the practicalities of complying with the Regulation are immense.

Given the amount of information that must be provided in the brochure it will not be long before some of it is found to be inaccurate and the agent informed of this. At this stage he will know that the information is inaccurate and he will be committing an offence if he *makes available* the brochure. The only escape then is either to take the drastic step of taking the brochures off display or ensuring a fail-safe errata system in the brochures themselves. The alternative is to avail themselves of the due diligence defence in Regulation 24 (see Chapter Fourteen). Whether this would work depends upon whether a court would accept the argument that even though an inaccurate or deficient brochure was made available it amounted to the taking of all reasonable care to prevent the commission of the offence if say the travel agent drew the consumer's attention to it before a booking was made. Although that may be the only practicable way to deal with brochures that rapidly become out of date it nevertheless means that agents will be racking brochures that they know are inaccurate and will be allowing consumers to walk out of the agency with bundles of such brochures. (See Nardi "Due Diligence: the Travel Agent's Perspective [1994] TLJ 13 on this issue.)

Multiple travel agencies have the added problem that once the company knows from one branch that a brochure is inaccurate then they will know that the same brochure in all its branches is inaccurate and they will have to take company-wide steps to address the problem. Knowledge of the inaccuracy might typically come from the tour operator himself, but might also come from information supplied by a client, or even by a different tour operator who features the same hotel and notifies the travel agent that, *e.g.*, the hotel swimming pool has closed. However, so long as the knowledge is confined to branch level the company can escape conviction by invoking the principle in *Tesco v Nattrass*, that no "directing mind" of the company knew of the inaccuracy. But once the branch manager has informed senior personnel at head office then the company will have the requisite knowledge. The way the offence is framed it is not unlikely that a factual situation, similar to the *Wings* case under the TDA could arise: A consumer returns from an early season holiday and complains to his travel agent that the brochure he booked his holiday from was inaccurate. At this stage no offence has been committed by the travel agent as the agent did not know or have reasonable cause to believe the brochure was inaccurate (the tour operator's position is different of course). Once the manager informs head office then the company faces potential prosecution unless it removes all the brochures from the racks or puts errata stickers on the offending passage. If however an offending brochure, despite the best efforts of the travel agent, is made available to a consumer, then the travel agent has probably committed a prima facie offence. He knows that the brochure is inaccurate and he has made it available. The mental element, as under *Wings*, relates to the inaccuracy not to the making available. The agent can of course still raise the due diligence defence and escape conviction (see Chapter Fourteen on defences.)

To assist travel agents and indeed tour operators in this situation, ABTA has recommended that all its travel agent members display the following notice prominently and close to the brochure racks:

> "Important notice: the prices or details contained within brochures displayed in this shop may have changed since the brochures were printed. Please ask our staff for details. You will be informed about any changes that we are aware of before you book as part of our commitment to quality customer service".

This so-called "Shelf Talker" would, with other measures, form part of a Due Diligence defence—see Chapter Fourteen."

PRE-CONTRACT—REGULATION 7

Although information about health formalities and visa requirements must be provided in the brochure if a brochure is made available there is an independent requirement in Regulation 7 that the tour operator provide the same kind of information before the contract is concluded. The wording is almost identical to the wording in Schedule 1 and there is no reason to believe that they impose different obligations. The rationale for having two identical requirements is presumably to cover the situation where the consumer books a holiday without the assistance of a brochure.

Regulation 7 provides:

> "7(1) Before a contract is concluded, the other party to the contract shall provide the intending consumer with the information specified in paragraph (2) below in writing or in some other appropriate form.
>
> (2) The information referred to in paragraph (1) is:—

(a) general information about passport and visa requirements which apply to Nationals of the Member State or States concerned who purchase the package in question, including information about the length of time it is likely to take to obtain the appropriate passports and visas;
(b) information about health formalities required for the journey and the stay; and
(c) the arrangements for security for the money paid over and (where applicable) for the repatriation of the consumer in the event of insolvency.

(3) If the other party to the contract contravenes paragraph (1) of this regulation he shall be guilty of an offence and liable:—

(a) on summary conviction, to a fine not exceeding level 5 on the standard scale
(b) on conviction on indictment, to a fine.

One difference between Regulation 7 and Schedule 1 is that not only must information be given about passport and visa requirements but also the length of time it is likely to take to obtain them.

Much of what is required in Regulation 7 is also required by Regulation 5 thus if a tour operator does provide a brochure which complies with Regulation 5 he will also be complying with Regulation 7 except for the time limits for passports and visas.

One problem that arises is for tour operators who do not publish brochures and who use telesales to sell their holidays. How are they to comply with Regulation 7? The requirement is to provide this information *in writing or in other appropriate form before the contract is made*. Generally in such a situation the contract is concluded over the phone so unless the contract is to be postponed until after the information is received putting the information in the post will slow things down considerably. It could be argued that the only practicable way to comply is to give the information orally. This could be justified on the ground that this would be an *appropriate* method of providing the information in the circumstances. If the consumer is prepared to contract over the phone in the first place then it would be difficult to argue that the information was not given in an appropriate form. It would be wise to ensure that in any subsequent written confirmation the information about health and visas is confirmed in writing. This will deflect later complaints that the information was not provided.

If it were just the health and visa requirements that were to be given over the phone this would probably not prove too burdensome. However, under Regulation 9, there is a requirement (albeit with civil not criminal sanctions) that *all* the terms of the contract are reduced to writing or other appropriate form *before* the contract is made. This obligation is one which telesales operators without brochures will have great difficulty complying with.

The penalty for not complying with Regulation 7 will be criminal and will be imposed on *the other party to the contract*. Usually this will be the operator but in some circumstances could be the agent. Indeed it has been widely assumed in the industry that the combined effect of the 1998 amendments to Regulations 5 and 7 is to impose the visa and passport requirements on travel agents, especially where the consumers are not British nationals—acceptance indeed that "the other party to the contract" can be the travel agent. However it may be that for the present at least Regulation 7(2)(b) is largely redundant. Although in certain cases it is highly advisable to take health precautions there are very few countries where there is a *requirement* to do so.

Technically, Regulation 7 also applies to domestic as well as foreign packages. This means that domestic tour operators and hoteliers selling packages ought to go through the motions of telling clients that they do not need passports or visas nor are there any health formalities for the journey or the stay.

Again, for defence and other provisions, see Chapter Fourteen.

In Good Time Before Departure—Regulation 8

In addition to all the contractual information to be provided and information on health and visa requirements there are certain other details which must be provided before travel.

Regulation 8 provides:

> "8(1) The other party to the contract shall in good time before the start of the journey provide the consumer with the information specified in paragraph (2) below in writing or in some other appropriate form.
>
> (2) The information referred to in paragraph (1) is the following:—
>
> (a) the times and places of intermediate stops and transport connections and particulars of the place to be occupied by the traveller (for example, cabin or berth on ship, sleeper compartment on train);
>
> (b) the name, address and telephone number—

(i) of the representative or other party to the contract in the locality where the consumer is to stay,

or, if there is no such representative,

(ii) of any agency in that locality on whose assistance a consumer in difficulty would be able to call,

or, if there is no such representative or agency, a telephone number or other information which will enable the consumer to contact the other party to the contract during the stay; and

(c) in the case of a journey or stay outside the United Kingdom by a child under the age of 16 on the day when the journey or stay is due to start, information enabling direct contact to be made with the child or the person responsible at the place where he is to stay; and

(d) except where the consumer is required as a term of the contract to take out an insurance policy in order to cover the cost of cancellation by the consumer or the cost of assistance, including repatriation, in the event of accident or illness, information about an insurance policy which the consumer may if he wishes, take out in respect of the risk of those costs being incurred.

(3) If the other party to the contract contravenes paragraph (1) of this regulation he shall be guilty of an offence and liable:—

(a) on summary conviction, to a fine not exceeding level 5 on the standard scale; and
(b) on conviction on indictment, to a fine.

Again, for defence provisions see Chapter Fourteen.

There is no definition of the words "in good time". The DTI recommend a minimum of seven days and ABTA urges on its members the minimum of 14 days. Obviously shorter periods will be appropriate in the case of last minute bookings.

Intermediate stops and transport connections

This may cause problems. The DTI considers that intermediate stops are those which significantly affect the nature of the package, and do not include meal or refreshment breaks. If travel is by a train, and it stops at intermediate stations, this would surely not be covered. What, however, of flights which stop to pick up or re-fuel en route? It could possibly make a difference if the passengers have to troop off the plane during this procedure, and then re-embark, although this seems rather a random test. Many passengers would argue that an extra landing and take-off makes a flight a more daunting proposition and is therefore significant; but what in fact is the difference in principle from the train that stops at an intermediate station?

Representative

It will be seen that this is a three step procedure. If there is a representative, his or her contact details must be supplied; if not, contact details for a local agency; and if there is no representative and no agency, a telephone contact number to enable the consumer contact with the organiser.

It is a matter of some astonishment to tour operators that it is considered a matter worthy of criminal penalty if they fail to give the name, etc., of their representative. In the nature of things, representatives come and go—does the law really require them to say to consumers:

> "Your Representative is Tracy and her telephone number is. . ."?

In practice the larger tour operators give the name and address of their local office. This does not strictly comply with the law, but the hope must be that Trading Standards Officers will consider the purpose of this regulation—that a consumer in difficulty will have somewhere to turn.

In the absence of these, there must be a telephone contact number, perhaps the operator's own office number. It does not say that the number must be manned. While this must be implied, the question is—between what hours must it be manned? Normal working hours or 24 hours? What about week-ends? In practice, the major tour operators maintain a 24 hour emergency contact service; the small operators do not (the very wide definition of an organiser must also be borne in mind here).

Insurance

The requirement to give insurance details will not create problems in practice—tour operators and travel agents make considerable commission out of the sale of holiday insurance and will be keen to draw its existence to the attention of consumers much earlier than is required by Regulation 8. The overwhelming majority of holiday insurance is in fact sold by travel agents at the booking stage. (See the 1997 MMC report on vertical integration in the travel industry.) In contrast to the much used Regulation 5, the writers are unaware of any actual prosecutions which have been launched under Regulation 8.

Comparison of TDA and the Regulations

There will be many instances when a Trading Standards Officer could prosecute an organiser under both s.14 of the TDA and Regulations 5, 7 and 8, particularly Regulation 5. In deciding which to choose, the officer will bear in mind the following distinctions:

(1) The 1968 Act is a prohibitory provision covering any type of statement, spoken, written, pictorial or computerised, about almost any subject to do with a package which is false to a material degree. The trader simply must not make such a statement, but there is no positive requirement to say anything at all.

The Regulations are mandatory—certain statements about a package, on a limited express range of topics, must be made. Regulation 5 applies only to brochures.

(2) To prove an offence under the TDA, the prosecution must show that the offender has a guilty mind in that either he knew he was making a false statement, or he was reckless about it. The Regulations do not require proof of any guilty mind but create offences of strict liability, subject to the statutory defences (note: offences by travel agents under Regulation 5(2) are an exception).

(3) The positive requirement for *accurate* information in Regulation 5 may impose a greater burden on the trader for precision in his statements, than does the prohibition of statements *false to a material degree* under the TDA.

Therefore, subject to the defence provisions described in Chapter Fourteen, it may be easier for a Trading Standards Officer to obtain a conviction under Regulation 5 than under the TDA, providing the statement is in a brochure and is within the range of information required by Schedule 1.

In practice, many Trading Standards Officers issue Summonses under both the Trade Descriptions Act and Regulation 5 as alternatives, withdrawing one of them at a "plea bargain" stage; or at a trial, inviting the Court to convict under one or the other. (See Slee, "The Camera Never Lies" [1997] ITLJ 21 for a discussion of the decision to prosecute under the TDA or the PTR.)

Chapter Fourteen
Defences

Introduction

Each of the three statutory provisions which impose criminal liability on tour operators or travel agents which we have examined—The Trade Descriptions Act 1968 (the TDA), the Consumer Protection Act 1987 (the CPA) and the Package Travel Regulations 1992 (the Regulations) contain similar, though not identical, defence provisions—known for convenience as the "due diligence" defence.

We will now examine the rules in detail, and explain why, in fact, they are sometimes of very little help to travel companies in practice.

The Trade Descriptions Act

Section 24 (1) of the TDA provides as follows:—

> "In any proceedings for an offence under this Act it shall, . . . be a defence for the person charged to prove:—
>
> (a) that the commission of the offence was due to a mistake or to reliance on information supplied to him or to the act or default of another person, an accident or some other cause beyond his control; and
>
> (b) that he took all reasonable precautions and exercised all due diligence to avoid the commission of such an offence by himself or any other person under his control."

It is further provided that where the defendant alleges that the offence was due to the act or default of another person, or information supplied by another person, he must serve notice not less than seven clear days before the hearing on the prosecution by identifying or assisting in identifying the other persons.

The Consumer Protection Act

Section 39 of the CPA provides:—

> "(1) Subject to the following provisions of this section, in proceedings against any person for any offence to which this section applies it shall be a defence for that person to show that he took all reasonable steps and exercised all due diligence to avoid committing the offence.
>
> (2) Where in any proceedings against any person for such an offence the defence provided by sub-section (1) above involves an allegation that the commission of the offence was due:—
>
> (a) to the act or default of another; or
>
> (b) to reliance on information given by another, that person shall not, without the leave of Court, be entitled to rely on the Defence unless, not less than 7 clear days before the hearing of the proceedings, he has served a notice under sub-section (3) below on the person bringing the proceedings;
>
> (3) A notice under this sub-section shall give such information identifying or assisting in the identification of the person who has committed the actual default or gave the information and is in the possession of the person serving the notice at the time he serves it.
>
> (4) It is hereby declared that a person shall not be entitled to rely on the defence provided by sub-section (1) above by reason of his reliance on the information supplied by another, unless he shows that it was reasonable in all the circumstances for him to have relied on the information, having regard in particular:—
>
> (a) to the steps which he took and those which might reasonably have been taken, for the purpose of verifying the information and
>
> (b) to whether he had any reason to disbelieve the information".

It is further provided that this section applies to an offence under Section 20(1). Note that it does not apply to an offence under section 20(2) which in effect has its own self-contained defence.

The Regulations

Regulation 24 of the Regulations provides a defence in virtually identical terms to s.39 of the CPA. Regulation 24 applies this defence to offences under Regulations 5, 7 and 8 (which requires certain information to be given to consumers) and also to Regulations 16 and 22 (information relating to security of monies, and bonding).

In General

It will be seen that under the TDA, the burden is on the defendant to prove (on the balance of probabilities) that the commission of the offence was due to one of the specific factors namely:

- a mistake, or
- reliance on some information supplied to him, or
- the act or default of another person, or
- an accident, or
- some other cause beyond his control.

But it is a two stage test. *In addition*, the defendant has to show that he took all reasonable precautions and exercised all due diligence to avoid the commission of the offence.

The CPA and the Regulations differ in that they do not give a list of specific defences that can be pleaded, but merely provide a general defence of due diligence. There is no reason to believe that the five specific defences cannot be raised under the CPA or the Regulations, however. In fact there is clear recognition of this because they provide that if the defendant attempts to show the commission of the offence was due to the act or default of another or due to reliance on information provided by another, then notice must be given to the prosecution.

The leading case on the statutory defence is *Tesco v Nattrass* [1972] A.C. 153. It was a TDA case, not under section 14, but under the now repealed section 1 for making a false claim about prices. However, the case remains relevant on the issue of the defence. The facts were that Tesco displayed a poster in one of their supermarket windows stating that packets of soap powder were available inside the store for 2/11d each. In fact the packets inside cost 3/11d each. Tesco's defence was that the commission of the offence by them was due to "the act or default of another" namely their store manager. The House of Lords agreed that the store manager was sufficiently junior for him not to be regarded as the company:

> "The acts or omissions of shop managers were not the acts of the company itself." (Lord Reid)

Thus a Company can in many instances cast the blame on their employees. Likewise, it may be relatively easy to show that a mistake was made or that the defendant relied on information supplied to him. To do this is only to satisfy half of the defence. The defendant has to go on to show that he took all reasonable precautions and exercised all due diligence. Lord Diplock said that the law would not penalise:

> "... an employer or principal who has done everything that he can reasonably to be expected to do by supervision or inspection, by improvement of his business methods or by exhorting those whom he may be expected to control or influence to prevent the commission of the offence ..."

In the same case Lord Reid said that a "paper system" operated in a "perfunctory" fashion would not be good enough. A system has to more than just a pious expression of policy without any substance to it.

One CPA case already mentioned *Berkshire CC v Olympic* (1993, Divisional Court, unreported) (see Chapter Thirteen) was decided in the tour operator's favour on the basis of the due diligence defence. The Magistrates decided that the software which caused the wrong price to be displayed on the screen had been substantially tested before going live and that its accuracy could not have been checked further. The error was due to an unexplained fault unconnected to the software. They held that Olympic had taken all reasonable steps and exercised all due diligence, *i.e.* they had a proper system. The Divisional Court confirmed this decision. It is interesting to note however that they did so less than enthusiastically. Essentially they said that the Magistrates' decision was a decision on the facts that they could not disturb unless it was patently wrong. As the decision fell within a spectrum of what a reasonable bench could decide then the decision would stand but they hinted that they might have come to a different decision themselves.

For tour operators who are prosecuted under s.14 of the TDA, this is largely academic because in most cases they will not be able to satisfy the "due diligence" test. As has been said in section one the TDA requires the Court to be satisfied that the Defendant has *knowingly* or *recklessly* made a false statement. If the Court is satisfied, how can the tour operator turn round and say that nevertheless he took all reasonable precautions to prevent the offence occurring in the first place? Clearly to do so is a contradiction in terms, and this has been recognised in the case law. Lord Widgery CJ said in *Coupe v Guyett* [1973] 2 All E.R. 1058 (a non-tour operator case):

> "... the defence under Section 24 will *rarely*, if ever, be appropriate to a charge under Section 14. I say that because, if I am right, in order to establish the charge under Section 14 you have to show knowing falsity or recklessness, which themselves are inconsistent with the statutory defence." [Emphasis added]

Lord Widgery was correct to qualify his words because in the *Wings* case it is possible to see the defence being applicable. The tour operator in that case knew that the statement in the brochure was false but did not know it was being made. However they had taken steps to prevent that statement being repeated. The question arose as to whether those steps would have been sufficient to convince a court that they had taken all reasonable precautions and exercised all due diligence to prevent the occurrence of the offence. For reasons which were not explained (but can be guessed at) Wings chose not to reply on the Section 24 Defence. The House of Lords however did speculate on what the outcome might have been if they had chosen to do so. Lord Templeman said:

> "the respondents [Wings] did not attempt to put forward a defence under Section 24. In order to succeed in any such defence the respondent would first have been obliged to explain the introduction of a false statement into the brochure. There was a vague suggestion that this was a typographical error. The Magistrates were not asked to decide and had no evidence on which to decide whether the Respondent 'took all reasonable precautions and exercised all due diligence' in the employment and supervision of the blundering typist and the blundering proof-reader. Moreover it was certainly not clear that the Respondent 'took all reasonable precautions and exercised all due diligence to avoid the commission' of an offence under Section 14 after it was discovered that the brochure contained a false statement. By relying on an oral correction being made by the sales agent and transmitted by the travel agent, the Respondent accepted the risk of committing an offence under Section 14. The Respondents exposed Mr Wade to the serious risk that he would not be made aware of the correction and the added risk that he would not be able to prove that he had not been made aware of the corrections. It may or may not have been practicable to send out correction slips to travel agents".

The tenor of this passage is not favorable to Wings and it may be that even if they had raised a Section 24 defence it would not have been effective. However the possibility remains that if a similar situation arises a tour operator may escape liability if he takes the right kind of precautions to correct the error once he knows of it.

In Chapter Eleven we looked at the case of *Airtours v Shipley* (1994, Divisional Court, unreported) where the tour operator escaped liability on the basis of the system they employed to detect misdescriptions in their brochures. It is important to note that this was *not* an example of the due diligence defence being used. The importance of having a proper system was not that it established due diligence *defence* on Airtours' part but that it enabled them to demonstrate that they had not been reckless in the first place, *i.e.* there had been no breach of the Act because the elements of the *offence* could not be established by the prosecution.

The position under the CPA and the Regulations is, however, different. In these cases, (with one exception for travel agents under Regulation 5 where it must be shown that the travel agent *knew* or *had reasonable cause to believe* that the brochure did not comply with the Regulations), it is not necessary for the prosecution to show that the defendants committed the offences knowingly or recklessly. Therefore, it is more logically consistent for the defendants to set up the statutory defence of due diligence.

In practice, the same type of evidence will have to be put before the Court by the Defendant whether under the Trade Descriptions Act, the Consumer Protection Act or under the Regulations.

The difference is where the burden of proof lies. Under the TDA the prosecution must prove recklessness beyond a reasonable doubt; the defendant theoretically needs to prove nothing; whereas under the CPA/Regulations the burden is on the defendant to prove all due diligence on a balance of probabilities.

Under s.39 of the CPA, the travel agent may have more success than tour operators, given that most prices they quote are not their own but those of others. If they do plead that it was the act or default of the tour operator or reliance upon information supplied by the tour operator, they will still have to show that they took all reasonable precautions and exercised all due diligence. Also section 39(4) states that in deciding whether the due diligence defence will apply, a court can take into account what steps were taken or could reasonably have been taken, to verify the information from the tour operator and whether the travel agent had reasons for disbelieving the information. This suggests that it would be dangerous for a travel agent just to sit back and say there was nothing he could do apart from rely on the prices printed on the brochure or displayed on the screen.

This presents a dilemma for the travel agent. It is not practicable to check all the holiday prices. What then should he do? He will of course deal diligently with notified errata, but what about all the other thousands of prices in the brochure? One way may be to set up a system of random sampling as other major retailers do. If so the information should be recorded and could be used as evidence that steps are taken to prevent the commission of an offence. At any rate it would certainly look better that saying nothing had been done. (See Nardi, "Due Diligence—The Travel Agent's Perspective" [1994] TLJ 13 for an excellent discussion of this problem.)

In the case of cards in travel agency windows, a stricter checking regime will be needed because these are the travel agents own documents. From time to time Trading Standards Officers in many parts of the UK have "blitzed" travel agencies searching for cards which were out of date or misleading. (See "The Bulletin" [2003] ITLJ vii for an example of this being done by the OFT in relation to travel websites).

All Reasonable Steps?

It will be noticed that all the defences require proof by the defendant, on a balance of probabilities, not just that diligence was used and reasonable steps taken, but that *all* due diligence and *all* reasonable steps were used. In practice, this has proved a very heavy burden for travel companies to discharge. The tour operator will find his system subjected to minute examination in court. If the prosecution can think of one idea, which is reasonable, which the defendant could have used but did not, the defence will fail. Even under the CPA and the Regulations, it remains a conundrum. If the system the tour operator describes is good, how come the offence was committed in the first place? Of course, the law does not require perfection, only that all *due* diligence and all *reasonable* steps are used. Tour operators however often feel that the burden in court in reality is a great deal higher than that.

This was illustrated by the case of *Buckinghamshire County Council v Crystal Holidays Limited* (Divisional Court, January 26, 1993) in which Kennedy LJ said:

> "... it seems to me that once one is able to identify a precaution which can properly be described as a reasonable precaution which was not taken, such as the different wording ... being put in the brochure in this case, then that really is the end of the case so far as reliance upon Section 24 (1)(b) is concerned."

In that case the defendants had advertised that the resort had an 18 hole golf course. The brochure said: "The pride of the village *is* the new 18 hole Bernhard Langer golf course." [Emphasis added] When holidaymakers arrived they found that the course had not been built yet. Bulldozers were still on the site. Extreme weather conditions had caused the site to become waterlogged and delayed the completion of the course. The court accepted the prosecution's contention that it would have been a reasonable precaution to have altered the wording. The words suggested by the prosecution were: "The pride of the village will be a new golf course which is scheduled to be open."

However, the larger tour operators in particular now have very sophisticated systems, often highly computerised, and have found it easier in the last couple of years to establish due diligence. In *Airtours PLC v Shipley* (1994) 158 JPN 319 the Airtours system was praised as "excellent" by the Court.

A number of non-travel cases have illustrated the point that merely relying upon a supplier, however reputable, is not due diligence. For instance in *Sherratt v Geralds The American Jewellers* (1970) 114 SJ 147 D.C. waterproof watches sold by the Defendants had been purchased from an impeccable source but were not waterproof. It was held that the shop should have carried out its own tests. In *Garratt v Boots the Chemists Limited* (1980 unreported, DC) Boots sold pencils with an illegal level of lead. They had informed their supplier of the relevant law and made compliance with the law a term of the contract. But Lane LCJ said:

> "All reasonable precautions are strong words. One obvious and reasonable precaution which could have been taken in the present case was to take random samples of the various batches of pencils ... of course I scarcely need to say that every case will vary in its facts; but what might be reasonable for a large retailer might not be reasonable for a village shop. One does not know whether the random sample would have in fact produced detection of the errant pencils. It might have, it might not have. But to say that it was not a precaution which had reasonably to be taken does not seem to me to accord with good sense."

It follows that relying on hotel descriptions supplied by the hotelier, or a local agent with little attempt to check the truth, will not be due diligence—and the bigger the operator the greater the responsibility to check.

Sunworld Ltd v London Borough of Hammersmith & Fulham (Divisional Court, November 23, 1999) (See [2000] ITLJ 67 for a report) is a case where the tour operator escaped conviction under s.14 of the TDA on a technicality but where the court had some harsh words to say on their brochure checking system. Sunworld had a system which, on the face of it was quite sophisticated and which they described to the court as working "extremely well". It consisted of a four part process for ensuring the accuracy of the information in the brochure. An area manager was sent a Product Information Form (PIF) on which he had to enter the details of any property which went into the brochure. This had to be certified as correct by him and also by the property manager. When these details were ready to go into the brochure galley proofs were sent to the resort manager which again had to be certified as correct by him and the property manager. The process was repeated twice more—when the brochure was published and at the commencement of the season. However, despite all this, errors crept into the brochure due to the fault of an employee, Ms Mittroyani. This is what Simon Brown LJ had to say about the system:

> "Mr James said in his evidence that 'the system works extremely well'; nobody apparently asked him even whether the errors here were the only ones ever to have been made. No one asked whether Ms Mittroyanni had proved to be an unusually unreliable area manager. No one asked what instructions were given to the copywriters. No one asked what if any sanctions attended were visited upon copywriters who departed from the PIF, or area managers who failed to correct such departures."

The CPA Code of Practice

Alone of the three provisions we are looking at, the CPA provides another line of defence. Section 25 provides for the publication of a Code of Practice for the guidance of traders. The purpose of the Code is to indicate what amounts to good and bad practice. It is open to both the prosecution and the defence to make use of the Code in appropriate circumstances—either to assist in proving the commission of an offence or to show that an offence has not been committed. Section 25(2) provides:

> "A contravention of a Code of Practice approved under this section shall not of itself give rise to any criminal or civil liability, but in any proceedings against any person for any offence under Section 20(1) or (2) above—
>
> (a) any contravention by that person of such a Code may be relied on in relation to any matter for the purpose of

establishing that that person committed the offence or of negativing any difference; and

(b) compliance by that person with such a Code may be relied on in relation to any matter for the purpose of showing that the commission of the offence by that person has not been established or that that person has a defence".

The Code contains a great deal of sensible and clear advice in relation to such matters as sale prices, special offers, introductory offers, comparison with other Companies prices, the use of the terms "value" or "worth" and the use of the word "free". On this last point, the Code advises that traders must make clear to consumers at the time of the offer for sale, exactly what they will have to buy to get the "free offer". If there are any conditions attached to the "free offer", at least the main points must be given with the price indication and consumers must be made clearly aware where they can get the full details. Traders must not claim that an offer is free if they have imposed additional charges they would not normally make, or reduce the price to consumers who do not have to take up the free offer. In one case, a tour operator offered "free car hire" with a holiday. The consumer asked whether he could get the holiday cheaper if he did not take up the car hire, and was told that this was possible. Thus the tour operator unwittingly fell foul of the Code, and therefore the Act.

Offers of the type "from £99" or "up to 60% off" are required by the Code to offer at least 10 per cent of the product on offer at the cheapest price.

The Code has specific advice for travel companies. Tour operators are told:

"If you offer a variety of prices to give consumers a choice (for example paying more or less for a holiday depending on the time of year or the standard of accommodation) make clear in your brochure—or any other price indication—what the basic price is and what it covers. Give details of any optional additional charges and what those charges cover, or of the place where this information can be found, clearly and close to the basic price. Any non-optional extra charges which are for fixed amounts should be included in the basic price and not shown as additions, unless they are only payable by some consumers. In that case you should specify, near to the details of the basic price, either what the amounts are and the circumstances in which they are payable, or where in the brochure, etc., the information is given. Details of non-optional charges which may vary (such as holiday insurance) or of where in the brochure the information is given should be made clear to consumers near to the basic price."

As a result of this provision, the price panels in brochures commonly contain a battery of cross references to the pages where flight supplements, child offers, etc., etc., are set out in detail. This has the paradoxical effect of increasing the complexity of the price panels.

In 1997, controversy arose over the way in which Air Passenger Duty (APD) is shown in brochures. Following the Code of Practice, most tour operators correctly include it in the basic price. For some time at least one major operator refused to do so, arguing that airlines always showed taxes separately and thereby gained an apparent price advantage. However following a complaint to the Advertising Standards Authority by the Air Transport Users Council in 1997 the ASA required airlines to consolidate their prices and most airlines complied immediately. (See ASA Monthly Report for December 1997.) The penalty for not doing so could be a successful prosecution as in the case of *Toyota (GB) Ltd v North Yorkshire County Council* (Div. Ct., March 11, 1998; (1998) 162 J.P. 794 referred to in Chapter Twelve).

A similar controversy arose in 2001/2 over the addition of a security levy by airlines to pay for counter-terrorism measures.

The Code has interesting advice errata which is dealt with in the next section.

Are Errata Effective?

One of the most hotly debated issues in the travel industry of recent years is this:

A tour operator issues a brochure. He may send over a million copies of it out to several thousand travel agents. Immediately, the public will come and remove some of those brochures from the travel agency racks, often without asking the travel agency staff any questions about holidays. The tour operator discovers a completely innocent mistake which has crept in, perhaps, say, a half board supplement, or the official classification of a hotel. Is the tour operator bound to be guilty of an offence (subject to proving one of the defences described below), or is there anything at all that he can do at this stage to render himself not guilty? An interesting case took place before the Stipendiary Magistrate at Liverpool on July 26, 1993 involving Thomson Tour Operators Limited. Thomson had innocently misstated the amount of a supplement. As soon as they discovered it, and before the complainant booked the holiday, they placed the correct information on the viewdata system. Therefore, the travel agent was able to advise the complainant of the correct price before he booked the holiday. Nonetheless it was held that the company was still guilty of an offence. The court held that correcting an error by viewdata was the best possible means available, and that it showed that the Company had used all due diligence after it discovered the mistake. That alone was not enough. It still had to demonstrate that the original mistake was caused despite all due diligence and all reasonable steps. The Company was unable to do this. There was, however, the strongest possible mitigation and a fine of only £100 was imposed.

By contrast another Stipendiary Magistrate sitting at Oldham in 1996 found First Choice Holidays guilty of an offence purely because (as she found) viewdata correction on its own was not enough (*R v First Choice*, February 27, 1996, Oldham Magistrates' Ct, unreported).

Readers may decide for themselves which decision they prefer. Much overlooked however are some further words of Lord Templeman in *Wings v Ellis* above:

> "If all had gone according to plan, the respondent [Wings] *would not have committed an offence*. The sales agent would have told the travel agent. In turn the travel agent would have told Mr. Wade and the statement made by the Respondent to Mr. Wade would have been the statement in the brochure as orally corrected.
>
> . . .
>
> It may or may not have been practicable to send out correction slips to travel agents. In any event if the respondent, on receiving the booking form signed by Mr. Wade, had written to Mr. Wade, if necessary through the travel agent, confirming the oral correction which ought to have been conveyed to Mr. Wade, and explaining that since the publication of the brochure the respondent had discovered that the Seashells Hotel was equipped with overhead fans but not with air conditioning, then Mr. Wade could have withdrawn the booking or accepted the correction and the Respondent *would not have committed an offence*". [Emphasis added]

A further straw in the wind was the case of *Marshall v Airtours* (1994), an unreported Magistrates' Court decision. On similar facts to the *Thomson* case and after hearing expert evidence from ABTA the magistrates had acquitted Airtours. The prosecution appealed, raising two essential points, (i) was a viewdata correction too late to correct an offence which had been committed when the brochure was read? (ii) is due diligence relevant *after* an offence is committed? However shortly before the Divisional Court hearing the prosecution dropped the appeal.

Needless to say, tour operators are not very happy with this situation under the CPA, which can be characterised as a conflict at the interface of the old print technology and the new viewdata technology. And this is exacerbated by Regulation 5 of the PTR which appears on one view to disallow any change to the brochure price.

One attempt to marry legality with commercial sense is so-called (but mis-named) "fluid pricing", first introduced into the UK in late 1995. The price in the brochure is the highest price that can be charged but the tour operator reserves the right to move prices up and down up to that ceiling

The DTI 1995 Guidelines on the PTR places a responsibility on travel agents, saying that they would be culpable if they failed to use "shelf talkers" to draw the attention of potential clients to the fact that there were errors or changes in the brochure. Clients could then ask at the desk where the viewdata screen could be used to shown them. Subsequently, ABTA have drafted a Notice which they strongly urge all agents to display prominently. It reads:

> "The prices or details contained within brochures displayed in this shop may have changed since the brochures were printed. Please ask our staff for details. You will be informed of any changes that we are aware of before you book as part of our commitment to quality customer service".

The purpose is for it to be used as part of a due diligence defence by agent or operator. (Note that LACORS have also published guidance on fluid pricing.)

A different way of looking at this argument is to say that the errata notification is a "disclaimer". The defence of a disclaimer is not to be found in the statutes, but has been created by the courts (mostly to deal with second-hand car dealers disclaiming mileage reading on cars). The principle is that the disclaimer nullifies the effect of any misleading statement by overriding it. To achieve this, the disclaimer must be as "bold, precise and compelling" as the original mis-statement (*Norman v Bennett* [1974] 3 All E.R. 351). The disclaimer must also be brought to the attention of the consumer before he is committed to the contract. The difficulty for tour operators is that the consumer may well have read the uncorrected brochure at home before learning of any viewdata errata. If there was also a "shelf talker" as described above it may well be argued that this would be an effective disclaimer. In the

First Choice case referred to earlier one of the defences raised before the magistrate was that the brochure contained a disclaimer. It was held however that this was ineffective on the grounds that it did not satisfy the criteria in *Norman v Bennett*—it did not refer to prices at all and was badly sited in the brochure. It did not do enough to "flag up" the possibility of price inaccuracies.

An interesting variation on these concepts is provided by the DTI Code of Practice on misleading prices, primarily in the context of prices which were originally correct but have become misleading (s.20(2) of the CPA). These are provided by the Code, to supplement the fact that the due diligence defence does not apply to Section 20(2). The Code says that tour operators selling direct to the public should make clear to anyone who orders the holiday to which any brochure applies that a price indication has become misleading. This must be done before the consumer is committed to buying the holiday.

Tour operators selling through agents are advised as follows:—

> "If a price indication becomes misleading while your brochure is still current, make this clear to the travel agents to whom you distributed the brochure. Be prepared to cancel any holiday bookings consumers have made on the basis of a misleading price indication. (3.4.2)
>
> Travel agents should ensure that the correct price indication is made clear to consumers before they make a booking. (3.4.3)"

Some prosecuting authorities have tried to argue that this advice applies only to offences under section 20(2), where prices were originally correct but changed. By this they also exclude the possibility of deliberate price increases by a tour operator while the brochure is current. However, in the case of *Oldham MBC v Sun Express Holidays Limited t/a Suntours* 1997 Oldham Magistrates Court, unreported, one Magistrates' Court at least was persuaded that these passages can be used to illustrate compliance with the Code of Practice following a deliberate price rise. After selling many holidays at the brochure price (a fact Suntours were able to prove to the Court), they decided to put the price up but in doing so complied with the above advice. The Court found them not guilty. One of the reasons is that the passage from the Code quoted above is introduced in this way, namely that the advice does not apply to Surcharges (the right to extract more money from a customer who has already booked), but applies to "a price indication [which] becomes misleading for *any other reason*".

The question arises as to whether compliance with the Code of Practice can be used as a defence to an allegation under Regulation

5 of the PTR of failing to state accurately the price in any brochure? The answer is probably yes, for two reasons:

1. Section 25 of the Consumer Protection Act 1987 defines the Code of Practice as not only giving practical advice about Section 20 of the Act, but also as "promoting what appear to be desirable practices as to the circumstances and manner in which any person gives an indication as to the price at which any goods, services, accommodation or facilities are available."—in other words the Code is of general application; and
2. Because in any event compliance with the Code could be said to be part of a due diligence defence under the Regulations.

A Due Diligence System

Each company must devise its own system appropriate to its size and operations but we offer the following as common features of the better "due diligence" systems we have encountered.

(a) All the company's quality control systems should operate according to written guidelines. Ideally there should also be a manual, especially for brochure production and accuracy of brochure information.

(b) Compliance with the manual should be regularly monitored and documented.

(c) No accommodation or transport should be sold to clients unless the company first has a contract with the supplier.

(d) All accommodation should be personally inspected by a company employee who completes a detailed questionnaire about the hotel.

(e) Brochure copy should be approved by the hotelier who should be required to sign an approval form.

(f) The brochure proofs should be carefully checked including all price information. The checking process should be documented.

(g) There should be regular updates from resorts throughout the season.

(h) There should be an effective errata system to catch new customers before they book and to notify existing customers without delay. The system should be activated by consumer comment as well as by resort reports.

(i) All personnel should be properly trained in their tasks, particularly as to the impact of the law on their work; the attendance at training should be documented.

Finally, there is now the prospect that repeated offending against any of the provisions in the PTR and the CPA can result in action being taken by the Office of Fair Trading and a number of other bodies, including Trading Standards Departments and the CAA, under the "Stop Now" or Enforcement Order powers. Stop now orders can be used to restrain further breaches and if not complied with can lead to further penalties. (see below.)

The Position of the Employees

It can been seen from the *Tesco* case that it is possible for companies to use that aspect of the statutory defence involving placing the blame on "the act or default of another", if the other is an employee of the company, provided that the employee is sufficiently junior so as to render him not part of the "directing mind" of the Company. (In the *Wings* case, this argument was used successfully to negative the *recklessness* of the company, rather than as part of the statutory defence. For the company to be reckless the "directing mind" of the Company must be shown to be reckless).

Under the TDA there has been a reluctance by companies to blame their employees. This is because under section 23, where it is shown that the commission of an offence was due to the act or default of some other person, that other person shall also be guilty of the offence.

However the position is rather brighter under the CPA and the Regulations. Section 40 (1) of the CPA provides:

> "Where the commission by any person of an offence to which Section 39 above applies is due to an act or default committed by some other person *in the course of any business of his*, the other person shall be guilty of the offence and may be proceeded against and punished by virtue of this sub-section whether or not proceedings are taking against the first mentioned person." (Emphasis added).

There is a similar provision in the Regulations under Regulation 25(1).

An employee of a Company, in the ordinary sense, is not guilty of any act or default in the course of any business of *his*, and therefore cannot be prosecuted in addition to or instead of the Company itself. This point has been confirmed by the House of Lords in the case of *R v Warwickshire County Council ex parte Johnson* (1993) already mentioned in Chapter Twelve.

Directors and senior staff are, however, not so happily placed. There are virtually identical provisions under s.20(1) of the TDA, s.40(2) of the CPA, and Regulations 25 (2) which provide that:

> "Where an offence has been committed by a body corporate and is proved to have been committed with the consent and connivance of, or to be attributable to any neglect on the part of, any director, manager, secretary or other similar officer of the body corporate, or any person who was purporting to act in any such capacity, he as well as the body corporate shall be guilty of that offence."

In practice what happens is that if a Trading Standards Department takes the view that offences are being committed by the deliberate policy of the board of the company (for example a deliberate policy of over-booking hotels), the directors as well as the company may be prosecuted. Where however the offence is committed by a company "doing its incompetent but obvious best", and in spite of the desire of the management to obey the law, then it is extremely rare for any director to be prosecuted. Indeed, prosecutions under these provisions are surprisingly uncommon altogether. Prosecutions of employees below the rank of director are virtually unheard of.

Procedure

All the offences we have been discussing are to be prosecuted by Trading Standards departments, attached to the local authority. Many of these are under-resourced, and they have many responsibilities beyond holidays. Enforcement of the law is therefore patchy at best although from time to time there are flurries of prosecutions. Each of the offences we have discussed can be dealt with in the Magistrates Court where there is a maximum fine of £5,000 for each offence. Compensation can also be ordered. Each of the matters can also be dealt with in the Crown Court where there is the possibility of an unlimited fine. However courts must always have regard to the means of a defendant in fixing the level of a fine. In addition, under the TDA only, there is power in the

Crown Court to imprison any non-corporate defendants for a period of up to two years.

In the case of each offence, the prosecution must commence proceedings no later than three years from the commission of the offence, or one year from its discovery by the prosecutor, whichever is the earlier. In each case a wide variety of powers is given to Trading Standards Officers to investigate the offence, and it is a separate offence to obstruct a Trading Standards Officer in the course of his duty. Some tour operators have over the years discovered to their horror that, in a serious case, Trading Standards Officers will use their power to seize some or all of their working documents to take away, by the lorryload if necessary, to examine them at their own offices for evidence of offences. Full details of all these powers are set out in the Schedules of the relevant statutes, *e.g.* Schedule 3 of the PTR which is set out in an Appendix to this book. The powers are not however limitless, and an officer must have reason to believe an offence has been committed before seizing documents—see *Dudley MBC v Debenhams PLC, The Times,* August 16, 1994—the Police & Criminal Evidence Act 1984 and its Codes apply, so far as relevant, to Trading Standards Officers, including the provisions the provisions on powers of search, and tape recording of interviews. (See Kerrigan "Trading Standards Officers must comply with Search Code" [1996] TLJ 91.) Note that the Codes have been amended since this case was decided so caution is required in applying it.

Enforcement Orders

This powerful tool in the hands of the enforcement authorities has been the subject of rapid progress in recent times. It enables the authorities to put a stop to traders whose conduct in the sale of goods or services to consumers harms the collective interest of consumers in the United Kingdom (and indeed there is provision for EU wide enforcement in respect of some misconduct).

In our last edition we noted the limited powers of the OFT under the Fair Trading Act 1973. The first enhancement of the powers of the authorities was by way of The Stop Now Orders (EC Directive) Regulations 2001, which came into force on June 1, 2001, and should be read together with The Stop Now Orders Guidance published by the OFT in April 2002. The new "Stop Now Orders" permitted a range of enforcement authorities—which included the Office of Fair Trading, Local Trading Standards Offices, and other authorities such as the Civil Aviation Authority and the Information Commissioner—to apply to Court for an order stopping the trader from the conduct which was harmful to the collective interest of consumers. The point to note about these powers is that they are related to infringements of a specific list of European directives as required by the European Injunctions Directive (97/27/EC) of 1998. For the purposes of this book, the most relevant directives, infringements of which could lead to a Stop Now order, were those brought into force by the following English legislation namely:

Package Travel, Package Holidays and Package Tours Regulations 1992, the Timeshare Act 1992, the Consumer Protection (Distance Selling) Regulations 2000, the Control of Misleading Advertisements Regulations 1988 and the Unfair Terms in Consumer Contracts Regulations 1999.

The type of infringement which might therefore lead to a Stop Now order includes:

- A fluid pricing policy which may infringe Regulation 5 of the PTR;
- Excessive cancellation charges;
- Repeated failure to give consumers the requisite holiday information, or giving misleading information;
- Repeated failure to warn consumers in advance of changes to holiday arrangements;
- Repeated failure to perform the holiday properly;
- Repeated failure to allow transfers of packages;
- Repeated failure to observe the surcharge rules;
- A system of window cards which is not kept up to date or omits compulsory charges;
- Continuing to sell holidays without proper bonding/security arrangements in place.

By virtue of the Regulations, and in particular the April 2002 Guidance booklet, the following enforcement policy was to be adopted:—

- Businesses are given a reasonable opportunity to put matters right by discussion (at least 14 days except in emergencies);
- The OFT co-ordinate action so that the most appropriate enforcement body takes the action;
- There is proper regard for other statutory regulatory means

(*e.g.* criminal prosecution by Trading Standards) and for non statutory mechanisms (*e.g.* the Advertising Standards Authority enforcement procedures);

- Regard be had for the Home Authority principle;
- In summary, all action taken would be necessary and proportionate.

The Regulations provided for interim orders to be made. Thus, for example, the tour operator whose brochures were thought by the authorities to be harming the interest of consumers by an unfair pricing policy could be forced to withdraw its brochures from sale pending the final hearing by the High Court or County Court of the Application for a Stop Now order. It is not clear whether the authorities could be ordered by the Court, as a condition of granting an interim order, to give an undertaking to be responsible for any losses suffered by the trader as a result of an interim order, in circumstances where ultimately the authorities failed to get a Stop Now order.

Then the authorities spotted a defect in the new procedure; these wider powers are available only for breaches of the specified list of legislation; it did not cover, for example, breaches of the Trade Descriptions Act 1968 or the Consumer Protection Act 1987 or a whole raft of other conduct harmful to the interest of consumers.

The result has been Part 8 of the Enterprise Act 2002, scheduled to come into force in Spring 2003. This has the following effect:

- Stop Now orders are abolished and replaced by new wider Enforcement Orders (no-one will miss the somewhat clumsy name "Stop Now orders" anyway!);
- Despite the new name, nothing will change in respect of EU Wide Enforcement, which will be limited to the legislation already mentioned;
- However for "domestic infringements" harmful to the collective interests of consumers in the United Kingdom, Enforcement Orders can be used to back up a much wider range of situations in addition. These include any contravention of any enactment which imposes a duty or restriction enforceable by criminal proceedings (therefore now including the TDA and CPA); and
- any act done or omission made in breach of contract;
- there are a number of additional areas covered which are perhaps less relevant to the contents of this book.

It can now be seen that the authorities have wide powers to prevent travel companies abusing consumers, whether by misleading descriptions, misleading price campaigns whether in a brochure or not; and even breaches of contract. Thus an airline which repeatedly abandons its passengers at some foreign location, because of technical difficulties and an insufficiently large fleet of planes to respond to the problem, could find itself the subject of an enforcement order procedure to stop this happening; and one can think of many other examples besides.

The OFT have indicated that the same policy on enforcement will be adopted as described in their April 2002 Stop Now Guidance Booklet, and briefly described above. Thus enforcement orders are seen as a weapon of last resort, where individual prosecution by trading standards is inadequate, and the trader will not undertake voluntarily to "mend his ways". It should be noted that where the infringer is a company, enforcement action can also be taken against a director, manager, secretary or other similar officer or a person who is a controller of the company, where any such person have consented to or connived in the infringement. An order made against one company in a group can be extended to cover all companies within that group.

It perhaps goes without saying that failure to comply with an enforcement order, or breach of an undertaking, is a contempt of Court punishable by imprisonment or unlimited fines.

Chapter Fifteen
Travel Agents

Introduction

We have already seen in Chapter One how travel agents fit into the structure of the industry. Because they are by name "agents", it is tempting to think that they can never be liable for anything. However, as we have already seen in Chapter Two and Chapter Five, this is very far from the case; furthermore, we have seen in Chapters Eleven to Thirteen how travel agents can fall foul of the criminal law.

For ease of reference, we set out here the various ways in which a travel agent may be liable for any problems which might arise from a package, with cross references where necessary to places in the book where this topic is more fully explored. Potential liability can arise either because they are seen by the law as in fact being an organiser in certain circumstances; or, secondly, whilst their position as an agent is accepted, nonetheless there is still potential liability attaching to them.

Liability as an Organiser

There are three potential ways in which an agent can become liable as an organiser:—

(i) By allowing themselves to be held out as organiser

(ii) A "split contract" arrangement

(iii) As "the other party to the contract"

Held out as an organiser

If the consumer is reasonably led to believe that the travel agent is in fact the organiser of a package, the agent will have the liability of an organiser for the package. To escape this risk, the travel agent must make it clear to the consumer, before the contract is entered into, that they are "only an agent".

An alternative analysis of this type of situation would be to say that the law holds an agent liable where the existence of a principal is undisclosed.

In looking at all these situations regarding agents, it should be borne in mind that as well as the traditional travel agent, the term also includes newspapers and magazines offering "reader's offers" type holidays.

Many references have been made in this book to the Court of Appeal decision in *Hone v Going Places* [2001] EWCA Civ. 947—see especially Chapter 5. In the High Court (November 16, 2000 QBD unreported) an important issue had been the potential liability of Going Places, a well known travel agent, as organiser. This issue was not the subject of any appeal, and therefore the decision of Douglas Brown J on this issue remains good law.

He set out the facts as follows:

> "The Defendant is a very well known travel agent with many high street shops but also invites business through advertisements on the ITV teletext service. This branch of the Defendant's enterprise is called Late Escapes and specialises in late or last minute holiday bookings. It is now agreed that the Defendant acts as a retail agent for tour operators but there was an issue as to whether the Defendant had made it known to, or clear to the Claimant or his brother who actually made the holiday booking that they were acting as retail agents for a tour operator. On 22 September 1996 the Claimant saw a holiday advertised on the teletext message for 14 nights at a hotel at Gumbet in Turkey on a date convenient for him and at an acceptable price .... The following day his brother Mr Duncan Hone, booked the holiday by telephone. Mr Hone himself looked at the teletext message and then telephoned the numbers shown. He did not remember the details save that the holiday was through Going Places. He knew that his brother, then a serving police officer, was particular anxious about booking through a reputable and well known concern. A telephone sales representative now known only as Gillian dealt with Mr Hone. He asked if the holiday advertised was still available and it was. He gave the visa number of the joint card held by himself and his wife and booked for four persons ... he is certain ... that there was no mention of Suntours during the conversation. Gillian told him that a confirmation of the booking would be sent by post and the tickets were to be collected at the airport ... all the sample pages [from teletext] contain the words 'retail agent ATOL holder'. The case put forward before me by the Defendants is that their advertisements make it clear that they were acting as agents for tour

operators who are the holders of the appropriate licence. The sample pages in evidence show nothing of the kind. . . . When the holiday documents arrived, the vouchers to be exchanged for the tickets was headed in large print 'GOING PLACES DIRECT' and 'LATE ESCAPES'. In the top left hand corner in the representative's handwriting against the printed word operator 'SUNTOURS' was written and the collection point for the air tickets was Suntours desk . . . I accept that if [the Claimants] saw the word Suntours written, it meant nothing to them and as far as they were concerned they were dealing with Going Places or Late Escapes".

We have set out this passage at some length because there is nothing unusual about the transaction. Many holidays or travel arrangements are booked this way. The Judge held Going Places liable as the organiser under Regulation 15, although, as we have seen elsewhere, in the end they escaped liability on the facts of this particular claim.

Split contract arrangements

We have already seen in Chapter Two how the European Court of Justice, in *Club Tour v Garrido* held a Portuguese travel agent liable as organiser, under the Package Travel Directive. Club Tour had put together a "package" of flights and a Club Med Holiday in Greece at the request of the consumer. The Club Med Resort was overrun by wasps. Club Tour argued that the holiday sold was outside the scope of the Package Travel Directive. But the European Court of Justice held:

"The term 'package' must be interpreted so as to include holidays organised by travel agents at the request of and in accordance with the specifications of the consumer . . . the term 'pre-arranged combination' must be interpreted so as to include combinations of tourist services put together at the time when the contract is concluded between the travel agents and the consumer".

Despite this ruling, many English travel agents will continue to argue that the different way in which the English travel industry is set up means that this Judgment does not apply to them.

In this context note:

- because of the defect with the holiday, the consumer had refused to pay for it. It was Club Tour who were suing the consumer for non payment. In those circumstances it is hardly surprising that the question of whether a contract existed between the parties seems to have been taken as read.

- Hence the Judgment is framed in terms of "the contract concluded between the travel agent and the consumer".

An English agent would say that even if they put together a combination of flights and accommodation for a holiday or a business trip, they clearly do so in each case as agent for the airline/ATOL holder and as agent for the accommodation company. Therefore there never is any contract between the travel agent and the consumer; and therefore the Club Tour case is completely irrelevant.

Whilst it is still possible for an English Court to accept that analysis, the trend of the times, and the desire to give consumers protection and avoid easy circumvention of the regulations, seem to be against this. A further important step down the road is the change to the ATOL Regulations, in effect from April 2003; this has the effect that if a package is sold under a split contract arrangement, and it includes a flight, the whole package must be protected by the ATOL bond, and not just the flight. (Note that the Package Travel Regulations do not refer to "principals" or "agents" but to "organisers".)

Other party to the contract

The possibility that the agent might be "the other party to the contract", and indeed the definition of "contract", have been fully dealt with in Chapter Two. There are hints, although not entirely clear ones, that the High Court and the Court of Appeal in *Hone v Going Places* felt that the travel agent could be liable by this route, as well as by dint of holding themselves out as the organiser. (See also *Minhas v Imperial Travel* [2003] ITLJ 69).

Liability as an Agent

What is an agent?

Several learned works have been written on this subject, and our readers are referred to them for a detailed examination of the law (*e.g.* Fridman *The Law of Agency*; Bowstead on Agency) For our purposes, it suffices to say that an agent is someone authorised to do certain acts on behalf of his principal. When he has carried out those acts, the effect will be that his principal is legally bound by the acts. For example, if a tour operator authorises a travel agent to sell certain holidays, then if the agent sells those holidays, the tour operator must fulfil the agreement with the customers. (But see Grant "An Agent but not a Retailer" [1996] TLJ 29.)

In return, an agent in the commercial world will be entitled to be paid, usually by way of commission, by his principal.

Even if the agent oversteps his authority, but this was not obvious to a third party, the principal will still be bound. For example, an airline authorises a travel agent to sell flight tickets. After a while the airline tells the agent that the flight is fully booked, but the agent carries on selling the tickets. The agent is in possession of tickets and appears to a validly appointed agent for the airline. The airline will be bound to honour the contract with the innocent member of the public, by performing it or paying compensation for breach of it.

Whose agent is a travel agent?

It is one of the most extraordinary features of holiday law that there is no authoritative answer to this question. Is the travel agent the customer's agent or the tour operators agent? If the travel agent is the customer's agent, he will owe duties to the customer and if he fails in those duties, the customer will be able to sue him. If the travel agent is agent of the tour operator, then he does not owe any duty to the customer (certainly not in contract, but we will look at the position in negligence later)—and the customer will have to sue the tour operator, and not the travel agent, if things go wrong.

However, piecing together all the evidence, we now feel confident enough to offer this rule of thumb: the travel agent is agent for the consumer up until the time that a contract is made between the consumer and the tour operator; and from that time on the agent is agent for the tour operator. We emphasise that this is a rule of thumb; the courts will look at each situation and make their own judgment based on all the circumstances.

So what is the evidence?

(i) The Nature Of The Transaction

Useful guidance can be obtained from the world of insurance. It is settled law that an insurance agent, who is hired to recommend one particular company, is agent for the company; whilst an insurance broker is for most purposes the agent of the proposer. (See *Chitty on Contracts*).

Unlike an insurance agent, but more akin to a broker, a travel agent will stock the brochures of a large number of different tour operators. How can it then be said that he is agent for any one of them? His first duty, upon the customer entering the shop, may be to guide the customer towards some brochures and positively to discourage the customer from other brochures. The next customer who walks in might be given a totally opposite recommendation. The answer appears to be that in this stage of the transaction, the agent is certainly not the agent of the tour operator.

Some guidance on this is given in the Court of Appeal decision of *Kemp v Intasun Holidays Limited* (1988) 6 Tr.L. 161. In that case, Mrs Kemp went into her local Thomas Cooks to book a holiday. Before she had homed in on Intasun as the holiday she would definitely book, she informed the Thomas Cook staff that her husband was ill with asthma. Subsequently she booked the Intasun holiday. If Thomas Cook were acting as agents for Intasun, then the knowledge they had about Mr Kemp's medical condition would, in law, be treated as knowledge that Intasun had. Intasun would then be aware that they were carrying a passenger with a health problem and could be liable for additional compensation if, as happened to Mr Kemp was put in a dusty bedroom. Lord Justice Kerr put it this way:

> "Special circumstances ... must be brought home to a tour operator before damages in respect of injury to health are also to be recoverable. The only possible basis for the latter conclusion is the casual conversation which Mrs Kemp had with one or more of the ladies at Thomas Cook before this holiday was booked. In my view there can be no doubt at all, with all due respect to the Judge, that he was in error in attributing any contractual consequences, at any rate so far as Intasun are concerned, to that conversation. One can put the matter in many different ways, but there is none whereby this casual conversation can possibly have any contractual consequences for these Defendants. *At the time of that conversation, Thomas Cook were not the agents of the Defendants*, let alone for the purpose of receiving or passing on the contents of the conversation. Whether they became their agent at a later stage and, if so, for what purpose, it is unnecessary to decide". [Emphasis added].

Mr Kemp's Barrister had pointed out that the Thomas Cook witness had said at court that while she could not remember the conversation, if it had occurred she would have made a note of it. Lord Justice Kerr went on:

> "I cannot see that he derives any benefit from that."

Either, as the Judge appears to have thought, the conversation was too casual to make any impact on Miss Hodge's mind, or it may be—though I express no view about it—that some note should have been made of it by her. But in any event that would have no bearing on any liability of Intasun.

The Judge in the original court in Worcester had said that Thomas Cook had been given the information about Mr Kemp's health, and he had held that this knowledge was attributable to Intasun. He had said:

> "The fact that it is not given for practical purposes, or to make special arrangements, is neither here nor there. If I go into a travel agent in a wheelchair, I am entitled to rely on that agent's knowledge".

Lord Justice Kerr in the Court of Appeal commented on this view saying:

> "Without expressing any view about a point which was not argued, it may be that a client going into a travel agent's in a wheelchair is for certain purposes entitled to rely on that agent's knowledge of his condition. But that would be a matter between the travel agent and the customer, and Thomas Cook are not parties to this action".

The other Judge in the Court of Appeal, Lord Justice Parker, commented somewhat testily, about this argument:

> "It may be that it is part of what appears to occur in this industry—that the customer finds that everybody he turns to says "It's not my fault—it's somebody else's".

A later case goes right to the point. *Brewer v Best Travel Limited* [1993] 10 CL 10 is a decision of Swansea County Court and therefore of "persuasive" and not "binding" authority. On the other hand, the decision was by the Circuit Judge on an appeal on a point of law from the District Judge, with a Reserved Judgment, so that it can be said that the matter was very carefully considered.

Mr Brewer had told the Court that he wanted to stay on holiday in some particular apartments. It was common ground that what the travel agents actually booked, for him, with Best Travel Limited, was a "late availability" type of package where the accommodation is allocated on arrival in resort by the tour operator. Needless to say, Mr Brewer did not get his chosen apartment. He sued the tour operator, Best Travel. The travel agents gave evidence that they had booked what Mr Brewer had requested, but the District Judge ruled that this was not correct, and Mr Brewer had made his wishes quite clear. He held Best Travel Limited liable for not providing the correct accommodation. Best Travel appealed on the ground that the travel agents were acting as agents for the customer at the time the booking (and the mistake) were made and that therefore they as the tour operator were not to blame and their appeal succeeded. Best Travel had not broken their agreement, because there never had been a proper agreement between them and Mr Brewer, thanks to the failure of Mr Brewer's travel agent.

Similarly in *Williams v Cosmos* (1995, Newport County Court, unreported), before booking a holiday the plaintiff told his travel agent that he was a keen marksman and was taking two shotguns with him on holiday. The tour operator was never told this, nor was the sub-contracted airline, and at check-in the Plaintiff was told the guns could not be carried. He refused to travel, and sued Cosmos for his lost holiday. It was held that the travel agent was his agent and any failure to take necessary steps to ensure carriage of the guns was their responsibility, not that of Cosmos. (It was by the way also held that the airline was entitled to refuse to to carry the guns and ammunition under the Air Navigation Order 1985 and Cosmos were not in breach of contract by reason of this refusal).

But does this mean that the consumer can sue the travel agent for breach of contract?

(ii) Payment

For there to be a contract to be breached, there must be some consideration passing from the consumer to the travel agent. Well, who does pay the travel agent? The most obvious answer is the tour operator, who will pay the agent a fixed commission. But some customers, who wish to hold the travel agent liable, would argue differently. They would say that in effect they pay the travel agent, because they hand their money to the travel agent who keeps some of it and passes the balance on to the tour operator. But surely the truth is that the customer pays the price demanded by the tour operator, and it is the tour operator who arranges for some of that price to be paid/retained by the travel agent by way of commission. If that is right, no consideration passes from the consumer and there is no contract between consumer and travel agent—and, logically, no possible breach of contract. The consumer will have to rely on his rights in the law of negligence, which we will look at shortly. (But see also the analysis by Wohlmuth referred to below.)

An agent by definition cannot make a secret profit at the expense of his principal. It is clear that an agent who feels free to set his own price, and does not merely rely upon commission, is not acting as an agent at all, but is acting as a principal in his own right—*ex parte White, re Neville* 1871 LR 6 CH App 397. It is common to find in practice that, if an agent has hiked up the price himself, he does not send to the customer a copy of the tour operators confirmation invoice in order to hide his own covert charges. This is further evidence that they are not acting as an agent, particularly as the ABTA Code of Conduct requires that such documentation be sent on, and within four working days of receipt. There are legal requirements within the ATOL Regulations to a similar effect with criminal sanctions.

It is interesting to note that airlines are cutting the amount of commission received by travel agents and one can imagine that tour operators may not be far behind. There is an increasing trend among travel agents to charge their customers a service charge. Such a move certainly clarifies the legal relationships, as plainly then there would be a contract between the customer and travel agent, at least leading up to the completion of a booking between the customer and the tour operator.

(iii) When, If At All, Does The Agency Switch?

The standard ATOL terms provide some assistance on this issue. The significance of ATOLs is explained in Chapters One and Sixteen. Where a holiday or travel arrangements are protected by an ATOL, then the contract between consumer and tour operator is subject to the standard ATOL terms, which have legal force through a statutory instrument.

Standard Term 8 reads: "The licence holder shall not enter into a contract through an agent to make available flight accommodation pursuant to the license unless he has made it clear in writing to the agent and to the customer that any money paid by the customer to the agent under or in contemplation of the contract is held by the agent as agent for the license holder until the date on which the agent pays the money to the license holder".

This term, last revised in April 1997, replaced an earlier rule whereby such money (commonly called "pipeline money") was held as agent for the license holder once a confirmation of the booking was issued, but the parties were free to contract as to the position before the confirmation. So far as the holding of money is concerned, the position is now clear; but during the consultation period which led to the revised rule, all parties were at pains to express that the position of the travel agent in all regards except as the holding of money was to be unaffected by the changed rule.

Who Can Sue for Breach of Contract, and When?

The customer

We have seen that the Courts will be reluctant to construe a contract between the consumer and the travel agent where his position as agent is clear. Despite this, the writers have seen innumerable examples whereby the consumer sues the travel agent, usually as co-defendant with the tour operator. The writers have never known any such claim to succeed. An exhaustive test took place in the unreported case of *Edwards v Intasun and Lunn Poly*, Guildford County Court 1991. In a trial that lasted no less than four days, the Plaintiffs tried to claim that Lunn Poly were in breach of contract for the alleged shortcomings of Intasun Holidays. However by the fourth day, Counsel for the Plaintiffs had to concede, under pressure from the Judge, that in fact there was no contract at all between the customers and Lunn Poly.

However, in one very, important, though limited, way, the Package Travel Regulations do impose civil liability on the retailer. This is under Regulation 4, where the consumer has suffered loss as a result of relying on any misleading descriptive matter concerning the package supplied by the retailer. This has been dealt with in detail in Chapter 5. The result is that a retailer will be liable to the consumer if, for example, the swimming pool promised in the tour operator's brochure was not actually there; but will not be liable if the pool did exist, but was (say) unusable because the filter pump had broken. The loss of enjoyment suffered by the holidaymaker will however be the same in both cases!

This right of action against retailers is of particular importance to consumers in two circumstances:—

- where the tour operator has become insolvent shortly after the holiday—none of the bonding schemes in operation currently offer any security for claims for compensation made after a holiday has taken place.
- where the tour operator takes a hard line in opposing the claim, the retailer may, for various commercial reasons, prove to be more of a "soft touch".

The travel agent

If there is no contract, can the travel agent sue the customer?. The nature of the relationships involved are highlighted by an unreported case called *Tony Iredale Travel Centre Limited v Holt and Alta Holidays Limited t/as Speedbird* 1991—Huddersfield County Court. H, an important business house client of the travel agent plaintiff, booked an expensive holiday just before departure and persuaded the agent that he would pay for the holiday immediately upon his return. The agent thereupon forwarded his own money to the tour operator in order to obtain travel documents, etc., for the customer. H then returned from the holiday complaining that it had been badly sub-standard. He refused to pay the travel agent. The travel agent sued H in the High Court and applied for Summary Judgment. The Court refused, saying that the contract position was far from clear and that it was arguable that the travel agent was responsible for the alleged shortcomings of Speedbird Holidays. This decision may have been wrong—however, Speedbird were joined as Second Defendants. In the end, when the matter came before a Judge, he threw up his hands in horror at the legal difficulties and dealt with the matter on a very practical level. He said that obviously the travel agent should be paid in full and sent the two Defendants out of Court to work out between themselves who would pay and in what proportions. They agreed privately that the customer should pay the travel agent in full while Speedbird paid some compensation to the customer. While this was a satisfactory result, it clearly illustrates how ill-defined the precise legal relationships in operation are.

Following the *Club Tour* case, above, it is now more likely that the Court was correct to view the agent as potentially responsible for the holiday—it will be recalled that Club Tour were also suing on an unpaid invoice.

An Alternative View

As can be seen from all the above, the precise legal position and responsibilities of a travel agent have been surprisingly resistant to analysis. Could this be because the wrong questions are being asked? Is the whole question "whose agent is the travel agent?" a red herring? Certainly there has been thinking in America to that effect. Paul Wohlmuth in his article "The Liability of Travel Agents: a study in the selection of appropriate legal principles" 1966 Temple Law Quarterly 29 has argued that in reality there is a contract between consumer and travel agent. He concludes:

> "the question of travel agents' liability is very much an open one. The few available decisions on the subject are not very infor-

mative, ... [my approach] has led to the following conclusions:—

(1) The travel agent resembles more closely an independent middleman than an agent.
(2) The interaction between the travel agent, client and hotel or carrier is best viewed as an interweaving of contractual relations.
(3) Even if the travel agent could be considered an agent, it merely clouds the issue to treat him as such for the purpose of liability. The issue is: should the travel agent be held liable to the client under various circumstances? This question, aside from the problem of negligence, can best be answered by treating the travel agent as one who contracts with his client and then, by determining what the travel agent expressly impliedly and as a matter of legal imposition, undertakes to do in his relations with the client".

Wohlmuth identifies three contracts in the client/tour operator/travel agent relationship. First, a contract between client and tour operator for the provision of the holiday. Second a contract between tour operator and travel agent whereby the tour operator agrees to pay the travel agent commission for each of the tour operator's holidays the travel agent sells. Thirdly a contract between client and travel agent whereby the travel agent agrees to exercise reasonable care and skill on the clients behalf to secure the reservations and handle the documentation etc and in return the client agrees to abide by his contract with the tour operator—thus permitting the agent to earn his commission.

There is no doubt that the American courts have been prepared to adopt this analysis—see the case of *Pellegrini v Landmark Travel* reported in [1998] ITLJ 22. However it must be said that there is no English case which supports this approach. The English courts continue to analyse the position of the travel agent by reference to the law of agency, or by reference to negligence, the subject to which we now turn.

Liability in Negligence

Fortunately for disgruntled consumers, the law of negligence offers a more helpful route to enforcing rights against the travel agent. It is worth remembering here that travel agents conduct a much wider range of business than just package holidays including flights, rail tickets, hotels, business travel, etc. Many problems arise in those areas also (*e.g.* mistakes in ticketing).

Negligence—the duty of care

The concept that negligence which causes damage should result in a right of legal action is surprisingly young in English law—indeed it does not pre-date the package holiday by so many years. It was properly established in the famous "Snail in the Ginger Beer Bottle" case of *Donoghue v Stevenson* [1932] A.C. 562. One of the best known passages from an English Judgment is the following from Lord Atkin:—

> "The rule that you are to love your neighbour becomes in law you must not injure your neighbour; and the lawyers question, who is my neighbour? receives a restricted reply. You must take reasonable care to avoid acts or omissions which you can reasonably foresee would be likely to injure your neighbour. Who, then, in law is my neighbour? The answer seems to be—the persons who are so closely and directly affected by my act that I ought reasonably to have them in my contemplation as being so affected when I am directing my mind to act or omissions which are causing question".

This case established the test to discover whether a duty of care exists in law which, if broken, gives rise to a claim for compensation. However, a normal travel agent's business would still not have been subject to legal action. Why not? Because the type of damage which was recoverable was physical, *e.g.*, damage to property or injury to a person. Mere loss of money, economic loss, was not recoverable in 1932 for negligence. However substantial inroads have been made into that proposition since the case of *Hedley Byrne & Co Limited v Heller & Partners Limited* [1964] A.C. 465. The Defendants were bankers who negligently gave a good reference about a worthless company, one of their customers. The Plaintiffs lost a lot of money by relying on the reference and sued the Defendant Bank. In the House of Lords, Lord Morris said:

> "It should now be regarded as settled law that if someone possessed of a special skill undertakes, quite irrespective of the contract, to apply that skill for the assistance of another person who relies upon such skill, a duty of care will arise. The fact that the service is to be given by the means of or by the instrumentality of words can make no difference. Furthermore if in a

sphere in which a person is so placed that others could reasonably rely upon his Judgment or skill or upon his ability to make careful enquiry, the person takes it upon himself to give information or advice to, or allows his information or advice to be passed on to another person who, as he knows or should know, will place reliance upon it, then a duty of care will arise".

Whilst it should be noted that the Plaintiffs lost their claim on other grounds, and that the Courts have been somewhat reluctant to extend the scope of this head of claim, nonetheless Lord Morris could almost have had travel agents and their customers, in mind. If therefore a travel agent's advice is careless and the person who relies on it suffers an economic loss, then he will be liable in negligence.

Furthermore, as other cases show, all the staff of a travel agency will be expected to show the requisite skill—so young trainees had better be kept under close supervision!

Common Problems in Practice

Passports and visas

Where package travel is involved, we have already seen in Chapter Five that the Package Travel Regulations put specific legal obligations on "The Other Party to the Contract", normally the organiser. In practice, many tour operators expect travel agents to give this advice, and of course the duty falls on travel agents when they are selling non-packages, *e.g.*, flight tickets. Also, as we have seen, the legal requirement only applies to information required for British Citizens. What if a travel agent sells a package to the USA, for which a Visa is no longer required by British nationals—but fails to establish that one of the party is, for example, an Irish Citizen who may still need a Visa? There could well be liability here. See the section on Regulation 7 in Chapter Thirteen above in the light of amendments to that Regulation. (See also *Bagley v Intourist Moscow* [1984] CLY 1024).

Health requirements

The same comments apply here. An interesting point arises in this way: the 1992 Regulations require information to be given accurately in the brochure and in the contract—but what if things change after the contract is made—*e.g.*, an outbreak of illness—in the resort. The tour operator may have some liability (see *Davey v Cosmos* [1989] C.L.Y. 2561), but does the travel agent have too? The answer is "probably not" as this extends too far the concept of "careless mis-statement" in the *Hedley Byrne* case. In *Spencer v Lotus* 2000, Manchester County Court, unreported, a travel agent stated that he did not know whether vaccinations were recommended for the Dominican Republic. In fact they were. A Circuit Judge on appeal held Lotus not liable where the customer took a risk and booked the holiday anyway. The answer "I do not know" cannot ground an action for negligent misstatement.

Outbreaks of violence

If a holiday area is affected by violence whether political or criminal, whether aimed at tourists or not, does the travel agent have a duty to advise? The current stand taken by the travel industry is that the British Foreign Office is in the best position to make judgments about these matters, and that a small high street travel agency cannot be expected to have greater knowledge and insight into the situation. Therefore advice is given purely on the basis of current Foreign Office warnings. See also in this context: Dickerson "The Liability for Tour Operators and Suppliers for Physical Injuries sustained by Travellers on Tour" [1995] TLJ 44)).

Mistakes on ticketing or timing

Clearly the travel agent can be liable for writing the wrong times in airline tickets, or for giving customers wrong timings for flight departures (especially where, in a late booking, tickets are to be collected on departure at the airport).

Other regular problems

Overselling holidays by making promises beyond what the tour operator has promised, advising that a holiday is suitable for the disabled where it is not, making mistakes in the booking by pressing the wrong Viewdata button, selling inadequate holiday insurance, failing to advise as to the best prices available for flight seats; in all these cases, there is potential liability for the travel agent.

It sometimes happens that travel agents fail to pass on to their customers a change to holiday arrangements notified to the travel agent by the tour operator. As we have seen, however, by this time the travel agent will almost certainly have become the agent of the tour operator, and therefore it will be possible for the customer to sue the tour operator, who may however join in the travel agent as a third party. This leads us conveniently on to the relationship between travel agent and tour operator.

Travel Agent and Tour Operator

As travel agents and tour operators are both commercial entities, the law is much less ready to jump in with implied terms to assist one or the other. The relationship between the two is therefore generally governed in two ways: by a written agency agreement, or by ABTA's Code of Conduct (but see Chapter One and the reference to The Foreign Package Holidays (Tour Operators and Travel Agents) Order 2001 (SI 2001/2581)). Despite the abolition of the rule known as "stabiliser" by ABTA (which used to have the effect of creating what was largely a closed shop in the travel industry), it remains the case that most high street travel agencies are ABTA Members and therefore bound by its Code. Furthermore, the Code is often expressly incorporated into agency agreements, so we will examine the Code first.

ABTA code of conduct

Travel agents are required by virtue of this code to do the following:—

- to comply with all relevant law (*e.g.* the Trade Descriptions Act), and to ensure that clients are sold tour holiday and travel arrangements compatible with their individual requirements. For example, selling a "Club 18-30" holiday to an elderly couple, as has happened, would fall foul of this rule;
- to notify the clients immediately they are advised of any change to their bookings and to supply to ABTA an emergency telephone number where they may be contacted outside office hours;
- to study carefully the brochures from which they sell and draw the attention of clients to the booking conditions applicable—a rule which is too often honoured in the breach in practice, leaving the tour operator carrying the can (but

with a right of indemnity against a travel agent if he chooses to use it);

- to check all documentation received from tour operators before sending them to clients within 4 days of receipt—in this way any changes or errors in flight timings, for example, should be picked up and notified;
- in the event of a dispute with a client, to make every effort to reach an amicable and speedy solution. Minor complaints should be dealt with by the travel agents themselves, without recourse to the tour operator; and where it is necessary to refer the matter to the tour operator, the travel agent is to act as intermediary to bring about a satisfactory conclusion. In practice, too many travel agents still merely act as a posting house sending on letters between customer and tour operator without any help or comment.
- there are many other requirements in the code, often joint with tour operators, *e.g.* re health/visa requirements, and telling consumers about the availability of Foreign Office Advice.

Agency agreements

Agency agreements between travel agent and tour operator have become increasingly complicated. As it is a commercial agreement between commercial entities, Courts generally will enforce the agreement without reference to the Unfair Contract Terms Act. In 1997 the Office of Fair Trading investigated the relationships between tour operators and travel agents in a market where many of the leading travel agencies are owned by, or under common ownership with, leading tour operators, causing possible market distortion (so called "vertical integration" which also involves airlines). The potential for market abuse can clearly be seen and was declared to be a "complex monopoly" by the OFT (see Chapter One). The result was the Foreign Package Holidays (Tour Operators and Travel Agents) Order 1998 which outlawed (a) the tying of travel insurance policy sales to the purchase of discounted holidays and (b) "most favoured customer" clauses whereby a tour operator won't sell through or discriminates against an agent who does not match for his holidays any offers he makes for other tour operator holidays. Greater transparency in the common ownership of the constituent parts of vertically integrated groups was also required; hence we now have *e.g.* "World of TUI" common branding for Thomson, Lunn Poly, Britannia, etc.

Common terms to be found in modern agency agreements are:—

- for the agent to promote and sell the tour operator's products and display its brochures prominently;
- for the agent to obtain a signed backing booking form and to ensure that the tour operator's booking conditions are brought to the attention of the consumer. With the increasing use of technology, the marketing forces within the industry have sought to create a "paper free" booking transaction. Unfortunately, in many ways, the Package Travel Regulations make it more important than ever that there should be a signed booking form. For example:—

  (i) how else does the tour operator prove compliance with Regulation 9?

  (ii) it will be very difficult for a tour operator to prove that he is entitled to rely upon the Warsaw Convention limits for compensation in the absence of a signed booking form. Regulation 15 makes the tour operator liable for the improper performance of all the components of the package, including the air travel; and it is only by terms in the contract that the tour operator is permitted to take advantage of the limitations on damages in the conventions. One can easily foresee a situation in which there is a major airline accident, where the customers or their executors sue the tour operator for millions of pounds in damages and are able to recover this (instead of the few thousand pounds currently allowed under the Convention) because there is no signed booking form (see *Lee & Lee v Airtours*, 2002 Central London County Court unreported, discussed in Saggerson "That Sinking Feeling—Psychiatric Injury, Lost Valuables and the Demise of the Cruise Ship Sun Vista" [2002] ITLJ 198 where exactly this problem arose under the Athens Convention). The tour operator will probably not be able to claim indemnity against the airline because his agreement with the airline will be subject to very strict limitations on damages, probably the Convention limits; and so the tour operator will claim indemnity against the travel agent for breach of the agency agreement by not obtaining a signed booking form. Such a claim would wipe out many travel agencies, whose liability insurance may well be inadequate; and yet, in our experience, travel agents remain remarkably cavalier about obtaining signed booking forms or making any proper notes that the booking conditions have been explained to customers, for example in the case of telephone bookings.

- for the agent to obtain the deposit and send on the tour operator's confirmation and invoice, and to recover the balance due from the customer and collect any cancellation or amendment charges.
- for the operator to pay the agent's commission.
- for both parties to comply with the Rules and Code of Conduct of ABTA. For the agent this includes displaying prominently the "Due Diligence" notice described in Chapter Fourteen.
- for the agent to notify all customers who have booked or enquire about booking in respect of any corrections or alterations made by the tour operator to brochures or literature. Some agreements recite that the agent is responsible for giving health, passport and visa requirements to consumers. Whilst it is not possible for tour operators to pass on to someone else the duty to comply with the criminal law (Trade Descriptions Act, and Regulations 5, 7 and 8), such a provision accords with general practice and should be made part of a "due diligence" system. The clause may also impose on the agent the duty to advise the tour operator of any special requirements of the customer, *e.g.*, a customer in a wheelchair.
- for the agent not to oversell the holiday by making representations about it beyond those appearing in the tour operator's brochure or other literature.
- for either party to indemnify the other where appropriate. This usually states that the travel agent indemnifies the tour operator in respect of any claims which the tour operator faces as a result of the breach of the agreement by a travel agent, as we have discussed; and the tour operator indemnifies the travel agent vice versa, this latter provision being particularly important in view of Regulation 4.
- for the operator to comply with certain quality standards. Some of the major chains of travel agencies, the so called multiples, having realised their own financial muscle in the market place, impose quality control provisions over the tour operator in the agency agreement, for example: the speed at which the tour operator answers the telephone, the

accuracy of price information given, the ratio of complaints by customers, and, most controversially of all, a right to the travel agent to compensate a dissatisfied customer almost in their own discretion, and then recoup the money from the tour operator.

Chapter Sixteen
Insolvency and Security

For the average consumer, there are not many transactions in a lifetime for which he is required to hand over large sums of money so far in advance of receiving the goods or services as he does with a package holiday. The dangers are obvious and the holiday industry, which enjoys a high media profile, has often found itself the centre of attention when a holiday company collapses. The media coverage generally focuses upon:

- The large numbers of consumers who have not yet taken their holidays but have paid over their hard earned savings to the now insolvent company.
- Other consumers who are stranded overseas at the time of the insolvency, with unpaid hotels threatening to eject them onto the street, and airlines threatening not to carry them home.

Within limits, the industry has responded very well to this challenge. Driven partly by the self-interest of wishing to restore public faith in the industry, and partly by a genuine concern for consumers, a mixture of statutory and voluntary schemes to protect holidaymakers against a tour operator's insolvency has grown up during the last three decades, and these remain important today, within the more comprehensive framework established by the Package Travel Regulations 1992.

The statutory scheme is the ATOL scheme operated by the Civil Aviation Authority, which covers (in effect) any package holiday or package arrangements which includes a flight as one of its elements. A package covered by the scheme is known as a "Licensable Activity".

The voluntary schemes have arisen piecemeal for members of certain organisations. We have already discussed the structure of the industry in Chapter One, and the various bodies in it. The best known scheme is operated by ABTA for its members, and it is the proud boast of ABTA that no customer who has booked with an ABTA operator has ever lost their money or been stranded. The Federation of Tour Operators runs a similar scheme for its large tour operator members, and AITO also runs a scheme for its generally smaller independent operators. Lesser known but important schemes were also set up for members of the Passenger Shipping Association (PSA), the Confederation of Passenger Transport Bonded Coach Holiday Scheme (BCH), and the Yacht Charter Association.

All the above schemes impose strict quality controls. All require that its members be, or be run by, fit persons, persons who have not had a history of company failures, personal insolvencies or dishonest behaviour. A fairly rigorous examination of the Company accounts is also carried out. The CAA imposes its "ATOL Standard Terms" on ATOL Holders, (including personal guarantees by directors in many cases) whilst ABTA imposes its strict Codes of Conduct.

The advantage of these schemes is that they have worked extremely well. The disadvantage used to be that any package not involving a flight, where the operator was not a member of ABTA, etc., was not protected. So it was still possible for a company such as Land Travel to collapse in 1992, leaving consumers with shattered dreams and no money.

Theoretically, this should never happen again in the case of packages. (It must be said that non-packages, *e.g.* the simple rental of a holiday villa in France, are not protected, and consumers are advised to examine what, if any, protection has been put in place by companies offering such holidays. Frequently the only protection in such cases is where the payment was made by credit card and s.75 of the Consumer Credit Act 1974 applies although this protection may be disappearing soon when EU rules on consumer credit are harmonised). We will examine the details of the Regulations shortly, but let it be said straight away that there are three major disadvantages to the regime:

- The way the Regulations are drafted leaves plenty of opportunity for abuse.
- They are enforced by overworked and underfunded Trading Standards Departments who have little training or experience to help them understand what is and what is not adequate protection—*e.g.* in spotting "creative accountancy" in company accounts.
- They resulted in the abolition of ABTA's "stabiliser" rule, which used to be at the heart of the voluntary consumer protection which worked so well.

Stabiliser

This rule which appeared in ABTA's Articles of Association provided:

- No ABTA tour operator could sell its packages through any retail outlet other than an ABTA travel agency (but sales direct to the public were permitted).
- No ABTA travel agency could sell the packages put together by any organiser other than an ABTA member.

Clearly this was a restrictive trade practice, but when it was challenged through the Courts the practice was held to be for the public good, and therefore permitted to remain *(Re Association of British Travel Agents Ltd's Agreement* [1984] ICR 12).

Once the Package Travel Regulations had come into effect, however, the picture was transformed. Now all organisers of packages have to protect consumers" money and, providing these rules work, it could no longer be argued by ABTA that their restrictive practice was necessary for public protection. In anticipation of a further court challenge, ABTA voluntarily repealed its stabiliser rule in 1993. The result was that even the major ABTA tour operators became free to sell their holidays through any retail outlet—although predictions of holidays being sold through retail fashion chains, petrol stations and even with the daily milk delivery have proved rather fanciful to date. In practice the status quo has largely survived intact. The other side of the coin is that ABTA travel agents can sell the packages of non-ABTA tour operators. It is interesting to note however that such is the reputation of ABTA that at least one local authority we know of prohibits schools in the authority from booking school trips with non-ABTA operators—which has prompted complaints from such operators.

The Rules Under the Package Travel Regulations

Regulation 16(1) provides that:

> "The other party to the contract shall at all times be able to provide sufficient evidence of security for the refund of money paid over and for the repatriation of the consumer in the event of insolvency."

Note that:

- The words "shall at all times be able to provide" suggests that Trading Standards Officers have a right to demand the evidence at any time; but the effect of Schedule 3, Paragraph 3 is that a Trading Standards Officer can only demand to see the evidence of adequate security if he has reasonable grounds for suspecting that an offence has been committed.
- The security has to cover two things, the refund of money paid over and the repatriation of the consumer. The remainder of Regulations 16 to 21 provide a set of rules, in some detail, as to how security for the refund of money paid over is to be provided; but are (surprisingly) completely silent as to how security for the repatriation of the consumer is to be organised. Whilst the major bonding organisations have, through ABTA and other bodies, got repatriation down to a fine art, the situation may be very different where security is provided by a trust account under Regulations 20 or 21. One wonders how the trustee, who may be a local accountant or banker, can ever have the expertise to persuade hotels and airlines far away overseas to continue services for the customers of the failed company.

Note also that by Regulation 16(5) the security is required until the contract has been fully performed. This means "until the holiday or travel is over", and it expressly does not require the organiser to provide security in respect of claims for improper performance of the contract under Regulation 15. Therefore, as has always been the case, consumers who have had a disastrous holiday will only be unsecured creditors against their failed holiday company. There is no security for such claims.

There are various methods set down whereby the necessary security can be provided.

Other European jurisdictions

Security will be sufficient if the package is covered by measures adopted by another member state of the EU under Article 7 of the Directive—see Regulation 16(2)(a).

ATOL

Where the package is one in respect of which the organiser is required to hold an ATOL under the Civil Aviation (Air Travel

Organisers Licensing) Regulations 1995 or is covered by such arrangements, no further security needs to be provided. Therefore, no new provision was necessitated by the 1992 Regulations for companies selling air based packages, a large part of the traditional package market. Note the proposals to amend the ATOL Regulations to include "split contract" arrangements with effect from April 2003—see Chapters Two and Fifteen.

Bonding—Regulations 17 and 18

Two methods of bonding are provided whereby a bond is entered into by an authorised institution under which the institution binds itself to pay an approved body (of which the organiser is a member) a particular sum in the event of the insolvency of the organiser. Bonds have to be renewed at least every 18 months.

The difference between Regulations 17 and 18 turns on whether the approved body does or does not have a reserve fund or insurance cover to cover prepayments by consumers. The approval of the Secretary of State is required for all approved bodies and/or the reserve fund itself.

Where no reserve fund or insurance exists, then Regulation 17 provides that the sum which the bonding institution must pay shall be such sum as may reasonably be expected to enable all the monies paid over by consumers under or in contemplation of the contracts for relevant packages which have not been fully performed to be repaid and in any event not less than 25 per cent of all the payments which the organiser estimates he will receive under or in contemplation of contracts for packages in the 12 months from the start date of the bond, or the maximum amount of all payments which the organiser expects to hold at any one time in respect of contracts which have not been fully performed, whichever sum is the smaller. Because of the seasonal nature of the holiday industry, the first of these two calculations may produce the smaller sum. For example, a traditional summer holiday package company will hold maximum prepayments in about June or early July, just before the peak season, and these indeed may well exceed 25 per cent of all payments it will receive in a year; but on the other hand, it is also the time of year when in normal trading circumstances that company is least likely to become insolvent, because its cash flow will be very good.

Where the approved body does have a reserve fund or insurance, then Regulation 18 provides the method of calculating the size of the bond required; in effect it is the same calculation which we have just described under Regulation 17, except that the percentage of all payments which the organiser estimates he will receive during the 12 month period is reduced from 25 per cent to 10 per cent, making it even more likely that this is the lesser of the two sums.

In practice, bonding, by whatever method, is extremely expensive for tour operators, a major part of their overheads. Furthermore the bonding authorities, for good reasons, insist on seeing a healthy balance sheet with large capital resources, often to be provided in hard cash (and personal guarantees from the directors). This can be backbreaking for a tour operator after a difficult year's trading, but of course the object of all these rules is consumer protection.

A number of well established bodies including ABTA, FTO and AITO together with PSA and BCH (see above) have acquired approved body status for the purposes of these regulations. As a rule of thumb, ABTA typically require 10–15 per cent bonding for tour operators (2–3 per cent for retailers).

In a recent case ABTA's famous "consumer promise" has been held by the Court of Appeal to create a right in the consumer to sue ABTA for reimbursement following the insolvency of an ABTA member—*Bowerman and Wallace v ABTA 1995 The Times* November 24. (ABTA subsequently altered the wording of its promise slightly, but probably not to the extent of altering the principle. See Chapter Three for a fuller discussion of this case.)

Insurance

Regulation 19 permits security to be provided under one or more appropriate policies of insurance under which the insurer agrees to indemnify consumers, who shall be the insured persons under the policy, against the loss of money paid over by them under or in contemplation of contracts for packages, in the event of the organiser becoming insolvent. It is required that the organiser makes it a term of every contract with the consumer that the consumer acquires the benefit of such an insurance policy in the event of the insolvency. There are further provisions to prevent the insurance policy being avoided by the Insurer on technical grounds.

This appeared, at first sight, to be an attractive method of providing security for smaller companies. Unfortunately this option has been little used. The major reason has been the unavailability of suitable insurance products in the market, although in recent times a "supplier insolvency" form of insurance has begun to emerge and is now commonly available to cover scheduled airline insolvency. It is likely that any insurer would, like a bonding authority, require a high level of capitalisation in any company which was insured, so that the benefit for smaller companies would be illusory.

Further problems are highlighted by two Austrian cases before the European Court.

In *Verein Fur Konsumenteninformation v Osterreichische* Case 364/96 ECJ, May 14, 1998, the Austrian Tour Operator Karthago went bust, and hoteliers in Crete insisted that consumers pay again or they would not be allowed to leave their hotels! The insurers refused to reimburse the consumers on the grounds that had not been legally obliged to pay the hotelier a second time. However the Court held that consumers must be compensated under Article 7, which protects the "money paid over and . . . the repatriation of the consumer in the event of insolvency".

In the other case, *Rechberger v Austria* Case 140/97, June 15, 1999, insurance was based on 5 per cent of turnover over three months. This proved insufficient to reimburse consumers. The Court held that Austria had not sufficiently implemented Article 7, and it was not a defence for Austria to say that the losses only happened because of unexpected and unwise trading by the tour operator. (it is interesting to note that the holidays in this case were offered as a prize by a newspaper, and that the only payment made by consumers was either for airport taxes only, or in some cases for a single room supplement as well. Austria argued this was not a package; the Court said that the services sold were a package, and it made no difference that payment was only required for part).

Trust accounts

If there was one provision in the Package Travel Regulations 1992 which drew universal cries of "rubbish!" it was Regulation 20 which allowed package organisers to provide security by placing money in a trust account. As we shall see, anyone can be a trustee, there is no effective checking procedure, there is no means by which a consumer can tell whether a trust account is being properly operated and, in short, the system was wide open to abuse by unscrupulous operators. On December 31, 1992, when the Regulations came into effect, it was widely expected that Regulation 20 had so little credibility that it would fall into instant disuse.

In fact, despite the obvious hazards, and continuing misgivings, trust accounts are alive and flourishing. The reasons are that they provide the only legal method of compliance with Regulation 16 for many companies. Small tour operators, people running coach tours, hotels offering bargain break weekends and the like are excluded from other methods of providing security by the prohibitive costs or the unwillingness of bonding and insurance companies to take them on.

So what are the rules? All monies paid by a consumer must be held by a person as trustee for the consumer until the contract has been fully performed (or money forfeited as cancellation charges). There are no rules as to who should be the trustee, and theoretically it could be the managing director's wife or husband, or the office junior. A reputable company will appoint a bank, accountant or solicitor. It could not of course be the company's own solicitors—the solicitor holds the money as trustee for consumers—and this would create a conflict of interest with the company.

The cost of administering the trust is to be paid by the organiser. Any interest earned on the monies held by the trustee accrue to the organiser.

Regulation 20(4) provides that the trustee shall release to the organiser the appropriate sum of money from the trust account when he receives a statement signed by the organiser to the effect that:

- a contract for a package the price of which is specified in the statement has been fully performed; or
- the organiser has repaid to the consumer a sum of money specified in the statement which the consumer had paid in respect of the package; or
- the consumer has on cancellation of the package forfeited a sum of money specified in the statement.

Paragraph 5 permits the trustee to require the organiser to provide further information or evidence before releasing any sum mentioned in the statement.

In the event of the insolvency of the organiser, the monies held in trust by the trustee are to be applied to meet the claims of consumers who are creditors of the organiser in respect of contracts for packages for which the arrangements were established and which have not been fully performed and, in the unlikely event that there is a surplus after those claims have been met, it shall form part of the estate of the insolvent organiser. (It will be noticed that nothing is said about the need to repatriate consumers.)

In the more likely event that the money in trust is insufficient to meet the claim of consumers, payments to those consumers are to be made by the trustee on a pari passu basis.

Such has been the popularity of this method that organisations such as the Travel Trust Association (TTA) have become an established part of the scene. They aim to bring legitimacy and credibility to organisers using this method of providing security on payment of a fee, and on submitting accounts and brochures. The tour organiser can claim to be a member of the Association which, they hope, will bring comfort to consumers. The Association does not act as trustee itself, but has created TTA Trustees UK Ltd, operated by Chartered Accountants; each member has a dedicated trust account, currently with NatWest Bank. In addition fidelity insurance of (currently) £11,000 per passenger is arranged to cover any shortfall in the trust account, on insolvency.

The most obvious disadvantage for an organiser using the trust account method of bonding is a cash flow problem; they cannot touch the customer's money until the holiday is over, and yet may well have to pay suppliers such as airlines, "up front". (Rules of the TTA, however, permit a certain amount of payment of suppliers under strict conditions).

This cash flow implication does not apply under Regulation 21, another method of providing security by way of a trust account—but in this case only available to organisers acting "otherwise than in the course of business". A small number of voluntary organisations (and perhaps a large number of schools—see Chapter Two on the definition of organiser) may be able to take advantage of these rules, which are similar to those already set out except that:

- The costs of administering the trust can be paid for out of the monies held in trust.
- The statement signed by the organiser and produced for the trustee can require money to be paid over to the organiser because a sum is required for the purpose of paying for a component or part of a component of a package.

See also Brown—"Trust Me—I'm a Tour Operator" [1994] 3 TLJ 11 and Sheen "Is consumers" money really safe in a trust?" [1998] ITLJ 57.

Offences

An organiser who fails to provide sufficient evidence of security as required by Regulation 16 is guilty of an offence and liable on summary conviction to a fine not exceeding level five (£5,000 at the current time); or the matter can be dealt with in the Crown Court where an unlimited fine can be imposed. Further identical penalties are imposed by Regulation 22 for any organiser who makes a false "statement" to a trustee under Regulations 20 or 21 requiring the release of monies. The defence of due diligence is available to defendants under Regulation 16 and 22. (The due diligence defence has been discussed at length in Chapter Fourteen.)

The first prosecution under Regulation 16, in Humberside, resulted in a fine of £250 which was condemned as too low by industry and consumer groups. Several further cases have seen higher fines imposed but the feeling persists that enforcement is too sporadic to be really effective—especially for package holidays within the UK (see Grant, "When is a package not a package" [1996] TLJ 4). For comment on the ATOL system see Simpson "The new ATOL Regulations: What will they mean in practice?" [1996] TLJ 87; "Recent Developments on the ATOL Regulations [1997] ITLJ 113; and "Financial Protection for Scheduled Airline Passengers" [2002] ITLJ 15.

Chapter Seventeen
Practical Litigation

This chapter is addressed to consumers and their advisers who may wish to pursue a claim against a travel company; and also to tour operators, travel agents and their advisers who receive such a claim. Firstly we will examine what can be expected from the court system; and then we will pass on some practical tips on conducting the litigation.

In our last edition we foreshadowed the arrival of the so called "Woolf Reforms", the Civil Procedure Rules 1998 (CPR). April 1999 was the date when these changes took effect, and there have been no less than 29 sets of amendments to them since then, at the time of writing this. They have revolutionised the way in which the Civil Courts operate. All cases must be dealt with in a way which is just and proportionate to their importance.

At the same time, legal aid was withdrawn from almost all civil proceedings. Therefore legal aid is rarely available to consumers wishing to sue a holiday company whether for breach of contract or for personal injury. Instead, lawyers are able to conduct all litigation on a "no win no fee" basis (conditional fee arrangements, or CFA's). If the case is lost, the lawyer receives nothing; but if it is won, the lawyer will normally expect an enhanced fee. An insurance policy is, available at (in theory) a reasonable price to guard against the risk of having to pay the defendants costs in the event of losing. Bearing in mind the likelihood that the vast majority of package holidays are purchased by people in the middle income bracket who would not normally have qualified for legal aid, the changes to these rules are likely to have found favour among holidaymakers as increasing access to justice. Unfortunately, the complexity of the regulations governing Conditional Fee Agreements is such that satellite litigation challenging the validity of various forms of CFA, has proliferated. The anger and despair this has generated, combined with a strange judicial antipathy to litigation, has probably in fact reduced access to justice. The authorities regard it as healthy that many fewer cases are brought, and settlement of disputes is on the rise; and they are right, as long as the reason for settlement is positive and not borne out of a fear that the Courts will no longer willingly assist claimants or defendants to enforce their rights.

As an alternative a consumer who wishes to avoid recourse to lawyers at all can do so by limiting the size of his claim within the limits of the ABTA Arbitration Scheme or the small claims track of the County Court.

Court Or Arbitration?

The consumer is faced with a choice—to start a court action or to submit his claim to arbitration. Arbitration in this context means arbitration that exists outside the ordinary court system.

There are several arbitration schemes administered by the Chartered Institute of Arbitrators of which the best known is the ABTA scheme. Indeed it is by far the most heavily used consumer arbitration scheme in the UK. This allows claims of up to £5,000 per person or £15,000 per booking form to be referred to arbitration, to which ABTA members have to agree. Small personal injury claims of up to £1,000 can be handled under this scheme, as part of a general quality complaint. From April 2003 there are proposals to bring all personal injury claims within the scheme.

The scheme has several advantages:

- It is cheap. Fees are comparable with going to court and indeed less where the claim is at about the average value of £1500.
- It is relatively quick.
- As the arbitrator decides the case merely by reading the papers, there is none of the ordeal of giving live evidence in Court; about 80 per cent of claims result in an award to the consumer.
- An appeal (a review by a senior arbitrator) can be made by either party for any reason; in the Courts, appeals need permission and can only be on the grounds of error of law or serious procedural error.

There are, however, two disadvantages for a claimant:

- Merely reading the papers will almost certainly not have the same emotional impact upon the arbitrator as seeing and hearing the holidaymaker live in court will have for the judge. Also, many people have difficulty expressing themselves cogently in writing.
- "HolidayWhich?" magazine conducted a survey which

> showed that if there is a good claim, judges will generally award higher compensation on average than arbitrators. (Holiday Which, September 1996, pp.184–187.)

Travel companies, of course, do not get a choice—they must deal with whichever procedure the consumer has elected to pursue. Perhaps surprisingly, many travel companies prefer the court system feeling that, if they have a valid defence, it is easier to persuade a judge who is sitting in front of them. The judge will invariably draw attention to any particular points that concern him, and these can then be addressed. By contrast, one never knows what points impress or upset an arbitrator.

If the consumer chooses arbitration, he or she must write out a full account of all their complaints and submit this together with copies of all supporting documents. The respondent travel company then writes out its full defence, again with any relevant documents, and submits these. The claimant is allowed to respond to any points a rising out of the defence. Then all the papers are placed in front of the arbitrator, who issues a written decision. Any award made can be enforced, if necessary, through the courts. (See [1994] TLJ 35–42 for three separate accounts of the arbitration process—allowance should be made for the now increased ambit of the scheme as set out above. See also Munro, "Arbitration Review Procedure: Fear of the Unknown", [2002] ITLJ 195 for an account of the review.)

As an alternative to taking action themselves some consumers will complain to their trading standards department. Should the case be suitable for a criminal prosecution, and the travel company is found guilty, the prosecution can ask the magistrates to order the defendant to pay compensation. Whether the court does this, and if so, in what amount, is something of a lottery. (Powers of Criminal Courts Act 2000.)

The Road To Court

The days when parties could simply rush off to Court are gone. The procedure laid down by the Pre-Action Protocols must be followed before proceedings are issued. The purpose of the Protocols is, by early exchange of information, to encourage settlement; but if settlement proves impossible, then at least the parties are better prepared for the speed of the timetable which a Court will fix in proceedings.

The most relevant Protocols for our purposes are the personal injury Pre-Action Protocol, and the new Disease and Illness Protocol. Although work has been done on the preparation of a dedicated holiday claims Pre-Action Protocol, that work has not been completed and its future is uncertain at the time of writing.

The Protocols encourage:

- The Claimant to set out the reasons for his claim (and particulars of his loss or injury) in detail.
- The Defendant to admit liability where appropriate. If denying liability, the Defendant must state why and also disclose all relevant documents in his possession at that stage.
- The Defendant to formally admit/deny liability within three months. Where however the incident complained of took place overseas, that period is extended to a maximum of six months.
- The joint selection of experts wherever possible. Parties who fail to find common ground in the choice of expert are likely to have to explain their reasons to a Court at a later date, if the case does not settle.
- The adoption of a standard form of directions for holiday claims (set out in the CPR—Practice Direction 27) brought within the small claims track and, in summary, provides for disclosure of documents including photographs and videos, and the exchange of signed witness statements.

There is a County Court in almost every town of substance. There are somewhat fewer offices (Registries) of the High Court. Every personal injury action where the claim is valued at £50,000 or less must be started in the County Court and not the High Court. If a claim for personal injuries is issued in the High court, it must contain a statement that the claim is worth £50,000 or more. There are penalties laid down for abusing this system. In practice, claims well into six figures are routinely started in the County Court. The unified rules of the CPR make the difference between Courts negligible anyway.

It follows that almost every claim against holiday companies will proceed in the County Court.

The claim can be started in any County Court—usually the one most convenient for the Claimant's home or work. Holiday claims are generally what is called "unliquidated", *i.e.* not a claim for a fixed sum of money, but for compensation which the court must assess. The action should therefore continue in the Claimant's home court.

On receipt of a Claim Form, the Defendant has 14 days in which to lodge at Court his Defence—28 days if he lodges at Court the Acknowledgement of Service form received with the Claim Form, within 14 days. The Defence (and indeed the Particulars of Claim before it) must be verified by a "Statement of Truth". This makes the parties accountable for the truth of their claim or Defence. Signing (or authorising the signature of) a Statement of Truth without an honest belief in the facts stated is a contempt of Court punishable by imprisonment.

The Court will then send out an Allocation Questionnaire to each party, with a strict time limit for completion and return. This is a vital document. On the basis of the answers given, the District Judge will decide, often without a hearing, what steps are to be taken in the action. These will include:—

(a) Allocation to one of the three tracks. This is usually done on the basis of the true value of the claim as assessed by the District Judge, although there are other criteria. The small claims track is the normal track for claims valued at £5,000 or less. This includes personal injury claims, but on a more limited basis—they can only be referred to the small claims track if the amount of compensation (general damages) for pain and suffering will not exceed £1,000 as part of an overall claim not exceeding £5,000.

Claims which exceed the small claims limit but have a value of less than £15,000 are normally allocated to the fast track. Claims too large or complex for the fast track will be allocated to the multi track.

(b) Orders will be made for disclosure by each party to the other of relevant documents, and a mutual exchange of witness statements; and for limits on the number of expert witnesses, indeed frequently directing that any expert evidence should be given by a jointly selected or instructed expert. Expert evidence is rare on the small claims track; on the fast track any expert evidence at trial will normally be in the form of a written report, and therefore it is important for the parties to take advantage of the right to challenge written expert evidence by asking the expert questions in writing. In the multi track it is still quite common for experts to attend Court and be cross examined, and it is more common for each party to be allowed their own choice of expert.

In ordinary cases, the most common type of experts needed are medical experts to deal with injury/illness claims, and also engineering or other liability expert evidence as to whether the hotel complied with local standards, or whether, *e.g.* a lift, or a swimming pool filter, were operating properly.

(c) A hearing date (with a time limit given by the Court) will normally be fixed in the small claims track; in the other tracks a "trial window", usually a period of three weeks, will be fixed (which in the fast track will be not more than 30 weeks away) and, at a later date, the parties must indicate any days within the trial window which are inconvenient for the trial to take place. Fast track trials will not exceed one day.

A Claimant must in practice decide whether to limit the claim to a figure within the small claims procedure. Sometimes the decision is easy—for example, a minor complaint about a cheap package. Often it is not so clear cut.

The major advantage of using the small claims system is that, unlike the usual case in English law, the loser does not have to pay the legal costs of the winner. The maximum which the losing party can be ordered to pay is a sum up to £50 of the loss of earnings of the opposite party or a witness, plus the actual travel and subsistence expenses of the opposite party or witness. In addition, if the defendant loses, he can be ordered to pay a court fee or other costs which are marked on the claim form (there are some rare exceptions to these rules—see CPR, Pt 27. 14).

This means that in most cases the consumer can safely launch proceedings for up to £5,000 without having to fear the fact that he or she is taking on a large corporation which can afford lawyers. On the other hand, if the case turns out to be quite difficult, the Claimant will still have to soldier on without legal assistance, or pay for it out of his own pocket. On balance, however, the advantages outweigh the disadvantages providing the claim is not worth substantially more than £5,000.

It is not possible for a defendant to make a payment into court in a small claims case; not even a formal so-called "Part 36 offer"; but presumably the court will still take into account any "without prejudice" written offer of settlement made by the defendant in deciding what orders for witnesses expenses, etc., to make at the end of the hearing.

The hearing itself is generally very informal but there is an enormous variety in approach from court to court, and indeed from District Judge to District Judge within the courts. However, some judges conduct a matter in a fairly formal way, so that the only difference from a full trial is that it takes place in a private room and without fancy legal robes (but note: the public can attend if there is room). Other judges take the case by the scruff of the neck and virtually say to one party or the other, "Well I've read the papers and you are going to have a job to persuade me that you are in the right—what have you got to say?". Most judges come somewhere between these two extremes. It is a fairly rough and ready form of justice, and litigants should not arrive expecting a really thorough examination of the issues. Many courts list a number of hearings to take place at the same time, and the District Judge is under enormous pressure to complete the hearings quickly. At the very least, the judge must allow cross-examination of the other party and his witnesses (*Chilton v Saga Holidays plc* [1986] 1 All E.R. 841, CA) although this can be limited. Furthermore, the judge must give reasons for his decision. As we have already seen there are limited rights to appeal to the Circuit Judge, the only grounds being that the District Judge made an error of law or serious error of procedure. Permission to appeal is needed, and should be sought in the first instance from the District Judge at the end of the hearing.

Preparing For Trial

Fast or Multi–Track Trials are a formal business. Unlike in small claims witnesses give evidence on oath. They will be cross-examined, and there will be full opening and closing speeches, (though with time limits), legal submissions, etc. Subject to obtaining permission, there are the same limited rights of appeal as we saw above from the District Judge to the Circuit Judge and from the Circuit Judge to a High Court Judge (in Fast Track) or to the Court of Appeal.

The loser can expect to be ordered to pay the legal costs of the winner. The costs are often likely to be a four figure sum in Fast-Track, or five in Multi-Track. Accurate costs estimates must be filed in advance. Costs therefore become a significant consideration in deciding the tactics of the case. Most defendants will, if they feel there is weakness in their case, make a payment into court (a Part 36 Payment) and the Claimant will recover legal costs only up to the date of the payment in if the judge ultimately awards less than the payment in; and thereafter the Claimant will be ordered to pay the defendant's costs. As these latter costs include the costs of trial, by far the most expensive part of any litigation, the Claimant ends up substantially out of pocket. A carefully calculated payment into court is therefore the greatest weapon in the hands of the defendant travel company, as it is only a brave or foolhardy Claimant who presses on in the face of it. If of course the Claimant is awarded more than the payment into court, the defendant will have to pay all his legal costs throughout. Please note that although we use the phrase "all his legal costs", in fact the costs you can recover from the other party rarely exceed 75 per cent to 80 per cent of the bill the Claimant may receive from his own lawyers. There are several reasons for this, some more worthy than others, but they tend to underline the wise words of a Court of Appeal judge who commented "litigation is not an activity which has contributed markedly to the happiness of mankind". (For advice on how to calculate or judge a payment into court see Chapter 10 on remedies which deals in some detail with damages.)

In cases run under a Conditional Fee Agreement (see above), the amount of percentage uplift allowed to a successful Claimant's lawyer, and of the insurance premium, fall to be argued about. At present there are widely differing views as to appropriate figures.

Additional Points

- Specific rules deal with class or group actions, which the Courts used to struggle to fit within their existing rules. This is of particular interest in holiday law, where there is an increasing trend towards class actions where for example a large number of people have been affected by a bad holiday hotel, or given food poisoning or injured in a coach accident.
- A Defendant tour operator can usually join in a supplier, *e.g.* a foreign hotel (or say the parents of a child Claimant, *cf. Roberts v Ibero Travel* 2001 dealt with in Chapter Five), as an additional party (Part 20 Defendant) and thereby obtain an indemnity for a contribution to the claim.
- There is greater emphasis on encouraging parties to refer their dispute to alternative dispute resolution (ADR), *cf. Dunnett v Railtrack* [2002] 2 All ER 850 where a successful party in the Court of Appeal was refused costs because it had declined to participate in a mediation.

Practical Tips To Help You Win Your Case

(i) Photographs

Judges frequently joke in holiday cases that it would be advisable to take a "judicial view" of the site—in other words the whole court travel out to see the location being complained of. Mercifully for the purses of those funding the litigation, this rarely actually happens (but see *Osborne & Others v Malta Sun Holidays* August 18, 1998, Birmingham County Court, where the parties and the judge and their advisors all visited the hotel in Malta at the centre of the dispute. For comment see Mason "Consumer Claims—The Worm Turns" [1998] ITLJ 106). The next best evidence available to the judge is photographs—indeed they are often the most compelling evidence available.

Many consumers are already aware of how important it is to take photographs of their complaints. This is so if they wish to demonstrate a dirty room, or intrusive building works, or a scruffy beach; it is doubly so if the claim concerns injuries sustained in an accident. Photographs should be taken immediately before the scene changes. Take for example an accident or near drowning in the deep end of the swimming pool. There may be no notices up with depth markings, or sudden hidden changes of depth. After the accident has happened, hotel management may well move quickly to put these things right—so immediate photographs are essential.

Of course the same applies for a defending tour operator. Perhaps there are notices up with depth markings, or notices warning parents that children should not swim without supervision. Consumers may deny that they ever saw any such signs. If photographs are taken well after the event, it gives the plaintiffs (and some willing judges) an opportunity to suggest that things were altered after the accident.

Video evidence is frequently used by both sides too, in particular if it is important to show perspective, or to pan round a wide area, or of course if any moving parts were involved in an accident, *e.g.* a chairlift to the beach which malfunctioned in one case. Because videos have a soundtrack too, consumers often use them to demonstrate building work or traffic noise. In addition, many cameras, video and still have the valuable feature that they automatically put the date on the film.

Ironically, the Claimant's photographs can be a useful weapon for the defendants, particularly in quality complaints. It is all too easy for the Claimant to stand in the witness box complaining bitterly about what a miserable time they had on holiday. Their holiday of a lifetime was ruined by some trivial defects in their bedroom. It is all too difficult for the travel company to contradict this in evidence, and the judge is left with not much option but to accept the Claimant's evidence. However, if the defendant insists upon the Claimants disclosing all their holiday photographs, and not just the one or two showing the bare wires in the bedroom, they may show a very different story of happy faces, sun drenched beaches, excursions, nightclubs, etc. giving the judge a true picture of what the holiday was like. (The second author once asked for all the plaintiff's photographs to be disclosed only to receive an extremely abusive response for wanting to view snaps of the Claimant's wife topless on the beach!)

(ii) Physical Evidence

It may be important to preserve physical evidence, possibly for an eventual trial. In the case of *Hoffman v Intasun Holidays Limited* (1990, High Court, unreported) the plaintiff was a young lady who badly injured her leg on what she claimed to be defective swimming pool steps. The steps themselves mysteriously disappeared shortly afterwards. Fortunately for Intasun, this case was decided before the extended liability in the 1990 ABTA Code of Conduct and the PTR, and they won the case. Nowadays, the absence of the steps might have made all the difference between winning and losing.

In one case also attended by the second author, a Claimant giving evidence was complaining that the window in her bedroom had been too small to let in decent light. To emphasise her point she delved into the bag she had with her in the witness box and suddenly pulled from it, with a flourish, the window itself, which she had removed from the hotel! This may be going to extremes.

(iii) Witnesses

Many consumers are very organised. If a major quality problem (*e.g.* damp or cold) affects a holiday hotel, mass meetings of guests are held, committees are formed, petitions written out and names and addresses exchanged for future mutual aid as witnesses. Such evidence can be very telling at trial, although evidence by Mr Smith that his own bedroom was defective is not really evidence in support of a breach of contract as alleged by Mrs Jones about her bedroom—it is better if Mr Smith has first hand experience of the plaintiff's bedroom himself. As has already been said, there is an increasing trend towards class actions by groups of dissatisfied or injured holidaymakers.

Holiday companies, by contrast, face a number of difficulties in this area. If an accident occurs in a factory in front of a group of workers, most of that group may still be together months or even years later. It is in the nature of holidays that witnesses are together for only a short time. In one case, a young man told the representative in front of a number of other clients that he injured his ankle while dancing in a disco. Subsequently he claimed in court that he sustained the injury because of a rocky flagstone around the swimming pool. By the time the action commenced, the representative could not remember who the other clients were. For the judge, it would be simply one person's word against another.

Another problem travel companies face is the expense and difficulty of bringing overseas witnesses to trial in England—hoteliers, swimming pool maintenance staff, even the defendant's own representatives. Technology, allowing video link evidence from overseas, would be an answer if the Courts ever receive their long promised funding. Even identifying visitors in this seasonal business can be difficult after the event. A particular difficulty surrounds the eviction of holidaymakers from their hotel for misbehaviour. The burden of proof lies on the tour operator to prove that the eviction was justified—*Spencer v Cosmos*, *The Times*, December 6, 1989 (CA) (See also Chapter Ten). Inevitably, the incident giving rise to the eviction has happened in the middle of the night when the only person on duty was a seasonal night porter whose entire name (to the best of anyone's recollection) was Jose. Fortunately, for them, tour operators are becoming more aware of the need to plan for litigation. Training courses for overseas representatives explain the need to obtain statements immediately from the people concerned, without waiting several months to see if a claim is issued by the consumer.

In travel cases, as in any litigation, favourable evidence you can obtain from "the other side" is worth ten times as much as evidence from your natural supporters. Look at it this way: when a judge looks at his list for the day and sees a holiday case on it he knows even before the case starts what he is in for. He is going to hear a Claimant whinging on about what a miserable time he had, and then he is going to hear a holiday representative say how absolutely fantastic everything was. He knows he is probably going to find for the Claimant unless the Claimant is intrinsically unbelievable, but he will probably reduce the damages to allow for probable exaggeration by the Claimant. All this the judge knows before he starts. What, however, is really going to wake the judge up is the unexpected—for example, a statement put in evidence by the Claimant and signed by the defendant's representative confirming that everything was truly awful—or by an official of the local Tourist Board; or on the other side, if the defendant calls another consumer who was there at the time who will say that they had a fantastic holiday, spoilt only the endless whinging of Mr and Mrs Claimant. Such evidence is gold dust to the tour operator.

It is, of course, possible to serve in written form the evidence of any witness who is overseas, under the provisions of the Civil Evidence Act 1995. Indeed the rule against hearsay in civil proceedings was virtually abolished when this Act came into force for actions commenced after January 1997. This can be useful for filling in one or two fringe details. As the major defence evidence, it is useless. Imagine: there in the court room are the Claimants shedding tears in the witness box about what a terrible time they had, and the only thing the defendants have to put against this is a piece of paper! Which way is the judge going to decide the case? Come to that, which way would you decide the case? One should never underestimate the extent to which holiday cases are an emotional experience for all concerned.

(iv) Expert witnesses

In ordinary holiday cases, these are almost unknown—after all we are all experts on holidays. In an illness or injury claim, medical evidence is required. This point is sometimes missed by a Claimant where there are a large number of allegations, one of which is that they suffered sickness and diarrhoea, or an attack of asthma, as a consequence of some problem with the holiday; or suffered depression afterwards (as distinct from mere disappointment). Engineers or other experts may be required to explain the reasons for an accident, or the appropriate local standards.

(v) Witness statements

It will be remembered that for County Court (and High Court) trials, the exchange of witness statements is compulsory. No party is allowed to call a witness unless the substance of what that witness is to say is contained in an exchanged witness statement. This rule applies equally to fast track and multi-track cases. This puts a very high premium on early preparation of witness statements which should also be thorough. In theory, the statements should be prepared by lawyers. This will generally be possible for the Claimants, but often not practicable for the defendants where witnesses live or work overseas. This is why holiday representatives are usually trained in writing statements themselves. The defendant statements must deal positively with each of the complaints of the consumer. There is a tendency to respond in detail to the first four or five complaints, at which point the witness appears to get bored and ignore the remaining 12 complaints. This is not good enough. It is a mistake to assume that the Claimant's complaints appear in decreasing order of seriousness. The judge will look at each complaint separately, and will also look at the effect on the holiday of the totality of the complaints.

In practice it is difficult to persuade a court to allow new witness statements to be served after the formal exchange has taken place. This entails making an application and attending court, a considerable extra expense. "Difficult" becomes "impossible" if a trial date would have to be adjourned as a result of the new evidence.

Exchange of witness statements at an early stage adds markedly to the cost of litigation. It is part of the trend of costs being "front loaded" now, which concerns the judiciary. Receiving the other side's statements is an exciting moment. You either suffer that sinking feeling on discovering some point completely overlooked in one's own statements; or there is the elation of realising how thin the opponent's case really is.

It is normal for the judge to order that witness statements shall stand as the witness' evidence in chief, thereby shortening the trial. In practice a few supplementary questions are asked, to deal with the other side's case—or at least to allow the witness to find his/her voice in the witness box prior to the ordeal of cross-examination.

(vi) Documents

The booking form invoice and brochure will generally be available, if relevant. Other types of document commonly relevant to holiday claims are menus, sketch plans and vouchers for out of pocket expenses (*e.g.* restaurant bills or at least credit card statements for meals eaten out where the allegation is that the hotel restaurant was abysmal). An accident might happen during a risky excursion (jeep safari, midnight tobogganing, etc). In that case, a leaflet which did (or did not) mention the risks involved or indeed the identity of the excursion promoter would be relevant. Such documents are in circulation for a very short time and need to be preserved immediately. The tour operator by contrast may have prepared a health and safety report on a hotel which is relevant to prove or disprove allegations. (See *Patrick v Cosmosair*, March 5, 2001, Manchester CC as discussed in Chapman, "Excursions: Tour

Operators and the Negligence of Local Suppliers" [2002] ITLJ 123).

Computer print-outs from the travel company showing that the low or non-existent number of other complaints about a hotel are sometimes used. They may influence a judge who is not sure what to make of the Claimant's evidence.

Finally, many tour operators, from an excess of caution or a fear of the laws trickeries, mark every single letter which they send out "without prejudice". If in fact the letter does not consist of an attempt to resolve the dispute outside the court it can still be referred to in court by the Claimant at the hearing.

Chapter Eighteen
Air and Sea Travel

Introduction

Air travel

Although this book is primarily about package holiday law and a consumer's rights in relation to tour operators and travel agents it will have become apparent that it is necessary to have at least an elementary grasp of holidaymakers' rights in respect of air travel in order to have a complete picture of their legal position. The reason for this is twofold. First, the great bulk of holidaymakers travel to their destinations by air, whether as part of a package or independently, and this will directly or indirectly give rise to a legal relationship with the air carrier that carries them. Secondly, the Package Travel Regulations make specific reference to the Warsaw Convention in Regulation 15 in order to permit tour operators to limit their liability.

With this in mind it is our intention in the first section of this chapter to sketch out briefly two major areas of air law that are relevant to holidaymakers. These are the Warsaw Convention and the Denied Boarding Regulations. The Warsaw Convention sets out a passengers rights against a carrier in respect of death or injury, delay to passengers or baggage and loss, damage or delay to baggage. The Denied Boarding Regulations provide compensation to passengers who are "bumped" when their plane is overbooked.

It must be said at the outset that at the time of writing the Warsaw Convention is about to be superseded by the Montreal Convention. It is our intention therefore not only to set out the law as it stands at present but also to indicate briefly what changes will be taking place. It also needs to be said that air law consists of a vast body of law in its own right and this chapter only scratches the surface. For more detailed coverage you are referred to the highly respected standard text—"Shawcross and Beaumont on Air Law" by Martin, McLean, Martin, Margo and Balfour or to "Warsaw Convention" by Giemulla, Schmid and Ehlers both of which are highly recommended and which we drew on heavily when writing this chapter. A more manageable text is "Contracts of Carriage by Air" by Malcolm Clarke.

Sea travel

Given the growing importance of the cruise industry we have also added a short section on the Athens Convention which covers international carriage by sea. The Athens convention, while not identical in format to the Warsaw Convention, has many similarities, but interestingly there is a the paucity of case law in this area compared to Warsaw. A search for reported cases in the last 20 years revealed only a handful of cases.

The Warsaw System

1. An overview

Air travel is predominantly international in nature and as a consequence it has come to be regulated by a series of international treaties stretching back to the Warsaw Convention. Where non-international carriage is concerned that will be regulated by the domestic law of the country within which the flight takes place.

The Warsaw Convention was agreed in Warsaw in 1929 at a conference of 32 states. It entered into force in 1933. Since then approximately 130 states have become signatories—referred to in the Convention as "High Contracting Parties". The Convention created a comprehensive code of liability for death and injury to passengers, loss of or damage to baggage, and delay to passengers and baggage based upon the presumed fault of the carrier. However the price to be paid for this reversed burden of proof was that carriers were allowed to limit their liability to relatively small sums—the value of which has been eroded further by inflation in the ensuing years.

The original Convention was amended in 1955 by the Hague Protocol which entered into force in 1963. The Hague Protocol made two important changes. First it changed the rules on claiming limitation of liability. Under the Warsaw Convention a carrier would lose the benefit of the limitations on liability in the Convention if it had acted with wilful misconduct. Under the amended Convention the benefit would be lost if the carrier intended to cause damage or acted recklessly with knowledge that damage would probably result. Secondly it doubled the limits of liability. So for personal injury or death the limit was raised from 125,000 "Poincare" francs to 250,000 "Poincare" francs. As this unit of currency no longer exists the response of the UK government is to base liability upon the SDR (Special Drawing Right), a unit of currency based upon a basket of international currencies. The current conversion rates are to be found in The Carriage by Air (Sterling Equivalents) Order 1999 SI/2881. Using the SDR as the basis of conversion the figures arrived at are:

Amount in francs	**Sterling Equivalent (£)**
250	19.54
5000	390.71
125000	9,767.83
250000	19,535.66

Unfortunately the US government did not feel that enough had been done to raise limits and therefore it refused to sign the Hague Protocol. This has had the effect of creating two liability regimes under the Convention. There are those states which have signed both the Warsaw Convention and the Hague Protocol and therefore international flights between those countries are subject to the Warsaw/Hague regime. Then there are those states such as the US which have signed only the Warsaw Convention and therefore international carriage to and from such states is subject only to the unamended Warsaw regime. (There is a minority third regime consisting of states which have signed none of the treaties.) Superimposed on both treaties is the Guadalajara Convention of 1961 which came into force in 1964. This convention is designed to clarify the meaning of "carrier", a term which was not defined in either of the other conventions.

Subsequent to 1955 there were a number of initiatives around the world which attempted to address the problem of the low limits of liability. The US government for instance imposed the "Montreal Agreement" on carriers flying to and from the US under which they agreed to higher limits. European governments did much the same to their carriers and in 1995 IATA carriers agreed the IATA Intercarrier Agreement under which IATA carriers also agreed to raise the limits of liability and adjust the burden of proof in the passenger's favour. As a consequence a patchwork of liability regimes emerged dependent upon which airline a passenger was flying and to which countries. At one end of the scale a passenger might find themselves limited to the sums found in the original Warsaw Convention while at the other end liability was strict and almost unlimited. Also having the status of international conventions are the four Montreal Protocols of 1975 which have only recently come into effect and which make some amendments to the Warsaw Convention, both the amended and unamended versions.

In an attempt to bring some uniformity to this increasingly complex situation the International Civil Aviation Organisation, ICAO, called an international conference in 1999 which agreed a new convention—the Montreal Convention (not to be confused with the Montreal Agreement or indeed the Montreal Protocols). This convention has widespread support, including that of the US, and it is hoped that sufficient ratifications will be obtained in the near future for it to enter into force soon.

Prior to this, however, the EU, impatient with progress, made a unilateral decision to move forward on reforming the liability limits and in Council Regulation on Air Carrier Liability in the Event of Accidents (No. 2027/97) it imposed a much more onerous liability regime on "community air carriers", *i.e.* carriers licensed by member states of the EU. The scheme of the Regulation closely follows the Warsaw Convention and has already been prospectively amended so that when the Montreal Convention comes into force the amended Regulation (No. 889/2002) can be immediately implemented. In the UK the Regulation has been implemented by the Air Carrier Liability Order 1998 (SI 1998/1751).

2. Universality

The full title of the Warsaw Convention is the Convention for the Unification of Certain Rules Relating to International Carriage by Air. It is this aspect of the Convention that is perhaps its greatest success. Most nations of the world have become signatories to the Convention and this has had the effect of creating an international regime where if a plaintiff wishes to bring an action against an airline he can do so in the knowledge that the rules on liability will be the same wherever the action is brought.

In the words of Professor Bin Cheng.

> "The effectiveness of this international code is ensured by its being comprehensive, mandatory and exclusive. It is comprehensive in that it covers the carriage of passengers, baggage and cargo, and does so in detail. It is mandatory in the sense that its terms are applicable to a Warsaw carriage irrespective of the wishes or conduct of the parties and may not be modified even by consent, except in favour of the passenger or shipper in specified instances. It is exclusive in the sense that it excludes other grounds of recovery in law." (Air Transport and the Consumer: A need for change, National Consumer Council, HMSO, 1986, p. 208.)

Much of what Professor Bin Cheng said remains true despite the difficulties created by the manoeuvrings over the limits of liability. It is still the case that the basic rules of liability apply to the vast majority of international flights. The controversy that the Warsaw system generates is over the fact that it has become a lottery as to the level of compensation one receives in the case of an accident.

Much less controversial but nonetheless of great concern to those who are affected is the issue of compensation for loss, damage and delay to baggage where the universally applied limits are derisory but where the Montreal Convention will offer much more generous compensation when it is implemented.

As well as having universal application the Convention is also exclusive. Once a case falls within the Convention then no remedy will be availabel at common law (*Sidhu v British Airways* [1997] A.C. 430).

3. The position for UK-based travellers

The UK is party to both the Warsaw Convention and the Hague Protocol. The Warsaw Convention was originally incorporated into English law by the Carriage by Air Act 1932 and the Hague Protocol by the Carriage by Air Act 1961. The 1961 Act repealed the 1932 Act when it was brought into force in 1967 by the Carriage by Air Acts (Application of Provisions) Order 1967—so that Warsaw Convention carriage was replaced by Warsaw/Hague carriage. However in order to take account of those nations such as the US that had not ratified the Hague Protocol a Schedule to the 1967 Order preserved the unamended Warsaw Convention rules for travel to such countries.

As far as domestic carriage is concerned and carriage to countries which are not party to either Warsaw or the Hague the 1967 Order effectively makes such carriage subject to the Warsaw/Hague rules.

Thus as far as UK law is concerned there are two regimes:

Warsaw Carriage Rules which apply to flights to:

- countries which have only ratified the Warsaw Convention, and

Warsaw/Hague Carriage Rules which apply to flights to:

- countries which have ratified both the Warsaw Convention and the Hague Protocol

- purely domestic flights, and
- countries which have ratified neither Convention.

Grafted on top of these rules however are the Montreal Protocol amendments and the EU Regulation on Air Carriers' Liability which imposes different liability rules on community carriers.

Thus for travellers flying from or within the UK the first problem is to ascertain which set of rules applies—a task which is not easily accomplished.

4. The meaning of "international carriage"

The Warsaw Convention only covers "international carriage". This is defined in Article 1 of the Convention as

> "(2) ... any carriage in which, according to the agreement between the parties, the place of departure and the place of destination, whether or not there be a break in the carriage or a transhipment, are within the territory of a single High Contracting Party if there is an agreed stopping place within the territory of another State, even if that State is not a High Contracting Party. Carriage between two points within the territory of a single High Contracting Party without an agreed stopping place within the territory of another State is not international carriage for the purposes of this Convention.
>
> (3) Carriage to be performed by several successive air carriers is deemed, for the purposes of this Convention, to be one undivided carriage if it has been regarded by the parties as a single operation, whether it had been agreed upon under the form of a single contract or of a series of contracts, and it does not lose its international character merely because one contract or a series of contracts is to be performed entirely within the territory of the same State."

Thus a flight from England to France would be covered by the Convention because both parties are signatories to the Convention—or High Contracting Parties to use the terminology of the Convention. Likewise flights from England to Spain, Greece, Turkey and Italy, all popular holiday destinations, would be covered by the Convention. However Thailand, another popular destination for British holidaymakers, is not a signatory to the Convention. One's immediate reaction to that might be to conclude that it is not covered by the Convention. This would be the case if it was just a one way flight. However if it was a round trip, as most holiday flights are, then it would be covered. This is because the definition of international carriage encompasses those flights where the place of departure and the place of destination are within the territory of a High Contracting Party so long as there is an agreed stopping place outside the territory of that state—even if the agreed stopping place is not within the territory of a High Contracting Party.

Similarly if the flight to Thailand was just one leg of a journey from London to Sydney then the flight would be international carriage covered by the Convention because the definition of successive carriage in Article 1(3) would cover it. Equally, so long as the parties agreed that it was a single operation, the feeder legs of the London-Sydney journey would also be international carriage—for instance the connecting flights from Newcastle upon Tyne to Heathrow and Sydney to Newcastle NSW. For a discussion of the meaning of "international carriage" in an English court see *Grein v Imperial Airways, Limited* [1937] 1 KB 50 (C.A.) where it was held that a return flight from Croydon to Brussels via Antwerp was international carriage even though at the time Belgium was not a party to the Warsaw Convention.

Purely domestic carriage and international carriage to a state which is not a High Contracting Party is not covered by the Convention. The liability in such cases will be decided by domestic law or according to the principles of private international law—but see the section above on how this is treated in the UK.

One further complication as already indicated is that some states have signed up to both the Warsaw Convention and the Hague Protocol but there are other states that are only signatories to Warsaw but not the Hague. Thus if I am travelling on a one-way flight to the US from the UK then my rights are determined by Warsaw alone, not Warsaw/Hague. However if the flight is a return trip from London to London via New York then this is Warsaw/Hague.

5. Main provisions of the Warsaw Convention

The carriers liability to passengers, the limitations on that liability and the defences available are set out in Chapter III of the Convention. We will examine the main provisions in turn. Note that the provisions cited in this section are those of the Warsaw Convention as amended by the Hague Protocol and the Montreal Protocol No. 4. The reason for this is that the book is aimed primarily at UK tourists and that is the regime that will apply to most of them. However we also set out in square brackets and italics below each provision the corresponding provision from the Montreal Convention, in the hope that it will come into force before the next edition of the book is published and will therefore be of some assistance to readers. The changes brought about by the EU Regulation on Air Carrier liability are set out in a separate section.

(a) Death and Injury

Liability

Article 17 provides:

> "The carrier is liable for damage sustained in the event of the death or wounding of a passenger or any other bodily injury suffered by a passenger, if the accident which caused the damage so sustained took place on board the aircraft or in the course of any of the operations of embarking or disembarking.
>
> *[Montreal Convention*
>
> *Article 17.1*
>
> *The carrier is liable for damage sustained in case of death or bodily injury of a passenger upon condition only that the accident which caused the death or injury took place on board the aircraft or in the course of any of the operations of embarking or disembarking.]*"

Note that this is a strict liability, subject to the available defences and the limitation on liability provisions.

To establish liability on the carrier's part to the passenger it has to be established that

- death, wounding or other bodily injury was caused;
- by an accident;
- on board the aircraft or in the course of embarking or disembarking.

The meaning of death and wounding are relatively straightforward but "other bodily injury" has caused problems. The particular problem arises in cases where passengers have suffered mental injury unaccompanied by any physical injury—where there has been an emergency landing or inflight incident etc. International authorities are now predominantly in favour of the view that psychiatric harm or mental injury is not covered by Article 17. In the American case *Eastern Airlines v Floyd* 499 US 530 (1991) it was held by the Supreme Court that there was no liability for purely mental injury. In that case all three engines on an aircraft had simultaneously failed and passengers had been told that the aircraft would have to ditch. In the event the pilot regained control and no one was injured. *Floyd* was followed by *El Al Israel Airlines v Tseng* 119 S Ct 662 (1999) in which the Supreme Court confirmed the decision in *Floyd*. More recently the House of Lords has also come to the same conclusion in two appeals heard at the same time, *Philip King v Bristow Helicopters Limited* and *Kelly Morris v KLM Royal Dutch Airlines* [2002] 2 All E.R. 565. (See Goh, "The Meaning Of 'Bodily Injury' In International Carriage By Air" [2002] ITLJ 139 for a discussion of these cases.)

Accident is another word that has caused problems. It clearly covers crashes and collisions, but will also cover extreme turbulence, sudden unexpected de-pressurisation, and violent touch-downs. It will not cover light or moderate turbulence, routine depressurisation during landing or a merely bumpy or hard landing. Articles falling from overhead lockers, hot drinks being spilled, or the collapse of a seat would all be accidents. The authorities are split on cases of food poisoning.

What would not be an accident is where the passenger faints or suffers a heart attack or an asthmatic attack during the flight where this is not triggered by some external unexpected event. Although in popular terms these might be regarded as accidents they are not classified as accidents under the Convention because they are not caused by something external to the passenger. In *Chaudhari v British Airways* (1997, CA) the plaintiff was a passenger on board one of the defendant's flights. He was a disabled person who already suffered from paralysis to the left side of his body. He sustained further injury when attempting to leave his seat. The court held that the injury was not caused by any unexpected or unusual event external to him, but by his own personal, particular or peculiar reaction to the normal operation of the aircraft. He fell as a result of his pre-existing medical condition and therefore his injury was not caused by an accident within the meaning of Article 17.

Morris v KLM, discussed above in the context of mental injury, also raised the issue of what amounts to an accident. The claimant, a girl of 15, had travelled unaccompanied, on a KLM flight from Kuala Lumpur to Amsterdam and had been indecently assaulted during the flight by a male passenger in the adjoining seat. She suffered clinical depression as a result of the assault and brought an action for damages against the defendant airline claiming that the assault was an "accident" within the ambit of article 17. Referring to the US case of *Air France v Saks* (1985) 470 US 392 in which a similar incident had occurred the Court of Appeal in *Morris* held that the incident was an accident and this decision was not appealed in the House of Lords.

There have been a number of cases recently in which claims have been make against airlines for causing DVT. With one or two exceptions these have all been rejected on the grounds that DVT is not an "accident" within the meaning of the Warsaw Convention. In the UK this was the decision in *Re: Deep Vein Thrombosis and Air Travel Group Litigation* [2002] EWHC 2825 (QB). (For a commentary see Khan "DVT Litigation Fails" [2003] ITLJ 80). Nelson J had this to say:

> "The agreed factual matrix does not disclose an accident under article 17 of the Warsaw Convention. The definition of accident which is to be applied is that set out by the U. S. Supreme Court in *Saks*, followed here in the Court of Appeal in *Morris*, in *Chaudhari*, and approved by the House of Lords in *Morris*.
>
> . . .
>
> The test to be applied is 'a simple criterion of causation by an accident'. That is to be defined as:—
>
> > 'an unexpected or unusual event or happening that is external to the passenger'
>
> The agreed factual matrix does not satisfy this definition. It reveals that no event or happening occurred on the flight which was not ordinary and unremarkable and involved no actions of anyone save for the passenger's reaction to that normal and unremarkable flight. There was no unexpected or unusual event or happening. A culpable act or omission by itself which does not amount to an unusual or unexpected event or happening does not come within the definition of accident."

What amounts to the operations of embarking or disembarking and at what stage they begin and end is not as simple as it appears at first glance. The problem is summed up by Leland:

> "Despite a substantial volume of litigation on the interpretation of Article 17 in both common and civil law jurisdictions, the question has remained clouded in some complexity. One of the greatest impediments to a clear vista has been the strategy of airlines in dealing with actions for compensation for injuries incurred by clients. Essentially the terms of Article 17 have proved to be a chameleon, providing both shield and sword to

potential defendants. If for example an airline thinks it has a very strong defence to a claim of negligence against it then it is in their interest to prove that the Convention does not apply, thus placing an onus on the plaintiff to prove negligence. If, on the other hand, the defendant airline's case is a weak one, they will argue that the Convention does apply, thus limiting the amount of compensation recoverable by the passenger." ([1997] ITLJ 162)

Another reason adding to the complexity is that the limitation period is only two years under the Convention whereas for personal injury at common law it is three years. Thus a plaintiff commencing an action after two years but before three would need to bring his case at common law rather than within the Convention. Proposed changes in the limits of liability under the Convention and in the burden of proof will probably also result in a change of tactics by plaintiffs and defendants.

An Irish case, cited by Leland, contains a statement of the law as it is commonly understood to be at present:

"To make a prima facie case that a particular claim is within Article 17 it must be established (i) that the accident to the passenger is related to a specific flight and (ii) that it happened while the latter was actually entering or about to enter the aircraft, or (iii) if it happened in the terminal building, or otherwise on the airport premises, that the location of the accident is a place where the injured party was obliged to be while in the process of embarkation. Whether or not the location as so defined is within the ambit of Article 17 will depend upon the circumstances of each individual case. The location of the accident is just one of the factors for consideration in determining the scope of the phrase 'any of the operations of embarking" within the meaning of the article.' (Barr J in *Galvin v Aer Rianta*, Irish High Court, October 13, 1993)

The same issue arose in *Phillips v Air New Zealand* [2002] EWHC 800 (Comm), [2002] 1 All E.R. (Comm) 801 where the judge applied the same tests as in the *Galvin* case. (See Saggerson, "Case Comment: *Susan Phillips v Air New Zealand*, [2002] ITLJ 144 for a discussion of this case.)

Defences

Article 20 provides:

"In the case of passengers and baggage, and in the case of damage occasioned by delay in the carriage of cargo, the carrier shall not be liable if he proves that he and his servants and agents have taken all necessary measures to avoid the damage or that it was impossible for him or them to take such measures."

The wording of this provision is significant. It requires that the carrier take *all necessary measures* to avoid the damage. This imposes a greater burden upon the carrier than to take all *reasonable care*. (Note that there is no equivalent to this defence in the Montreal Convention.)

Circumstances where the defence could be invoked would include situations where the aircraft was hit by lightning or affected by clear air turbulence but Shawcross and Beaumont comment that the defence is rarely established. However in *Chisholm v British European Airways* [1963] 1 Lloyd's Rep. 626 the plaintiff failed in her action for personal injuries caused during turbulence after she had left her seat. The crew had warned passengers and told them to remain seated and to fasten their seatbelts. By contrast in *Goldman v Thai Airways International Ltd* [1983] 1 All E.R. 693 the defence failed because no warning had been given to passengers to wear seatbelts despite the presence of turbulence.

A further defence is provided in Article 21:

"If the carrier proves that the damage was caused by or contributed to by the negligence of the injured person the court may, in accordance with the provisions of its own law, exonerate the carrier wholly or partly from his liability.

[Montreal Convention

Article 20—Exoneration

If the carrier proves that the damage was caused or contributed to by the negligence or other wrongful act or omission of the person claiming compensation, or the person from whom he or she derives his or her rights, the carrier shall be wholly or partly exonerated from its liability to the claimant to the extent that such negligence or wrongful act or omission caused or contributed to the damage. When by reason of death or injury of a passenger compensation is claimed by a person other than the passenger, the carrier shall likewise be wholly or partly exonerated from its liability to the extent that it proves that the damage was caused or contributed to by the negligence or other wrongful act or omission of that passenger. This Article applies to all the liability provisions in this Convention, including paragraph 1 of Article 21.]"

Failure to wear a seatbelt after having been warned to do so would fall within this defence. Blackshaw gives the example of a passenger burnt in a fire in the lavatory caused by lighting a cigarette, despite being prohibited from doing so, being caught by this defence.

Exclusion of Liability

Article 23 contains a blanket prohibition on the use of exclusion clauses. It provides:

"(1) Any provision tending to relieve the carrier of liability or to fix a lower limit than that which is laid down in this convention shall be null and void, but the nullity of any such provision shall not involve the nullity of the whole contract, which shall remain subject to the provisions of this convention.

[Montreal Convention

Article 26—Invalidity of Contractual Provisions

Any provision tending to relieve the carrier of liability or to fix a lower limit than that which is laid down in this Convention shall be null and void, but the nullity of any such provision does not involve the nullity of the whole contract, which shall remain subject to the provisions of this Convention.]"

This would be effective to combat most varieties of exclusion clause including those that set short time limits or impose onerous conditions. Shawcross and Beaumont draw attention to the practice of some airlines which require disabled passengers to sign a waiver and suggest that they would be of doubtful effectiveness.

Limitation of Liability

Article 22 provides:

"(1) In the carriage of persons the liability of the carrier for each passenger is limited to the sum of two hundred and fifty thousand francs. . . .

[Montreal Convention

Article 21—Compensation in Case of Death or Injury of Passengers

1. *For damages arising under paragraph 1 of Article 17 not exceeding 100 000 Special Drawing Rights for each passenger, the carrier shall not be able to exclude or limit its liability.*
2. *The carrier shall not be liable for damages arising under paragraph 1 of Article 17 to the extent that they exceed for each passenger 100 000 Special Drawing Rights if the carrier proves that:*
   - *(a) such damage was not due to the negligence or other wrongful act or omission of the carrier or its servants or agents; or*
   - *(b) such damage was solely due to the negligence or other wrongful act or omission of a third party.]*"

According to the The Carriage by Air (Sterling Equivalents) Order 1999 SI/2881 250,000 francs is equivalent to £19,535.66. Thus the maximum recoverable by a passenger is less than £20,000—a sum which is risibly small by today's standards. Fortunately in most cases, either by government action or by voluntary agreement, this limit is not applicable. For UK travellers flying on a "community carrier" there is no limit to liability by virtue of Council Regulation No. 2027/97 on Air Carrier Liability.

When the Limitations do not Apply

Article 3 provides:

"(1) In respect of the carriage of passengers a ticket shall be delivered containing:

- (a) an indication of the places of departure and destination;
- (b) if the places of departure and destination are within the territory of a single High Contracting Party, one or more agreed stopping places being within the territory of another State, an indication of at least one such stopping place;
- (c) a notice to the effect that, if the passenger's journey involves an ultimate destination or stop in a country other than the country of departure, the Warsaw Convention may be applicable and that the Convention governs and in most cases limits the liability of carriers for death or personal injury and in respect of loss of or damage to baggage

(2) The passenger ticket shall constitute *prima facie* evidence of the conclusion and conditions of the contract of carriage. The

absence, irregularity or loss of the passenger ticket does not affect the existence or the validity of the contract of carriage which shall, none the less, be subject to the rules of this Convention. Nevertheless, if, with the consent of the carrier, the passenger embarks without a passenger ticket having been delivered, or it the ticket does not include the notice required by paragraph (1)(c) of this Article, the carrier shall not be entitled to avail himself of the provisions of Article 22.

[Montreal Convention

Article 3—Passengers and Baggage

1. *In respect of carriage of passengers, an individual or collective document of carriage shall be delivered containing:*

   (a) *an indication of the places of departure and destination;*
   (b) *if the places of departure and destination are within the territory of a single State Party, one or more agreed stopping places being within the territory of another State, an indication of at least one such stopping place.*

2. *Any other means which preserves the information indicated in paragraph 1 may be substituted for the delivery of the document referred to in that paragraph. If any such other means is used, the carrier shall offer to deliver to the passenger a written statement of the information so preserved.*
3. *The carrier shall deliver to the passenger a baggage identification tag for each piece of checked baggage.*
4. *The passenger shall be given written notice to the effect that where this Convention is applicable it governs and may limit the liability of carriers in respect of death or injury and for destruction or loss of, or damage to, baggage, and for delay.*
5. *Non-compliance with the provisions of the foregoing paragraphs shall not affect the existence or the validity of the contract of carriage, which shall, nonetheless, be subject to the rules of this Convention including those relating to limitation of liability.]*"

Broadly speaking this requires the carrier to provide the passenger with a ticket containing certain information on it and if either the ticket is not provided or the information is not included than the carrier loses the right to limit his liability.

Given the low limits applicable under the Convention there has, understandably, grown up an extensive body of case law around this provision which we can only hint at in a book of this nature. Cases have turned on *who* the ticket should be delivered to (*Ross v Pan American Airways Inc* (1955) 2 Avi Cas 14,911); *when* it should be delivered (*Mertens v Flying Tiger Line Inc* (1965) 9 Avi Cas 17,475) and *Warren v Flying Tiger Line Inc* (1965) 9 Avi Cas 17,848); *what* constitutes a ticket (*Chan v Korean Airlines Ltd* (1989) 24 Avi Cas 18,221); and *how legible* the notice should be (*Chan*; *Lisi v Alitalia-Linee Italiana SpA* ([1968] 1 Lloyd's Rep. 505).

A further exception to Article 22 is found in Article 25:

> "The limits of liability specified in Article 22 shall not apply if it is proved that the damage resulted from an act of omission of the carrier, his servants or agents, done with intent to cause damage or recklessly and with knowledge that damage would probably result; provided that, in the case of such act or omission of a servant or agent, it is also proved that he was acting within the scope of his employment."

Thus intentional or reckless conduct on the part of the carrier or his servants or agents will deprive him of his ability to limit his liability. In *Goldman v Thai Airways International Ltd* [1983] 1 All E.R. 693 the Court of Appeal held that the test of recklessness was a subjective test, *i.e.* that the pilot had to have actual knowledge that damage would result from his act. It was not enough to show that he should have known. Other jurisdictions however have applied an objective test.

(b) Loss and Destruction of Baggage

Liability for Registered Baggage

Article 18 provides:

> "(1) The carrier is liable for damage sustained in the event of the destruction or loss of, or of damage to, any registered baggage, if the occurrence which caused the damage so sustained took place during the carriage by air.
>
> . . .
>
> (4) The carriage by air within the meaning of the preceding paragraphs comprises the period during which the baggage or

cargo is in the charge of the carrier, whether in an airport or on board an aircraft or in the case of a landing outside an airport, in any place whatsoever.

[Montreal Convention

Article 17—Death and Injury of Passengers—Damage to Baggage

. . .

2. *The carrier is liable for damage sustained in case of destruction or loss of, or of damage to, checked baggage upon condition only that the event which caused the destruction, loss or damage took place on board the aircraft or during any period within which the checked baggage was in the charge of the carrier. However, the carrier is not liable if and to the extent that the damage resulted from the inherent defect, quality or vice of the baggage. In the case of unchecked baggage, including personal items, the carrier is liable if the damage resulted from its fault or that of its servants or agents.*
3. *If the carrier admits the loss of the checked baggage, or if the checked baggage has not arrived at the expiration of twenty-one days after the date on which it ought to have arrived. the passenger is entitled to enforce against the carrier the rights which flow from the contract of carriage.*
4. *Unless otherwise specified, in this Convention the term 'baggage' means both checked baggage and unchecked baggage."*

Note again that, subject to the defences and limitations, this is a strict liability. The elements of the liability are that the carrier is liable if:

- damage or destruction is caused
- to registered baggage
- during the carriage by air.

There must be damage or destruction of the baggage if an action is to fall within this article. Delay to baggage is covered by separate provisions in Article 19.

Registered baggage needs to be distinguished from cargo and from unregistered baggage. As far as holidaymakers are concerned the distinction between baggage and cargo will rarely if ever concern them. In practice, where the distinction does arise, the matter is usually conclusively decided by reference to the documentation provided by the carrier. If a baggage check is issued it is baggage. If an air waybill is issued then it will be cargo. The need to make the distinction arises because different limitations of liability apply and there are different periods of notice for making complaint.

The distinction between registered baggage and unregistered baggage is between that baggage for which the passenger receives a baggage check and hands over control of it to the carrier and that baggage which he retains control of himself and takes onto the aircraft—usually referred to as hand luggage. Again, the reason for needing to make the distinction is because there are different liability limits.

The period during which the liability will arise is defined as the period where the baggage is in charge of the carrier. Usually this will be the period between handing over the baggage at check-in and then recovering it from the carousel at the destination airport. It clearly covers those periods during which the baggage is being dealt with by ground handlers and for whom the carrier is responsible.

Liability for Unregistered Baggage

There is no provision in the Convention which expressly creates liability for damage to, or destruction of, unregistered baggage, although there is a limitation applied to this liability by Article 22(3). The question of liability is therefore a little obscure. Where a passenger has been killed or wounded and there has been incidental damage to baggage Shawcross and Beaumont suggest that this amounts to "damage sustained in the event of death or wounding of a passenger" and therefore there would be liability for the damage to the baggage under Article 17. They also find attractive the reasoning in *Kabbani v International Total Services* 807 F Supp 1073 (DC DofC, 1992) where the court held that where the baggage was in the care of the passenger Article 17 would apply, *i.e.* there would be liability if damage occurred on board the aircraft or during embarkation or disembarkation. However, where the carrier took charge of the baggage, *e.g.* for security purposes then Article 18(2) would apply, *i.e.* the carrier would be liable if the damage took place on board the aircraft or in the airport.

Claiming for Damage to Baggage

In order to recover compensation for damage to baggage the passenger must comply with certain formalities and time limits. Article 26 provides:

"(1) Receipt by the person entitled to the delivery of baggage or goods without complaint shall be prima facie evidence that the same have been delivered in good condition and in accordance with the document of transportation.

(2) In the case of damage, the person entitled to delivery must complain to the carrier forthwith after the discovery of the damage, and, at the latest, within seven days from the date of receipt in the case of baggage and fourteen days from the date of receipt in the case of cargo. In the case of delay the complaint must be made at the latest within twenty-one days from the date on which the baggage or cargo have been placed at his disposal.

(3) Every complaint must be made in writing upon the document of transportation or by separate notice in writing dispatched within the times aforesaid.

(4) Failing complaint within the times aforesaid, no action shall lie against the carrier, save in the case of fraud on his part.

[Montreal Convention

Article 31—Timely Notice of Complaints

1. *Receipt by the person entitled to delivery of checked baggage or cargo without complaint is prima facie evidence that the same has been delivered in good condition and in accordance with the document of carriage or with the record preserved by the other means referred to in paragraph 2 of Article 3 and paragraph 2 of Article 4.*
2. *In the case of damage, the person entitled to delivery must complain to the carrier forthwith after the discovery of the damage, and, at the latest, within seven days from the date of receipt in the case of checked baggage and fourteen days from the date of receipt in the case of cargo. In the case of delay, the complaint must be made at the latest within twenty-one days from the date on which the baggage or cargo have been placed at his or her disposal.*
3. *Every complaint must be made in writing and given or dispatched within the times aforesaid.*
4. *If no complaint is made within the times aforesaid, no*

action shall lie against the carrier, save in the case of fraud on its part.]"

One important point to note is that in the case of destruction of baggage, as opposed to damage, no notice is required. In other cases the passenger must adhere to strict requirements:

- the complaint must be made in writing
- to the carrier
- within seven days, or in the case of delayed baggage, within 21 days of receipt.

It is important therefore for holidaymakers to make prompt complaint about any damage or risk losing their rights altogether. These conditions will apply to both registered and unregistered baggage as Article 26(2) makes no distinction between the two.

One trap for the unwary is that Article 26(2) covers partial loss as well as damage. In *Fothergill v Monarch Airlines Ltd* [1980] 2 All E.R. 696 the plaintiff complained within the time limit about damage to his suitcase but did not complain about the loss of contents which he only discovered later. It was held that he could not recover for the contents.

Defences

The defences in Article 20 (all necessary measures) and Article 21 (contributory negligence) apply to baggage as they do to death or injury. In *Goldman v Thai Airways* [1983] 3 All E.R. 693 contributory negligence was raised as a defence against a passenger who had not fastened his seatbelt but it failed on the grounds that he had not been warned to fasten it. In a French case quoted by Clarke, *Araluce v Air France*, CA, Paris December 18, 1987, the airline succeeded in the defence against an asthmatic passenger who embarked on a long flight but refused to disembark at an intermediate stop and died on board. In a German case it was held that the passenger was contributorily negligent when he put important papers in his registered baggage instead of keeping them with him in his hand baggage (1988 ZLW 265).

[The Montreal Convention provides the new Article 20 defence of contributory negligence and also the defence in Article 17.2 quoted above based upon any inherent defect, quality or vice of the baggage.]

Exclusion of Liability

Article 23 applies to the exclusion of liability for baggage as it does to liability for personal injury or death, *i.e.* there is a blanket prohibition—as does the Montreal Convention in Art. 26.

Limitation of Liability for Registered Baggage

Limitation on liability for loss or destruction of registered baggage is found in Article 22

> "22(2)(a) In the carriage of registered baggage, the liability of the carrier is limited to a sum of two hundred and fifty francs per kilogramme, unless the passenger or consignor has made, at the time when the package was handed over to the carrier, a special declaration of interest in delivery at destination and has paid a supplementary sum if the case so requires. In that case the carrier will be liable to pay a sum not exceeding the declared sum, unless he proves that that sum is greater than the passenger's or consignor's actual interest in delivery at destination.
>
> (b) . . .
>
> (c) In the case of loss, damage or delay of part of registered baggage or cargo, or of any objects contained therein, the weight to be taken into consideration in determining the amount to which the carrier's liability is limited shall be only the total weight of the package or packages concerned. Nevertheless, when the loss, damage or delay of a part of the registered baggage or cargo, or of an object contained therein, affect the value of other packages covered by the same baggage check or the same air waybill, the total weight of such package or packages shall also be taken into consideration in determining the limit of liability.

[Montreal Convention

> *Article 22—Limits of Liability in Relation to Delay, Baggage and Cargo*
>
> 2. *In the carriage of baggage, the liability of the carrier in the case of destruction, loss, damage or delay is limited to 1000 Special Drawing Rights for each passenger unless the passenger has made, at the time when the checked baggage was handed over to the carrier, a special declaration of interest in delivery at destination and has paid a supplementary sum if the case so requires. In that*

case the carrier will be liable to pay a sum not exceeding the declared sum, unless it proves that the sum is greater than the passenger's actual interest in delivery at destination.]"

Two hundred and fifty francs converted into sterling is equivalent to £19.54 per kilo. (Carriage by Air (Sterling Equivalents) Order 1999 SI/2881.) This is a relatively small sum by modern standards and ought to be supplemented by insurance cover whenever possible. Note however that it is not unknown for insurers to include a clause in their policies excluding liability while the baggage is in the care of a carrier. Passengers have the alternative of declaring a higher value and paying extra in which case they will be able to claim the higher sum.

Despite the low sums these are not paid automatically. The passenger must still prove the value of the contents in order to recover up to the limit—which in most cases will probably not be difficult. In situations when suitcases suffer considerable delay but are ultimately recovered intact it is a source of constant amazement for airlines and insurance companies the disparity between the contents declared by the passenger and the contents the case actually contained.

Complications arise when more than one piece of baggage is checked but one of the pieces is lost. Article 26(2) deals with this by stating that only the weight of the package or packages concerned can be taken into account. However it is for the airline to prove the weight of the packages concerned. In the case of *Bland v British Airways Board* [1981] 1 Lloyd's Rep. 289 (CA) the plaintiff had checked in six pieces of luggage totalling 75kg but one of the cases had been lost. The airline acquired a suitcase of the same type as the plaintiff's and filled it with the items similar to those she had lost. The weight came to 13.5kg. The Court of Appeal accepted that this was an acceptable way of proving the weight of the missing item and awarded her damages based on the 13.5kg weight. (See also *Reid v Ski Independence* 1999 SLT (Sh Ct) 62 on this point, below.)

However there is a proviso to Article 26(2). If the lost case or the lost contents affect the value of what is in the other cases then the value of the other cases can be taken into account also. So if a woman travelling by air packed all her suit jackets in one case and all her skirts in another and the one with the jackets in was lost then the value of the other could be taken into account.

Limitation of Liability for Unregistered Baggage

This too is covered by Article 26:

> "(3) As regard objects of which the passenger takes charge himself the liability of the carrier is limited to five thousand francs per passenger."

The sterling equivalent of 5,000 francs is £390.71 which is considerably more generous than the registered baggage limitation but again pitifully small. It would not cover the cost of even an average video camera or a laptop computer which are items you might wish to carry with you rather than put in the hold. If there is any justification for such low figures it is to emphasise the responsibility on the passenger to have adequate insurance cover; we have often seen in this book how the availability of insurance affects the attitudes of courts to where the risk should lie.

When the Limitations do not Apply

As with liability under Article 17 the passenger must be given notice of the limitations on liability and if the carrier fails to do so he will lose the benefit of the limits. The relevant provisions are to be found in Article 4:

> "(1) In respect of the carriage of registered baggage, a baggage check shall be delivered, which, unless combined with or incorporated in a passenger ticket which complies with the provisions of Article 3, paragraph (1), shall contain:
>
> (a) an indication of the places of departure and destination;
> (b) if the places of departure and destination are within the territory of a single High Contracting Party, one or more agreed stopping places being within the territory of another State, an indication of at least one such stopping place;
> (c) a notice to the effect that, if the passenger's journey involves an ultimate destination or stop in a country other than the country of departure, the Warsaw Convention may be applicable and that the Convention governs and in most cases limits the liability of carriers in respect of loss of or damage to baggage.
>
> (2) The baggage check shall constitute *prima facie* evidence of the registration of the baggage and of the conditions of the contract of carriage. The absence, irregularity or loss of the

baggage check does not affect the existence or the validity of the contract of carriage which shall, none the less, be subject to the rules of this Convention. Nevertheless, if the carrier takes charge of the baggage without a baggage check having been delivered, or if the baggage check (unless combined with or incorporated in the passenger ticket which complies with the provisions of Article 3, paragraph (1)(c)) does not include the notice required by paragraph (1)(c) of this Article, he shall not be entitled to avail himself of the provisions of Article 22.

[Montreal Convention

Article 3—Passengers and Baggage

...

3. *The carrier shall deliver to the passenger a baggage identification tag for each piece of checked baggage.*
4. *The passenger shall be given written notice to the effect that where this Convention is applicable it governs and may limit the liability of carriers in respect of death or injury and for destruction or loss of, or damage to, baggage, and for delay.*
5. *Non-compliance with the provisions of the foregoing paragraphs shall not affect the existence or the validity of the contract of carriage, which shall, nonetheless, be subject to the rules of this Convention including those relating to limitation of liability.]*"

As with passenger tickets there has been extensive litigation worldwide as to what constitutes a baggage check, when it must be delivered and how legible it must be. In the leading English case, *Collins v British Airways Board* [1982] 1 All E.R. 302, the Court of Appeal held that so long as a baggage check was delivered at the outset of the journey it was not necessary to deliver one at the intermediate stages. Nor was it necessary to detail the weight and number of the pieces of baggage. The failure to record the baggage might be an irregularity but it did not contravene Article 4 so as to deprive the carrier of its limitation of liability.

Modern practice is for carriers to combine the passenger ticket with the baggage check in one document so that the passenger is not provided with a separate baggage check—although he may be handed a receipt which he can use to retrieve his baggage at his destination.

Under Article 25 recklessness or intent to cause damage will also deprive the carrier of the limitations on liability. In *Newell v Canadian Pacific Airlines Ltd* (1976) 74 DLR 3d 574 the carrier placed the passengers' two pet dogs in the hold—this despite an offer by the passengers to purchase all the seats in first class to accommodate themselves and their pets! One dog was killed and the other became severely ill when carbon dioxide was given off by a consignment of dry ice carried in the same hold. The carrier was held to have been reckless in the circumstances; they knew that harm would result from their actions. Note that this case is interesting for the fact that damages were also awarded for distress and disappointment.

(c) Delay of Passengers or Baggage

Liability for Delay

Article 19 provides:

> "The carrier is liable for damage occasioned by delay in the carriage by air of passengers, baggage or cargo.
>
> *[Montreal Convention*
>
> *Article 19—Delay*
>
> *The carrier is liable for damage occasioned by delay in the carriage by air of passengers, baggage or cargo. Nevertheless, the carrier shall not be liable for damage occasioned by delay if it proves that it and its servants and agents took all measures that could reasonably be required to avoid the damage or that it was impossible for it or them to take such measures.]*"

There are some difficulties about the definition of delay in the Warsaw Convention. For instance does it cover the situation where the delay occurs before the passenger has checked in or before he has boarded the plane or does it just cover delays while the aircraft is airborne? Different views have been expressed on these matters and none seems to prevail but it seems reasonable to measure the delay in terms of arrival time. If the airline timetable states a particular arrival time then the flight is delayed if it arrives later than the time scheduled in the timetable. This was the perspective taken by two leading aviation lawyers at a conference in London in 1987. Professor Bin Cheng and Peter Martin suggested the following definition of delay:

> "Delay occurs when passengers and their belongings of which the themselves have charge have not been carried to their immediate or final destination or when checked baggage or cargo has not been delivered within the time expressly agreed upon or, in the absence of such agreement, within the time which it would be reasonable to require of a diligent carrier, having regard to the circumstances of the case." (The "Alvor Draft", Bin Cheng and Peter Martin, Lloyd's of London 4th International Aviation Law Seminar, London, 1987.)

English case law suggests that so long as the delay is not unreasonable then there will be no breach of Article 19. What is reasonable is of course a question of fact and this will have to be measured in terms of the scheduled time of arrival, the length of the flight and the fact that passengers choose to fly primarily because of its speed—and they are prepared to pay substantial sums for this.

Note that if the flight is cancelled altogether this is not a delay and therefore not dealt with by the Convention. In such cases the liability is dealt with under the terms of the contract and the common law. (See Grant "The Unfair Terms in Consumer Contracts Regulations and the IATA General Conditions of Carriage—A United Kingdom Consumer's Perspective" [1998] JBL 123 for a discussion of such issues.)

Measuring whether baggage has been delayed will in most cases be relatively straightforward. If it was intended to be carried on the same aircraft as the passenger but fails to do arrive at the same time then prima facie it will be have been delayed. However this may not be the case where the passenger has excess baggage and it is carried on a later aircraft.

Damages Recoverable for Delay

According to Giemulla, Schmid and Ehlers:

> "Damage in this context could be, for example, the costs of accommodation and transportation if the passenger missed his only connecting flight because the arrival of his flight was delayed, or additional expenses (*e.g.* additional fee for a first-class ticket) in order to reach the destination in time by a different flight." ("Warsaw Convention" WC Art. 19. II Liability for Delay. 1. The Damage)

For delay to baggage it is common practice for airlines to offer a sum of money to replace essential items of clothing until the baggage arrives. The low limitations on damages in these cases means that there may be little difference in compensation between baggage merely delayed or totally destroyed. Because of this courts sometimes feel it right to scale down delay damages.

In *Reid v Ski Independence* 1999 SLT (Sh Ct) 62 the pursuers claimed damages from their tour operator for the improper performance of their package holiday contract, namely considerable delays in the arrival of their baggage. The tour operator claimed to be able to limit its liability as permitted by Regulation 15(3) of the PTR by invoking the limitation in Article 19 of the Convention. The court held that as their was no evidence of the weight of the bags then it would be difficult to assess the maximum amount that could be claimed. However, even if the permitted maximum of 20 kg per person was taken as the correct sum it was more than the pursuers were claiming. If that was all that was decided the case would be unexceptional but the pursuer's claim was largely for distress and disappointment and the defendant claimed that such a claim was not permissible because Article 19 did not cover this head of damages. The court then went on to decide, probably unnecessarily, that Article 19 did indeed cover such damages. (See Clarke, *Contracts of Carriage by Air*, p.120 for a contrary view. For a small claims arbitration where these issues were discussed see 'Case Note: *Marshall & Dixon v KLM* [2002] ITLJ 63.)

Defences

[Note that the Montreal Convention defence in Art. 19 quoted above is not as strict as in the Warsaw Convention.]

Can the carrier invoke the Article 20 defence that they took all necessary measures to avoid damage or that it was impossible for them to take such measures?

Delays can occur for many reasons—weather, air traffic control problems, mechanical problems, industrial action, etc. If the airport is completely snowbound or the ATC computer system has crashed and aircraft simply cannot take off then on the face of it the airline has a defence. However this is not as simple as it appears. The requirement in Article 20 is to avoid *damage*. If the flight is say a Heathrow-Paris flight then the airline might be able to re-route its passengers on Eurostar. This is an option that can be found in the General Conditions of Contract issued by IATA and adopted by most scheduled carriers. Under the General Conditions airlines can at their option re-route passengers on the flights of other carriers or even by surface transportation (GCC Article 10.2). This would not be possible of course on long-haul routes but it should be considered for short-haul domestic routes in cases where it appears the delay will be at all significant.

Even in cases where re-routing cannot be undertaken the requirement is still to avoid the damage—which could mean providing meals and even overnight accommodation.

Where the problem is mechanical three issues arise. First, can the airline argue that the delay could not have been avoided because mechanical problems are not predictable. The answer to this may lie in the purchasing and maintenance policies of the airline concerned. If the airline buys or leases second-hand aircraft, only maintains them to the minimum standard required and has no back-up aircraft standing by in case of difficulties then one could argue forcibly that the delay was preventable. Compared to the best-practice of other airlines such a policy is simply courting disaster.

Secondly, if other airlines have departures to the passengers' destination then why cannot these passengers be re-routed on the flights of others. This may not be possible in small provincial airports but in major international airports there will often be seats available on alternative flights—subject of course to price—which may be the real stumbling block when it comes to re-routing.

Thirdly, is it possible to hire in an alternative aircraft? This may not be a realistic alternative, *i.e.* it goes beyond what is reasonably necessary in circumstances where the delay is likely to be short term but where the delay is likely to be longer or where perhaps there is a history of mechanical failures then this may be an option the airline should consider—and if it doesn't then it is failing to take all necessary measures to prevent the damage.

The view of the Department of Transportation in the US on the question of delays can be seen in this extract from a letter written to the chief executives of 59 US airlines by Secretary of Transportation Federico Pena in December 1994:

> "Carriers with few backup aircraft or crews should be conservative in scheduling their flights in order to limit inconvenience to consumers. Routine lengthy flight delays or frequent flight cancellations that result from unavailability of aircraft or crew will be considered unrealistic scheduling, which is actionable under [the Federal Aviation Act]. Also, to the extent that such airlines have a limited ability to accommodate overbooked passengers, they must be especially cautious in applying their overbooking procedures."

As in the UK, the DoT maintains records of flight delays. The yardstick in the US for determining whether a flight is late is whether it lands within 15 minutes of its scheduled arrival time.

All this seems to suggest that delays for mechanical problems do not necessarily give the carrier an automatic defence—either because the problems can be attributed to the carrier in the first place or because other means can be found to get the passengers to their destination—and in any case steps should be taken to alleviate the damage to passengers by the provision of appropriate refreshments and accommodation. According to Clarke (p.131) the airline must, at the very least, have a contingency plan for when mechanical failures occur.

For an interesting comparison of how charter (as opposed to scheduled) airlines compare in terms of delay see the league table issued by the Air Transport Users Council in April 1997 (and subsequently) and discussed in [1997] ITLJ 117. The significant feature of this table is that external factors such as weather and air traffic control are neutral, they do not affect the rankings. What the table demonstrates is that some airlines are just better than others at reducing delays. In other words the airlines at the bottom of the table would probably not be able to demonstrate that they had taken all necessary measures to avoid the delay.

Contributory negligence is a defence under Article 21. The usual example cited is of the passenger who turns up so late at check-in that he misses his flight. In such cases any delay would be caused solely by the passenger's own negligence and would afford a complete defence.

Exclusion of Liability for Delay

On the face of it Article 23 [and Article 26 of the Montreal Convention] precludes exclusion of liability for delay. However, passengers may still be faced with a term like this in their contract of carriage based upon IATA's General Conditions of Carriage:

> "Carrier undertakes to use its best efforts to carry the passenger and his or her baggage with reasonable dispatch and to adhere to published schedules in effect on the date of travel."

According to Miller:

> "The object of such clauses is to deny to the passenger/shipper the right to expect the performance of the carriage at a particular time. Since there is nothing with which the actual time of performance can be compared, no delay can appear.
>
> . . . the actual conditions of carriage do not openly contradict the terms of Article 19, but they deprive the article of any real meaning. The principle of liability for delay is respected, but the condition precedent to the application of the text *i.e.* the exis-

tence of delay, is made unattainable." (Liability in International Air Transport, Kluwer, 1978, pp. 154–56.)

However later, after a review of case law, she concludes:

"... the only effect produced by the provision of the Conditions of Carriage dealing with delay is to exonerate the carrier for cases of slight delay."

Limits of Liability for Delay

Liability for delay of passengers is limited by Article 22(1) and for the delay of baggage by Article 22(2) which are set out above.

[Montreal Convention

Limits of liability for delay to passengers is set out above.

Article 22—Limits of Liability in Relation to Delay, Baggage and Cargo

1. *In the case of damage caused by delay as specified in Article 19 in the carriage of persons, the liability of the carrier for each passenger is limited to 4,150 Special Drawing Rights.]*

As we have seen, the present UK value of 250,000 francs is about £16,000. The irony here is that the limit is so high that it is difficult to conceive of a delay to a passenger giving rise to a claim which would not be met by this limit—effectively allowing claims for delay in full while denying all but the smallest claims for death or personal injury.

For delay to baggage the limit is very low (£19.54 per kilo) and holidaymakers should always ensure that they are covered by insurance.

When the Limitations do not Apply

The Article 25 provisions on intent and recklessness also apply to delay of passengers and baggage as do the provisions in Articles 3 and 4 on giving notice.

The EU Regulation On Air Carrier Liability In The Event Of Accidents

The European Commission, having tired of waiting for a revision of the Warsaw Convention, decided that it would enact its own provisions on liability for accidents. In October 1997 it enacted Council Regulation No. 2027/97 on Air Carrier Liability in the Event of Accidents which came into force in October 1998. The main purpose of the Regulation is to waive the limits of liability currently payable and to restrict the defences available to carriers. As far as possible it does so by working within the framework created by the Warsaw Convention. Article 2.1 specifically provides that concepts in the Regulation not defined shall be equivalent to those used in the Convention. However it does include the novel element of requiring carriers to make advance payments to persons entitled to compensation before liability has been settled.

The scope of the regulation

Article 1 provides:

> "This Regulation lays down the obligations of Community air carriers in relation to liability in the event of accidents to passengers for damage sustained in the event of death or wounding of a passenger or any other bodily injury suffered by a passenger, if the accident which caused the damage so sustained took place on board an aircraft or in the course of any of the operations of embarking or disembarking."

The Regulation applies, except in one minor detail, to "Community air carriers" (Article 1). This is defined in Article 2 as meaning an air carrier granted a licence by a Member State. Thus non-EU carriers are not generally bound by it.

Note that the provisions only apply in the case of accidents causing death or wounding of a passenger or any other bodily injury—so liability for delay to passengers and baggage, and damage, loss or delay of baggage are not covered. Moreover the language used is identical to the language of the Convention so the same problems of interpretation will apply although thankfully no new ones seem to have been created. So for instance the recent decisions on recovery for mental injury and DVT will apply to the Regulation.

Waiving the limits

Article 3 provides

> "1.(a) The liability of a Community air carrier for damages sustained in the event of death, wounding or any other bodily injury by a passenger in the event of an accident shall not be subject to any financial limit, be it defined by law, convention or contract."

Thus in one fell swoop the Commission has swept away any limits of liability for death or injury. Claimants will still of course have to prove loss under the normal rules relating to personal injury—pain, suffering, loss of amenity, loss of earnings etc.

Defences

Article 3 goes on to provide:

> "2. For any damages up to the sum of the equivalent in ecus of 100,000 SDR, the Community air carrier shall not exclude or limit his liability by proving that he and his agents have taken all necessary measures to avoid the damage or that it was impossible for him or them to take such measures.
>
> 3. Notwithstanding the provisions of paragraph 2, if the Community air carrier proves that the damage was caused by, or contributed to by, the negligence of the injured or deceased passenger, the carrier may be exonerated in whole or partly from its liability in accordance with applicable law."

Thus for the first 100,000 SDR's of damage the carrier's liability is absolute rather than strict. All that the passenger has to show is that damage was caused and the carrier will be liable, subject only to the defence that the passenger caused or contributed to his own damage.

Advance payments

Article 5 provides:

> "1. The Community air carrier shall without delay, and in any event not later than fifteen days after the identity of the natural person entitled to compensation has been established, make such

advance payments as may be required to meet immediate economic needs on a basis proportional to the hardship suffered.

2. Without prejudice to paragraph 1, an advance payment shall not be less than the equivalent in ecus of 15,000 SDR per passenger in the event of death.

3. An advance payment shall not constitute recognition of liability and may be offset against any subsequent sums paid on the basis of Community air carrier liability, but is not returnable, except in the cases prescribed in Article 3(3) or in circumstances where it is subsequently proved that the person who received the advance payment caused, or contributed to, the damage by negligence or was not the person entitled to compensation."

This provision requires carriers to make immediate payments to victims of air accidents regardless of liability. It sets a basic minimum of 15,000 SDR but more will be payable if the victim's needs are greater. Although the sum can be offset against any subsequent payment of compensation it is not recoverable by the carrier unless they can prove fault on the part of the victim or the person who received the payment was not entitled at all.

The rationale for this provision, found in the preamble, is that such advance payments can considerably assist injured passengers and their relatives to meet the immediate costs following an air accident.

It is possible to envisage a scenario where the payment may exceed any damages that would be recoverable. For instance in the case of the death of an unaccompanied minor the damages payable at common law are very low but it might cost considerable sums for parents fly out to the scene of the accident to identify the body and then arrange for the burial.

Information requirements

To combat the problem of different liability limits between Community and non-Community carriers, to ensure that consumers are properly informed of this, and to ensure that Community carriers are not at a competitive disadvantage as a result Article 6 provides:

"1. The provisions contained in Articles 3 and 5 shall be included in the Community air carrier's conditions of carriage.

2. Adequate information on the provisions contained in Articles 3 and 5 shall, on request, be available to passengers at the Community air carriers's agencies, travel agencies and check-in counters and at points of sale. The ticket document or an

equivalent shall contain a summary of the requirements in plain and intelligible language.

3. Air carriers established outside the Community operating to, from or within the Community and not applying the provisions referred to in Articles 3 and 5 shall expressly and clearly inform the passengers thereof, at the time of purchase of the ticket at the carriers's agencies, travel agencies or check-in counters located in the territory of a Member State. Air carriers shall provide the passengers with a form setting out their conditions. The fact that only a liability limit is indicated on the ticket document or an equivalent shall not constitute sufficient information."

This imposes obligations on both Community and non-Community carriers. Community carriers must put the new provisions in their conditions of carriage and make the information available at travel agencies and check-in counters. There is also a requirement to put a summary of the provisions on tickets. The first and third of these requirements should not be too difficult but the second is more debatable. Anyone who has tried acquiring this kind of information from travel agents or check-in counters knows that it is rarely available and the immediate reaction of counter staff is either one of puzzlement or defensiveness.

The obligation placed on non-Community carriers is more onerous. There is a requirement that at the point of sale the information be given clearly and *expressly*. Thus the carriers must ensure that all the travel agencies they use within the EU inform passengers that the carrier has a limitation on liability. Furthermore the carriers must provide passengers with a form setting out what their limitations are and it is not sufficient for this information to be conveyed by a simple statement on the back of tickets that they have a liability limit.

Denied Boarding Compensation

1. Introduction

One of the risks of air travel, and one of which many passengers are unaware, is that even when you have a confirmed reservation you can still be denied boarding or "bumped" from a flight because the airline has overbooked. Put simply, the airline has sold more tickets for the flight than there are seats available on the plane.

Overbooking is a practice used by airlines to counteract the effects of "no shows"—those passengers who do not turn up for flights on which they have confirmed reservations. Sophisticated computer systems enable airlines to predict the percentage of passengers who are likely to be no-shows with some accuracy, however there is always the possibility of an incorrect prediction resulting in some passengers being bumped.

Prior to 1991, airlines avoided paying compensation to passengers who were bumped by citing Clause 9 of the Conditions of Contract, which are printed inside ticket jackets. This states that the "carrier undertakes to use its best efforts to carry the passenger and baggage with reasonable dispatch. Times shown in timetables or elsewhere are not guaranteed and form no part of this contract". Once alternative transport arrangements were made for overbooked passengers to reach their final destination the airlines claimed they had fulfilled their obligations, irrespective of any inconvenience caused.

In recognition of the problem the EC introduced Regulation 295/91 which established common rules for a denied boarding compensation (DBC) scheme in scheduled air transport. The rationale behind introducing a compensation scheme, rather than making overbooking illegal, is because overbooking is considered a necessary evil of air transport. If airlines did not overbook, flights would depart with empty seats and the airlines would have to increase their fares to recover the shortfall in revenue. The Commission's Regulation therefore represented a compromise—airlines would be allowed to overbook, however they must ensure that their passengers are adequately compensated for the inconvenience caused.

2. EC regulation 295/91

EC Regulation 295/91 applies to all scheduled flights departing from any country of the European Union, irrespective of the country of registration of the airline, the nationality of the passenger who has been bumped or the point of destination (Article 1). Note however that it does not apply to passengers bumped on the return journey from a country outside the EU. In those circumstances the passenger would have to look to the rules of the country he was departing from or to the carrier's conditions of carriage.

For the purposes of Regulation 295/91 "denied boarding" means a refusal to accommodate passengers on a flight although they have a valid ticket, a confirmed reservation on that flight, and have presented themselves for check-in within the required time limit (Article 2(a)).

According to Article 2 (c) a "scheduled flight" means a flight possessing the following:

- it is performed by aircraft for transport of passengers for remuneration, in such a manner that seats are available to the public, either directly from the carrier or from its agents;
- it is operated between two or more points, either according to a published timetable or with flights so regular or frequent that they constitute a recognisable series.

The Regulation allows airlines to ask for volunteers who are prepared not to board an overbooked flight, in exchange for cash compensation or travel vouchers (Article 3(3)). Clearly, there will be occasions when there are no volunteers, and the Regulation therefore makes provisions for those passengers who are involuntarily bumped (Article 4).

These provisions allow the passenger to choose between:

- reimbursement of the cost of the ticket for the part of the journey not made, or
- re-routing to the final destination at the earliest opportunity, or
- re-routing at a later date at the passengers convenience.

Irrespective of the passenger's choice, the airline must also pay compensation to passengers who are involuntarily bumped. The amount of compensation depends on the length of the flight and how much later any alternative flight arrives.

For flights up to 3,500 km the minimum DBC is ECU 75 (about £60) where the alternative flights offered arrives within two hours of the original time and ECU 150 (about £120) for flights arriving over two hours later.

On flights over 3,500 km airlines must pay ECU 150 for flights arriving within four hours of the original time and ECU 300 for flights where the delay is over four hours.

Compensation may be paid in travel vouchers, however passengers are entitled to insist on cash. The amount of compensation need not exceed the price of the ticket in respect of the final destination.

In addition to the minimum compensation levels, passengers who are denied boarding must be offered the following, free of charge, by the airline (Article 6):

- expenses for a telephone call and/or telex/fax to the point of destination;
- meals and refreshments in a reasonable relation to the waiting time;
- hotel accommodation where an additional stay of one or more nights is necessary.

Many package holidays include scheduled flights which would therefore be covered by the Regulation. Often, however, the question arises as to how the Regulation affects package holidays and charter flights. Article 5 states that if a passenger is denied boarding on a flight which has been sold as part of a package, the airline is obliged to compensate the tour operator, who must then compensate the passenger. However, charter flights are generally not overbooked as the restricted nature of the tickets (no changes, no refunds) means that it is unusual for passengers to be no-shows. If a passenger does not turn up for a charter flight the airline still receives its money, which means that charter airlines do not have to cover themselves by overbooking.

3. EC regulation 295/91 in practice

Not surprisingly, there were teething problems as details of the new Regulation took time to filter down to the airlines' check-in staff.

In the early days, passengers were still being bumped but not informed of the Regulation, and although some approached the Air Transport Users Council (AUC) for advice, many others must have gone away without compensation. Some airlines were simply not aware of the Regulation. And some non-EU carriers claimed that it did not apply to them.

Over time, however, application of the Regulation has become much more consistent. Indeed, some airlines pay denied boarding compensation above and beyond the minimum stipulated by the Regulation. Furthermore, many of the major airlines also compensate passengers who are bumped in non-EU countries which are outside the jurisdiction of the Regulation.

Nevertheless, there are several recurring problems worth mentioning. Some airlines who know that a flight is overbooked contact their passengers the day before the intended flight and change their reservation. Using the Regulation's definition of an overbooked flight (see above) the airlines are not obliged to pay denied boarding compensation to these passengers as they have not presented themselves for check-in.

Article 8 of the Regulation states that "air carriers shall provide each passenger affected by denied boarding with a form setting out the denied boarding compensation rules". Not only do many carriers ignore Article 8, but some also only pay compensation when asked to by those who know of the Regulation, rather than immediately advising overbooked passengers of their rights.

As many passengers are not aware of the existence of the Regulation, let alone the fact that they can insist on cash compensation when overbooked, some airlines still get away with paying in travel vouchers. However most airlines, once pressed to do so, will pay up in cash.

It is important to remember that compensation need not exceed the price of the ticket to the final destination, which is described in the Regulation as "the destination on the flight coupon presented at the check-in counter or, in the case of successive flights, on the last flight coupon of the ticket". Problems sometimes arise with multi-sector tickets and the calculation of the price of the ticket for the sector that is overbooked, which is often a lot less than the passenger expects.

As compensation is linked to ticket price, it follows that children who have not paid the full adult fare might not be entitled to the same amount of compensation. At least one airline only pays half the statutory DBC to children who are overbooked, although the Regulation does not differentiate between adults and children. If the child fare is equal to or more than the denied boarding compensation then the child should be paid the full entitlement.

In parts the Regulation only offers guidance to airlines, which can cause confusion. For example, Article 3 states that the airlines "should take into consideration the interests of passengers who must be given boarding priority for legitimate reasons, such as handicapped persons and unaccompanied children". In practice, the selection of passengers to be bumped appears to be entirely at the airlines' discretion, and Article 3 needs elaboration to ensure consistency amongst airlines.

One final, less common problem is the entitlement of those passengers who agree to be downgraded on an overbooked flight. Whilst the Regulation is clear that they must be reimbursed the difference in price between the classes of travel (which might be minimal with promotional fares), it does not state whether they are entitled to compensation in addition to this.

4. Proposed revisions to the denied boarding regulation

In January 1998 the Commission published a proposal to amend Regulation 295/91 (COM (1998) 41 final) but it failed to become law. In December 2001 the Commission issued another proposal—COM(2001) 784 final and this is currently still being considered, having been out to consultation. The difference between this proposal and the earlier one is that it covers not only denied boarding but extends to flight cancellations as well.

Carriage By Sea

The increasing popularity of cruising as a form of holiday makes it more relevant than formerly to consider the Law on international carriage by sea. As we shall see, the basic scheme is similar, but not identical, to the position in carriage by air.

The Athens Convention 1974 governs the position. It has been in force in the UK since 1996 by virtue of the Merchant Shipping Act 1995.

Who is the carrier?

Article 1 of the Convention distinguishes "carrier" from "performing carrier". The carrier means a person by or on behalf of whom a Contract of carriage has been concluded, whether the carriage is actually performed by him or by a performing carrier. A performing carrier means a person other than the carrier, being the owner, chartered or operator of the ship, who actually performs the whole or a part of the carriage.

As we have seen, there is much debate as to whether in the context of carriage by air, a tour operator can be a carrier. It is much clearer that the tour operator could take the risk (and benefit) of being a carrier under the Athens Convention, even though not a performing carrier.

Limitation period

By Article 16, any action for death, personal injury or loss or damage of luggage must be issued within two years of the date of disembarkation (as it was contracted to be). In very limited circumstances this can be extended to three years (and not at all thereafter) if domestic rules allow for suspension or interruption of the limitation period. (Note that this is not the same as the discretion to disapply the limitation period contained in Section 33 of our own Limitation Act 1980). In *Higham v Stena Sealink* [1996] 2 Lloyd's Rep. 26 the claimant, while a passenger on the defendants' ferry *Stena Cambria* sailing between Holyhead and Dunlaoghrie in the Republic of Ireland, suffered injury when she slipped on some broken glass on the deck and fell. She disembarked later the same day but failed to issue proceedings within the two year period and thus failed in her action.

Note that for claims for lost or damaged luggage there are additional requirements for written notice to be given at or immediately after the occurrence.

International carriage

The Athens Convention applies to any international carriage by sea where the ship is flying the flag of a Convention country, or the Contract was made in a Convention country. The "International" element of the carriage is defined in accordance with common sense and includes carriage which starts and ends in the same place, as many cruises do, but has least one port of call in another country.

Liability

This is defined by Article 3(1) of the Athens Convention which says:—

> "The Carrier shall be liable for the damage suffered as a result of the death of or personal injury to a passenger and the loss of or damage to luggage if the incident which caused the damage so suffered occurred in the course of Carriage and was due to the fault or neglect of the Carrier or of his servants or agents acting within the scope of their employment".

There are three points to note from this definition:—

- Note the reference to personal injury as distinct from "bodily injury" in the Warsaw Convention. It is clear that psychiatric damage *is* included under the Athens Convention.
- Note the word "incident" as distinct from the words "accident" which appears in the Warsaw Convention. Incident is of course a much wider word. Having said that, it is not clear that in practice there is going to be much difference. One can speculate whether DVT is any more the result of an "incident" than it is of an "accident"; but in the real world DVT appears to be an unlikely result of a cruise anyway!

- At first blush it looks as though the definition requires the Claimant to prove fault; however, article three goes on to presume fault in cases of injury or damage to cabin luggage which arise from or in connection with shipwreck, collision, stranding, explosion, fire or defect in the ship. This appears to cover all the most serious situations likely to arise. In any other situation—perhaps for example food poisoning—the Claimant will have to prove fault (note however that in case of stored luggage, fault is presumed in every case).

Limits on damage

Limits on damage are somewhat more generous, though still unsatisfactory, than under the Warsaw Convention. The limits for personal injury and death are defined in units of account; approximate value in sterling is £38,000. (For cabin luggage it is £140, for other luggage about £228).

A trap for consumers is that valuables (*e.g.* jewellery) are not covered unless deposited with the carrier for the agreed purpose of safekeeping.

For consumers there are two pieces of good news:—

- For British registered carriers/ships, the limit on damages for personal injuries is raised to approximately £250,000.
- Just as with the Warsaw Convention, there are proposals to substantially increase, if not abolish all together, the limitations in the Athens Convention. However these proposals appear to be a considerable distance from enactment.

A practical example

Many issues arose in the unreported case of *Lee v Airtours* October 2002, Central London County Court (See Saggerson, "Case Comment: That Sinking Feeling—Psychiatric Injury, Lost Valuables And The Demise Of The Cruise Ship 'Sun Vista'. *Lee & Lee v Airtours Holidays Limited*" [2002] ITLJ 198).

The Claimants suffered psychiatric damage and the loss of valuables when their cruise ship caused fire and sank. The points to be noted in this case are:

- Airtours were held to be a carrier within the definition set out above
- Psychiatric injury is recoverable

- The valuables were in their cabin safe, not deposited with the carrier for safekeeping
- The Airtours Booking Conditions provided for damages to be limited in accordance with International Conventions. However the Claimants had booked on the telephone and had never seen the conditions therefore the Judge held them to be irrelevant to this case
- Article 14 of the Athens Convention stipulates that the Convention provides exclusive remedies against the carrier—the position is therefore similar to that seen under the Warsaw Convention in *Sidhu v British Airways* [1997] AC 430
- Surprisingly in view of the exclusivity of the Convention (and surely wrongly?) the Judge held that there was a parallel remedy under Regulation 15 of the Package Travel Regulations against Airtours as tour operator, as distinct from Airtours as a carrier. Financial limits for injury or lost property therefore did not apply (presumably it would follow that the two year limitation period also did not apply).
- In any event, held the Judge, financial limits on the lost valuables did not apply because the Claimants had asked the ship to look after the valuables, but this request was declined.

Chapter Nineteen
Accidents Abroad

In the course of this book we have seen that the tour operator is potentially responsible for injury or illness caused to a consumer during the course of the package holiday in a wide variety of situations ranging from the flight, the coach, the hotel and even in some cases an excursion.

In such circumstances, the claim can be brought by the consumer in the Courts of England and Wales (or Scotland or Northern Ireland if appropriate to the consumer). Unfortunately not all accidents or problems abroad fit into this easy category. In other cases, the first question arises; where can any Court action be brought, in the UK or overseas? What law applies? And how can a foreign action be funded? In this chapter we aim to explore these topics. Before doing so it is worth remembering that currently, despite threats of a repeal, s.75 of the Consumer Credit Act 1974 may give to a consumer a legal claim in the UK against his credit card company for the defaults of foreign suppliers.

Jurisdiction

It is unfortunately the fact that there are a wide variety of circumstances in which a consumer may become ill or be injured whilst overseas, but no claim is possible against a tour operator. Here are a few examples:—

- Whilst crossing the road in resort, a consumer is knocked down and injured by a speeding motorist
- A consumer decides to visit a local restaurant and suffers food poisoning as a result
- A consumer purchases an excursion locally (*e.g.* jeep safari, water park, banana boat) and is injured while on the excursion.
- A consumer is injured whilst participating in arrangements which turn out not to be a "package" under the Regulations, *e.g.* a split contract which is successful from the trader's

stand point; or perhaps the rental of accommodation only, *e.g.* a French villa with dangerous steps; or simply renting a hire car which is defective and causes injury

- Arrangements are made by a consumer directly, either by telephone or over the internet, with an foreign supplier such as a French villa owner, hotel or transport provider, and the consumer is injured by the service.

Of course the damage suffered by the consumer may not be injury or illness; a French villa contracted direct with its French owner have turn out to dirty and disappointing and the consumer wishes to bring a claim. As we shall see, however, the hurdles which lie in the path of such actions make the typical "small claim" are uneconomic, and it is only going to be a larger sort of claim, *e.g.* injury/illness, which justifies action against an overseas Defendant.

This chapter will concentrate upon accidents etc suffered within the European Union, or contracts made with suppliers in the EU. As we shall see, these situations are quite difficult enough. We will indicate where the remarks we make are of international application, rather than merely European.

Even within Europe, one must be careful of the precise position. All the EU countries except Denmark are now governed by EU Council Regulation Number 44/2001 ("the Judgments Regulation"), which came into force on March 1, 2002. Denmark is still covered by the Brussels Convention 1968; whilst Norway, Switzerland and Iceland (together with Poland) are governed by the Lugano Convention 1988.

The good news is that the general principles in the Judgments Regulation, and the Brussels and Lugano Conventions, are the same; where the differences of detail are significant, we will note them below.

The basic rule

It has to be realised that the basic rule, whether under the Judgment Regulation, Brussels, Lugano—or even the Hague Convention which deals with international matters outside the EU—is this; that Defendants are entitled to be sued in their own jurisdiction.

Thus, in our above example of the villa rented direct from the French owner, the basic rule is that the French owner is entitled to be sued in the Courts of France. The Spanish restaurant which has poisoned a consumer is entitled to be sued in the Courts of Spain; and so on (and of course, as a daunting non EU example, if that illness is caused by a restaurant in Peru or Zaire, then those are the Courts where any claim must be pursued.)

It follows that, if a consumer is searching for an opportunity to commence proceedings in his own home Court, say the Courts of England and Wales, it is always the case that he will have to uncover and establish one of the exceptions to the basic rule. There are a number of exceptions, of which the most relevant are set out below. Some are more helpful than others.

Exceptions to basic rule—possible UK jurisdiction

Contract Claims

In a case of breach of contracts Article 5 of the Judgments Regulation provides an exception to the basic rule, namely that action may be commenced in the Courts where the place of performance of the obligations in question is. Unfortunately, this rule (replicated in Brussels and Lugano) is not much help. The place of performance will generally be the same country as the Defendant's home Court. Thus the rental of the French Villa was to take place in France, and the poisonous meal was served in Spain.

Claims in Tort

The same problem arises here; the exception to the basic rule is that proceedings may be commended in "the Courts of the place where the harmful event occurred". If the Italian driver has run over the consumer in Italy, then again this is the same Court. (If of course the driver who knocks you down in Italy, or anywhere else, is in fact British—which happens more often than you might imagine—then you can sue the Defendant in his home Court in the appropriate part of the UK, although interesting questions of applicable law, the measure of damages, etc can arise).

Consumer Contracts

This may be more useful in some circumstances. Article 15 of the Judgments Regulation permits the consumer to bring an action in his own jurisdiction if it concerns a contract for the supply of goods or the supply of services, and the contract was "concluded with a person who pursues commercial and professional activities in the Member State of the consumer's domicile or, by any means, directs such activities to that member state or to several countries including the Member State, and the contract falls within the scope of such activities". Any contract for the supply of transport only is excluded; but included is a contract which "for an inclusive price, provides for a combination of travel and accommodation". So the traditional package holiday, including transport and accommodation, and purchased from a supplier in a foreign EU country, is covered, and the consumer can commence a claim in his own Court. In fact, basically, any consumer contract which fulfils the rules and is not just for transport, is covered. One need not therefore be too exercised by the omission of "other tourist services" from this pared down definition of a "package".

Indeed, the wording of Article 15 has clearly taken into account the increasing use by consumers of the internet as a means of ordering goods and services from overseas suppliers. Non internet contacts are of course covered too. A French villa owner who advertises in the *Sunday Times*, resulting in an English consumer making a booking, will therefore find himself subject to English jurisdiction under Article 15.

Where Brussels or Lugano still apply, then their Article 13 provides that the contract is covered by this exception if "the conclusion of the contract was preceded by specific invitation addressed to him or by advertising, and the consumer took in his own state the steps necessary for the conclusion of the contract." This older wording predates the Internet and may exclude Internet based contracts. Contracts for transport only are again specifically excluded.

Of course, contracts for a meal in a restaurant in Spain could not possibly come within this exception, or any other contract entered into *whilst overseas*.

Choice of Jurisdiction Clauses

A significant exception to the basic rule is that where the parties have agreed exclusive jurisdiction to the Courts of a particular country, such agreement overrides any other provisions of the Regulation (or Conventions). Article 23 of the Regulation states that; "if the parties, one or more of whom is domiciled in a Member State, have agreed that a Court or the Courts of a Member State are to have jurisdiction to settle any disputes which have arisen or which may arise in connection with a particular legal relationship, that Court or those Courts shall have jurisdiction. Such jurisdiction shall be exclusive unless the parties have agreed otherwise".

There is a requirement that such agreement be in writing or evidenced in writing. Writing includes e-mail.

This provision can benefit both consumers and travel companies. The difficulty for consumers is that they are unlikely, at the time of making any contract for any travel or holiday service, to write a term into the Contract for English jurisdiction. There is certainly a case for greater education of consumers on these matters!

Where a tour operator is sued over, for example, an accident in a hotel, then as we shall shortly see, it is possible for the tour operator to join the hotel as a Third Party (Part 20 Defendant) into the proceedings—but not if, for example, the hotel contract provides for exclusive Spanish jurisdiction. In the latter event, the tour operator will have to defend the English proceedings as best it can. If he loses, or reaches a compromise settlement, he will then have to start new proceedings in Spain against the hotel to effect recovery.

Third Party or Additional Defendant

Following on from the above, Article 6 of the Regulation says that a Defendant in an EU State may be sued:

1. Where he is one of a number of Defendants, in the Courts for the place where any one of them is domiciled, provided the claims are so closely connected that it is expedient to hear and determine them together to avoid the risk of irreconcilable judgments resulting from separate proceedings.
2. As a Third Party in an action under warranty or guarantee or in any other Third Party proceedings, in the Court seized of the original proceedings, unless these were instituted solely with the object of removing him from the jurisdiction of the Court which would be competent in his case.

We have already seen how the Third Party provision can assist a tour operator, with a properly drawn supplier contract, to effect recovery/indemnity from a hotel or other supplier as part of English proceedings started against the tour operator by a consumer.

In addition, however, this provision can benefit the consumer. If he can find one sensible and meaningful Defendant in England and Wales to sue, then he can join in a Defendant from any other part of the EU (or the other Convention Countries) as a second Defendant in the English proceedings, under this provision. The overriding criteria of the Courts is to try to avoid at all costs the possibility that, on the same set of facts, a Court in one Country might reach one decision, whilst the Court in another Country reaches a different decision.

There has been recent case law as to whether a claim in contract and a claim in tort can be said to be "so closely connected" that they can be joined together under this provision. See *Watson v First Choice* [2001] 2 Lloyd's Rep. 339.

But there is no doubt that where, for example, a consumer is injured in a road accident which is the fault of two different vehicles, one driven by an English driver (or a driver employed by an English corporation) and the other from say Spain, that both can be made co-Defendants in English proceedings.

EU Fourth Motor Insurance Directive

This exception may assist those injured in a road traffic accident overseas. The European Fourth Motor Insurance Directive 2000/26/EC dated May 16, 2000, came into effect on January 19, 2003. It will assist a British consumer injured in a road traffic accident elsewhere within the EU in two ways:—

1. It introduces a streamlined system for dealing with claims. Within each EU country there is required to be an information centre, enabling victims to discover details of insurance of the foreign vehicle/driver. Secondly, each motor insurer within the EU is required to appoint a claims representative in each EU country empowered to negotiate settlements; thirdly, within each EU country a compensation body is set up to pay compensation (recoverable from the compensation body in the country of the driver/vehicle) where a Third Party driver is uninsured or unidentified.

2. Even more dramatically, article three of the Directive states that; "each Member State shall insure that injured parties . . . in accidents . . . enjoy a direct right of action against the insurance undertaking covering the responsible person against civil liability".

   Within the UK, this was brought into force by the European Communities (Rights against Insurers) Regulations 2002—other EU countries have similar provisions, and indeed many already allowed direct actions against insurers, unlike the UK.

   One then has to turn to articles 9 and 11 of the Judgments Regulation (EC No. 44/2001)—the same Regulation has already been discussed in this chapter in other contexts. The effect of Articles 9 and 11 is that where an insurer can be sued direct, the insurer can be sued either in the insurer's home Court, or in the claimant's home Court. If an English consumer is injured in a road accident in France or Spain, he can sue the insurer of the French or Spanish driver in the English Court.

   We should add a note of caution; this is the view of the UK government in its consultation paper on the Fourth Motor

Directive issued in 2002, and is also the view of the authors based on a purposive interpretation of the Judgments Regulation. There are those who argue that the strict wording of Articles 9 and 11 do not achieve English jurisdiction against foreign insurers.

Foreign limitation periods

It is worth pointing out that, just because English jurisdiction is possible against an overseas Defendant, it does not necessarily follow that English Law will apply. Foreign Law may well apply, either because the contract says so, or because foreign Law is the most applicable Law following the rules in the Rome Convention. Of most relevance to consumers is the risk that foreign limitation periods might apply to a claim. These vary widely from country to country, even within the EU. Any consumer bringing a claim of this nature must urgently therefore check the appropriate limitation period. Particularly short ones include Switzerland (one year from date of knowledge) and California (one year). By contrast, Denmark, Greece and the Netherlands allow five years (but only two for direct actions against insurers).

If Overseas Proceedings Are Necessary

It may well be that a particular claim cannot be brought within one of the exceptions listed above to the basic rule. In such circumstances there may be no alternative but to commence action in the Defendant's home Court (even where an English Judgment can be obtained, it may still need to be pursued by way of enforcement through the foreign Court, if the Defendant does not pay up voluntarily).

For example, the second author has a friend who, whilst on holiday in Corfu, went to the beach and booked to go on a "banana boat" ride. She was injured through the negligence of the driver/owner of the banana boat. This does not come within any of the above listed exceptions, and there was therefore no alternative but to pursue the claim in Greece.

In these circumstances the very first point to look out for the is the foreign limitation period, which will certainly apply. The second point to note is that no such action will be simple to pursue. Much work remains to be done within the EU (let alone the wider international community, mostly governed by the less consumer friendly Hague Convention 1965), to ease the burden on consumers/victims in cross border cases.

Funding

The logistics and finance of such a case dictate that no small claim is likely to be worth pursuing in a foreign Court. If one books an excursion whilst overseas, and it fails to live up to its description, then frankly the trader is likely to get away with it.

The services of a foreign lawyer in the appropriate country are likely to be needed. How can a lawyer be chosen, and how can he/she be funded? As to a choice of lawyer, it is possible to consult the Law Society, or a directory such as Chambers Global Directory (3rd ed. 2002/2003). APIL (the Association of Personal Injury Lawyers www.apil.com) keep a list. If the consumer has travelled with the tour operator, but it is not the tour operator whom he wishes to sue, then the tour operator may be able to provide details of their own legal contacts in the country in question. Finally, the International Bar Association (IBA) has a travel and tourism section.

Possible sources of funding include:—

- Possible availability of some type of legal aid or conditional/contingency fee arrangement in the country in question.
- If a consumer travelled with the tour operator but it is not the tour operator who is to be sued, then ABTA members at least are required in their reasonable discretion to lend up to £5,000 by way of legal expenses in such cases—this topic is explored more fully in Chapter Five.
- Many travel insurance policies contain legal expenses cover.
- Some credit cards bring, with their use, insurance of this nature.
- Household insurance may include this cover.
- Failing the above possibilities, private funding of the foreign lawyer may be necessary. A clear statement of hourly rates, likely costs etc, together with regular budget reports, should be required.

It should be remembered that few countries adopt as clear a model of fee shifting or "loser pays" as exists in the UK. The resulting economics of pursuing a claim therefore also need investigation.

Appendix One
Council Directive on Package Travel, Package Holidays and Package Tours

COUNCIL DIRECTIVE

of 13 June 1990

on package travel, package holidays and package tours

(90/314/EEC)

THE COUNCIL OF THE EUROPEAN COMMUNITIES, Having regard to the Treaty establishing the European Economic Community, and in particular Article 100a thereof,

Having regard to the proposal from the Commission,[1]

In cooperation with the European Parliament,[2]

Having regard to the opinion of the Economic and Social Committee,[3]

Whereas one of the main objectives of the Community is to complete the internal market, of which the tourist sector is an essential part;

Whereas the national laws of Member States concerning package travel, package holidays and package tours hereinafter referred to as 'packages', show many disparities and national practices in this field are markedly different, which gives rise to obstacles to the freedom to provide services in respect of packages and distortions of competition amongst operators established in different Member States;

Whereas the establishment of common rules on packages will contribute to the elimination of these obstacles and thereby to the achievement of a common market in services, thus enabling operators established in one Member State to offer their services in other Member States and Com-

[1] O.J. No. C 96, 12. 4. 1988, p. 5.
[2] O.J. No. C 69, 20. 3. 1989, p. 102 and O.J. No. C 149, 18. 6. 1990.
[3] O.J. No. C 102. 24. 4. 1989, p. 27.

munity consumers to benefit from comparable conditions when buying a package in a Member State;

Whereas paragraph 36(b) of the Annex to the Council resolution of 19 May 1981 on a second programme of the European Economic Community for a consumer protection and information policy[4] invites the Commission to study, *inter alia*, tourism and, if appropriate, to put forward suitable proposals, with due regard for their significance for consumer protection and the effects of differences in Member States' legislation on the proper functioning of the common market;

Whereas in the resolution on a Community policy on tourism on 10 April 1984[5] the Council welcomed the Commission's initiative in drawing attention to the importance of tourism and took note of the Commission's initial guidelines for a Community policy on tourism;

Whereas the Commission communication to the Council entitled 'A New Impetus for Consumer Protection Policy', which was approved by resolution of the Council on 6 May 1986,[6] lists in paragraph 37, among the measures proposed by the Commission, the harmonization of legislation on packages;

Whereas tourism plays an increasingly important role in the economies of the Member States; whereas the package system is a fundamental part of tourism; whereas the package travel industry in Member State would be stimulated to greater growth and productivity if at least a minimum of common rules were adopted in order to give it a Community dimension; whereas this would not only produce benefits for Community citizens buying packages organized on the basis of those rules, but would attract tourists from outside the Community seeking the advantages of guaranteed standards in packages;

Whereas disparities in the rules protecting consumers in different Member States are a disincentive to consumers in one Member State from buying packages in another Member State;

Whereas this disincentive is particularly effective in deterring consumers from buying packages outside their own Member State, and more effective than it would be in relation to the acquisition of other services, having regard to the special nature of the services supplied in a package which generally involve the expenditure of substantial amounts of money in advance and the supply of the services in a State other than that in which the consumer is resident;

Whereas the consumer should have the benefit of the protection introduced

[4] O.J. No. C 165, 23. 6. 1981, p. 24.
[5] O.J. No. C 115, 30. 4. 1984, p. 1.
[6] O.J. No. C 118, 7. 3. 1986, p. 28.

by this Directive irrespective of whether he is a direct contracting party, a transferee or a member of a group on whose behalf another person has concluded a contract in respect of a package;

Whereas the organizer of the package and/or the retailer of it should be under obligation to ensure that in descriptive matter relating to packages which they respectively organize and sell, the information which is given is not misleading and brochures made available to consumers contain information which is comprehensible and accurate;

Whereas the consumer needs to have a record of the terms of contract applicable to the package; whereas this can conveniently be achieved by requiring that all the terms of the contract be stated in writing or such other documentary form as shall be comprehensible and accessible to him, and that he be given a copy thereof;

Whereas the consumer should be at liberty in certain circumstances to transfer to a willing third person a booking made by him for a package;

Whereas the price established under the contract should not in principle be subject to revision except where the possibility of upward or downward revision is expressly provided for in the contract; whereas that possibility should nonetheless be subject to certain conditions;

Whereas the consumer should in certain circumstances be free to withdraw before departure from a package travel contract;

Whereas there should be a clear definition of the rights available to the consumer in circumstances where the organizer of the package cancels it before the agreed date of departure;

Whereas if, after the consumer has departed, there occurs a significant failure of performance of the services for which he has contracted or the organizer perceives that he will be unable to procure a significant part of the services to be provided; the organizer should have certain obligations towards the consumer;

Whereas the organizer and/or retailer party to the contract should be liable to the consumer for the proper performance of the obligations arising from the contract; whereas, moreover, the organizer and/or retailer should be liable for the damage resulting for the consumer from failure to perform or improper performance of the contract unless the defects in the performance of the contract are attributable neither to any fault of theirs nor to that of another supplier of services;

Whereas in the cases where the organizer and/or retailer is liable for failure to perform or improper performance of the services involved in the package, such liability should be limited in accordance with the international conventions governing such services, in particular the Warsaw

Convention of 1929 in International Carriage by Air, the Berne Convention of 1961 on Carriage by Rail, the Athens Convention of 1974 on Carriage by Sea and the Paris Convention of 1962 on the Liability of Hotel-keepers; whereas, moreover, with regard to damage other than personal injury, it should be possible for liability also to be limited under the package contract provided, however, that such limits are not unreasonable;

Whereas certain arrangements should be made for the information of consumers and the handling of complaints;

Whereas both the consumer and the package travel industry would benefit if organizers and/or retailers were placed under an obligation to provide sufficient evidence of security in the event of insolvency;

Whereas Member State should be at a liberty to adopt, or retain, more stringent provisions relating to package travel for the purpose of protecting the consumer,

HAS ADOPTED THIS DIRECTIVE:

Article 1

The purpose of this Directive is to approximate the laws, regulations and administrative provisions of the Member States relating to packages sold or offered for sale in the territory of the Community.

Article 2

For the purposes of this Directive:

1. 'package' means the pre-arranged combination of not fewer than two of the following when sold or offered for sale at an inclusive price and when the service covers a period of more than twenty-four hours or includes overnight accommodation:

(a) transport;

(b) accommodation;

(c) other tourist services not ancillary to transport or accommodation and accounting for a significant proportion of the package.

The separate billing of various components of the same package shall not absolve the organizer or retailer from the obligations under this Directive;

2. 'organizer' means the person who, other than occasionally, organizes packages and sells or offers them for sale, whether directly or through a retailer;

3. 'retailer' means the person who sells or offers for sale the package put together by the organizer;

4. 'consumer' means the person who takes or agrees to take the package ('the principal contractor'), or any person on whose behalf the principal contractor agrees to purchase the package ('the other beneficiaries') or any person to whom the principal contractor or any of the other beneficiaries transfers the package ('the transferee');

5. 'contract' means the agreement linking the consumer to the organizer and/or the retailer.

Article 3

1. Any descriptive matter concerning a package and supplied by the organizer or the retailer to the consumer, the price of the package and any other conditions applying to the contract must not contain any misleading information.

2. When a brochure is made available to the consumer, it shall indicate in a legible, comprehensible and accurate manner both the price and adequate information concerning:

(a) the destination and the means, characteristics and categories of transport used;

(b) the type of accommodation, its location, category or degree of comfort and its main features, its approval and tourist classification under the rules of the host Member State concerned;

(c) the meal plan;

(d) the itinerary;

(e) general information on passport and visa requirements for nationals of the Member State or States concerned and health formalities required for the journey and the stay;

(f) either the monetary amount or the percentage of the price which is to be paid on account, and the time-table for payment of the balance;

(g) whether a minimum number of persons is required for the package to take place and, if so, the deadline for informing the consumer in the event of cancellation.

The particulars contained in the brochure are binding on the organizer or retailer, unless:

— changes in such particulars have been clearly communicated to the consumer before conclusion of the contract, in which case the brochure shall expressly state so,

— changes are made later following an agreement between the parties to the contract.

Article 4

1. (a) The organizer and/or the retailer shall provide the consumer, in writing or any other appropriate form, before the contract is concluded, with general information on passport and visa requirements applicable to nationals of the Member State or States concerned and in particular on the periods for obtaining them, as well as with information on the health formalities required for the journey and the stay;

(b) The organizer and/or retailer shall also provide the consumer, in writing or any other appropriate form, with the following information in good time before the start of the journey;

(i) the times and places of intermediate stops and transport connections as well as details of the place to be occupied by the traveller, *e.g.* cabin or berth on ship, sleeper compartment on train;
(ii) the name, address and telephone number of the organizer's and/or retailer's local representative or, failing that, of local agencies on whose assistance a consumer in difficulty could call.
Where no such representatives or agencies exist, the consumer must in any case be provided with an emergency telephone number or any other information that will enable him to contract the organizer and/or the retailer;
(iii) in the case of journeys or stays abroad by minors, information enabling direct contact to be established with the child or the person responsible at the child's place of stay;
(iv) information on the optional conclusion of an insurance policy to cover the cost of cancellation by the consumer or the cost of assistance, including repatriation, in the event of accident or illness.

2. Member States shall ensure that in relation to the contract the following principles apply:

(a) depending on the particular package, the contract shall contain at least the elements listed in the Annex;

(b) all the terms of the contract are set out in writing or such other form as is comprehensible and accessible to the consumer and must be communicated to him before the conclusion of the contract; the consumer is given a copy of these terms;

(c) the provision under (b) shall not preclude the belated conclusion of last-minute reservations or contracts.

3. Where the consumer is prevented from proceeding with the package, he may transfer his booking, having first given the organizer or the retailer reasonable notice of his intention before departure, to a person who satisfies all the conditions applicable to the package. The transferor of the package and the transferee shall be jointly and severally liable to the organizer or retailer party to the contract for payment of the balance due and for any additional costs arising from such transfer.

4. (a) The prices laid down in the contract shall not be subject to revision unless the contract expressly provides for the possibility of upward or downward revision and states precisely how the revised price is to be calculated, and solely to allow for variations in:

- transportation costs, including the cost of fuel,
- dues, taxes or fees chargeable for certain services, such as landing taxes or embarkation or disembarkation fees at ports and airports,
- the exchange rates applied to the particular package.

(b) During the twenty days prior to the departure date stipulated, the price stated in the contract shall not be increased.

5. If the organizer finds that before the departure he is constrained to alter significantly any of the essential terms, such as the price, he shall notify the consumer as quickly as possible in order to enable him to take appropriate decisions and in particular:

- either to withdraw from the contract without penalty,
- or to accept a rider to the contract specifying the alterations made and their impact on the price.

The consumer shall inform the organizer or the retailer of his decision as soon as possible.

6. If the consumer withdraws from the contract pursuant to paragraph 5, or if, for whatever cause, other than the fault of the consumer, the organizer cancels the package before the agreed date of departure, the consume shall be entitled:

(a) either to take a substitute package of equivalent or higher quality where the organizer and/or retailer is able to offer him such a substitute. If the replacement package offered is of lower quality, the organizer shall refund the difference in price to the consumer;

(b) or to be repaid as soon as possible all sums paid by him under the contract.

In such a case, he shall be entitled, if appropriate, to be compensated by either the organizer or the retailer, whichever the relevant Member State's law requires, for non-performance of the contract, except where:

(i) cancellation is on the grounds that the number of persons enrolled for the package is less than the minimum number required and the consumer is informed of the cancellation, in writing, within the period indicated in the package description; or

(ii) cancellation, excluding overbooking, is for reasons of *force majeure*, *i.e.* unusual and unforeseeable circumstances beyond the control of the party by whom it is pleaded, the consequences of which could have not have been avoided even if all due care had been exercised.

7. Where, after departure, a significant proportion of the services contracted for is not provided or the organizer perceives that he will be unable to procure a significant proportion of the services to be provided, the organizer shall make suitable alternative arrangements, at no extra cost to the consumer, for the continuation of the package, and where appropriate compensate the consumer for the difference between the services offered and those supplied.

If it is impossible to make such arrangements or these are not accepted by the consumer for good reasons the organizer shall, where appropriate, provide the consumer, at no extra costs, with equivalent transport back to the place of departure, or to another return-point to which the consumer has agreed and shall, where appropriate, compensate the consumer.

Article 5

1. Member States shall take the necessary steps to ensure that the organizer and/or retailer party to the contract is liable to the consumer for the proper performance of the obligations arising from the contract, irrespective of whether such obligations are to be performed by that organizer and/or retailer or by other suppliers of services without prejudice to the right of the organizer and/or retailer to pursue those other suppliers of services.

2. With regard to the damage resulting for the consumer from the failure to perform or the improper performance of the contract, Member States shall take the necessary steps to ensure that the organizer and/or retailer is/are liable unless such failure to perform or improper performance is attributable neither to any fault of theirs nor to that of another supplier of services, because:

- the failures which occur in the performance of the contract are attributable to the consumer,
- such failures are attributable to a third party unconnected with the provision of the services contracted for, and are unforeseeable or unavoidable,

— such failures are due to a case of *force majeure* such as that defined in Article 4(6), second subparagraph (ii), or to an event which the organizer and/or retailer or the supplier of services, even with all due care, could not foresee or forestall.

In the cases referred to in the second and third indents, the organizer and/or retailer party to the contract shall be required to give prompt assistance to a consumer in difficulty.

In the matter of damages arising from the non-performance or improper performance of the services involved in the package, the Member States may allow compensation to be limited in accordance with the international conventions governing such services.

In the matter of damage other than personal injury resulting from the non-performance of improper performance of the services involved in the package, the Member States may allow compensation to be limited under the contract. Such limitation shall not be unreasonable.

3. Without prejudice to the fourth subparagraph of paragraph 2, there may be no exclusion by means of a contractual clause from the provisions of paragraphs 1 and 2.

4. The consumer must communicate any failure in the performance of a contract which he perceives on the spot to the supplier of the services concerned and to the organizer and/or retailer in writing or any other appropriate form at the earliest opportunity.

This obligation must be stated clearly and explicitly in the contract.

Article 6

In cases of complaint, the organizer and/or retailer or his local representative, if there is one, must make prompt efforts to find appropriate solutions.

Article 7

The organizer and/or retailer party to the contract shall provide sufficient evidence of security for the refund of money paid over and for the repatriation of the consumer in the event of insolvency.

Article 8

Member States may adopt or return more stringent provisions in the field covered by this Directive to protect the consumer.

Article 9

1. Member States shall bring into force the measures necessary to comply

with this Directive before 31 December 1992. They shall forthwith inform the Commission thereof.

2. Member States shall communicate to the Commission the texts of the main provisions of national law which they adopt in the field governed by this Directive. The Commission shall inform the other Member States thereof.

Article 10

This Directive is addressed to the Member States.

Done at Luxembourg, 13 June 1990.

For the Council

The President

D. J. O'MALLEY

Appendix Two

The Package Travel, Package Holidays and Package Tours Regulations 1992

1992 No. 3228

Amendments in square brackets inserted by SI 1995/1648 and SI 1998/1208

CONSUMER PROTECTION

The Package Travel, Package Holidays and Package Tours Regulations 1992

Whereas the Secretary of State is a Minister designated for the purposes of section 2(2) of the European Communities Act 1972 in relation to measures relating to consumer protection as regards package travel, package holidays and package tours;

And whereas a draft of these Regulations has been approved by a resolution of each House of Parliament pursuant to section 2(2) of and paragraph 2(2) of Schedule 2 to that Act;

Now, therefore the Secretary of State in exercise of the powers conferred on him by section 2(2) of that Act hereby makes the following Regulations:

Citation and commencement

1. These Regulations may be cited as the Package Travel, Package Holidays and Package Tours Regulations 1992 and shall come into force on the day after the day on which they are made.

Interpretation

2.—(1) In these Regulations—

"brochure" means any brochure in which packages are offered for sale;
"contract" means the agreement linking the consumer to the organiser or to the retailer, or to both, as the case may be:
"the Directive" means Council Directive 90/314/EEC on package travel, package holidays and package tours; ["member State" means a member

State of the European Community or another State in the European Economic Area;]
"offer" includes an invitation to treat whether by means of advertising or otherwise, and cognate expressions shall be construed accordingly;
"organiser" means the person who, otherwise than occasionally, organises packages and sells or offers them for sale, whether directly or through a retailer;
a "the other party to the contract" means the party, other than the consumer, to the contract, that is, the organiser or the retailer, or both, as the case may be;
"package" means the pre-arranged combination of at least two of the following components when sold or offered for sale at an inclusive price and when the service covers a period of time more than twenty-four hours or includes overnight accommodation:—

(a) transport;

(b) accommodation;

(c) other tourist services not ancillary to transport or accommodation and accounting for a significant proportion of the package,

and

(i) the submission of separate accounts for different components shall not cause the arrangements to be other than a package:
(ii) the fact that a combination is arranged at the request of the consumer and in accordance with his specific instructions (whether modified or not) shall not of itself cause it to be treated as other than pre-arranged:

and

"retailer" means the person who sells or offers for sale the package put together by the organiser.

(2) In the definition of "contract" in paragraph (1) above, "consumer" means the person who takes or agrees to take the package ("the principal contractor") and elsewhere in these Regulations "consumer" means as the context requires, the principal contractor, any person on whose behalf the principal contractor agrees to purchase the package ("the other beneficiaries") or any person to whom the principal contractor or any of the other beneficiaries transfers the package ("the transferee").

Application of Regulations

3.—(1) These regulations apply to packages sold or offered for sale in the territory of the United Kingdom.

(2) Regulations 4 to 15 apply to packages sold or offered for sale on or after 31st December 1992.

(3) Regulations 16 to 22 apply to contracts which, in whole or part, remain to be performed on 31st December 1992.

Descriptive matter relating to packages must not be misleading

4.—(1) No organiser or retailer shall supply to a consumer any descriptive matter concerning a package, the price of a package or any other conditions applying to the contract which contains any misleading information.

(2) If an organiser or retailer is in breach of paragraph (1) he shall be liable to compensate the consumer for any loss which the consumer suffers in consequence.

Requirements as to brochures

5.—(1) Subject to paragraph (4) below, no organiser shall make available a brochure to a possible consumer unless it indicates in legible, comprehensible and accurate manner the price and adequate information about the matters specified in Schedule **1** to these Regulations in respect of the packages offered for sale in the brochure to the extent that those matters are relevant to the packages so offered.

(2) Subject to paragraph (4) below, no retailer shall make available to a possible consumer a brochure which he knows or has reasonable cause to believe does not comply with the requirements of paragraph (1).

(3) An organiser who contravenes paragraph (1) of this regulation and a retailer who contravenes paragraph (2) thereof shall be guilty of an offence and liable:

(a) on summary conviction, to a fine not exceeding level 5 on the standard scale;

and

(b) on conviction on indictment, to a fine.

(4) Where a brochure was first made available to consumers generally before 31st December 1992 no liability shall arise under this regulation in respect of an identical brochure being made available to a consumer at any time.

Circumstances in which particulars in brochure are to be binding

6.—(1) Subject to paragraphs (2) and (3) of this regulation, the particulars in the brochure (whether or not they are required by regulation 5(1) above to be included in the brochure) shall constitute implied warranties (or, as regards Scotland, implied terms) for the purposes of any contract to which the particulars relate.

(2) Paragraph (1) of this regulation does not apply:

(a) in relation to information required to be included by virtue of paragraph 9 of Schedule 1 to these Regulations: or

(b) where the brochure contains an express statement that changes may be made in the particulars contained in it before a contract is concluded and changes in the particulars so contained are clearly communicated to the customer before a contract is concluded.

(3) Paragraph (1) of this regulation does not apply when the consumer and the other party to the contract agree after the contract has been made that the particulars in the brochure, or some of those particulars, should not form part of the contract.

Information to be provided before contract is concluded

7.—(1) Before a contract is concluded, the other party to the contract shall provide the intending consumer with the information specified in paragraph (2) below in writing or in some other appropriate form.

(2) The information referred to in paragraph (1) is:

(a) general information about passport and visa requirements which apply to [nationals of the member States or States Concerned] who purchase the package in question, including information about the length of time it is likely to take to obtain the appropriate passports and visas;

(b) information about health formalities required for the journey and the stay; and

(c) the arrangements for security for the money paid over and (where applicable) for the repatriation of the consumer in the event of insolvency.

(3) If the intending consumer is not provided with the information required by paragraph (1) in accordance with that paragraph the other party to the contract shall be guilty of an offence and liable:

(a) on summary conviction, to a fine not exceeding level 5 on the standard scale:

and

(b) on conviction on indictment, to a fine.

Information to be provided in good time

8.—(1) The other party to the contract shall in good time before the start of the journey provide the consumer with the information specified in paragraph (2) below in writing or in some other appropriate form.

(2) The information referred to in paragraph (1) is the following:

(a) the times and places of intermediate stops and transport connections and particulars of the place to be occupied by the traveller (for example, cabin or berth on a ship, sleeper compartment on train);

(b) the name, address and telephone number—

(i) of the representative of the other party to the contract in the locality where the consumer is to stay,
or, if there is no such representative,

(ii) of an agency in that locality on whose assistance a consumer in difficulty would be able to call,
or, if there is no such representative or agency, a telephone number or other information which will enable the consumer to contract the other party to the contract during the stay;

and

(c) in the case of a journey or stay abroad by a child under the age of 16 on the day when the journey or stay is due to start, information enabling direct contact to be made with the child or the person responsible at the place where he is to stay;

and

(d) except where the consumer is required as a term of the contract to take out an insurance policy in order to cover the cost of cancellation by the consumer or the cost of assistance, including repatriation, in the event of accident or illness, information about an insurance policy which the consumer may, if he wishes, take out in respect of the risk of those costs being incurred.

(3) If the consumer is not provided with the information required by paragraph (1) in accordance with that paragraph the other party to the contract shall be guilty of an offence an liable:

(a) on summary conviction, to a fine not exceeding level 5 on the standard scale; and

(b) on conviction on indictment, to a fine.

Contents and form of contract

9.—(1) The other party to the contract shall ensure that—

(a) depending on the nature of the package being purchased, the contract contains at least the elements specified in Schedule 2 to these regulations;

(b) subject to paragraph (2) below, all the terms of the contract are set out in writing or such other form as is comprehensible and accessible to the consumer and are communicated to the consumer before the contract is made; and

(c) a written copy of these terms is supplied to the consumer.

(2) Paragraph (1)(b) above does not apply when the interval between the time when the consumer approaches the other party to the contract with a view to entering into a contract and the time of departure under the proposed contract is so short that it is impracticable to comply with the sub-paragraph.

(3) It is an implied condition (or, as regards Scotland, an implied term) of the contract that the other party to the contract complies with the provisions of paragraph (1).

(4) In Scotland, any breach of the condition implied by paragraph (3) above shall be deemed to be a material breach justifying rescission of the contract.

Transfer of bookings

10.—(1) In every contract there is an implied term that where the consumer is prevented from proceeding with the package the consumer may transfer his booking to a person who satisfies all the conditions applicable to the package, provided that the consumer gives reasonable notice to the other party to the contract of his intention to transfer before the date when departure is due to take place.

(2) Where a transfer is made in accordance with the implied term set out in paragraph (1) above, the transferor and the transferee shall be jointly and severally liable to the other party to the contract for payment of the price of the package (or, if part of the price has been paid, for payment of the balance) and for any additional costs arising from such transfer.

Price revision

11.—(1) Any term in a contract to the effect that the prices laid down in the contract may be revised shall be void and of no effect unless the contract provides for the possibility of upward or downward revision and satisfies the conditions laid down in paragraph (2) below.

(2) The conditions mentioned in paragraph (1) are that—

(a) the contract states precisely how the revised price is to be calculated;

(b) the contract provides that price revisions are to be made solely to allow for variations in:

(i) transportation costs, including the cost of fuel,
(ii) dues, taxes or fees chargeable for services such as landing taxes

or embarkation or disembarkation fees at ports and airports, or

(iii) the exchange rates applied to the particular package; and

(3) Notwithstanding any terms of a contract.

(i) no price increase may be made in a specified period which may not be less that 30 days before the departure date stipulated; and

(ii) as against an individual consumer liable under the contract, no price increase may be made in respect of variations which would produce an increase of less than 2%, or such greater percentage as the contract may specify, ("non-eligible variations") and that the non-eligible variations shall be left out of account in the calculation.

Significant alterations to essential terms

12. In every contract there are implied terms to the effect that—

(a) where the organiser is constrained before the departure to alter significantly an essential term of the contract, such as the price (so far as regulation 11 permits him to do so), he will notify the consumer as quickly as possible in order to enable him to take appropriate decisions and in particular to withdraw from the contract without penalty or to accept a rider to the contract specifying the alterations made and their impact on the price; and

(b) the consumer will inform the organiser or the retailer of his decision as soon as possible.

Withdrawal by consumer pursuant to regulation 12 and cancellation by organiser

13.—(1) The terms set out in paragraphs (2) and (3) below are implied in every contract and apply where the consumer withdraws from the contract pursuant to the term in it implied by virtue of regulation 12(a), or where the organiser, for any reason other than the fault of the consumer, cancels the package before the agreed date of departure.

(2) The consumer is entitled—

(a) to take a substitute package of equivalent or superior quality if the other party to the contract is able to offer such a substitute; or

(b) to take a substitute package of lower quality if the other party to the contract is able to offer him one and to recover from the organiser the difference in price between the price of the package purchased and that of the substitute package; or

(c) to have repaid to him as soon as possible all the monies paid by him under the contract.

(3) The consumer is entitled, if appropriate, to be compensated by the organiser for non-performance of the contract except where—

(a) the package is cancelled because the number of persons who agree to take it is less than the minimum number required and the consumer is informed of the cancellation, in writing, within the period indicated in the description of the package; or

(b) the package is cancelled by reason of unusual and unforeseeable circumstances beyond the control of the party by whom this exception is pleaded, the consequences of which could not have been avoided even if all due care had been exercised.

(4) Overbooking shall not be regarded as a circumstance falling within the provisions of sub-paragraph (b) of paragraph (3) above.

Significant proportion of services not provided

14.—(1) The terms set out in paragraphs (2) and (3) below are implied in every contract and apply where after departure, a significant proportion of the services contracted for is not provided or the organiser becomes aware that he will be unable to procure a significant proportion of the services to be provided.

(2) The organiser will make suitable alternative arrangements, at no extra cost to the consumer, for the continuation of the package and will, where appropriate, compensate the consumer for the difference between the services to be supplied under the contract and those supplied.

(3) If it is impossible to make arrangements as described in paragraph (2), or these are not accepted by the consumer for good reasons, the organiser will, where appropriate, provide the consumer with equivalent transport back to the place of departure or to another place to which the consumer has agreed and will, where appropriate, compensate the consumer.

Liability of other party to the contract for poor performance of obligations under contract

15.—(1) The other party is liable to the consumer for the proper performance of the obligations under the contract, irrespective of whether such obligations are to be performed by that other party or by other suppliers of services but this shall not affect any remedy or right of action which that other party may have against those other suppliers of services.

(2) The other party to the contract is liable to the consumer for any damage caused to him by the failure to perform the contract or the

improper performance of the contract unless the failure or the improper performance is due neither to any fault of that other party nor to that of another supplier of services, because—

(a) the failures which occur in the performance of the contract are attributable to the consumer;

(b) such failures are attributable to a third party unconnected with the provision of the services contracted for, and are unforeseeable or unavoidable; or

(c) such failures are due to—

(i) unusual and unforeseeable circumstances beyond the control of the party by whom this exception is pleaded, the consequences of which could not have been avoided even if all due care had been exercised; or

(ii) an event which the other party to the contract or the supplier of services, even with all due care, could not foresee or forestall.

(3) In the case of damage arising from the non-performance or improper performance of the services involved in the package, the contract may provide for compensation to be limited in accordance with the international conventions which govern such services.

(4) In the case of damage other than personal injury resulting from the non-performance or improper performance of the services involved in the package, the contract may include a term limiting the amount of compensation which will be paid to the consumer, provided that the limitation is not unreasonable.

(5) Without prejudice to paragraph (3) and paragraph (4) above, liability under paragraphs (1) and (2) above cannot be excluded by any contractual term.

(6) The terms set out in paragraphs (7) and (8) below are implied in every contract.

(7) In the circumstances described in paragraph (2)(b) and (c) of this regulation, the other party to the contract will give prompt assistance to a consumer in difficulty.

(8) If the consumer complains about a defect in the performance of the contract, the other party to the contract, or his local representative, if there is one, will make prompt efforts to find appropriate solutions.

(9) The contract must clearly and explicitly oblige the consumer to communicate at the earliest opportunity, in writing or any other appropriate form, to the supplier of the services concerned and to the other party

to the contract any failure which he percieves at the place where the services concerned are supplied.

Security in event of insolvency—requirements and offences

16.—(1) The other party to the contract shall at all times be able to provide sufficient evidence of security for the refund of money paid over and for the repatriation of the consumer in the event of insolvency.

(2) Without prejudice to paragraph (1) above, and subject to paragraph (4) below, save to the extent that—

(a) the package is covered by measures adopted or retained by the member State where he is established for the purpose of implementing Article 7 of the Directive; or

(b) the package is one in respect of which he is required to hold a licence under the Civil Aviation (Air Travel Organiser's Licensing) Regulations 1972 or the package is one that is covered by the arrangements he has entered into for the purposes of those Regulations.

The other party to the contract shall at least ensure that there are in force arrangements as described in regulations 17, 18, 19 or 20 or, if that party is acting otherwise than in the course of business, as described in any of those regulations or in regulation 21.

(3) Any person who contravenes paragraph (1) or (2) of this regulation shall be guilty of an offence and liable:

(a) on summary conviction to a fine not exceeding level 5 on the standard scale; and

(b) on conviction on indictment, to a fine.

(4) A person shall not be guilty of an offence under paragraph (3) above by reason only of the fact that arrangements such as are mentioned in paragraph (2) above are not in force in respect to any period before 1 April 1993 unless money paid over is not refunded when it is due or the consumer is not repatriated in the event of insolvency.

(5) For the purposes of regulations 17 to 21 below a contract shall be treated as having been fully performed if the package or, as the case may be, the part of the package has been completed irrespective of whether the obligations under the contract have been properly performed for the purposes of regulation 15.

Bonding

17.—(1) The other party to the contract shall ensure that a bond is entered into by an authorised institution under which the institution binds itself of pay an approved body of which that other party is a member a sum calculated in accordance with paragraph (3) below in the event of the insolvency of that other party.

(2) Any bond entered into pursuant to paragraph (1) above shall not be expressed to be in force for a period exceeding eighteen months.

(3) The sum referred to in paragraph (1) above shall be such as may reasonably be expected to enable all monies paid over by consumers under or in contemplation of contracts for relevant packages which have not been fully performed to be repaid and shall not in any event be a sum which is less than the minimum sum calculated in accordance with paragraph (4) below.

(4) The minimum sum for the purposes of paragraph (3) above shall be a sum which represents:

(a) not less than 25% of all the payments which the other party to the contract estimates that he will receive under or in contemplation of contracts for relevant packages in the twelve month period from the data of entry into force of the bond refereed to in paragraph (1) above; or

(b) the maximum amount of all the payments which the other party to the contract expects to hold at any one time, in respect of contracts which have not been fully performed.

whichever sum is the smaller.

(5) Before a bond is entered into pursuant to paragraph (1) above, the other party to the contract shall inform the approved body of which he is a member of the minimum sum which he proposes for the purposes of paragraph (3) and (4) above and it shall be the duty of the approved body to consider whether such sum is sufficient for the purpose mentioned in paragraph (3) and, if it does not consider that this is the case, it shall be the duty of the approved body so to inform the other party to the contract and to inform him of the sum which, in the opinion of the approved body is sufficient for that purpose.

(6) Where an approved body has informed the other party to the contract of a sum pursuant to paragraph (5) above, the minimum sum for the purposes of paragraphs (3) and (4) above shall be that sum.

(7) In this regulation—

"approved body" means a body which is for the time being approved by the Secretary of State for the purposes of this regulation;
"authorised institution" means a person authorised under the law of a member State [, of the Channel Islands or of the Isle of Man] to carry on

the business of entering into bonds of the kind required by this regulation.

Bonding where approved body has reserve fund or insurance

18.—(1) The other party to the contract shall ensure that a bond is entered into by an authorised institution, under which the institution agrees to pay to an approved body of which that other party is a member a sum calculated in accordance with paragraph (3) below in the event of the insolvency of that other party.

(2) Any bond entered into pursuant to paragraph (1) above shall to be expressed to be in force for a period exceeding eighteen moths.

(3) The sum refereed to in paragraph (1) above shall be such sum as may be specified by the approved body as representing the lesser of—

(a) the maximum amount of all the payments which the other party to the contract expects to hold at any one time in respect of contracts which have not been fully performed; or

(b) the minimum sum calculated in accordance with paragraph (4) below.

(4) The minimum sum for the purposes of paragraph (3) above shall be a sum which represents not less than 10% of all the payments which the other party to the contract estimates that he will receive under or in contemplation of contracts for relevant packages in the twelve month period from the date of entry referred to in paragraph (1) above.

(5) In this regulation "approved body" means a body which is for the time being approved by the Secretary of State for the purposes of this regulation and no such approval shall be given unless the conditions mentioned in paragraph (6) below are satisfied in relation to it.

(6) A body may not be approved for the purposes of this regulation unless—

(a) it has a reserve fund or insurance cover with an insurer authorised in respect of such business in a member state [, the Channel Islands or of the Isle of Man] of an amount in each case which is designed to enable all monies paid over to a member of the body of consumers under or in contemplation of contracts for relevant packages which have not been fully performed to be repaid to those consumers in the event of insolvency of the member; and

(b) where it has a reserve fund, it agrees that the fund will be held by persons and in a manner approved by the Secretary of State.

(7) In this regulation, authorised institution has the meaning given to that expression by paragraph (7) of regulation 17.

Insurance

19.—(1) The other party to the contract shall have insurance under one or more appropriate policies with an insurer authorised in respect of such business in a member State under which the insurer agrees to indemnify consumer's who shall be insured persons under the policy, against the loss of money paid over by them under or in contemplation of contracts for packages in the event of insolvency of the contractor.

(2) The other party to the contract shall ensure that it is a term of every contract with a consumer that the consumer acquires the benefit of a policy of a kind mentioned in paragraph (1) above in the event of the insolvency of the other party to the contract.

(3) In this regulation:

"appropriate policy" means one which does not contain a condition which provides (in whatever terms) that no liability shall arise under the policy, or that any liability so arising shall cease:

(i) in the event of some specified thing being done or omitted to be done after the happening of the even giving rise to a claim under the policy;

(ii) in the event of the policy holder no making payments under or in connection with other policies; or

(iii) unless the policy holder keeps specified records or provides the insurer with or makes available to him information therefrom.

Monies in trust

20.—(1) The other party to the contract shall ensure that all monies paid over by a consumer under or in contemplation of a contract for a relevant package are held in the United Kingdom by a person as trustee for the consumer until the contract has been fully performed or any sum of money paid by the consumer in respect of the contract has been repaid to him or has been forfeited on cancellation by the consumer.

(2) The costs of administering the trust mentioned in paragraph (1) above shall be paid for by the other party to the contract.

(3) Any interest which is earned in the monies held by the trustee pursuant to paragraph (1) shall be held for the other party to the contract and shall be payable to him on demand.

(4) Where there is produced to the trustee a statement signed by the other party to the contract to the effect that—

(a) a contract for a package the price of which is specified in that statement has been fully performed;

(b) the other party to the contract has repaid the consumer a sum of money specified in that statement which the consumer had paid in respect of a contract or a package; or

(c) the consumer has on cancellation forfeited a sum of money specified in that statement which he had paid in respect of a contract for a relevant package,

the trustee shall (subject to paragraph (5) below) release to the other party to the contract the sum specified in the statement.

(5) Where the trustee considers it appropriate to do so, he may require the other party to the contract to provide further information or evidence of the matters mentioned in sub-paragraph (a), (b) or (c) of paragraph (4) above before he releases any sum to that other party pursuant to that paragraph.

(6) Subject to paragraph (7) below, in the event of the insolvency of the other party to the contract the monies held in trust by the trustee pursuant to paragraph (1) of this regulation shall be applied to meet the claims of consumers who are creditors of that other party in respect of contracts for packages in respect of which the arrangements were established and which have not been fully performed and, if there is a surplus after those claims have been met, it shall form part of the estate of that insolvent other party for the purposes of insolvency law.

(7) If the monies held in trust by the trustee pursuant to paragraph (1) of this regulation are insufficient to meet the claims of consumers as described in paragraph (6), payments to those consumers shall be made by the trustee on a pari passu basis.

Monies in trust where other party to contract is acting otherwise than in the course of business

21.—(1) The other party to the contract shall ensure that all monies paid over by a consumer under or in contemplation of a contract for a relevant package are held in the United Kingdom by a person as trustee for the consumer for the purpose of paying for the consumer's package.

(2) The costs of administering the trust mentioned in paragraph (1) shall be paid for out of the monies held in trust and the interest earned on the monies.

(3) Where there is produced to the trustee a statement signed by the other party to the contract to the effect that—

(a) the consumer has previously paid over a sum of money specified in that statement in respect of a contract for a package and that sum is required for the purpose of paying for a component (or part of a component) of the package;

(b) the consumer has previously paid over a sum of money specified in that statement in respect of a contract for a package and the other party to the contract has paid that sum in respect of a component (or part of a component) of the package;

(c) the consumer requires the repayment to him of a sum of money specified in that statement which was previously paid over by the consumer in respect of a contract for a package; or

(d) the consumer has on cancellation forfeited a sum of money specified in that statement which he had paid in respect of a contract for a package,

the trustee shall (subject to paragraph (4) below) release to the other party to the contract the sum specified in the statement.

(4) Where the trustee considers it appropriate to do so, he may require the other party to the contract to provide further information or evidence of the matters mentioned in sub-paragraph (a), (b), (c) or (d) of paragraph (3) above before the releases to that other party any sum from the monies held in trust for the consumer.

(5) Subject to paragraph (6) below, in the event of the insolvency of the other party to the contract and of contracts for packages not being fully performed (whether before or after the insolvency) the monies held in trust by the trustee pursuant to paragraph (1) of this regulation shall be applied to meet the claims of consumers who are creditors of that other party in respect of amounts paid over by them and remaining in the trust fund after deductions have been made in respect of amounts released to that other party pursuant to paragraph (3) and, if there is a surplus after those claims have been met, it shall be divided amongst those consumers pro rata.

(6) If the moies held in trust by the trustee pursuant to paragraph (1) of this regulation are insufficient to meet the claims of consumers as described in paragraph (5) above, payments to those consumers shall be made by the trustee on a pari passu basis.

(7) Any sums remaining after all the packages in respect of which the arrangements were established have been fully performed shall be dealt with as provided in the arrangements or in default of such provision, may be paid to the other party to the contract.

Offences arising from breach of regulations 20 and 21

22.—(1) If the other party to the contract makes a false statement under paragraph (4) of regulation 20 or paragraph (3) of regulation 21 he shall be guilty of an offence.

(2) If the other party to the contract applies monies released to him on the basis of a statement made by him under regulation 21(3)(a) or (c) for a purpose other than that mentioned in the statement he shall be guilty of an offence.

(3) If the other party to the contract is guilty of an offence under paragraph (1) or (2) of this regulation shall be liable—

(a) on summary conviction to a fine not exceeding level 5 on the standard scale; and

(b) on conviction on indictment, to a fine.

Enforcement

23. Schedule 3 to these Regulations (which makes provision about the enforcement of regulations 5, 7, 8, 16 and 22 of these Regulations) shall have effect.

Due diligence defence

24.—(1) Subject to the following provisions of this regulation, in proceedings against any person for an offence under regulations 5, 7, 8, 16 or 22 of these Regulations, it shall be a defence for that person to show that he took all reasonable steps exercised all due diligence to avoid committing the offence.

(2) Where in any proceedings against any person for such an offence the defence provided by paragraph (1) above involves an allegation that the commission of the offence was due—

(a) to the act or default of another; or

(b) to reliance on information given by another.

that person shall not, without the leave of the court, be entitled to rely on the defence unless, not less than seven clear days before the hearing of the proceedings, or, in Scotland, the trial diet, he has served a notice under paragraph (3) below on the person bringing the proceedings.

(3) A notice under this paragraph shall given such information identifying or assisting in the identification of the person who committed the act or default or gave the information as is in the possession of the person serving the notice at the time he serves it.

(4) It is hereby declared that a person shall not be entitled to rely on the defence provided by paragraph (1) above by reason of his reliance on information supplied by another, unless he shows that it was reasonable in all circumstances for him to have relied on the information, having regard in particular—

(a) to the steps which he took, and those which might reasonably have been taken, for the purpose of verifying the information; and

(b) to whether he had any reason to disbelieve the information.

Liability of persons other than principal offender

25.—(1) Where the commission by any person of an offence under regulations 5, 7, 8, 16 or 22 of these Regulations is due to an act or default committed by some other person in the course of any business of his, the other person shall be guilty of the offence and may be proceeded against and punished by virtue of this paragraph whether or not proceedings are taken against the first-mentioned person.

(2) Where a body corporate is guilty of an offence under any of the provisions mentioned in paragraph (1) above (including where it is so guilty by virtue of the said paragraph (1) in respect of any act or default which is shown to have been committed with the consent or connivance of, or to be attributable to any neglect on the part of any director, manager, secretary or other similar officer of the body corporate or any person who was purporting to act in any such capacity he, as well as the body corporate, shall be guilty of that offence and shall be liable to be proceeded against and punished accordingly.

(3) Where the affairs of a body corporate are managed by its members, paragraph (2) above shall apply in relation to the acts and defaults of a member in connection with this functions of management as if he were a director of the body corporate.

(4) Where an offence under any of the provisions mentioned in paragraph (1) above committed in Scotland by a Scottish partnership is proved to have been committed with the consent or connivance of, or to be attributable to neglect on the part of, a partner, he (as well as the partnership) is guilty of the offence and liable to be proceeded against and punished accordingly.

(5) On proceedings for an offence under regulation 5 by virtue of paragraph (1) above committed by the making available of a brochure it shall be a defence for the person charged to prove that he is a person whose business it is to publish or arrange for the publication of brochures and that the received the brochure for publication in the ordinary course of business and did not know and had no reason to suspect that its publication would amount to an offence under these Regulations.

Prosecution time limit

26.—(1) No proceedings for an offence under regulation 5, 7, 8, 16 or 22 or these Regulations or under paragraphs 5(3), 6 or 7 of Schedule 3 thereto shall be commenced after—

(a) the end of the period of three years beginning within the date of the commission of the offence; or

(b) the end of the period of one year beginning with the date of the discovery of the offence by the prosecutor,

which ever is the earlier.

(2) For the purposes of this regulation a certificate signed by or on behalf of the prosecutor and stating the date on which the offence was discovered by him shall be conclusive evidence of that fact; and a certificate stating that matter and purporting to be so signed shall be treated as so signed unless the contrary is proved.

(3) In relation to proceedings in Scotland, subsection (3) of section 31 of the Criminal Procedure (Scotland) Act 1975 (date of commencement of proceedings) shall apply for the purposes of this regulation as it applied for the purposes of that section.

Saving for civil consequences

27. No contract shall be void or unenforceable, and no right of action in civil proceedings in respect of any loss shall arise, by reason only of the commission of an offence under regulations 5, 7, 8, 16 or 22 of these Regulations.

Terms implied in contract

28. Where it is provided in these Regulations that a term (whether so described or whether described as a condition or warranty) is implied in the contract it is so implied irrespective o the law which governs the contract.

Denton of Wakefield
Parliamentary Under-Secretary of State,
Department of Trade and Industry

22 December 1992

SCHEDULE 1 — Regulation 5

Information to be included (in addition to the price) in brochures where relevant to packages offered

1. The destination and the means, characteristics and categories of transport used.

2. The type of accommodation its location, category or degree of comfort and its main features and, where the accommodation is to be provided in a member State, its approval or tourist classification under the rules of that member State.

3. The meals which are included in the package.

4. The itinerary.

5. General information about passport and visa requirements which apply for [nationals of the member State or State in which the brochure is made available] and health formalities required for the journey and the stay.

6. Either the monetary amount or the percentage of the price which is to be paid on account and the timetable for payment of the balance.

7. Whether a minimum number of persons is required for the package to take place and, if so, the deadline for informing the consumer in the event of cancellation.

8. The arrangements (if any) which apply if consumers are delayed at the outward or homeward points of departure.

9. The arrangements for security for money paid over and for the repatriation of the consumer in the event of insolvency.

SCHEDULE 2 Regulation 9

Elements to be included in the contract if relevant to the particular package

1. The travel destination(s) and, where periods of stay are involved, the relevant periods, with dates.

2. The means, characteristics and categories of transport to be used and the dates, times and points of departure and return.

3. Where the package includes accommodation, its location, its tourist category or degree of comfort, its main features and, where the accommodation is to be provided in a member State, its compliance with the rules of that member States.

4. The meals which are included in the package.

5. Whether a minimum number of persons is required for the package to take place and, if so, the deadline for informing the consumer in the event of cancellation.

6. The itinerary.

7. Visits, excursions or other services which are included in the total price agreed for the package.

8. The name and address of the organiser, the retailer and, where appropriate, the insurer.

9. The price of the package, if the price may be revised in accordance

with the term which may be included in the contract under regulation 11, an indication of the possibility of such price revisions, and an indiction of any dues, taxes or fees chargeable for certain services (landing, embarkation or disembarkation fees at ports and airports and tourist taxes) where such costs are not included in the package.

10. The payment schedule and method of payment.

11. Special requirements which the consumer has communicated to the organiser or retailer when making the booking and which both have accepted.

12. The periods within which the consumer must make any complaint about the failure to perform or the inadequate performance of the contract.

SCHEDULE 3 Regulation 23

ENFORCEMENT

Enforcement authority

1.—(1) Every local weights and measures authority in Great Britain shall be an enforcement authority for the purposes of regulations 5, 7, 8, 16 and 22 of these Regulations ("the relevant regulations"), and it shall be the duty of each such authority to enforce those provisions within their area.

(2) The Department of Economics Development in Northern Ireland shall be an enforcement authority for the purposes of the relevant regulations, and it shall be the duty of the Department to enforce those provisions within Northern Ireland.

Prosecutions

2.—(1) Where an enforcement authority in England or Wales proposes to institute proceedings for an offence under any of the relevant regulations it shall be as between the enforcement authority and the Director General of Fair Tradings be the duty of the enforcement authority to give to the Director General of Fair Trading notice of the intended proceedings, together with a summary of the facts on which the charges are to be founded, and to postpone institution of the proceedings until either—

(a) twenty-eight days have elapsed since the giving of that notice; or

(b) the Director General of Fair Trading has notified the enforcement authority that he has received the notice and the summary of the facts.

(2) Nothing in paragraph 1 above shall authorise a local weights and measures authority to bring proceedings in Scotland for an offence.

APPENDIX TWO

Powers of offices of enforcement authority

3.—(1) If a duty authorised officer of an enforcement authority has reasonable grounds for suspecting that an offence has been committed under any of the relevant regulations, he may—

(a) require a person whom he believes on reasonable grounds to be engaged in the organisation or retailing of packages to produce any book or document relating to the activity and take copies of it or any entry in it, or

(b) require such a person to produce in a visible and legible documentary form any information so relating which is contained in a computer, and take copies of it,

for the purpose of ascertaining whether such an offence has been committed.

(2) Such an officer may inspect any goods for the purpose of ascertaining whether such an offence has been committed.

(3) If such an officer has reasonable grounds for believing that any documents or goods may be required as evidence in proceedings for such an offence, he may seize and detain them.

(4) An officer seizing any documents or goods in the excerise of his power under sub-paragraph (3) above shall inform the person from whom they are seized.

(5) The powers of an officer under this paragraph may be exercised by him only at a reasonable hour and on production (if required) of his credentials.

(6) Nothing in this paragraph—

(a) requires a person to produce a document if he would be entitled to refuse to produce it in proceedings in a court on the grounds that it is the subject of legal professional privilege or, in Scotland, that it contains a confidential communication made by or to an advocate or a solicitor in that capacity; or

(b) authorises the taking possession of a document which is in the possession of a person who would be so entitled.

4.—(1) A duly authorised officer of an enforcement authority may, at a reasonable hour and on production (if required) of his credentials, enter any premises for the purpose of ascertaining whether an offence under any of the relevant regulations has been committed.

(2) If a justice of the peace, or in Scotland a justice of the peace or a sheriff, is satisfied—

(a) that any relevant books, documents or goods are on, or that any relevant information contained in a computer is available from, any premises, and that production or inspection is likely to disclose the commission of an offence under the relevant regulations; or

(b) that any such offence has been, is being or is about to be committed on any premises,

and that any of the conditions specified in sub-paragraph (3) below is met he may by warrant under his hand authorise an officer of an enforcement authority to enter the premises, if need be by force.

(3) The conditions referred to in sub-paragraph (2) above are—

(a) that admission to the premises has been or is likely to be refused and that notice of intention to apply for a warrant under that subparagraph his been given to the occupier;

(b) that an application for admission, or the giving of such a notice, would defeat the object of the entry.

(c) that the premises are unoccupied; and

(d) that the occupier is temporarily absent and it might defeat the object of the entry to await his return.

(4) In sub-paragraph (2) above "relevant", in relation to books, documents, goods or information, means books, documents, goods or information which, under paragraph 3 above, a duly authorised officer may require to be produced or may inspect.

(5) A warrant under sub-paragraph (2) above may be issued only if—

(a) in England and Wales, the justice of the peace is satisfied as required by that sub-paragraph by written information on oath;

(b) in Scotland, the justice of the peace of sheriff is so satisfied by evidence on oath; or

(c) in Northern Ireland, the justice of the peace is so satisfied by compliant on oath.

(6) A warrant under sub-paragraph (2) above shall continue in force for a period of one month.

(7) An officer entering any premises by virtue of this paragraph may take with him such other persons as may appear to him necessary.

(8) On leaving premises which he has entered by virtue of a warrant under sub-paragraph (2) above, an officer shall, if the premises are unoccupied or the occupier is temporarily absent, leave the premises as effectively secured against trespassers as he found them.

(9) In this paragraph "premises" includes any place (including any vehicle, ship or aircraft) except premises used only as a dwelling.

Obstruction of officers

5.—(1) A person who—

(a) intentionally obstructs an officer of an enforcement authority acting in pursuance of this schedule;

(b) without reasonable excuse fails to comply with a requirement made of him by such an officer under paragraph 3(1) above; or

(c) without reasonable excuse fails to give an officer of an enforcement authority acting in pursuance of this Schedule any other assistance or information which the officer may reasonably require of him for the purpose of the performance of the officer's functions under this Schedule,

shall be guilty of an offence.

(2) A person guilty of an offence under sub-paragraph (1) above shall be liable on summary conviction to a fine not exceeding level 5 on the standard scale.

(3) If a person, in giving any such information as is mentioned in sub-paragraph (1)(c) above,—

(a) makes a statement which he knows is false in a material particular; or

(b) recklessly makes a statement which is false in a material particular,

he shall be guilty of an offence.

(4) A person guilty of an offence under sub-paragraph (3) above shall be liable—

(a) on summary conviction, to a fine not exceeding level 5 on the standard scale; and

(c) on conviction on indictment, to a fine.

Impersonation of officers

6.—(1) If a person who is not a duly authorised officer of an enforcement authority purports to act as such under this Schedule he shall be guilty of an offence.

(2) A person guilty of an offence under sub-paragraph (1) above shall be liable—

(a) on summary conviction, to a fine not exceeding level 5 on the standard scale; and

(b) on conviction on indictment, to a fine.

Disclosure of information

7.—(1) If a person discloses to another any information obtained by him by virtue of this Schedule he shall be guilty of an offence unless the disclosure was made—

(a) in or for the purpose of the performance by him or any person of any function under the relevant regulations; or

(b) for a purpose specified in section 38(2)(a), (b) or (c) of the Consumer Protection Act 1987.

(2) a person guilty of an offence under sub-paragraph (1) above shall be liable—

(a) on summary conviction, to a fine not exceeding level 5 of the standards scale; and

(b) on conviction on indictment, to a fine.

Privilege against self-incrimination

8. Nothing in this Schedule requires a person to answer any question or give an information if to do so might incriminate him.

Appendix Three

Code of Conduct of the Association of British Travel Agents

This Code of Conduct has been prepared and approved by the Board of Directors in accordance with Article 13 of the Articles of Association of the Association of British Travel Agents Limited.

This Code of Conduct is binding upon all Members of the Association.

AIMS OF THIS CODE OF CONDUCT

- To ensure that the public receive the best possible service from Members.
- To maintain and enhance the reputation, standing and good name of the Association and its membership.
- To encourage initiative and enterprise in the belief that properly regulated competitive trading by and between Members will best serve the public interest and the well being of the travel industry.
- To ensure that Members and their staff are familiar with this Code and the Articles of Association.

PRINCIPLES OF THIS CODE OF CONDUCT

- This Code is designed to regulate the activities of Members between (i) themselves and members of the public; (ii) themselves and other Members; and (iii) themselves and agents or Principals or other persons who are not members of the Association.
- This Code recognises and embodies the relevant parts of those Acts of Parliament and Government Regulations which relate to the regulation of the travel industry and its constituent parts and the codes or regulations of Recognised Organisations or Associations such as the Advertising Standards Authority, Trust UK, the Code of Advertising Practice Committee, the Independent Broadcasting Authority, the Independent Television Companies Association, the Association of Independent Radio Contractors and the Civil Aviation Authority which regulate the standards and practices of Members in relation to advertising.
- This Code embodies definitions of commercial practices and terminology used by Members. These definitions are designed to

specify and clarify beyond reasonable doubt the intentions of the Code.

- This Code recognises the necessity for enforcement of its standards and practices and embodies measures and procedures by which Members can uphold observance of the Code under the authority of the Board of Directors.
- This Code provides facilities to deal with consumer complaints by a system of arbitration.

DEFINITIONS

For the purposes of this Code, definitions are as follows:

Advertising: a means of promoting Travel Arrangements by any printed, viewable, audible or other form other than a Brochure as defined below.

Association: the Association of British Travel Agents Limited.

Basic Price: the price of Travel Arrangements shown in the price panel of a Brochure, in Advertising or elsewhere, before the addition of any supplements or other optional charges necessary to arrive at the total price of the Travel Arrangements.

Brochure: a communication in any printed, viewable, audible or other form which specifies the contents of Travel Arrangements offered by a Member in sufficient detail to allow a Client to reliably book the Travel Arrangements without obtaining additional information from the Member.

Client: a Consumer or prospective Consumer of the Travel Arrangements offered by a Member.

Code: this Code of Conduct.

Consumer: a person, company or firm acting in a personal or business capacity.

***Force Majeure*:** circumstances where performance and/or prompt performance of the contract is prevented by reasons of war or threat of war, riot, civil strife, industrial dispute (as defined below), terrorist activity, natural or nuclear disaster, fire or adverse weather conditions.

Incentives: offers in cash or kind to a Member to sell a holiday.

Industrial Dispute: a dispute which affects the services to be provided under a Package which the Principal cannot reasonably be expected to overcome by substituting comparable alternative arrangements other than a dispute between the Principal and his employees.

APPENDIX THREE

Member: a member of the Association.

Package: a pre-arranged combination of at least two of the following three items:

(a) transport;

(b) accommodation;

(c) other services not ancillary to transport or accommodation and forming a significant part of the package.

The submission of separate accounts for different components will not cause the arrangements to be other than a package.

Principal: a Member or other person, company or firm who enters into a contract with, or who holds himself out as being able to enter into a contract with, the Client under which he agrees to supply services, or a Member or other person, company or firm who supplies services, or who holds himself out as being able to supply services, under the terms of an ATOL.

Promotions: activities designed to stimulate the sale or purchase of a tour, holiday or Travel Arrangements offered by a Member by means other than Advertising as defined above.

Recognised Organisations or Associations: those organisations and associations referred to in the Principles of this Code.

Retailer: a Member or other person, company or firm when carrying on business as an agent for a Principal.

Travel Arrangements: all services sold by or on behalf of Members including, but not exclusively, transport services, accommodation services, other travel services and Packages as defined above.

On-line: websites (which term shall include individual web pages) and electronic or digital media accessible by consumers, including software, whether or not a live communication link is established.

1. CONDUCT BETWEEN MEMBERS AND BETWEEN MEMBERS AND CLIENTS

1.1 Standard of Service

(i) Members shall maintain a high standard of service to Clients.

(ii) Members shall not conduct their business in a manner which does not maintain or enhance the reputation, standing and good name of the Association and its membership.

(iii) Members shall make every effort to ensure that accurate information is provided to enable Clients to exercise an informed judgement in making their choice of Travel Arrangements.

(iv) Members shall make every effort to ensure that the Travel Arrangements sold to their Clients are compatible with their Clients' individual requirements.

(v) Members shall comply with all relevant statutory and regulatory requirements.

1.2 Minimum Standards on Brochures

(i) A Member shall ensure that his Brochure complies with the principles, rules and procedures contained in "ABTA's Standards on Brochures" as published by the Association from time to time.

(ii) A Member shall ensure that his booking conditions do not conflict with this Code and comply with the principles, rules and procedures contained in "ABTA's Standards on Brochures".

(iii) Every Brochure published by or in the name of a Member shall comply with all statutory or regulatory requirements from time to time in force.

1.3 Advertising and Promotion

(i) No Advertising or Promotion or any other publication, whether in writing or otherwise, shall contain anything which is likely to mislead the public.

(ii) All Advertising and Promotion by Members shall observe the requirements of all such Acts of Parliament and Government Regulation as may be enacted from time to time and the codes, regulations and rulings of the Recognised Organisations or Associations.

(iii) Where a Member is convicted of an offence in respect of a proven breach of any of the statutory provisions as contained in Clause 1.3(ii) above he shall be deemed to be in breach of this Code.

(iv) Where a Member is reported to have breached the codes, regulations or rulings referred to in Clause 1.3(ii) the Code of Conduct Committee retains the right to consider the alleged complaint and to decide if the Member has or has not breached this Code.

(v) A Member shall not advertise in such a manner as to suggest that other Members of the Association are or may become insolvent.

(vi) (a) A Member shall show or indicate his ABTA number in all his Advertising for travel business but, subject to paragraph (b) below, shall not be obliged to do so where press Advertising is in classified run-on form unless such Advertising contains any reference to ABTA.

(b) A Member whose press Advertising in classified run-on form contains any reference to an ATOL, whether held by that Member or any other party, shall make reference to ABTA but shall not be obliged to show his ABTA number.

(vii) A Member shall include within the Basic Price quoted in Advertising and Promotions for all Travel Arrangements, all non-optional costs for example, but not limited to, all airport and seaport fees, charges and taxes (except those that cannot be paid in advance by the Principal) insurance and ticketing costs.

(viii) No Member shall, directly or indirectly, publish a Brochure or Advertise in such a way as to encourage, cause or incite Clients to make use of the services or facilities offered by another Member (for example, but not exclusively, the supply of Brochures) in respect of any Travel Arrangements without, in the same Brochure or Advertising, encouraging, causing or inciting such Clients to book such Travel Arrangements through that other Member.

(ix) No Member shall indicate that a price is payable for a service or facility (such as a ticket on departure) or charge a fee to a Client for the provision of a service or facility, where that service or facility is not then provided. Where the service or facility to be provided is a ticket on departure a Member shall not impose any charge more than 14 days before the date of departure unless that Member can show that other means of distribution were not practicable.

1.4 Booking Procedure

(i) Members shall ensure that satisfactory booking procedures are followed and, where appropriate, that such booking procedures are in accordance with the procedures laid down by the Principal.

(ii) Members shall ensure that any special requests relating to disabilities or medical conditions are noted and, where appropriate, passed on to Principals effectively and in accordance with any agency agreement.

(iii) When dealing with Principals, Members shall ensure that they obtain confirmation from the Principal that all statutory or other financial protection requirements are met.

(iv) Members shall ensure that details of the arrangements that are in place for the financial security of the Client (*e.g.* ABTA/ATOL bonding) are communicated to the Client before any contract is made.

1.5 Booking Conditions

(i) Members shall ensure that their Clients are aware of booking and other published conditions applicable to their Travel Arrangements before any contract is made.

(ii) Members shall ensure that at least the relevant details given in the Appendix 1 to this Code shall be communicated to the Client before the contract is made. With regard to Packages, Members shall ensure that all Clients have access to a set of booking conditions in written or other appropriate form on or before confirmation of the booking. Additionally, in the case of on-line transactions members shall ensure that clients are given a clear opportunity to view and obtain a hard copy of any booking conditions that apply to the transaction before any contract is made.

(iii) Members shall ensure that their booking conditions comply with all relevant statutory provisions including the Unfair Terms in Consumer Contracts Regulations 1999. Where a Member is reported to have breached any such statutory provisions the Code of Conduct Committee retains the right to consider the alleged complaint and to decide if the Member has or has not breached this Code.

1.6 Passports, Visa and Health Requirements

(i) Before a contract is made, Members shall inform their Clients of health requirements which are necessary for the journey to be undertaken and shall draw to the attention of Clients travelling abroad the availability of the D.O.H. leaflet Advice on Health for Travellers.

(ii) Before a contract is made, Members shall advise their Clients of passport and visa requirements for the journey to be undertaken where it is reasonably practicable for the Members to obtain this information. In other cases, Members shall offer Clients reasonable assistance in obtaining such information.

(iii) Before a contract is made, Members shall advise their Clients of the availability of any advice issued by the Foreign and Commonwealth Office.

1.7 Insurance Facilities

(i) (a) Members shall draw their Client's attention to the availability of insurance cover to suit their Client's requirements.

(b) Where a Member issues an insurance policy to a Client that policy shall be appropriate for the Client's requirements in relation to the nature of travel booked by the Client and any hazardous activities that may be undertaken during such travel that are known to the Member.

(c) Members shall ensure that Clients are aware of the need to comply with the insurance company's requirements and of their duty to disclose to the insurance company all relevant information, *e.g.* pre-existing illness.

(d) Members shall comply strictly with the terms of business with insurance companies, whether such terms are evidenced in writing or not, and shall make prompt sales and other financial returns as required under these agreements.

(ii) (a) Retailers when providing insurance which is not arranged through the Principal concerned, shall ensure that within 48 hours of the booking being made, Clients are given an insurance document showing the effective start date of cover, the premium paid whether by Client or agent on his behalf and the insurance company's name, address and reference number. Written details of cover and claims procedures including an emergency contact number shall normally be given to Clients prior to departure.

(b) In respect of Packages, Retailers shall use their best endeavours to ensure that in cases where the Principal requires insurance and where neither the Principal's nor their own insurance is taken by the Client, details of the insurance taken by the Client are obtained and passed onto the Principal.

(iii) (a) Principals, when providing insurance to Clients, shall ensure that Clients are given a document showing the effective start date of cover, the premium paid and the insurance company's name, address and reference number. Full written details of cover shall be provided to Clients with the Principal's confirmation invoice. In respect of late bookings where it is not possible to issue a confirmation to the Client, Principals shall ensure that full written details of cover are provided to the Client with tickets and documentation provided at the point of departure.

(b) Where a Client is insured under a master policy held by the Principal under which cover is provided as soon as a confirmation invoice is issued then, for the purposes of this Clause, such confirmation invoice will provide evidence of cover. Where the effective start date of cover is other than the date of issue of the confirmation invoice, this shall be clearly indicated in writing to the Client.

(c) Principals shall ensure that insurance policies detailed in their Brochure are appropriate to any Packages or other Travel Arrangements detailed within that Brochure.

1.8 Confirmation of Bookings, Tickets and other Documentation

(i) It shall be the duty of a Principal to pass on without delay to the Retailer confirmation of bookings, tickets and other relevant documents relating to the Travel Arrangements booked, to enable the Retailer to transmit these to the Client within a reasonable period before departure.

(ii) Where Clients have booked Travel Arrangements direct with a Principal it shall be the duty of the Principal to pass on to the Client confirmation of bookings, tickets and other relevant documents a reasonable period before departure.

1.9 Travel Documents

(i) Retailers shall ensure that all documentation received from Principals is checked before delivery to Clients and that any points requiring clarification are investigated and explained to their Clients.

(ii) Retailers shall, as required by the Principals, pass on to Clients, within 4 working days of receipt, all relevant documents and in particular shall assist the Principals in complying with the requirements of their Air Travel Organisers' Licences.

(iii) Retailers shall not materially alter, amend or delete, any part of any Principals' documentation or fail to pass on any documentation from a Principal intended for the Client.

1.10 lterations to Travel Arrangements and Emergency Contact

(i) When alterations are made to Travel Arrangements for which bookings have already been accepted, Members shall inform their Clients immediately they are advised of the situation and Retailers shall act as intermediaries between their Principals and Clients in any subsequent negotiations.

(ii) To facilitate emergency contact by Principals, Retailers shall on request supply to the Association a telephone number where they may be contacted outside office hours.

1.11 Privacy and Data Protection

(i) Members shall comply with the Data Protection Act 1998 and shall ensure that they have in place an effective policy for protecting the privacy of Clients which shall be available to Clients on request and, in respect of on-line transactions shall be available on-line.

(ii) In accordance with the Data Protection Act 1998 members shall ensure that:

(a) their collection and use of personal information from Clients is fair;
(b) they take responsibility for all personal information held and used and that appropriate security measures are in place to protect Client information;
(c) a clear, prominent statement is available to Clients before any information is collected explaining what type of information is required and as far as possible by whom. Where information may be passed to entities outside the countries of the EEA this should be made available to the Client at the time of collection of the information;
(d) a clear prominent statement is available to the Client that in order to process the transaction information about that Client, including sensitive information (such as any disabilities, dietary/religious requirements etc.) must be passed to other entities;
(e) a clear prominent statement should be available to Clients prior to the time that information is collected explaining whether information will be used, or passed to third parties for

any purpose other than effecting the transaction (such as marketing). Any personal information which is not required to process the transaction shall be identified as optional;

(f) Clients are given the right to opt out of future marketing approaches at the time of information collection;

(g) databases are kept up to date and that information is held only as long as is necessary for the purposes for which it was collected;

(h) that Clients are given access, on request, to information held about them, and that incorrect information is amended or deleted without delay. Clients shall be clearly informed of their rights in this respect.

(iii) Members shall not send unsolicited electronic mail to Clients unless;

(a) the message is clearly identifiable as unsolicited before it is opened by a Client; and

(b) a check has been carried out against a register for opting out of such transmission (such as the e-mail preference service) at a reasonable time before the message is sent.

(iv) Members shall not send any random, untargeted, unsolicited commercial electronic mail (*i.e.* "Spam").

(v) Members shall not seek to obtain information from persons under the age of 14 years without first securing parental consent.

2 CONDUCT OF PRINCIPALS IN RESPECT OF CONFIRMED TRAVEL ARRANGEMENTS

2.1 Cancellation by Principal

(i) A Principal shall not cancel Travel Arrangements after the balance due date unless it is necessary to do so as a result of *force majeure*, or unless the Client defaults in payment of such balance.

(ii) Notwithstanding Clause 2.1(i), if Travel Arrangements are cancelled for reasons other than *force majeure* on or after the balance due date the Principal shall, in addition to the requirements of Clause 2.1(iii), below also offer that Client reasonable compensation. Such compensation may be offered in accordance with a rising scale of payments calculated so that the nearer to the time of departure that the cancellation occurs, the higher the level of compensation to be paid.

(iii) If a Principal cancels previously confirmed Travel Arrangements he shall inform the Retailers and direct Clients without delay and shall offer Clients the choice of either:

(i) alternative Travel Arrangements of comparable standard, if available; or

(ii) a full refund of all monies paid. Such refunds shall be sent to

Retailers and direct Clients within 10 days of the Client's decision being notified to the Principal.

2.2 Significant Alterations to Travel Arrangements by Principals

(i) Except for reasons of *force majeure*, a Principal shall not make a significant alteration to previously confirmed Travel Arrangements unless he does so in time to inform agents and direct Clients not less than 14 days before the departure date of the Travel Arrangements.

(ii) Notwithstanding Clause 2.2(i), if a Principal makes a significant alteration to previously confirmed Travel Arrangements for reasons *other than force majeure* on or after the balance due date, the Principal shall, in addition to the requirements of Clause 2(iii) below, also offer Clients reasonable compensation. Such compensation may be offered in accordance with a rising scale of payments calculated so that the nearer to the time of departure that the alteration occurs, the higher the level of compensation to be paid.

(iii) If a Principal makes a significant alteration to previously confirmed Travel Arrangements he shall inform Retailers and direct Clients without delay and shall offer Clients the choice of either:

(i) accepting the alteration; or
(ii) cancelling the Travel Arrangements and receiving a full refund of all monies paid. Such refund shall be sent to Retailers and direct Clients within 10 days of receipt of the notification to cancel; or
(iii) alternative Travel Arrangements of comparable standard, if available.

2.3 Cancellation and Amendment of Travel Arrangements by Clients

(i) A Member shall clearly state in his booking conditions or terms of trading the amount of, or the basis for calculating, any cancellation and amendment fees which the Client might incur, as well as the terms and conditions under which the Client might incur such fees.

(ii) A Principal, as soon as reasonably practicable, shall issue any cancellation or amendment invoice.

2.4 Overbooking

(i) A Principal shall exercise reasonable care and skill to ensure that Travel Arrangements are not cancelled or altered as a result of overbooking.

(ii) Where Travel Arrangements are cancelled or altered as a result of overbooking by a supplier, a Principal shall only be deemed to have exercised reasonable care and skill to prevent the cancellation or alteration if he can show that the overbooking occurred for reasons beyond his control. A Principal shall produce evidence concerning the reasons for an overbooking to the Association upon request by the Association.

(iii) Subject to clause 2.4(v) below, if, despite sub-clause (i) and (ii) above, an element is overbooked and a Principal knows this before the departure of the affected Clients, he shall immediately inform those Clients and shall offer them the choice of an alternative holiday of at least comparable standard, if available.

(iv) If, despite sub-clause (i) and (ii) above, an element is overbooked and a Principal does not know this before the departure of the affected Clients, such Clients shall be offered suitable alternative accommodation.

(v) Where circumstances arising under sub-clause (iii) above result in the cancellation of, or significant alteration to, the Client's Travel Arrangements, Clauses 2.1 and/or 2.2 of this Code shall apply.

2.5 Building Works

Where a Principal becomes aware or ought reasonably to have become aware of building works which may reasonably be considered to seriously impair the enjoyment of Travel Arrangements he must, without undue delay, notify Clients of the situation, provide them with accurate information about the extent of the building works and offer them the opportunity to transfer to alternative Travel Arrangements at the price of the original Travel Arrangements or to cancel without penalty. Furthermore, he must ensure that all prospective Clients are alerted to the situation.

2.6 Principals' Liability

(i) A Principal shall include, as a term of any contract for the sale of Packages, a provision accepting responsibility for the proper performance of the contract. A Principal shall not be required to accept responsibility where the failure to perform the contract or the improper performance of the contract is due neither to the fault of the Principal nor to that of his employees, agents, sub-contractors or suppliers because the failure—

(a) is attributable to the Client, or
(b) is attributable to a third party unconnected with the provision of the services contracted for *and* is unforeseeable or unavoidable, or
(c) is due to—

(i) unusual and unforeseeable circumstances beyond the control of the Principal the consequences of which could not have been avoided even if all due care had been exercised, or
(ii) an event which the Principal, his employees, agents, suppliers and subcontractors could not, even with all due care, have foreseen or forestalled.

Except in the case of damage involving death or personal injury a Principal is entitled to limit his liability under this Clause 2.6 to a reasonable level provided he states such a level expressly within his conditions.

(ii) Subject to clause 2.6 (vi)(c) below a Principal shall include, as a term of any contract for the sale of Packages, a provision obliging the Client to communicate to the Principal and to the relevant supplier at the earliest opportunity any failure which he perceives in the provision of the services contracted for.

(iii) Where the contract services referred to in Clause 2.6(i) consist of carriage by air, by sea, or by rail or the provision of accommodation, the Principal shall be entitled to limit his liability in accordance with the international conventions which govern such services.

(iv) A Principal shall include as a term of any contract for the sale of a Package, provisions stating that, where appropriate and subject to the Principal's reasonable discretion:

(a) general assistance shall be afforded to Clients who, through misadventure, suffer illness, personal injury or death during the period of their holiday arising out of an activity which does not form part of the contracted services nor of an excursion offered through the Principal;
(b) where legal action is undertaken by the Client, with the prior agreement of the Tour Operator, initial costs associated therewith shall be met by the Principal, always provided Clients request such assistance within 90 days from date of misadventure; and
(c) the aggregate costs for the Principal in respect of Clause 2.6(iv)(a) and (b) above shall not exceed £5,000 per booking form. Furthermore, in the event of there being either a successful claim for costs against a third party or suitable insurance policy/ies in force, costs actually incurred by the Principal shall be recoverable from the Client.

(v) A Principal shall ensure that he obtains liability insurance to cover claims made by Clients under Clause 2.6(i). Principals shall complete Form E (attached as appendix 6) and return this to the Association to evidence that liability insurance has been obtained, within 28 days of the commencement of such insurance policy. Acceptance by the Association of such evidence is not an acceptance by the Association of the adequacy of such insurance.

(vi) A Principal shall not include as a term to any contract relating to the sale of any travel arrangement, clauses which purport to:

(a) exclude liability for misleading statements made by the Principal, his employees or agents; or
(b) exclude liability for the Principal's contractual duty to exercise care and skill in making arrangements for a Package other than

as provided by the Package Travel, Package Holidays and Package Tours Regulations 1992; or

(c) exclude liability for any alleged cause of dissatisfaction by stipulating that such cause must be made known to the Principal within a fixed period which is unreasonably short.

(vii) A Principal shall indicate which law and jurisdiction will apply to claims brought under the provisions of Clause 2.6.

2.7 Package Travel Regulations

In addition to the obligations set out in Clauses 2.1, 2.2, 2.4, 2.5 and under the ABTA Standards on Surcharges, Members shall comply with the requirements of Regulation 13 and 14 of the Package Travel Regulations.

3 CONDUCT BETWEEN MEMBERS AND CLIENTS AND BETWEEN MEMBERS AND THE ASSOCIATION

3.1 Transactions and Correspondence

(i) Transactions with Clients shall be treated as confidential.

(ii) In the event of a dispute between a Member and a Client or member of the public, all correspondence shall be dealt with within the following time limits:

(a) an acknowledgement shall be sent not later than 14 days from the date of receipt of correspondence (not later than 5 days in the case of an email): and

(b) a detailed reply, or a reply containing a detailed explanation for any delay, shall be sent not later than 28 days from the date of receipt of correspondence.

If a matter which comes within the scope of this Clause is dealt with other than in writing, the Member shall nevertheless produce evidence in writing or other appropriate form that the matter has been dealt with in accordance with the time limits stated above.

3.2 Correspondence from the Association

(i) Subject to (ii) below, all correspondence from the Association shall be answered within the same time limits shown in Clause 3.1.

(ii) Where the Association requires a response to correspondence from a Member within a specified period, the Member shall ensure that such response is sent within that period.

If a matter which comes within the scope of this Clause is dealt with other than in writing, the Member shall nevertheless produce evidence in writing or other appropriate form that the matter has been dealt with in accordance with the relevant time limit.

3.3 Disputes

(i) (a) In the event of a dispute with a Client, Members shall make every reasonable effort to reach a speedy solution.

(b) Where a transaction has taken place on-line Members shall accept on-line complaints from Clients and deal with them within an appropriate period of time, which time period shall be no longer than that set out in Clause 3.1.

(ii) Retailers shall make every reasonable effort to deal with complaints of a minor and general character with a view to avoiding recourse to Principals. When complaints are of such a nature that reference to the Principal is necessary, a Retailer shall use his best endeavours acting as an intermediary to bring about a satisfactory conclusion.

(iii) Any dispute arising out of an alleged breach of contract or negligence by a Member may be referred to arbitration arranged with the Chartered Institute of Arbitrators. It shall be subject to such time, financial and other restrictions as from time to time shall apply.

(iv) Where a Client wishes to refer an unresolved dispute to arbitration, the Chartered Institute of Arbitrators will forward the Client's application form and Statement of Claim to the Member. Within 21 days of receipt the Member shall ensure that the application form is signed and returned to the Chartered Institute of Arbitrators, together with a Defence to Claim and the appropriate arbitration fee.

(v) The Member shall comply with the terms of the Arbitration Scheme referred to in sub-clause (iii) above and in particular with all the relevant rules and regulations of the Chartered Institute of Arbitrators for the time being in force.

3.4 Arbitration

A Principal shall include as a term of any contract relating to the sale of his Travel Arrangements a provision whereby any dispute arising out of, or in connection with, such sale which is not amicably settled, may be referred for resolution by arbitration under a special scheme devised for the travel industry by the Chartered Institute of Arbitrators.

It shall also be stated that:

(a) the scheme provides for a simple and inexpensive method of arbitration on documents alone with restricted liability for the Client in respect of costs;

(b) the scheme does not apply to claims for an amount greater than £5,000 per person or £15,000 per booking form. Where a claim includes in part a claim for personal injury or illness a limit of £1,000 per person applies to this part of the claim.

(c) the scheme does not apply to claims that are solely in respect of physical injury or illness

(d) the Client must return a completed application for arbitration and Statement of Claim to the Chartered Institute of Arbitrators within nine months of completion of the return journey or of the events giving rise to the dispute, whichever is the later; and

(e) the scheme provides a right for either party to have the arbitrators decision reviewed and details are set out in the rules of the Scheme.

(f) details of the scheme will be supplied on request.

Note: A recommended clause for inclusion in booking conditions is set out in the ABTA's Standards on Brochures.

4 GENERAL CONDUCT

4.1 Misleading Use of the ABTA Symbol etc.

(i) A Member shall not, directly or indirectly, cause, permit, assist, encourage or in any other way provide any person, company or firm not in membership of the Association with the opportunity to represent itself as a Member or as being associated with or connected to the Member or the Association in any way that is likely to mislead any person by the use of the ABTA symbol or any ABTA number or by any other means.

(ii) A Member shall not, directly or indirectly, represent any person, company or firm not in membership of the Association as a Member or as being associated with or connected to the Member or the Association in any way that is likely to mislead any person by the use of the ABTA symbol or any ABTA number or by any other means.

Where a Member is alleged to be in breach of this provision the Member shall comply with any requirement placed upon it by the Association within any time limit that may be specified.

4.2 Trading & Website Names

(i) Before employing a trading name a Member shall notify ABTA in writing of such trading name. For the purposes of this Clause, trading name means a name which is not the correct legal name under which ABTA membership is registered and includes any website address or domain name which is owned by a Member and used for the advertising, promotion or sale of Travel Arrangements.

(ii) When notifying ABTA of any website address or domain name a Member must sent to ABTA an accurately complete Website Information Form as set out in Appendix 5 to the Code, Form D.

Further completed Forms D must be sent to ABTA on each subsequent anniversary of the original notification of any website address or domain name.

4.3 Notice to Customers—Financial Protection

Retailers shall display in a prominent position at each of their offices which is open to the public, their certificate of membership currently in force and a financial protection notice in the form set out in the Appendix 2 to this Code or in such other form as the Board of Directors may from time to time approve but which shall include the words "we act as agent only for selected operators".

4.4 Payments of Debts

Members shall settle all debts due without delay or within any period agreed with the creditor. A continued failure to do so shall constitute *prima facie* evidence of an inability to meet liabilities under Article 14(1) of the Articles of Association.

4.5 Refunds

(i) Where a refund is due to a Client Members will, where appropriate, apply for the refund on behalf of the Client without delay.

(ii) Where a Principal is due to make a refund to a Client such refund shall be dispatched to the Client within 10 days of the refund being due.

(iii) Where Retailers receive refunds that are due to Clients they shall, unless there are exceptional circumstances, remit such refunds to Clients within six working days of their receipt.

4.6 Vouchers

Where a voucher is published by or on behalf of a Member or made accessible on-line and it contains any reference to ABTA, it must include the appropriate statement as listed below. This statement must feature in capital letters and bold print in a size no smaller than 10 point.

(i) Where the voucher is given away for free or offers a discount, the following phrase must be used:

"THIS VOUCHER IS NOT COVERED BY THE ABTA FINANCIAL PROTECTION SCHEME"

(ii) Where the Member is paid the face value of the voucher, it must carry the following phrase:

"THIS VOUCHER IS ONLY COVERED BY THE ABTA FINANCIAL PROTECTION SCHEME ONCE IT HAS BEEN REDEEMED AGAINST A SPECIFIC HOLIDAY BOOKING"

4.7 ABTA Gold Training Award

(i) Any Member that has joined or applied to join the ABTA Gold Training Award Scheme shall comply fully with the rules of that scheme whose rules are incorporated in their entirety into this Code of Conduct.

(ii) No Member shall display the logo of the ABTA Gold Training Award or make any reference to the award unless he is entitled to do so under the rules of the scheme.

4.8 Single Payment Scheme

Members operating under the Single Payment Scheme shall comply with the Code of Practice as agreed by the Board of Directors from time to time.

4.9 Surcharges

A Principal shall ensure that his conduct complies with the principles, rules and procedures contained in "ABTA's Standards on Surcharges" as published by the Association from time to time.

4.10 Incentives

Any Incentives shall only be offered by a Principal to the Head Office of a Retailer and shall not be offered direct to a Retailer's staff.

4.11 On-line Transactions

(i) In addition to the other provisions of this Code any Member transacting business on-line shall ensure that adequate on-line system security exists to protect client information, payment details and unauthorised access to the Member's system.

(ii) Members shall ensure that on-line system security is kept up-to-date in an appropriate manner.

(iii) Members shall take reasonable steps to authenticate parties to an on-line transaction in a secure manner.

(iv) In the event of an apparent breach of sub-clauses (i), (ii), (iii) above it shall be for the Member to show that adequate security existed; was kept up-to-date and/or that authentication steps were taken as the case may be.

(v) Members shall ensure that any external on-line code accreditation logo adopted by ABTA, the ABTA logo and the Member's ABTA number are shown upon any websites together with a summary of the details of the accreditation which may be achieved by a link to the accrediting body website where one exists.

(vi) Members shall make clear reference to ABTA membership upon any website and provide a summary of protection and consumer services provided by ABTA which may be provided by a link to the ABTA website.

(vii) Members providing links to sites of third parties who are not members of ABTA or framing such sites shall ensure that clients are made aware of this fact before any such link is followed or frame created.

(viii) Members framing sites of third parties shall ensure that clients are aware of the existence of the frame and the identity of the content owner of the framed site.

(ix) Where Members provide Travel Arrangements through websites owned by third parties the Members shall be responsible for ensuring that all information provided on that website in respect of the Travel Arrangements complies with the provisions of this Code.

5. INFRINGEMENT AND ENFORCEMENT

5.1 If any infringement of this Code is alleged against a Member, the facts shall be reported to the Secretariat for preliminary investigation.

5.2 The Member against whom the allegation has been made shall provide, at the request of the Secretariat, such further information or documents as may be required within such a period as may be specified.

5.3 If, after the preliminary investigation, the facts alleged against the Member appear to the Secretariat to constitute infringement of this Code, the matter shall be dealt with in accordance with Clause 5.4 below or submitted to the Code of Conduct Committee (hereinafter called the Committee) in accordance with Clause 5.5 below.

5.4 (i) Where the Secretariat, after due investigation, have reason to believe that a Member has committed a fixed penalty offence as set out herein below, the Secretariat may issue the Member with a fixed penalty notice in respect of the offence.

(ii) The following breaches of this Code by a Member constitute a fixed penalty offence and attract a fine of £300 which may be varied by the Board of Directors from time to time:

1.2(i), (ii), (iii)	Brochure Standards
1.3(vi), (vii), (ix)	Advertising Requirements
1.8 (i), (ii)	Confirmation of Bookings
1.9	Requirements Relating toTravel documents
2.3(i), (ii)	Cancellation and Amendment Fees
3.1(ii)(a), (b)	Dealing with complaints and correspondence from Clients
3.2(i), (ii)	Complaints and correspondence from the Association
4.2(i), (ii)	Failure to advise of trading or website name
4.3	Requirement to display membership certificate and financial protection notice
4.4	Payment of Debts
4.5(i), (ii), (iii)	Requirement to remit refunds

4.6(i), (ii)	Requirements Relating to Vouchers
4.9	Standards on Surcharges
4.11 (v), (vi), (vii), (viii)	Requirements relating to on-line transactions

Apparent breaches of the remaining Clauses of this Code are not fixed penalty offences and therefore shall be referred to the Committee in accordance with Clause 5.5 below.

(iii) The Secretariat has at all times the discretion to refer directly to the Committee in accordance with the procedures laid down at Clause 5.5 below all alleged breaches of this Code including breaches of this Code which would normally constitute a fixed penalty offence.

(iv) Where the Secretariat issues a fixed penalty notice in the standard form as set out in the Appendix 3 to the Code, the Member may:

(a) pay the fine within 28 days as set out in the fixed penalty notice; or

(b) request in writing to the Secretariat that the matter be referred to the Committee.

(v) Where the Member fails to pay the fine within the specified period, or requests the matter be referred to the Committee, or fails to respond to the fixed penalty notice, the Secretariat shall refer the matter to the Committee in accordance with the procedures laid down in Clause 5.5 of this Code. The Secretariat shall not refer the matter to the Committee until the period specified in the fixed penalty notice has expired. The Committee has the powers granted by Clause 5.5 below and may impose a penalty higher than the £300 imposed by the fixed penalty notice.

5.5 Where the Secretariat, after due investigation, has reason to believe that the facts alleged against the Member constitute infringement of this Code, the facts may be submitted to the Committee who shall give the Member at least 14 days notice in writing of the time and place of hearing of the complaint. The Member shall be entitled to make representations at the hearing either personally (with or without legal representation) or in writing. The Committee shall have the power to impose a reprimand or a fine or to suspend or terminate membership of the Association.

5.6 The decision of the Committee shall be notified to the Member, who shall have the right, exercisable within 14 days after the service of the notice upon him, to appeal against such decision to the Appeal Board which shall make such arrangements as it thinks fit for the conduct of the appeal. The decision of the Committee to reprimand a Member or to suspend or terminate a Member's membership of the Association shall take effect on the expiration of the period for appeal. If the Member has not then appealed, he shall thereupon be liable to sustain the reprimand or pay the fine or his membership of the Association shall be suspended or terminated.

5.7 If the Member shall appeal against a reprimand or a fine or against suspension or termination of membership, the decision shall not take effect unless and to the extent that it is confirmed or varied by the Appeal Board, which shall determine the appeal by exercising the powers of the Board of Directors in such manner as it, in its discretion, thinks fit.

5.8 The Appeal Board shall be constituted in accordance with Article 15 of the Articles of Association.

5.9 After the decision of the Appeal Board has been made known to the appellant, that decision shall be communicated to the Board of Directors.

5.10 The Board of Directors shall arrange for decisions to penalise a Member and the reasons therefore to be published.

Appendix 1—Clause 1.5

Details to be given to Clients before a contract is made if relevant to the particular Travel Arrangements.

1. The travel destination(s) and, where periods of stay are involved, the relevant periods, with dates.
2. The means, characteristics and categories of transport to be used and the dates, times and points of departure and return.
3. Where the Travel Arrangements include accommodation, its location, its tourist category or degree of comfort.
4. The meals which are included in the Travel Arrangements.
5. The itinerary.
6. Visits, excursions or other services which are included in the total price of the Travel Arrangements.
7. The name and address of the Principal, the Travel Agent and, where appropriate, the insurer.
8. The price of the Travel Arrangements, if the price may be revised in accordance with any contract term, an indication of the possibility of such price revisions and an indication of any dues taxes or fees chargeable for certain services where such costs are not included in the price of the Travel Arrangements.
9. The payment schedule and method of payment.
10. Special requirements which the consumer has communicated to the Principal or Travel Agent when making the booking and which both have accepted.

11. The possibility of the consumer canceling or amending the booking and the method of so doing and the costs involved to the consumer.

12. In respect of on-line transactions:

    (a) the payment mechanism(s), its level of security and any risks to the Client of undertaking the transaction.
    (b) details of how document delivery to/collection by the Client will be effected.
    (c) Information on any applicable cooling-off period offered to the Client and the method for using this
    (d) Clients shall have easy access to applicable terms and conditions applying to the transaction which shall be down-loadable.
    (e) clear details which are easy to locate, to enable the Client to contact the Member both on and off-line, including the full legal name of the Member, its head office address, contact address (if different), e-mail address, company registration number (or national equivalent), place and country of registration and establishment (if this is not the UK), telephone number for enquiries and usual hours of business.
    (f) information on how to complain and the ABTA Arbitration Scheme together with contact details for ABTA, including a link to the ABTA website.

MODEL BOOKING CONDITIONS

YOUR CONTRACT IS WITH [*insert legal identity of your business*], a member of ABTA.

1. Your Holiday Contract

When you make a booking you guarantee that you have the authority to accept and do accept on behalf of your party the terms of these booking conditions. A contract will exist as soon as we issue our confirmation invoice[1]. This contract is made on the terms of these booking conditions, which are governed by English Law, and the jurisdiction of the English Courts. You may however, choose the law and jurisdiction of Scotland or Northern Ireland if you wish to do so[2].

[If you had not seen these terms and conditions when you made your booking and you are not happy to proceed with the booking now that you have seen them please return all documentation to us or to your travel agent, within 7 days of receiving these booking conditions. Your booking will be cancelled and your monies will be returned in full, provided you

[1] Members taking bookings over Viewdata or CRS may wish to specify a different time for the coming into existence of the contract. Please contact the Legal Department for advice.

[2] You may amend the default jurisdiction to Scottish, Northern Irish or any other appropriate system as required.

have not commenced your travel. This clause does not apply if your booking was made within 10 weeks of travel][3].

2. Your Financial Protection

We are a member of ABTA, [Holding ATOL No [. . .] issued by the Civil Aviation Authority,] which provide for your protection in the event of our insolvency.

3. Your Holiday Price

When you make your booking you must pay a deposit of £[*insert amount*][*insert percentage % of the holiday cost*] per person. The balance of the price of your travel arrangements must be paid at least [. . .] weeks before your departure date. If the deposit and/or balance is not paid in time, we shall cancel your travel arrangements. If the balance is not paid in time we shall retain your deposit. All monies you pay to the travel agent are held by him on our behalf at all times.[4] [All monies you pay to the travel agent are held by him on your behalf until we issue our confirmation invoice. After this the travel agent holds the monies on our behalf.]

The price of your travel arrangements was calculated using exchange rates quoted in the "Financial Times Guide to World Currencies" on [*insert* date] in relation to the following currencies:[list currencies]

[The price of your travel arrangements is fully guaranteed and will not be subject to any surcharges.] **OR**

The price of your travel arrangements can be varied due to changes in transportation costs such as fuel, scheduled airfares and any other airline cost changes which are part of the contract between airlines (and their agents) and the tour operator or organiser]. Also [government action such as changes in VAT or any other government imposed changes] and [currency changes in relation to an exchange rate variation].

In the case of any small variation, an amount equivalent to 2% of the price of your travel arrangements, which excludes insurance premiums and any amendment charges, will be absorbed or retained. For larger variations this 2% will still be absorbed for increases but not retained from refunds. In either case there will be an administration charge of £1.00 per person together with an amount to cover agents' commission. If this means that you have to pay an increase of more than 10% of the price of your travel arrangements, you may cancel your travel arrangements and receive a full refund of all monies paid, except for any amendment charges. We will consider an appropriate refund of insurance premiums paid if you can show that you are unable to transfer or reuse your policy. Should you

[3] [optional clause] please see guideline.

[4] This clause is drafted to comply with the ATOL Regulations. Members conducting non-licensable business do not have to accept immediate responsibility for monies paid to an agent and alternative wording is given within the square brackets.

decide to cancel for this reason, you must exercise your right to do so within 14 days from the issue date printed on your final invoice. Whether you cancel or not you will also be entitled, on the terms set out in respect of major changes in paragraph 6 below, to accept an offer of alternative travel arrangements from us if we are able to do so and compensation as set out below. Please note that travel arrangements are not always purchased in local currency and some apparent changes have no impact on the price of your travel due to contractual and other protection in place.

4. If You Change Your Booking

If, after our confirmation invoice has been issued, you wish to change your travel arrangements in any way, for example your chosen departure date or accommodation, we will do our utmost to make these changes but it may not always be possible. Any request for changes to be made must be in writing from the person who made the booking or your travel agent. You will be asked to pay an administration charge of (£), and any further cost we incur in making this alteration. You should be aware that these costs could increase the closer to the departure date that changes are made and you should contact us as soon as possible.

Note: Certain travel arrangements (*e.g.* Apex Tickets) may not be changeable after a reservation has been made and any alteration request could incur a cancellation charge of up to 100% of that part of the arrangements.

5. If You Cancel Your Holiday

You, or any member of your party, may cancel your travel arrangements at any time. Written notification from the person who made the booking or your travel agent on your behalf must be received at our offices. Since we incur costs in cancelling your travel arrangements, you will have to pay the applicable cancellation charges up to the maximum shown in clause 6.

Note: If the reason for your cancellation is covered under the terms of your insurance policy, you may be able to reclaim these charges.

6. If We Change or Cancel Your Holiday

It is unlikely that we will have to make any changes to your travel arrangements, but we do plan the arrangements many months in advance. Occasionally, we may have to make changes and we reserve the right to do so at any time. Most of these changes will be minor and we will advise you or your travel agent of them at the earliest possible date. We also reserve the right in any circumstances to cancel your travel arrangements. For example, if the minimum number of clients required for a particular travel arrangement is not reached, we may have to cancel it. However, we will not cancel your travel arrangements less than [...] weeks before your departure date, except for reasons of *force majeure* or failure by you to pay the final balance. If we are unable to provide the booked travel arrangements, you can either have a refund of all monies paid or accept an offer of alternative travel arrangements of comparable standard from us, if available (we will refund any price difference if the alternative is of a lower value). If it is necessary to cancel your travel arrangements, we will pay to you compensation as set out in this clause.

Please note that carriers such as Airlines used in the brochure may be subject to change. Such a change is deemed to be a minor change. Other examples of minor changes include alteration of your outward/return flights by less than 12 hours, changes to aircraft type, change of accommodation to another of the same standard.

If we make a major change to your holiday, we will inform you or your travel agent as soon as reasonably possible if there is time before your departure. You will have the choice of either accepting the change of arrangements, accepting an offer of alternative travel arrangements of comparable standard from us if available (we will refund any price difference if the alternative is of a lower value), or cancelling your booked holiday and receiving a full refund of all monies paid. In all cases, except where the major change arises due to reasons of *force majeure*, we will pay compensation as detailed below:

	IF WE MAKE A MAJOR CHANGE TO YOUR HOLIDAY	IF WE CANCEL YOUR HOLIDAY	IF YOU CANCEL YOUR HOLIDAY
Period before departure within which notice of Cancellation or major change is received by us or notified to you		Amount you will receive from us	Amount of cancellation charge
More than [......] days	£...	Deposit only	Deposit only
More than [......] days	£...	100% of holiday cost [+£...]	[...]% of holiday cost/£...
More than [......] days	£...	100% of holiday cost [+£...]	[...]% of holiday cost/£...
Less than one day	£...	100% of holiday cost [+£...]	[...]% of holiday cost/£...

The compensation that we offer does not exclude you from claiming more if you are entitled to do so.

***Force Majeure*: This means that we will not pay you compensation if we have to cancel or change your travel arrangements in any way because of unusual or unforeseeable circumstances beyond our control. These can include, for example, war, riot, industrial dispute, terrorist activity and its consequences, natural or nuclear disaster, fire, adverse weather conditions.**

7. If You Have A Complaint

If you have a problem during your holiday, please inform the relevant supplier (*e.g.* your hotelier) and our resort representative immediately who will endeavour to put things right. If your complaint is not resolved locally, please follow this up within 28 days of your return home by writing to our Customer Services Department at [*insert address*] giving your booking reference and all other relevant information. Please keep your letter concise and to the point. This will assist us to quickly identify your concerns and speed up our response to you.

It is strongly suggested that you communicate any complaint to the supplier of the services in question as well as to our representative without delay and complete a report form *whilst in resort.*

If you fail to follow this simple procedure we will have been deprived of the opportunity to investigate and rectify your complaint whilst you were in resort and this may affect your rights under this contract.

8. What Happens To Complaints

Disputes arising out of, or in connection with, this contract which cannot be amicably settled may be referred to arbitration, if the customer so wishes, under a special Scheme arranged by the Association of British Travel Agents, and administered independently by the Chartered Institute of Arbitrators.

The scheme provides for a simple and inexpensive method of arbitration on documents alone with restricted liability on the customer in respect of costs. Full details will be provided on request or can be obtained from the ABTA website (*www.abta.com*).

The Scheme does not apply to claims for an amount greater than £5,000 per person. There is also a limit of £15,000 per booking form. Neither does it apply to claims which are solely in respect of physical injury or illness or their consequences. The Scheme can however deal with compensation claims which include an element of minor injury or illness subject to a limit of £1,000 on the amount the arbitrator can award per person in respect of this element.

The application for arbitration and Statement of Claim must be received by the Chartered Institute of Arbitrators within nine months of the date of return from the holiday. Outside this time limit arbitration under the Scheme may still be available if the company agrees, but the ABTA Code does not require such agreement.

9. Our Liability to You

(i) We accept responsibility for ensuring that your travel arrangements, which you book with us, are supplied as described in this brochure. If any part of your travel arrangements are not provided as promised, due to the fault of our employees, agents or suppliers we will pay you appropriate compensation if this has affected the enjoyment of your travel arrangements. Subject to paragraph (ii) below our liability in all cases shall be limited to a maximum of [. . . . .] the costs of your travel arrangements.

(ii) We accept responsibility for death, injury or illness caused by the negligent acts and/or omissions of our employees or agents, our suppliers and sub-contractors, whilst acting within the scope of, or in the course of their employment in the provision of your travel arrangements. We will accordingly pay to you such damages as might have been awarded in such circumstances under English Law or the law you have chosen under clause 1 above.

(iii) In respect of travel by air, sea and rail, and the provision of accommodation our liability will be limited in the manner provided by the relevant international convention. You can ask for copies of these international conventions from our offices (*Address & Telephone)*

10. Personal Injury Unconnected With Your Booked Travel Arrangements

If you, or any member of your party, suffer death, illness or injury whilst overseas arising out of an activity which does not form part of your package travel arrangements or an excursion arranged through us, we shall at our discretion, offer advice, guidance and assistance. Where legal action is contemplated and you want our assistance, you must obtain our written consent prior to commencement of proceedings. Our consent will be given subject to you undertaking to assign any costs, benefits received under any relevant insurance policy to ourselves. We limit the cost of our assistance to you or any member of your party to £5,000.

11. Conditions of Carriage

The Contractual terms of the companies that provide the transportation for your travel arrangements will apply to this contract. These may contain terms which affect your rights to compensation. You may ask for copies of the relevant conditions of carriage from our offices.

This brochure is our responsibility, as your tour operator. It is not issued on behalf of, and does not commit the airlines mentioned herein or any airline whose services are used in the course of your travel arrangements. Please note that in accordance with Air Navigation Orders in order to qualify for infant status, a child must be under 2 years of age on the date of its *return* flight.

GUIDELINES

When you are using these model-booking conditions there are a number of points to be considered. You will notice straightaway that there are a number of blanks which you are required to fill in.

Contracting Business

The first line of the model booking conditions states that "Your contract is with . . .". In the space provided you must state the correct legal identity of your business: if you are a partnership, you should state who the partners are; if you are a limited company then the correct company name as registered at Companies House should be inserted. This is in fact a legal requirement.

Clause 1: Your Holiday Contract

This clause relates to the law and jurisdiction of the contract. This is normally stated to be English, Scottish or Northern Irish, whichever is appropriate to your business. It is now a requirement that the UK consumer should choose his law and jurisdiction. We therefore suggest a default position but with the consumer having the option to change this but only within the UK. You can, of course, make the contract subject to another jurisdiction, but the Package Travel Regulations state that all the rights of the consumer will be implied into the contract irrespective of which jurisdiction is chosen.

Please note that in the case of bookings made using Viewdata / CRS, you may wish the contract to come into existence earlier than when you issue your confirmation invoice eg. when the booking is confirmed on the computer system.

We suggest you consider including the optional "cooling off period" if your clients have not seen your booking conditions at the time of booking. You should, of course, always ensure that the core parts of your booking conditions eg. cancellation charges are made known to your client at time of booking. You can vary the wording to give a number of days from issue of the invoice rather than receipt by the consumer if you wish to do so. Some members find this approach brings more certainty.

Clause 2: Your Financial Protection

In order to comply with the Package Travel Regulations details of your financial protection must be passed onto the consumer before the contract is concluded. Here you need to fill in your ATOL number in the blank space.

Clause 3: Your Holiday Price

Here you need to place the amount of deposit you will be seeking from the client. This can be a flat fee or a percentage.

You should also state the date you require the balance of the monies to be paid by the client. Please note that this time period can have a major impact on your other rights and obligations. Under the Association's Code of Conduct, travel arrangements cannot be cancelled for commercial reasons once the balance due date has passed. Therefore, the period you state in this clause will impact on Clause 6. In addition, please note that if the consumer fails to pay the balance by the balance due date, you reserve the right to retain their deposit. You may not have a right to apply any further cancellation charges since when you allow the consumer greater time to pay you are impliedly waiving your right to cancel the contract

If you charge a relatively low deposit it is more likely to be seen as fair to retain this amount if your client cancels. Deposits are viewed as evidence of the client's good faith when entering the agreement. It is more difficult to justify retaining a high deposit, as that deposit will then be seen as part-payment for the holiday, and you would have to justify your loss.

If you do wish to set a high deposit and retain the deposit when your client cancels, you may be able to do this and justify it if you balance this action by paying your client compensation when you cancel the travel arrangement at deposit stage.

You should include exchange rates used in calculating brochure prices in your brochure, website or conditions. You do not have to include this information in the conditions themselves if it is not practical to do so. It is recognised that the conditions may be printed on invoices and documentation stocks that could be used for varying programmes that are costed differently. Wherever the rates are displayed, they must be easily accessible and transparent.

This clause also contains the mandatory surcharge paragraphs: Please delete as appropriate, depending on whether or not you are going to reserve the right to surcharge, and depending on what matters you wish to surcharge. Note that a surcharge of over 10% of the client's travel cost entitles the client to the same options and compensation as a major change. This also allows clients to be refunded for favourable changes in costs in respect of which members reserve the right to surcharge. This does not apply if a no surcharge guarantee is given or to changes which are less than 2% of the cost of the holiday. Favourable changes above 2% of the holiday cost are refundable *in full*. There is a proviso to this at the end of the clause to make it clear to consumers that an operators ability to hedge against cost changes etc may mean there is no refund even if costs appear to go down. Finally the clause provides for consumers to be able to claim refunds of their insurance premiums if they can show the policy cannot be transferred / used / refunded by the insurer.

Clause 4: If You Change Your Booking

Please note that the client has a legal right pursuant to Regulation 10 of the Package Travel Regulations which will be implied, even if it is not expressly stated in your booking conditions. This right relates to a consumer who is *prevented* from travelling and allows him to transfer his travel arrangements to another person without having to pay the cancellation charges set out in Clause 4. However, this is subject to certain restrictions in the Regulations:

(i) the client must be prevented from travelling. He cannot simply change his mind; however, we recommend that you consider expressly allowing clients to transfer holidays in most circumstances if this is possible.

(ii) the replacement client must be a suitable consumer for your product;

(iii) both the original client and his replacement will be equally liable for all the costs incurred in making the transfer; ("Costs incurred in making the transfer" does not mean your cancellation charges unless they are imposed by the suppliers of the various elements of the package. It has to be an accurate reflection of all the costs incurred by you).

(iv) the client must give reasonable notice of his intention to make such a change. What is reasonable will depend on the individual circumstances.

If you have a fixed period within which changes, either to client or any of the travel arrangements, will be impossible you can state this in the conditions, giving the length of time. Otherwise the contract will be balanced by not being restrictive as to final amendment date. As drafted the term gives flexibility to you.

If you know that a client will not be able to make any changes to their travel arrangements after they have been confirmed, this should be made clear at the time of booking and shown on the invoice.

Clause 5: If You Cancel Your Holiday

Here you can state the cancellation charges which will apply depending on the time period before departure that notice of cancellation is given. Please note that in order for you to rely on the cancellation charges they must be an accurate reflection of the costs that you might incur, and a genuine pre-estimate of the loss you would suffer if you could not re-sell the product within the remaining time period. We would suggest that you carry out a review of the costs to your company of cancellations in order to be in a position to justify your cancellation charges.

In order to reflect more accurately the relationship between your cancellation charges and compensation paid to clients we have decided to set both out in the form of a percentage. If you cancel the holiday and you have to pay the client compensation you would do so by refunding 100% of the holiday price plus an amount for compensation shown as a percentage of the holiday price or as a fixed amount.

By showing the cancellation charges and compensation as percentages of the holiday price we hope to emphasise the relative fairness of the amounts.

Clause 6 & 7: If We Change or Cancel Your Holiday

Certain minor changes are stated within this clause as examples. You may wish to refine these. They are not items specifically stated within the Association's Code of Conduct, but are rather customs within the industry (see the Guidelines to the Tour Operators' Code of Conduct). Your business may of course be more generous, *e.g.* a six hour flight time change instead of 12 hours (and indeed a change of less than 12 hours may in certain circumstances be deemed to be a major alteration). However, the law states that if the change is "significant" the client can withdraw from the contract. Therefore, any unreasonable limits are open to challenge by the consumer.

Please note that should your conditions specify different levels of compensation being payable to the consumer depending on the option chosen by the consumer, this may be viewed as an unfair term and therefore void. Also this clause is not binding on consumers. They could claim more compensation. This prevents your term from being viewed as unfair by OFT but should make no difference in most cases where clients accept your offer.

The figure within this clause should correspond with your balance due date as specified in Clause 3.

Delay

The Office of Fair Trading (OFT) has questioned whether consumers should be entitled to compensation if their flights are delayed for less than 12 hours. It is certainly possible that consumers could suffer significant inconvenience where their flight is delayed for less than 12 hours and we suggest, therefore, that you set out your policy where there is any delay. For scheduled flights you can state that the individual airline policy will apply.

Clause 8: If You Have A Complaint

You will note that the client ought to make his complaint on the spot. He should also take it up in writing within a reasonable period upon his return. The code no longer sets out a 28 day minimum period. You must not impose an unreasonably short period to complain on the client. Our clause recommends your client to set out their complaint within 28 days and is a request, not a mandatory requirement, which would automatically exclude them from any legal action. However the clause also clearly tells the consumer that if he fails to complain IN RESORT then he may reduce his rights under the contract. This is a basic failure to mitigate point recognised in law. If the client does not give you or your supplier the chance to put things right he only increases his loss and he cannot claim any such increased loss back from you in most cases.

Clause 9: Our Liability to You

You will note a space within Clause 9(i). This is to allow for a limitation permitted by Regulation 15 of the Package Travel Regulations. You can place a limit on the compensation you will pay where the travel arrangements are not supplied as specified. There are two important limitations:

(i) the limit must be reasonable *e.g.* 2–3[1] times the value of the original cost of the travel arrangements; and

[1] Twice the value of the original cost of the travel arrangements is the minimum a tour operator should choose. However, the Association's advice is that it should be three times the value of the original cost of the travel arrangements. You may take the view that you do not need this provision at all, as any compensation is usually less than the holiday cost itself and a court can always override the contract limitation.

(ii) the limit does not apply to injury, illness or death.

ABTA'S STANDARDS ON SURCHARGES

1. INTRODUCTION

These Standards form Clause 4.9 of the Code of Conduct. This issue now replaces all previous issues. These Standards apply to all Packages and, as provided for in Section 8, to seat only arrangements. In addition Members must comply with Clause 2.7 of the Code of Conduct

2. DEFINITIONS

For the purposes of these Standards, a surcharge is defined as a supplementary amount requested from clients after the booking has been confirmed by the Member, and which is levied in addition to the original confirmed package price.

3. BASIC PRINCIPLES

The basic principles are:

- A surcharge in respect of currency rates, fuel or transportation cost variations or as a result of *government action shall only be made if the Member can show that his booking conditions provide for it.
- Members must absorb increased costs up to an amount equivalent to 2% of the original holiday price. In this context the "holiday price" does not include separately itemised insurance premiums and amendment charges. The "holiday price" amount is by reference to the invoice total and not an individual clients' price. Furthermore, if the surcharge levied exceeds 10% of the holiday price, after the absorption of the 2% referred to above, the client has the right to cancel within 14 days of the issue date printed on his surcharge invoice and be reimbursed any monies paid towards the holiday price, excluding amendment fees and, in some cases insurance premiums.
- Consumers are entitled to a refund if costs in respect of which members reserve the right to surcharge move favourably. This is subject to a 2% (of the holiday price) threshold. Any price change in the consumers' favour within the 2% is not passed on. However, if the change is over 2% the **whole** of the change is refunded. The note at the end of the paragraph makes it clear to consumers that apparent changes do not necessarily affect the holiday price either way. For example buying fuel or currency forward or certain costs not being paid in local currency. If there is no actual impact on cost then no refund is payable just as no surcharge could be imposed.
- A Member who levies a surcharge shall give written notice to the client (which must be dated) of the additional charge detailing the main cost headings. He shall also provide, or have available to provide on request, reasonable written explanation of the reasons

and calculations of the additional charge by reference to each cost heading.

- Members shall not surcharge a client within 30 clear days of departure. Members must bear in mind that time must be allowed for the raising and despatching of surcharge invoices. Where evidence clearly shows surcharge invoices have not been despatched in good time, permission to surcharge will be withdrawn. It is recommended that surcharge invoices be sent 35 days before departure as a minimum to comply with the 30 day rule.

* GOVERNMENT ACTION

For the sake of clarity Members should note that government action relates to the imposition of new taxes and the variation of existing taxes or any other government imposed increase such as an increase in VAT. Government action does not cover currency variations and Members should specify the exact items for which they reserve the right to surcharge as shown in the mandatory paragraph in Clause 9 of these Standards.

4. IMPOSITION OF SURCHARGES

(i) All Members must submit to ABTA a copy of each Brochure they publish, within 7 days of publication.

If a Member does not publish a Brochure they should submit their booking conditions.

It should be noted that failure to submit Brochures or booking conditions to ABTA will constitute a breach of clause 4.9 of the Code which may result in the issue of a Fixed Penalty Notice.

(ii) All Members must notify ABTA in the event that they wish to impose a surcharge. This is done by means of Forms B and C which are described below and attached as appendices to this document.

Form B: Notification of Intention to Surcharge (Appendix 1)

This form must be completed and forwarded to ABTA at least seven days prior to the intended date of despatch to clients of the invoice containing the surcharge. All relevant supporting information must accompany this form. For example, where surcharges arise through currency variations, the supporting information must include reference to the relevant rate of exchange as published in the Financial Times "Guide to World Currencies" on the date closest to which the surcharge calculations have been made. Furthermore, this form must state all currencies affected by adverse fluctuations which necessitate the surcharge.

Alternatively it may be in the form of a letter from a bank indicating the rate at which the currency has been purchased for the holiday concerned. Such currency purchases must be made at or around the time of surcharge calculations. In respect of other surcharges, letters or invoices from suppliers seeking increases must also accompany Form B.

Members who tailor-make packages must bear in mind that if they put together a package the client must have in writing the rate of exchange used when costing their holiday, if it is not shown in the booking conditions. Otherwise permission to surcharge cannot be granted as there will be no proof of the rate of exchange used when the client first booked his arrangements.

Form C: Surcharge Calculations (Appendix 2)

This form demonstrates the calculation of a specific surcharge and is a random example of how one client's surcharge has been calculated. ABTA reserves the right to request the specific details of any surcharge imposed. Members should note that surcharges are based on gross cost increases alone and "marking up" is not permitted.

5. AUTHORISATION TO SURCHARGE

Members are reminded that, until authorisation is received from ABTA, they cannot pass on any surcharges. ABTA has the right to require any Member to withdraw or reduce any proposed surcharge if the Member has failed to demonstrate the surcharge is due to a verifiable cost increase or where the surcharge calculation is inconsistent with previously submitted information. ABTA can require a Member to refund any unauthorised surcharges already collected. Any Member who attempts to pass on surcharges without prior authorisation or who obtains approval for a surcharge which is subsequently found to be in excess of the original advice from the supplier will be in breach of these Standards and automatically referred to the Code of Conduct Committee. A list showing all Members who have been given permission to surcharge, with dates and routes, is normally available on ABTEL and the ABTA members' website. It should be noted that as soon as the departure dates shown on Form B have expired, the Member's company name and details are removed from the system.

6. MONITORING OF SURCHARGES

Routine monitoring of surcharges is undertaken by the Legal Department of ABTA. Where discrepancies arise the matter is referred to a Monitoring Committee, which may in turn seek advice from a Surcharge Advisory Panel.

(i) **Surcharge Monitoring Committee**

This Committee exists to investigate inconsistent or inaccurate information supplied by the Member in support of a proposed surcharge. Additional information may be sought by the Committee which must be supplied by the Member. Failure or refusal to do so will result automatically in a denial to levy the proposed surcharge.

(ii) **Surcharge Advisory Panel**

A Surcharge Advisory Panel has been formed to address issues in relation to surcharges which are not adequately covered in these Standards. They shall also identify areas on which guidance from the Board of Directors is required on the implementation of these Standards.

7. SURCHARGEABLE ITEMS

The surchargeable items are as follows:

(a) transportation costs, *e.g.* fuel, increases in scheduled fares and any other airline surcharges which are part of the contract between airlines (and their agents) and the Member;

(b) government action as defined in Section 3 of these Standards; and

(c) currency in relation to exchange rate variations.

8. SEAT ONLY ARRANGEMENTS:

With the exception of Sections 5, 6 and 7 herein, these Standards shall apply to seat only charter arrangements covered by a Civil Aviation Authority ATOL.

Tour Operators shall provide evidence of any surcharge to the Association upon request. Where adequate evidence cannot be provided by the Tour Operator the Association may require the Tour Operator to withdraw the surcharge and may refer the matter to the Code of Conduct Committee

9. MISCELLANEOUS

Consumer Protection Act: Members are reminded that it is a criminal offence to give a client a misleading price indication. It is incumbent on each Member to ensure that a client is informed at the time of booking of any price increases that may occur.

Advertising: Any Member who knowingly misleads clients into entering into contracts without informing them of the possibility of surcharges may not only be in breach of the above Act, but also these Standards, resulting in referral to the Code of Conduct Committee..

Special Offers/Late Bookings: For special offers or late bookings, where all monies are payable at the time of booking, prices must be quoted all inclusive i.e. the surcharge must be included in the price quoted at the time of booking and not requested at a later date.

Administration Charge and Agents' Commission For Surcharges: Members must state in their brochures the level of any administration fee per passenger actually made in respect of surcharges. The maximum administration fee is £1 per person. Where applicable, reference must also be made to agents' commission.

Final Invoices: Members should note that if an invoice states "final invoice", this means it is the last, therefore surcharges cannot be requested after the issue of a final invoice.

Surcharge For Late Payment: Some Members have reserved the right to pass surcharges on for late payment, in the form of a penalty clause, which is not permitted. It should be noted that if a Member finds it necessary to surcharge, but only wishes to pass on surcharges to clients who are late in paying, he must clearly state in what circumstances surcharges will be passed on in his booking conditions.

It should also be noted that if a client is late in paying, then the booking should be treated as cancelled and the appropriate cancellation charges (in most cases this will be limited to the deposit) should be applied.

10. RECOMMENDED PARAGRAPHS

One of the following paragraphs or, as a minimum, the principles set out within them, must be shown in all booking conditions. Failure to incorporate the recommended surcharge paragraph or its principles may constitute a breach of Clause 4.9 of the Code of Conduct and may be subject to the issue of a Fixed Penalty Notice.

(a) **Full Price Guarantee**

"The price of your holiday is fully guaranteed and will not be subject to any surcharges."

A full price guarantee is the only situation where terms such as "No surcharges" or "Guaranteed no Surcharges" or similar phrases can be used. It should be noted that Members cannot guarantee prices then go on to make an exception.

(b) **Right To Surcharge Paragraph**

"The price of your travel arrangements can be varied due to changes in: *transportation costs e.g. *fuel, *scheduled airfares and *any other airline surcharges which are part of the contract between airlines (and their agents) and the tour operator/organiser, *Government action such as increases in VAT or any other Government imposed increases, *currency in relation to adverse exchange rate variations.

In the case of any small variation, an amount equivalent to 2% of the price of your travel arrangements, which excludes insurance premiums and any amendment charges, will be absorbed or retained. For larger variations this 2% will still be absorbed for increases but not retained from refunds. In either case there will be an administration charge of £1.00 per person together with an amount to cover agents' commission. If this means that you have to pay an increase of more than 10% of the price of your travel arrangements, you may cancel your travel arrangements and receive a full refund of all monies paid, except for any amendment charges. We will consider an appropriate refund of insurance premiums paid if you can show that are unable to transfer or reuse your policy. Should you decide to cancel for this reason, you must exercise your right to do so within 14 days from the issue date printed on your final invoice. Whether you cancel or not you will also be entitled, on the terms set out in respect of major changes in paragraph 6 below, to accept an offer of alternative travel arrangements from us if we are able to do so and compensation as set out below. Please note that travel arrangements are not always purchased in local currency and some apparent changes have no impact on the price of your travel due to contractual and other protection in place.

Members, as required by these Standards should also include a suggested statement as follows:

"The price of your holiday was calculated using exchange rates quoted in the "Financial Times Guide to World Currencies" on .... in relation to the following currencies: (list currencies)".

*Please delete as appropriate. It should be noted that these items are the only items on which surcharges may be applied.

Any Member who requires assistance or advice on the implementation of surcharges should telephone the Legal Department.

Bibliography

The following sources are referred to in the text or were used in the preparation of the book.

Blackshaw, C, Aviation Law and Regulation, Pitman, 1992

Bone, S, Rutherford, L & Wilson, S, Unfair Terms in Consumer Contracts Regulations: The New Law, Northumbria Law Press, 1996

Bragg, Richard, Trade Descriptions, Clarendon Press, Oxford, 1991

Butterworths Trading and Consumer Law, 1993-2003

Clarke, Malcolm A, Contracts of Carriage by Air, LLP, 2002

Collins, H, The Law of Contract, Butterworths, 3rd ed., 1997

Cordato, A, Australian Travel and Tourism Law, Butterworths, Australia, 3rd ed., 1999

Dickerson, T, Travel Law, Law Journals Seminars Press, New York, 1981-2003

Diederiks-Verschoor, IHPh, An Introduction to Air Law, Kluwer Law International, 6th ed., 1997

Furmston, MP, Cheshire, Fifoot & Furmstons Law of Contract, Butterworths, 14th ed., 2001

Giemulla, E, Schmid, R, Ehlers, N & Muller-Rostin, W, Warsaw Convention, Kluwer Law International, 1994-2003

International Travel Law Journal (ITLJ), Travel Law Centre, University of Northumbria, 1997-2003, (formerly the Travel Law Journal)(http://tlc.unn.ac.uk)

Lowe, R & Woodroffe, GF, Consumer Law and Practice, 5th ed., Sweet & Maxwell, 1999

Martin, P, McLean, D, Martin, E, Margo, R & Balfour, J, Shawcross and Beaumont on Air Law, Butterworths, 4th ed.

McKendrick, Ewan, Contract law, 4th ed., Palgrave, 2000

Nelson-Jones, J & Stewart, P, Package Holiday Law and Contracts, 3rd ed., Tolley

Oughton, D & Lowry, J, Textbook on Consumer Law, 2nd ed., 2000, Blackstone Press

Poole, Jill, Textbook on Contract, 6th ed., Blackstone, 2001

Saggerson, Alan, Travel Law and Litigation, CLT Professional Publishing, 2nd ed., 2000

BIBLIOGRAPHY

Travel Law Journal (TLJ), Travel Law Centre, University of Northumbria, 1994-1996, (now the International Travel Law Journal)
Treitel, G, The Law of Contract, Sweet & Maxwell, 10th ed., 1999
Vrancken, Patrick et al, Tourism and the Law, Butterworths, 2002
Yates, D, Exclusion Clauses in Contracts, Sweet & Maxwell, 2nd ed., 1982

Index

INDEX

INDEX

INDEX

INDEX

INDEX

INDEX

INDEX

INDEX

INDEX

INDEX

INDEX

INDEX

INDEX